# Internationalizing Cultural Studies

# Internationalizing Cultural Studies

*An Anthology*

*Edited by*

Ackbar Abbas and John Nguyet Erni

**Blackwell** Publishing

BLACKWELL PUBLISHING
350 Main Street, Malden, MA 02148-5020, USA
108 Cowley Road, Oxford OX4 1JF, UK
550 Swanston Street, Carlton, Victoria 3053, Australia

First published 2005 by Blackwell Publishing Ltd

*Library of Congress Cataloging-in-Publication Data*

Internationalizing cultural studies: an anthology / edited by Ackbar Abbas and John Nguyet Erni.
   p. cm.
  Includes bibliographical references and index.
  ISBN 0-631-23623-6 (hardcover: alk. paper)—ISBN 0-631-23624-4 (pbk.: alk. paper)
1. Culture—Study and teaching/ I. Abbas, M. A. (M. Ackbar) II. Erni, John Nguyet.

HM623. I573 2005
306′.071—dc22

2004015387

A catalogue record for this title is available from the British Library.

Set in 10.5/13pt Minion
by Kolam Information Services Pvt. Ltd, Pondicherry, India
Printed and bound in the United Kingdom
by TJ International Ltd, Padstow, Cornwall

For further information on
Blackwell Publishing, visit our website:
www.blackwellpublishing.com

# Contents

# Alternative Contents:
# Speaking Positions

This table of contents categorizes the chapter according to many different voices and the vantage points from which they speak. These are intellectual and political vantage points, not necessarily places from which the chapters were authored.

The diverse speaking positions include:

- Anthropological/Ethnographic Position
- Indigenous Local Position
- Critical Counternationalist Position
- Comparative Local Position
- Postcolonial/Subaltern Position
- Diasporic Position
- Transnational Position
- Regionalist Position

## Anthropological/Ethnographic Position

## Indigenous Local Position

## Critical Counternationalist Position

## Postcolonial/Subaltern Position

# Alternative Contents: Localities

This third table of contents facilitates learning and teaching the materials by categorizing the chapters according to geographical divides. Localities, however, represent more than geographies; they fall under the grid of cultural, political, and historical coordinates.

## Africa

## South Asia

## Transnational

# Preface: How To Use This Book

## ▨ Basic Purposes ▨

This anthology uses the term "cultural studies" to include all critically grounded, interdisciplinary, multimethod, politically oriented scholarships on the relations among culture, society, and power, scholarships which are found in both national and international contexts, in the recognition of diverse intellectual and historical trajectories. A mere half century after the politico-intellectual movement of cultural studies was born out of the specific contour of British society, the "Birmingham tradition" informs both the practice and theory of international work that has, by now, gone far beyond cultural studies' Britishness. Although the dominance of cultural studies as a North Atlantic ideal or ideology or educational practice is evident, that ideal has become a part of international consciousness, a lens through which to see the development of critical cultural studies movements elsewhere in the world, as well as a discourse capable of potent reflexivity and self-challenge.

The anthology critically samples the forms, tendencies, and achievements of cultural studies in national(ist) vs. postnational(ist) frames, canonical vs. dialogical frames, North Atlantic vs. diasporic vs. postcolonial frames. These various frames now form an indelible part of our international landscape of cultural studies. The failures as well as the dilemmas in seeking to work on cultural studies projects across these diverse frames (diverse cultures?) are equally instructive for an understanding of that landscape. Today's university curriculum evidences the significance of including international works in cultural studies for fields of study as diverse as philosophy, government, communication and media, gender studies, sociology, public health, world finance, ecology, racial and ethnic conflict, religion, education, and anthropology.

The anthology builds on the premise that a basic course in cultural studies today should educate students to see the "big international picture." Of course it should enable students to understand the histories, doctrines, and institutional structures of North Atlantic, canonical cultural studies. But it should also persuade students to think critically about the subject as a whole. Thus the topics and chapter selections here describe, analyze, criticize, propose, provoke, and engage, without imposing any dominant dogma, direction, or method for thinking about the development of cultural studies in the international arena. The student must reflect on those vexing questions. The knowledge and conceptual framework provided by the anthology prepares the student seriously engaging with it to work with commitment and critical reflection in a range of positions to articulate cultural studies internationally – postnationalist, postcolonialist, diasporic, and so on – regardless of which parts of the world the student is studying. The same applies to the contributing editors of the various Parts, whose primary charge was to advance an assortment of positions for a specific theme of cultural studies, regardless of where these editors reside and work, or their ethnic/racial/national belongings.

## ▓ Principal Features of the Anthology ▓

The conceptual framework for the Anthology is set forth in the Introduction and each topical part introduction. The framework in each part consists, with no intention of "total coverage" whatsoever, of some of the historical development and character of cultural studies work found in different parts of the world; the dilemmas of theoretical universalism vs. particularism; the architecture of local cultural institutions/industries as well as their powers and interplay with politics; and the relationships between North Atlantic and non-North Atlantic formations. Some major themes run through the different sections of the anthology – for example, changing notions of the "local" and "localities" in the times of globalization, the changing configuration of modernity/postmodernity, the play of identities in the gradual expansion of cultural studies (especially in places where cultural studies articulate with rights-based social movements), the striking adaptation, modification, and challenge of ideas about the nature and purposes of cultural studies itself.

Some understandings informing the entire anthology thus follow:

1. Cultural politics are politics within local contexts, not in outer space. One might therefore argue that the study of cultural studies should concentrate on different locales – say, cultural studies *in* Africa, *in* Pakistan, China, the United States, Egypt, France. Such an approach could offer contextual studies drawn from different national histories and political cultures. This anthology wants to suggest a different path. The distinctive aspect of cultural studies has been its development on the international level (hence, admittedly, a certain redundancy in the anthology's title). It therefore wants to stress reading the local *in* the international landscape, as well as the vital relationships between that international landscape

and a local society's internal struggles. Although many chapters throughout the anthology focus on cultural politics as experienced within one or another local setting, we encourage the students to use these "cases" to address cross-national processes, struggles, and politics.

2. What are the sensible boundaries of an anthology that is about a field or a movement that has sprung from so many different disciplines? Clearly it could not achieve its goals if it held to a positivist conception of culture, society, or politics that blocked out deeply related fields of inquiry. The diverse "case studies" presented in the chapters come from diverse disciplines (anthropology, performance studies, political economy, media studies, literature, cinema studies, etc.), which interact with broad theoretical materials (on identity politics, on epistemology, on modernity, on resistance, and so on) to form a network of related "scenarios" for international cultural studies. Thus, this range of readings should be readily accessible to university students from varied academic backgrounds in the humanities and social sciences. Cultural Studies courses benefit greatly by including students from such diverse disciplinary backgrounds, as well as from diverse cultural or national backgrounds.

3. An anthology that attempts to present important exemplars of cultural studies work from different parts of the world would bear the characteristic of giving attention to the work of key intellectual figures beyond those "usual suspects." Admittedly, this plays into a visible tendency found in the Western academy. But where critical political work is born out of places that are not usually referenced in typical bibliographies of cultural studies, key figures – both those established and those who are emergent – are a relevant point of attention for such an anthology.

## ▪ Suggestions for Use of the Anthology ▪

International cultural studies materials are too extensive to be covered in most courses. Choice will surely vary among teachers, depending on the time available for a course and the purposes for which the course is offered. Some suggestions follow.

Although the topical sections are designed to serve as a whole as a general map and conceptual framework for international cultural studies, they need not be taught in lock-step. The chapters within each section can be studied independently outside that section, and in a different order from that presented here. Teachers, for example, may prefer more or less stress on questions of "modernity/postmodernity," as they are engaged in cultural studies work from diverse locales, on institutional formations as opposed to the analysis of texts, or on particular regions of the world. Hence there is more than one table of contents in the anthology: the first one arranges the chapters according to topical sections, the second one does so according to estimated intellectual positions represented in the chapter selections, and still a third is arranged through regional categories.

# Acknowledgments

The impetus of this daunting project came several years ago upon my return to Hong Kong, from a generously funded international cultural studies conference held in Hong Kong in June 2001, entitled "Hong Kong and Beyond: East–West Critical Dialogues in Cultural Studies." I thank Prof. Matthew Chen, former Dean of the Faculty of Humanities and Social Sciences at City University of Hong Kong, who offered his tremendous support and enthusiasm for endorsing and advancing cultural studies scholarship at the University. A number of good friends and colleagues have also been supportive of this endeavor wholeheartedly or implicitly, by challenging me over the years to polish my work and thought processes as I moved between national contexts of living and working. They include Larry Grossberg, Lisa Henderson, Toby Miller, Cindy Patton, Chin-chuan Lee, Meaghan Morris, Chua Siew Keng, Alex C. K. Lee, Stephen Chan, Sheila McNamee, Eric Ma, Anthony Fung, Angel Lin, Paula Salvio, Ted Striphas, Anthony Spires, and all of you in the Conjunctures Group. Flaws of judgment and other inadequacies are of course mine. Jayne Fargnoli of Blackwell has offered her deep support and comradeship; without her this project would not have come to fruition. I also thank Ken Provencher and Cameron Laux on the Blackwell team for pushing me to the finish line. My whole family has been an understated source of strength in my life. A warm thank-you, finally, goes to Tony, who has been a real "comfort zone" to me.

*JNE*

## ■ Text Acknowledgments

The editors and publisher gratefully acknowledge the permission granted to reproduce the copyright material in this book. This material is ordered below by chapter number. Any material not listed is © 2005 by Blackwell Publishing Ltd.

1 Ashis Nandy, "Science as a Reason of State," pp. 1–12 and 22–3 (notes) in Ashis Nandy (ed.), *Science, Hegemony and Violence: A Requiem for Modernity.* Delhi: Oxford University Press, 1988. Reprinted with permission of Oxford University Press India, New Delhi.

2 Vandana Shiva, "Biotechnological Development and the Conservation of Biodiversity," pp. 193–213 (excerpts) in Vandana Shiva and Ingunn Moser (eds.), *Biopolitics: A Feminist and Ecological Reader on Biotechnology.* London and New Jersey: Zed Books, 1995. Reprinted with permission of Zed Books.

3 Ravi Sundaram, "Recycling Modernity: Pirate Electronic Cultures in India," pp. 93–9 in S. Sengupta and G. Lovink (eds.), *Sarai Reader 01: The Public Domain.* Delhi/Amsterdam: Sarai and The Society for Old and New Media, 2001.

4 Akiko Ōtake and Shūhei Hosokawa, "Karaoke in East Asia: Modernization, Japanization, or Asianization?" pp. 191–201 in Tōru Mitsui and Shūhei Hosokawa (eds.), *Karaoke Around the World: Global Technology, Local Singing.* London and New York: Routledge, 1998. Reprinted with permission of Routledge/Taylor and Francis Books, Inc.

6 Dwight Conquergood, "Health Theatre in a Hmong Refugee Camp: Performance, Communication, and Culture," *TDR: The Drama Review* 32 (1988), pp. 175–6; 180–91; 193; 195–9; 202; 205–8. Reprinted with permission of MIT Press Journals.

8 Smadar Lavie, "The Fool," pp. 219–24, 229–39, and 352–3 (notes) from *The Poetics of Military Occupation: Mzeina Allegories of Bedouin Identity Under Israeli and Egyptian Rule.* Berkeley: University of California Press, 1990. Reprinted with permission of University of California Press.

9 Jennifer Robertson, "East Asian Bouquet: Ethnicity and Gender in the Wartime Japanese Revue Theatre." Adapted from chapter 5 (pp. 89–139) in *Takarazuka: Sexual Politics and Popular Culture in Modern Japan.* Berkeley: University of California Press, 1998. Reprinted with permission of the author.

10 Diana Taylor, "The Theatre of Operations: Performing Nation-ness in the Public Sphere," pp. 91–102, 104–9, and 276–8 (notes) from her *Disappearing Acts: Spectacles of Gender and Nationalism in Argentina's "Dirty War."* Durham: Duke University Press, 1997. © 1997 by Duke University Press. All rights reserved. Reprinted with permission of the publisher.

11 Erica Carter, "Frontier City Berlin: The Post-War Politics of Space," *Art Papers* (July–Aug. 1992), pp. 3–9.

12 Jennifer Robertson, "Gender-Bending in Paradise: Doing 'Female' and 'Male' in Japan," *Genders* 5 (Summer 1989): 50–69.

13   Lila Abu-Lughod, "The Marriage of Feminism and Islamism in Egypt: Select-ive Repudiation as a Dynamic of Postcolonial Cultural Politics," pp. 244–59, 261–4, and 265–9 (notes) in Lila Abu-Lughod (ed.), *Remaking Women: Feminism and Modernity in the Middle East*. New Jersey: Princeton University Press, 1998.

14   Donald L. Donham, "Freeing South Africa: The 'Modernization' of Male–Male Sexuality in Soweto," *Cultural Anthropology* 13:1 (1998), pp. 3–21. © 1998 by the American Anthropological Association. All rights reserved. Re-printed with permission.

15   Ding Naifei, "Very Close to *yinfu* and *ënu*, Or How Prefaces Matter for *JPM* (1695) and *Enu Shu* (Taipei, 1995)," © 2002 by Duke University Press. All rights reserved. Reprinted with permission of the publisher.

16   Jenine Abboushi Dallal, "Hizballah's Virtual Civil Society," *Television & New Media* 2:4 (2001), pp. 367–72. © 2001 by Sage Publications Inc. Reprinted with permission.

17   Umberto Eco (trans. Paola Spendore), "Towards a Semiotic Inquiry into the Television Message," *Working Papers in Cultural Studies* 3 (1972): 103–21.

18   Richard Fung, "Looking for My Penis: The Eroticized Asian in Gay Video Porn," pp. 145–60 in Bad Object-Choices (ed.), *How Do I Look? Queer Film and Video*. Seattle: Bay Press, 1991.

19   Néstor García-Canclini (trans. George Yúdice), "From the Public to the Private: The 'Americanization' of Spectators," pp. 109–22 and 178–9 (notes) in *Consumers and Citizens: Globalization and Multicultural Conflicts*. Minne-apolis: University of Minnesota Press, 2001.

20   Faye Ginsburg, "Embedded Aesthetics: Creating a Discursive Space for Indi-genous Media," *Cultural Anthropology* 9:3 (1994), pp. 365–82. © 1994 by the American Anthropological Association. All rights reserved. Reprinted with permission.

21   Olatunde Bayo Lawuyi, "The World of the Yoruba Taxi Driver: An Interpret-ative Approach to Vehicle Slogans, " *Africa* 58:1 (1998), pp. 1–12. Reprinted with permission of Edinburgh University Press.

22   Angel M. Y. Lin, "Doing Verbal Play: Creative Work of Cantonese Working Class Schoolboys in Hong Kong." Portions of this chapter have previously appeared in "Resistance and Creativity in English Reading Lessons in Hong Kong," *Language, Culture and Curriculum* 12:3 (2000), pp. 285–96, and in "Lively Children Trapped in an Island of Disadvantage: Verbal Play of Can-tonese Working Class Schoolboys in Hong Kong," *The International Journal of the Sociology of Language* 143 (2000), pp. 63–83.

23   Keith Breckenridge, "Love Letters and Amanuenses: Beginning the Cultural History of the Working Class Private Sphere in Southern Africa, 1900–1933," *Journal of Southern African Studies* 26:2 (2000), pp. 337–48. Reprinted with permission of Taylor & Francis Journals. www.tandf.co.uk/journals.

24   Mark McLelland, "Live Life More Selfishly: An On-line Gay Advice Column in Japan," *Continuum: Journal of Media and Cultural Studies* 15:1 (2001),

pp. 103–16. Reprinted with permission of Taylor & Francis Journals. www.tandf.co.uk/journals.

25    Igor Cusack, "African Cuisines: Recipes for Nation-Building?" *Journal of African Cultural Studies* 13:2 (Dec. 2000), pp. 207–25. Reprinted with permission of Taylor & Francis Journals. www.tandf.co.uk/journals.

26    Kwame Anthony Appiah, "Racisms," pp. 10–17 in David Theo Goldberg (ed.), *Anatomy of Racism.* Minneapolis: University of Minnesota Press, 1990.

27    Cornel West, "Race and Social Theory," pp. 251–70 in his *Keeping Faith: Philosophy and Race in America.* London and New York: Routledge, 1993. Reprinted by permission of Routledge/Taylor & Francis, Inc.

28    Paul Gilroy, "The End of Antiracism," pp. 191–209 in W. Ball and J. Solomon (eds.), *Race and Local Politics.* Basingstoke: Macmillan, 1990.

29    Partha Chatterjee, "Whose Imagined Community?" pp. 4–11 from his *The Nation and its Fragments.* Princeton: Princeton University Press, 1993. Reprinted with permission of Princeton University Press.

30    Arjun Appadurai, "Patriotism and Its Futures," pp. 172–7 from his *Modernity at Large.* Minneapolis: University of Minnesota Press, 1996. All rights reserved. Reprinted with permission of the publisher.

32    Simon During (1993). "Popular Culture on a Global Scale: A Challenge for Cultural Studies?" Adapted from his "Toward the Global Popular?: Knowledge, Strength and Magic," pp. 133–55 in David Bennett (ed.), *Cultural Studies: Pluralism and Theory.* Melbourne: University of Melbourne Literary and Cultural Studies, 1993. An extended argument concerning the institutional (both governmental and academic), economic, and technological aspects of the global popular – along with extended bibliographic references – had to be removed due to the exigencies of space in this present volume.

33    Rachel Hughes,"The Abject Artefacts of Memory: The 1997 Museum of Modern Art New York Exhibition of Photographs from Cambodia's Genocide," *Media, Culture and Society* 25:1 (2003), pp. 23–44.

34    L. H. M. Ling (1999), "Sex Machine: Global Hypermasculinity and Images of the Asian Woman in Modernity." This is adapted from an article published in *Positions: East Asia Cultures Critique* 7:2 (1999), pp. 277–306. Extensively referenced footnotes have been edited out of this current version in the interests of space. All rights reserved. Reprinted with permission of the publisher.

36    Benedict Anderson, "Exodus," from *Critical Inquiry* 20:2 (1994), pp. 314–27. Reprinted with permission of the University of Chicago Press.

37    James Clifford, "Diasporas," pp. 244–77 from *Routes: Travel and Translation in the Late Twentieth Century.* Cambridge, Mass.: Harvard University Press, 1997.

38    David L. Eng, "Out Here and Over There: Queerness and Diaspora in Asian (-)American Studies," pp. 215–24 and 264–6 from *Racial Castration: Managing Masculinity in Asian America.* Durham: Duke University Press, 2001. All rights reserved. Reprinted with permission of the publisher.

39   Hamid Naficy, "Situating Accented Cinema," pp. 10–39 from *An Accented Cinema: Exilic and Diasporic Filmmaking. Princeton: Princeton University Press, 2001. Reprinted with permission of the publisher.*

40   Zeynep Çelik, "Cultural Intersections: Re-visioning Architecture and the City in the Twentieth Century," pp. 190–203, 216–21, and 222–6 in Russell Ferguson (ed.), *At the End of the Century: One Hundred Years of Architecture.* New York: Harry N. Abrams, 1998 (in association with the Museum of Contemporary Art, Los Angeles).

41   Manuel Castells, "Grassrooting the Space of Flows," pp. 18–27 in James O. Wheeler, Yuko Aoyama, and Barney Warf (eds.), *Cities in the Telecommunication Age.* New York and London: Routledge, 2000. Reprinted with permission of Routledge/Taylor & Francis Books, Inc.

42   Rem Koolhaas, "The Generic City," pp. 1238–64 in his *S, M, L, XL,* ed. Jennifer Sigler. New York: Monicelli Press, 1995.

43   Mario Gandelsonas, "Scene X: The Development of the X-Urban City," pp. 36–43 in *X-Urbanism.* New York: Princeton Architectural Press, 1999. Reprinted with permission of Princeton Architectural Press.

44   Ziauddin Sardar, "On the Political Economy of the Fake," pp. 82–90 in *The Consumption of Kuala Lumpur.* London: Reaktion Books, 2000. Reprinted with permission.

Every effort has been made to trace copyright holders and to obtain their permission for the use of copyright material. The publisher apologizes for any errors or omissions in the above list, and would be grateful if notified of any corrections that should be incorporated in future reprints or editions of this book.

# General Introduction

## Ackbar Abbas and John Nguyet Erni

There is a moment in Nietzsche's *The Birth of Tragedy* (1956/1990) worth recalling when we think about Cultural Studies today and the reasons for putting together a new anthology on the field. It is the moment when (according to Nietzsche) a voice enjoins Socrates, just when he is about to give up his life rather than his convictions, to "practice music." It is a thoroughly ambivalent moment, because throughout the book, Nietzsche has with characteristic iconoclasm described Socrates not as an intellectual hero but as a kind of intellectual monster who takes to extremes the idea that the beautiful is synonymous with the intelligible, that thought can separate true knowledge from illusion and error. Socrates becomes preeminently a teacher who teaches a powerful critical method of guarding against error. Hence, the Socratic spirit is optimistic and serene, devoid of self-doubt.

Nevertheless, Nietzsche concedes that there is another side to Socrates which makes him "the most problematic figure among the ancients." We remember Socrates' famous *diamonon*, that divine *voice* that spoke to him during those moments when even his magnificent intelligence faltered. It is true that for the most part, the Socratic *daimonon* is a negative inhibitory agent, speaking to dissuade, a kind of nagging Xanthippe, nothing if not critical. Nevertheless, there was one important instance when the voice spoke to him in order to persuade: during Socrates' last days, the voice said to him in a dream: "Practice music, Socrates!" "These words heard by Socrates in his dream," Nietzsche comments, "are the only indication that he ever experienced any uneasiness about the limits of his logical universe" (p. 90). It is said that in prison Socrates composed a song to Apollo and versified several of Aesop's fables.

"Music" in the above anecdote suggests at least two things for Cultural Studies. Firstly, it suggests the value of taking a powerful and dominant line of thought *elsewhere*, of opening oneself to other cultures and other orders of things. But it also suggests even more importantly that this "elsewhere" should not be taken too literally. For example, a music-practicing Socrates will have to do more than versify Aesop, just as Cultural Studies is more than just an interest in popular culture. Cultural Studies needs to speak not only against domination but, in order to do this with any success, it needs also to ensure that the hard-earned insights of the field – about marginality, otherness, local contexts and so on – should not be foreclosed by literal-minded applications. In Cultural Studies as in other terrains of study, literal-mindedness is the original sin.

And this brings us back to the aims of this anthology. One of our aims is indeed to take Cultural Studies elsewhere, to internationalize the field a little further. While Cultural Studies has long been conducted in various national and inter-national contexts, it is unclear how the active and proliferating practices of Cultural Studies in other regions of the world are taken up, circulated, used, valued, or taught. A certain parochialism continues to operate in Cultural Studies as a whole, whose objects of and languages for analysis have had the effect of closing off real contact with scholarship conducted outside its (western) radar screen. In the current moment of what we call the "postcolonial predicament" of Cultural Studies, in which a broad hegemony of western modernity is increasingly being questioned among Cultural Studies scholars from around the world, we must consider any form of internationalization as an effort – and a critical context – for facilitating the visibility, transportability, and translation of works produced out-side North America, Europe, and Australia. This proposed anthology is an attempt to make a political and intellectual intervention into a state of unevenness in the flow and impact of knowledge within Cultural Studies, to clear a space for an introduction to, and pluralization of, Cultural Studies work from diverse locales and intellectual traditions.

However, we need to remind ourselves that in order to achieve any kind of genuine plurality, we must allow the notion of "elsewhere" to retain its critical and interrogative edge. "Elsewhere is a negative mirror," Italo Calvino makes the traveler Marco Polo remark, and this is as true of travel as it is of Cultural Studies. If the aim is to reveal and topple an underlying universalism, the means for doing so cannot be to revert to parochialism. Thus "Asia" cannot simply be opposed to North America, Europe, or Australia. Benjamin Lee (1995) makes a similar point when, in arguing for the need to resituate area studies to a critical internationalist framework, he suggests that debates over such things as multiculturalism or other conceptions of difference can "only be decentered by being examined from another perspective. This does not mean that the other perspectives will provide solutions to our problems, or that ours can solve their problems, but that they may suggest strategies for disaggregating issues which may appear to go together naturally... We have reached a time when no values from any single cultural perspective can provide frameworks adequate to understanding the changes affecting all of us" (p. 588). These observations are in line with a flurry of critical debates that have confronted the question of whether the broad proliferation of Cultural Studies work in many parts of the world really means anything at all to the whole political ethos of Cultural Studies (see Birch, 2000; Chen, 1996, 2000; Cevasco, 2000;

Desmond & Dominguez, 1996; Grossberg, 1994; Mato, 2000; Stratton & Ang, 1996). Practical articulations of an internationalist Cultural Studies have appeared in the form of journals and series with "postdisciplinarity" and even "postnational" and "heterolingualism" as their explicitly stated goals (e.g. *International Journal of Cultural Studies, Communal/Plural* [now defunct], *Inter-Asia Cultural Studies, Traces: A Multilingual Series of Cultural Theory and Translation*), in international conferences (e.g. the Dismantle/Fremantle Conference held in Australia in 1991, the Trajectories: Toward an International Cultural Studies conference held in Taipei in 1992, the International Crossroads Conferences in Cultural Studies held since 1997 in Europe, UK, and the US, and the Critical Dialogues in Cultural Studies Conference held in Hong Kong in 2001), and in the recent establishment of an International Association of Cultural Studies. If these initiatives have contributed to the establishment of critical internationalism, it is partly because they have implicitly or explicitly subjected the notion of elsewhere to critical and often contentious scrutiny.

The same attention will have to be directed to other important and historically complex notions like "otherness" or "the local." Radical otherness is also radically incomprehensible, as Lévi-Strauss has shown some time ago in *Tristes Tropiques* (1976). Lévi-Strauss's argument can be formulated in a question: how can we know others, without in the process surreptitiously reducing them to versions of ourselves? This is the theme of knowledge as betrayal, known in another guise as ethnocentrism. In the encounter with otherness, something is inevitably lost. "I had only to succeed in guessing what they were like," Lévi-Strauss writes about natives in the jungles of Brazil never seen before by the white man, "for them to be deprived of their strangeness" (p. 333). The right distance is never achieved: you are always standing either too near or too far. And the result of this stand-off is a kind of *tristesse* or scholarly melancholy. We also know Lévi-Strauss's solution to the problem, which was presented to the world as structuralism, the bold face put on *tristesse*.

There are different reasons why Lévi-Strauss is relevant for Cultural Studies. To begin with, after *Tristes Tropiques*, Cultural Studies will have to avoid speaking about otherness the way TV evangelists speak about god – as our familiar. But this should not blur the fact that the trajectories and positions of Cultural Studies are very different from Lévi-Straussian anthropology. Even a highly sympathetic text like *Tristes Tropiques* shows that in the encounter with the natives, the anthropologist never loses her/his position as observer and the privilege that the position bestows. The other is always an object of study, which is why the central issue in the text has more to do with epistemology (knowledge-as-betrayal) than with ethnocentrism. In Cultural Studies, these priorities are reversed and reversible. We find there a different mode of otherness, where the other is not merely an epistemological problem, but capable of looking back and talking back. We can mention here yet another perspective on otherness, that of Roland Barthes, a reader of both Marx and Saussure, a lover of cities and of signs, who sees an erotic dimension in cities because they are "sites of an encounter with the other." The city-as-other is erotic because it makes possible exchange, discourse, and intercourse. In a text like

*Empire of Signs* (1982) about Japan, written admittedly from a position of ignorance, Barthes is not a privileged observer or ambassador of "cultural exchange" or
emissary of the West. Rather, it is at the moment when cultural understanding
breaks down, when cultural translation fails, that insights are gained. Such insights
are never epiphanies of knowledge about the other, but rather negative epiphanies
that do not pretend to pose themselves as universality. Instead of the universal,
they move us towards a politics of knowledge and culture, which we believe is the
major trajectory in Cultural Studies.

We can briefly examine how the diverse meanings of otherness in different
specific contexts can give rise to different kinds of cultural politics. A number of
important voices – all occupying Third World, subaltern speaking positions –
provide the relevant points of illumination here. Kuan-Hsing Chen, who co-edits
the first Asian-based journal entitled *Inter-Asia Cultural Studies*, reflects on the
critical trajectory he took in navigating the politics of Cultural Studies as an Asian
scholar/subject:

> After a long period of training in Anglo-American Cultural Studies, I went back to
> Taiwan in 1989 and have witnessed the most turbulent transformations. My critical
> training has driven my involvement in these changes. Meanwhile, the mood of
> "indigenization" (*ben-tu-hua*) provokes me to reflect on the necessity of decolonizing
> my intellectual work. But it also makes me realize that exclusive indigenization is a
> sheer dead end. Wavering constantly between a local critical theoretical stand and my
> personal historical experiences, I have been searching for a workable position,
> without which no research is possible. Compared with my theoretical writings
> abroad, discourse on "popular democracy" and "new internationalist localism" are
> harbingers of the results of my attempts. (Chen, 2000: 10)

Chen's concern about "decolonizing [his] intellectual work" highlights the importance of seeing "Cultural Studies" as a politico-theoretical project that contests any
leaning towards intellectual imperialism. Echoing a Fanonian analytic, Chen's
reservation towards both "Anglo-American Cultural Studies" and "indigenization"
movements suggests the need to open up another space for Cultural Studies today.
Politically speaking, then, the challenge for a critical internationalist Cultural
Studies entails a workable definition of this other space, where "the canonical"
must be recast (and not abandoned altogether) and "the international/local nexus"
must be rigorously contextualized in relation to various historical, geopolitical, and
intellectual positions. This is why in dealing with various thematic concerns being
selected for this anthology (e.g. Cities, Technocultures, Gender and Sexual Politics,
and so on), we will ensure that the selections will be sufficiently *diverse* (in terms of
origins of work and in terms of covering both canonical and noncanonical works)
and *self-reflexive* (in terms of attempts to offer theoretical reflections on the various
operating positions of Cultural Studies, such as "international," "global," "local,"
"indigenous," "subaltern," and so on).

A clear and necessary strategy provoked by Chen's convictions is to perform
comparative Cultural Studies work. While a seemingly banal strategy, doing com-

parative work is especially crucial under the name of globalization, so as to resist forms of universalism and particularism.

Much of Cultural Studies work around the world has been concerned with the problem of globalization, including the globalization of Cultural Studies. One such articulation by a Brazilian literary critic, Maria Elisa Cevasco, takes the global transportability of Cultural Studies as a positive opportunity to perform critical comparative thinking. For instance, in tracing the transnational appeal of Raymond Williams's work, Cevasco describes her borrowing of Williams in this way: "In peripheral countries like mine, conditions of living are undisguisedly marked by the contradictions of a devastatingly unfair system. Under such conditions, it is more difficult to leave aside the thought that intellectual work cannot keep any sense of human relevance unless it sets out to oppose existing relations. Hence the respect for work such as Williams'" (Cevasco, 2000: 433). Yet she does not stop there, for ultimately part of the struggle is over the relevance of Williams's critical humanism for Brazil. She continues:

> Reading Williams from Brazil enables me to trace the lines of convergence between the moment of the British New Left and a Brazilian tradition of cultural criticism, associated with the same University of Sao Paulo where all that reading was going on ... Take, for example, what went on in the faculty of Letters: literary criticism was to view literature not only as another import from elsewhere – the place which issued the standards that everything had to achieve so as to "exist" in the so-called civilized world – but ... analyses of literary works were to be viewed as potent means of discovering and interpreting Brazilian reality. (2000: 434–5)

Practicing Cultural Studies for Cevasco (and by extension, for many other Third World intellectuals), then, has the effect of "counteract[ing] the seemingly endless proliferation of particularisms and random difference that marked much contemporary cultural theory, and show[ing] that different projects were determined by the same world order, which helps explain their structural similarities" (2000: 436). One of the advantages of opening up the space for international Cultural Studies, as this anthology is attempting to do, is therefore to cultivate the ground for comparisons over *structured* differences (rather than random differences) under the conditions of globalization. But of course to do that means that we need to embark on a critical project that can satisfy two interrelated necessities: (a) the need to rediscover neglected voices and (b) the need to challenge the constructed singular origin of Cultural Studies.

A story was told about an occasion when, during an International Congress of the Latin American Studies Association, Néstor García Canclini, a well-known Mexican cultural theorist and public intellectual today, was asked whether his book *Hybrid Cultures* (1995) was ever influenced by Homi Bhabha's work. Canclini answered that he had not read Bhabha at that time. It remains doubtful, as the story tries to indicate, whether Bhabha was at any time asked about the influence of Canclini on his work.

Daniel Mato, of the Universidad Central de Venezuela, told this story as part of his effort to topple the monolingual and monodiscursive tendencies of Cultural Studies, which according to him, conflates the diasporic with the indigenous. As a result, it continues to misrecognize critical intellectual work from Latin America as "Latin American Cultural Studies." The Bhabha–Canclini "encounter," as it were, illustrates an important lesson for a critical international Cultural Studies: a diasporic voice wedged in a western Cultural Studies institution and an indigenous voice active in a Third World Cultural Studies practice tell very different stories, about such things as "hybrid cultures" or any other business. Mato argues that whether or not any of the local intellectual voices concerned with issues of culture and power can be appropriated as Cultural Studies from Latin America, remains a matter of strategic articulation.

Mato's position is similar to Chen's, for both are concerned with finding ways to decolonize Cultural Studies. Mato's strategy is twofold. First, through redefining Cultural Studies work across Latin America as critical intellectual social movements, Mato offers key exemplary figures who have developed their work independently of those initiatives in the English-speaking world, but which have shared with them some of their most significant characteristics. He offers a long list of Latin American intellectual figures as examples, e.g. besides Canclini, Rex Nattleford (Jamaican), Jesus Martin Barbero (Mexican), Manuel Garreton (Chilean), Lourdes Arizpe (Mexican), Gustavo Lins Ribeiro (Brazilian), Gioconda Espina (Venezuelan), Ana Maria Ochoa (Colombia), Angel Quintero Rivera (Puerto Rico), and so on. Under the name of *Estudios Culturales*, their work takes the framework that "[f]irst, Latin America doesn't exist, at least not a sort of more or less homogenous unit; and second 'Latin American Cultural Studies' as a field does not exist in Latin America" (Mato, 2000).

Mato's second strategy is to attack the constructed singular "origin" of Cultural Studies. What we need, he implies, is to write alternative genealogies. He cites Jesus Martin Barbero from Mexico as saying, "I did not begin to speak of culture because of ideas that came from abroad. It was reading the work of [Jose] Marti, and [Jose Maria] Arguedas that I discovered [the significance of] culture, and with it the process of communication that I had to study. I did not think of the media, the media were there: in the parties ['fiesta'], at home, in the 'cantina,' in the stadium . . . We had done Cultural Studies well before this label appeared" (Barbero cited in Mato, 2000). Canclini too has stated, "I became involved in Cultural Studies before I realized this is what it was called" (cited in Mato, 2000). Similarly, some years ago, in an effort to argue for the specificity of Cultural Studies in Australia, John Frow and Meaghan Morris also provided an alternative genealogy:

> Our first encounter with a "culture and society" approach in the late 1960s came not from reading Raymond Williams but from attending WEA [Workers Educational Association] summer schools on film run at Newport Beach in Sydney by John Flaus. Flaus works as a teacher in university and adult education contexts, as a critic who uses radio as fluently as he writes for magazines, and as an actor in a variety of media from experimental film to TV drama and commercials . . . we can say that Flaus (like

Sylvia Lawson) helped to create a constituency for the project of Cultural Studies as well as train a generation of film and media critics. Yet his work, along with the socially mixed but intensely familial urban subculture and small journals networks which sustained it (both of which were historically deeply-rooted in the inner-city life of Sydney and Melbourne), has been erased from those Australian accounts of Cultural Studies which take bearings from the British tradition – and then pose problems for application. (Frow & Morris, 1993: xxvi)

That the alternative reference points mentioned by Barbero, Mato, Canclini, Frow, and Morris are relevant to a critical internationalist Cultural Studies is obvious, but significant. However, the current state of knowledge is that these are largely occluded reference points. It's time that a pluralization of Cultural Studies, including its varied intellectual inheritances, be brought to light.

Whether it is about combating academic imperialism, performing critical comparisons, or rediscovering alternative traditions, Cultural Studies need to be inclusive of a wide array of diverse speaking positions. At the risk of reductivism, let us outline some of these speaking positions that inhabit and move across the international sphere of Cultural Studies:

1   The canonical speaking positions, either from the metropoles or from the peripheries;
2   The alternative local, contextually specific position lodged in an indigenous intellectual tradition;
3   The alternative local, contextually specific position framed in a national intellectual tradition, or one lodged in a nationalist tradition;
4   The alternative local position couched in an "east–west" comparative framework (thereby possibly redeploying an anachronistic, outdated, Cold War framework);
5   The alternative local position lodged in a regional, comparative framework asserting regional alliances (thereby possibly redeploying the "triumphalist" rhetorics of such entities as ASEAN or EU);
6   The subaltern position that critiques either one or both of the hegemony of western modernity and local nationalist modernity;
7   The relocalizing speaking position after encountering and interacting with the metropole (with the possible variety of localist positions mentioned above);
8   The diasporic speaking position situated in the metropole but concerned with issues at the periphery, with or without a critique of the hegemony of the metropole;
9   The nomadic speaking position that performs critiques of alterity and difference on a continuous basis, with no privileging of any form of particularism.

What is clear in this list of speaking positions that have appeared in Cultural Studies around the world is the condition of tension between positionality as well as the condition of unknowability discussed above. These positions embody a sense of geographical and politico-intellectual tension (e.g. between universalism and particularism, metropole and periphery, nationalist and internationalist, internationalist and local internationalist, and so on). It is within such conditions of tension that we are arguing for the proper space for a critical international Cultural Studies. It is through these possible forms of critique that we name the "*postcolonial predicament of Cultural Studies*" (which is different from "postcolonial Cultural Studies"). To paraphrase Stuart Hall, it is when Cultural Studies is dislocated that some of the openness to cultural politics that underlies it can be recovered, like a "rush of cultural/political blood to the head" (cited in Chen, 1996: 407). What we have here, then, isn't a book that captures all possible speaking positions, once and for all. We are not interested in producing a volume that positions itself as "World Cultural Studies" (cf. the pitfalls of the Norton Anthologies on World Literature; see Hassan, 2000). We resist the multiculturalist logic that fantasizes about a supermarket book along the line of "The United Colors of Cultural Studies." What we have is a book that, through a reasonable and careful sampling of different works representing a variety of speaking positions, would clear a space for a research, resource, and teaching text that can illuminate the necessary tensions and incommensurabilities across area-based Cultural Studies. What this does is to help locate what Lawrence Grossberg calls the "complexly determined and determining contexts" of cultural practices (1996: 141).

Significant in our goal is that we are not interested in producing a "definitive" volume that pretends to offer a totalizing coverage. Rather, we see this clearing of space as a modest beginning, as a way to whet the appetite of Cultural Studies scholars and teachers to begin to discuss and use a broader canvas of work. This is therefore meant as a resource book and a kind of textbook. The chapters to be included will infer for the readers (a) some of the paths of development of Cultural Studies in various locations under specific local intellectual traditions; (b) key exemplars; (c) key problematics in the practice of Cultural Studies in the locations concerned; and/or (d) how these works contribute to a "decentering" of Cultural Studies. Regarding the scope and organization of the anthology, our thinking has been to stay away from geographical sections – too simplistic and insufficiently dynamic, and too laden with massive political flaws (e.g. over the question of "equity of coverage," and so on). Rather, we shall have topical sections, with coverage of regional works within each section. Such coverage will have flexibility depending on actual selections from as many parts of the world as possible. The principle of selection here is to find exemplary, and not representative, works. We have selected a set of broad thematics for the book and invited section editors who are knowledgeable about international works to make a selection based on the principle of exemplarity – and not representativeness. Some of these section editors may work and reside in North America, but their locations of choice for their work (and implied professional trajectories) should not be viewed as a deficit to the project. Each editor has provided an introduction to their section. The sections (or parts) in this book are:

- Technocultures (edited by J. Macgregor Wise)
- Performance and Culture (edited by Della Pollock)

- Gender and Sexuality (edited by Cindy Patton)
- Media Production and Consumption (edited by Toby Miller)
- Popular Practices (edited by John Nguyet Erni)
- Race, Ethnicity, and Nation (edited by Wimal Dissanayake)
- Visual Cultures (edited by Dominic Pettman)
- Global Diasporas (edited by Ping-hui Liao)
- Cities and the Urban Imaginary (edited by Ackbar Abbas)

Moving between and across different speaking positions – some of which are mentioned above – the section editors present their own take on what "internationalizing Cultural Studies" means. Let us highlight some of their perspectives here. For instance, Cindy Patton reminds us that with *or without* Cultural Studies, critical intellectual works that bear a different frame of reference than the Euro-American coordinates often cohabit with the postcolonial critique. It is therefore not Cultural Studies *per se*, Patton hints, but the broad and dispersed project of cultural decolonization around the world that shapes many critical initiatives, small and large, that can be referred to as Cultural Studies. Similarly, J. Macgregor Wise warns us about the desire of looking for alternatives. He argues that this desire often leads to a fetishization of the other, and therefore blinds us to cultural traffic, including the trafficking of Cultural Studies works. What we need is a more dynamic understanding of the "international." Della Pollock emphasizes that the "inter/national" is a product and struggle of performance, i.e. of strategic evocations of the "inter" and the "national" through rituals, body politics, memories, and other violent acts. The "inter" and the "national" often trouble each other; hence a volatile frontier for Cultural Studies.

One of the important sites of this volatile encounter in the inter/national sphere today is cross-border cultural labor. Toby Miller maintains that labor issues – the substance of Marxian internationalism in the first place – cut across the entire chain of cultural production, distribution, and consumption, prompting him to reassess the current state of media studies within Cultural Studies. An internationalist Cultural Studies of the media, Miller argues, must move away from textual obsessions and engage with the spatial and temporal circuit of cultural labor that links different locales in uneven connections, along with habitats, tastes, cultural policies, and so on around the globe.

Together, 44 chapters are included in this anthology, representing diverse works about – and many hailing from – India, Mexico, Berlin, Taiwan, South Africa, Hong Kong, St. Petersburg, Egypt, Palestine, Toronto, Italy, the US, Cambodia, Japan, Argentina, the UK, and Nigeria. Ultimately, we hope this anthology will be taken up as a resource – and a symbolic space – that brings together transnationally transportable and contextually specific works in Cultural Studies from diverse locales and intellectual traditions. Several transnational Cultural Studies academic groups have been formed to overcome Cultural Studies' Anglo- and Eurocentrism, such as the Public Culture groups interested in the studies of alternative modernities, the Inter-Asia group, the Traces group, and the Latin American Working Group on Globalization, Culture and Social Transformations.

In addition, discussions and debates over the recent establishment of an International Association of Cultural Studies have been active for a number of years. This anthology does not only testify to the significance and rapidity of these developments, it also contributes a tangible resource and reference book to assist in further opening up the critical intellectual space for the international future of Cultural Studies. With this in mind, we want to proceed with a few important axiomatic assumptions that underline the conception of this anthology.

## ■ Five Axioms for a "Critical International Cultural Studies" ■

*Axiom 1: Critical international Cultural Studies is a political and intellectual intervention into a state of unevenness in the flow and impact of knowledge.*

This intervention involves an effort to *renarrativize* the foundational assumptions behind the "canonical" work in Cultural Studies, so as to encourage a new articulation between "the west and the rest," the universal and the particular.

*Axiom 2: Concomitantly, in its effort to locate international work, critical international Cultural Studies must render visible the nationalist assumptions behind nation-based and area-based work.*

Even critical theorists committed to internationalizing Cultural Studies tend to romanticize the periphery's perspectives, forgetting about the diffused hegemony that governs local traditions. Often, the nation-state is the most powerful chauvinistic enunciator of the hegemonic logic, producing its own system of power through a triumphalist denouncing of western modernity. Many voices, such as those of Canclini, Chen, and Mato, have already laid the ground for countering the political and epistemological power assumed by the nation-state. Such voices will have to be made more visible.

*Axiom 3: Translation, whether formal or informal, conscious or unconscious, is a necessary but complex political component in the performance of critical international Cultural Studies.*

Put simply, we need skillful translators. The formal practice of linguistic translation is itself a testimony to the historically unequal relations between Anglophonic and Francophonic Cultural Studies on the one hand and Cultural Studies written in other languages on the other hand. By positioning English/French as languages to translate *from*, and rarely languages to translate *to*, the normative practice of translation already calls attention to the incommensurability of different systems/ spaces of knowledge. Yet another politics of translation exists at a more diffused but no less practical level, which concerns the relaying, citation, absorption, paraphrasing, and recontextualization of theories into diverse regions of the world. Implicit in this second practice of translation is a politics of "transplanted authority" through which local works struggle for legitimacy through a borrowed canon.

*Axiom 4: The pragmatics and logistics of a critical international Cultural Studies are daunting, but listening to each other is a crucial first step.*

A decentering of Cultural Studies requires multiple levels of coordination and experimentation, including the overlapping tasks of (a) engendering a dialogical spirit and actual opportunities for conversation; (b) building a system of regular and even exchange of works; (c) developing and sustaining cross-border collaborative projects; (d) facilitating the actual visibility of diverse local and regional works through the publishing industry; and (e) altering and expanding pedagogical curricula and reading lists. In these endeavors, speech is secondary to the listening and reading faculty, because more than speech, listening and reading summon a space of interaction.

*Axiom 5: Critical international Cultural Studies takes situated optimism.*

It requires a new "imagined community" that is more performative and experimental than we have seen. Situated optimism is built upon imagining the conditions of possibility, seeing that a critical internationalism in Cultural Studies – as a contested terrain – is worth struggling over.

REFERENCES

Barthes, Roland (1982). *Empire of Signs*. Trans. Richard Howard. London: Cape.

Birch, David (2000). Transnational Cultural Studies: What price globalisation? *Social Semiotics* 10(2): 141–56.

Cevasco, Maria Elisa (2000). Whatever happened to Cultural Studies: Notes from the periphery. *Textual Practice* 14(3): 433–8.

Chen, Kuan-Hsing (1996). Cultural studies and the politics of internationalization: An interview with Stuart Hall. In David Morley and Kuan-Hsing Chen (eds.), *Stuart Hall: Critical Dialogues in Cultural Studies*. New York: Routledge, 392–408.

Chen, Kuan-Hsing (2000). The imperialist eye: The cultural imaginary of a subempire and a nation-state. *Positions: East Asia Cultures Critique* 8(1): 9–76.

Cultural Studies Listserv: www.cas.usf.edu/communication/rodman/cultstud/.

Desmond, Jane C. and Dominguez, Virginia R. (1996). Resituating American Studies in a critical internationalism. *American Quarterly* 48(3): 475–90.

García Canclini, Néstor (1995). *Hybrid Cultures: Strategies for Entering and Leaving Modernity*. Trans. Christopher L. Chiappari and Silvia L. López. Minneapolis: University of Minnesota Press.

Grossberg, Lawrence (1994). Something is happening here and you don't know what it is, do you, Mr. Jones? In David Birch (ed.), *Cultural Studies in the Asia Pacific*, a special double issue of *Southeast Asian Journal of Social Science* 22(1–2): v–x.

Grossberg, Lawrence (1996). Toward a genealogy of the state of Cultural Studies. In Cary Nelson and Dilip Gaonkar (eds.), *Disciplinarity and Dissent in Cultural Studies*. New York: Routledge, 131–48.

Hassan, Wail (2000). World literature in the age of globalization: Reflections on an anthology. *College English* 63(1): 38–47.

Lee, Benjamin (1995). Critical internationalism. *Public Culture* 7(3): 559–92.

Lévi-Strauss, Claude (1976). *Tristes Tropiques*. Trans. John and Doreen Weightman. Harmondsworth: Penguin Books.

Mato, Daniel (2000). Towards a transnational dialogue and context specific forms of transnational collaboration: Recent studies on culture and power in Latin America, and what our English speaking colleagues call Cultural Studies. Plenary Speech at the Third Crossroads Conference in Cultural Studies, University of Birmingham, UK, July (www.crossroads-conference.org/2000/Daniel_mato_speech.html).

Nietzsche, Friedrich (1956/1990). *The Birth of Tragedy; and, The Genealogy of Morals*. Trans. Francis Golffing. New York: Anchor Books.

Stratton, Jon and Ang, Ien (1996). On the impossibility of a global Cultural Studies: "British" Cultural Studies in an "international" frame. In David Morley and Kuan-Hsing Chen (eds.), *Stuart Hall: Critical Dialogues in Cultural Studies*. New York: Routledge, 361–91.

Striphas, Ted (1998). Cultural studies' institutional presence: A resource and guide. *Cultural Studies* 12(4).

# Part I

## Technocultures

# Introduction

## J. Macgregor Wise[1]

The range of work that could fall under the title "Technoculture" is potentially quite broad, encompassing all forms of culture that are somewhat technologically intensive. Technology itself can be thought of broadly, as Vandana Shiva does in her essay (chapter 2), as "ways of doing," which would make "technoculture" quite broad indeed. But as an academic discourse, technoculture is restricted to narrower views of technology. For example, the germinal book *Technoculture* (1991), edited by Constance Penley and Andrew Ross, tends to focus on communication technologies (pornographic Japanese computer software, popular video, cyberpunk, popular music, the mediated discourse of reproduction and also of AIDS treatment, and so on), and Donna Haraway's notion of the cyborg (which, though it is fairly flexible in its concerns, is usually about certain forms of advanced technology, computers, and prosthetics rather than looms and shovels). Kevin Robins and Frank Webster, in their book *Times of the Technoculture: From the Information Society to the Virtual Life* (1999), narrow the range of work even more to refer to computer-mediated communication technologies such as the internet. Indeed, it is in this latter sense that technoculture is most often understood in the western academy. Technoculture and cyberculture become synonymous terms.

The purpose of this selection is to re-broaden our sense of technoculture by addressing alternative discourses about "ways of doing" that speak to different concerns, and perhaps do not assume (or do not take uncritically) a certain level and type of prevalent technology. Wired into our offices on well-connected college campuses, it is easy to forget that the level of connectivity and technology that one may be used to is not common to all either nationally or globally. In short, I would want to broaden the idea of technoculture so that we aren't simply looking at the role of computers and the internet in contemporary society, but at a variety of ways of doing in everyday life. This is not to say that we should abandon work on computers and the internet (indeed, much more critical international work needs to be done in this area[2]), but rather that these are not the only technologies that we should be looking at.[3]

In what has proven to be a remarkably generative essay, Arjun Appadurai addresses the process of globalization in terms of the disjunctions between "five dimensions of global cultural flows that can be termed (a) *ethnoscapes*, (b) *mediascapes*, (c) *technoscapes*, (d) *financescapes*, and (e) *ideoscapes*" (1996: 33). The flow most germane to our discussion here is that of the technoscape. "By *technoscape*, I mean the global configuration, also ever fluid, of technology and the fact that technology, both high and low, both mechanical and informational, now moves at high speeds across various kinds of previously impervious boundaries" (1996: 34). The global *flow* of technology is obviously an important dimension of critical Cultural Studies of technology. Such flows could be that of technologies of colonialist nation-building (for example, railways in India and Africa), of economic exploitation (sneaker factories in southeast Asia, sweatshops in Central America), or other more ambiguous movements of technology like that of computer hardware and software globally, or even karaoke technologies across southeast Asia. Such global flows of technology have been researched under the ostensibly benign term "technology transfer," a seemingly apolitical, technocratic body of work. More commonly such flows occur under the heading of "development," a problematic term with a contentious 50-year history. Historically the term has come to be associated with the imposition of western technologies (farming techniques and equipment, water management, electrification, communication technology, and so forth) on relatively impoverished countries with the goal of enabling these countries to "develop" so that they can be just like the industrialized west. The term has thus become associated with (neo- and post-) colonialism as well as discourses on nationalism (for example in the context of India, see the work of Ashis Nandy and also Sundaram, 2000).[4] But along with Ashis Nandy in his following essay (chapter 1), should we not ask: "Can one not go beyond shedding tears copiously over the misuse of modern science by wicked politicians, militarists and multinational corporations, and scrutinize the popular culture and philosophy of modern science?"

A first step in scrutinizing the popular culture of both science *and technology* is the recognition of the radical contextuality of these terms (*science, technology, culture*); that is to recognize the fact that such terms do not have universal, fixed meanings but have specific histories. We can think of concepts as having trajectories through cultural spaces, trajectories which will be different in different contexts. For example, in the North American context the term technology has been articulated to other concepts such as progress, efficiency, and profit. But in the context of India the term is articulated to nation, development, and science, so that perhaps "nothing is more distinctive about Indian modernity than the intense, highly charged relationship it embodies between science and politics" (Prakash, 1999: 11). In another example, the view that Japanese technology and production is an expression of Japanese culture (a view prevalent in Japan but also picked up in the west as a form of techno-orientalism, according to Morley & Robins, 1995) is a historical articulation of the post-Second World War era, as Tetsuo Najita (1989) argues. Prior to the Second World War, culture and technology were thought distinct: technology coming to mean western industrialization and culture thought to be a shrinking premodern site of creativity and resistance to technology. So technology and politics end up being articulated differently in the United States, India, and Japan. However, we also have to map the trajectories of western (North American and European) technology, science, and their accompanying philosophies, *across* India, Japan, and the rest of the world where, as noted above, these can be read as forms of imperialism.

Critical approaches to technology often seek alternatives to these colonizing machines, processes, and knowledges (which are seen as violent, inhumane, and destructive to the environment), and in doing so look to indigenous technologies based on alternative ethical, often religious, assumptions. Thus, E. F. Schumacher writes the germinal book for the alternative technology movement, *Small is Beautiful: Economics as if People Mattered* (1973), based on what Schumacher calls Buddhist Economics. Likewise, Arnold Pacey, in the influential book *The Culture of Technology* (1983), sets out an alternative value structure for technology also based on Buddhist principles. And Jerry Mander turns to Native American culture in his critique of western technology, *In the Absence of the Sacred: The Failure of Technology and the Survival of the Indian Nations* (1991). In seeking out such alternatives, we must be careful not to strip such principles of their context and history, mining the Other to solve our problems, and reinforcing orientalist assumptions about the Other as holistic, natural, primitive, or even as completely separate from the west. This is not to say that the above volumes are orientalist, but rather that this is a subtle danger with which they flirt. The search for alternatives often reifies the Other in an unchanging, uniform cultural context. As Nandy warns, "[t]hey see in such a culture not merely an alternative civilization, but also a negation of the dominant culture in their own societies" (1980: 14). The fetishization of the alternative as completely different, as completely outside the modern west, allows us to ignore commonalities, shared histories and values which muddy such clear dichotomies. In other words, our response to modernization cannot simply be to abandon the modern for something else. We (and this includes almost all of the world to greater or lesser extents) are for the foreseeable future entangled with the modern in ways that are complex, if not messy, and critiques must be posed from within this messy context.

It is impossible to survey or sample such broad-ranging work as discussed above in the space given to this section. And so rather than being representative (either in terms of regions discussed, disciplinary approaches, or technologies addressed) in these selections, I intend these selections to be generative of future work. The first three selections all focus on India, and we can see these authors build and respond to different aspects of Indian modernity. The first selection is by Ashis Nandy, a founding figure in south Asian Cultural Studies. This essay is an excerpt from his introduction to an edited volume on science, hegemony, and violence. In it he discusses the collapse of the distinction between science and technology and the use of science as a political tool in the hands of the nation-state. He provides the extended example of nuclear scientists in India to illustrate on the one hand the nondemocratic nature of the culture of modern science and technology, but on the other "the global problem of knowledge and power in our times." The selection ends with his challenge to generate new knowledges, in some cases by mobilizing traditional systems of knowledge still struggling to exist today, against the hegemony of modern science (and technology). Vandana Shiva, a well respected and widely published physicist, philosopher, and activist, in her essay excerpted below, critiques the hegemony of modern science and technology from feminist and environmentalist perspectives. She discusses the colonization of Indian manufacture and later agriculture by national and international forces of development. In doing so she uncovers the real effects of the so-called Green Revolution which destroyed the diversity of local crops and farming techniques and made agriculture dependent on industrial seed, fertilizer, and pesticide companies. But at the core of these debates she places the controversial claim that life-forms can be owned and patented, which she sees as the industrialized nations claiming ownership of what had been communal indigenous seed, exploiting the poorer nations. Scientific and technological decisions, she concludes, need to be made with human rights and environmental responsibility as their core criteria, not profit. Ravi Sundaram, one of the founders of the Sarai New Media Collective in New Delhi (www.sarai.net), addresses the more recent turn of Indian modernity to the booming computer industry in India. Countering nationalistic, class-centered myths of India's technofuture, Sundaram focuses on the everyday realm of technology "recycling." Recycling refers to those practices of scrounging and building computer systems and networks well outside of the glare of the spotlight of multinational cyberculture. Often illegal, these practices create a "pirate electronic space" within India, a space not directly oppositional to modernity, not even organized or coherent in its purpose, but a space created out of necessity. As such, these pirate spaces open up as yet unrealized possibilities for resistance at the level of the everyday.

The final two essays chosen for this section present quite different means of addressing modern technoculture. The first, on Karaoke in east Asia, by Akiko Ōtake, a writer and essayist, and Shūhei Hosokawa, a historian of Japanese popular music, maps a specific technoscape: the diffusion of karaoke technology and practices from Japan to other countries in east Asia. In the longer essay from which this essay is excerpted, the authors trace local responses to karaoke in Taiwan, Hong Kong, China, Vietnam, Korea, and Okinawa. Our excerpt begins after these summaries, where the authors consider karaoke as a cultural technology that transforms public and private spaces. Karaoke becomes a point of articulation for local practices of leisure (singing in public), the distribution of Japanese technology, and discourses of Japanese modernity. The result is a regional globalization, called Asianization, a complex interchange of culture, technology, and music.

Our final essay is by Viktor Mazin, editor-in-chief of the journal *Kabinet*, and founding director of Freud's Dreams Museum, both located in St. Petersburg, Russia. Mazin's essay, written especially for this collection, sketches an approach to technoculture based on the disciplines of psychology and art which sees human beings as the result of the co-evolution of technology and psychology. As an example of work that contributes to this body of knowledge, Mazin describes a recent exhibit, called "The Electromirror," that took place at the Freud's Dreams Museum in January, 2002. In the end, Mazin argues, what we are facing is a "dissolution of man in its machine," made possible by contemporary technologies of digital hardware and pharmacology.

## NOTES

1   I need to thank a number of people who responded to my email queries on global technocultures. Some provided suggestions of scholars whose work would be relevant to this area, and with others I've been engaged in conversations on this topic both extended and brief, but all have stimulated my thinking and energized this project: Gayatri Chatterjee, Greg Elmer, Myungkoo Kang, Viktor Mazin, Mehdi Semati, David Silver, Jennifer Slack, Ravi Sundaram, Keyan Tomaselli, and Yukhiko Yoshida.
2   See, for example, the special issue of the journal *Third Text* on the Third Worldwide Web (Summer, 1999).
3   For a more extended discussion of contemporary Cultural Studies approaches to technology, see Slack & Wise, 2002.
4   More recently the term has been rearticulated to indicate grassroots-level activities to improve the quality of life for impoverished populations.

## REFERENCES

Appadurai, A. (1996). Disjuncture and difference in the global cultural economy. In *Modernity At Large: Cultural Dimensions of Globalization*. Minneapolis: University of Minnesota Press, 27–47.

Mander, J. (1991). *In the Absence of the Sacred: The Failure of Technology and the Survival of the Indian Nations*. San Francisco: Sierra Club Books.

Morley, D. and Robins, K. (1995). Techno-orientalism: Japan panic. In *Spaces of Identity: Global Media, Electronic Landscapes and Cultural Boundaries*. New York: Routledge, 147–73.

Najita, T. (1989). On culture and technology in postmodern Japan. In M. Miyoshi and H. D. Harootunian (eds.), *Postmodernism and Japan*. Durham, NC: Duke University Press, 3–20.

Nandy, A. (1980). *Alternative Sciences: Creativity and Authenticity in Two Indian Scientists*. New Delhi: Allied Publishers.

Pacey, A. (1983). *The Culture of Technology*. Cambridge, MA: MIT Press.

Penley, C. and Ross, A. (1991). *Technoculture*. Minneapolis: University of Minnesota Press.

Prakash, G. (1999). *Another Reason: Science and the Imagination of Modern India*. Princeton: Princeton University Press.

Robins, K. and Webster, F. (1999). *Times of the Technoculture: From the Information Society to the Virtual Life*. New York: Routledge.

Schumacher, E. F. (1973). *Small is Beautiful: Economics As If People Mattered.* New York: Harper & Row.

Slack, J. D. and Wise, J. M. (2002). Cultural studies and technology. In L. Lievrouw and S. Livingstone (eds.), *The Handbook of New Media.* London: Sage, 485–501.

Sundaram, R. (2000). Beyond the nationalist panopticon: The experience of cyberpublics in India. In J. T. Caldwell (ed.), *Electronic Media and Technoculture.* New Brunswick, NJ: Rutgers University Press, 270–94.

# 1

# Science as a Reason of State

## Ashis Nandy

The thinking person cannot but notice that since the Second World War, two new reasons of state have been added to the traditional one of national security. These are science and development. In the name of science and development one can today demand enormous sacrifices from, and inflict immense sufferings on, the ordinary citizen. That these are often willingly borne by the citizen is itself a part of the syndrome; for this willingness is an extension of the problem which national security has posed over the centuries.

Defying protests by (and to the mortification of) pacifists and anti-militarists, a significant proportion of ordinary citizens in virtually every country have consistently and willingly died for king and country. There are already signs that at least as large a proportion of citizens is equally willing to lay down their lives heroically for the sake of science and development. In 1985, one Japanese doctor praised the atomic bombing of Hiroshima and Nagasaki for the indirect benefits they have brought to Japan. In an election held soon after the gas tragedy in 1984, the affected citizenry of Bhopal returned the same regime to power that shared the responsibility for the disaster. Likewise, demands for new steel mills and large dams often come from the very regions and sectors in the third world which are most likely to be the first victims of industrialization.

What are the sources of such commitment to the development of science, and the science of development? Can one identify and challenge the philosophical and ideological framework within which the commitment is located? Can one not go beyond shedding tears copiously over the misuse of modern science by wicked politicians, militarists and multinational corporations, and scrutinize the popular culture and philosophy of modern science? May the sources of violence not lie partly in the nature of science itself? Is there something in modern science itself which makes it a human enterprise particularly open to co-optation by the powerful and the wealthy?

These questions have been with us ever since Archimedes devised new weapons for his city state with the hope that they would remain the monopoly of his country and not also become the property of the ungodly. But the questions had a different ring for a long, long time. From the halcyon days of Archimedes to the heady days of early colonialism, science was primarily an instrument, not an end; certainly not the end of any nation or state. Even the states which drew the most handsome economic dividends from the discoveries of modern science and technology, or justified global dominance by referring to their scientific and technological power – I have in mind the nineteenth century colonial powers – did not see science as a reason of state. The reader may remember popular anecdotes about colonial adventurers, or scientifically-minded explorers who sometimes scared off or impressed the natives of Asia and Africa with new forms of black magic based on the discoveries of modern science. The civilizing mission of colonialism thrived on this folklore of encounter between western science and savage superstitions. But in each such instance, it was science that was put to the use of the colonial state; the state was not put to the use of science.

The nature of science has since then changed, and so has the nature of human violence. [ ... ] It is the contention of [this essay] that these changes can be understood with reference to the mediatory role played by the modern nation-state, the invitation which the culture of modern science extends to state power to use scientific knowledge outside the reaches of the democratic process and, above all, the growth of institutionalized violence in place of the personalized, face-to-face, impassioned violence associated with traditional concepts of sacrifice and feuds.[1]

Ivan Illich has traced the contemporary idea of development to a speech President Harry S. Truman made in 1945.[2] Till then, the word 'development' had had other associations which had very little connection with what we understand by development today. But such was the latent social need for a concept akin to development that, once Truman gave it a new meaning, not only did it quickly acquire wide currency, it was also retrospectively applied to the history of social change in Europe during the previous three hundred odd years.

In a similar way, we can trace the idea of science as a reason of state to a speech made by President John F. Kennedy in 1962. The speech declared one of America's major national goals to be the scientific feat of putting a man on the moon. Though mega-science had already become an important concern of the state during the Second World War, science was, for the first time, projected in Kennedy's speech as a goal of a state and, one might add, as a substitute for conventional politics. A state for the first time on that occasion sought to out-rival another state not in the political or military arena, nor in sports, but in science redefined as dramatic technology. The formulation might have been older and might have been tried out haphazardly earlier but never had it been made so directly a part of the mainstream idiom of politics as in Kennedy's speech. Perhaps

Kennedy was reacting to the Russian claim that the Sputniks showed the superiority of the socialist system and, especially, that of 'scientific socialism'. Perhaps he was trying to strengthen his political image as a leader who could help American society to cope with the scientific age. Whatever the reason, for the first time Kennedy's speech showed that a wide enough political base had been built in a major developed society for the successful use of science as a goal of state and, perhaps, as a means of populist political mobilization. Spectacular science could be now used as a political plank within the United States in the ideological battle against ungodly communism.

Kennedy's speech had another implication. The boundary between science and technology had been softening for about two hundred years. The histories of science and technology could at one time be written separately. But since the early years of the Royal Society, modern scientists had intermittently been seeking legitimacy not only from the philosophical implications of their theories but also from the practical pay-offs of science. The process reached its symbolic culmination in Kennedy's concept of science – a concept which not merely incorporated technology; it gave spectacular technology the central place in science. The speech in fact anticipated the vision which occupies so much space in the popular culture of our day, namely, the image of a science which, by the beginning of the twenty-first century, will be coterminous with technology. By the mid-1980s the proportion of pure scientists to all scientists in the world had fallen to less than five per cent, and the proportion is reportedly falling at a faster rate now. The pure scientist today is an even rarer species than the scientist who does not participate in military research and development.

Yet, at the same time, we can be reasonably sure that the concept of pure science and the conceptual difference between science and technology will be carefully retained. It will be retained not because of the demands of the philosophers of science but because it is only by distinguishing between science and technology that all social criticism of science can continue to be deflected away from science towards technology. A shadowy, ethereal concept of science that has little to do with the real-life endeavours of practising scientists can then be politically defended as the pursuit of truth uncontaminated by human greed, violence and search for power.

The studies assembled in this volume [*Science, Hegemony, and Violence: A Requiem for Modernity*] have these two basic issues – science as a new justificatory principle, and science as technological intervention – as their points of theoretical departure. However, these issues also intersect with a cultural dimension: all the studies are by Indian scholars and have primarily the Indian experience as their backdrop. This is only partly due to the accident of having an Indian editor for this volume. I shall argue that things could hardly have been otherwise.

India has been a remarkable example of an open society in which, since the early years of independence, the political élites have deliberately chosen to see science as the responsibility of the state and have, at the same time, treated it as a sphere of knowledge which should be free from the constraints of day-to-day politics. Every society decides what content to give to its politics and what to keep out of politics. The Indian state, representing the wishes of a powerful section of the nationalist movement and being led in the early years of independence by Jawaharlal Nehru, a gentleman Fabian steeped in the nineteenth-century vision of human liberation through science, decided to keep the practice of science outside politics but ensured that the scientific estate had a direct, privileged access to the state. It was as a part of this 'double vision' that Nehru, the modern élites which gathered around him, and the Indian state began to build science as a major source of justification for the Indian state as well as for their political dominance. That the formula did not keep science out of politics but only introduced another kind of politics into science is one of those paradoxes which lie at the heart of the distinctive relationship between science and society in contemporary India.

Thus, [ ... ] the powers and freedoms that were given to nuclear scientists in India since the days of Homi Bhabha, India's first nuclear boss, were near-total. Firstly, nuclear scientists were freed from all financial constraints. The budget of the nuclear programme – the entire budget, not the budget devoted to research and development – was routinely pushed through parliament without any scrutiny whatsoever. And the expenditures – the entire expenditure, not only the expenditure on laboratories – were never publicly audited. [ ... ]

Secondly, nuclear scientists were given enormous scope for research if they moved out of the universities into special research institutions. While universities were starved of funds and allowed to decay, research institutions were richly funded. This might not have been a matter of deliberate policy but it certainly set a context to India's nuclear policy, because what scientists gained in research opportunities in the new institutions, they lost in personal political freedom. [ ... ]

Thirdly, once some of the finer minds of India were netted by the state in this manner and some of the less scrupulous among them were given access to power, the Indian nuclear programme could be safely handed over to the civilians; the army or the defence ministry did not need to be in the picture at all. The nuclear scientists could be their unofficial proxies. Thus, India's first nuclear explosion in 1974 was a civilian enterprise, with the army only playing second fiddle. Civilian scientists planned, initiated and executed the programme; the army and defence scientists played a peripheral role, providing organizational back-up, on-site security, and control or management of the villagers to be uprooted.

In fact, contrary to popular stereotypes, modern science or scientists in India have not been used by blood-thirsty generals, scheming politicians, and greedy businessmen. Rather, the science establishment, on its own initiative, has taken advantage of the anxieties about national security and the developmental aspirations of a new nation to gain access to power and resources. Not surprisingly, the record of mainstream scientists in India has been particularly poor in the matter of protecting democratic rights in the country. In fact, in recent years the privileged among Indian scientists have often been the most vigorous critics of civil rights groups struggling for protection against the hazards of a callous nuclear establishment.

I give the example of the Indian nuclear establishment not to make a scapegoat out of it but to draw attention to the manner in which the link between science and violence in India has been strengthened by forces within the culture of Indian science, forces which in other cultures of science in some other parts of the world have been either less visible or less powerful.

The curious case of the nuclearization of India has not one but three morals to it. First, as modern science gets more and more incorporated into technology, it necessarily has to be increasingly justified in terms of technology. The frequent exhortations to have a more 'scientific temper' (exhortations to which all Indians, but particularly the 'less civilized' traditional Indians, are subjected by the scientific and political establishments) and the repeated references to the scientific world-view as a philosophical venture in learned seminars in India are not taken seriously by 'normal' scientists (who do 'normal' science *à la* Thomas Kuhn), or by their political patrons and their admirers. For both, the slogan of the 'scientific temper' is a means of legitimizing their new-found status in Indian society. Both like to define the 'temper' as the spirit of technology and the instrumentalism which is an inescapable part of that spirit. The invocation of the 'temper' almost invariably goes with a negative reading of India's traditional cultures and ways of life, seen as impediments to a modern technological order, and with the search for uncritical legitimacy for all forms of technology – seen as an undifferentiated mass of knowledge, institutions and persons.

As a result, conspicuous technology has become gradually the official goal of science in India, as well as the main source of legitimacy for science among the Indian middle classes. Thanks to the media, government-controlled as well as uncontrolled, and thanks to the values propagated by the westernized education system, the Indian middle classes have come to see science as primarily spectacular technology. They expect this technology to allow the country to tackle its basic political and social problems and thus ensure the continued political domination of an apolitical, that is technocratic, modern élite over the decision-making process, defying the democratic system. This expectation partly explains why science is advertised and sold in India the way consumer products are sold in any market economy, and why it is sought to be sold by the Indian élites as a cure-all for the ills of Indian society.[3] Such a public consciousness moves from one euphoria to another. In the 1950s and 1960s, it was Atom for Peace, supposedly the final solution of all energy problems of India; in the '60s and '70s it was the Green Revolution, reportedly the patented cure for food shortages in the country; in the '70s and '80s it is Operation Flood, the talisman for malnutrition through the easy availability of milk for every poor household in the country. In this environment it does not matter whether the technology is innovative or replicative, moral or immoral, obsolete or new. For technology comes to represent an escape from the dirtyness of politics; it becomes an indicator of Brahminic purity, a form of social change which ensures a place in the sun for portions of the middle classes whom the democratic process otherwise tends to marginalize, an anxiety-binding agent in the public realm, and often a media-based exercise in public relations. That is why, as with nuclear science, the adaptations in India of decades-old western technologies are advertised and purchased as great leaps forward in science, even when such adaptations turn entire disciplines or areas of knowledge into mere intellectual machines for the adaptation, replication and testing of shop-worn western models which have often been given up in the west itself as too dangerous or as ecologically non-viable.

The second moral of the story is more disturbing. Because the concept of science in this model of scientific growth is that of the ultimate key to all problems facing the country, scientists subscribing to the model can lay claims to the charisma which in some other political cultures belongs exclusively to god-kings. In the process, scientists become one of the two ultimate sources of legitimacy for the Indian state among the middle classes – the others, as I indicated at the beginning, are development experts and experts on national security. These three kinds of specialists – the scientists, the developmentalists and the security experts – are the ones to assess and pass final judgement on Indian culture, on what is good in it and what is defective. Generally it turns out that what is good in the Indic civilization, according to these specialists, is exactly that which is good for modern science and what is defective in the civilization is exactly that which impedes modern science. Predictably, this presumption of a total fit between the needs of a good society and the needs of modern science leaves no scope for any assessment and evaluation of scientists by non-scientists, particularly by those rooted in the 'little cultures' of India. Nor does it give any scope for instituting controls on the scientific establishment through a competitive political process and democratic participation.[4]

The political asymmetry or inequality between the scientist and the laity is endorsed not only by the concept of expertise which dominates the culture of modern science globally, but also by a philosophy of science which allows the laity to criticize modern science only in terms of its use value, that is, its social and political deployment and not in terms of its end values, that is, the social and philosophical goals and assumptions built into the heart of the culture and the text of modern science. Even this limited criticism of the social and political relationships of science has to be ventured, to be audible to the modern world, in terms of the criteria specified by the dominant philosophy of modern science itself. Thus, a plethora of critical evaluations of the practice of modern science in recent times have ended up by arguing, rather pathetically, that they, the evaluations, are motivated more by the spirit of modern science than the normal practitioners of modern science themselves, that the criticisms are in fact congruent with the latest discoveries of post-Einsteinian physics, microbiology and post-Freudian social psychiatry. From Erich Fromm to Fritjof Capra to Maharishi Mahesh Yogi, it is roughly the same story.

The third moral of the story is even more painful. By the very nature of its instrumental-managerial orientation to Indian society, modern science has established a secure relationship with the philosophy and practice of development in India. Indian developmentalists are now faced with the obvious fact that the developmental vision cannot be universalized, for the earth just does not have the resources for the entire world to attain the consumption levels of the developed west. It does not have such resources now, nor will it have them in the distant future. The developmentalists, therefore, have a vested interest in linking up with the drive for theatrical science to create the illusion of spectacular development which, in essence, consists of occasional dramatic demonstrations of technological capability based on a standard technology-transfer model. Under this model, highly visible short-term technological performance in small areas yields nation-wide political dividends. This model includes a clearly delimited space for 'dissent', too. While some questions are grudgingly allowed about the social consequences of technology – about modern agronomy, large dams, hydel projects, new dairy technology, modern health care systems, space flights, Antarctica expeditions, et cetera – no question can be raised about the nature of technology itself.

Roughly similar links have grown between science and the élite perceptions of the security needs of India. Like other third-world societies such as Brazil, India too has begun to show a high growth rate and export potentials in defence-related industries and, like some developed societies such as France and the United States, India, too, is perfectly willing to make security anxieties a central plank of its political identity.

Apparently, what Robert Jungk says about nuclear energy holds good for modern science in general.[5] Namely, that modern science has the capacity within it to sustain a culture of science which is incompatible with democratic governance as well as with the democratic rights of those who are turned into the subjects of modern science and technology. In India at least, the culture of modern science *has* built an inverse relationship with the culture of open politics and has began to produce new forms of secrecy, centralization, disinformation and authoritarian organizational structures. Nuclear science in this respect has only been true to the overall cultural design of modern science and technology in the country.[6]

Science, I have said, has become a new reason of state. The state and its various arms can kill, maim or exploit in the name of science. Science in turn, as a *raison d'état*, can inflict violence in the name of national security or development and – this is the change – increasingly under its own flag and for its own sake. There are now scientists, political leaders and intellectuals in India – as in other similarly placed societies – who are perfectly willing to close the polity if that ensures faster scientific growth. And there are now scientifically-minded Indian citizens who are as willing to sacrifice millions of ordinary Indians to advance the cause of science and science-based development.

In such a world, the intellectual challenge is to build the basis of resistance to militarization and organized violence, firstly by providing a better understanding of how modern science or technology is gradually becoming a substitute for politics in many societies, and secondly by defying the middle-class consensus against bringing the estate of science within the scope of public life or politics.[ ... ]

Contemporary India, by virtue of its bicultural experience, manages to epitom-ize the global problem of knowledge and power in our times. There is a continuity between the Indian experience of an increasingly violent modern science, en-croaching upon other traditions of knowledge and social life, and the western experience with modern science as the dominant cultural principle resisting the emergence of new cultures of knowledge. There is a continuity between the experiences of the two civilizations even at the level of élite and middle-class responses to the situation. The modern Indian élites and middle classes have a fear of the present, explained away, with the help of some forms of history, as only a fear of the past. The western élites and middle classes have a fear of the future, explained away, with the help of some forms of futurology, as only the fear of a future unrestrained by or disjunctive with the present. Evidently, the élites of both worlds have in common the ambition of containing the future by controlling the present politics of knowledge. The former fear the process of democratization of India which is marginalizing them; the latter fear the possibility of future democratization of the world which will marginalize *them*. And, as if to spite those who pin their hopes in matters such as this on generational changes, on the expectation that the youth will liberate them from the certitudes of the past, in India the emerging middle-class élites seem to nurture the same hope of substituting science for politics, because politics for them is irrational and messy, and science is rational, neat and controllable. Meanwhile in the west a project takes shape which seeks to derive all politics from science for roughly the same set of reasons.

Put simply, the challenge for the movements for alternative science and technology in the west is to generate new knowledge in the future by participating in the politics of knowledge today. But to participate meaningfully in the politics of knowledge today, they must take into account and build upon the ongoing intellectual and political battles in societies where alternatives, or at least alternative baselines, exist in the present, in the form of traditional systems of knowledge that have survived and are struggling against the hegemony of modern science. In India, traditional systems of knowledge may not have provided ready-made solutions to the present crisis of knowledge and power, but they have certainly become a part of the repertoire of the dissenting movements of science. Seen thus, the crisis of science in India becomes, for all practical purposes, coterminous with the crisis of science globally. And the crisis of global science, in turn, becomes an extension of the Indian experience with modern science over the last 150 years.

## NOTES

1 Veena Das and Ashis Nandy, 'Violence, Victimhood and the Language of Silence', *Contributions to Indian Sociology*, 1985, 19, pp. 177–94. Also Ashis Nandy, 'Science, Authoritarianism and Culture: On the Scope and Limits of Isolation Outside the Clinic', in *Traditions, Tyranny and Utopias: Essays in the Politics of Awareness* (New Delhi: Oxford University Press, 1987), pp. 95–126.
2 Ivan Illich, 'The Delinking of Peace and Development', *Gandhi Marg*, 1981, 3, pp. 257–65.
3 For instance, P. N. Haksar et al., 'A Statement on Scientific Temper' (Bombay: Nehru Centre, 1981).
4 See a brief discussion of this in Nandy, 'Science, Authoritarianism and Culture'.

5   On nuclear energy see, for instance, Praful Bidwai, 'Atomic Power on the Run', *The Times of India*, 13–15 October 1986; and Dhirendra Sharma (ed.), *The Indian Atom: Power and Proliferation* (New Delhi: Philosophy and Social Action, 1986). On modern agronomy see, for example, the assessments by J. K. Bajaj, 'Green Revolution: A Historical Perspective', *PPST Bulletin*, 1982, 2, pp. 87–112; and Claude Alvares, 'The Great Gene Robbery', *The Illustrated Weekly of India*, 23 March 1986. On dairy technology see Claude Alvares (ed.), *Another Revolution Fails* (Delhi: Ajanta, 1984); Shanti George, *Operation Flood: An Appraisal of Current Indian Dairy Policy* (New Delhi: Oxford University Press, 1986); and 'Faulty Lactometers', *Economic and Political Weekly*, 31 May and 7 June 1986, 21, pp. 963–71, 1020–8.

6   See note 5 above. Also see Sharma, *India's Nuclear Estate*; Ashis Nandy, 'The Bomb', *The Illustrated Weekly of India*, 4 August 1985; Jatinder K. Bajaj, 'The Bhopal Tragedy: The Responsibility of the Scientific Community', and Sunil Sahasrabudhey, 'Bhopal: Science Must Share the Blame', *PPST Bulletin*, 1985, 5, pp. 6–14, 25–9; Shiv Visvanathan 'Bhopal: The Imagination of a Disaster', *Alternatives*, 1986, 11, pp. 147–65.

# 2

# Biotechnological Development and the Conservation of Biodiversity

## Vandana Shiva

In the dominant paradigm, technology is seen as being above society both in its structure and evolution, in its offering technological fixes, and in its technological determinism. It is seen as a source of solutions to problems that lie in society, and is rarely perceived as a source of new social problems. Its course is viewed as self-determined. In periods of rapid technological transformation, it is assumed that society and people must adjust to change, instead of technological change adjusting to the social values of equity, sustainability and participation.

There is, however, another perspective which treats technological change as a process that is shaped by and serves the priorities of whoever controls it. In this perspective, a narrow social base of technological choice excludes human concerns and public participation. The interests of that base are protected in the name of sustaining an inherently progressive and socially neutral technology. On the other hand, a broader social base protects human rights and the environment by widening the circle of control beyond the current small group.

The emergence of the new biotechnologies brings out these two tendencies dramatically. The technocratic approach to biotechnology portrays the evolution of the technology as self-determined and views social sacrifice as a necessity. Human rights, including the right to a livelihood, must therefore be sacrificed for property rights that give protection to the innovation processes. Ironically, a process based on the sacrifice of human rights continues to be projected as automatically leading to human well-being.

The sacrifice of people's rights to create new property rights is not new. It has been part of the hidden history of the rise of capitalism and its technological structures. The laws of private property which arose during the fifteenth and sixteenth centuries simultaneously eroded people's common rights to the use of forests and pastures while creating the social conditions for capital accumulation through industrialization. The new laws of private property were aimed at protecting individual rights to property as a commodity, while destroying collective rights to commons as a basis of sustenance. The Latin root of private property, *privare*, means 'to deprive'. The shift from common rights to private property rights is therefore a general social and political precondition for exclusivist technologies to take root in society. The scene for such a shift is now being set to allow the emergence of a biotechnical era of corporate and industrial growth.

In the narrow view, science and technology are conventionally accepted as what scientists and technologists produce, and development is accepted as what science and technology produce. Scientists and technologists are in turn taken to be that sociological category formally trained in Western science and technology, either in institutions or organizations in the West, or in Asian institutions miming the paradigms of the West. These tautological definitions are unproblematic if one leaves out people, especially poor people, and if one ignores the cultural diversity and distinct civilizational histories of our planet. Development, in this view, is taken as synonymous with the introduction of Western science and technology in non-Western contexts. The magical identity is development = modernization = Westernization.

In a wider context, where science is viewed as 'ways of knowing' and technology as 'ways of doing', all societies have had their diverse and distinct science and technology systems on which development has been based. Technologies or systems of technology bridge the gap between nature's resources and human needs. Systems of knowledge and culture provide the framework for the perception and utilization of natural resources. Two changes occur in this shift of definition of science and technology – they are no longer viewed as uniquely Western but as a plurality associated with all cultures and civilizations. And a particular science and technology does not automatically translate into development everywhere. Ecologically and economically inappropriate science and technology can become causes of, not solutions to underdevelopment. Ecological inappropriateness is a mismatch between the ecological processes of nature which renew life support systems and the resource demands and impact of technological processes, which can lead to higher withdrawals of natural resources or higher additions of pollutants than ecological limits allow. In such cases they contribute to underdevelopment through the destruction of ecosystems.

Economic inappropriateness is the mismatch between the needs of society and the requirements of a technological system. Technological processes create demands for raw materials and markets, and control over these becomes essential to the politics of technological change.

Lack of theoretical cognition of the two ends of the technological process, its beginning in natural resources and its end in basic human needs, has created the current paradigm of economic and technological development which demands the increasing withdrawal of natural resources and generates the increasing addition of pollutants, while marginalizing and dispossessing increasing numbers from the productive process. These characteristics of contemporary scientific industrial development are the primary causes of current ecological, political and economic crises. The combination of ecologically disruptive scientific and technological systems in terms of resource-use efficiency and capability for basic needs satisfaction has created conditions that increasingly propel society towards ecological and economic instability, in the absence of a rational and organized response to arrest and curtail these destructive tendencies.

The introduction of ecologically and economically inappropriate science and technology leads to underdevelopment instead of development. Modernization based on resource-hungry processes materially impoverishes communities which use those resources for survival, either directly, or through their ecological function. Growth under these conditions does not ensure development for all, but creates underdevelopment for those affected negatively by resource diversion or destruction. Conflicting demands on resources thus lead to economic polarization through growth. The growing extent of popular ecology movements is a symptom of this polarization and a reminder that for many people natural resources play a vital role in survival. Their diversion to other uses or their destruction through other uses therefore creates increasing impoverishment and an increasing threat to survival.

Underdevelopment is commonly projected as a state created by the absence of modern Western science and technology systems. However, poverty and underdevelopment are, more often than not, conditions created by the externalized and invisible costs of resource-intensive and resource-destructive technological processes which support the livelihood of millions.

The experience of all industrial revolutions illustrates how poverty and underdevelopment are created as an integral part of the whole process of contemporary growth and development, in which gains accrue to one section of the society or nation and the costs, economic or ecological, are borne by the rest.

The first industrialization was based on the mechanization of work, with its focus on the textile industry. The second industrialization was based on the chemicalization of processes in agriculture and other sectors, and the emerging third industrialization is based on the engineering of the life process. We can draw some lessons from history about how technological change initiated by a special interest brings development to that interest group while creating underdevelopment for others.

## ▪ Colonization and the Spinning Wheel ▪

The mechanization of textile manufacture was the leading technological transformation of the first industrial revolution. By the time that technological innovations made their full impact on the British textile industry in the early nineteenth century, England had gained full political control over the resources and markets of its colonies, including India. India until then had been a leading producer and exporter of textiles in the world market. The industrialization of England was based in part on the de-industrialization of India. The development of England was based in part on India's underdevelopment. It is no coincidence that India's independence movement was based in large measure on seeking liberation from the control over Third World resources and people that were part of the process of Europe's industrialization. Two symbols of India's independence struggle were the Champaran *satyagraha* and the *charkha*. The Champaran *satyagraha* was a peaceful revolt against the forced cultivation of indigo as a dye for the British textile industry. The *charkha* or spinning wheel was the technological alternative that created self-reliance instead of dependence, and generated livelihoods instead of destroying them.

While the rapid technological innovations in the British textile industry were made possible only through the prior control over resources and the market, the stagnation and decay of this industry in India was a result of the loss of political control first over the market and later over the raw materials. The destruction of India's textile industry necessitated the destruction of the skills and autonomy of India's weavers. Often this destruction was extremely violent. For instance, the thumbs of the best Bengal weavers were cut off to prevent market competition when Indian hand-woven textiles continued to do better than the British mill products.[1] The impact of the violent manipulation and control of Indian weavers by English merchants was first felt when the East India Company (EIC) became a territorial power by defeating Nawab Sirajuddaula in the battle of Plassi in 1757. Before that, Indian weavers were independent producers and had control over their produce. The EIC replaced indigenous merchants by a 'body of paid servants receiving instructions from them with coercive authority over weavers that none had before. They had virtual monopoly of the market and had effectively exercised control over raw materials and began to extend this control over the weavers' tools. Under the company, weavers had virtually become wage workers on terms and conditions over which they had no control.'[2]

In the context of such erosion of the control of resources and the market, the traditional weavers of India were displaced. There was an exodus out of the weaving trade. New textile technology was imported into India from England in the mid-nineteenth century by the cotton traders of India who were involved in export of cotton to England. This new group of powerful merchants-turned-mill-owners competed with the handloom weavers for the common market and the raw material base. The establishment of textile mills in Lancashire and later in India deprived the Indian weaver both of the market and the raw material. When American cotton supply to the English textile industry was disturbed by the American civil war, the famous cotton famine of the 1860s broke out and the English instantly reacted by grabbing cotton in India. The cotton famine was transferred to India. [ ... ]

Gandhi's critique of the industrialization of India on the Western model was based on his perception of the poverty, dispossession and destruction of livelihood which resulted from it. [ ... ]

It was to regenerate livelihood in India that Gandhi thought of the spinning wheel as a symbol of liberation and a tool for development. Power-driven mills were the model of development in that period of early industrialization. However, the hunger of mills for raw materials and markets was the reason for a new poverty, created by the destruction of livelihood either by diverting land and biomass from local subsistence to the factory, or by displacing local production through the market.

Gandhi had said that 'anything that millions can do together, becomes charged with unique power'. The spinning wheel was a symbol of such power. 'The wheel as such is lifeless, but when I invest it with symbolism, it becomes a living thing for me.'[3] [ ... ]

Gandhi's spinning wheel is a challenge to notions of progress and obsolescence that arise from absolutism and false universalism in concepts of science and technology development. Obsolescence and waste are social constructs that have both a political and ecological component. Politically, the notion of obsolescence gets rid of people's control over their lives and livelihoods by defining productive work as unproductive and removing people's control over production in the name of progress. It would rather waste hands than waste time. Ecologically, too, obsolescence destroys the regenerative capacity of nature by substituting manufactured uniformity in place of nature's diversity. This induced dispensability of poorer people on the one hand and diversity on the other constitutes the political ecology of technological development guided by narrow and reductionist notions of productivity. Parochial notions of productivity, perceived as universal, rob people of control over their means of reproducing life and rob nature of her capacity to regenerate diversity.

Ecological erosion and destruction of livelihood are linked to one another. Displacement of diversity and of people's sources of sustenance both arise from a view of development and growth based on uniformity created through centralized control. In this process of control, reductionist science and technology act as handmaidens for economically powerful interests. The struggle between the factory and the spinning wheel continues as new technologies emerge.

## ■ Colonization of the Seed ■

The changes that took place in the textile industry during colonialism were replayed in agriculture after India's independence through the green revolution. Whether we consider the chemicalization of agriculture through the green revolution or its transformation through the new biotechnologies, the seed is at the centre of all recent changes in agricultural production.

All technological transformation of biodiversity is justified in the language of 'improvement' and increase of 'economic value'. However, 'improvement' and 'value' are not neutral terms. They are contextual and value-laden. What is improvement in one context is often regression in another. What is value added from one perspective is value lost from another.

The 'improvement' of the seed is not a neutral economic process. It is, more importantly, a political process that shifts control over biological diversity from local peasants to transnational corporations and changes biological systems from complete systems reproducing themselves into raw material. It therefore changes the role of the agricultural producer and the role of ecological processes. The new biotechnologies follow the path of hybridization in changing the location of power as associated with the seed. As Jack Kloppenburg has stated, 'It decouples seed as "seed" from seed as "grain" and thereby facilitates the transformation of seed from a use value to an exchange value.'[4]

Agricultural research is primarily a means of eliminating barriers to the penetration of agriculture by capital. The most important barrier is the nature of the seed, which reproduces itself and multiplies. The seed thus possesses a dual character that links both ends of the process of crop production: it is both means of production and, as grain, the product. In planting each year's crop the farmers also reproduce a necessary part of that means of production. The seed thus presents capital with a simple biological obstacle: given appropriate conditions the seed will reproduce itself manifold.

The seed has therefore to be transformed materially if a market for seed is to be created. Modern plant breeding is primarily an attempt to remove this biological obstacle to the market in seed. Seed reproducing itself stays free, a common resource and under the farmer's control. Corporate seed has a cost and is under the control of the corporate sector or under the control of agricultural research institutions. The transformation of a common resource into a commodity, of a self-regenerative resource into mere 'input', changes the nature of the seed and of agriculture itself. Since it robs peasants of their means of livelihood, the new technology becomes an instrument of poverty and underdevelopment.

The decoupling of seed from grain also changes the status of seed. From being finished produce which rises from itself, nature's seeds and people's seeds become mere raw material for the production of corporate seed as commodity. The cycle of regeneration of biodiversity is therefore replaced by a linear flow of free germ plasm from farms and forests into labs and research stations, and the flow of modified uniform products as priced commodities from corporations to farmers. Diversity is destroyed by transforming it into mere raw material for industrial production based on uniformity, which necessarily displaces the diversity of local agricultural practice. [ ... ]

As Claude Alvares has said, 'for the first time the human race has produced seed that cannot cope on its own, but needs to be placed within an artificial environment for growth and output'.[5] This change in the nature of seed is justified by creating a framework that treats self-regenerative seed as 'primitive' and as new germ plasm, and the seed that is inert without inputs and is non-reproducible as a finished product. The whole is rendered partial, the partial is rendered whole. The commoditized seed is ecologically incomplete and ruptured at two levels:

1  It does not *reproduce* itself, while, by definition, seed is a regenerative resource. Genetic resources are thus, through technological transformation, transformed from renewable into non-renewable.

2   It does not *produce* by itself. It needs the help of inputs to produce. As the seed and chemical companies merge, the dependence on inputs will increase, not decrease. And whether a chemical is added externally or internally, it remains an external input in the ecological cycle of the reproduction of seed.

It is this shift from the ecological processes of reproduction to the technological processes of production that underlies both the problem of dispossession of farmers and genetic erosion. [ . . . ]

Biotechnology can thus become an instrument of dispossessing the farmer of seed as a means of production. The relocation of seed production from the farm to the corporate laboratory relocates power and value between the North and South; and between corporations and farmers. It is estimated that the elimination of home-grown seed would dramatically increase the farmers' dependence on biotech industries by about US$6 billion annually.

It also becomes an instrument of dispossession by selectively removing those plants or parts of plants that do not serve the commercial interests but are essential for the survival of nature and people. 'Improvement' of a selected characteristic in a plant is also a selection *against* other characteristics which are useful to nature, or for local consumption. Improvement is not a class- or gender-neutral concept. Improvement of partitioning efficiency is based on the 'enhancement of the yield of desired product at the expense of unwanted plant parts'. The desired product is, however, not the same for rich people and poor people, or rich countries and poor countries, nor is efficiency. On the input side, richer people and richer countries are short of labour and poorer people and poorer countries are short of capital and land. Most agricultural development, however, increases capital input while displacing labour, thus destroying livelihoods. On the output side, which parts of a farming system or a plant will be treated as unwanted depends on what class and gender one is. What is unwanted for the better off may be the wanted part for the poor. The plants or plant parts which serve the poor are the ones whose supply is squeezed by the normal priorities of improvement in response to commercial forces.

In the Indian context, plants that have been displaced by plant improvement in the green revolution are pulses and oilseeds, which are crucial to the nutrient needs of people and the soil. Monocultures of wheat and rice spread through the green revolution have also turned useful plants into weeds, as is the case with green leafy vegetables which grow as associates. Herbicide use has destroyed plants useful for the poor, and pesticide use has destroyed the fish culture usually associated with paddy cultivation in the Asian rice farming system. These losses through biodiversity destruction resulting from increasing yields of monocultures are never internalized in the productivity measure of technological change. Instead, both increased inputs and decreased outputs are externalized in measurement of productivity. Productivity is a measure of output per unit input. A typical subsistence farm in an Asian village produces more than 20 crops and supports animals. Individual crops are also multi-purpose. Rice, for instance, is only partially food. The residue after removal of the grain is not a nuisance to be disposed of as it would be on a farm in the developed world. The straw is used to feed work animals, to cook food, or even to help fertilize the field for the next year's crops. The straw and husk are important construction material. Traditional rice varieties produced five times as much straw as grain, and were an important source of food, feed, fuel, fertilizer and housing material.

Plant breeders, however, saw rice only as food and created a science and technology to increase grain yields. Traditional crop varieties, characterized by tall and thin straw, typically convert the heavy doses of fertilizer into overall growth of the plant, rather than increasing the grain yield. Commonly, the excessive growth of the plant causes the stalk to break, lodging the grain on the ground, which results in heavy crop losses. The 'miracle seeds' or 'high-yielding varieties' which started the process of the green revolution were biologically engineered to be dwarf varieties. The important feature of these new varieties is not that they are particularly productive in themselves but that they can absorb three or four times higher doses of fertilizer than the traditional varieties and convert it into grain, provided proportionately heavy and frequent irrigation applications are also available. They also have high susceptibility to insect and pest attacks.

For equivalent fertilization, the high-yielding varieties produce about the same total biomass as the traditional rice. They increase the grain yield at the cost of the straw. Thus while traditional rice produces four to five times as much straw as grain, high-yielding varieties of rice typically produce a one-to-one ratio of grain to straw. Thus a conversion from traditional to high-yielding rice increases the grain available but decreases the straw. Abundance creates scarcity. Output as total biomass does not increase, but the input increases dramatically. High-yielding varieties of wheat, for example, need about three times as much irrigation as traditional varieties. If water is considered a critical input, the productivity of the new seeds is only a third of the productivity of traditional varieties. In terms of water use, the green revolution is clearly counter-productive. Increased irrigation intensity has further costs associated with it in terms of waterlogging and salinity, as the experience in India's Punjab has shown. In other regions such as Maharashtra and Tamil Nadu, the green revolution is causing large-scale mining of ground water. Large-scale desiccation of the regions of the world now supporting the green revolution is thus a real possibility. Abundance again generates scarcity. [ ... ]

The higher productivity and efficiency of industrial agriculture is contextually determined, by selecting those inputs and outputs which suit the endowments of rich people and rich countries. Before we push through new agricultural technologies, it would be wise to pause and look at the other paths that were available for increased production but were never considered. Alternatives in agriculture have been based on conserving nature and people's livelihoods, while improving yields, not on destroying them. [ ... ]

Worldwide examples of successful alternative agriculture exist and are growing, even while they continue to be ignored by the dominant world view of agriculture. And it is these initiatives that carry the seeds of a sustainable agriculture. Blindness to these alternatives is not a proof of their non-existence. It is merely a reflection of the blindness.

## ◼ Biotechnological Development and the Conservation of Biodiversity ◼

The central paradox posed by the green revolution and biotechnological development is that modern plant improvement has been based on the destruction of the biodiversity which it uses as raw material. The irony of plant and animal breeding is that it destroys the very building blocks on which the technology depends. When agricultural modernization schemes introduce new and uniform crops into the farmers' fields, they push into extinction the diversity of local varieties. In the words of Garrison Wilkes of the University of Massachusetts, it is analogous to taking stones from a building's foundations to repair the roof. [ ... ]

The paradox arises from the foundational errors of assignment of value and utility, which then make the 'modern' varieties look inherently superior, whereas they are superior only in the context of increased control over plant genetic resources and a restricted production of certain commodities for the market.

The challenge of the 1990s is based on our getting rid of false notions of obsolescence and productivity which legitimize the extinction of large parts of nature and society. The push for homogenization and uniformity comes both from the transnational corporate sector, which has to create uniformity to control markets, and from the nature of modern research systems which have grown in response to the market. Since most bio-technology research is dictated by TNCs, the sought-out solutions must have a global and homogeneous character. TNCs do not tend to work for small market niches, but aim at large market shares. In addition, researchers prefer tasks that can be simplified enough to be tackled systematically, and that produce stable and widely applicable outcomes. Diversity goes against the standardization of scientific research.

However, more production of partial outputs as measured on the market and in a monoculture is often less production when measured in the diversity of nature's economy or people's sustenance economy. In the context of diversity, increased production and improved productivity can be consonant with biodiversity conservation. In fact it is often dependent on it.

There is, however, a prevalent misconception that biotechnology development will automatically lead to biodiversity conservation. The main problem with viewing biotechnology as a miracle solution to the biodiversity crisis is related to the fact that biotechnologies are, in essence, technologies for the breeding of uniformity in plants and animals. Biotechnology corporations do sometimes talk of contributing to genetic diversity – as when John Duesing of Ciba Geigy states: 'Patent protection will serve to stimulate the development of competing and diverse genetic solutions with access to these diverse solutions ensured by free market forces at work in biotech ecology and seed industries.'[6] However, the 'diversity' of corporate strategies and the diversity of life-forms on this planet are not the same thing, and corporate competition can hardly be treated as a substitute for nature's evolution in the creation of genetic diversity. [ ... ]

The main challenge to biodiversity conservation is the removal of reductionist blinkers which make more look less and less look more. The social construction of growth and productivity is achieved (1) by excluding crops and parts of crops as unwanted and (2) by creating a false hierarchy of resources and knowledge, splitting diversity into dichotomy.

Not till diversity is made the logic of production can diversity be conserved. If production continues to be based on the logic of uniformity and homogenization, uniformity will continue to displace diversity. 'Improvement' from the corporate viewpoint, or from the viewpoint of Western agricultural research is often a loss for the Third World, especially the poor in the Third World. There is therefore no inevitability that production acts against diversity. Uniformity as a pattern of production becomes inevitable only in a context of control and profitability. [ ... ]

Diversity as a pattern of production, not merely of conservation, ensures pluralism and decentralization. It prevents the dichotomizing of biological systems into 'primitive' and 'advanced'. As Gandhi challenged the false concepts of obsolescence and productivity in the production of textiles by his search for the spinning wheel, groups across the Third World are challenging the false concepts of obsolescence in agricultural production by searching for seeds used by farmers over centuries and making them the basis of a future-oriented, self-reliant and sustainable agriculture.

## ▪ Patents, Intellectual Property and Politics of Knowledge ▪

As the spinning wheel was rendered backward and obsolete by an earlier technological revolution, farmers' seeds are rendered incomplete and valueless by the process that makes corporate seeds the basis of wealth creation. The indigenous varieties or land races, evolved through both natural and human selection, and produced and used by Third World farmers worldwide, are called 'primitive cultivars'. Those varieties created by modern plant breeders in international research centres or by transnational seed corporations are called 'advanced' or 'élite'. The tacit hierarchy in words like 'primitive' and 'élite' becomes an explicit one in the process of conflict. Thus the North has always used Third World germ plasm as a freely available resource and treated it as valueless. The advanced capitalist nations wish to retain free access to the developing world's storehouse of genetic diversity, while the South would like to have the proprietary varieties of the North's industry declared a similarly 'public' good. The North, however, resists this democracy based on the logic of the market. [ ... ] The corporate perspective views as valuable only that which serves the market. However, all material processes serve ecological needs and social needs, and these needs are undermined by the monopolizing tendency of corporations.

The issue of patent protection for modified life forms raises a number of unresolved political questions about ownership and control of genetic resources. The problem is that in manipulating life forms you do not start from nothing, but from other life forms which belong to others – maybe through customary law. Second, genetic engineering and biotechnology do not create new genes, but merely relocate genes already existing in organisms. When genes are made the object of value through the patent system, a dangerous shift takes place in the approach to genetic resources.

Most Third World countries view genetic resources as part of the common heritage. In most countries animals and plants were excluded from the patent system until recently when the advent of biotechnologies changed concepts of ownership of life. With the new biotechnologies life can now be owned. The potential for gene manipulation reduces the organism to its genetic constituents. Centuries of innovation are totally devalued to give monopoly rights on life forms to those who manipulate genes with new technologies, placing their contribution above that of generations of Third World farmers for over 10,000 years in the areas of conservation, breeding, domestication, and development of plant and animal genetic resources. As Pat Mooney has said, 'the argument that intellectual property is only recognizable when performed in laboratories with white lab coats is fundamentally a racist view of scientific development'.[7] [ ... ]

There is no epistemological justification for treating some germ plasm as valueless and part of the common heritage, and other germ plasm as a valuable commodity and private property. The distinction is not based on the nature of the germ plasm, but on the nature of political and economic power. Putting value on the gene through patents makes biology stand on its head. Complex organisms which have evolved over millennia in nature, and through the contributions of Third World peasants, tribal cultivators and healers, are reduced to their parts, and treated as mere inputs into genetic engineering. Patenting of genes thus leads to a devaluation of life forms by reducing them to their constituents and allowing them to be repeatedly owned as private property. This reductionism and fragmentation might be convenient for commercial concerns but it violates the integrity of life as well as the common property rights of the Third World people. On these false notions of genetic resources and their ownership through intellectual property rights are based the 'biobattles' at the FAO and the trade wars at GATT. Countries like the US are using trade as a means of enforcing their patent laws and intellectual property rights on the sovereign nations of the Third World. The US has accused countries of the Third World of engaging in 'unfair trading practice' if they fail to adopt the US patent laws which allow monopoly rights in life forms. Yet it is the US which has engaged in unfair practices related to the use of Third World genetic resources. It has freely raided the biological diversity of the Third World to spin millions of dollars of profits, none of which have been shared with Third World countries, the original owners of the germ plasm. A wild tomato variety (*Lycopresicon chomrelweskii*) taken from Peru in 1962 has contributed US$8 million a year to the American tomato-processing industry by increasing the content of soluble solids. Yet none of these profits or benefits have been shared with Peru, the original source of the genetic material.

According to Prescott-Allen, wild varieties contributed US$340 million per year between 1976 and 1980 to the US farm economy. The total contribution of wild germ plasm to the American economy has been US$66 billion, which is more than the total international debt of Mexico and the Philippines combined. This wild material is 'owned' by sovereign states and by local people.[8]

Patents and intellectual property rights are at the centre of the protection of the right to profits. Human rights are at the centre of the protection of the right to life, which is threatened by the new biotechnologies as they expand the domain of capital accumulation while introducing new risks and hazards for citizens. The words 'freedom' and 'protection' have been robbed of their humane meaning and are being absorbed into the double-speak of corporate jargon. With double-speak are associated double standards, one for citizens and one for corporations, one for corporate responsibility and one for corporate profits. [ ... ]

All life is precious. It is equally precious to the rich and the poor, the white and the black, to men and women. Universalization of laws for the protection of life is an ethical imperative. On the other hand, private property and private profits are culturally and socio-economically legitimized constructs holding only for some groups. They do not hold for all societies and all cultures. Laws for the protection of private property rights, especially as related to life forms, cannot and should not be imposed globally. They need to be restrained.

Double standards also exist in the shift from private gain to social responsibility for environmental costs. When the patenting of life is at issue, arguments from the concept of 'novelty' are used. Novelty requires that the subject matter of a patent be new, that it be the result of an inventive step, and not something existing in nature. On the other hand, when it comes to legislative safeguards, the arguments shift to the concept of 'similarity', to establishing that biotechnological products and genetically engineered organisms differ little from parent organisms.

To have one law for environmental responsibility and another for proprietary rights and profits is an expression of double standards. Double standards are ethically unjustified and illegitimate, especially when they deal with life itself. However, double standards are consistent with and necessary for the defence of private property rights. It is these double standards which allow the lives and livelihoods of the people and the planet to be sacrificed for the protection of profits.

Resistance to such anti-life technological shifts requires that we widen the circle of control and decision-making about technology, by treating technology in its social and ecological context. By keeping human rights at the centre of discourse and debate, we might be able to restrain the ultimate privatization of life itself.


NOTES

This chapter was originally presented as a paper at a conference on the 'Conservation of Genetic Resources', Norway, September 1990.

1 Vandana Shiva and J. Bandyopadhyay (1982), 'Political Economy of Technological Polarisations', *Economic and Political Weekly*, Vol. XVII, No. 45, 6 November, pp. 1827–32.
2 Arasarathnam, S., 'Weavers, Merchants and Company: The Handloom Industry in South Eastern India', *The Indian Economic and Social History Review*, Vol. 17, No. 3, p. 281.
3 Quoted in Pyarelal, *Towards New Horizons*, Navjivan Press, Ahmedabad, 1959, p. 150.
4 Jack Kloppenburg (1988), *First the Seed: The Political Economy of Plant Biotechnology 1492–2000*, Cambridge University Press, New York.
5 Claude Alvares, 'The Great Gene Robbery', *The Illustrated Weekly of India*, 23 March 1986.
6 Statement of John Duesing, in meeting on patents of the European Parliament, Brussels, in February 1990.
7 Pat Mooney (1989), 'From Cabbages to Kings: Intellectual Property vs Intellectual Integrity', Proceedings of Conference on Patenting of Life Forms, ICDA Report, Brussels.
8 Hugh Iltis (1986), 'Serendipity in Exploration of Biodiversity: What Good Are Weedy Tomatoes?' in E. O. Wilson (ed.), *Biodiversity*, National Academy Press, Washington, DC.

# 3

# Recycling Modernity: Pirate Electronic Cultures in India

## Ravi Sundaram

Marx, now long forgotten by most who spoke his name but a decade or two ago, once said the following in his brilliantly allegorical essay on the Eighteenth Brumaire of Louis Bonaparte. "Bourgeois revolutions...storm quickly from success to success; their dramatic effects outdo each; men and things set in sparkling brilliants; ecstasy is the everyday spirit; but they are short-lived; soon they have attained their zenith, and a long crapulent depression lays hold of society before it learns soberly to assimilate the results of its storm-and-stress period".

In Asia, reeling under the current crisis, the moment of ecstasy has long passed, and the 'long crapulent depression' is here to stay. India, a poor cousin of the East Asians, tried to ignore the crisis through its traditional west-centeredness. But the crisis has finally arrived in South Asia, the Indian rupee has dived steadily since last year and inflation is raging. But in the area of electronic capitalism, the mood is buoyant. Software stocks have risen 120 percent and soon software will become India's largest export.

Many fables have emerged as a response to the irruption of electronic capitalism in a country where 400 million cannot still read or write. The first fable is a domesticated version of the virtual ideology. In this Indianised version, propagated by the technocratic and programming elite, India's access to western modernity (and progress) would obtain through a vast virtual universe, programmed and developed by 'Indians'. The model: to develop techno-cities existing in virtual time with US corporations, where Indian programmers would provide low-cost solutions to the new global techno-space.

The second fable is a counter-fable to the first and quite familiar to those who live in the alternative publics of the net. This fable comes out of a long culture of Old-Left politics in India and draws liberally from 1960's dependency theory. The fable, not surprisingly, argues that India's insertion in the virtual global economy follows traditional patterns of unequal exchange. Indian programmers offer a low-cost solution to the problems of transnational corporations. Indian software solutions occupy the lower end of the global virtual commodity chain, just as cotton farmers in South Asia did in the nineteenth century, where they would supply Manchester mills with produce.

All fables are not untrue, some more 'true' than others. Thus the second fable claims, not unfairly, that most Indian software is exported, and there is very little available in the local languages (ironically the Indian language versions of the main programs are being developed by IBM and Microsoft!).

The alternative vision posed by the second fable is typically nationalist. Here India would first concentrate on its domestic space and then forge international links. In a sense both fables suffer from a yearning for perfection. While the first promises a seamless transition to globalism, the second offers a world that is autarchic. Both are ideological, in the old, nineteenth-century sense of the term, which makes one a little uncomfortable. "Down with all the hypotheses that allow the belief in a true world", once wrote Nietzsche, angrily.

There is no doubt that for a 'Third World' country, India displays a dynamic map of the new techno-cultures. The problem for both the fables mentioned above is that they remain limited to the elite domains of techno-space in India. This domain is composed of young, upper-caste, often English-speaking programmers in large metropoles, particularly emerging techno-cities like Bangalore and Hyderabad. This is the story that Wired loves to tell its Western audiences, but in a critical, innovative sense most of these programmers are not the future citizens of the counter net-publics in India.

What is crucial in the Indian scenario is that the dominant electronic public has cohered with the cultural-political imagination of a belligerent Hindu-nationalist movement. Hindu nationalism in India came to power using an explosive mix of anti-minority violence and a discourse of modernity that was quite contemporary. This discourse appealed to the uppercaste elites in the fast-growing cities and towns, using innovative forms of mechanical and electronic reproduction. Thus it was the Hindu nationalists who first used cheap audiocassette tapes to spread anti-Muslim messages; later giant video-scapes were used to project an aestheti-sized politics of hate. Some of the first Indian web sites were also set up by the Hindu nationalists. To this landscape has been added that terrifying nineteenth century weapon, the nuclear bomb.

This is an imagination that is aggressive, technologically savvy, and eminently attractive to the cyber-elites. The cyber-elites may be uncomfortable with the Hindu nationalists' periodic rhetoric of 'national sufficiency', but such language is hyper-political and has less meaning on the ground.

Outside the universe of the cyber-elite, is another one, which speaks to a more energetic techno-culture. This is a world of innovation and non-legality, of ad-hoc discovery and electronic survival strategies. But before I talk about this, a story of my own.

Some years ago, I was on a train in Southern India where I met Selvam, a young man of 24, who I saw reading used computer magazines in the railway compartment. Selvam's story is fascinating, for it throws light on a world outside those of the techno-elite. Selvam was born in the temple town of Madurai in Southern India, the son of a worker in the town court. After ten years in school, Selvam began doing a series of odd jobs, learnt to type at a night school after which he landed a job at a typists shop. It was there that Selvam first encountered the new technoculture – Indian-style.

From the late 1980's, India witnessed a unique communicative transformation – the spread of public telephones in different parts of the country. Typically, these were not anonymous card-based instruments as in the West or other parts of the Third World, but run by humans. These were called Public Call Offices (PCOs). The idea was that in a non-literate society like India the act of telecommunication had to be mediated by humans. Typically literates and non-literates used PCOs, which often doubled as fax centres, photocopy shops and typists' shops. Open through the night, PCOs offered inexpensive, personalised services that spread rapidly all over the country.

Selvam's typing shop was such a PCO. Selvam worked on a used 286, running an old version of WordStar, where he would type out formal letters to state officials for clients, usually peasants and unemployed. Soon Selvam graduated to a faster 486 and learnt programming by devouring used manuals, and simply asking around. This is the world of informal technological knowledge existing in most parts of India, where those excluded from the upper-caste, English-speaking bastions of the cyber-elite learn their tools.

Selvam told me how the textile town of Coimbatore, a few hours from Madurai, set up its own BBS, by procuring used modems, and connecting them later at night. Used computer equipment is part of a vast commodity chain in India, originating from various centres in India but the main centre is Delhi.

Delhi has a history of single-commodity markets from the days of the Mughal Empire. Various markets would specialise in a single commodity, a tradition that has continued to the present. The centre of Delhi's computer trade is the Nehru Place market. Nehru Place is a dark, seedy cluster of grey concrete blocks, which is filled with small shops devoted to the computer trade. Present here are the agents of large corporations, as also software pirates, spare parts dealers, electronic smugglers, and wheeler-dealers of every kind in the computer world.

This cluster of legality and non-legality is typical of Indian technoculture. When the cable television revolution began in the 1990s, all the cable operators were illegal, and many continue to be so even today. This largely disorganised, dispersed scenario makes it impossible for paid cable television to work in India. This is a pirate modernity, but one with no particular thought about counter-culture or its likes. It is a simple survival strategy.

The computer trade has followed the pirate modernity of cable television. Just as small town cable operators would come to the cable market in the walled city area of Delhi for equipment, so people from small towns like Selvam would come to Nehru Place to source computer parts, used computers, older black and white monitors, and mother-boards out of fashion in Delhi.

This is a world that is everyday in its imaginary, pirate in its practice, and mobile in its innovation. This is also a world that never makes it to the computer magazines, nor the technological discourses dominated by the cyber-elite. The old nationalists and Left view this world with fascination and horror, for it makes a muddle of simple nationalist solutions. One can call this a recycled electronic modernity. And it is an imaginary that is suspect in the eyes of all the major ideological actors in techno-space.

For the Indian proponents of a global virtual universe, the illegality of recycled modernity is alarming and 'unproductive'. Recycled modernity prevents India's accession to WTO conventions, and has prevented multinational manufacturers from dominating India's domestic computer market. For the nationalists, this modernity only reconfirms older patterns of unequal exchange and world inequality. In cyber-terms this means smaller processing power than those current in the West, lesser bandwidth, and no control over the key processes of electronic production.

I suspect that members of the electronic avant-gardes and the counter net-publics in the West will find recycled modernity in India baffling. For recycled modernity has no discrete spaces of its own in opposition to the main cyber-elites, nor does it posit a self-defined oppositional stance. This is a modernity that is fluid and mocking in definition. But is also a world of those dispossessed by the elite domains of electronic capital, a world which possesses a hunter-gatherer cunning and practical intelligence.

The term 'recycling' may conjure up images of a borrowed, unoriginal modern. Originality (the eternal search for 'newness') was of course Baudelairian modernity's great claim to dynamism. As social life progressed through a combination of dispersion and unity, the Baudelairian subject was propelled by a search for new visions of original innovation, both artistic and scientific. A lot of this has fallen by the wayside in the past few decades, but weak impulses survive to this day.

It is important to stress too that recycled modernity does not reflect a thought-out post-modern sensibility. Recycling is a strategy of both survival and innovation on terms entirely outside the current debates on the structure and imagination of the net and techno-culture in general. As globalists/virtualists push eagerly for a new economy of virtual space, and the nationalists call for a national electronic self-sufficiency, the practitioners of recycling keep working away in the invisible markets of India.

In fact given the evidence, it could even be argued that recycling's claim to 'modernity' is quite fragile. Recycling practices (today at least) lack modernity's self-proclaimed reflexivity, there is no sense of a means-ends action, nor is there any coherent project. This contrasts with the many historical legacies of modernity in India – one of which was Nehruvian. The technological side of this modernity was monumental and future-oriented; it spoke in terms of projects, clear visions, argued goals. And the favourite instrument of this modernity was a state Plan, borrowed from Soviet models. Nehruvian modernity has been recently challenged by Hindu nationalism, which too, has sought to posit its own claims to the modern, where an authoritarian state and the hegemony of the Hindu majority ally with a dynamic urban consumption regime.

Recycling practices' claim to modernity relies less on any architecture of mobility, but on an engagement with speed. Speed constitutes recycling's great reference of activity, centred on sound, vision and data. This is the pirate modern's 'eternal present' (Benjamin), one that is historically situated and mediated through various registers of difference. Speed in the time of the 'now' is the effort at acceleration propelled partly by global techno-capital. Temporal acceleration, which Reinhart Koselleck claims is one of modernity's central features, speaks to the deep yearnings of recycling's praxis. But this is a constantly shifting universe of adaptation to available tools of speed, the world info-*bahn* being but an infrequent visitor. Consider the practice of speed in a Third World country like India, where both the given-ness of access to the net and the purchase of processing power do not exist in simultaneity. They have to be created, partly through developing new techniques, and partly through breaking the laws of global electronic capital.

Recycling's great limitation in the computer/net industry is content. This actually contrasts with the other areas of India's culture industry – music and cinema. In the field of popular music, a pirate culture effectively broke the stranglehold of multinational companies in the music scene and opened up vast new areas of popular music that the big companies had been afraid to touch. Selling less from official music stores but from neighbourhood betel-leaf (*paan*) shops, the pirate cassettes have made India into one of the major music markets in the world. In the field of cinema and television, content has never been a problem with a large local film industry that has restricted Hollywood largely to English-language audiences.

What accounts for this great limitation in the net and the computer components of recycled modernity? Recycling practices have, as we have shown, been very successful in expanding computer culture, by making it inexpensive and accessible. Most importantly recycling provided a practical education to tens of thousands of people left out of the upper-caste technical universities. But content providers are still at a discount. But perhaps not yet. The last time I went to Nehru Place I met a young man from Eastern India busy collecting Linux manuals. In a few years the recyclers, bored with pirating Microsoft ware, will surely begin writing their own.

■ Thinking Through the Transitions: The City
and the Pirate Modern ■

The emergence of a large 'pirate' electronic space in India gestures to a number of emergent practices in India in the 1980s and the 1990s. Though 'globalisation' is usually held out as a representational shorthand to capture this era, one can argue that in fact a number of complex, often unintended factors cohered in making the 'contemporary'.

Globalisation discourses in the public sphere have tended to focus on the state and its regulatory regime as a major reference point. While neo-liberal critics of the old regime of state-centred accumulation have pushed, often successfully, for a dismantling of state controls, critics from both the right and the left have tended to defend a nationalist economic model which would retain regulatory controls.

In fact, one of the most interesting aspects of the 1990s in India has been the dramatic retreat of the state at the level of the everyday. The magnified imaginary of the regulatory national state which informed the architecture of Nehruvianism is little in evidence, with a number of competing actors on the ground.

The 'everyday' is something that needs to be clarified here. The state, for example, continues to retain a close grip on the means of legal violence, and the regulatory model has not been allowed to disappear. In fact this model has been grafted onto a corrupt liberalisation regime to award the larger contracts in infrastructure.

I would like to speak of the 'everyday' as a space where practices of quotidian consumption, mobility, and struggle are articulated. It is this space that has been largely absent even in the cultural discourses on technological globalisation which have tended to look at elite domains of consumption and identity.

Looking back at the 1990s without the benefit of long-term hindsight, one can posit a number of preliminary formulations on the transitions of the decade. For clarity, I will limit my argument to the electronic everyday, the world of phones, computers, communication, television and music cultures.

The first would be that this everyday has emerged within a distinct urban space, in India's fast growing metropolitan centres and small towns. The notion of a distinct urban culture has lacked a public register in the Indian case, but this 'new' everyday has in a sense announced the arrival, albeit hesitantly, of a wide-ranging cluster of forms which we could organise under the term 'urban experience'. Unknown to many of us who lived through the decade, the urban arrived in India in the 1990s. To be sure, the multiple crises of the Third World City are also reflected in this 'urban experience' – large-scale inequalities, violence, collapse of infrastructure, and the rise of elite suburbia based on automobile transport. In the midst of all this is a pirate electronic space speaking to the new phone, television, and communication cultures that offer a new mobility and employment to thousands in the grey economy.

Thus the second aspect of this everyday would be of its preponderant non-legality. Operating at the level of techno-cultural services to the vast majority of the population in cities and towns, the actors in this space have simply ignored the state as the regulator of everyday life. The thousands of small cable television operators; pirate audiocassette shop owners; and grey market computer companies have, with significant success evaded state controls on their operations. Part of the problem has been the state's slow response to impose regulatory mechanisms due to an inability in understanding the new technologies. But when regulation has come, success has been uneven, with only the larger firms falling in line.

The third aspect of the everyday is that the networks of quotidian consumption are dominated by those who, in the older Marxist language would be called 'petty-commodity-producers'. Much of twentieth-century Marxism from Lenin to the structuralists has puzzled over the reproduction of petty-commodity production in contemporary capitalism. Often this sector has been seen as a derivative category distinguished from the main dynamic of capitalist production, a form that is mired in 'circulation', not production. In fact in the expansion of the electronic everyday in India's cities in the 1990s, it is precisely this petty-commodity-sector that was crucial. Dominated by small entrepreneurs often focused in their own locality, this sector laid non-legal cable television networks, set up small PCO and computer shops, and distribution outlets of music cassettes. Along with this expansion came a host of other interventions in the locality: community advertising through inexpensive desktop-published flyers, and informal credit networks that give liquidity for low-cost consumption goods like black and white television sets sold in poor parts of the city.

Many years ago, before he joined the academic star-system, Jean Baudrillard wrote *The Mirror of Production*, a critique of Marxist political economy. Despite its problems, some of which anticipate his later shifts, Baudrillard's text nevertheless managed to point to the anthropomorphic core of Marxism's critique of political economy. Marxism's primacy of production (the 'realm of the concrete') led to a devaluing of the circuits of exchange and consumption. Exchange was always seen as exhibiting a lack, a space where labour-power was reified, and often generating 'false needs'. In the Indian case many of the critics of globalisation, by focusing on the elite consumption spaces (with their effects of waste and violence), tended to miss out on the profound transformations that were taking place in daily life in cities and towns. The Marxisant/nationalist heritage with its hostility and moral suspicion towards consumption in general, played no small part in this.

The last feature of the electronic everyday has been the insertion of a spatio-temporal experience in the locality through speed. As urban neighbourhoods get connected through phone lines, television, and increasingly PCO/internet access points, we can speak of flashes of what Paul Virilio has called the possibility of arrival without departure in late modernity. Virilio argues that temporal experiences have been fundamentally transformed with the arrival of the new telecommunication networks. Central to the transition is the transformation of modes of travel, thus for Virilio the audio-visual is the 'last vehicle' in modernity, after the railway, the automobile and the aeroplane. Further, a new form of chrono-politics is increasingly displacing the older forms of geo-politics.

Virilio's model is too extreme for the Indian case, but one can surely detect a transformation of the 'local' in the city with the spread of techno-cultural density. With the generalisation of modes of simultaneity through new technologies of transmission (live telecasts, sport events, long distance phone use by sections of the migrant poor), the 'locality' loses the old form of spatial security. The abolition of distance has of course been the great motive force of speed. In India this was pioneered by television (one can recall Heidegger's comments on television: "The peak of the abolition of every possibility of remoteness"), but also through the phone network.

## ▩ The 'Asian' Modern? ▩

Are pirate/recycling electronic cultures the defining mark of the 'Asian' engagement with contemporary modernity? 'Asia', is of course a violent abstraction, but one can surely detect the chain of non-legal electronic markets from Hong Kong to Shanghai, from Singapore to Delhi. Non-legality has been a major feature of all East Asian computer cultures where Western electronic commodities are re-sold in the world market, particularly the Third World. In the Indian case, the mimetic act is less punctual; the copy is not crucial to pirate culture. Rather, it is the insertion into the non-legal local, cultural commodity chains, and the unintended mocking of the state that define 'pirate' cultures in India. It is this mode that opens a wide spectrum of possibilities, many of which remain unrealised.

# 4

# Karaoke in East Asia: Modernization, Japanization, or Asianization?

## Akiko Ōtake and Shūhei Hosokawa

### ■ Karaoke in an Asian Context[1] ■

*Karaoke as cultural technology*

Our research has focused upon the local differences in the reception and appropriation of a Japanese-made entertainment machine in five East Asian countries/regions. The differences reflect the pre-existing culture of people's singing and socializing, and the organization of the entertainment industry (music, television, restaurants, sex, and so on). International copyright control (in the cases of Taiwan and Viet Nam), the American occupation (Okinawa) and national antagonism to Japan (Korea) also play important roles in the karaoke scenes in each region. Furthermore, Japanese governance of Taiwan up to 1945 made old people's desire for Japanese songs precede its popularity among the young. The radical change in the economic system in China stimulated new kinds of individualism that is in turn symbolized by such things as karaoke and hamburgers, that is, 'global' commodities born of capitalism. Karaoke at first appealed to the urban upper-middle class in China, as in Hong Kong and Viet Nam. The prosperity of karaoke in restaurants is common in China and Viet Nam.

This contrasts with the other two cases of Taiwan and Okinawa that show more similarity with the history of karaoke in Japan. In both societies, karaoke was at first found in small bars for middle-aged and old men who sang Japanese songs. In Taiwan, the tradition of small-room entertainment seems to have been of importance for karaoke to reach a wider audience, whereas in Okinawa, local people supported the 'juke–karaoke', a symbolic product appropriating the relic of American occupation, without abandoning the unplugged performance. In Korea, the first karaoke bars for local people were set up in small bars, too. In spite of national rivalry, Korean businessmen started to use the equipment in a similar way to their Japanese counterparts. It is partly because of this association with Japaneseness that the Korean authorities tend to frown on karaoke establishments.

In every case in question except for the Okinawan, the karaoke space is apt to be associated with delinquency and prostitution. Almost axiomatically, the introduction of visual karaoke and the karaoke box, no matter how varied they may be from region to region, ignited the boom with the youth participation. The exploding popularity of the karaoke box, although usually regarded as a place for delinquency by the authorities, is brought about by dissociating the young from adult entertainment (old songs, alcohol and/or hostesses). In many countries, karaoke consumption is a key factor in pop production and distribution.

What is at stake is the production of space correlated with a form of technology, the structure of industry and the articulation of singing and listening bodies. It is misleading to think that there exist audiovisual products separate from the space they occupy and the bodies they are addressed to. Crucial to this idea is the complex intertwining of the production and consumption of products, the spaces and the sound-and-vision effects, that is to say, 'cultural technologies' as Jody Berland defines them. She emphasizes by this concept the mediation between the processes of 'producing texts, producing spaces, producing listeners' (1992: 39). This concept, she continues,

> draws our attention to the ways that pop culture represents a mediation between technologies, economics, spaces, and listeners: or in other words, to the often paradoxical dynamics of contemporary culture as it is technologically articulated with the changing spatiality of social production. (1992: 39)

The shift of cultural technologies used in the space in Taiwan – from Music TV to Movie TV and Karaoke TV – provides a conspicuous case of the 'mediation between technologies, economics, spaces, and listeners'. The small room itself is an old spatial arrangement for men's entertainment and the installation of a monitor in it, realized by the growing economic power and the development of consumer technology of Taiwan, transformed not only the ways of using the space but also the relationships between sound-and-vision and audience.

Consider, for example, the Taiwanese case and the way technologies transform the private to the public, and reflect on the spatial signification of headphones, speaker and microphone. The experience of viewing VCR tape with headphones is private, and thus structurally different from the use of speakers, a more public event. Whether the viewers receive sound scattered from speakers and shared with co-viewers or addressed exclusively to their ears is a significant difference. Similarly, when a singer's voice is mechanically amplified (with echo) and shared with the anonymous audience, it becomes more 'publicized' than an unamplified singing voice. Speakers can produce, we infer, a more communal feeling in the space than with headphones. Headphones and microphone – these immediate objects attached to the body of the viewer/singer occupy a special position in spatiality because they transmit the final sound the viewers receive or the singers emit. While the former (headphones) enclose the ready-made sound in an extremely private 'head space' (privatization of the public), the latter (the microphone) scatters the individual voice to an open space (publicization of the private). As J. Fornäs (1998) remarks, the significance of the visual in karaoke lies in the subjective and collective participation in it in order to 'fill the gap' rather than in viewing it from outside as ready-made and the interpretation of it as work established by others. The transition of compartments in Taiwan would need further research with respect to the shift in technology and the construction of subjective experience.

The transition from juke-box to karaoke in the 1970s should not be interpreted in the same way. For the difference between these two sound machines is found not in the meaning of sound-and-vision experience (e.g., the difference between MTV and KTV) but in the theatricalization of space by separating the 'stage' from the 'floor' (although the 'stage' is not always an elevated area physically distinguishable from the 'floor'). The amplified voice of the standing singer is the focus of the karaoke space just as the bodies and voices of actors in the theatre are. Just like 'free-style' rapping, however, all the listeners can in turn pick up a microphone and make their own 'spectacle'. This 'egalitarian' feature of 'participatory consumption' characteristic of karaoke behaviour is echoed in the video game centre in Pusan. Individual players of various electronic games take turns instead to be engaged in the transitory but communal relationship between singers and audience. The interaction between these occupants–participants is certainly born out of the pervasiveness of amplified sound and the act of singing to the listeners. How cultural technologies such as karaoke transform the spatial arrangement is clear-cut in these cases.

Cultural technologies produce not only the content of precedent media as McLuhan formulated but also 'material practices with their own structural effects and tensions' (Berland 1992: 45). In other words, no cultural products exist *per se*, isolated from the 'structural effects and tensions' specific to the 'material practices' in particular socio-political and economic settings. These effects and tensions include gender relationships, family formation, spatial arrangements, racial/ethnic segregation, the commodity economy, and so on. The concept of 'material practice' in Berland's quote may designate more properly the agent's intervention with cultural technologies than that of 'use': when we 'use' specific products, we are forced to appropriate ourselves to the *mode of operation* intrinsic to the materiality of them (see de Certeau 1980: 75–82). This does not mean, however, a deterministic view of technology. On the contrary, we would insist, 'material practices' (singing with pre-recorded sound, for example) vary depending on the localities, ethnicities and subjectivities involved. New cultural technologies raise questions 'addressed specifically to their place in the technological proliferation, cumulative privatization, and spatial expansion of global capitalization' (Berland 1992: 47). Our comparative study addressed these questions and we now turn to the question

PART I: TECHNOCULTURES

of the 'modernization' of East Asia emphasizing the three problematics mentioned here – proliferating technology, private space and increasing capitalization.

## Modernization, Japanization and Asianization

In all the cases we have dealt with, karaoke is regarded as something related to modernity and Japan, an Asian country that can allegedly say 'No' to the West. The Japanese 'No' (Ishihara 1991) is followed up by *The Asia That Can Say No* by the Malaysian Prime Minister Mohama Mahathir (1994) and by *The China That Can Say No* by Chinese journalists (Zhang 1996). These authors generally emphasize the economic independence of 'Japan', 'Asia' and 'China' respectively from the Western system and argue for the establishment of a third economic bloc after North America and the European Union, centred in East Asia. Their common scenario is roughly as follows: if Japan's advanced technology (or Asia's or China's advancing technology) and the huge market of workers and consumers in the most populated area on our planet co-operate with one another, then Japan (Asia, China) may be able to threaten (or finally end) the Western (more precisely, American) domination of the twentieth century.

Coincidentally, Japan, Malaysia and China (and their nearby countries) all have thriving karaoke scenes and the local people *in grosso modo* take karaoke more seriously than people in the West. Of course we do not claim that karaoke and economic growth in East Asia are causally related. Instead, we will pursue the triangular connection between Japan, the West and 'East Asia' (excluding Japan) with respect to the phenomenon of 'global karaoke'. Japan is ambiguous in the sense that it is geographically situated on the fringes of East Asia and has much more biological, historical and cultural affinity with Asia than with the West, but at the same time in terms of the economy it is closer to and much more competitive with the West than East Asia. The triangle we are dealing with has much to do with the triple interconnected processes of Japanization, modernization and Asianization.

To begin with, we fly to Lhasa, Tibet, with an American anthropologist to see how karaoke bars are operated under the repressive Chinese politics against Tibet and under the disinterested gaze of Western tourists. According to Vincanne Adams, in spite of the desire of Western visitors to keep Tibet Tibetan (more generally, to keep Tibetan religiously and exotically authentic), the local people who can afford to spend a certain amount of money on dancing, drinking and singing are fond of going to karaoke, where Chinese songs are predominant and sometimes MC Hammer clones are dancing. It symbolizes the modernizing façade for the Chinese government, and at the same time the Western contamination for tourists. Adams thinks that 'karaoke may in fact be an indicator of how important it is to not efface modernity but to acquire, participate in, and benefit from modernity' in Lhasa and 'to do so, for some Tibetans, can mean eroding the boundaries between Chinese, Tibetan, and Western that are used to define *difference*' (1996: 537). Therefore Tibetan karaoke singers can become, even if for only three minutes, Western and Chinese simultaneously 'while still remaining Tibetan and modern' (ibid.: 538). Karaoke accomplishes this because fundamentally it produces simulacra.

It is likely that the karaoke equipment in Lhasa is mostly imported from Japan via Beijing or Shanghai by Chinese proprietors. We presume so because in China, as noted above, karaoke machines are almost always Japanese-made. Furthermore, karaoke is affectively as well as economically associated with 'modernity' after the introduction of the free-market system. However, the Japaneseness of the technology does not figure in Tibetan karaoke and is thus combined with the modernity, at least in Adams' interpretation. This erasure of origin interests us when we ask why Japan massively exports hardware while hardly selling any of its cultural products except animated films and computer games. The dissemination of karaoke apparatus abroad does not mean disseminating Japanese popular songs.

As far as karaoke is cultural technology, it is irrelevant to conceive it as the product itself and we have to examine the 'structural effects and tensions' (Berland) intrinsic to it. In this context, Koichi Iwabuchi, in his work on Japanese technology and mass media in the Asian audiovisual market, remarks that 'what Japanese cultural industries try to export are not products *per se*, but items of urban middle-class culture constructed through an *indigenization of "the West"*' (1995: 95, our emphasis).

It is precisely the 'urban middle class' that constitutes the karaoke main stage in East Asia. Unlike other consumer technologies such as cassette tapes and television, karaoke apparatus has hardly penetrated the rural and/or underprivileged life in Asia. Theories concerning modernization of the formerly colonized countries generally claim that the economic and social growth of the 'middle class' can indicate proximity to the hegemonic countries, although the definition of 'middle class' may vary from one author to another. The rising middle class can consume new cultural products for their private pleasure and as status symbols and thus stimulate the national commodity economy. Different from the consumption by the upper class, whose economic effect is usually seen only in limited sectors of the country, the middle class can bring about the amplification (or emergence) of domestic markets and thus reinforce domestic capitalization.

In East Asia as well as in Europe and North America, it is with video or laser karaoke that the boom exploded (with the exception of Taiwan and Okinawa). It was generally oriented to the urban middle class. They may not know that the first decade of karaoke had no visuals. Karaoke is not only a sing-along machine but also a variation of image consumption for Asian (and Western) people. Not coincidentally, the middle class in various countries accepted karaoke when home video viewing was becoming more popular to them. The 'hi-tech' image of karaoke equipment is as crucial for its middle-class consumption as the evocation of a desire to sing in front of an audience, though the technology applied to karaoke is itself no more 'hi-tech' than other audiovisual technology such as video, laser disc and stereo. The technological image of karaoke may result from its contrast with pre-existent forms of non-professional singing. Unlike television and cassette tapes, cultural technologies that deeply penetrate mass music consumption in Asia and other areas (see Manuel 1993; Wong 1995; El-Shawan

Castelo-Branco 1987; Sutton 1985), karaoke cannot for the moment receive *nationwide* support in East Asia except for Japan, Korea and Taiwan, and it remains an urban middle-class leisure activity (in Viet Nam and China, for example). Although in Japan karaoke has almost wiped out singing without pre-recorded sound, in East Asia, 'unplugged' singing still co-exists and continues to thrive among the rural, the destitute and/or the older strata of society. We may infer that the nationwide diffusion of karaoke in Japan is related to the predominance of 'middle-class' consciousness.[2]

*Re-made in Asia*

Now we turn to the (non-)Japaneseness of karaoke. None of the basic parts of the karaoke apparatus – microphone, magnetic tape, video, laser disc, PA system – is a Japanese invention: what Japan created is a new combination and style of use in a certain spatial setting. In this, it resembles the Walkman whose uniqueness is clearer in its outdoor use of headphones than in its mechanism itself (Hosokawa 1984). Street use of headphones was possible before the ground-breaking release of Sony's Walkman in 1979. But nobody thought to do so because street walking and listening were conceived as two different acts. What Sony created was the desire and imagination *par excellence*: a new gadget that merged walking and listening into one simultaneous act.

This discussion relates to the case of karaoke. The two 'Japanese-made' cultural technologies create the playful theatricality in music consumption as well as bringing about the instant transformation of private/public spatiality. They are more intimately linked with Japaneseness than other technological products such as video decks and televisions not only because of the semi-monopolization by Japanese manufacturers but also because it is a particular mode of material practice. Both karaoke and Walkmans doubtless use Western technology, however, far from the realm of Western desire and imagination. These inventions and the image evoked by their use in public space are certainly modern but not necessarily Western. They were, at least to the first Western beholders, alien, bizarre and 'Japanese'. They did not represent striking technological progress one might envy (e.g. digital movies, giant video monitors, streamlined automobiles) but material practices twisted, material practices originating from the 'Orient'. In the domain of audiovisual consumption, they show that modernization is not always related to some forms of Westernization but sometimes to Japanization.

Like the Walkman, karaoke embodies both Japaneseness and modernity. They are 'transcending and displacing western modernity' as Japan asserts itself (Morley and Robins 1992: 153). This connotation, however, depends on the local images of Japan and modernity. For example in Korea, a country whose nationalism is founded on the difference from its neighbouring colonizer, Japaneseness is downplayed or even erased by renaming it in the local language and manufacturing it domestically. In Tibet, a country which has little cultural connection with Japan, the image of modernity is put to the fore.

The integration of Japaneseness and modernity is certainly tied up with the 'indigenisation of "the West"' characteristic of Japanese consumer technologies. Iwabuchi notes,

> I would argue that if there is anything attractive for Asians about Japanese culture, it would be precisely its habit of hyperactive indigenisation and domestication of 'the West', which makes modern Japanese culture scandalous to and subversive of 'the West'. In other words, I suggest that it is the *process* of indigenisation rather than the product *per se* that captures the attention of Asian people ... [W]hat Asian audiences are consuming is no longer 'the West' or 'a Westernised Asia', but an 'indigenised (Asianised) West'; they are fascinated neither by 'originality' nor by 'tradition', but are actively constructing their own images and meanings at the receiving end. (1995: 103)

To sum up, Japanese consumer technologies are trying to promulgate in Asia neither a 'Western way of life' nor a 'Japanese way of life' but a Japanized version of the 'American way of life' (see Tobin 1992), that is more simply 'Japanese middle-class material life'. This is in turn domesticated by Asian people and becomes, for example, a Malaysian version of a Japanized American way of life mixed with a Malaysianized American way of life imported by Chinese-Malaysian American repatriates. This situation of double domestication is typically found in karaoke bars in Kuala Lumpur (or in Hong Kong or Bangkok, if you like) where they sing not only locally made melodies but also many Japanese pop songs in one of the local languages, and some American and British oldies in English.

## Karaoke and 'Asian' pop

Asian pop songs[3] are unambiguous examples of the double indigenization of Japan and the West by local musicians. Many Japanese Top 10 tunes that usually consist of Western-borrowed sound are today covered in Cantonese and Taiwanese, and, with more luck, in Mandarin, Vietnamese, Thai, Burmese, Indonesian, Malay, and so on. They may in turn inspire local composers and arrangers. Not only the songs but also the formation of Japanese pop groups such as five handsome boys, three cute girls, or one female lead singer with four male backing vocalists–instrumentalists are sooner or later followed up in East Asia. Some Japanese singers make extensive promotional tours in China, whereas a Filipino singer's debut in Japan was publicized all over East Asia with the expectation of the positive effect of earning a reputation in Tokyo. The above-mentioned karaoke talent-search in China organized by Hori Production shows the new direction of Japanese show-biz to Asia in the 1990s.

Synchronized with the expansion of the Asian karaoke scene towards the end of the 1980s, Asian pop became known to some Japanese listeners at least inasmuch as there are currently two specialized monthly magazines, *Pop Asia* and *Asian Pops Magazine*, in Japan. Large CD retailers in Tokyo have as much space for Asian pop as for the rest of 'world music'. We do not intend to causally relate the formation of the Asian karaoke scene with the increasing interest in Asian pop in Japan, and in Japanese pop in East Asia. Instead, these two phenomena are, we suppose, triggered by the intensified cultural intercourse inside Asia through telecommunications, satellite TV, film, tourism, and so on. It is economic growth and political links in East Asia that encourage musical communication. The pan-Asian popularity of Japanese pop songs may in part be due to their karaoke play. Certainly, they are translated into local languages and interpreted by local singers. In this sense, to call the phenomenon simply the 'Japanese invasion' misses the point. If the Hong Kong-based STAR TV broadcasts those songs, for example, in Cantonese or Mandarin from above, karaoke bars and boxes on each corner follow it up from below. Japanese karaoke software manufacturers are trying to establish their local subsidiaries in the capitals of Asian countries in order to enhance copyright control and probably hoping for taste standardization as well.

It is important to note that the exportation of karaoke to East Asia has been accompanied by the increasing concern of JASRAC (the Japanese Society for the Rights of Authors, Composers, and Publishers) over illegal covers of Japanese songs and piracy in Asia. In the end, Asia is the market-place for Japanese record labels and was discovered as a potential source for royalties for Japanese authors, composers and publishers. It is because of pressure from Japanese record companies that JASRAC strives to raise copyright consciousness in East Asia. On the other hand, JASRAC is criticized for rental CD shops, and the unauthorized re-release and re-compilation of Western artists (e.g. Paul McCartney) by the Western copyright society. This double-edged situation may reflect the *ambiguous* (in terms of Kenzaburō Ōe, the Nobel Prize-winning novelist) position of Japan *vis-à-vis* Asia and the West.


■ Conclusion ■


As discussed above, Japan geographically belongs to East Asia but in terms of economy and politics, it is much closer to the West. This ambiguity makes karaoke – or by extension, mass culture in general – in East Asia more complicated than that in the West because it obliges us to reflect not upon two binary relationships (Japan–West, Japan–East Asia) but upon the triple one between the West, Japan and East Asia. The dynamic at work in this triangle is itself a sub-process of what is now called globalization. If we call the globalization within the region *Asianization*, karaoke is 'Asianizing' Asian popular music by way of Japanese intervention in music production, distribution and consumption.

It should be noted that *Asianization* has two dimensions: indigenization of foreign cultures and Pan-Asianization of indigenous cultures. For example, the former is related to the domestication of Japanese-made products like the karaoke machine in each region. The latter is concerned with the rising middle class and their non-Western non-national awareness through transnational technologies such as satellite TV. This Pan-Asian enterprise is often led by the official institutions like broadcasting stations and record companies. Since the mid-1980s,

Pan-Asian song festivals have been held in various countries in the area. Their form is more or less akin to that of the Eurovision Song Contest: one singer (or group) represents one nation and the jury elect the best Asian song and artist of the year under a slogan like 'Asia is one'. The artists are usually middle-of-the-road with little local flavour except for their language. The organizers expect the artists to receive Pan-Asian applause. Another example is given by the Asian karaoke contest organized by Pioneer in seven Asian countries. This suggests that the Japanese music industry is trying to create an 'Asian' market under its control.

Unlike the West where Japanese influence is usually limited to audio-visual technology and transnational capitalization, East Asia, in addition to these two factors, receives and appropriates Japanese popular music as well. For example, Japan sells technological products to the West but not Japanese music, just as the purchase of Columbia Pictures and MCA-Universal by Sony and Matsushita respectively will never mean that Hollywood will make samurai movies.

In East Asia, the situation is not the same. Karaoke is an indispensable tool for Asianizing popular music in East Asia because it is basically targeted at the urban middle class, the most influential sector for 'hi-tech'-related consumer culture in the country. Asianization for that class throughout East Asia inevitably implies modernization but results in Japanization since it is this 'economic leader of Asia' who demonstrates to East Asia more effectively than any other country how one 'Far Eastern' state can be economically competitive with the United States and Europe while domesticating the overwhelming material culture originated in the West. Karaoke in East Asia empowers the triple process of modernization, Japanization and Asianization of East Asia.

As suggested earlier, however, this does not mean that Asian music cultures are homogenized by the loud singing voice from the speakers. It is true that karaoke by necessity institutionalizes non-professional performance in front of bar or box audiences through pre-recorded sound, cheap images and amplified voice; it does not erase the local differences in which the material practice of singing is embedded.

## NOTES

1   This chapter is based on Ōtake's fieldwork conducted between 1994 and 1996 (Ōtake 1997) and our subsequent discussion thereupon.
2   Some 90 per cent of the Japanese nation identify themselves as 'middle class' and the economic discrepancy between the affordable and the unaffordable is smaller than in many other countries.
3   There exists no 'Asian' pop but various forms of pop music in Asia. Because of linguistic variety and ethnic diversity, it is unlikely to create pop music that can appeal to the whole nations in the area. The only *lingua franca* in pop music in East Asia may be English, a global but foreign language for everyone. Just like TV programmes, songs in a foreign language may appeal only to a limited sector of the people. Whether the lyrics are poetic or banal, the sound of familiar words is indispensable for nationwide popularity.

## REFERENCES

Adams, Vincanne (1996) 'Karaoke as modern Lhasa, Tibet: western encounters with cultural politics', *Cultural Anthropology*, vol. 11, no. 4, pp. 510–46.

Berland, Jody (1992) 'Angels dancing: cultural technologies and the production of space', *Cultural Studies*, vol. 6, no. 1, pp. 38–55.

de Certeau, Michel (1980) *L'invention du quotidien*, Paris: UGE.

El-Shawan Castelo-Branco, Salwa (1987) 'Some aspects of the cassette industry in Egypt', *World of Music*, vol. 29, vol. 2, pp. 32–45.

Fornäs, Johan (1998) 'Filling voids along the by way: identification and interpretation in the Swedish forms of Karaoke', in Tōru Mitsui and Shūhei Hosokawa (eds.), *Karaoke Around the World: Global Technology, Local Singing*. New York: Routledge, pp. 118–35.

Hosokawa, Shūhei (1984) 'The Walkman effect', *Popular Music*, vol. 4, pp. 165–80.

Ishihara, Shintaro (1991) *The Japan That Can Say No: Why Japan Will Be First Among Equals*, New York: Simon and Schuster.

Iwabuchi, Koichi (1995) 'Return to Asia? Japan in the global audiovisual market', *Media International Australia*, no. 77, pp. 94–106.

Mahathir, Mohama (1994) *Nō to Ieru Ajia* [The Asia That Can Say No], Tokyo: Kōbunsha.

Manuel, Peter (1993) *Cassette Culture: Popular Music and Technology in North India*, Chicago and London: University of Chicago Press.

Morley, David and Robins, Kevin (1992) 'Techno-orientalism: futures, foreigners and phobias', *New Formation*, no. 16, pp. 136–56.

Ōtake, Akiko (1997) *Karaoke Umi o Wataru* [Karaoke crosses over the sea], Tokyo: Chikuma Shobō.

Sutton, R. Anderson (1985) 'Commercial cassette recordings of traditional music in Java: implications for performers and scholars', *World of Music*, vol. 27, no.3, pp. 23–45.

Tobin, Joseph J. (ed.) (1992) *Re-Made in Japan: Everyday Life and Consumer Taste in a Changing Society*, New Haven and London: Yale University Press.

Wong, Deborah (1995) 'Thai cassettes and their covers: two case histories', in John Lent (ed.) *Asian Popular Culture*, Boulder, CO: Westview Press, pp. 43–60.

Zhang, Xiao Bo (ed.) (1996) *Nō to Ieru Chūgoku* [The China That Can Say No], Tokyo: Nihon Keizai Shinbunsha.

# 5

# Techno-Being

## Viktor Mazin

### ■ 1. Introduction: Psycho/Techno ■

Human being is always already a techno-being, a co-product of two evolutions – psychological and technological ones. Human being is much less a result of the Darwinian transmutations, than a product of drives and (their) techne. However, the history of humankind has been dominated by technological evolution, which is both a technical and logical mechanism of survival. The human psyche does not work and develop on its own as supposed, but is subjected to technological development. The human psyche in itself – if there could be such a thing – hasn't changed much for the last thousand years or so.

Human being appears on the planet Earth if not as a cyborg, then as a proto-cyborg, a being articulated by indispensable relations between organic and non-organic matters. Its appearance and existence are strictly connected with two types of devices: symbolic (language, anticipation, fantasy, memory) and material (from a stone knife to a space ship). Both devices function as prostheses or extensions, as a medium between inner and outer space. One could say that a human lives in-between inner and outer. In other words, the human appears through a differentiation of inner and outer. The evolution of extensions (McLuhan, 1964) presupposes virtual mastery over the outer. The notion of prosthesis (Freud, 1961/1930) presupposes not only an improvement of an organic organ by an inorganic supplement (an eye + eyeglasses, a foot + a car, an ear + a telephone, etc.), but also a process of anesthetization of the reality principle.

The obvious change in the evolution of the human is an exteriorization of psychic reality. A human is nothing but a process of exteriorization, a process in which access to time and culture is developed through memory as a form of relations between the "human" and the "technical object." The last century was especially successful in this sense: the oneiro-reality, the reality of desires, fantasies, hallucinations, made some serious breakthroughs: from cinema to computer games and virtual reality, from analog to digital technology.

Human evolution is epiphilogenetic, to use a notion of Bernard Stiegler (1998). This evolution develops itself not so much according to genetic and central nervous system types of memory, but rather according to cultural-technological memory, from books to computer archives, from cave drawings to media installations.

This techno-logical evolutional process became the subject matter of the journal *Kabinet* when it was established in St. Petersburg, Russia, in 1991, and of Freud's Dreams Museum, established there in 1999. To understand what's going on with humans on this planet, to get the idea of who we are, to master ourselves, we have to understand the relations between psyche and techne. And there is not just one true approach to working through this question. That is why *Kabinet* is based on the platform of multidisciplinary investigation, where artists, psychiatrists, poets, philosophers, critics, and psychoanalysts can contribute their ideas, dreams, and visions. That is why Freud's Dreams Museum was established, not to show something to the public but to create the conditions for subjective visions to be projected by its visitors.

## ■ 2.  Moebius Strip ■

On January 6, 2002, an artist, Julia Strauss, and a scholar, Philipp von Gilgers, created an event called *The Electromirror*, which took place in the spaces of Freud's Dreams Museum. Julia Strauss is a Berlin-based media artist working on the subject of psycho–techno, art–science, and human–machine correlations. Philipp von Gilgers is a scientist from Helmholz University for Techniques of Culture (Berlin). He is known as the inventor of the Discourse Analyzing Machine.

The *Electromirror* event was dedicated to the Moebius strip [a looped strip of paper that is twisted so that the resulting loop has only one surface; there is no front or back, inside or outside]. The key notions of the event were the relations between psychology and technology, inside and outside, and psychic apparatus and the computer machine. The figure of the Moebius strip was the connecting motif between the three main areas of the *Electromirror* media installation. In the informational hall of the museum one could see two partial objects: a sculptural figure of a fragment of Moebius strip with a small mirror; and a small element of the strip, a section representing a portrait of Jacques Lacan, a key figure for this event. In the dream hall of the museum Julia Strauss performed between a painting representing the Moebius strip with images of famous mathematicians on the one side, and images of famous psychoanalysts on the other, and a computer station that displayed the same painting. In another small room the Discourse Analyzing Machine combined mathematics and psychoanalysis in a Moebius way.

The name of the whole media installation, *The Electromirror*, derives from a small mirror put on the sculptural fragment of the Moebius strip in the informational hall (see figure 5.1). This mirror functions as an epigraph. It works as an entrance to an abyss of narcissistic reflection. The figure of Freud's shadow is heading towards the mirror entrance. There is an inscription over the mirror, *Hotel Esplanade*. Freud's shadow is running into the door of the building where Alan Turing was born, the man who is famous for his Turing Machine [an early theoretical version of the digital computer]. Here, in the deformed space and time of the Moebius strip Freud's Psycho-Logical Apparatus meets Turing's Cyber-Logical Apparatus. The two sides of the Moebius strip are only distinguished by the dimension of *time*, the time it takes to traverse the whole strip. The fragment of the Moebius strip mirrors the two apparatuses. Freud and Turing are two fathers of the human. The shadow of one father is running beyond the mirror surface where another father "is."

The Moebius strip illustrates ways to problematize different binary oppositions, such as inside/outside, love/hate, signifier/signified, truth/appearance, mathematics/psychoanalysis. While the two terms in these oppositions are presented in everyday life as radically distinct, Lacan tried to present such oppositions in terms of the topology of the Moebius strip. The opposed terms are thus seen to be not discrete but continuous with each other. Likewise, the discourse of the artist is continuous with the discourse of the viewer.

In the dream hall, Julia Strauss performs between two representations, an analog representation of the Moebius strip which is the painting and its digital copy which is on the computer screen (see figure 5.2). While she performs with the painting

FIGURE 5.1

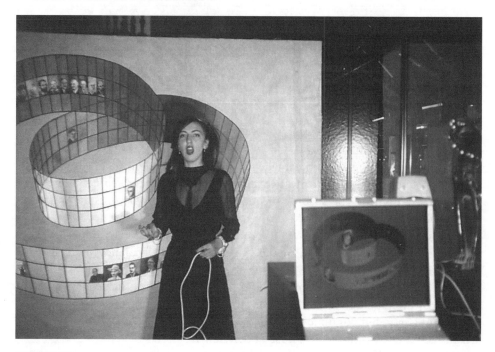

FIGURE 5.2

she is attached to the computer by a cable. When someone from the audience moves to the computer and makes a mouse-click on one of the portraits of famous mathematicians and psychoanalysts, a mechanical voice starts talking about the figure selected. Julia Strauss opens her mouth, repeating soundlessly the text she knows by heart. She looks like a programmed TV weather reporter, and she behaves like a marionette that is completely dependent on the instructive computer voice. "Organic" human is becoming an appendix of the "non-organic" machine. The machine speaks! The human just opens her mouth. The machine becomes an industrial unconscious of the human. Lacan reminds us: the human speaks, and that's why s/he is unconscious. Now the function of speech is readdressed to a machine, a computer.

The problematization of inner and outer in the Moebius strip fundamentally challenges the notion of borders, and therefore of bodies as well, and thus challenges our means of self-representation. This same question is raised quite prominently when we consider virtual reality. In virtual reality what appears is an outer representation of an inner psychic space. Cyberreality and psychic reality are two forms of reality narcissistically representing each other, like two sides of a Moebius strip.

While Freud's shadow is frozen in his run on the Moebius fragment, and while Julia Strauss is animating computer voices, Philipp von Gilgers is presenting his Discourse Analyzing Machine. He is working in a study beyond the analog-digital portrait of Jacques Lacan. (See figure 5.3.) Why Lacan? Not only because of his interest in the figure of Moebius, but also because he is tries to join mathematics

FIGURE 5.3

and psychoanalysis, to combine two fields of human knowledge which seem so distant. Lacan introduces fundamental algebraic mathemes to psychoanalysis.

What is the Discourse Analyzing Machine? While seated in front of a computer monitor, an attached video camera focuses on your eye. You see your eye on the computer screen. You see the eye staring at you. Does it remind you of something? Sure: it is the gaze. More than that, you see a blindspot nearby, a point you can't see because it is the point the gaze is controlling you from. Then a few words appear on the screen. They split and move to different parts of the screen. Your eye starts chasing and choosing a word. Not you, but your eye. Every involuntary choice brings the next words to the screen to bifurcate once more (see figure 5.4).

Where do the words come from? From a collection of texts downloaded onto the computer, including Leibnitz's *Monadology*, Lacan's *Seminars*, Astrompsychosis's *Book of Dreams*, and *The Interpretation of Dreams in the Epoch of Mass Communication* by Mazin and Pepperstein. In fact, from the psychoanalytic point of view it is not so important what kind of texts are "there," in the machine's programs. What is important is the choice of your eye. It is like John Cage's chance operations. It is a nonstop bifurcation, which you are not able to stand after 10–15 minutes. It is too fast for day-reality; it is too close to the dream world. Words immediately bring other words in chains of associations. Every signifier is a set of references of virtual paths to different directions. And your eye is responsible for this choice. Every time the path of associations is dependent on the eye's choice. Every time we are confronted by new possibilities.

In the end we are presented with one more partial object of *The Electromirror*: a digital video-projection of Freud's death mask, or, more correctly, Freud's Ghost-Mask. Since there is no death mask of Freud, Julia Strauss took a photograph of him as a 12-year-old boy and transformed this image into a 3-D mask. Thus, one

FIGURE 5.4

has the ability to make Freud's death mask some decades after his death and without his corporeal presence. Digital technology doesn't need "the original." Not only a partial object, but also even a transitional object is enough to restore the virtual presence.

Thus, Freud's image itself became one of the pieces of his own collection of death masks; his image transforms itself into one of the ghosts in the collection of human-inherited archives. This ghost is very much unlike his physical prototype. This ghost is haunting us. But we don't recognize him any longer.

The mask of the 12-year-old Freud appears from out of visual noise, opens its mouth and speaks with the voice of an 82-year-old man, Freud's voice, and then disappears again in the microbits of the noise. He dissolves himself in the noise of the medium. No figure, no background. No inside, no outside. No chronology. No boy, no man. Just a machine.

■ 3. Man-machine ■

We are witnessing the moment of this dissolution of the man into his machine. And in a paradoxical way the reason for this transformation is more ideological than technological. The idea of man-machine isn't a new one. One can find its very different representations from Golem to Lamettrie's *L'homme machine*, from Frankenstein to Cyborg. Nowadays the man-machine is a product of at least two factors: scientific ideology and the pharmacological industry's ideology of the so-called consumer society.

The scientific ideology describes human as a man-machine, as a behavioral man, not only in magazines like *Scientific American* and on TV channels like *Discovery*, but – and this is much more efficient – in science-fiction movies. In *Blade Runner*, *Johnny Mnemonic*, *Total Recall*, *The Cell*, *The 6th Day*, and so on, the human – in contrast to different types of human-like nonhumans – is the one who has true memory, that is, subjective true history. Memory is the last residue of the subject. The thing is that this memory is industrialized. If beforehand it was possible to exploit human memory as a data archive (like Mr. Memory in Hitchcock's *39 Steps*), to use the human unconscious as an information container in itself, nowadays it is allegedly possible to transfer data directly from psyche to a machine. According to this ideology, they are compatible, and it is easy to translate psychic processes onto digital hardware. They are compatible, for computer hardware is an analogue of the human brain, and brain is psyche. Memory is produced as a set of archives analogous to computer memory. It is possible to download, erase, reinscribe, and reduplicate memory. It is possible to clone the psyche as it is possible to clone cells. This is the ideology of mechanical memory reproduction based on the substitution of psychic processes with electric-chemical brain processes. Psychic activity is reduced to the work of the brain. Thus if you have problems with your memory you can fix them with the help of pharmacological production. Your aim is to function. If you have problems with your "normal" functioning, you have to be repaired with a magic pill. If you wish to change your thoughts use pills, if you wish to find your desire use hormones. Welcome to the world of the man-machine of the chemical generation.

## REFERENCES

Freud, S. (1961/1930). *Civilization and its discontents*. Trans. J. Strachey. New York: W. W. Norton. (Original work published 1930: *Das Ubehagen in der Kultur*. Vienna: Internationaler Psychoanalytischer Verlag.)

McLuhan, M. (1964). *Understanding Media: The Extensions of Man*. New York: Signet.

Stiegler, B. (1998). *Technics and Time*. Trans. R. Beardsworth and G. Collins. Stanford: Stanford University Press. (Original work published 1994: *La technique et le temps. Vol. 1. La faute d'Epiméthée*. Paris: Galilee.)

# Part II

## Performance and Culture

# Introduction

## Della Pollock

The nation, for Diana Taylor (see chapter 10 below), is a "theatre of operations." It is a militarized zone defined by defensive stratagems. Among these are spectacular reiterations: elaborately staged representations of itself to itself, securing by rehearsing identification. The primary battle is an internal and symbolic one, played out on the bodies – often tortured, dead, or disappeared – that make up the "nation."

Performance – as a practice and as an analytic – shows the antagonistic insecurities at the heart of the "nation." In each of the essays in this section, the nation is unstable and anxious. It requires elusive cohesion – elusive to the very extent that it is performed: each performance, disappearing into time and strife, needs another. Each, moreover, underscores the extent to which performance may repeat, suspend, critique, and transform the normative values and practices of (self-) colonization.

These essays articulate performance, international, and Cultural Studies, suggesting above all the praxical significance of performance for Cultural Studies. Each sees the nation as a "theatre of operations." But as such, each also sees the limits of what Judith Butler calls "performativity" or the compulsive repetitions of disciplinary order that congeal ideology into "nature." Performative repetition materializes order. And yet materialization occurs in time among embodied subjects as performance. The embodied performative process is risky, precarious, fraught with contextual desires, dangers, and implications – to the extent that in the same moment that performative histories become real, their reality becomes shaky.

Performativity rests at best uneasily in performance. As Elin Diamond argues:

When performativity materializes as performance in that risky and dangerous negotiation between a doing (a reiteration of norms) and a thing done (discursive conventions that frame our interpretations), between someone's body and the conventions of embodiment, we have access to cultural meanings and critique. (1997: 5)

Performance does not merely execute what is conventional or *done*. To the contrary, the tension between *the act of doing* and *what is done* suggests an essential ambivalence in the order of things. Performance at once enacts and contests reiterations of the past in ongoing negotiations and re-creations of *what matters now*. In its amplified versions as drama, ritual, show, and spectacle (whether as points of description or deliberate practice) performance thus becomes culturally salient as a way of *knowing* the past, *doing* the present, and *intervening* on the future.

The scholarship on performance, culture, and nation is wide-ranging and complex. The essays in this section are by no means representative. They are, however, exemplary investigations into such diverse forms of performance as stage shows, classical and vernacular traditions, popular raids on state theatricality, the composition of self in dialogue, and corporeal dogma. Each reflects the power of performance to press at the borders of nationality, suggesting their porousness and plasticity and focusing questions of inter/nationality at specific regional sites; in conditions of exile (internal and external), refuge, diaspora; and from the performative place of "in-betweeness, the shared spaces of the border itself" (Taylor, 1997: x).

Jennifer Robertson's study of the gender-bending Japanese theater revue, Takarazuka, shows the collaboration of colonial anthropology and popular entertainment in "Japanization." A massively produced theater spectacle, Takarazuka inverts the traditional practice of all-male Kabuki. Characterized by an all-female cast engaged in cross-dressing and "cross-ethnicking," the revue gained its popularity in part on the proposition of female drag. Conservative defenders argued that the ambivalence inherent in women-playing-men glorified masculinity and reified the facticity of women's bodies. Government censors and female fans, however, agreed that the performance (as performance) exceeded its conservative agendas. The government found the female player or *otokoyaku* sufficiently offensive to ban her from the stage in 1939; for similar reasons, female fans savored the sense of radical possibility she seemed to represent:

> Watching the otokoyaku onstage, (female) fans enjoy vicariously what they too might be able to do *if* – magically – they were someone else: not male, but players of men's roles. The key to liberation, as it were, involves not a change of sex but a new gender identity, and by extension, a transformation in gender ideology. (Robertson, 1998: 86–7)

The imperialist state also found Takarazuka useful. It deployed the ambivalence at the heart of the revue, drawing gender and colonial mis/identification into a homologous relation that rendered the state "androgynous" – itself and not itself, nation and empire, Japan and Greater East Asia. The wartime revue, characterized by collage representations of "other" cultures, assimilated pan-Asian ethnologies

into gender play, simultaneously elaborately marking and deflating cultural difference. In this way, hybridity did not so much signify the duplicity of apparently
fixed identity positions as much as "the composite construction of Japanese
national cultural identity, the 'Japanization' of Asian peoples incorporated into
the Greater East Asia Co-Prosperity Sphere ... and the embodiment of 'outsiders'
(*gaijin*) by certain Japanese" (Robertson, ch. 12 below). Accordingly, Takarazuka,
despite its all-female cast and related controversies, was a powerful means
of expanding and consolidating imperial Japan. Unlike the spare, socialist-
realist theater to which other emerging regimes turned in the 1930s and 1940s,
Takarazuka eschewed the dramatization of apparently "transparent" populist
values. It overhauled tradition and reveled in the twin virtuosities of its female
players and anthropological displays. It took its imperial force precisely, ironically,
from the pleasures of seeing supposedly "authentic" bodies mixed and crossed
on stage.[1]

For Taylor, gender is also the contested ground of national identity. Excerpted
from her ground-breaking work, *Disappearing Acts: Spectacles of Gender and
Nationalism in Argentina's "Dirty War"* (1997), Taylor's essay concerns the psychosocial claims of public spectacle in the wake of Peron's death in 1974 and the
military coup and establishment of Argentina's National Security Doctrine in 1976.
Working from the Gramscian premise that myth is a "concrete phantasy which acts
on a dispersed and shattered people to arouse and organize its collective will,"
Taylor refuses the disarticulation of psychoanalysis and social theory, pursuing
instead the essential question of how sight compels desire (Gramsci, qtd. Taylor,
1997: 30).

What Taylor finds is the implacable compression of myths of the nation and
gender, implemented through state control of what can and cannot be seen or,
more insidiously, what is "disappeared" by spectacles of terror. The junta performed what Michael Taussig calls the "magic of the state" through disappearing
acts. It inscribed the rule of a new national family on and through the bodies of
women who were always already condemned for excess and treason:

> The nocturnal raids on homes, the abduction of family members, the practice of
> raping and torturing loved ones in front of each other revealed the armed forces'
> uneasiness with the family as a separate space and organizational unit. As the junta
> had warned, all the interior/private spaces were turned inside out. (Taylor, 1997: 88)

Introducing the critical notion of "percepticide," Taylor argues that the military
dictatorship protected its jealous claims to the motherland or *Patria* through the
totalizing representation of military/masculine power. By destroying conventionally feminine spaces, effacing any remnant of "flesh-and-blood" feminine power,
and vanishing the bodies of feminized – weak or dissident – males, it sought to
stabilize the symbolic value of the virgin mother, disappearing real bodies under
the rule of national/Oedipal myth. One effect was to reproduce people as non-
subjects, to "disappear" subjectivity altogether. Taylor cites one military leader's
justification: "It wasn't people that disappeared, but subversives" (1997: 148).

*Disappearing Acts* is an act of witness. It is allied with the now widely celebrated mothers of the Plaza de Mayo who refuse the elision of (virgin) maternity with the state and violate rules of assembly to claim visual, public space for their lost children. The mothers stand in for the bodies of the disappeared. They are metonymic representations of bodies that have been removed even from the cultural encodings of death. As such, they are haunted and haunting. Silently carrying placards emblazoned with old photographs of sons and daughters, the mothers materialize ghosts. Their bodies signify absent bodies, figments, whose absence is marked by their presence.

In her central chapter on "Disappearing Bodies: Writing Torture and Torture as Writing," Taylor represents her own struggle with testifying to bodies that appear to the reader only as signs. How can she perform witness through writing? How can writing intervene on policy through its own haunting presence? Taylor insists on the power of critical witness to clear the ground for questions of "'real' biological and historical materiality":

> only by disentangling the gendered tropes constructed in terms of individual, social, and political bodies from the master narrative on the "authentic national being" can we begin to examine the significance of the "real" biological and historical materiality of the victimized women, men, and children. (1997: 149)

Taylor wants to disentangle the myth of the state (with its claims for authenticity) from the material bodies made to bear and signify that myth. But between flat claims on the material facticity of the body and the terrifying rule of the body-as-sign – so easily and evidently appropriated by military rule – Taylor asks: "how to hold onto the materiality of the individual body even as we accept the social production of subjectivity?"[2]

This is the defining question of performance. Insofar as performativity works itself out through "the materiality of the individual body" in performance, performance is always a hybrid composition of the material and social. It mediates myth and matter while it (1) following Diamond, exceeds performativity in the immediacies of contest and critique, (2) enacts the power of the "individual body" to signify prevailing myths, whether by presence or marked absence, and (3) suggests possibilities for *re*producing social subjectivity through poetics of resistance, such as those described by Lavie and Conquergood in chapters 8 and 6 below.

Smadar Lavie's path-breaking work, *The Poetics of Military Occupation: Mzeina Allegories of Bedouin Identity Under Israeli and Egyptian Rule* (1990), is perhaps most remarkable for its cautious and yet insistent claims on the power of the performer to exert "symbolic defiance." Lavie's work complements others' attempts to qualify what Lila Abu-Lughod has called the "romance of resistance" by focusing on the necessary deferral of resistance to allegory.[3] As Lavie argues:

> the constant military occupation of the South Sinai precluded for the Mzeina the identity that both turn-of-the-century travelers' accounts and contemporary nostalgic literature or media accounts inscribed for the Bedouin: fierce romantic nomads

on loping camels in the vast desert. On the contrary, the military occupation had penetrated Mzeini daily life so deeply and so long that it had become much more than soldiers, developers, settlers, and tourists impinging on the external political and economic relationships between the indigenous tribe and the state. The omnipresent occupations had permeated not only internal inter- and intratribal affairs, but also discourses as delicate and intimate as those between husbands and wives. Given that the Mzeina were helpless objects of external political processes, I argue that their Bedouin identity could be little more than literary allegory: tribal identity appeared as moralistic, multilayered narratives transcending the spatial and temporal boundaries of military occupation through symbolic defiance only, because for Mzeinis to openly confront any armed or unarmed occupier could mean beatings, jail, even death.

Lavie recounts cultural conditions so shredded by occupation that they could no longer support regular, ritual practices much less direct resistance. To the extent that the Mzeina resisted, it was through occasional, impromptu evocations of Bedouin identity. These performances "would unfold during the fragile interstices of a tense, discontinuous conversation" (1990: 6–7). They would disappear as quickly as they began, almost as if they hadn't happened at all. For a few moments, performance would brace open liminal spaces in which participants reflected on current circumstances in faint echoes (or simulations) of traditional, ritual forms. These performances – as sudden and slight as they may have been – enabled participants to renew, practice, and adjust their identification as Mzeinis. At the same time, the performers and participants hid within the symbolic framework of performance. They protected themselves and their culture against further incursion by marking performance as such, by identifying a story as "just a story," not real, not effective (1990: 335). They quarantined story in allegory, ironically attaching cultural survival to the poetics of performance.

The fool is one of six symbolic types around which Lavie structures *The Poetics of Military Occupation*. The Mzeini Fool is a comic figure: a joker, wild card, and shape-shifter, who embodies the contradictions inherent in cultural practice generally and the paradoxes of living under shifting Israeli and Egyptian domination specifically. As Lavie shows, he is at once discounted and gains his power as a fool, typically trumping normative systems with performative wit, often opportunistically. The fool is a marginal character who nonetheless *works the borders*. He greases the forces of contradiction that may otherwise hold a culture – vice-like – in its grip. Performing the "fool," he evokes a traditional role in Bedouin culture. But in so doing he does not renew old, traditional, or subordinate identities as much as he models the survival value of light-footed, shifting, hybrid identifications. He not only parodies prevailing conditions but embraces the contingencies of contradiction, paradox, and duplicity that would otherwise prove oppressive.

Dwight Conquergood's "Health Theatre in a Hmong Refugee Camp" (chapter 6 below) is a landmark study in what it can mean to mobilize indigenous knowledge. The camp at Ban Vinai was for Conquergood a "crucible of refugee crisis." It was a site of equally intense displacement and performativity. Western oversight groups attributed mounting hygiene problems in the camp to stubbornly "primitive" practices among the Hmong inhabitants, reinforcing the conventional divide between Western scientific presumption and traditional wisdom. Conquergood worked with the Hmong to break open the middle ground of cultural difference: to articulate modern and traditional knowledge systems in order to identify infra-structural problems, develop alternative practices, and implement massive change. The result was a fast-expanding health theater program, a parade-style social movement that drew its alchemical force from dialogic interaction and that ultimately allowed Hmong cultural tradition to perform its adaptive function.

For Conquergood, "as a medium of exchange, performance draws us to the margin, the borders between Self and Other." It is a site of barter, a boundary practice, that makes the Self vulnerable to transformation by the Other. Conquergood relies on Bakhtin's sense that "the most intense and productive life of culture takes place on the boundaries" (1986: 2, 202). The health theater was a boundary practice, a large-scale effort in tricksterism, that not only initiated but changed the very terms of exchange, dissolving conventional distinctions between Self and the primitive Other into a vibrant, effective reinvention of camp culture that was quickly taken up by other camps along the Pacific rim.

Judith Hamera's study of the Sem family (chapter 7 below), survivors of the Khmer Rouge living in exile in LA, however, points to the limits of dialogue. The Sems' survival depends on the performance of amnesia. In order to escape the Khmer and to survive in exile, they must forget their most essential traditions, ties, and histories. And yet, as members of an elite class of Thai classical dancers, they cannot forget the esoteric techniques and ideals of the "Apsara" so deeply impressed on their rigorously trained bodies. In LA they are ghosts of a tradition all but wiped out by the Khmer.

They are consequently caught, Hamera argues, in a dynamic of "answerability." They must account for their individual survival, even while survival brings them to the edge of disappearing into their host culture. Their bodies moreover speak what they can't: "For the Sems, what personal silence foreclosed, dance enabled; through the solace of good form, it offered an answer back – albeit a problematic one – to their pervasive sense of goneness" (Hamera, p. 98, below). And yet the Sems' performances – in dance and life narrative – are riven by the "truth in trauma": the evident knowledge that the genocidal wound cannot be closed, that the utopian promise of the Apsara – the promise of transcendence and immortality – has been irreparably degraded. The Sems' fragmentary attempts to remember and renew Thai dance only underscore the incommensurability of art, life, and "goneness" they are meant to resolve:

> What we are left with is not only a palimpsest of answerability in which the body of the dancer writes over the invisible text of the refugee and is, in so doing, written over by the ideal body of the Apsara, but also a dance in which each move is a partial erasure and a contestatory deferral of the previous move. The net result is not unity but the mutual destabilization of art, life, and goneness, an exposure of their incommensurability, a destabilization and exposure the Sems sought to shore up through the dance. (Hamera, p. 102, below)

In this case, the performance of self and tradition materializes loss. It yields unassimilable gaps in history and experience to which performance nonetheless must continue to "answer."

In each of these chapters, performance troubles the terms of nation-making, challenging *empire* with *androgyny, disappearance* with *witness, oppression* with *paradox, dogma* with *dialogue,* and the promise of *continuity* with *discontinuity* and *incommensurability.* Performance variously extends, asserts, breaks, and refuses the boundaries necessary to secure a national "self." In each of these essays, performance involves crossing borders, magically and violently. In each, perform-ance exceeds itself in material *contingencies* and *instabilities.* As a poetics of political practice, it introduces *ambivalence* even into those places where it would install the unitary vision of military dictatorship or even traditional dance, risking in turn the gaps, division, contradiction, paradox, mimicry, parody, and play that com-prise countermemory.[4] It configures the ground of ongoing *answerability,* continu-ally deferring closure while re-marking loss, "goneness," disappearance, and displacement. And yet as a means of *invention* and *intervention,* performance may be a specific, strategic practice of negotiating boundaries, articulating differ-ence, and *re*producing (colonial) subjectivities. It challenges inter/national Cultural Studies to answer to "the materiality of the individual body" while it initiates a sense of material possibility and change.

## NOTES

1  Note that drag is Judith Butler's premiere example of the subversive power of the performative in performance: "Bodily Inscriptions, Performative Subversions," in *Gender Trouble* (New York: Routledge, 1991).

2  See also Taylor's recent essay on third-generation witnessing in Argentina, "'You Are Here': The DNA of Performance," *TDR: The Drama Review* 46(1) (2002): 149–69, as well as her co-edited volume, *Negotiating Performance: Gender, Sexuality, and Theatri-cality in Latin/o America,* eds. Taylor and Villegas (Durham, NC: Duke University Press, 1994).

3  See Lila Abu-Lughod, "The Romance of Resistance: Tracing Transformations of Power Through Bedouin Women," *American Ethnologist* 17(1) (1990): 41–55.

4  See Homi Bhabha on the "Janus-faced discourse of the nation": "Introduction: Narrat-ing the Nation," in *Nation and Narration,* ed. Bhabha (New York: Routledge, 1990), as well as Bhabha's more recent conceptualization of the performative "beyond" in *The Location of Culture* (New York: Routledge, 1994).

## REFERENCES

Bakhtin, Mikhail M. (1986). *Speech Genres.* Eds. C. Emerson and M. Holquist, trans. V. W. McGee. Austin: University of Texas Press.

Diamond, Elin (1997). *Unmaking Mimesis: Essays on Feminism and Theater.* New York and London: Routledge.

Lavie, Smadar (1990). *The Poetics of Military Occupation: Mzeina Allegories of Bedouin Identity Under Israeli and Egyptian Rule.* Berkeley: University of California Press.

Robertson, Jennifer (1998). *Takarazuka: Sexual Politics and Popular Culture in Modern Japan.* Berkeley: University of California Press.

Taussig, Michael (1996). *The Magic of the State.* New York and London: Routledge.

Taylor, Diana (1997). *Disappearing Acts: Spectacles of Gender and Nationalism in Argentina's "Dirty War."* Durham, NC: Duke University Press.

# 6

# Health Theatre in a Hmong Refugee Camp: Performance, Communication, and Culture

## Dwight Conquergood

I arrived in Thailand in February 1985 having just completed, with Taggart Siegel, a documentary on Hmong shamanism and the Sudden Unexpected Death Syndrome that has reached epidemic proportions among the Hmong resettled in the United States (Siegel and Conquergood 1985).[1] My intention was to do straightforward field research on cultural performance in refugee camps, particularly shamanism, but the refugee situation had become so politically sensitive in Thailand that all camps were closed to outsiders, particularly researchers. Therefore, I sought employment with the international aid voluntary agencies that administer health care and services to the camps. Fortunately I was hired by the International Rescue Committee (IRC) as a health worker in Ban Vinai, a hilltribe camp not far from the Mekong River that divides Thailand from Laos, and the oldest and largest refugee camp in Thailand. During the time of my fieldwork the official population of the camp was 45,231 with an additional 2,000–3,000 undocumented "illegals" living in the camp without rice rations. I offered my services as an ethnographic consultant in exchange for the official papers that would legitimize my presence in the camp. My major assignment was to help design and direct an environmental health education program for this camp which was represented in many agency reports as the "filthiest," most "primitive," and "difficult" in Thailand.

Working with the refugees and a local Thai IRC employee, I helped design and direct a health education campaign based on native beliefs and values and communicated in culturally appropriate forms. Specifically, we started a refugee performance company that produced skits and scenarios drawing on Hmong folklore and traditional communicative forms, such as proverbs, storytelling, and folksinging, to develop critical awareness about the health problems in Ban Vinai.

### ■ The Ban Vinai Performance Company ■

Camp Ban Vinai may lack many things – water, housing, sewage disposal system – but not performance. The Camp is an embarrassment of riches in terms of cultural performance. No matter where you go in the camp, at almost any hour of the day or night, you can simultaneously hear two or three performances, from simple storytelling and folksinging to the elaborate collective ritual performances for the dead that orchestrate multiple media, including drumming, stylized lamentation, ritual chanting, manipulation of funerary artifacts, incense, fire, dancing, and animal sacrifice. Nearly every morning I was awakened before dawn by the drumming and ecstatic chanting of performing shamans. During the day women everywhere would sew *pa ndau* (flower cloth), an intricate textile art that sometimes takes the form of embroidered story quilts with pictorial narratives drawn from history and folklore. Performance permeates the fabric of everyday life in Ban Vinai.

A high level of cultural performance is characteristic of refugee camps in general. Since my work in Ban Vinai I have visited or lived for short periods of time in 11 refugee camps in Southeast Asia and the Middle East, not counting a shantytown for displaced people in Nigeria. In every one of them I was struck by the richness and frequency of performative expression. One explanation for this is that refugees have a lot of time on their hands to cultivate expressive traditions. But I think there are deeper psychological and cultural reasons for the high incidence of performance in the camps. Refugee camps are liminal zones where people displaced by trauma and crisis – usually war or famine – must try to regroup and salvage what is left of their lives. Their world has been shattered. They are in passage, no longer Laotian, certainly not Thai, and not quite sure where they will end up or what their lives will become. Betwixt and between worlds, suspended between past and future, they fall back on the performance of their traditions as an empowering way of securing continuity and some semblance of stability. Moreover, through performative flexibility they can play with new identities, new strategies for adaptation and survival. The playful creativity of performance enables them to experiment with and invent a new "camp culture" that is part affirmation of the past and part adaptive response to the exigencies of the present. Performance participates in the re-creation of self and society that emerges within refugee camps. Through its reflexive capacities, performance enables people to take stock of their situation and through this self-knowledge to cope better. There are good reasons why in the crucible of refugee crisis, performative behaviors intensify.

And, of course, even before the Hmong became refugees, oral traditions and cultural performance were the primary ways of educating the young and promoting beliefs and values among adults, as is the case in most third world cultures (see Ong 1982). Any communication campaign that ignored the indigenous cultural strengths of performance would be doomed to failure.

There is always the danger, however, of appropriating performance and using it as an instrument of domination. I wanted no part of the puppet theatre approach used by some expatriates as simply another means to get refugees to do what bureaucrats think best for them. Instead, I hoped that performance could be used as a method for developing critical awareness as an essential part of the process of improving the health situation in the camp. My project was aligned with the popular theatre approach to development and political struggle that is being used with success throughout the third world, particularly Africa, Latin America, and Asia. [ ... ]

I hoped to break the pattern of importing the knowledge of "experts" and distributing it to the refugees, who were expected to be grateful consumers. I wanted to help demonstrate to both expatriates and refugees that *dialogical* exchange between the two cultures, the two worldviews and sensibilities, was possible (see Bakhtin 1981; Todorov 1984; Conquergood 1985).

One of the things that worked well for me as a health worker was to barter recommendations and health practices with traditional healers. [ ... ] What I tried to do in my fieldwork was enact an example of dialogical exchange, or barter, wherein each culture could benefit from the other, approaching health care issues within a both/and embrace instead of an either/or separation of categories; this approach was particularly important because the refugees were accustomed to having expatriates undermine, even outrightly assault, their traditions.

The first test was whether or not the Hmong would accept a popular theatre approach. Quite simply, could we gather an audience? That test came earlier than I had planned when five rabid dogs rampaged through the camp biting several children. The solution proposed by the camp commander was to go to the Thai market, buy five machetes, and kill all the dogs. To his great credit, the director of the International Rescue Committee in Ban Vinai persuaded the colonel against this course of action. He proposed instead that IRC use its funds to buy rabies vaccine and inoculate all the dogs in camp. The vaccine was purchased and IRC personnel were at their stations ready and poised with needles to vaccinate the dogs. No dogs arrived. The problem centered on communication. The Hmong were not boycotting the rabies program. They simply were baffled by this strange procedure, or unaware of it. There was no effective way of getting the word out as to where, when, and why dogs should be brought to the IRC stations for injections.

I had just arrived in camp and was beginning to establish rapport, recruit, and work with refugee performers/health workers. We had developed some characters based on stock figures in Hmong folklore and were designing and constructing costumes and masks. We had started improvisation and confidence-building exercises, but everything was still very tentative. The group was very young; all but one were under 20. We were just beginning to mesh as a group when the IRC director approached me and asked for help with the rabies vaccination project. Time was running out. The camp dogs would have to be vaccinated soon or Ban Vinai might have a serious rabies epidemic.

I certainly did not feel confident about putting the fledgling actors to this kind of major test so soon. We met and discussed the seriousness of the situation and collectively decided what would be the best strategy for quickly communicating this important message to as much of the camp population as possible. We soon agreed on a grand, clamorous, eye-catching "Rabies Parade" that would snake its way through all the sections of the camp. The tiger costume – appliquéd cotton fabric with a long rope tail – was almost finished, so it was agreed that the tiger would be the lead figure in the parade. The tiger is a trickster figure in Hmong folklore and mythology, a very dramatic and evocative character. We knew the tiger would draw attention, inspire awe. The tiger would be followed by a nature-spirit, a ragged costume with long colored strings for hair, that would sing and bang on a drum. That noise, we hoped, would reach the people inside their huts and bring them out to see the commotion. We agreed that the chicken, a feathered costume with a striking cardboard mask that covered the entire head, would be the pivotal figure. After the dancing tiger and the clamorous nature-spirit got people's attention, the chicken would talk through a bullhorn and explain in terms the Hmong would understand the seriousness of rabies and why it was important for every family to round up the dogs and bring them for injections. The chicken couched all this in an appeal toward protecting the children and then gave specific instructions for each neighborhood in the camp as to where and when they should bring the dogs. It was culturally appropriate for the chicken to be the leading speaker because in Hmong lore chickens have divinatory powers. They are frequently offered up in spirit ceremonies as guides to lead the way to the sky kingdom. Three days after a baby is born, chickens are used in an augury ceremony to determine the child's future. Hmong naturally associate the chicken with divination because, as was explained to me, "Who is the one who knows first when the sun comes up every morning?" [ ... ]

In terms of ability to gather an audience, the Rabies Parade was a huge success. Also, the novice performers had acquitted themselves beyond my highest expectations. However, the real test of our communication effectiveness was whether or not the Hmong would bring their dogs to the vaccination stations.

The next morning, full of nervous anticipation, I staked out the first vaccination station. It was a heartwarming sight. Dogs came pouring in – on rope leashes, in two-wheel pushcarts, and carried in their owners' arms. We could not vaccinate them fast enough. I myself vaccinated scores of dogs. The vaccination stations became a sort of street theatre. As you can imagine, the dogs did not submit willingly to these injections. It is a rather intricate operation to hold a struggling dog up in the air – we had no veterinary tables – and get it injected properly. There was a lot of scuffling and abortive thrusts of the needle – the stuff of farce. Also, with so many nervous dogs concentrated in one area, fights broke out. For a week this part of the rabies program performed before rapt audiences, drawing crowds equal to those for the parades. We vaccinated almost 500 dogs. [ ... ]

Throughout the development of our health theatre programs we actively solicited feedback from Hmong elders. We received excellent, helpful criticism. After we had rehearsed our first set of acted scenarios we showed them to a Hmong leader. He critiqued the performers on three points: (1) the performers and stage managers not in costume should wear traditional Hmong clothes, and not Western-style T-shirts and trousers available in the camp through charity outlets; (2) the backup music for the dances should be authentic Hmong, not Thai or Western-influenced melodies; (3) the rhymed chants were a little off from the traditional Hmong prosody, he taught the young performers the correct speech patterns. These criticisms were very useful because many of the members of the performance company were quite young and had grown up in the camp, exposed to outside influences. Moreover, the critique demonstrated the concern of Hmong leaders for maintaining their cultural integrity against the forces of assimilation.

There was one other criticism regarding the masks and the tiger. The oldest member of the performance company declined to wear a mask of any kind. The masks were too real for him. He was unable to frame the wearing of a mask as make-believe and worried about problems with spirits as a consequence of wearing the mask. We, of course, gave him roles that did not require wearing a mask and he remained a dedicated and important member of the performance company. But, soon after the Rabies Parade, a few of the people said that the masks and the tiger were scary and worried that some of the children's spirits might be scared away and they would fall sick. This response struck terror in me. As many anthropologists have noted, the political influence and power of shamans lies in their role as interpreters of the source and cause of illness. Shamanic ceremonies for a patient are in two phases: first, the divination/diagnosis, then the cure (see Conquergood forthcoming a). A shaman can influence the politics of a village by interpreting certain actions as the cause of illness or calamity. There is no lack of children falling sick every day in Ban Vinai. Fever and diarrhea are prevalent. Hundreds of children had enjoyed our parades. If one shaman attributed the sickness of one child to spirit-flight precipitated by the parade, the Ban Vinai health and performance company would be destroyed. One accusation could ruin us.

It was a tense week for me, but no accusations came. However, we decided to modify our staging techniques based on this feedback. Powerful characters like the tiger would no longer play directly to the audience in open form. Using theatre-in-the-round staging, we would direct the energies of the tiger and other masked characters inside the circle, using onstage focus. We would have these dramatic characters interact in an animated way with one another, but not directly confront the audience.

However, we did not want to lose the power of open-form communication, so we needed a narrator character who could safely and directly address audiences. Proverbs are an important communication form in all oral cultures and particularly popular with the Hmong (see Conquergood forthcoming b). We wanted to use a character who could recite health proverbs and tell stories and who would have a special rapport with small children. Almost a quarter of the camp's population is under the age of five, the most vulnerable group with a high rate of disease and death. Appealing to them would also be a way of involving their parents; Hmong families are tightly knit and children are greatly loved. This led to the creation of our most successful character who became the symbol for the entire health communication program: the beloved Niam Tsev Huv (Mother Clean), our cleanliness clown. She was the collective creation of the entire performance company. Inspired by Peter Schumann's Bread and Puppet Theatre, I introduced the idea of a huge muppet figure constructed on a bamboo frame. The performance company took it from there. Someone designed her face, a pleasant smile painted on a cloth-stuffed dummy's head tacked atop the bamboo frame; someone else did her costume, a colorfully striped dress that made her look larger than life; another member made her hair out of dyed yarn. The performance company worked collectively on all phases of the performance process, from research for scenarios to composing songs and proverbs to costume construction. Except for the tiger's mask which I purchased in Loei, the provincial capital, all of the costumes and props were handmade from local materials.

The performer who eventually assumed the role of Mother Clean was a late starter – not one of the precocious three who emerged during the Rabies Parade. Several members of the company tried out the role, but he was the one who brought Mother Clean to life. Mother Clean, as he created her, was as gentle and loving as she was physically huge and imposing. She was a narrator-character who set the stage for the performance and, during the performance, could negotiate back and forth between direct address to the audience and dialog with onstage characters. Mother Clean particularly loved little children and always had special words for them. They adored her; sometimes during a performance they would run on stage to peek underneath her muppet skirts. Mother Clean always handled these moments with tender dignity, improvising skillfully. She also was very, very funny. Adults would double over with laughter at her antics. The incongruity between her size and her feigned daintiness was very farcical. Mother Clean grew in popularity so that the sight of her coming down the camp road would immediately draw a huge crowd for a performance. As she would walk through the camp, small children would shout her name. Hundreds of T-shirts were printed with her image in the Ban Vinai Print Shop run by a Japanese Refugee Relief Agency. The camp literacy project used her image on posters. She was perhaps the most visible figure with the highest name recognition in the camp and she became the linchpin of our communication campaign. People believed that Mother Clean was on their side and the side of their children and they listened to what she told them about health and sanitation.

## ■ Performance, Garbage, and the Environmental Setting ■

Once we had demonstrated that performance was an appropriate and successful way of communicating with the Hmong, we set out to work on the environmental health problems of the camp. Ban Vinai has serious hygiene and sanitation problems. The cause, however, lies in the environmental circumstances, not any innate character flaw of the Hmong. Simplistic health messages imported from Western middle-class notions of cleanliness simply would not work for Ban Vinai. What was needed was a health education and consciousness-raising program that was sensitive to the history and specific environmental problems and constraints of the camp.

Ban Vinai is located in an isolated, hilly region of northeast Thailand, the poorest sector of the country. The camp has a population larger than any city in this remote area of Thailand, surpassing even Loei, the provincial capital. It is the most populous refugee camp in Asia. All these people are crowded onto about 400 acres of undeveloped land. The camp space is intensively used because refugees are forbidden to go outside the camp without the express permission of Colonel Vichitmala, the Thai camp commander. Armed guards enforce this policy. During the time of my fieldwork more than one refugee was shot for venturing outside the camp. [ … ]

Camp Ban Vinai is the largest gathering of Hmong in the world. The tragic events of war and global politics have led to this artificial urbanization of the Hmong with dizzying speed. Traditionally, the Hmong lived in small mountaintop villages in the forbidding terrain of northern Laos where they tended their animals and grew dry rice and corn in fields cleared from the forest. F.M. Savina reported that the Hmong in Laos "do not seem to like big settlements. They prefer to live in little groups making up hamlets rather than real villages" (1930:182). A peaceful mountain people who kept to themselves, they had little contact with even the lowland-dwelling Lao, much less the rest of the world, until they were pulled into the war in Southeast Asia. In the 1960s they were recruited by the CIA and trained by the Green Berets as anticommunist guerilla fighters.[2] In proportion to their population, they suffered casualties 10 times higher than those of Americans who fought in Vietnam (Cerquone 1986). When US forces withdrew in 1975, Laos collapsed and came under the rule of a government hostile to the Hmong who were viewed as collaborators with the hated enemy. Thousands fled their beloved mountain homes to seek asylum in Camp Ban Vinai, just across the Mekong in Thailand. Almost overnight they were thrown into a densely populated camp with no time to develop the adaptive cultural traditions and folkways, not to mention garbage disposal systems, that societies in the West have had centuries to evolve. It is any wonder, then, that there would be severe environmental health problems in Ban Vinai?

Moreover, there is no running water or adequate sewage disposal in the camp. The camp commander lists the water shortage as one of the major problems. Water has to be carried long distances in buckets balanced on shoulder yokes or in 10-gallon cans strapped to the back, a job usually done by teenagers. Sewage disposal is also a chronic problem. There are not enough pit toilets for the camp population. The latrines are distributed unevenly throughout the camp and are clustered together in long rows – convenient if you happen to live close to a cluster but the trade-off is the overwhelming stench. Because there is a shortage of toilets, they are kept locked and families have to obtain keys from the camp administration. Keys get lost, and there are never enough keys to go around, particularly for all the children. Further, you need to bring along a bucket of water to flush the shallow pit, water that is scarce and has to be carried on the back of some family member. Obviously, there are many disincentives for using the pit toilets; the stench alone is often a deterrent. Because gaining access to and using the pit toilets is a rather complex operation, most small children (one-fourth the population) simply cannot manage.

I go into detail about the camp toilets in order to give an infrastructural explanation for what has become a topos in reports about Ban Vinai from Western journalists and visiting relief workers. Ban Vinai is notorious for the image of refugees relieving themselves in the open space. This act, so shocking to "sophisticated" sensibilities, functions discursively as a sign of "the primitive." Before I left Bangkok en route to Ban Vinai, I heard stories about this behavior from other aid workers and came across this motif in written reports as well as oral anecdotes. This recurrent image is psychologically and rhetorically interesting for what it reveals about our discursive projections of the Other. [ ... ]

Instead of blaming the Hmong for the poor health conditions, our performance company situated the problem in the environmental setting. Instead of didactic health messages instructing the Hmong to change their behavior, we developed performances that would stimulate critical awareness about the camp environment, particularly how it differed from the natural mountain villages of the Hmong in Laos. Once their radically changed living conditions could be brought to consciousness through performance, the Hmong might understand the need for changing some of their habits to adapt to this altered situation. Such a line of thinking was not alien to them. One man offered me an environmental explanation for the high suicide rate in Ban Vinai. He argued that, in their homeland, family tensions and pressures could be relieved by the troubled person leaving home temporarily to stay with relatives or friends in the next village until the situation cooled down. Without this outlet in Ban Vinai, pressures sometimes mount until suicide seems the only escape. Also, there is a traditional Hmong proverb that encourages adjustment to change of venue: "When you cross a river, take off your shoes/When you move to another place, you must change your headman" (Conquergood forthcoming b).

We mounted a series of performances focused on the problem of garbage in the camp. The first thing we had to do was problematize "garbage." In a traditional Hmong village, garbage would not be the problem it was in Ban Vinai. If all disposable waste is organic, and you live in a small hamlet on a windswept mountain slope, then pitching waste out the door is not a problem. It becomes instant feed for the household pigs or is biodegradably reabsorbed into the natural ecology of the environment. Within the context of a crowded refugee camp, however, traditional ways of waste disposal entail radically different consequences. We wanted to get this message across without demeaning the people, suggesting that they were dirty.

Our "Garbage Theme" month featured Mother Clean in one of our most successful scenarios. Drawing on the *poj ntxoog* evil ogre character from Hmong folklore, we created an ugly Garbage Troll in soiled ragged clothes and a mask plastered with bits of garbage and dirt. The Garbage Troll would lumber into the center of the playing space and begin dramatizing the behavior we wanted to discourage – peeling eggs and other food and throwing the waste on the ground, picking up dirty food from the ground and putting it into his mouth, and so forth. After a few minutes of this improvisation, the tiger would charge on stage and rebuke the troll for such unseemly behavior. The tiger would growl and snarl and pounce at the impassive troll, all the while making verbally explicit how bad this behavior was. The tiger would give up and leave but then the pig would run out on stage and fuss at the troll for his disgusting conduct. The young performer who played our pig was a gifted clown and there would be much farcical business between the pig and the Garbage Troll until the troll drove the pig away. Then the chicken would follow suit and sagely admonish the troll about the environmental consequences of his behavior and how he would make children sick by throwing garbage all about. The troll would respond by throwing more garbage on the ground and at the chicken, driving the latter away.

From a considerable distance, Mother Clean would slowly sweep toward the dirty Garbage Troll. The children forming a circle around the playing space would have to open up their ranks to permit Mother Clean's passage. They would call out, warning her to beware of the nasty Garbage Troll. But Mother Clean would be unaware of the danger; absorbed in sweet thoughts she would sing to herself and dance as daintily as her bulk would permit. The children in the audience would increase the volume of their warning cries until Mother Clean heard and caught sight of the Garbage Troll. Unafraid, slowly, triumphantly she would sweep toward the nasty troll huddling in the dirt making menacing noises. She'd reach down, pull him up by his hands, then, in a moment of redemptive grace, remove his dirt-face mask and wash his face and hands. Transformed, the troll and Mother Clean danced as music was played from our battery-operated cassette player. Tiger, pig, and chicken rushed back on stage to dance and sing with Mother Clean and the redeemed troll. Our health workers, wearing sandwich-board posters with the health theme boldly lettered, would join the circle, and Mother Clean would slowly spell out and read the poster proverbs for those in the audience who were nonliterate. She would talk and invite comment and discussion about the theme.

The theme we developed in proverb form and painted on the sandwich-board posters was this:

> Thaum peb nyob pem roob cua thiab nag
> Tshoob yam khoom qias neeg pov tseg.
> Tam sim no muaj neeg coob coob nyob hauv zos vib nai,
> Peb txhua leej txhua tus yuav xyuam xim
> Cheb yam khoom qias neeg kom huv si

> [When you lived in the mountains
> The wind and the rain cleaned the garbage.
> Now with so many people in Ban Vinai
> We all must be careful to clean up the garbage]

Mother Clean would lovingly amplify the message of the proverb, explaining how a small village on a mountain slope with plenty of space for everyone could absorb organic refuse naturally through the elements of wind and rain. She pointed out that Ban Vinai is very different from the mountaintop villages in which the Hmong used to live. Consequently, customs and habits, particularly regarding garbage, needed to change accordingly. She exhorted a change in behavior without degrading the people whom she was trying to persuade, locating responsibility in the environmental circumstances. Everyone could agree that indeed Ban Vinai was very different from their former home. After establishing that premise, Mother Clean then could make the point about the need for adaptive response to this new situation. [ ... ]


## ▪ Expatriate Health Professionals and the Hmong: Perceptions of Difference, Disorder, Dirt, and Danger ▪

The more I learned about the history and cultural dynamics of the camp, the more I came to believe that the expatriate health professionals needed consciousness-raising messages as much as the Hmong. The Hmong are perceived by Western officials and visiting journalists as the causal, producing agents of the unsanitary and unhealthy conditions in the camp. Instead of seeing the Hmong as struggling within a constraining context of historical, political, and economic forces that have reduced them from proud, independent, mountain people to landless refugees, the Hmong are blamed for their miserable condition. In her brilliant and incisive analysis of refugee assistance programs, Barbara Harrell-Bond notes this sad pattern: "[I]t is alarming to observe that assistance programmes are dominated by an ethos in which the victims of mass exodus are treated as the villains" (1986:305). It is easier to scapegoat than to historicize a complex problem.

I began to collect the phrases used regularly to describe the Hmong by agency officials who worked in Ban Vinai. The word I heard most often was "filthy," followed closely by "dirty," and often part of a cluster of terms that included "scabies," "abscesses," "feces," and "piles of garbage." A phrase regularly employed to cover a multitude of perceived sanitation sins was the following, "They're one step out of the Stone Age, you know." A meaning-packed word heard about the Hmong almost every day was "difficult," and its ramified derivatives: "difficult to work with," "the most difficult group," "set in their ways," "rigid," "stubborn," "you cannot get through to them," "backward." One dedicated humanitarian agency employee who had worked with the Hmong for several years told me that "the hand of God is on this place," but as for the Hmong living here, "they're a fearful lot...you cannot work with them." These perceptions surface in official discourse as well. Senator Alan Simpson, ranking minority member of the Senate Subcommittee on Immigration and Refugee Affairs, visited Ban Vinai for a day during the time of my fieldwork. He introduced a new metaphor into this complex of discursive denigrations of the Hmong. He called the Hmong "the most indigestible group in society" (1987:4). Ambassador Jonathan Moore, the new US Coordinator for Refugee Affairs, was more diplomatic when, in a 1987 interview, he singled out the Hmong as "the people with special problems" (1987:5).

The dialectic between the perception of "difference" and "dirt" is interesting. I suggest that so much focus on the "dirtiness" and "difficulty" of the Hmong is actually an expression of Western expatriates' uneasiness when confronted with Difference, the Other. A Western aid official's encounter with the Hmong is a confrontation with radical difference – in cosmology, worldview, ethos, texture of everyday life. The difference is exacerbated if the relief workers are devout Christians. The three relief agencies that have been in charge of the camp hospital have all been Christian organizations which have perceived the animism of the Hmong as "devil worship."

For medical health officials with a professional commitment to the tenets of Western science, the equally strong Hmong belief in spirits and shamans challenges fundamental Western assumptions about the nature of the world. What is frustrating for agency workers is that the acceptance and cooperation of the Hmong are essential for the successful delivery of health care programs and services. The Hmong are the clear majority in Camp Ban Vinai, of course, and they continue to control their symbolic universe. Much to the distress of agency workers, they have not acquiesced to the new scientific epistemology presented to them as a "superior" form of knowledge. Visible affirmations of their traditional way of understanding the world are displayed everywhere. Here are excerpts from a report by Dr. Ronald Munger, an epidemiologist who did research in Ban Vinai:

> The striking issue in regard to traditional Hmong health practices is how visible these practices are in Ban Vinai Refugee camp in Thailand. [ . . . ] Shamanism was widely practiced. [ . . . ] There were other more common everyday rituals which reflected pervading belief in the spirits in every aspect of life. Ritual figures or heads of sacrificed animals set on poles were common. Wooden boards on the floor at the doorway of a home were intended to confuse unwanted spirits and prevent them from entering the house. [ . . . ] Pleasing the spirits was a primary goal. For example, bracelets, necklaces, and other devices were often placed on babies and small children to contain the spirit of that person and avoid its loss. [ . . . ] Many Hmong homes [ . . . ] contained small altars with the items needed to interact with spirits. There were buffalo horns [ . . . ] rings and rattles used during rituals (1984).

All this display of "difference" and "strangeness" is quite dramatic to Western eyes and makes a vivid impression. Unfortunately, as Tzvetan Todorov reminds us, "The first, spontaneous reaction with regard to the stranger is to imagine him as inferior, since he is different from us" (1984:76). All too easily, "difference is corrupted into inequality" (1984:146).

Mary Douglas' ideas about the social relativity and symbolic functions of dirt help explain how "Difference" and "Dirt" are conjoined in perceptions of the Hmong. Inspired by William James' insight that dirt is "matter out of place" (Douglas 1966:164), she argues:

> [D]irt is essentially disorder. There is no such thing as absolute dirt: it exists in the eye of the beholder. [ . . . ] Dirt offends against order. Eliminating it is not a negative movement, but a positive effort to organise the environment (1966:2).

Perceptions of what is clean and unclean are contextually variable and culturally specific. Habits of cleanliness and rites of purification are the manifest expressions and protections of deep structures and fundamental classificatory schemes that maintain order and help hold a society together. People and actions that disturb order, violate categories, mess up the system are branded unclean: "The unclear is the unclean" (Turner 1967:97). Labeling someone or something "dirty" is a way of controlling perceived anomalies, incongruities, contradictions, ambiguities – all that does not fit into our categories, and therefore threatens cherished principles. "Dirt," then, functions as the mediating term between "Difference" and "Danger." It is the term that loads the perception of "Difference" with a moral imperative, and enables the move from description to action, from "is" to "ought." Defining something as unhealthy, harmful, dangerous establishes the premise for "moving in," for control, making it "licit to intervene [ . . . ] in order to exercise the rights of guardianship [ . . . ] to impose 'the good' on others" (Todorov 1984:150). Perception, language, and politics cathect in the encounter with the Other. [ . . . ]

One of the motives that would prompt doctors and nurses to volunteer for stressful work in an alien, harsh environment is concern for the refugees' souls as well as their physical bodies. I heard horror story after horror story from the refugees about people who went to the hospital for treatment, but before being admitted had their spirit-strings cut from their wrists by a nurse because "the strings were unsanitary and carried germs." Doctors confidently cut off neck-rings that held the life-souls of babies intact. Instead of working in cooperation with the shamans, they did everything to disconfirm them and undermine their authority. Shamans were regarded as "witch doctors." Here are the views of a Finnish nurse who worked in Ban Vinai: "They have their bark and root medicines and rites to appease the spirits. Most of it is worthless, and some of it is positively harmful" (Evans 1983:111). Is it any wonder that the Hmong community regarded the camp hospital as the last choice of available health care options? In the local hierarchy of values, consulting a shaman or herbalist, or purchasing medicine available in the Thai market just outside the entrance to the camp, was much preferred and more prestigious than going to the camp hospital. The refugees told me that only the very poorest people who had no relatives or resources whatsoever would subject themselves to the camp hospital treatment. To say that the camp hospital was underutilized would be an understatement.

As I critique my work in the camp I realize that I should have developed more consciousness-raising performances specifically for the expatriate health professionals. They needed to develop a critical awareness about health problems in the camp at least as much as did the Hmong. Directing most of the performances to the Hmong resulted in a one-sided communication campaign and subtly reinforced the prevailing notion that the Hmong were primarily responsible for the bad conditions.

I did develop one performance event that was designed especially for the agency health workers, the *IRC Health and Sanitation Celebration*. All the voluntary agency personnel were invited to a showcase of skits from the refugee performance company culminating in a shared meal. The ostensible purpose of this event was to let the other agency workers know what we were doing so that they would not be surprised if they came across one of our health shows in the camp. The implicit agenda was to promote better understanding of Hmong culture and traditions. To this end, we capped the series of performance sketches by bringing a Hmong shaman on stage who enacted a traditional soul-calling ceremony of blessing and tied string around the wrists of expatriate personnel who voluntarily came up to the stage. Given the history of hostility between shamans and the hospital, this was a radical move. Those who participated in this intercultural performance found it deeply moving. However, they were a small, self-selected group who were already the most open-minded. Most of the expatriate guests politely remained in their seats but observed attentively. The most dogmatic agency workers – for example, the Christian nurse who refused to allow any Thai calendars in her ward because they had pictures of the Buddha – did not even attend this event.

I should have been more assiduous in attempts to reach the expatriate personnel who were most ethnocentric in their dealings with the Hmong. My sympathies were with the refugees. My interests and energies were devoted to understanding and working with the Hmong. It was easier to identify with the Hmong; the dogmatic Christians became the Other for me.

It is important to speak out against the repressive practices of some refugee relief agencies, however, in the interest of searching for a solution to this sad situation, I do not want to substitute one scapegoat for another. I agree with Harrell-Bond that "it is unproductive to blame" the agency fieldworkers for the enormous communication breakdowns that occur in refugee camps. By nature a refugee camp is a highly volatile, stressful, politically intense, multicultural arena, usually located in a harsh environment. In matters of communication and intercultural sensitivity, relief workers "are not trained. Within the agency bureaucracy they are not rewarded for involving themselves with individuals. In fact, fieldworkers are often warned against 'getting involved'" (1986:305). The agency workers I met in Ban Vinai were all dedicated, caring people. Even though they commuted to the camp from a Thai village an hour away, their living conditions there were quite basic. Many of the workers were volunteers, working in the camp at considerable personal sacrifice. The problem cannot be so easily contained at the level of the agency personnel. The root of the problem goes much deeper into institutional bureaucratic practices and the ideologies that empower and sustain them.

The ideal is for the two cultures, refugees' and relief workers', to enter into a productive and mutually invigorating dialog, with neither side dominating or winning out, but both replenishing one another (see Bakhtin 1981). Intercultural performance can enable this kind of dialogical exchange between Self and Other. Eugenio Barba talks about performance as "barter":

Otherness is our point of departure. Imagine two very different tribes, each on their own side of the river. Each tribe can live for itself, talk about the other, praise or slander it. But every time one of them rows over to the other shore it is to exchange something. One does not row over to teach, to enlighten, to entertain, but rather to give and take: a handful of salt for a scrap of cloth. [ ... ] Otherness is our meeting point (1986:161).

As a medium of exchange, performance draws us to the margins, the borders between Self and Other. Bakhtin affirms: "The most intense and productive life of culture takes place on the boundaries" (1986:2). Conceived of as barter, a site of exchange, performance is a key to understanding "how the deeply different can be deeply known without becoming any less different" (Geertz 1983:48). The value of the exchange is in the encounter, the relations that are produced, not the objects: "It is the act of exchanging that gives value to that which is exchanged, and not the opposite" (Barba 1986:268). [ ... ]

## NOTES

1   More than 100 Hmong refugees, almost all men, have died suddenly. Autopsy reports show no cause of death (see Holtan 1984; Munger 1986).
2   Through the Freedom of Information Act a CIA film depicting the recruitment, training, and guerilla warfare of the Hmong in Laos is now available. This media text documents how the Hmong were recruited and used by the CIA during the war in Southeast Asia. It sets forth vividly the political-historical circumstances that led ultimately to the Hmong becoming refugees.

## REFERENCES

Bakhtin, Mikhail Mikhailovich (1981). *The Dialogic Imagination*. Edited by Michael Holquist, translated by Caryl Emerson and Michael Holquist. Austin: University of Texas Press.
—— (1986). *Speech Genres*. Edited by Caryl Emerson and Michael Holquist, translated by Vern W. McGee. Austin: University of Texas Press.
Barba, Eugenio (1986). *Beyond the Floating Islands*. New York: Performing Arts Journal Publications.
Boal, Augusto (1985 [1979]). *Theatre of the Oppressed*. Translated by Charles A. & Maria-Odila Leal McBride. New York: Theatre Communications Group.
Burke, Kenneth (1969). *A Rhetoric of Motives*. Berkeley: University of California Press.
Bustos, Nidia (1984). "Mecate, the Nicaraguan Farm Workers' Theatre Movement." *Adult Education and Development* 23 (September): 129–140.
Cerquone, Joseph (1986). *Refugees From Laos: In Harm's Way*. Washington, DC: US Committee for Refugees, American Council for Nationalities Service.
Conquergood, Dwight (1985). "Performing as a Moral Act: Ethical Dimensions of the Ethnography of Performance." *Literature in Performance* 5 (April): 1–13.
—— (Forthcoming a). *I Am a Shaman: A Hmong Life Story, with Hmong Text and Ethnographic Commentary*. Minneapolis, MN: Center for Urban and Regional Affairs, Southeast Asia Refugee Studies.
—— (Forthcoming b). "Hmong Proverbs: Texts and Ethnographic Commentary." In *The Hmong World*. New Haven, CT: Yale University, Council on Southeast Asia Studies.
Desai, Gaurav (1987). "Popular Theatre, Participatory Research and Adult Education in Africa: A Preliminary Bibliography." Unpublished manuscript, Northwestern University.

Douglas, Mary (1966) *Purity and Danger: An Analysis of the Concepts of Pollution and Taboo.* London: Routledge & Kegan Paul.

van Erven, Eugène (1987). "Philippine Political Theatre and the Fall of Ferdinand Marcos." *The Drama Review* 31, no. 2 (T114): 58–78.

Evans, Grant (1983). *The Yellow Rainmakers.* London: Verso.

Eyoh, H. Ndumbe (1986). *Hammocks to Bridges: Report of the Workshop on Theatre for Integrated Rural Development.* Yaounde, Cameroon: BET & Co.

Foucault, Michel (1973). *The Birth of the Clinic: An Archaeology of Medical Perception.* Translated by A. M. Sheridan Smith. New York: Pantheon.

—— (1977). *Discipline and Punish: The Birth of the Prison.* Translated by Alan Sheridan. New York: Pantheon.

Freire, Paulo (1986 [1970]). *Pedagogy of the Oppressed.* New York: Continuum.

Geertz, Clifford (1983). *Local Knowledge: Further Essays in Interpretive Anthropology.* New York: Basic Books.

Harrell-Bond, Barbara (1986). *Imposing Aid: Emergency Assistance to Refugees.* New York: Oxford University Press.

Holtan, Neal, ed. (1984). *Final Report of the SUNDS Planning Project.* St. Paul, MN: St. Paul-Ramsey Medical Center.

Kaitaro, Tsuno, ed. (1979). "Theater as Struggle: Asian People's Drama." *Ampo* 11, nos. 2–3 (special issue).

Kidd, Ross (1982). *The Popular Performing Arts, Non-formal Education and Social Change in the Third World: A Bibliography and Review Essay.* Hague: Centre for the Study of Education in Developing Countries.

—— (1984). *From People's Theatre for Revolution to Popular Theatre for Reconstruction: Diary of a Zimbabwean Workshop.* Hague: Centre for the Study of Education in Developing Countries.

Kidd, Ross, and Martin Byram (1978). *Popular Theatre and Participation in Development: Three Botswana Case Studies.* Gaborone: Bosele Tshwaraganang Publications.

Moore, Jonathan (1987). "Interview with Jonathan Moore: US Coordinator for Refugees." *Refugee Reports* 8 (June):1–5.

Munger, Ron (1984). "Synopsis of Comments to the Wilder Foundation Refugee Projects." *Final Report of the SUNDS Planning Project,* edited by Neal Holtan, 37–39. St. Paul, MN: St. Paul-Ramsey Medical Center.

—— (1986). "Sleep Disturbance and Sudden Death of Hmong Refugees: A Report on Fieldwork Conducted in the Ban Vinai Refugee Camp." In *The Hmong in Transition.* New York: Center for Migration Studies.

Ong, Walter (1982). *Orality and Literacy: The Technologizing of the Word.* London: Methuen.

Said, Edward (1979). *Orientalism.* New York: Vintage.

Savina, F.M. (1930). *Histoire des Miao.* Hong Kong: Société des Missions Étrangères de Paris.

Siegel, Taggart, and Dwight Conquergood, producers (1985). *Between Two Worlds: The Hmong Shaman in America.* Video-documentary. 28 mins. Siegel Productions.

Simpson, Alan (1987). Quoted in "Senate Holds Midyear Hearings on FY 87 Refugee Admissions." *Refugee Reports* 8 (July): 4.

Tapp, Nicholas (1986). *The Hmong of Thailand: Opium People of the Golden Triangle.* Indigenous Peoples and Development Series Report No. 4. London: Anti-Slavery Society.

Thiong'o, Ngugi wa (1981). *Detained: A Writer's Prison Diary.* London: Heinemann.

—— (1983). *Barrel of a Pen: Resistance to Repression in Neo-Colonial Kenya.* Trenton: Africa World Press.

—— (1986). *Decolonising the Mind: The Politics of Language in African Literature.* London: J. Currey.

Todorov, Tzvetan (1984). *The Conquest of America: The Question of the Other.* New York: Harper & Row.

Turner, Victor (1967) *The Forest of Symbols.* Ithaca, NY: Cornell University Press.

Werner, David (1977). *Where There Is No Doctor: A Village Health Care Handbook.* Palo Alto, CA: Hesperian Foundation.

Werner, David, and Bill Bower (1982). *Helping Health Workers Learn.* Palo Alto, CA: Hesperian Foundation.

# 7

# The Answerability of Memory: "Saving" Khmer Classical Dance

## Judith Hamera

### ■ Answerable Bodies/"Unclaimed" Experience ■

Scholars in performance studies are well equipped to engage the fraught relations between representation and trauma, to "constellate various approaches to the nexus of performance and history" (Pollock 1998: 1). The taxing, relentless, affective labors of introducing trauma into representation often lend themselves to hero stories of what performance overcomes. This account is not one of these. Rather, I suggest here that, while performance in/as a tactic of survival often overcomes, it is as likely to succumb to exhaustion, to deep personal anguish and profound social dislocation, and to the memories it has deployed as both blessing and goad.

Further, crises of truth so central to the relationship between trauma and representation (as in "speaking the truth back to power") undermine, at almost every turn, my attempts to narrate a coherent account of one family of Khmer survivors,[1] of how they told themselves that dance was the reason for their survival, and of the ways they tried and failed to find solace therein to performatively shore up survivorship and continuity. These crises of truth in trauma remind me that cultural gaps, as well as representational and methodological ones, are fundamentally human – that is to say affective, psychic – gaps, and they divide husband from wife, parents from children, and family from community, as well as researcher from the ease and stability of scholarly claims.

### Thresholds of secrecy

I met the Sem[2] family in the Los Angeles area in 1990. The children were fairly gregarious and suggested that, as I was interested in classical dance, I should meet their parents who, in their words, "danced *real* Cambodian dance in Cambodia and in [refugee] camp."

Father Ben Sem and his wife May were vague about details of their lives in Cambodia, the date of their arrival in Long Beach, California (1981 or 1982) and the organization that had sponsored them. As Feldman reminds us, it is a mistake to view thresholds of silence, like the Sems' tactical ambiguities, as purely individual matters, though they are that. Like virtually every other "first wave" Cambodian refugee family, the Sems did not escape the Khmer Rouge autohomeogenocide intact or unscathed, physically or psychically. Like most, the Sems' survival, and indeed, their sanity, depended upon relational amnesia and aphasia:

> *Ben Sem*: You had to forget yourself, understand? Forget you were student, forget you have family, tell them [Khmer Rouge] you are farmer, you are builder. Then more forget. Forget hungry, forget tired, forget scared.

In a very real way, the Khmer Rouge enforced a tyranny of forgetting, from the macro to the micro: the calendar began with Year Zero, monuments and archives of all sorts were systematically destroyed, families split apart.

The Sems' "inability to remember," and/or their unwillingness to divulge, key aspects of their autobiographies reflects a logic of memory in the "death world," a logic articulated by Edith Wyschogrod and Elaine Scarry. Wyschogrod uses the term "death world" to characterize a form of social existence "in which vast populations are subjected to conditions of life simulating imagined conditions of death, conferring upon their inhabitants the status of the living dead" (1985: 15). Intrinsic to this context is the image of the inhabitants of the death world as reduced to animated corpses, bodies without sentience, bodies, terrifyingly, wholly bodies. As Wyschogrod concludes, "At the level of vital existence, the life-world suffer[s] a severe condensation of meaning" (1985: 20). This radical reduction to the brute circumstances of survival, and particularly the emphasis on all-consuming hunger, runs through all published accounts of Khmer survivors.

This condensation of meaning is etched onto the body through pain, through beatings, rapes, torture that are the physical signifiers of the authorities in the death world. I use "signifiers" ironically for, as Elaine Scarry demonstrates, torture/pain undoes the very process of signification: "Physical pain does not simply resist language, but actively destroys it, bringing about an immediate reversion to a state anterior to language, to the sounds and cries a human being makes before language is heard" (1985: 4).

Nadezda Mandelstam observed, "If nothing else is left, one must scream. Silence is the real crime against humanity" (in Wyschogrod 1985: 21), and herein lies a minor triumph of the death world. Voice, language, even screams, may recuperate shards of the life world but pain precludes language and appropriates the scream as an object unto itself, indeed, particularly for the torturers, one that legitimates itself.

Simply put, in the death world, the discursive apparatus of memory is as likely to fall into a pit of irretrievable inwardness, inaccessible, as it is to generate an imperative to "tell." To say that, once freed from these immediate exigencies, the Sems' reluctance to present "coherent" autobiographies might be a simple, tactical performance of mistrust is both true and misses the point. Such a reading ignores the social surround which regulates and polices memory, which, indeed, makes memory possible. Ben and May Sem *had* to tactically manage memory because, in the words of Adrienne Rich, they always ran the risk of remembering their names and, in so doing, failing the strategic forgetfulness which kept them alive. In genocide's aftermath, memory does not always equal information retrieval or expressive force, much less solace. It was, rather, a wound and, moreover, one whose unique etiology was inextricable from deeply personal limits and frailties.

Once in this country, amnesia, the ability to become unstuck in personal narrative borne out of genocidal imperative and psychological necessity, proved difficult to abandon. Some stories could never be told.

> *Ben*: We don't talk [about] that time. Far away now. Then too. Far away then. Like not [points to himself], not us, understand? Here, not here. Not live, just move. Not see – like – say?
> *Rith*: Ghost?
> *Ben*: Yes.
> *Rith*: They were like ghosts.

In *Ghostly Matters: Haunting and the Sociological Imagination*, Avery Gordon writes:

> The ghost always registers the actual "degraded present" [...] in which we are inextricably and historically entangled AND the longing for the arrival of a future, entangled certainly, but ripe in the plenitude of nonsacrifical freedoms [...] The ghost registers AND it incites. (1997: 207)

Accounts of Khmer survivors are replete with this paradoxical ghostliness so characteristic of the death world: reduced to shades themselves, they are both haunted registers of atrocity and avenging angels, impelled by other ghosts, even in diaspora, to reimagine the generative possibilities of Khmer culture.

For May, this dual status – both ghost and haunted – was literal:

> *May*: I hear my teachers who did not get out. I hear them sometimes in the day. I don't see, just hear. I am scared but they tell me the steps [movements generally] to the dance. I am like a child, a baby. I listen to them tell me the step. At first I am so scared, I don't listen. Maybe go crazy like my neighbor I tell you. But I listen to them tell me the step, then I do. I do. Sometimes I do better, I think so, because they tell me.

As surely as the spacings of memory shrouded some texts in silence, it resurrected others and, in the Sems' case, these other texts were dances specifically and, more generally, classical dance as an ur-text of Khmer culture.

May's ghostly interlocutors recall James Brandon's observation that, while "performing arts do not die, performers do" (in Sam 1994: 47). Beginning in 1975, Pol Pot and his Khmer Rouge forces set out to systematically and ruthlessly destroy classical Cambodian performance and culture.

> *May:* They killed everybody. You can't even think so many. You old – killed. You student – killed. You dancer, play music – killed. We [referent unclear] are [relatively] strong, we run and walk to camp. Sometime we see other student in camp but [holds up two fingers] teachers. Why? Old, dance long time, look like dancers – killed. And I hear in camp, you know, so many did not get out. Dancers and teachers from the school. I see and I hear. They did not get out. Dead. All dead. Before I get to camp I – What if I am only left?

And so Ben and May deployed dance as a fictive ground from which they legitimized their survival and organized a sense of agency counterpoised against survivor and refugee status.

In *Spectacular Suffering: Theatre, Fascism, and the Holocaust*, Vivian Patraka engages Elin Diamond's notion of performativity and reimagines it in light of the Holocaust[3]:

> According to this model of the performative, "the thing done" is a kind of yardstick, a system of beliefs and presuppositions that has taken on an authority and become a hegemonic means of understanding. The "thing done," then, represents particular discursive categories, conventions, genres and practices that frame our interpretations, even as we try to perceive the present moment of doing. As we are in the doing, then, there is the pressure of the thing done. The doing is not knowable without the thing done, and the thing done is all the discursive conventions that allow us to think through a doing. (1999: 6)

In the case of "the Holocaust performative," Patraka identifies

> the thing done as *the thing gone* [ ... ] It is the goneness of the Holocaust that produces the simultaneous profusion of discourses and understandings [ ... T]he absoluteness of the thing done [gone] weighs heavily on any doing in the Holocaust performative. [ ... It] acknowledges that there is nothing to say to goneness and yet we continue to try and mark it, say it, identify it, memorialize the loss over and over. (1999: 7)

Yet, while the invocation of goneness is explicit in both general and highly personal "introductions of [Khmer Rouge] atrocity into representation" (Patraka 1999: 7; see especially Sophiline Cheam Shapiro's "Songs My Enemies Taught Me" in Pran 1997: 1–5), for the Sems, this animating sense of "goneness" was expressed in general, cultural terms ("so Khmer dance don't die too, like everything else beautiful in our country die"), and only rarely and obliquely in personal ones ("We don't talk that time."). For the Sems, what personal silence foreclosed, dance enabled; through the solace of good form, it offered an answer back – albeit a problematic one – to their pervasive sense of goneness.

Patraka writes that doing/performance is always accountable to the thing gone (1999: 7). It is also useful to imagine this accountability in Bakhtinian terms. Here, in the case of the Sems, dance becomes the vehicle through which Ben and May perform *answers* for their individual survival, and that of Khmer culture. At its simplest, Bakhtin's "answerability" is very like accountability, predicated on an interanimation of art and guilt, life and blame. In "Art and Answerability" (1990), his earliest known publication, he writes:

> I have to answer with my own life for what I have experienced and understood in art, so that everything I have experienced and understood would not remain ineffectual in my life. But answerability entails guilt, or liability to blame. It is not only mutual answerability that art and life must assume, but also mutual ability to blame [ ... ] Art and life are not one, but they must become united in the unity of my answerability. (1990: 1–2)

Answerability is ambivalent. At its most generative, it seems to offer an ethical opportunity to deploy art to speak back, both to life and to goneness. At its most impotent, answerability seems to circumscribe agency, limiting it to re-actions of singular subjects condemned to answer to, or "rent" meaning (Hitchcock 1993: 10). Central to this ambivalence is Bakhtin's emphasis on the mutuality of art and life congealed into a unity through answerability-in-practice. In the case of the Sem family, can answerability, as they deploy it congeal into such a unity? Can art, life, and goneness answer for or to each other? I suspect Ben and May, Ben in particular, would have it so. Yet it seems to me that this unitary emphasis in answerability, both in Bakhtin's terms and in Ben Sem's, can be held to a different light which reveals, instead, a palimpsest in which speech and silence, the dancing Apsara body and the precariously poised refugee–survivor body, etch themselves over and over onto each other, again and again, always incompletely, always in difference. I attribute this profoundly ambivalent palimpsest of answerability through performance in the Sem family to a peculiar relationship between a classical form and a fraught subject. Here, as I will explain, the dancer was always already too distinguishable from the dance, turning precisely on the pivot of guilt and blame so intimately linked, both to his own legitimation of his survival, and Bahktin's theoretical tool to describe it. Perhaps the most enabling way to explore this relationship is to examine specific technologies of answerability.

## ■ Technologies of Answerability ■

### Pure products

Joseph Brodsky observes:

> What the past and the future have in common is our imagination, which conjures them. And our imagination is rooted in our eschatological dread: the dread of thinking that we are without precedence or consequence. The stronger that dread,

the more detailed our notion of antiquity or of utopia. Sometimes [ ... ] they overlap [ ... ] (1994: 40)

This confluence of antiquity and utopia is particularly magnified for the refugee or the exile, who faces

two types of immanent and imminent threats simultaneously: the threat of the disappearance of the homeland and the threat of themselves disappearing in the host society. Fetishization [as a strategy for negotiating these threats...] entails condensing all the meanings of home [ ... ] into substitute fetishes and frozen stereotypes. (Naficy 1993: 129)

Hamid Naficy concludes, the net result of this fetishization of past and future is that "[t]hrough controlling 'there' and 'then,' the exile can control 'here and 'now'" (1993: 132).

The fetish of Cambodia as it was and never was has an especially acute pull for refugee survivor artists, for whom answerability to and through Khmer culture is seen as rooted in a sacred, utopian past while mired in a degenerate present. No matter that the exact nature of this past is unclear as Khmer traditions are, to a great degree, contested constructs among Khmer themselves (see Ebihara et al. 1994: 5–9). Juxtaposition between sacred past and degenerate present permeates Khmer discourse, as does the sense that the future may hold only greater remove from utopian antiquity and, ultimately, perhaps abyss, though this has been modified considerably by the death of Pol Pot and the collapse of the remaining Khmer Rouge forces. Still, in the early 1990s, when I met the Sems, the rhetoric of these juxtapositions between present and past was both radically essentialist and pessimistic. If answerability, predicated on the reconstitution of Khmer culture, seemed logistically problematic if not doomed, this did not keep Ben and May from trying, or from modelling their efforts on a "pure product," a cultural fetish, even if their approach to it was necessarily asymptotic.

In Bakhtin's view, the ethical, answerable performance is effective, regardless of contextual contingencies. Indeed answerability rehabilitates such contingencies and reinvigorates them, generating a coherent, unitary assemblage that is concrete and historical, affective and ideological. In *Toward a Philosophy of the Act* (1993), which I see as a companion to, and elaboration on, "Art and Answerability," Bakhtin writes:

This answerability of the performed act is the taking-into-account in it of all factors [ ... ] as well as of its factual performance in all its concrete history and individuality. The answerability of the actually performed act knows a unitary place, a unitary context in which this taking-into-account is possible – in which its theoretical validity, its historical factuality, and its emotional-volitional tone figure as moments in a single decision or resolution. All these moments, moreover [ ... ], are not impoverished, but are taken in their fullness, and in all their truth. (1993: 28)

That is, within the architectonics of answerability, individuals, from our own unique spatio-temporal perspectives, perform, consummate, and, in so doing, unite moments of content, context, affect, etc., in all their truths, as acts of authorship for which we are then answerable and for which we have no alibi. From this perspective, the relationship between authorship, answerability and performance in the Sem's deployment of the Khmer cultural fetish is especially complex and peculiar.

Ideally, the visible body of the dancer, as author of the pure product, attempts to write itself over an invisible personal text ("we don't talk that time"). At the core of this act of authorship is mimesis. The sems' oldest daughter explains:

> *Sandy*: There is only one right way, only one right way. You learn like in a mirror, repeat it like the teacher is your mirror, okay? It's hard cause there's just one right way, like math.

This is not an idiosyncratic view. Cambodian dance functions linguistically, with an extensive vocabulary and syntax. It is as much sign language as dance, and it functions as a narrative technology to embody and reproduce both sacred classical, and secular folk, texts and images.

> *Ben*: We are book. Not just pictures like [holds up a magazine]. Not to look at only. We are – dance story, stories, not only nice good pictures.

To reproduce these stories, the body of the dancer becomes a complex intertext as the eyes, head, fingers, wrists, torso, legs, and feet all speak – through their specific, fixed repertory of poses – at the same time. These positions and poses are highly stylized, demanding a level of precision and artifice that makes ballet seem naturalistic by comparison. For example, fingers and wrists are generally both fully flexed *and* fluid, with the former curving back away from the palms in a manner similar to, but seemingly even more stylized and extreme that Indian mudras.

Yet, as Elin Diamond observes, incommensurability lies at the heart of mimesis: "[t]he body is never fully subsumed in impersonation" (1997: 180), or in mirrors or stories, however compelling. And between the utopian antiquity of Khmer dance and the trauma and goneness that the Sems deployed dance to answer, this incommensurability was especially acute. In contrast to Bakhtin's "unitary principle," in contrast to an answerable unity between art, life, and goneness, the Sems depended on an answerability which reiterated the deferral of life to the transcendent rhetoric of the dance. Mimesis became too full and too empty at the same time.

## Virtual bodies

For this incommensurable element of answerability to become clear, it is useful to look even more specifically at the virtual body ventriloquated through the material body of the dancer, at the referent of this mimesis. Khmer dancers, particularly the women, embody "Apsaras," celestial dancers who guard the heavens, serve as intermediaries between the sacred and the secular through their dances, and epitomize the beauty of Khmer culture. Male dancers, and women as well, perform acrobatic "monkey roles" in sacred epics, or ogres and trolls in folk pieces called Lakhon Khol. Their movements are both more forceful and somewhat less refined than those of women's roles. In representing and ventriloquating the Apsara ideal, the body of the dancer becomes the narrative container of the cosmos, a microcosm of myriad, nuanced interrelationships between the physical and the spiritual. This microcosmic body, in turn, has consequences for the visible, answerable body of the dancer. Susan Stewart observes that, in order for the body to "stand in" for the universe, "it must itself be exaggerated into an abstraction of the ideal. The *model* is not the realization of a variety of differences. As the word implies, it is an abstraction or image and not a presentation of any lived possibility" (1993: 135). In Bakhtinian terms, this is not a novelistic body, but an epic one (1981: 15).

As a technology predicated on and maintained by the epic body, the Apsara "implicitly denies the possibility of death – it attempts to present a realm of transcendence and immortality" (Stewart 1993: 133). And herein lies an additional ambivalence embedded in the Apsara ideal and classical dance as an answerable act of Khmer survivors. The Apsara, as a technology of answerability, is set in motion by the materiality of that which it implicitly defers, if not denies: death and displacement in the degraded present. Further, the Sems, the individual bodies who employ this technology, defer this too ("We don't talk that time. Far away."). Yet both death and displacement do make their contestory presences felt in "What if I am only left?" What we are left with is not only a palimpsest of answerability in which the body of the dancer writes over the invisible text of the refugee and is, in so doing, written over by the ideal body of the Apsara, but also a dance in which each move is a partial erasure and a contestory deferral of the previous move. The net result is not unity but the mutual destabilization of art, life and goneness, an exposure of their incommensurability, a destabilization and exposure the Sems sought to shore up through the dance.

### Incommensurable biographies

If the epic body of the Apsara belies a simple answerability to goneness, the material bodies and biographies of the dancers themselves complicate this further, though, to be sure, not all Khmer Rouge survivor artists face these complications equally. In the case of the Sems, however, these complications were profound.

Even by the fraught standards of survival crises and refugee status, Ben Sem seemed to me to be a particularly damaged person. He drank heavily, though not with his contemporaries in the Khmer neighborhood but at a relatively out of the way bar frequented almost exclusively by Mexican and Mexican-American laborers. He was easily angered and would fly into rages, shrieking and pounding the walls or the furniture with his fists. While I never saw or heard any evidence of him striking members of the family, it was clear that his rages were a kind of affective tyranny permeating the household. May intimated that they had lost friends due to these outbursts. Indeed, though I was told they rehearsed and performed for friends, I did not see a single adult visitor in the apartment in the years I knew the family which, based on what I knew about the affective and logistical interdependence in refugee communities, struck me as strange.

Certainly part of Ben's frustration was that the art which, in his mind, so clearly legitimated his survival would not, it appeared, insure continuity across generations. Rith, Sandy, and Jennie simply were not as invested in classical dance as their parents. This break in the continuity of answerability across generations was made all the more painfully visible by my presence, an unmistakable indicator that the pure audience for the pure product of Khmer culture was polluted, corrupted by the reality of somewhere else and someone other. My interest in the dance, over against his children's relative disinterest, could probably only be, for Ben, an index of his failure.

In her introduction to *Trauma: Explorations in Memory*, Cathy Caruth notes that "what trauma has to tell us – the historical and personal truth it transmits – is intricately bound up with its refusal of historical boundaries; [...] its truth is bound up with its crises of truth" (1995: 8); this seems equally relevant to Apsara bodies, which transcend historical boundaries, and to material ones which do not. I am not able, and have no desire, to determine the specifics of Ben Sem's damage. Still, it was clear from family dynamics and May's oblique and cryptic references that perhaps, in complex, painful and unknowable ways, the "guilt and liability to blame" inherent in answerability might conjure ghosts independent of, and antithetical to, the monkeys, ogres and trolls of the Lakhon Khol, and to the transcendent, celestial Apsara, as Ben and May tried to inhabit and impart them. Perhaps, in the final turn, for the Sems, the palimpsest of answerability I have described, already precarious, became a chasm between two impossible bodies: one ideal and redemptive, the other material, historical, answerable to both utopian voices and darker sounds.

Bruno Bettleheim once observed that psychoanalysis explains why we go crazy, not why we survive. Despite the Sems' insistence to the contrary, the daily rituals and invocations of performance didn't appear to explain it either. Perhaps this is because this "why" is often permeated by exhaustion, by crises of truth and thresholds of silence. Ben and May were fragile people. In 1992, they abruptly left the Los Angeles area.

Technique makes dance go. It is both the animating principle and the core ambivalence housed in every studio and manipulated by every performer: both task master and mastered, both warden and liberator. In Khmer classical dance, no less than ballet or butoh, technique, like language, reaches out to meet us as we are birthed into dance. It is, however pliable and enabling, a pre-existing conversation between bodies, history and desire. Yet it is also true that, however monumental, however rigorously drilled into new generations of little Apsaras, all technique is, finally, local. It's conversations are uniquely affected and inflected by the exigencies of those who keep it in play, set it to music, or deploy it to remake both it and themselves. The archives of technique, like closets filled with the clothes of a dead relative or memories not to be spoken of, beckon with the promise of answerability or beg for exorcism. For Ben and May Sem, saving Khmer classical dance as a daily legitimation of their survival offered both and, at least in the time of our acquaintance, delivered neither.

## NOTES

1 In the words of fellow survivor Dith Pran:

> the Khmer Rouge surrounded Phnom Penh, and on April 17, 1975 [ ... ] they took control [ ... ]. Until January, 1979, they forced all Cambodians to live in labor camps and work 14 to 18 hour days. They fed us one daily bowl of watery rice; they separated families; they destroyed all Cambodian institutions and culture; they systematically tortured and killed innocent people. It is estimated that during this time nearly a third of the Cambodian population was killed due to disease, starvation, or execution. (1997: x)

2 "Sem" is a pseudonym and my decision to use it requires both an acknowledgment of, and my complicity in, the "thresholds of secrecy" (Feldman 1991: 11) that characterized my relationship with this family. I use the pseudonym, in part, because I am not able to ask the family directly for permission to represent them and their stories. Beyond this, I have been unable to account for and confirm key details about the family, which has led me to suspect that the name they lived under in Long Beach, CA was itself an enabling fiction. The name used by the family while in Long Beach is a common one; this is true of the pseudonym I have chosen as well. I have used the Sems' daughters' "American" names, Sandy and Jennie, which, at the time I knew them, they preferred. This choice also reflects the distance between parents and children, a distance which figures prominently in Ben's and May's deployment of dance to theorize their own survival and legacy. I have used a shortened version of a Khmer name, "Rith," similar to that of the Sems' son and oldest child, in keeping with what was, at the time, his preference.

3 While I do not want to understate in any way the specificity of Patraka's theorizing the Holocaust performative (per her observations on p. 3), it is striking to note how forcefully it resonates with the testimony of Khmer Rouge survivors, and with the Sems' commitment to dance, over against the goneness of classical Khmer culture in the aftermath of the Pol Pot regime.

## REFERENCES

All material from the Sem family is taken from fieldnotes spanning 1990–2. These excerpts were not edited for grammar. They do not, however, reflect paralinguistic elements like pauses, etc.

Bakhtin, M. M. (1981). *The Dialogic Imagination: Four Essays*. M. Holquist (ed.), C. Emerson and M. Holquist (trans.). Austin: University of Texas Press.
——(1990). *Art and Answerability: Early Philosophical Essays*. M. Holquist and Vadim Liapunov (eds.), V. Liapunov (trans.). Austin: University of Texas Press.

——(1993). *Toward a Philosophy of the Act*. V. Liapunov and M. Holquist (eds.), V. Liapunov (trans.). Austin: University of Texas Press.

Brodsky, J. (1997). Homage to Marcus Aurelius. In *On Grief and Reason*. New York: Farar, Straus, Giroux.

Caruth, C. (1995). Introduction: trauma and experience. In C. Caruth (ed.), *Trauma: Explorations in Memory*. Baltimore: Johns Hopkins University Press.

Diamond, E. (1997). *Unmaking Mimesis*. London: Routledge.

Ebihara, M. M., et. al. (eds.) (1994). *Cambodian Culture since 1975: Homeland and Exile*. Ithaca: Cornell University Press.

Feldman, A. (1991). *Formations of Violence: The Narrative of the Body and Political Terror in Northern Ireland*. Chicago: University of Chicago Press.

Gordon, A. (1997). *Ghostly Matters: Haunting and the Sociological Imagination*. Minneapolis: University of Minnesota Press.

Hitchcock, P. (1993). *Dialogics of the Oppressed*. Minneapolis: University of Minnesota Press.

Naficy, H. (1993). *The Making of Exile Cultures: Iranian Television in Los Angeles*. Minneapolis: University of Minnesota Press.

Patraka, V. (1999). *Spectacular Suffering: Theatre, Fascism, and the Holocaust*. Bloomington: Indiana University Press.

Pollock, D. (1998). Introduction: making history go. In D. Pollock (ed.), *Exceptional Spaces: Essays in Performance and History*. Chapel Hill, NC: University of North Carolina Press, pp. 1–45.

Pran, D. (1997). *Children of Cambodia's Killing Fields: Memoirs by Survivors*. New Haven: Yale University Press.

Sam, S. (1994). Khmer traditional music today. In M. M. Ebihara, et. al. (eds.), *Cambodian Culture since 1975: Homeland and Exile*. Ithaca: Cornell University Press, pp. 39–47.

Scarry, E. (1985). *The Body in Pain: The Making and Unmaking of the World*. New York: Oxford University Press.

Stewart, S. (1993). *On Longing: Narratives of the Miniature, the Gigantic, the Souvenir, the Collection*. Durham, NC: Duke University Press.

Wyschogrod, E. (1985). *Spirit in Ashes: Hegel, Heidegger, and Man-Made Mass Death*. New Haven: Yale University Press.

# 8

# The Fool

## Smadar Lavie

FOOL. Truth's a dog must to kennel; he must be whipped out, when the Lady Brach
   may stand by th' fire and stink...Prithee, nuncle, keep a schoolmaster that can
   teach thy fool to lie. I would fain learn to lie.
LEAR. An you lie, sirrah, we'll have you whipped.

William Shakespeare, *King Lear*

"Every dog has its day [to get a beating], and every place has its Fool." So goes
the Mzeini saying. And the day young Manṣūr left for Zurich, to marry his love
whom he had met on ʿAqaba Gulf nude beach,[1] his father declared him *mesham-
mas*, disowned from both family and tribe by the father's statement that from
this day forth, his son was dead. During the week of ritual mourning that followed,
the father kept repeating, "The day has come when iron talks back and the Fool
rules."

Indeed, the Fool, a Mzeini character present in almost every encampment or
sedentarized settlement, was the agent who expressed clearly and succinctly,
though perhaps with deliberate awkwardness, the paradoxes of the local South
Sinai hybridization of two contradictory cultures: the Mzeina qua traditional
Bedouin, with their Islamic religion and nomadic-pastoralist ideology, and the
Western culture imposed on them by international politics.

The Fool himself would usually be a reification of this hybridized juncture. He
typically looked like a klutz, with a dirty patched caftan and a headdress only half-
tied around his head, and with uncut fingernails and beard, which the Mzeinis
consider pollution. "We Bedouin are almost waterless, very poor," remarked one
Fool, "so we'd better look like it."

"Don't believe him," some who were listening warned me later. "He's made lots of money since the Eilat-Sharm road was opened. He keeps it all in that khaki pouch hanging diagonally from his shoulder."

The handful of Fools I knew were talented businessmen who accumulated wealth from pioneering entrepreneurial activities. If a Fool lived in the heavily toured coastal areas, he would venture into building and renting out traditional-style Bedouin palm-frond huts to the many tourists who wanted to vacation in what they envisioned as authentic desert settings. He also sold them food, drink, and touristy simulations of traditional Bedouin attire imported from the West Bank, and later from Cairo. He was among the first to organize and market Desert Tours on Camelback, and to produce Bedouin-style celebrations for the tourists' amusement and edification. In addition, the Fool would be a money changer, at better rates than the bank, illegally converting the tourists' hard currency (preferably German marks, Swiss francs, or American dollars) into the notoriously inflation-ridden Israeli and later Egyptian currencies. In a case where the Fool lived away from the main tourist routes, he would usually be the one to win the hearts and pockets of Israeli or Egyptian developers, who conceived of him as both nonthreatening, due to his use of humor, and cheap to employ, due to his shabby appearance. So they would appoint him as a subcontractor or labor supervisor, the foreign developers' go-between in their relations with their Mzeini blue-collar laborers.

Unlike the typical nouveaux riches, the Fool did not invest his money in conspicuous consumption of semidilapidated pickup trucks or jeeps. Nor did he buy fancy Japanese transistor radios and cassette recorders, or elegant Swiss watches. Rather, he generously donated the money he made to the building of hewn-stone mosques that mushroomed in all the heavily toured communities. These replaced the spaces on the rough ground made sacred by marking, only with laid-down stones or conch shells, the *miḥrāb* pointing toward Mecca. Perhaps this building of permanent mosques was a response to the presence of so many scantily clad tourists intruding into the everyday life of the Mzeini encampments and settlements, as if visiting some sort of human zoo.

The Mzeinis repeatedly organized delegations that went to plead with the peninsula's Israeli military governor to put up signs requesting the tourists to wear bathing suits. But the military governor merely advised the Mzeinis to make the best of it and learn to enjoy the show, and refused to take any further action aside from choosing an occasional one-night stand from among the naked bodies on the beach. The Mzeinis had no choice but to acquiesce.

When the Egyptians got the 'Aqaba Gulf Coast back in 1982, they immediately responded to the Bedouin request and erected those long-hoped-for signs on the South Sinai beaches. But the more signs, the fewer tourists. Every tourist also had to register with the Egyptian Tourist Police and could be subject to occasional questioning. A few women were subjected to sexual harassment. The Egyptians also outlawed individual and spontaneous small group backpacking by putting up signs along the peninsula's asphalt roads announcing that tourists were prohibited from leaving them. Perhaps the Egyptians, fearing the desert themselves, feared also for the tourists' safety. But the Bedouin thereby lost a relatively hefty source of income. Once again they organized delegations to the governing authorities of the South Sinai, this time requesting the Egyptians to ease the no-nudity and no-hiking regulations. And once again they were instructed to make the best of the new situation and had to acquiesce.

"I am a merchant of sins," confessed one Fool. "I sell the tourists alcohol and rent them huts where unmarried people have tabooed sex." (One of his own brothers later announced, for all but this Fool to hear, "That's why he was the first to sign up and pay the large deposit the first year the Israelis organized the holy pilgrimage to Mecca.") "In Mecca I went to see a holy man. I asked him whether selling alcohol to non-Muslims was *ḥarām* (taboo for Muslims) or *ḥalāl* (religiously permitted). He told me I should cease this at once. But what can I do instead? Make money cleaning toilets in non-Muslim hotels?"

From the remarks I heard by and about the Fool, and given his no-win situation, it is clear that, like other figures of sacred clowns or tricksters, the contradictions built into the composition of the Fool's persona were never resolved.[2] But in contrast to the textually prescribed roles of those other clowns or tricksters, the Mzeini Fool did not make his debut on the societal stage during the spatially and temporally bounded domains that characterize communal ritual performances. Rather, the Mzeini Fool, if present and only if he chose to perform, might spontaneously rise up during awkward breaks in the conversation, interrupting the spatially and temporally unbounded flow of ordinary quotidian discourse. Such fissures would occur when the conversation got stuck in a circular, reductionist argument pitting the Mzeini identity qua Bedouin against the hybridizations in their identity forced on them by their local compromises with Western influences. At this point, the people might all just get up and leave the conversation circle. But sometimes a Fool could save the situation for the time being at least, bridging the textual and contextual discontinuities by embodying them in his own persona and performing a solo ritual with its own farcical logic, allegorizing his own experiences into a moral exemplar that clarified for his listeners their own identity.

The Fool had "ill-formed unity" (Handelman 1987: 548): a bright, rich merchant dressed in rags and acting silly, miming the antics of those naked Others on the beach even while his audience was well aware of his conspicuous Muslim piety. His own paradoxical existence enabled him to draw for his audience a clear boundary between themselves qua traditional Bedouin, and themselves qua workers, many of whom preferred the creative, clever job of running their own enterprises marketing their culture to sinful foreigners, when the only apparent alternatives were miserable unskilled jobs in similar enterprises run by their occupiers. The Fool's staging of his own paradoxes, therefore, temporarily solved the Mzeinis' contradiction between their yearning to embody their traditional Bedouin lifestyle, and their reality of having to perform this lifestyle they had never really had in front of exotica-hunting tourists, whom they could not restrain into civility because they were not the ones to decide on the rules and regulations in their own land. [ ... ]

■ II. ■

Dahab, Spring 1978, seven years earlier

Evening at this main sedentarized oasis along the ʿAqaba Gulf, a community of 89 nuclear households live here permanently. Dinner smells, still in the air, mingle with the salty sea breeze softly blowing among the fronds of the date trees scattered in clusters on the coastline. A mother's undulating melancholy voice, singing a lullaby, tenderly echoes the cry of the muezzin calling for the ʿasha after-dinner prayer. Answering the call, fourteen men from the northern neighborhood's magʿad enter the newly built nearby mosque. After about ten minutes, some of them begin to go back to the magʿad, where they sit in a circle around the embers of a small fire. The older men stay a few minutes longer for pious individual prayer. Moonlight glows on the faces of people tranquil because they have fulfilled another duty of their religious routine. The youngest of the men serves small glasses of sweet dark tea that was heated on the embers. A quiet conversation emerges from the silence.

The conversation focuses on the hippies in al-Billij, called by the Mzeinis "Batānka," a *nisba* (group name) for "Beatniks." Since the Mzeinis considered the hippies to be sort of an international clan, they gave them a group name ending in "-a," like their own clan names. They were sure that the word "Beatnik" was derived from the Arabic *nīk*, meaning, "to fuck." This made sense to them because the Mzeinis, both women and men clad in their traditional attire, observed the Batānka from close range, doing it on the beach daily.

ʿĪD: By Allah, today there was such a fat, healthy girl on the beach. Did you see her? The one with that dark, skinny guy.

KHDEIR: Yes, I think I know who you are talking about. They are in Hammūda's hut, under the palms he shares with Freij.

ʿĪD: Too bad she sunbathes. Her beautiful milky skin has turned red like a roasted lobster.

JUMʿA: Yeah, she came to me asking for tobacco. I told her I smoke only *banjo*, and asked her if she would like to buy some.

The listeners grin with amusement, knowing that Jumʿa was offering the woman cheap homegrown green tobacco, which smells very much like marijuana but of course lacks its active ingredient.

When the first Batānka arrived in the South Sinai, they asked the Bedouin for marijuana. When it became clear that the Bedouin did not know that word, the hippies resorted to the exotic term "ganja," which the Bedouin misheard and then mispronounced as "banjo." The local folk wisdom has it that one day a naked beatnik sniffed the smoke from an ordinary rolled green tobacco cigarette a Bedouin was smoking, and instead of shouting "Eureka!" he pointed and gleefully exclaimed, "Ganja! Ganja!" Whereupon the Bedouin realized they had a common product with extraordinary commercial possibilities.

JUMʿA: I sold her three cigarettes at four American bucks a shot.

*The circle is sprinkled with wry smiles.*

RĀSHED: I saw her too. I think she dyes her hair. Her pubic hair is black and her hair is kind of red.

ABU-MŪSA [*muttering in dismay*]: Oh evil of disaster!

Everyone but Abu-Mūsa is snickering as if at a dirty joke, but also with embarrassment, because not only have they all seen the young woman naked, but she didn't at least follow the proper custom of removing her body hair, which the Mzeinis considered religious pollution.

ʿĪD: I swear by my life, I can't figure out what she sees in that guy, he's so dark and skinny.

People laugh again. For the Mzeinis, being dark meant a person had to work hard in the sun, and being skinny meant that the person did not get enough to eat – so he was poor and ugly.

SWĒLEM: This summer the Batānka increased like the amount of rubbish they throw on the beach. They throw themselves on the sand, too – dirty.

*The atmosphere sobers at this distressing reality.*

JUMʿA [*raising his voice*]: What do you want? It's their vacation. This is how they enjoy themselves. Tell me, isn't it fun to take your girlfriend, or even come by yourself – everybody's naked, and you – just pick the one you like? And with their exchange rate, a vacation like that is pretty cheap.

ABU-MŪSA [*loud*]: Pray to the Prophet! You two have turned into Beatniks. Aren't you fed up with staring at the genitals of heretic girls? Do we have to discuss it every evening here in our magʿad by the holy mosque?

ʿAWAYED [*louder*]: All of us are gradually joining the Batānka. Today when I was praying the noon prayer to myself near the hut I rent out in al-Billij, two guys with their uncircumcised penises dangling – tphooo [*he spits on the ground in disgust*] – and wearing only their cameras – they took pictures of me, just like that, without asking and without paying me. [*very upset, beating his hands on the air*] Who do they think we are? Their free picture show? It's bad enough they put on *their* free picture show for us all over our beach.

KHḌEIR [*just as loud, with gestures that punctuate the air*]: Other places don't have this mess that we do. People still follow the old ways. The hell with money – what kind of a life are we living?

ABU-MŪSA [*firmly*]: Have you ever seen or heard of an Arab praying right in the middle of a bunch of naked ladies and their lovers?

The anthropologist, in spite of hearing the pain in Abu-Mūsa's voice, barely manages to suppress a grin at the incongruity of this image.

ʿAWAYED: Allah the Great! The Bedouin live in the desert, in Egypt, in Saudi Arabia, everywhere, without being touched by this pollution. Why do we have the bad luck to have to do this for a living?

ʿĪD [*with deliberate calmness, to tone down the argument in tempo and volume*]: You think you got problems? Just try raising goats in this desert and see how far you get. Within a week all your money will have gone for their food. Our desert has lots of the wrong kind of grass.

ʿĪd meant to end the argument with a funny pun: both pasture grass and dope were referred to by the word "hashish." But by now, the men are so demoralized by the subject that the joke musters only a few weak smiles.

JUMʿA [*flares up*]: We are all Batānka now. Living on as little money as they, spending no more than they do. What property do we own? Our land is all bare rugged mountains and jagged corals, good for nothing except attracting crazy tourists to dive and climb and risk their necks for the fun of it. Real Bedouin have fields and flocks. Every once in a while they go to the market and exchange some goats for [consumer] goods. But these dollars are killing us.

ʿAWAYED [*with conviction*]: The Bedouin are people of honor. They believe in God and His Disciple. They disdain money-grubbing!

ʿĪD [*with a voice of sugarcoated poison*]: Oh yes, we all saw you yesterday haggling with those scumbags over exchange rates of Israeli and German money down to the last penny, nervously counting your sheaf of bills. Oh Great Lord, we're not like the rest of 'em, the Bedouin.

RĀSHED [*furiously jumps into the conversation*]: Who needs money anyway? The Bedouin need freedom. Let them roam around in the desert like they used to, riding their camels, singing *hejēnis* (caravan songs), courting the veiled goatherds.

SWĒLEM [*with authority*]: The Bedouin don't put their heart in money. One helps the other: the father his sons, the sons their old father, everyone their uncles and cousins. They are organized better than the Eged Corporation.

The anthropologist is startled to hear this comparison made between the classic agnatic-corporate tribe and Eged, the powerful transportation monopoly that owns and runs almost every bus in Israel and the Occupied Territories.

ABU-MŪSA [*with finality*]: For the Bedouin, *al-damm dhamm, ma fi khramm!* (The blood is protected – there are no holes).

"Al-damm dhamm, ma fi khramm" was a legal statement taken from the codex of Blood Vengeance Law. It meant that, in a social network based on blood relationship, there could not be any gaps. When such a statement was uttered in everyday discourse, it meant that the conversation had reached a moment of crisis and could no longer proceed.

All of a sudden, out of the silence following this weighty declaration, a very short, skinny, sharp-boned and sloppily dressed figure rises, waving his hands.

"Ho!" exclaims this Shgēṭef, the local Fool.

The others, realizing he has not spoken yet and has something to say, turn their heads in his direction.

With all solemnity he declares, "The Bedouin pee in a squat and so do we."

After initial puzzlement, the group bursts into hearty laughter. The Mzeinis believed that squatting was the proper way Muslims should urinate in order not to become polluted with drops of urine. The Fool's remark drew a sharp line between the magʿad and al-Billij. In that absurd context, peeing while squatting meant existing in the world qua Bedouin.

After the last peals of laughter fade away, the Fool starts speaking in the calm and measured voice that signifies a shift into a storytelling mode.

*

"Yesterday a couple came to me. They wanted to rent one of my huts. I think they were from a kibbutz because they wore those plaid flannel shirts. But the guy looked Swedish."

"You mean, he had those devil-colored eyes?" asks ʿĪd, to show he is listening attentively.

"Yes, his eyes were as green as the eyes of those accursed cats. And believe it or not, *she* was driving the car and *he* unloaded it."

The Fool stops to give his audience a chance to laugh at the ridiculous gender-role reversal of the Batānka tribe. When the Mzeinis migrated, or even just went away with the family for a couple of days to visit friends and relatives, it was the husband who loaded and drove the pickup truck, and the wife who unloaded it.

"That devilish guy shut up, and *she* haggled with me over the price of the hut and then tried to cheat and pay less."

The Fool again pauses to let his audience savor yet another role reversal that delineates the boundaries between the Batānka and themselves.

"So finally, after all that, they took all their clothes off and went for a walk on the beach, like Adam and Eve in the Garden."

And then the Fool stands up, violating the convention of the magʿad and starts miming an imitation of a Batānka woman delicately prancing on the beach.

"Wait a second," he suddenly says, still jogging around the amused circle. "I forgot my tits!" He holds his open hands under the places where his size D breasts would have been, and with huge motions moves them up and down. The men crack up. The Fool stops to catch his breath and again violates convention by wiping the sweat off his brow with the hem of his long caftan, deliberately raising it to an immodest height and revealing his undergarment.

ʿĪd, the youngest among the men, whistles with his fingers, but immediately stops because of Abu-Mūsa's piercing look.

"And that Swede, he had the biggest foreskin I've ever seen in my life." And the fool jabs his elbow into his navel and dangles his arm from side to side, using his whole forearm to represent the tourist's penis, with the hand being the huge foreskin. The men roar with laughter.

"There really is some difference between the Batānka tribe and the Mzeina tribe," chokes Jumʿa through his guffaws.

"There is indeed a difference," agree ʿAwayed and Khḍeir.

"In the afternoon she pulled the guy by his hand from the water and shoved him into the hut. There they did all sorts of things that people never do." And the Fool mimes hugging the air, kissing it, and mounting around it.

These gestures were all varieties of sexual foreplay foreign to the Mzeinis, though they had seen them many times on their own beach. Nevertheless they now cheerfully volunteer lots of free advice to the Fool, just as they had gotten into the habit of doing when they walked on the beach among the bodies of the Batānka.

"Hey, give her another kiss there."

"No, no, above, on her neck."

"Don't forget her navel..."

"And believe it or not, by the end of it all, she was on top," Shgēṭef proclaims.

Everyone is weeping with laughter at this final proof of the topsy-turvy world of Batānka.

"And that's the way it is," the Fool concludes, using this formulaic statement typical of codas for solo performances.

"And that's the way it is," all the men repeat in unison.

After several moments of awkward silence, which the anthropologist is careful to record, the conversation begins to flow again. Now the topic is the prices, and amount of stock on hand, of the tourists' favorite designs for Bedouin caftans and so on, as if the bitter argument had never happened.

I look around for the Fool, but it seems he has already left the circle. "Where is Shgēṭef?" I ask Jumʿa, sitting on my right.

"He's already gone back to his Billij huts, to make some more money off the tourists just arriving on the evening bus."

So the Fool has walked right back into the source of all the tension played out just now on the stage of the magʿad. But where did it go? This quirky tension-dissolver has taken it with him until his next performance.

### ■ III. ■

In the summer of 1979, the same dispute kept arising in Dahab's northern magʿad. The Mzeinis juxtaposed their Muslim, Bedouin identity with that of their drifting Batānka neighbors, and the Fool had to keep reassuring them in his farcical, convoluted way, that there were clear boundaries between them and their neighbors. A couple of days after one of these performances, I was sitting on the beach, leaning my back against a date-palm trunk. These were the smudgy hours of dusk, when the sharp red-granite cliffs seemed to glide into the Red Sea and be mirrored in its reddish-blue water. These were also the soon-to-be sacred moments when men washed in the tidal zone, purifying themselves for the *maghreb* prayer, while smells of poached fish, black pepper, and cumin drifted in the air. Jumʿa and

Rāshed completed their ritual purification and seated themselves near me beneath the palms, silently waiting for the muezzin cry.

The anthropologist dropped a casual remark, as if to herself: "This Shgēṭef is an incredibly funny guy. I have notebooks and rolls of film full of his antics."

There were almost 60 seconds of silence – a very long pause in a regular Mzeini conversation. Then Jumˤa said, somehow baffled: "You came all the way here just to write and picture some fool?"

After another very long pause, Rāshed slowly and carefully chose his words. "No, ya Jumˤa," he said frankly, "Shgēṭef is no fool. His mind is sharp as a sword. This summer he earned more than any of the rest of us off the tourists. And if it had not been for Shgēṭef's generosity, we would not have our mosque. But let me tell you, ya Smadar," Rāshed went on, turning his head towards me, "at times, this Fool's mind goes with the *tarāwa* (early evening breeze). His mind and his tongue then go separate routes, and he thinks of himself as if he's one of those Batānka."

"Poor Shgēṭef," added ˤAwayed, who had just joined our little group after finishing his ritual washing while half-listening to the conversation. With matter-of-fact finality he declared, "The Fool is a *fool*."

"Is *he* a fool?" Rāshed immediately responded, "*All* of us have become fools!"

"All of you? Fools?" The anthropologist perked up. "What do you mean?"

"The tourists have made us into fools," Rāshed replied at once. "They photograph us, they even make movies of us. There's no mountain left they didn't climb, no wadi they didn't hike, no coral reef they didn't scuba. They want to drink our tea and eat our bread and then complain of constipation and *we* are to blame." Then he stopped his diatribe. His deeply lined face grimaced, and he continued: "Our children, our own children, they don't know this desert, their own land, as well as some of these Batānka tourists do. They just want to hang around Eilat, and eat white bread soaked in factory milk. And all they dream of is owning Mercedes taxis and screwing in the foreign style."

There were five whole minutes of silence. In that moody limbo of the waning day, I mourned how so many romantic pasts are dissolving into the transnational future, and the anthropologist wanted me to stop being sentimental and try to rescue this disappearing culture by getting it into text.

"The Fool is a *fool*," Jumˤa, Rāshed, and ˤAwayed said in quiet unison, and then ˤAwayed proceeded with a slow, monotonous recitation of a traditional *gaṣīda* (poem) about the Fool, careful to note that I had turned on my cassette recorder while the men repeated the rhymed syllables.

> *Al-Ahabal la shāf al-deif ma yewanni,*
> *Ya ḥasrati minno la leginā.*
> *Damm al-ḍabāyeḥ jamb beit'ho yejanni –*
> *Mabsūṭ ill ˤind'ho we-illi ḥawelā.*
>
> *Ya karwato tishbaˤ al-ḍeif watethanni!*
> *Wasamn al-mebahhar minho ganā.*
> *Wenghāb ˤanna gheibto ma temanni!*
> *Kul ḥayii yugˤud ˤala darbo yetaḥarrā.*

*Wanwagef ʿindok tegūl ghazāl mit'ḥanni,*
*Waṭarrad al-fagr ʿannok – weyaglaʿ mada'ā.*
*Wankheito lel-molma yeẓarret ma yewanni,*
*Mithel al-beʿīr illi khabrīn ma ʿashā.*

*Walā lo ma al-ḥayii min al-maḥalīg ḥanni,*
*Middat ḥayāti – wana māshi warrā.*

The fool jumps up to greet his guest,
But each time we meet, it's the end of rest.
Such lavish sacrifices – too much blood to clean –
He thinks he makes everyone glad and free of sin.

So many guests his hospitality stuffs!
Spiced ghee rivers from him gush.
How we'll miss him when he leaves!
But waiting on his path is all that lives.

He tries to visit like a delicate gazelle,
Wishing poverty away from you – he throws it to hell.
But he gives communal feasts only fearless farts
Like those of a camel before his dinner starts.

All God's creatures can live without his strife
But me – I'll follow his footsteps the rest of my life.

## NOTES

1  Generally I describe the hippies as naked, as distinguished from nude, since "nude" connotes asexuality; the tourists' shedding of clothes on the South Sinai beaches had definite sexual overtones.
2  The unresolved contradictions built into the composition of fools or tricksters are discussed in Charles (1945), Cox (1970), Crumrine (1969), Fellini (1976), Handelman (1981, 1987), Klapp (1949), Makarius (1970), Parsons and Beals (1934), Radin (1956), Stevens (1980), Willeford (1969), and Zucker (1969).

## REFERENCES

Charles, L. G. (1945). "The Clown's Function." *Journal of American Folklore* 58: 25–34.
Cox, Harvey (1970). *The Feast of Fools: A Theological Essay on Festivity and Fantasy.* New York: Harper and Row.
Crumrine, N. Ross (1969). "Capakoba, the Mayo Easter Ceremonial Impersonator: Explanations of Ritual Clowning." *Journal of Scientific Study of Religion* 8: 1–22.
Fellini, Federico (1976). "Why Clowns?" In *Fellini on Fellini.* New York: Delacorte Press, 115–39.
Handelman, Don (1981). "The Ritual Clown: Attributes and Affinities." *Anthropos* 76(1/2): 321–70.

—— (1987). "Clowns." In *Encyclopedia of Religion*, vol. 3, ed. M. Eliade. New York: Macmillan, 547–51.

Klapp, Orrin E. (1949). "The Fool as a Social Type." *American Journal of Sociology* 55(2): 157–62.

Makarius, Laura (1970). "Ritual Clowns and Symbolical Behavior." *Diogenes* 69: 44–73.

Parsons, Elsie Clews and Ralph L. Beals (1934). "The Sacred Clowns of the Pueblo and Mayo-Yaqui Indians." *American Anthropologist* 36: 491–514.

Radin, Paul (1956). *The Trickster: A Study in American Indian Mythology*. London: Routledge and Kegan Paul.

Stevens, Phillip, Jr. (1980). "The Bachama Trickster as Model for Clowning Behavior." *Rice University Studies* 66(1): 137–50.

Willeford, William (1969). *The Fool and His Sceptre*. London: Edward Arnold.

Zucker, Wolfgang M. (1969). "The Clown as the Lord of Disorder." In *Holy Laughter*, ed. M. C. Hyers. New York: Seabury Press, 75–88.

# 9

# East Asian Bouquet: Ethnicity and Gender in the Wartime Japanese Revue Theater

## Jennifer Robertson

The "playing" of ethnography is a genuinely interdisciplinary enterprise, for if we are to satisfy ourselves of the reliability of our script and our perform- ance of it, we will need advice from various nonanthropological sources. Professionals in the field of drama in our own culture – scriptwriters, directors, actors, even stagehands – draw on centuries of professional experi- ence in performing plays. Ideally, we need to consult, better still, bring in as part of the cast, members of the culture being enacted.

Turner 1982: 90

### ■ Playing Ethnography ■

Japanese theater directors and critics active in the 1930s and 1940s "played" ethnography for the dual purposes of wartime recreation and the cultural assimi- lation of Japanese colonial subjects. They sought to create a "cultural weapon" by fusing theater and ethnology. It was an ambitious – and in retrospect, chilling – plan for which they sought advice from various anthropological sources, including from the very peoples who themselves who were targeted for assimilation. One theater critic, Endô Shingo, writing in 1943 about Japanese theatrical productions about and for export to the "southern regions" (*nanpô*), urged playwrights and directors to collaborate closely with anthropologists in order to create plausible representations of and for Asian and Pacific peoples (Endô 1943: 1).

I shall explore in this essay the affective, aesthetic, and cultural dimensions of Japanese colonialism that have been neglected relative to the more bureaucratic, military, and political dimensions of that expansionist project. Specifically, drawing from several of my earlier publications, I shall examine the relationship, during the 1930s and 1940s primarily, between colonial anthropology and the revue theater in Japan, focusing in particular on the representation on stage of the various peoples and cultures subjected to Japanese domination. The revue theater in question is the all-female Takarazuka Revue, founded in 1913, which I introduce in greater detail below. The Revue's opportunistic founder, playwrights, and directors collaborated with the state to create a popular drama that had the didactic potential to shape public impressions about the peoples and cultures under Japanese rule.

Beginning with the colonization of Okinawa in 1874 followed by that of Taiwan in 1895, Korea in 1910, Micronesia in 1919, Manuchuria in 1931, North China by 1937, and much of Southeast Asia by 1942, the state consolidated through military force a vast Asian-Pacific domain, the so-called Greater East Asia Co-Prosperity Sphere (*daitôa kyôeiken*), a rubric coined in August 1940. The core literature on Japanese empire-building details four of the means through which Japanization of Asia was pursued: the education of children, the exaltation of state Shintô, the organization of youth, and observation tours to Japan (Peattie 1988: 104). To these I would add an overarching fifth means, entertainment, which, like the preceding four, was also deployed within Japan as a means of incorporating the public into the imperialist project and ethos. An abundance of archival evidence suggests that theater was regarded by the state and its agents as a particularly efficacious form of entertainment toward this end both within and outside of Japan.[1]

Takarazuka playwrights were especially keen on incorporating ethnographic details into wartime revues for the purpose of providing the public with "culturally authentic," spectacular "infotainment" (information + entertainment). Although the relationship between the Takarazuka Revue, a private corporation, and the imperial state was one of mutual opportunism as opposed to seamless consensus, the "cross-ethnicking" performed by the cross-dressed actors was homologous to the official rhetoric of assimilation which equated Japanese expansion with a mission to "civilize" through Japanization the peoples of Asia and the South Seas (see Robertson 2001 [1998], ch. 3; cf. de Grazia 1981). The "civilizing mission" of the ethnographically informed revues was twofold. On the one hand, colonial subjects were represented on stage as objects and products of the dominant Japanese imagination of exotic yet inferior alterity. On the other hand, these representations were sometimes recirculated in performances staged abroad, as "culturally correct" models to be emulated by the very peoples objictified on the Takarazuka stage. In this way, the theater enacted a discourse of comparative otherness with the catalytic effect of enabling a broad spectrum of the Japanese viewing public to think that they were familiar with and knowledgeable about – and superior to – manifold other cultures and ethnic groups.

European cultures and societies were also performed on the wartime Takarazuka stage. In the fall of 1941, for example, the Revue produced *New Flag* (*Atarashiki Hata*), which glamorized the unification of Germany under the Third Reich. The play was described as the "staged performance" (*butaika*) of the information on

Germany available in newspapers and magazines (Hasegawa 1941: 14). A brief aside on the synergistic relationship between the print media and Takarazuka is relevant in this connection. The Revue was regularly reviewed in newspapers and magazines, and, during the wartime period in particular, was envisioned as a "living newspaper" instrumental in mobilizing and indoctrining people. The "living newspaper" was a dramaturgical form in which current events were editorialized through dramatic metaphors and visual effects. I am using the term "living newspaper" loosely with respect to the Takarazuka Revue in referring to the interwar practice of staging plays whose themes and subjects corresponded with those addressed in the print media.[2] The Revue's directors effectively harnessed the operatic power of these themes and subjects in an effort to both accommodate and extend the directives of the state.

## ■ Staging Colonialism ■

Founded in 1913 by Kobayashi Ichizô, an influential businessman and Minister of Commerce and Industry between 1940 and 1941, the Takarazuka Revue was conceived in part as a novel inversion of the all-male Kabuki theater. In 1919, Kobayashi established the Takarazuka Music Academy as part of the Revue complex and from which all actors must graduate. The 3,000-seat Takarazuka Grand Theater (Daigekijô) was completed in 1924, the largest Japanese theater of its kind at the time – the original theater was much smaller and quite rudimentary. The Grand Theater, rebuilt after a fire in 1935, and again in the late 1980s, remains one component of an expansive "wholesome entertainment" (*kenzen na goraku*) complex in Takarazuka, now a city near Osaka. In 1943, the complex included a hot springs spa, a library, a botanical garden, an entomology museum, and a zoo noted for its white tiger. A theater nearly as large was opened in Tokyo in 1935 and was rebuilt in 2000.

Approximately 700 people presently enable Takarazuka to function, and the literature suggests that about the same number were employed during the wartime period: 400 performers and 300 specialists including producers, directors, writers, costumers, set designers, instructors, and two 35-piece orchestras. The actors are divided into five troupes, four of which were established between 1921 and 1933, while a fifth troupe was added in 1998. Dividing the women into troupes facilitated organizing the growing number of actors (from 20 at the outset, to about 350 in 1931 [Hashimoto 1984: 118–20]), and enabled year-round performances at different venues throughout Japan. Each troupe is overseen by a (male) member of the Revue administration. The internal hierarchy consists of a troupe manager and a vice-manager appointed from among the senior actors. The Revue's patriarchal management, strict vertical social organization, and emphasis on hierarchy determined by age, sex, and gender was confluent with the social agenda of the wartime state (see Robertson 2001 [1998], ch. 3).[3]

A conservative estimate of the total annual number of spectators at both the original Takarazuka and Tokyo Takarazuka theaters in the wartime period produces a figure in the several millions, a significant audience that, in the eyes of the state, could not be ignored. Partly to increase business and partly to work with the state in mobilizing the Japanese people, mobile troupes of actors from the Takarazuka and other revues were dispatched, in the late 1930s, to factories, farm villages, hospitals, and even war fronts throughout China, Korea, Manchuria, Southeast Asia, and Micronesia to provide civilians and soldiers with "wholesome entertainment" and to weave together symbolically the disparate parts of the Japanese Empire (Matsumoto 1939; Shasetsu: engeki bunka to engekihô 1942; Shôchiku Kagekidan 1978: 45–48; Takagi 1942; Toita 1956 [1950]: 250–2; Uemoto 1941). Revue administrators even briefly entertained a plan of establishing an all-female revue in North China (Matsumoto 1939). A couple of years later the state pressured Takarazuka and other theaters into organizing the mobile troupes under the auspices of the Japanese Federation of Mobile Theaters (Nippon idô engeki renmei).

Since, as of 1934, the 1,934 drama theaters of widely varying sizes were concentrated in cities (Monbusho goraku chôsa 1932), regional tours by commercial theater troupes were important components in the process of national mobilization. The intensive activities of the mobile groups of actors further popularized theater among diverse audiences in Japan and abroad (Toita 1956 [1950]: 252) and helped to disseminate a military and imperialist ethos in the guise of entertainment. Although mobile theater troupes have a centuries-old history in Japan, the specific use of such troupes during World War Two was reinforced by the precedent set in Nazi Germany and fascist Italy, where portable stages brought sanctioned entertainment to the masses.

In 1944, under the auspices of an emergency economizing measure, the state closed nineteen commercial theaters, including Takarazuka and levied a stiff tax on them; the mobile units continued to be deployed (Toita 1956 [1950]: 243–4). Six theaters were reopened the following month for a maximum of two-and-a-half hours daily during which patriotic plays and films were scheduled (Hagiwara 1954: 150–1). Takarazuka revues were resumed in May 1945 at the Takarazuka Eigagekijô (movie theater), the main theater having been expropriated by the Navy as an educational facility for air corps trainees. The Tokyo branch, on the other hand, had been converted into a factory for the assembly of exploding balloons made from mulberry paper.[4]

Takarazuka revues from the outset included Japanese-style "classical" dramas and historical subjects, such as the *Tale of Genji*, Broadway-based and European-style performances, such as *Madama Butterfly* and *Mon Paris*, as well as folk dances from all over the world. Excepting of wartime revues, contemporary Japan and Japanese were and are not objectified on the Takarazuka stage. Generally speaking, it was during the wartime years that "plays dealing with the present (emergency) situation" (*jikyoku engeki*) were staged. In these dramas, time and space, history and geography were collapsed. The majority of revues produced during the late 1930s and early 1940s were about military and colonial policies and exigencies, such as the "southward advance" (*nanshin*) (e.g., *Saipan-parao: Waga nan'yô* [Saipan-Palau: Our South Seas], 1940), immigration to Manchuria (e.g., *Shunran hiraku koro* [When Spring Orchids Bloom], 1941), patriotic school girls (e.g., Gunkoku jogakusei [Schoolgirls of a military nation,], 1938), and intrepid nurses (e.g., *Kaigun byôin* [Navy Hospital], 1940).

The Takarasiennes, as the Revue's actors are nicknamed, include *otokoyaku*, or men's role players, and *musumeyaku*, or women's role players. Like the Kabuki actors before them, the cross-dressed actors clinched the popular appeal of the Revue among a very broad, multi-generational, mixed-sex audience.[5] In addition to "doing" a wide range of men and women, the Takarazuka actors also engage in "cross-ethnicking," that is, in the embodiment and performance of non-Japanese characters of diverse national and ethnic backgrounds. Just as gender is constructed on the basis of contrastive physical and behavioral stereotypes about females and males, so too were ethnic characters in the wartime theater based on reified images of "us" and "them."

In this connection, it is useful to comment briefly about the specifically Japanese "orientalism" which characterized both colonial policy and revues built around the theme of Japanese cultural superiority and military supremacy. Imperialist Japanese also engaged in orientalizing practices. Non-Japanese Asians and South Sea islanders were uniformly portrayed as inferior to the Japanese, although some were "good" or dependent, and others "bad" or resistant. I am using "orientalism" in a broader sense than Edward Said's initial formulation, according to which "the West" creates "the East" as its diametrical opposite. I find orientalism most useful as a processual theory of oppositional, essentialized constructions of others that work to intensify a dominant cultural or national image. It does this by dramatizing the "distance and difference between what is closer to it and what is far away" (Said 1979 [1978]: 55).[6] Orientalism in this generic sense has been deployed since the late nineteenth century by Japanese historians and ideologues in two apparently contradictory but actually mutually constitutive ways: to present *the Japanese* as culturally superior to other Asian peoples, and/or to claim an essential, mystifying uniqueness that distinguishes Japan from nation-states perceived as comparable in industrial and military power (i.e., "the West") (cf. Tanaka 1993).[7] On the one hand, New Japan (*shin'nippon*), as the imperial nation-state was called, was an imagined community constructed from select artifacts of western material culture; a nation whose western inflections would, theoretically, allow it to withstand the encroachments of European and American powers (cf. Feuerwerker 1989). On the other hand, New Japan was also imagined to be both the repository for and legacy of the products of Asia's ancient cultural histories, and thus bore the burden of salvaging Asia for the Asians.

The process of Japanese orientalizing was expressed in a two-part article on the production and goals of wartime revues published in 1942 by a Takarazuka administrator in *Gendai Engeki* (Modern Theater), an influential theater arts journal.

The Japanese revue theater is best described as a cultural engineering corps, and as such, has a role in teaching and guiding East Asian peoples. The Japanese revue must work toward purging from Asian cultures the bad influence of Euro-American revues which have all but eradicated local cultures with glorious histories spanning thousands of years. It is the responsibility of the Japanese to raise the standard of culture in East Asia; they [East Asians] are leaving that task to us. We must...pursue affirmative, spiritual ideals. The revue is a rich repository of cultural forms; [Asian] customs and manners must be incorporated into revues in order to capture the charm of ordinary people. The revue is a type of entertainment that can and will become deployed as war materiél (*gunjuhin*). (Komatsu 1942: 67)

The Takarazuka administrator provided an example of a hypothetical revue, *East Asian Bouquet* (*Tôa no hanataba*), inspired by the Greater East Asian theater of war. *East Asian Bouquet* was to present various colonized Asian nationals and ethnic groups and their cultures to Japanese audiences. The ten geographically-based scenes constituting the hypothetical revue were titled, Japan, Manchuria, New China, French Indo-China, Thailand, Luzon, Burma, Malaya, Java (Bali), and a multi-ethnic finalé (Komatsu 1942: 65).[8] The people involved in its production – lyricists, choreographers, costume designers, and so on – were to travel to the featured sites where they could study the local cultures in order to better recreate "authentic" local settings for their Japanese audiences (ibid.).

There is no record of *East Asian Bouquet* ever having been performed by either Takarazuka or Shôchiku. The closest equivalent to this hypothetical revue was *Children of East Asia* (*Tôa no kodomotachi*, 1943), a drama "dedicated to the juveniles of East Asia, especially the sons of Nippon who shoulder the future destiny of the East." The 18-scene revue was divided into three geographic parts: Manchoukou, with an emphasis on the founding of the puppet state in 1932; China, whose relationship with Japan is portrayed metaphorically as a father–son relationship; and the "Southern Area," represented as a utopian garden whose feathered inhabitants happily chirp praises of Asian unity (Matsumoto 1943b).

*East Asian Bouquet* may have been a hypothetical revue, but it accurately describes the conception, dramaturgical organization, and production of wartime revues in general. The Revue's staff in fact often traveled to the countries and colonies represented on stage to gather first hand, culturally relative material and ideas for their productions (Komatsu 1942: 65; Miyatake 1942). Some wartime revues staged by the Revue were even written by army and navy playwrights who had access to unpublished ethnographic and military intelligence. In addition to incorporating ethnographic data into their plays, the Takarazuka staff also wrote "anthropological" reports about the various cultural areas they visited. For example, the script anthology in which *New Flag* appeared included an article by the playwright, Hasegawa Yoshio, which supplied readers with background information on the relationship between Takarazuka and Germany; the geology and climate of Germany; German history, ethnic composition, agriculture and industry; and a review of the consequences of post-WWI inflation – Hasegawa defines "inflation" for the readers – which occasioned Hitler's emergence (Hasegawa 1941).

The Takarazuka playwrights and directors may have claimed to recreate specific cultural practices, but they often resorted to staging eclectic, pan-Asian spectacles, such as orchestrating Indonesian gamelan music and dances in plays set in Thailand (e.g., *Only One Ancestral Land*) (Matsumoto 1943a). Likewise, the revue *Saipan-Palau: Our South Seas* (*Saipan-Parao: Waga Nan'yô*), composed by a Takarazuka playwright following his research trip to the Japanese mandated islands, was described in a newspaper review as a "potpourri of the delicacies of South America, Mexico, Spain, and [North] America" (Matsumoto 1940). (It is not clear from the reviewer's comments that the play was actually set in Saipan or Palau.) The reviewer was disturbed not by the eclecticism of the spectacle, but by the "mistake" the playwright made in representing musically, "native peoples who had neither dances nor tunes of their own" (ibid.). His assertion was, of course, erroneous and inconsistent with the well-documented ethnographic and ethno-musicological interests of Japanese colonialists and professional and amateur scholars in the South Seas since the turn of this century, including Matsuoka Shizuo, Tanabe Hisao, Katsuma Junzô, and Hijikata Hisakatsu (Peattie 1988; Tsubouchi Hakase Kinen Engeki Hakubutsukan 1932: 482). Moreover, a South Seas cultural exhibition, sponsored by the South Seas Bureau (Nan'yôchô) – basically the Japanese colonial government in the South Seas (see Peattie 1988: 68–71) – was staged at the main theater complex in Takarazuka to augment the ethnographic "infotainment" contained in the play (Hagiwara 1954: 130).

Such cultural exhibitions tended to be held in conjunction with revues set in areas of national interest to imperial Japan. A good example is the Greater East Asia Co-Prosperity Sphere series of plays and exhibitions inaugurated at the main revue theater in Takarazuka in September 1941. *Mongol* (*Mongôru*, 1941), the first play in the series, was basically a love story in which was embedded Japanese colonial propaganda extolling Mongolia's natural resources (coal, livestock) and its entry into the Co-Prosperity Sphere. Japanese audiences were treated to actors dressed as Mongolians and to sets featuring the yurts inhabited by nomads. They could even learn a few key phrases in Mongolian which had been incorporated into the scripted dialogue in the *katakana* syllabary, such as *moroguchibaaina* (thank you) and *sain baaina* (how are you).[9] Mongolian folk songs and dances were also performed throughout the 18-scene revue (*Mongôru* 1941).

Appearing with the *Mongol* script in the October 1941 anthology, was a photo-journalistic essay by the playwright, Utsu Hideo, detailing his fact-finding visit to Mongolia earlier that year. Utsu rhapsodizes about the natural beauty of the vast landscape filled with abundant wildlife, but seems equally enthusiastic about encroaching modernization in the form of factories for the production of butter and homespun. The rest of the article details the typical Mongolian diet of goat meat and fermented goat and horse milk, clothing, housing, festivals, folk dances, and various other aspects of material and ritual culture (Utsu 1941). Extending and reinforcing the colonial anthropology lesson of both the revue and the playwright's essay, was a photograph exhibition of Mongolia at the Takarazuka complex that continued throughout the play's one-month run.

A similar multi-media presentation accompanied the other revues in the Co-Prosperity Series, which included *Peking* (*Pekin*, 1942) and *Return to the East* (*Higashi e kaeru*, 1942), the latter of which I shall discuss shortly. In addition, radio broadcasts of some Takarazuka performances were transmitted to Mongolia, China, Thailand, India, and Burma with the aim of "introducing Japanese theater culture to the peoples living within the area of the Co-Prosperity Sphere" (Hagiwara 1954: 141). Multiple ironies framed the transmission of the play *Peking* to Mongolia and China on June 5, 1942. Chinese listeners were treated to an ostensibly culturally authentic Japanese musical representation of Beijing and its apparently bilingual inhabitants, who spoke and sang in Japanese and Mandarin (rendered in *katakana*) about their "love" (*ai*) for Japan and the benefits of colonial rule, which included "progress and prosperity".[10]

Orientalism aside, the transmission of *Peking* to China was part of the colonial strategy of Japanization, which also referred to the strategic effect that Takarazuka, among other theatrical forms, was to exert on peoples subjected to some form of Japanese domination or direct colonial rule. One component of the Revue's Japanization policy involved having "real native" members of the audience vouch for the cultural authenticity of plays set in their respective countries. For instance, after watching *Peking* at the main Takarazuka thater, the Chinese ambassador remarked that

> *Peking* is superb. It weaves together skilfully the establishment of the Greater East Asia Co-Prosperity Sphere[11] and the awakening of Asian peoples. For us Chinese, what really clinches the play is the pan-Asian unity of the dancing and acting techniques. Whether staged in Hong Kong, Nanking, or wherever Asian peoples live, *Peking* will generate appreciative applause. (Takarazuka Kagekidan 1943: 37)

Similarly, the (Thai) director of the Thai Monopoly Bureau publicly declared about the play, *Return to the East*, that "the stage sets, acting style, and choreography were redolent with the aura of Thai culture ... I felt as though I had actually returned to my country" (Takarazuka Kagekidan 1943: 37).

The symbolically titled revue, *Return to the East* was the second drama in the Greater East Asia Co-Prosperity Sphere series. The series reflected, in part, Kobayashi's efforts as Minister of Commerce and Industry in the period 1940–1 to consolidate the newly conceived Co-Prosperity Sphere.[12] Based on a novel by a Thai official, a former finance minister, *Return to the East* promoted a vision of a Japan-centered New World Order (*sekai shinjitsujo*).[13] The novelist and a Thai choreographer were consulted in the creation and production of this play.

Briefly, the 15-scene play focuses on the short life of Rambha, the beautiful daughter of the deposed maharaja of Misapur in North India. Concerned for his infant daughter's safety, the maharaja had entrusted her upbringing to his best friend, the Thai ambassador to France and his wife, and the girl, unaware of her royal lineage, was educated at an elite French school. (The play opens with a formal reception at the school.) When she comes of age, the ambassador recounts her biography and urges her to return to the East and devote her life to restoring her late father's kingdom in Misapur. She travels to Japan, Thailand, and India in order to learn more about her ancestral domain, and soon finalizes plans to transform Misapur into "a strong country like Japan."

While still a student in France, Rambha had fallen in love with Paul Roy, like her an "Oriental" (*tôyôjin*) but unlike her raised in a Bombay orphanage. Paul was later adopted by a wealthy Indian who moved to France where the boy was educated. The two teenagers shared a sense of alienation from their Asian roots and bemoaned the fact that they knew little about "the East." When she is bitten by a poisonous snake in Thailand, Paul rushes to her side to spur her recovery. Rambha has already decided to choose her country over Paul, but just as she is about to break her decision to him, the two discover that they are siblings. Rambha, recovered and relieved, journeys to Misapur, ravaged by a cholera epidemic, and, as planned, manages to win the heart of the current maharaja, Ravana, son of the usurper. She poisons the cruel Ravana and then commits suicide by swallowing poisoned tea. Paul ascends the throne as Bhumindra, the rightful maharaja of the now liberated Misapur (*Higashi e kaeru*, 1942: 40–68).

The intertwined themes of western colonialism, patriotism, duty, imperialism, sibling incest, murder, and suicide form a present-day allegory of a pan-Asian past and future shared by Japan, Thailand, and India.[14] Let me digress here for a moment: The dominant racial ideology in Japan has it that the origins of the Japanese race were held to be mystically linked to the Imperial House and thus to constitute an "imperial family," a principle which could be extended outward to include new populations brought under Japanese dominion, so that these too could become "imperial peoples" (*kômin*) (Peattie 1984: 97; see also Robertson 2001). The relationship between Rambha and Paul/Bhumindra can be understood as an aestheticized refraction of the triangulated relationship Asia, Japan and Europe. Rambha's duty is to clear the way of obstacles (read, westernists and local anglophiles) in preparation for the emergence of pan-Asian co-prosperity spearheaded by Japan. Like Rambha and Paul, modern Japan had become alienated from its eastern roots, but would be able to regain its identity and preeminence through extreme sacrifices made by non-Japanese Asians who were, theoretically, incorporated into the imperial family-system. A review of the play published in the Japanese press recommended that *Return to the East* be presented throughout Asia as well as in Germany and Italy, where the Takarazuka Revue had toured in 1938 and 1939 (Matsumoto 1942).

## ▓ Colonialism and Montage ▓

A discussion of the distinctive features of the revue theater that made it an especially effective didactic, anthropological medium concludes this chapter. Japanese wartime ideologues were well aware that their success in claiming and containing national and colonialized peoples alike was contingent upon the state's instrumental deployment of the entertainment media through which to shape popular consciousness. The usefulness of Takarazuka in creating a vision of a global hierarchy headed by Japan was linked to the structure of the revue form itself. In keeping with its etymology, the "revue" theater represents a break from "the past"; that is, a break from a fixed, singular, canonical reading of events past and present. Like photomontage – a potent medium of social critique, commentary, and propaganda alike during the 1930s and 1940s – the revue offered "completely new opportunities... for uncovering [and also remaking] relationships, oppositions, transitions and intersections of social reality" (Joachim Büthe, cited in Ollman 1991: 34). Revues consist of a montage-like display and concatenation of different, even contradictory, images, lands, settings, peoples, and scenarios. Similarly, the Greater East Asia Co-Prosperity Sphere signified a new chain of historical associations and newly historicized memories; it represented a new system of cultural artifacts in the service of New Japan. The revue theater was to serve this new order as an important proving ground where the composite image of a New Japan could be crafted, displayed, and naturalized.

The meaning of montage, whether in photography or theater, operates through allegory, which is essentially fragmentary. Allegory depends on the separation and isolation of elements comprising the totality of the life context. To work as allegory, montage necessarily requires the viewer's or audience's concatenation of the fragmented and juxtaposed images and scenarios.[15] As Peter Bürger describes this process,

> [t]he allegorist joins the isolated fragments of reality and thereby creates meaning.
> This is posited meaning; it does not derive from the original context of the fragments.
> (in Buck-Morss 1991 [1989]: 225)

Like montage, ethnographies have also been described as recombinations of fragments of, at the very least, the reality of both anthropologists and their subjects. In his introduction to *Writing Culture: The Poetics and Politics of Ethnography*, James Clifford, for example, asserts that the maker of ethnographic texts cannot avoid allegories that select and impose meaning as they translate it. Power and history work through ethnographic texts, he cautions, in ways their authors cannot fully control, and notes that "ethnographic truths are thus inherently partial" (1986: 6–7).

The revue theater and ethnography alike share certain salient, montage-like features which were purposefully deployed in the context of colonialism. In the case of wartime revues in particular, such as *Mongol*, it was a common practice to call for a narrator, either a character in a play or an emcee-like figure, to emerge at regular intervals and synthesize the various dramatic fragments or scenes for the viewers. Theoretically, this action would reduce the degree of slippage between the performance, its reception, and its lasting effects. The simultaneous appearance of ethnographic essays written by Takarazuka playwrights and the cultural exhibitions staged at the complex, can also be interpreted as attempts to reduce – ironically, in light of Clifford's caution – through the overdetermined display or concatenation of select information, the slippage between the official message of a given revue and the message(s) extracted by individual members of the audience.

As a performative and spectacular extension adaptation of colonial ethnography, the revue theater helped to bridge the gap between perceptions of colonialized others and actual colonial encounters; it was one way of linking imperialist dreams and colonial realities. Takarazuka wartime productions functioned as a type of "human relations area file" or archive which, along with census reports, maps, photographs, ethnographies, statistics, and news reels, worked to create and naturalize among Japanese and colonized peoples alike, a warped but pleasurable vision of co-prosperity in the New World Order.

## NOTES

1 This chapter incorporates material from earlier publications (Robertson 1995, 1998 and 2001 [1998]). There is relatively little research on the ways in which theater interfaces with imperialism and colonialism. In the case of Japanese studies, the uses of film and radio as vehicles for the spiritual and physical mobilization of the Japanese and colonial peoples have been expertly documented and discussed (e.g., Dower 1993; Fukushima and Nornes 1991; Goodman 1991; Hauser 1991; Kasza 1988; Silverberg 1993). But there is a dearth of critical research on wartime theater, where staged performances operated as social metacommentaries on and motivators for such interconnected practices as nationalism, imperialism, racism, militarism, sexual politics, and gendered relations (cf. Bratton 1991; Pickering 1991: 229). Similarly, theater–state relations are overlooked or ignored in the otherwise excellent scholarship on the Japanese colonial empire (Beasley 1987; Dower 1986; Duus, Myers, and Peattie 1989; Myers and Peattie 1984; Peattie 1988; Shillony 1991 [1981]; et al.). Rimer (1974) offers a complementary overview of the New Theater (Shingeki) movement through the career of the playwright, Kishida Kunio. In this chapter, I will not examine the role of "guerrilla plays" staged in China, the Philippines, Indonesia, and elsewhere to oppose and resist Japanese imperialism and colonialist policies.

2 In the United States, the provocative use of the living newspaper form was associated with the American Federal Theater Project of the 1930s. The boundary between actor and audience was blurred by the practice of planting actors in the audience to ask questions during the play or challenge the ongoing action. Housing, health care, public utilities, labor organizing, and consumer unions were among the issues dramatized, and the plays "usually concluded that working people could (and should) solve the problems either by taking action themselves or by demanding that their elected representatives act for them" (O'Connor 1985: 179–80). As a movement, the "living newspaper" was initiated in 1923 by students from the Institute of Journalism in Moscow who formed the company Blue Blouse. A typical living newspaper program consisted of headlines, news items, editorials, cartoons and official decrees, the intention being to make current events and themes "penetrate the masses more deeply" (Stourac and McCreery 1986: 3, 30).

3 There were other all-female revue theaters established in the early twentieth century as well, notably the Shôchiku Revue founded in Tokyo (in Asakusa, a major working-class theater district) in 1928, which quickly became Takarazuka's main rival in every respect. Other, much smaller, Tokyo revues included the Casino Folies (opened in 1929) in Asakusa, and the Moulin Rouge (opened in 1931) in Shinjuku, a student and intellectual center at the time (see Seidensticker 1990: 68–87).

4 Although the main theater was reopened after the war in April 1946, the Tokyo facility fell under the jurisdiction of the Allied Powers General Headquarters headed by General Douglas MacArthur. It was renamed the Ernie Pyle Theater – after the popular

American war correspondent killed in action in 1945 – until reverting back to Kobayashi's control in April 1955 (Hashimoto 1993: 78, 84; Toita 1956 [1950]: 244). Throughout the Occupation period (1945–52), Tokyo Takarazuka performances were staged at other local theaters, and the Revue produced special shows for Occupation personnel at the Ernie Pyle (Hashimoto 1993: 142).

5  I have published extensively on the sexual politics and gender ideology operative in the Takarazuka Revue and shall not repeat that information here in the interest of focusing on the relationship between theater and colonial anthropology (see Robertson 2001 [1998]).

6  Unlike Carrier (1992), I find it unnecessarily complicated to divide O/orientalism into unmarked (what "the West" does) and marked (the ethno-orientalisms of the non-West) categories. In using the lower case form, I wish to draw a distinction between the products of Orientalism (i.e., "the West" and "the Other") and the orientalizing process through which a national or cultural dominant is constructed and dramatized. I have retained the term "orientalism" as both it and its overtones are salient in the context of Japanese imperialist expansion and colonial domination. As Stefan Tanaka notes in *Japan's Orient*, by the twentieth century, *tôyô* (lit., eastern seas) signified the opposite of "the Occident" in both a geopolitical sense and an ideological sense (Tanaka 1993: 4). He argues that the contested discourse of *tôyô*/the orient helped to occasion a new sense of national and cultural identity in Japan even as it revealed the ambiguity of Japan's place in Asia and the world (ibid.: 11–12).

7  Some scholars have argued that Japanese orientalism was so totalizing that it obviated the need for the concomitant deployment of an equally evolved Japanese occidentalism in order to dramatize and allegorize "original" differences. As Tanaka notes in this respect, "Whereas Romantic [European] historians looked to the Orient for their origins, Japanese historians found them in *tôyô* [the orient] (1993: 14). The widest line of difference was drawn not between Japan and "the West," but between Japan and the rest of the world.

8  New China, or *shinkô shina*, refers to parts of China under Japanese control. *Shina*, in use since the mid-eighteenth century as a name for European-dominated China, is regarded today as a pejorative term for China.

9  This transcription is the anglicized version of the Japanese syllabic rendition of the Mongolian expression as it appeared in the script.

10  Similarly, the "patriotic extravaganzas" staged in English music halls at the turn of this century invariably presented the British colonies as "willingly subservient," masking palpable tensions between the colonizers and the colonized (Summerfield 1986: 29).

11  *Daitôa kyôeiken*, or Greater East Asia Co-Prosperity Sphere, was an integral part of Prime Minister Konoe Fumimaro's idea of a "New Order" in which the Japanese would lead a Pan-Asian effort toward Asian self-sufficiency and stability, and resist both communism, and Western imperialism. The projected area of the Sphere covered Japan, China, Manchukuo, the former Dutch, French, and British colonies in Southeast Asia, and the Philippines. Some ideologues included Australia and New Zealand in the projected area (Hunter 1984: 42, 143–4).

12  Kobayashi traveled to Batavia (Jakarta) in the fall of 1940 to secure Indonesia's place in the Sphere by seeking, unsuccessfully, to obtain mineral oil and other concessions from the Dutch (Beasley 1987: 228–9; Hall 1981 [1955]: 858–9; Mook 1944: 42–65).

13  Phra Sarasas, a bureaucrat and proponent of Thai-Japanese entente who resided in Japan between 1939 and 1945. The original title of the novel, a "fable of political

morals" (Batson 1996: 156) written in "flowery English" (Matsumoto 1942) and first published in London in 1940, is *Whom the Gods Deny*. It was translated into Japanese as *Unmei no kawa* (river of fate).

14 It is striking how *Return to the East* also anticipates the militant nationalist Subhas Chandra Bose's path from India to Southeast Asia via Germany and Japan. In 1943, he proclaimed a Provisional Government of *Azad Hind* (Free India) and led the Japanese-supported Indian National Army, recruited before his arrival, in anticipation of an invasion of India. Bose's activity was followed closely in Japanese domestic and colonial newspapers.

15 Because a single concatenated meaning cannot be guaranteed, montage generates a tension between the dominant meaning and the subtextual, and potentially subversive, readings of the same performance. Moreover, once an audience disperses and re-enters the wider social realm, the two-fold problem remains of how to reinforce the official text of a play and how to measure accurately any influence that the performance may have had on their behavior (cf. Kershaw 1992: 2).

## REFERENCES

Asad, Talal. 1991. From the History of Colonial Anthropology to the Anthropology of Western Hegemony. In *Colonial Situations: Essays on the Contextualization of Ethnographic Knowledge*. George Stocking, Jr., ed. Madison: University of Wisconsin Press, pp. 314–24.

Batson, Benjamin. 1996. Phra Sarasas: Rebel With Many Causes. *Journal of Southeast Asian Studies* 27(1): 150–65.

Beasley, William. 1987. *Japanese Imperialism, 1894–1945*. Oxford: Clarendon Press.

Bratton, J. S. 1991. Introduction. In *Acts of Supremacy: The British Empire and the Stage, 1790–1930*. J. S. Bratton et al., eds. Manchester: Manchester University Press, pp. 1–17.

Buck-Morss, Susan. 1991 [1989]. *The Dialectics of Seeing: Walter Benjamin and the Arcades Project*. Cambridge, MA: MIT Press.

Carrier, Joseph. Occidentalism: The World Turned Upside-Down. *American Ethnologist* 19(2): 195–212.

Clifford, James. 1986. Introduction: Partial Truths. In *Writing Culture: The Poetics and Politics of Ethnography*. James Clifford and George Marcus, eds. Berkeley: University of California Press, pp. 1–26.

de Grazia, Victoria. 1981. *The Culture of Consent: Mass Organization of Leisure in Fascist Italy*. Cambridge: Cambridge University Press.

Dower, John. 1986. *War Without Mercy: Race and Power in the Pacific War*. New York: Pantheon.

Duus, Peter, Ramon Myers, and Mark Peattie, eds. 1989. *The Japanese Informal Empire in China, 1895–1937*. Princeton: Princeton University Press.

Endô, Shingo, 1943. Nanpô no engeki kôsaku. *Engei Gahô* 37(2): 1.

Feuerwerker, Albert. 1989. Japanese Imperialism in China: A Commentary. In *The Japanese Informal Empire in China, 1895–1937*. Peter Duus, Ramon Myers, and Mark Peattie, eds. Princeton: Princeton University Press, pp. 431–8.

Fukushima, Yukio and Marcus Nornes, eds. 1991. *Media Wars: Then and Now*. Yamagata International Documentary Film Festival 1991. Tokyo: Sôjinsha.

Goodman, Grant, ed. 1991. *Japanese Cultural Policies in Southeast Asia during World War 2*. New York: St. Martin's Press.

Hagiwara Hiroyoshi. 1954. *Takarazuka kageki 40nenshi*. Takarazuka: Takarazuka Kagekidan Shuppanbu.

Hall, D. G. E. 1981 [1955]. *A History of South-East Asia*. Fourth edition. New York: St. Martin's Press.

Hasegawa Yoshio. 1941. "Atarashiki hata" jôen ni tsuite. *Takarazuka Kagekidan Kyakuhon-shû* 24(11): 11–14.

Hashimoto Masao. 1993. *Sumire no hana wa arashi o koete*. Tôkyô: Yomiuri Shinbunsha.

——. 1984. *Takarazuka kageki no 70nen*. Takarazuka: Takarazuka Kagekidan.

Hauser, William. 1991. Women and War: The Japanese Film Image. In *Recreating Japanese Women, 1600–1945*. Gail Bernstein, ed. Berkeley: University of California Press, pp. 296–313.

Higashi e kaeru. 1942. *Takarazuka Kageki Kyakuhonshû* 25(3): 41–68.

Hunter, Janet. 1984. *Concise Dictionary of Modern Japanese History*. Berkeley: University of California Press.

Kasza, Gregory. 1988. *The State and Mass Media in Japan, 1918–1945*. Berkeley: University of California Press.

Kershaw, Baz. 1992. *The Politics of Performance: Radical Theater as Cultural Intervention*. London: Routledge.

Komatsu Saka. 1942. Rebyû seisaku soshiki (2). *Gendai Engeki* 5(5): 61–7.

Matsumoto Narao. 1939. Pick of 13 Zukettes is Going to China to Cheer Up Nippon Soldiers at Front. *The Osaka Mainichi and Tokyo Nichinichi*, 9 Aug.

——. 1940. 'Zuka in August. *The Osaka Mainichi and Tokyo Nichinichi*, 10 Aug.

——. 1942. Hukuko Sayo Shines in Grand Zuka Opera. *The Osaka Mainichi and Tokyo Nichinichi*, 8 March.

——. 1943a. Thai Foreign Chief's Drama Adapted for June Takarazuka Feature Item. *The Mainichi*, 13 June.

——. 1943b. 'Children of East Asia' in 18 Scenes Pleasing Takarazuka Fans in August. *The Mainichi*, 15 Aug.

Miyatake Tatsuo. 1942. Barî-shima no onna. *Takarazuka Kageki Kyakuhonshû* 25(8): 8–14.

Mongôru. 1941. *Takarazuka Kageki Kyakuhonshû* 24(10): 60–77.

Mook, Hubertus J. 1944. *The Netherlands Indies and Japan: Their Relations 1940–1941*. London: George Allen and Unwin.

Myers, Ramon and Mark Peattie, eds. 1984. *The Japanese Colonial Empire, 1895–1945*. Princeton: Princeton University Press.

O'Connor, John. 1985. The Federal Theatre Project's Search for an Audience. In *Theatre for Working Class Audiences in the United States, 1830–1980*. Bruce McConachie and Daniel Friedman, eds. Westport, CT: Greenwood Press, pp. 171–83.

Ollman, Leah. 1991. *Camera as Weapon: Worker Photography Between the Wars*. San Diego: Museum of Photographic Arts.

Peattie, Mark. 1984. Japanese Attitudes Toward Colonialism, 1895–1945. In *The Japanese Colonial Empire, 1895–1945*. Ramon Myers and Mark Peattie, eds. Princeton: Princeton University Press, pp. 80–127.

——. 1988. *Nan'yô: The Rise and Fall of the Japanese in Micronesia, 1885–1945*. Pacific Islands Monograph Series, No. 4. Honolulu: University of Hawaii Press.

Pickering, Michael. 1991. Mock Blacks and Racial Mockery: The "Nigger" Minstrel and British Imperialism. In *Acts of Supremacy: The British Empire and the Stage, 1790–1930*. J. S. Bratton et al., eds. Manchester: Manchester University Press, pp. 179–236.

Rimer, J. Thomas. 1974. *Toward a Modern Japanese Theater: Kishida Kunio*. Princeton: Princeton University Press.

Robertson, Jennifer. 1995. Mon Japon: Theater as a Technology of Japanese Imperialism. *American Ethnologist* 22(4): 970–96.

——. 1998. Staging Ethnography: Theater and Japanese Colonialism. In *Colonial Anthropology in East and South-East Asia: A Comparative View*. Jan van Bremen and Akitoshi Shimizu, eds. London: Curzon Press, pp. 266–84.

——. 2001 [1998]. *Takarazuka: Sexual Politics and Popular Culture in Modern Japan*. Berkeley: University of California Press.

——. 2001. Japan's First Cyborg?: Miss Nippon, Eugenics, and Wartime Technologies of Beauty, Body, and Blood. *Body and Society* 7(1): 1–34.

Said, Edward. 1979 [1978]. *Orientalism*. New York: Vintage Books.

Seidensticker, Edward. 1990. *Tokyo Rising: The City Since the Great Earthquake*. New York: Alfred A. Knopf.

Shasetsu: engeki bunka to engekihô. 1942. *Tôkyô Asahi Shinbun*, 22 Nov.

Shillony, Ben-Ami. 1991 [1981]. *Politics and Culture in Wartime Japan*. Oxford: Clarendon Press.

Shôchiku Kagekidan. 1978. *Rebyû to tomo ni hanseiki: shôchiku kagekidan 50nen no ayumi*. Tôkyô: Kokusho Kankôkai.

Silverberg, Miriam. 1993. Constructing a New Cultural History of Prewar Japan. In *Japan in the World*. Masao Miyoshi and H. D. Harootunian, eds. Durham: Duke University Press, pp. 115–43.

Stourac, Richard and Kathleen McCreery. 1986. *Theatre as a Weapon: Workers' Theatre in the Soviet Union, Germany and Britain, 1917–1934*. London and New York: Routledge and Kegan Paul.

Summerfield, Peggy. 1986. Patriotism and Empire: Music-Hall Entertainment, 1870–1914. In *Imperialism and Popular Culture*. John Mackenzie, ed. Manchester: Manchester University Press, pp. 17–48.

Takagi Shin'ichi. 1942. Kôba kokumin engeki juritsu e no teishin. *Gendai Engeki* 5(3): 22–4.

Takarazuka Kagekidan. 1943. *Takarazuka nenkan*. Ôsaka: Takarazuka Kagekidan.

Tanaka, Stefan. 1993. *Japan's Orient: Rendering Pasts into History*. Berkeley: University of California Press.

Toita Yasuji. 1956 [1950]. *Engeki gojûnen*. Tôkyô: Jijitsûshinsha.

Tsubouchi Hakase Kinen Engeki Hakubutsukan, ed. 1932. *Kokugeki yôran*. Tôkyô: Azusa Shobô.

Turner, Victor. 1982. *From Ritual to Theatre: The Human Seriousness of Play*. New York: PAJ Publications.

Uemoto Shazô. 1941. Manshû ni okeru engeki seisaku ni tsuite. *Gendai Engeki* 4(3): 48–50.

# 10

# The Theatre of Operations: Performing Nation-ness in the Public Sphere

## Diana Taylor

...it is how citizens *see* themselves and how they *see* those against whom they define themselves that determines national self-perception...the very idea of a nation is itself dependent on this visual realm.

Susan Jeffords, *Hard Bodies*

## ■ Performing Nation-ness ■

"Argentineans," a commentator noted, "were not born Argentineans; their nationality needed to be invented."[1] Rather than posit an essentializing notion of "national character" and attempt to "psychoanalyze" it, I look at how nation-ness is shaped through spectacle, that desiring-machine at work in the "imaginings" that hold a community together. "Nation-ness" captures the *idea* of nation that links disparate phenomenon such as nation, nationalism, and nationality.[2] But it is not just about politics and borders, it's about our way of *imagining* community, of creating and performing civil bonds. While citizens may envision the horizontal, fraternal community described by Benedict Anderson, identification is predicated on the internalization of a rigid hierarchy along the lines of gender, class, and race. Theatrical choreography situates members of the population in relation to each other. The visual arena allows a basis for identification, for in the public sphere "citizens" see themselves as somehow related to other citizens, most of whom (as Anderson notes) they will never meet.

Other scholars have focused on *writing* the nation, examining foundation fictions (as Doris Sommer does) or the literary traditions (as Josefina Ludmer did with the *gauchesca*) or national constitutions, grammar books, and comportment manuals (as the Venezuelan scholar Beatriz González Stephan has done).[3] Although language, literature, and any number of linguistic systems are key in aligning a citizen's sense of identity to a geographic place, becoming a "citizen" is also performative. We might look at theatre as one more stage on which nation-ness was played out. Just as gender is a performative act, what Judith Butler describes as an "identity tenuously constituted in time – an identity instituted through a stylized repetition of acts,"[4] nation-ness is also performative. Both gender and nation-ness (which, I will argue, are the product of each other's performance and therefore difficult to imagine separately) are oppositional and exclusionary – just as one is male as opposed to female, one is Argentinean as opposed to something else. Both are inscribed on physical bodies. This does not suggest that either can be "put on" or exchanged at will. But there is a certain range available in enacting them. National/gender characteristics may look "natural," though they become more visibly performative in situations that brutally impose acceptable embodiments of national identity. But even in their everydayness they're performative: discontinuous moments come to appear as constituting a cohesive "reality" that social actors believe in. Doing one's nation-ness/gender "correctly" promises privilege and a sense of belonging, yet involves coercive mechanisms of identification. National/gender identity is not so much a question of being as of doing, of being seen doing, of identifying with the appropriate performative model. This identity is forged in the public sphere – the way we see others and ourselves is key to the process of national recognition and identification. Identification is key to subject formation, though enactments vary from country to country and from period to period.

The performativity of nation-ness involves a double mechanism – on one hand, nation-ness as the sum total of diverse "imaginings" is possible only because very different people imagine they share commonalities and learn to identify as part of a group. On the other, the hegemonic "nation" tends to suppress or appropriate diversity; otherness either disappears or becomes absorbed as sameness. The Dirty War represents an extreme example of the double mechanism of imagining and imposing national/gender identity. The military promoted an image of the "authentic national being" and demanded that the population feel "Argentine" by identifying with their performance of national identity. Everyone had to act and dress a part in the new scenario – from the Mothers of the Plaza de Mayo to students walking to school. The military mandated strict controls on the physical body and on sexuality. Unlike the Brazilian military junta during the same period that encouraged the export of highly eroticized body images to suggest that sexual freedom equaled political freedom, the Argentine military clamped down on the body with a vengeance.[5] Surviving meant "being" Argentinean, or, more specifically, "being seen as" Argentinean in a brutal context that defined patriotism as conformity and nonconformity as subversion.

The performative aspect of the struggle to control Argentinean citizens in no way minimizes those factors that, traditionally, have been thought of as objective or real – that is, the political, economic, historical, social, or ideological tensions that provoked the country's instability and culminated in the Dirty War. On the contrary. I would argue that the way nation-ness has been formulated and enacted in the public arena affects the way politics have been conceptualized, orchestrated, and played out in Argentina throughout its history. Thus, the performative strategies are themselves key factors – ultimately inseparable – from the other, more "objective" events of the Dirty War.

During the Dirty War, the military's spectacle, like Perón's populist spectacles before it, staged national/gender identity in the social arena. The two performances showed two faces of authoritarian power. Both spectacles were undoubtedly displays of masculine domination, yet they looked different and, thus, so did Argentineans. The *peronist* simulacrum of democracy and mutuality seemed antithetical to the brutal dictatorship of the junta. The *peronist* spectacle was organized around the cult of the *Líder* – Perón's and Evita's names were inscribed on streets, buildings, and plazas; public space became associated with their persons. The same gesture, however, absorbed "private" space into the all-encompassing "public": "when one reaches the home of the people one is accompanied by, it is like being in one's own home... Speaking the same language, we understand each other easily."[6] Communal cohesion, as in theatre, emanated from *presencing*. Perón and Evita territorialized their followers, and made them at home in what was presented as a shared collective and expansive *peronist* space. Nation-ness became equivalent to *peronismo* – an umbrella that promised to unite even the most disparate members of this imagined community: ("You can't be a good Argentine without being a good *peronist*" was one slogan).[7] Desire for national unity coalesced with desire for the glamorous, powerful, and entwined figures of Perón and Evita. One got read as the other. The visibility of Evita not only intensified popular desire, it made it appear that women too could play a central role in Argentinean nation-ness. Furthermore, Perón specifically encouraged racial and ethnic minorities to join his following. Perón and Evita toasted the poor and the powerless (children, most specifically) as the most deserving of their constituents. As classes, ranks, and races co-mingled, the rowdy anti-elitist aesthetic signaled a provocation to the established oligarchy. The pseudo-carnivalesque quality of the *peronist* production promised an inversion of the status quo. The taunt went so far that *peronist* supporters vowed to "tocarles el culo a los oligarcas [touch the oligarchy's ass]," thereby defiantly transgressing all the bounds of class and good manners.

The spectacle of the Dirty War, on the other hand, was a theatre of panic, of isolation, silence, and unnaming. The junta's show of male dominance varied from the *peronist* in that it shattered the festivity, the mass demonstrations, the illusion of political participation, the questionable racial and gender inclusivity associated with the *peronist* spectacle. Instead of the physical commingling of bodies, the junta enforced strict separation and control. Public space was reduced and policed.[8] The population was physically compartmentalized and organized in spatial divisions – cells, units, zones. People were not only exposed to surveillance by the armed forces, they internalized the surveillance, monitoring themselves to ensure that they were acting correctly. Instead of an active *Líder* cult, the junta encouraged the population to passively identify with their leaders, who presented themselves as "gentlemen." Argentineans were assigned to spectatorship – watching themselves, looking up to (or out for) the military, scrutinizing others. Instead of encouraging people to demonstrate on the streets and overflow the plazas in shows of political support, the junta emptied the streets and plazas.

The meaning and function of spectacle had changed. The junta entrapped the population through the controls of seeing and being seen. People were pushed back into the supposedly private spaces and, again supposedly, out of politics. Women were confined to more traditional roles. The junta wanted no more Evitas. Racial minorities were disparagingly referred to as *cabecitas negras* (little black heads), revealing a deep racism that to this day continues to marginal-ize and even disappear indigenous and racially mixed people from the collective imaginary.

Military males alone occupied public space. Silence replaced clamor. Only the military sirens and screams of victims broke the imposed quiet of the Dirty War. All the limits and boundaries enforced on the population emphasized that the military males themselves recognized no boundaries. There was no limit, it seemed, to what they could do and get away with. Transgression became the property of the state. The paramilitary forces in their Ford Falcons would run wild through the streets of Argentina, driving up on curbs and knocking over fruit stands and kiosks, but the general population had to walk the straight and narrow. The *peronist* populist spectacle of national cohesion gave way to atomiza-tion. The abductions, disappearances, exile, and inner exile made this, quite literally, a theatre of absenting and deterritorialization. Instead of the pseudo-carnivalesque inversion, the junta imposed order, "national reorganization," stasis. The military attempted to stamp out the *peronist* spectacle – they despised and feared it as the spectacle of the unruly, the diverse, the inclusive. During the Dirty War, nation-ness was resemanticized: every gesture was broken down, isolated, scrutinized. The ideal citizens were those who self-consciously controlled their every act, every word, even as they attempted to create the appearance of a cohesive and natural reality.

## ■ The Theatre of Operations ■

[T]he city is…the site of the body's cultural saturation, its take-over and transformation by images, representational systems, the mass media, and the arts – the place where the body is representationally reexplored, transformed, contested, reinscribed. In turn, the body (as cultural product) transforms, reinscribes the urban landscape according to its changing (demographic, economic, and psychological) needs, extending the limits of the city, of the sub-urban, ever towards the countryside which borders it.

Elizabeth Grosz, "Bodies-Cities"

The performativity of nation-ness and gender and coterminous and mutually reenforcing. The sense of geographic expansion that underlines a nation (though is not identical to it) includes both city and rural scapes and has often been expressed in terms of gendered bodies. Sarmiento, for example, described Buenos Aires as a lady reclining comfortably over a vast territory. "She," with her river and her port, is the point of entry that allows the interior provinces contact with the European nations across the sea (12–13). The female body and Buenos Aires, with their respective deltas, conflate into the site of both danger and desire as well as the arena for economic and cultural exchange. The national/state body subsumes both spatial configuration and human embodiment into its larger project. The various discourses that equate human bodies, spatial bodies (such as cities), and state bodies (nations or other imagined communities) indicate the degree to which nation-ness and gender have been naturalized to shape, organize, and valorize space as well as human corporeality: outside versus inside; up versus down; private versus public; functionality (health) versus nonfunctionality (or disease), and so on. Each of the divides is gendered along the lines that assign the outside, up, public, and functioning position to the masculine and the inside, down, private, and nonfunctioning position to the feminine. Thus each "body" is constructed along the various coordinates of space (territory/nation-ness) and gender.

Different societies, in different historical moments, will need different kinds of bodies. Cities and other national spaces contain humans, much as those humans become the containers of social and national images and values. I've come to think of the Dirty War as a theatre of operations, for the expression emphasizes the theatricality, the medicalization, and the violence of the operation exercised simultaneously on social space and human bodies. The theatre of operations served the goals of a new economic age of privatization. The entry into a neoliberal economy required the creation of a social body that would accelerate production yet obediently dissociate itself from the financial fruits of its labor. Breaking bodies literally became a way of breaking unions.[9] Yet the assault was framed in the seemingly incongruous discourses of conquest and Christian "purity." Only by cleansing the social body could Argentina once again achieve glory. The military, the embodiment of the spirit of conquest (with all those historical antecedents) would undertake the heroic struggle.

The armed forces assaulted both civil society and the individual worker/dissident/political opponent at the same time and in the same way. The masculinist discourse on bodies – that feminizes interiority, depth, and malfunctioning/disease, for example – shaped the nature of their attack on both the human body and civil society.

The military unleashed a two-pronged offensive. The first was the "masculine," logical, and seemingly necessary implementation of strategies that were supposedly "up" and aboveboard. The military's control of space and bodies was justified by a rhetoric extolling national health and rational social functioning. The visible was made available to inspection through the official reorganization and redistribution of space into "zones" and the regimentation and surveillance of the human body. As in Bentham's *Panopticon*, power was "visible and unverifiable"[10] –

visible because the population could not get away from the military presence, unverifiable because people never knew when they were being watched. Combining militarized and medicalized language, the armed forces exerted authority over the enemy/disease. Medical terminology allowed them to target not only the "disease" but the entire population. Theories of contagion suggest that all people are at risk of catching and spreading the disease; everyone was a candidate for surveillance.

The other prong of the attack was aimed at "feminine" spaces and bodies – those dangerous interiors associated with femininity, occupied by the diseased and deranged subversives who hid underground. The military, while flaunting its visibility, also laid claim to invisibility, appropriating the tactics of the weak, those who, as de Certeau puts it, can never control but only insinuate themselves into, invade, or disrupt the space of the powerful. "The place of a tactic," he writes in *The Practice of Everyday Life*, "belongs to the other" (xix). They could see without being seen. Members of the armed forces wore disguises, carried volumes by Marx or Freud under their arms, and "penetrated" the hidden spaces associated with subversion. Their weapons included torture, bespeaking the sexualized character of the assault. These violations took place in nonvisible places, in the secret detention and concentration camps that the military hid from public view (in the interstices of the *Patria*'s "body," as they put it). There, the military tortured and murdered the disappeared who opposed their Frankensteinian efforts at (national) body building. The feminized underground was imagined as the other, that which was not readily available for scrutiny, the limit, the boundary, the extreme. (This gendering, I believe, partially explains the scopic and discursive insistence on displaying/exposing/violating the female body.) The junta vowed to *operar* and *limpiar* (to operate and clean) the public sphere, exterminating the germs that threatened the well-being of the fragile social organism.[11] The offending body was literally under the knife or *picana eléctrica* (electric cattle prod). Those who were not deemed recoverable died. The well-being of the nation/patient often called for drastic measures.

If spatial configuration participates in nation-ness by locating national identity in a given place, and by shaping and reflecting the way that citizens see themselves and each other, then clearly the sense of a national self undergoes change when space is partitioned and policed. The mechanisms are more visible, because they're extreme, during states of siege. The cities and countryside were divided up into zones that were searched in operations known as *rastrillos* ("to rake").[12] Entire neighborhoods were blocked off, one by one, as military forces searched homes asking for identification of all those present and the whereabouts of those absent. These invasive spatial tactics went so far as to reproduce the ghosts, if not the actual bodies, of those whom the military had already disappeared. When those absent from the home were among the disappeared, some Argentines confess to succumbing to the absurdity of making up stories explaining the disappeared person's absence to avoid provoking the irascible and brutal members of the armed forces.[13] Terrified individuals had to stay put; there was no place else to go that would not incriminate friends or family. Buses, cars, and all other forms of transportation were randomly stopped and searched. Messages on the radio and television reminded citizens that it was their patriotic duty to report suspicious-looking individuals. The regimented population, in military fashion, was reviewed, controlled, disciplined, and, at times, punished in full public view. Visibility was key to social control: people had to be available for inspection.

In this theatre of operations, there was a new semiotics of terror. The green light gave the go-ahead for paramilitary and military "task forces" (*grupos de tarea*) to carry out their raids and abductions. These were not, as the term *disappearance* might suggest, invisible affairs. Members of the armed forces in helicopters, military trucks, and jeeps cordoned off the area under siege. The victim was abducted, often yelling and screaming for help, by a group of heavily armed men. The victim would usually be thrown down on the back seat of the waiting car, and the group would drive away, recklessly, flaunting. Yet no one was supposed to "see" or, more specifically, admit to seeing what was going on.

The term *theatre of operations* connotes not only the performative nature of nation-ness, mediated through the visual sphere, but also the military's flagrant theatricality in destabilizing the population en masse. As if by magic, people disappeared into thin air. Then, just as suddenly, the bodies of disappeared people showed up all over the country – on sidewalks, in trash cans – as messages to the population. In one dramatic display, a group of corpses – all dressed up in suits, with shoes dangling around their necks like neckties – was found tied around the Obelisk, Argentina's national monument of independence, situated at *punto zero*, the dead-center of Buenos Aires. A new sense of communal identity was simultaneously forged and undone around a shared terror. Apprehensive spectatorship united a silent, atomized population. People no longer identified with the space they inhabited. They no longer saw themselves as members of a cohesive community. They felt like strangers in their country, in their city, in their own homes. The scenario became increasingly surreal as the junta disavowed the state terrorism that people saw with their own eyes. News reports failed to mention the escalating number of disappearances that occurred daily throughout the country. The make-believe world traditionally associated with theatre became the official version of reality and was relentlessly transmitted through the media. The military blinded and silenced the population, which had to accept and even participate in the production of fictions.

Each aspect of this theatre of operations – the military, the medical, the theatrical – reflected the same struggle and objectives: men struggled for control and supremacy over the feminized body (Motherland, population, woman). There was a constant crossover from the individual to the social through the attack on the "body." The invisible yet all too obvious practice of torture is just one example of how the three discourses fused into one – the torture was a hidden, hence obscene and fascinating, spectacle that paralyzed both the victim and the population. The performance of torture was medicalized, though of course it was a part of a military operation. Torture annihilated the victim's body and the social "body" simultaneously. One mutilated body, theatrically exposed for the population to see, undid the national sense of self and subverted the judicial, ethical, and social safeguards designed to protect individuals from atrocity. Just as bodies disappeared, so did civil society.

Both the city/country and its inhabitants showed the effects of terror. Parks and streets were empty. The once lively Buenos Aires failed to energize its inhabitants. Curfews were imposed; plazas, bars, and cafés came under surveillance. The "center" of Buenos Aires itself disappeared as movie- and theatregoers, restaurant patrons, and strollers abandoned what had been the city's cultural hub of Corrientes and Lavalle. (Upper-class neighborhoods such as Palermo and Belgrano, considered less resistant to the military project because they benefited economically from its agenda, became the new social centers.) The seemingly "natural" performativity of everyday life transformed into a command performance. The normally stylish and even flamboyant population now wanted to go unnoticed.

The *idea* of an "imagined" community underwent metamorphosis. Argentineans felt as if they were in exile, an internal exile, as the signs, sights, and codes of their familiar environment became progressively stranger and more terrifying. They could no longer read the signs.

The transformation of public space into militarized zone through systems of visual dominance and surveillance affected all social organizations. Military personnel took over positions of power. The universities, the cultural centers, the news services, and government agencies were all run by military men. Argentina's 44 radio stations and 18 television stations were state owned and operated. The military's goal was to "purify" the environment by cracking down on ideological contaminants. The vibrant intellectual life was stifled, and those who did not tow the official line were pushed out of universities into the intellectual underground of private tutorials, seminars, and group research projects.[14] With inquisitorial zeal, the junta oversaw book burnings. Theatres were burned; actors, writers, and technicians were threatened and blacklisted.

While officials claimed there was no censorship, they imposed "guidelines": "The programs should offer models of Argentineness for each inhabitant of our country...exalting the values that conform to the desirable models."[15] The portrayal of conflict on TV was deemed unpatriotic. Even though it is hard to imagine a soap opera without divorce, adultery, abortion, depression, generational problems, economic problems, attempted suicides, and violent offenses, unpleasant realities simply vanished from view. There were no live shows; everything was taped first, then submitted to the censors.[16] The dictatorship's propaganda clearly transmitted its version of the struggle to establish good over evil. The make-believe quality of the programming, presented in the social context of extreme brutality in which ordinary people were dragged screaming off the streets by military forces, endowed the national scenario with a ghostly spectacularity.

Boundaries collapsed between private and public spaces as the entire "private" domain became sucked up into the *proceso*. The junta coopted the language and space of domesticity. The Motherland was the "house" in which the military had to establish order. [ ... ]

And in this new militarized "home," families, like armies, were reorganized and hierarchized. There had to be a clear system of command: fathers had to occupy their place of authority; mothers were responsible for household affairs; children had to respect and obey their parents. Parents were designated military proxies and asked to police their children: "Parents are primordial agents in the eradication of this nightmare [leftist ideology]. They must keep watch, participate and report whatever complaint they deem necessary."[17] [ ... ]

As society became "reorganized," the physical semiology of the population changed. Adherence to the uniform roles proscribed by the military became synonymous with Argentineness. Political adherence, belonging, "being Argentine" were enacted daily in the public sphere. Being "seen" performing one's national identity correctly was key to survival. Guidelines dictating appropriate appearance and behavior for male and female students were issued and enforced throughout the entire educational system. [ ... ]

These prohibitions extended to professors and school administrators, who were made responsible for all infractions and were forced into policing their students.

The dramas of Argentineness were also enacted throughout the public sphere, particularly by the mass media that extended the military's capacity to invade domestic spaces and redo the body of its citizens:

> between one program and another, there was endless ideological propaganda in which a well-dressed youth with short hair and a tie arrives at the University; another youth, dirty and long-haired, making crazy and frightened gestures, hands him a subversive flyer; a father (the first boy's, of course) finds out about the situation. First, he hesitates, but then he calls the police to inform them of what is happening. A voice (from off) recommends "call the authorities *before* your son becomes involved in some *dangerous business*." (Adellach, *Argentina* 44)

In this spectacle of control, the "authentic" body (male) of the tidy young man was in sync with military aspirations of order and hierarchy. Conformity had to be visible. The principles of duty, generational trust, and openness were affirmed. Doubt and self-doubt were portrayed as debilitating. The father and son duo (in association with the police) triumphed. They showed the efficacy of the chain of (male) command while the crazy, frightened, structureless, fatherless son tumbled toward doom. The "subversive" boy was associated with femininity – the long hair and the frenzied manner conjured up the enemy as hysterical and effeminate. The image of safety within the system overrode the representation of chaos engulfing those outside it. Along with the idea of order, the ad also insinuated the quasi-fascist opposition of cleanliness and "health" versus dirt, disease, and disorder. The "subversive" boy was both dirty and unhealthy – situated on the brink of mental disintegration. The pamphlets he handled seemed contaminated by their infirm source. Ideas, clearly, were not to be aired and debated; they were categorized as life-threatening and therefore to be shunned unexamined. The population at large was in danger of contagion. The father–son–police alliance kept danger and violence at bay by being obedient citizens (calling the authorities), rather than by assuming protagonistic or active roles in the conflict.

Maintaining visible differences between the sexes, through the use of gender-appropriate uniforms, grooming, and comportment, became paramount. In-between-ness became the zone of deviancy in which homosexuals and independent women "naturally" fell and in which all enemies were cast. However, as in the military ranks, difference *between* males was rigorous and visible as well. Hierarchies such as status, age, and ideological positioning became immediately discernible – worn in one's attitude and attire. Discipline, as Foucault noted, was truly "the art of rank"; it fixed bodies in a militarized system while allowing them to circulate "in a network of relations" (*Discipline and Punish* 146). [ . . . ]

With the general population safely pushed into visible performative categories, the public arena became a theatrical space for the military and their opponents. While the general population dressed up as itself (in its role as obedient citizen), the military and its opponents needed disguises to infiltrate the *other's* space, the space of the "weak." They tried to look like average citizens or students or soccer fans in order to pick up information or identify and track down their opponents.

The opposition, too, often tried to look like "good" Argentineans so that they could successfully enter the spaces otherwise closed to them. However, the media played up the performativity of the enemy while denying that the military used the same tactics. Here too gender played a role, as women opponents were accused of being more deceptive and seductive than their male counterparts. In his article "Las guerrilleras: La cruenta historia de la mujer en el terrorismo" (Guerrilleras: The bloody story of women in terrorism), which appeared in the weekly magazine *Somos*, Carlos Penguin described the *guerrillera* as an accomplished actor, with multiple names and looks: "today she'll wear a blond wig, tomorrow clean cut, the day after tomorrow a red wig. She has an arsenal that includes a variety of items: sunglasses, a freshly washed face, heavy makeup, loose fitting dresses and tight pants. Men have far more limited resources" (13). One of the photographs accompanying the article shows two women's wigs hanging next to numerous pistols and assorted ammunition. The innocent-looking Ana María González was presented as a monster by the media not just because she was supposedly responsible for the death of the chief of police, but because she had tricked him: "she was able to introduce herself into the household, her youth was seductive, as was her manner of relating to the family" (17). She had acted as a friend of the officer's daughter; she had deceived him and his family; she had betrayed their trust. That is what makes this story so shocking that *Gente* claims "This [story] is terrifying. Stunning. It makes adjectives impossible."[18]

Everyone was performing. Everyone was trying to look the part that offered them security and relative invisibility (if they wanted to stay out of the fray) or access and information (if they were somehow involved). Even those who did not participate in the political struggle, but who wanted to effect some kind of social change, found that they too had to dress up.[19] Other people, as Griselda Gambaro's play *Decir sí* (*Saying Yes*) suggests, found themselves playing the stooge in a drama that they did not recognize as their own. The rigid state control and the hypertheatricality of the period deterritorialized the population, making people feel like strangers in their own bodies as well as in their own home, city, and country. [ . . . ]

## NOTES

1   Eduardo P. Archetti, "Masculinity and Football: The Formation of National Identity in Argentina," in Giulianotti and Williams, *Games without Frontiers* 236.

2   The term *nation-ness* was coined by Benedict Anderson in *Imagined Communities* to encompass concepts as disparate as nation, nationality, and nationalism. Though clearly the three are not synonymous, there is a certain slippage even in Anderson's use of the terms: "My point of departure is that *nationality*, or, as one might prefer to put it in view of the word's multiple significations, *nation-ness*, as well as *nationalism*, are cultural artifacts of a particular kind" (13; italics added). "Nation-ness," Anderson states, "is the most universally legitimate value in the political life of our time" (12). Although he doesn't define the term, I take it to mean the *idea* of nation, which includes everything from the bureaucratic fact of citizenship to the nationalist's mythical construct of nation as an eternal entity.

3   Beatriz González Stephan, "Las escrituras de la Patria: Constituciones, gramáticas y manuales," *Estudios: Revista de Investigaciones Literarias* 3.5 (January–June 1995): 19–46.

4   Judith Butler, "Performative Acts," in Case, *Performing Feminisms* 270.

5   I am indebted to my colleague, Rodolfo Franconi, who has shared his work on modern Brazilian Cultural Studies with me.

6   Qtd. in Rowe and Schelling, *Memory and Modernity* 170.

7   Qtd. in Rowe and Schelling, *Memory and Modernity* 170.

8   The film *Man Facing SouthEast* beautifully captures the isolation and compartmental-ization of space under the junta. Rantes, a patient who claims to be an alien from a more humanitarian planet, leaves the psychiatric ward and initiates a spectacle of joy and inclusivity at a concert. His transgression ultimately leads to his death.

9   David Rock notes that the brutality of the Dirty War went hand in hand with the economic restructuring undertaken by Martínez de Hoz: "the butt of both was the urban sectors: the unions, industry, and much of the middle class. The Army's task, with the war against subversion in part as pretext, was to shatter their collective bargaining power and their means of resistance; Martínez de Hoz's role was to weaken and ultimately destroy the economy on which they subsisted" (*Argentina* 369).

10  Foucault, *Discipline and Punish* 201.

11  Admiral César A. Guzzetti put this clearly: "My concept of subversion refers to terrorist organizations on the left. There is no right wing subversion or terrorism. The social body of this society is contaminated by a disease that erodes its entrails and forms antibodies. Those antibodies cannot be considered in the same way that one considers a microbe. As the government controls and destroys the guerrilla, the action of the antibodies will disappear. I am convinced that in the next few months there will be no more action from the right, something that is already underway. It is only a natural reaction to a social body" (*La Opinión*, March 10, 1976, qtd. in Frontalini and Caiati, *El mito* 21).

12  One example of the military exercises in population control, documented in the daily *La razón* on December 19, 1976, illustrates how the theatre of operations worked: "An operation of population control, similar to earlier ones, was carried out this morning by the joint forces of Villa Comunicaciones and Retiro. This included the identification of persons, the registration of documents, and an intense sanitary control of the

population. The operation, which began at five this morning, was completed by 1,500 men from the joint forces, and 500 collaborators from the Departments of Migration, Social Welfare, Public Health and the Municipality of Buenos Aires" (qtd. in Frontalini and Caiati, *El mito* 37).

13   Renee Epelbaum's three children were disappeared in 1976–7. Her cook, Ester, not only stayed with her during that period and up to the present but she and her young daughter were submitted to a terrifying raid by paramilitary forces after the children's abductions. The "task force" took everything – all the photographs of the children, the soap, the toilet paper. Ester remembers lying that the children were away on holiday so that the soldiers would not take out their anger on her and her child (interview with author, Buenos Aires, July 1994).

14   Private instruction was offered by some of Argentina's bravest and most eminent academics. Entire disciplinary groups, such as women's studies, moved to relatively hidden spaces, such as the *ático* Gloria Bonder describes, with its labyrinthine approach (interview with author, Buenos Aires, July 1994).

15   AIDA, *Argentina: Como matar la cultura* 19–20.

16   The controls did not let up even when the government started moving toward privatization as part of their effort to dismantle the unwieldy state bureaucracy and enter into a neoliberal economy. When the radio stations were privatized in 1980, for example, a new law was passed, containing 87 articles controlling the content of broadcasted materials.

17   AIDA (Asociación Internacional para la Defensa de los Artistas víctimas de la represión en el mundo), ed., *Argentina: Cómo matar la cultura* (Madrid: Editorial Revolución, 1981), 249.

18   "Algo que espanta," *Gente*, August 26, 1976, pp. 4–7.

19   The feminist scholar Gloria Bonder recounts how she and the group of women who organized an interdisciplinary seminar on women's studies were forced out of the university. In 1979 they founded the Centro de Estudios de la Mujer (CEM), which they located in an attic with a labyrinthine approach to it. The women felt relatively safe there. This was one of the "alternate" spaces that, when they did not entirely disappear, the junta pushed out of sight. When the women left their attic to speak in public or to organize work groups in the poor districts, they would dress up, put on furs and earrings like good *burgesas* to avoid being seen as active women by the military or as lesbian feminists (terms perceived as synonymous) by the nonpoliticized women they worked to help.

## REFERENCES

Anderson, B. (1991). *Imagined Communities: Reflections on the Origin and Spread of Nationalism*. London: Verso.

Case, S.-E. (1990). *Performing Feminisms: Feminist Critical Theory and Theatre*. Baltimore: Johns Hopkins University Press.

Foucault, M. (1977). *Discipline and Punish: The Birth of the Prison*. Trans. Alan Sheridan. New York: Pantheon.

Frontalini, D. and Caiati, M. C. (1984). *El mito de la guerra sucia* [The myth of the dirty war]. Buenos Aires: Edición CELS.

Giulianotti, R. and Williams, J., eds. (1994). *Games Without Frontiers: Football, Identity and Modernity*. Aldershot: Ashgate.

Rock, D. (1987). *Argentina 1516–1987: From Spanish Colonization to Alfonsin*. Berkeley: University of California Press.

Rowe, W. and Schelling, V. (1991). *Memory and Modernity: Popular Culture in Latin America*. London: Verso.

# Part III

## Gender and Sexuality

# Introduction

## Cindy Patton

The "woman question" has been posed in every human science discipline and in every department of the humanities, indeed, it has been an animating feature of Western inquiry since the Greeks and Romans set the Western mind on its quixotic journey. But the study of women, or of women's place or potential place, her sensation, her ethics, her thought, has only and always been a caveat, a set of descriptions and calculations to mark hers as different in some respect from that to which she is Other. Even when her difference exposed the particularity of his difference, and spawned gender as the object of inquiry, the question of woman, her femininity or masculinity, her body and its practices remained the most enduring quandary and yet still the most particular.

Similarly, sex, or rather, sexuality: for so long thought mainly as reproduction (in its heterosexual form) or fraternity (in its homosexual form); as in service of the corporate body of man, or a perversion of the objective uses to which its parts were said to be destined. Like gender, universal; like gender, an object of study; like gender, ubiquitous and yet, chimerical.

How can we mark the contribution of an interdiscipline, an approach, to a topic so worked on, worked over?

On one hand, Cultural Studies, as departments, or majors, or sets of academic journals and book series has been particularly hospitable to an integrative and politically engaged form of work on gender and sexuality. This work has demonstrably changed the contours of the academy, and perhaps, through its presentation in the modest space of our classrooms, promoted a useful kind of critical thinking more broadly.

But on the other hand, collecting together sentinel works runs the risk of claiming for Cultural Studies all that has gone well of late in the study of gender and of sexuality, without recognizing the independent contributions of specific contributing disciplines, or the work of vanguard scholars within disciplines who have reshaped the modes of inquiry that appear, in Cultural Studies, in hybrid forms. But most especially, collecting Cultural Studies risks forgetting the political complexity of being the bodies under study (or, the body's understudy), and of that peculiar and vital contribution of minority scholars who, by insisting on the validity of study of their gender, their sexuality, their point of view as, in their daily modes, objects of study, exposed the poverty of the objective gaze much more thoroughly than philosophical inquiry into the decline of scientific foundations has done.

This is not the occasion, nor am I the person, to detail an intellectual genealogy of Cultural Studies and its fellow travelers, women's studies – which spawned gender studies – and lesbian and gay studies – which buggered classic studies of deviance, and returned them as queer theory. What I can note, however, is that Cultural Studies, emerging as an interdiscipline, as a multimethod, from the Birmingham Centre during an especially exciting national period in the United Kingdom, shares many intellectual and political concerns, and even personnel, in common with the impulses that more diffusely promoted the emergence of gender studies and sexuality studies. Work on gender and sexuality were present from the outset at the Centre, especially in the study of youth forms of the 1960s and 1970s, themselves reactions to particular forms of masculinist and heterosexist domination in postwar England. While it is hard to disentangle what was contributed by feminists and gay liberationists from what was accomplished despite new forms of sexism and homophobia within Cultural Studies, two contributions are clear. Reading French poststructuralism and English marxism, practitioners at the Center for Cultural Studies, and the feminist and gay liberationist scholars working independently and, in the US, even innocent of the Centre's existence, arrived at a common insight: "essentialism," whether in its stark biologistic form or its culturalist and nationalist forms, made unintelligible what was most vital to understand about the relational and hybrid genesis of social life. A second line of unifying inquiry emerged from the (many forms of) anti-essentialist thinking and practice: a concern to understand and reconceptualize power, as relational and much more complex than liberal theories and many marxisms have claimed.

But this rhyzomatic power also located Cultural Studies practitioners within the beast they had hoped to slay. Once Cultural Studies looked abroad, it became obvious that the intellectual economy of the international academy entails differential knowledge production and distribution: on one hand, an open space for global dialog on gender and sexuality, the composite academy is at the same time a series of heirarchized centers of knowledge-power. Especially for academies in postcolonial spaces, "local knowledge" and its production work against the dominant modes of study – especially against "area" studies – but at the same time, such scholars must use the ill-fitting mode of their objectification as "Indian" or "Chinese" to read back new knowledge. In addition, the flow of knowledge elites from former client states to master states like America or Britain to acquire their higher degrees is in no way the reciprocal of researchers from the centers of going to the supposed intellectual peripheries and returning to the dominant academies with changed perspectives.

One more comment should be made about the relation of "gender" and "sexuality" studies to feminist and women's studies. All work on gender and sexuality is indebted to the activism and scholarship of feminisms over the past century or more. However, some particularly influential work happened in the 1970s and 1980s, as the gay liberation movement, like the student and "hippy" movements of the decade before, began to raise questions about the constitution of norms for sexuality, and simultaneously, lesbians within the women's movement began to raise questions about the universality of women's erotic and sexual experience. From this pressuring of feminist theory from two sides, new ways of asking questions about gender and sexuality emerged, sometimes as an outgrowth of feminist theory, and sometimes in antagonism to it. Scholarly work on men and masculinity, deeply influenced by the analysis of gender roles proposed by feminist researchers, began to appear alongside feminist work on women. In the university, several emergent departments chose to label themselves "gender" rather than "women's" studies. Lesbian and gay studies were more controversial and some distance behind (still) the emergence of women/gender studies, however; because they were interested in comparative analysis of gender roles, gender studies programs were often more receptive to a kind of "gay" research, even though women's studies programs were interested in research on lesbians.

I have chosen essays, then, with an eye to problematizing, rather than certifying, something called "Cultural Studies." I have tried to keep in view the contribution of areas of significance and emergent alongside Cultural Studies, but without reducing them to Cultural Studies, or diluting the meaning that Cultural Studies might, and I believe should, hold as an inheritance of mixed methods, rethought continental philosophy, and political investment, I think it is fair to say, in a humane postmodernity. Each piece represents the interdisciplinary, multi-method, and political approach that I think characterizes Cultural Studies, and yet has something else...a mark of their simultaneous habitation in postcolonial studies, or gender studies, or queer theory, or urban studies, or media studies. I have also tried to emphasize different ways of thinking about "international" – not just as not confined to the national or combining more than one nation, but more explicitly outlining the ways in which nation is and is not any longer a functional category.

Written in the wake of the crumbling Berlin Wall, as Germans and Germanists began to consider what a reunified nation would mean, Erica Carter's 1992 "Frontier City Berlin: The Post-War Politics" stands as the most ideal-type Cultural Studies work among my selections. Carter indeed trained at the Centre for Cultural Studies, and was among the most important theorists of the link between femininity and consumption. Combining rigorous historical analysis of the shopping riots of 1952 with sociology of migration within the post-Wall reunifying Germany, Carter is able to raise concerns about the plight of the actual women who now enter the capitalist "West" and to demonstrate the more diffuse gendering of economic participation in state communism and social-democratic capitalism;

indeed, she is able to interrelate the metanational economic discourse with local commercial practices precisely through an examination of the treatment of "shopping criminals" from the East in the immediate pre-Wall period and the dispersion of female black marketers to their new role as suburban consumers. In addition to its compelling use of history, autobiography, and media analysis, Carter's essay is important in presenting a relatively early and highly worked out analysis of the gendered constitution of geographical space. Before geography + X became a trendy formula, Carter had undertaken an intense engagement with the new materialism represented in the remarriage of political economy and geography post-Foucault, post-Bourdieu, post-deCerteau, post-Lefevbre.

Jennifer Robertson's "Gender-Bending in Paradise: Doing 'Female' and 'Male' in Japan" represents an early – and unsurpassed – analysis of the plasticity of the body in creating female and male personae both on and off the theatrical stage. Combining historical anthropology with feminist theory and then-emergent gender studies (which questioned the priority of sex over gender, and proposed more analytic attention to erotics and gender self-production), Robertson documents a theatrical world in which women played both male and female roles. Exploring the sense female fans made of, especially, the "male" characters, she reveals the contours of erotic subculture in which love between "women" both was and was not "homosexual."

Lila Abu-Lughod makes a similar move in her, "The Marriage of Feminism and Islamism in Egypt: Selective Repudiation as a Dynamic of Postcolonial Cultural Politics," analyzing the use of feminist thought at the level of both state and dissidents. Discrediting the duplicitous essentialism of political calls to cultural return, Abu-Lughod juxtaposes the content and style of progressive soap opera's treatment of women's place with the pamphlets and cassettes of celebrity actresses who have repudiated the secular objectification of their bodies and now taken the veil. Reconstructing the century-long history of secular political theorists' advocacy of women's rights, she is able to show that while the contemporary secularists and islamists constitute each other as political opposites, both agree on the basic modernist tenets of early twentieth-century theorist Qasim Amin, developed as national policy under Nasser during the 1950s and 1960s. By combining historical and textual methods and examining survey data of veiled and unveiled women college students' views on marriage, education, and work, Abu-Lughod is able to show both that progressives are not nearly so progressive as their construction of their Islamist Other suggests, and that Islamists, although they claim religious authority for their views on women, nevertheless tacitly accept the modernist premises of the Amin–Nasser project. While it is focused on a single nation, the implications of Abu-Lughod's analysis are much broader than an "area study" reading might suggest. Of all the religious-ethnic based cultural groups of the post-Second World War international scene, "Arab world" peoples have the most tenuous claims to the geographical spaces they do, or hope to, occupy. Thus, understanding the interpretation and use of "Western feminism" on behalf of and in order to contest the status of women and the very meaning of modernity has major implications for the conduct of state and national politics in a twenty-first century context in which bald nationalisms are frowned upon, and religious movements (other than the crypto-Christianity of capitalism itself) are thought inherently antimodern.

Donald Donham's historical ethnography of the emergence of a "gay" identity in a Soweto township reveals the historical importance of gender roles for gender nonconformists: effeminate boys could take up an intermediate category that, while closer to female, enabled them to form a positive relationship to family and church. Significantly, as exiled opposition members encountered the evolving contents of civil rights activism in Europe and the US, they began to perceive the importance of "gay liberation" and "gay rights," even in the absence of local persons so identifying and so agitating. AIDS activism also provided a fulcrum for the emergence of gay identity in the townships, alongside the "traditional" modes of understanding gender nonconformity.

Finally, Naifei Ding employs feminist and literary theory to produce a comparison of two "prefaces" written 400 years apart. Using Bourdieu's theory of fields – part of the sociological framework that underwrote the early Birmingham School work on subcultures – Ding shows how a literary interpretation of a "pornographic" Qing period novel founders on its claim that the (male) author has authentically represented the experience of "bad women": a claim that, retrospectively, exposes the author and the preface writers' gender and heterosexual panic. Similarly, in his attempt to place a contemporary collection of lesbian short stories, the male preface writer must "straighten out" his claims to access to the experience of the lesbian authors. Ding's clever reading of the vertiginous spaces of author and reader, and the strange space of author and reader occupied by the preface writer, queers reader response theory and raises important questions about the process of writing and promoting books about experiences deemed obscene. Far from exposing "other worlds" to the reader's eyes, Ding suggests that writing and reading such books entails complex circuits of desire that cannot be contained within the dominant representational modes, and that the preface writer, trying to situate the topic as well as the desires, teeters between morality and literary merit in legitimating the basis of their evaluation. Far from simply telling the reader how to read a book, prefaces constitute the book – and its audiences – as the kind of work they are; prefaces shift the meaning of text, constitute the markets for texts, and struggle to establish the preface writers as more authorized than the author her or himself to comment upon the social value of literature.

Together, these five essays offer a rich sense of the distance (between Carter's and Robertson's early work and Donham's and Ding's very recent work) that the studies of sexuality and of gender have gone, both with, and without, the aid of a formal academic space called "Cultural Studies." And yet, what has changed or "improved" is more significantly the working conditions of those undertaking these researches. Where the study of women or homosexuals was once a matter of the insertion of the "objects" into existing disciplinary fields of study, the center that once housed refugees from disciplines has enabled, even if it cannot claim full credit for, the hope of working together across disciplines, and as researchers who were also subjects in the study of worlds apart from the academy. The essays here demonstrate the grace with which authors have taken up the call in and across history, anthropology, literary, media, and postcolonial studies, to find ways of discovering and expressing knowledge about the gendered and desiring body.

# 11

# Frontier City Berlin: The Post-War Politics

## Erica Carter

On June 29, 1990, the populist pan-European weekly *The European* published a feature on Berlin as the future capital of a united Germany. Speculating on the city's projected status as capital of "by far the biggest and strongest economic power in Europe," *The European* noted:

> The city is destined to become a central European megalopolis, outstripping perhaps even London and Paris in cultural importance, diversity, and doubtless social and political tensions. A throwback to the heady, strife-torn capital of the 1920s and 1930s portrayed in Isherwood's *Goodbye to Berlin* and later in the epic film *Cabaret?* The song *Money, Money, Money* roared out by Liza Minnelli's Sally Bowles from a smoke-filled room in pre-war Berlin's fictitious Kit-Kat club is uncannily apt in today's city. Money, in the form of the mighty D-Mark, is the determining factor.[1]

There is certainly evidence to underpin *The European*'s portrayal of a future Berlin as inflated replica of the Weimar metropolis. Big business "has been quick to recognize the potential of metropolis Berlin,"[2] and in the course of the coming decade, the city seems set to become the crucible of regeneration for a Germany steering its way towards economic hegemony in a post-Cold War Europe. In the process, Berlin will undergo massive physical transformations: it will see the restoration of key sites – the Brandenburg Gate, the Reichstag, Potsdamer Platz – as the defining coordinates of a reconstructed metropolitan center: an expansionist housing program to accommodate an exploding population, urban development on grandiose scale to accommodate the incoming giants of big business and industry, and to house part of the apparatus of national government.[3]

But this is not the full story. Contemporary cultural critics from Roland Barthes[4] to the postmodern geographer Edward Soja[5] have drawn attention to the "discursive nature of the boundaries whereby we define ourselves in social space," in analyses that examine "what is at stake in representations of particular places: what is at stake in our imaginary constructions of significant encounters in significant places: (in) the relationship between the intermeshing architectures of the city and the psyche."[6] Critical work of this kind should remind us that, concomitantly with its physical regeneration, Berlin will be subject to processes of symbolic reconstruction, out of which will be forged a new socio-spatial identity for the city. Though it is perhaps unlikely that the Berlin that emerges will be quite the DM-glutted Sodom *The European* envisages, it will certainly be a Western consumer-capitalist value – the affirmation of economic might against "Eastern" indigence – that will define the symbolic contours of the future capital. *The European* again:

> Inside West Berlin's trendier bars and restaurants, a generation of young people weaned exclusively on the D-Mark swig Tequila cocktails and compare notes on their BMWs. Outside is an *army of East Europe's poor*; not only East Germans in stinking two-stroke Trabants, but whole families of Poles laden down with cheap beer, videos and tinned pineapple from cut-price supermarkets...Berlin has suddenly reverted to its original role as a metropolis at the crossroads of East and Western Europe...a city straddling the frontier between poverty and wealth.[7]

*The European*'s mobilization of crude stereotype – the assertion of West German cocktail-swigging sophistication against the tastelessness and excess of the Eastern poor – might be condemned as a particularly brutal manifestation of British prejudice, were the paper's comments not rooted in a longer-standing discursive tradition that defines the "West" (here, West versus East Berlin) by its symbolic opposition to poverty-stricken, stinking/unhygenic/life-threatening "Eastern" elements. It is this tradition which will be my focus in the following pages. Presented below is an historical case study in the formation of an exclusionary Western identity: a study of the city of West Berlin in the early 1950s, as it struggled to position itself symbolically (since geographical Westernization was impossible) within the boundaries of the capitalist West.

The source of the work presented here is a longer study of West Germany's post-war economic regeneration.[8] There, I draw on poststructuralist and psychoanalytic critical methods to "read" the post-war West German "social market economy," not purely as a field of economic relations, but as a construct in representation, crossed by specific relations of cultural difference and cultural power. The history traced below – a history of the symbolic reconstruction of West Berlin as consumer marketplace – offers perhaps one of the most palpable examples from that longer work of the political benefits of viewing macro-economic developments *simultaneously* as economic and cultural process: for what the micro-history of West Berlin begins to reveal is the intimate imbrication of post-war economic regeneration at the macro-level with the (re)establishment of hierarchies of cultural difference.

It is no secret that Western European economic recovery was made dependent in the post-war years on the affirmation of mass consumption as Western cultural value – defined, of course, in opposition to the production-oriented cultures of the socialist East. Less well known perhaps are the processes of cultural reconstruction in the course of which the boundary between East and West was consolidated by the symbolic encoding of figures of Eastern "otherness" with various manifestations of transgressive femininity. Before I examine the precise nature of the links between Cold War definitions of Easterners as dangerous figures of difference, and those more intimate mechanisms of projection and splitting that consign a libidinized femininity to the realm of the other, and thus of danger, I want first to comment briefly on recent political events in some sense contingent on earlier developments post-World War II. In the first free elections in the former GDR in 1990, the conservative Christian Democrats (CDU) adopted as their election slogan "Wohlstand für alle" (prosperity for all). The phrase was purloined from CDU political rhetoric 40 years earlier, when "Wohlstand für alle" was the banner under which the then Economics Minister Ludwig Erhard courted support for neo-liberalism – specifically for his model of the "social market economy."

The 1990 elections delivered a crushing defeat, both to the Social Democrats, and to the grass-roots democratic parties which had orchestrated the political revolution of 1989. That election result has been widely interpreted as an indication that, now as in 1949, personal prosperity – pitted against poverty in the East and South – remains the defining feature of Western political identities. Any account of West Berlin reconstruction must be seen in the context of a broader, post-World War II, East-West struggle over which side – the Federal Republic or the GDR – could claim to be the "true" inheritor of German nationhood and identity. I have argued elsewhere that, in the West, it was personal prosperity – access to consumer pleasures – that came to figure as a key defining feature of "German" identity.[9] As the political scientist Frank Unger recently argued, the affirmation of a German-ness founded in consumer freedom reached its apogee in the run-up to unification:

> What kind of nationalism was it that motivated the desire of East Germans to become citizens of the FRG as fast as possible, and at whatever cost? My impression ... is this: that no matter how much life has changed for them, no matter how much harder and more insecure it will be, they enjoy being elevated to the status of "real Germans," and one is tempted to say, of white Germans ... For many East Germans, unification implies the elevation of their collective identity, a symbolic entrance into the club of the master races as it were, even if they earn this admission by their status as white trash.[10]

But there is a second and final connection between post-war and 1990s cultural politics in Germany. Then as now – as I begin to show below – the struggle to define a new West German sense of self centered on the fight to contain within meaningful categories of identity ("economic" versus "political" refugee, etc.) an exploding population of refugees and displaced persons: a mass of migrants feared for their capacity to undermine hard-won West German economic might. Precisely these fears are reemerging in the early 1990s: the supposed "rising tide" of refugees, ethnic German settlers, and asylum seekers finds representation in the German mass media variously as a threat to economic stability, or more emotively, as an uncontrolled "assault of the poor"[11] on a beleaguered Germany. In a context where the preferred solution to the refugee crisis is an ever-tighter policing of the boundaries between West, East, and South ("Fortress Europe"), the case of West Berlin 40 years ago may provide a salutary reminder of the cultural-political dangers of a Western world constructed around bounded, fortress identities.

## ■ The Urban Fabric and its Symbolic Organization ■

The devastations of the final war years, and Berlin's division after 1949, stripped the city not only of its political role, but of the economic and demographic components of capital status. Physically and industrially, the Berlin of 1945 was devastated. The city center was a wasteland, and the Western zones had lost 75% of their 1936 industrial capacity.[12] In numerical terms alone, the population too had been decimated. By August 1945, it had shrunk from the 4,332,000 registered in the May 1939 census, to only 2,784,000. The 170,000-strong Jewish community had been wiped out, as had the greater part of the political opposition;[13] and demographic imbalances of gender and age were particularly sharply marked in a city where the proportion of men between the ages of 18 and 40 had sunk by almost 80% since 1939, while numbers of men over 60 remained constant.[14]

After 1949, West Berlin would emerge as the bastion of a much-vaunted Western consumer democracy. Yet the city remained haunted by the absence, both of a clearly definable physical center, and by extension, the lack of centered meaning. Slashed in two by the border, later the Wall dividing the city: rendered symbolically monstrous as the site of fascist crimes and transgressions – in the Reichstag, or on Potsdamer Platz, the former location of the SS torture chambers – the center of West Berlin was reconstituted on the displaced site of the Kurfürstendamm, as a shopping boulevard: a monument not to metropolitan grandeur, but to Western consumerism.[15]

The physical de-centering of post-war West Berlin may appear little more than an accident of history: yet it derives also from specific features of the will to modernization in post-war planning. The thrust of architecture and town planning in the early post-war years was precisely *not* to reconstitute the city as high bourgeois European metropolis organized around a monumental center as its transcendent source of meaning. For the post-war planners, wartime bomb damage offered a welcome opportunity to make good the "old sins"[16] of 19th and early 20th century planning, precisely by displacing the central axes of urban life from the core to the suburban periphery, "in an effort to achieve an equal distribution of the Berlin population across residential areas, each with a green belt at its periphery."[17] Thus when West Berlin reconstruction began in earnest after massive injections of US funds in 1949, what made the city "Western" was its regeneration, not from the center outwards, but from multiple points of origin on the urban margins: "Reconstruction in the Western sectors of Berlin has made the border visible . . . The metropolis is beginning to scatter and disperse."[18] The post-war architects and planners embraced a familiar modernist vision of the city as organic unity of the urban and the rural, to be achieved in West Berlin via the zoning of the city – its division by major roads into spaces of work, residence, and leisure – and by the construction of suburban residential areas as autonomous "cells,"[19] each with its own retail and business center. Thus though the city center would remain the "nucleus . . . the heart of every metropolitan organism,"[20] its functions as everyday site of consumption would be assumed by redeveloped shopping streets on the suburban margins: the Schloßstraße in Steglitz, Neukölln's Karl-Marx-Straße, the Tempelhofdamm, Mehringdamm, Bergmannstraße.[21] A 1951 report from the Economic Cooperation Office of the Special Mission to Germany described "the true centers of the city": "They are destined for the future. . . . Firms with fine old names have established themselves here, and an atmosphere of cosmopolitanism, indeed of luxury pervades the busy streets."[22]

What emerged out of the wartime rubble was, then, a *polycentric* city which achieved identity as a component of the "West," not solely through the conspicuous display of wealth and might in (geographically and symbolically) centered urban monument to free market democracy, from the Staatsbibliothek (State Library) to KaDeWe,[23] but crucially, via the proliferation and dispersal of sites of everyday consumption at its periphery.

It is important to note here that a cornerstone of CDU economic policy at the moment of West Berlin's reconstruction was the maxim that social equality should be achieved, not by state economic planning, but by free market mechanisms. In the early years of their 16-year period in government, the Christian Democrats espoused an economic-distributive (as opposed to political-participatory) model of a consumer democracy where equality was grounded in equal access to a slice of the cake of national prosperity ("Wohlstand für alle").[24] The urban fabric of post-war West Berlin became the physical manifestation of Erhard's distributive vision of consumer democracy. His ideal of universal equal access to post-war prosperity was actualized in the spatial proximity of West Berliners one and all to suburban shopping centers.

Importantly, the reconfiguring of the urban landscape produced a simultaneous recomposition of the masses on the street. In the immediate aftermath of war, commodity exchange had taken the primitive form of black market barter. Berlin's black market center was the Tiergarten, where illegal trading was quietly tolerated by Allied Command as an emergency solution to economic catastrophe. In the early post-war months, before returning soldiers regained control, it was Berlin's remaining female population that managed and regulated the black market economy: thus in one autobiographical account by Ruth Strege, the black market figures as the province of women:

> Every woman knows that a woman can work, a woman can slog. But people used to think that women were too stupid to understand anything financial. Then suddenly we realized that we could deal, haggle, cheat, barter.[25]

When reconstruction began after 1949, the women who had once populated the city center as black market traders reemerged in a new guise – as housewives – on the streets of the suburban periphery.[26] One of the first national market research surveys into shopping habits concluded in 1951 that, in around 70% of households, shopping was conceived as women's work, and housewives devoted an average of a half to one hour daily to the labor of consumption in its form as shopping. Thus the reconstruction of the metropolis as decentered suburban network – and here West Berlin was only one example of a more widespread development in the industrialized West through the 1950s[27] – both produced a multiplication of sites for the massed street presence of femininity, and at the same time ensured the containment of women-as-shoppers within a domesticated suburbia.

## ■ Refugee Femininity in Public Discourse, 1949–1953 ■

> The farmer driven from house and land, the refugee steering towards an uncertain future is the symbol of our city and of our time.[28]

West Berlin: a refugee city, and a city of refugees. Between September 1949 and December 1952, 1,376,843 refugees from the so-called "Soviet-occupied zones" were registered as entering West Berlin and the Federal Republic; the estimated real total, including non-registered immigrants, was around two-and-a-half million.[29] Whereas in the last three months of 1949, only 21.8% of registered migrants entered the West via Berlin, around 50% of all refugees and expellees passed through the city in the first half of 1952 alone, and no less than 92% in the first quarter of the "flood year" 1953, following the tightening of border controls along inter-German frontiers.[30] This statistical abstraction becomes more concrete when its spatial dimensions are specified. West Berlin covered an area of 480 km$^2$, the Federal Republic, 254,000 km$^2$. Thus in the first half of 1952, half the total number of migrants from the East passed initially through a city 500 times smaller than the country which received the remaining 50%.

In 1953, the Berlin Senate issued an 80-page report on the refugee situation, and appealed for financial aid from Bonn and the federal states to support the struggle West Berliners waged "not only for themselves but for the whole of the free world."[31] Though foregrounding the moral responsibility of West Berliners toward fellow Germans in need – "all Germans have a natural duty to help compatriots in need and danger"[32] – the report was typical of official discourse on the refugee problem in its portrayal of the threats perceived to emanate from this migrant population: the threat of disease and contamination ("the threatening specter of an epidemic"[33]), or of political infiltration: "This is a place where agents from the communist sector can cross the border at will and offer the refugee a 'good time.' He in turn is then recruited as a spy or kidnapper."[34]

The political menace was partially neutralized in the reception procedure which divided the refugee population into categories of risk and non-risk, and banished political outsiders ("economic" migrants, which is to say, those who failed to equate individual prosperity with the Adenauer model of parliamentary democracy) to the B-camps on the city's borders. But in so doing, the West Berlin government actively produced a second danger to the city: the threat of a dissipation of the work ethic on which its future prosperity and political security putatively depended. Once interned in the B-camps, refugees were stripped of the citizens' rights they might have enjoyed as Westerners: the right to welfare benefits, to state-funded accommodation, and crucially, to legal employment. Official alarm mounted through the early 1950s over the effects of the B-camp inmates enforced unemployment:

> It is above all the unofficial refugees who fall prey to a general discontent... With nothing to keep them occupied, they wander restlessly through brightly-lit city streets and loiter before tempting shop windows. Is it any wonder that envy grips them? The vulnerability of these tens of thousands of unofficial refugees represents a grave political and psychological problem for an island city such as ours, isolated from the rest of the world by a sea of totalitarianism.[35]

The reconstruction of West Berlin as consumer showcase, though conceived to ensure the island-city's safety in a "sea of totalitarianism," had generated its own sources of danger. Concealed amongst the shopping crowds that signalled the city's return to free market "normality" was an alien mass of "instable figures"[36] who threatened both the political security of the city and its identity as flagship of a meritocratic order grounded in the values of prosperity through work and personal achievement.

I noted above the preponderance of women in the shopping streets of the reconstructed city. The footloose refugee populace attracted to the consumer centers rendered the normative (housewifely) consumer indistinguishable from deviant (Eastern, criminal) femininity. The Senate monograph cited above goes on to present, by way of illustration of the dangers of the unofficial refugees, the case of Ruth Schramm, an unemployed refugee who had fallen into the hands of East German secret agents, and worked as a spy in the West. Her case is cited as typical of "the cunning methods used by the Eastern powers to turn to their advantage the over-crowding from which a West Berlin full of impoverished refugees now suffers."[37]

The ambivalence the report displays toward the consumer pleasures to which unemployed women such as Schramm fell prey (of the B-camp inmates in general, it claims "these are instable figures, more susceptible than most to the temptations of the big city"[38]) was common in public discourse on female consumption of the period. Women's participation in market processes, and thus their massed presence in urban public space, was viewed with alarm as a disruptive force in an already fragile socio-symbolic order. Other prominent "bad girls" of the city in the hot summer of 1952 were Dora M., a 36-year-old clerk accused in July 1952 of denouncing a West German male friend to the secret police across the border;[39] Hildegard Eipel, arrested in September on Potsdamer Platz under suspicion of denouncing newly-arrived refugees to the East Berlin police;[40] and Christa L., from Pillnitz near Dresden, caught shoplifting on a visit to the West Berlin sales one month later.[41] Caught red-handed at KaDeWe, Christa L. was accused of stealing "two fabric remnants, five scarves, several handkerchiefs, stockings, a purse, wash-cloths, a tin of fillet..."[42]

This meticulous inventorying of shoplifters' booty was a common feature in local media coverage of illicit concupiscence running rampant in the stores of West Berlin during the summer sales at the end of August 1952. Notes of alarm were sounded over shoppers' "enticement" into department stores with half-price bargains; the local press anxiously anticipated stampedes of female bargain hunters, unrestrained "Schaulustige" (literally, seekers after visual pleasure)[43] blocking doorways, spilling onto pavements, cramming exits and entrances. Two days into the sales season, those fears took palpable form in the specter of the voracious (Eastern, Communist) shoplifter; 19 women were caught red-handed, only two from West Berlin, the rest from the GDR and its East Berlin capital. *Der Abend* reports: "Twenty-nine-year-old Ruth P. from the Soviet sector had the biggest haul: one pair of shoes, three blouses, two shirts, a child's pullover, a lady's overcoat, and a child's jacket."[44]

■ The Dangerous Other of Mass Consumption:
Refugee Femininity ■

Feminist critics have regularly commented on the consequences for representations of femininity of the process by which the modern city in literary and media representation, though figured in part as the site of market exchange, political practice, communication flows or information circuits, becomes more centrally the terrain of subjectivity and identity, the domain of the other.[45] It is contended that, in a culture organized around the hegemony of the white, male, middle-class and heterosexual subject, the other will perpetually be encoded as feminine (alongside its representation as "proletarian," "non-white," "homosexual," etc.). This ascrip-tion to femininity of the characteristics of the threatening other is evident through-out the early 1950s in official discourse on the refugee problem in West Berlin, and in its popular media representation. What was perceived at the level of government as economic, political, and social crisis found expression in public discourse as a crisis in representation. What was at stake in the struggle to contain the refugee influx was, in part at least, the restoration of symbolic order to a city newly reconstructed (at least in the perception of the planners and architects) as holistic "metropolitan organism,"[46] an ordered synthesis of civilization and nature.[47] Some headlines of the period: "Yet More Refugees," "The Refugee Flood," "Refugee Flood Doubles," "Refugee Flood Continues Unabated," "Refugee Misery Makes Aid Imperative."

The representation of the forces of marginality as floods and streams that threaten to dissolve the structured hierarchies of social order is a familiar strategy in the conservative discourse of crisis. The encoding of those dangers as voracious/

castrating femininity (the female spy, the grasping shoplifter) was particularly prevalent in post-war West Berlin, not least because this was a city in which women were numerically dominant, and in which, in the immediate aftermath of war, they had visibly occupied masculine positions – as heavy manual laborers, as black marketeers, etc.[48] Added to the fears generated by this supposed imbalance in post-war gender relations were the specific dangers perceived to flow from the refugee mass. The refugees were seen to endanger political stability; in this context, the production of political categories-in-difference (political refugee versus economic migrant or Communist subversive) helped shore up the defenses of a city fearing inundation by the socialist East. Disease within the immigrant body threatened the organic integrity of the city; hence the vigilance of the Red Cross and camp medical staff, who were praised by the West Berlin Senate for their punctilious examination of refugee excreta, to which was attributed the successful banishment of the "threatening specter of an epidemic."[49]

Equally crucial to internal security was the management of the refugee mass in public space. We have seen above how the Westernization of West Berlin involved a reordering of public space, in which proliferating suburban shopping developments functioned as the decentered centers of organization for a newly constituted (and feminized) consumer public. Fabulous window displays and gleaming new buildings acted both as shopping magnets to draw in housewives and other emergent consumer constituencies, and as markers of West–East cultural difference, defiant challenges to the drabness of the city's *Doppelgänger* in the East.

The effects of urban reconstruction were, however, crucially ambivalent. Success in drawing the shopping crowds has always carried with it the danger of consumer deviance: thus Klaus Strohmeyer, parodying the presentation of the 19th century department store in common parlance as "the ladies' paradise," has dubbed it instead the kleptomaniac's Eden.[50] In West Berlin's summer sales of '52, that threat was amplified and given political inflection by the presence on the streets of a footloose and potentially malevolent ("communist") migrant population. And there is more. The punctilious inventories of shoplifters' loot: the mobilization of crude sexual stereotype – the scopophilic female as destructive force in the market order; the persistent naming of the socialist East as the point of origin of a deviant femininity – female spies and kleptomaniacs: all this positions an excessive and transgressive *femininity* as a key source of this *political* danger to the city.

I have tried to suggest that the physical regeneration of the consumer market place in post-war West Berlin was part of a broader reordering of gender identities: specifically, that women were positioned in public space on either side of a borderline between domesticated (housewifely) and deviant (illicit or excessive) consumer femininity. As Berlin is rebuilt through the 1990s, it is of course unlikely that the same gender patterns will be repeated: consumerism's contemporary spatio-symbolic order is arranged more centrally around the *family* than the housewife as consuming agent. I hope however I have begun to show how textual criticism may be used critically to "read" the politico-economic and urban environment, as the starting point for a politics that addresses the invidious contemporary reconstruction of fortress identities. The struggle for a new socio-economic order is simultaneously a struggle in representation – and one in which it will be necessary to engage anew as boundaries are redrawn for a post-'92 free market Europe.

## NOTES

1   *The European*, 29 June 1990, p. 3.
2   ibid.
3   Since this article appeared in *The European*, it has been decided that Berlin will be the seat of government in a unified Germany.
4   Roland Barthes, "Semiology and Urbanism." In: idem., *The Semiotic Challenge*, New York, 1988; and idem., *The Eiffel Tower and Other Mythologies*, New York, 1979.
5   Edward W. Soja, *Postmodern Geographies: Reassertion of space in critical social theory.* London, 1988.
6   cit. Dick Hebdige, "Subjects in Space." *New Formations*, 1990 (11) v–x: p. vi.
7   *The European*, op. cit.
8   Erica Carter, *How German Is She? National Reconstruction and the Consuming Woman in the Federal Republic of Germany and West Berlin 1945–1960.* Unpublished Ph.D. thesis.
9   ibid., esp. chs. 1 & 2.
10  Frank Unger, "Speaking of Unity." In: Geoffrey Nowell-Smith and Tara Wollen (eds.), *After the Wall: Broadcasting in Germany*, London 1991, 69–76: p. 72.
11  The German magazine *Der Spiegel* ran a special issue in 1991 (37/1991) under this title.
12  Tilman Fischer, "Berlin, eine sozialdemokratische Stadt." *Ästhetik und Kommunikation*, 1983, 14 (52), *Mythos Berlin* 65–84: p. 74.
13  see ibid.
14  Figures from Economic Co-operation Administration. Office of the Special Mission to Germany, Frankfurt. *Berlin baut auf. Berlin am Werk.* Berlin, 1951, p. 8.
15  In a special issue of the Cultural Studies journal *Ästhetik und Kommunikation* on the "myth" of Berlin, the sociologist Dieter Hoffman-Axthelm for example described the Kurfürstendamm as a "hothouse of bourgeois life," which was "in no sense equipped to become the center of today's half-city in the West." Dieter Hoffman-Axthelm, "Berlin Zentrum," *Ästhetik und Kommunikation*, 1983, 14 (52), *Mythos Berlin* 41–6: p. 42.
16  Economic Co-operation Administration, op. cit., p. 12.
17  ibid., p. 12.
18  ibid., pp. 10 and 12.
19  See Hans Högg, *Der Neuaufbau der zerstörten Städte als zentrale Aufgabe unserer Zeit.* Bremen, 1949, p. 11.
20  ibid., p. 13.
21  see Economic Co-operation Administration, op. cit., p. 23.
22  Ibid., p. 23.
23  The rebuilding of Berlin's premier pre-war department store, KaDeWe, was considered particularly symbolic of West Berlin's "will to reconstruction." In the words of the Economic Co-operation Administration's 1951 report, "an established enterprise has taken the courageous first step. The old Kaufhaus des Westens (Department Store of the West) has reemerged on its old site . . . a sign of the energy and will dedicated to the

reconstruction of this city." (Economic Co-operation Administration, op. cit, p. 28.) Nonetheless, the "true centers" of the city were seen to lie on its periphery: see ibid., p. 23.

24  The CDU slogan was also the title of a book by the Economics Minister Erhard, published in 1957 by the Econ Verlag.

25  Ruth Strege, "Machen Sie mal die Hintergründe einer Frau aus..." *Freibeuter*, 1979, (2) 57–71:p. 68. On the gender relations of post-war black markets, see also Annette Kuhn and Doris Schubert, eds., *Frauen in der deutschen Nachkriegszeit*. Vol. I. *Frauenarbeit 1945–1949*. Düsseldorf 1984, p. 38.

26  It should be stressed that the term "women" must be understood here as a category in discourse. I am not suggesting that the very same "real" women who had figured immediately after the war as black marketeers were transformed after currency reform into suburban shoppers. Although in many cases, precisely such an empirical transformation occurred, our concern here is more centrally with femininity as *symbolic* presence on the streets of West Berlin.

27  For a view of this development from a town planner who describes himself as a pioneer of post-war shopping development in the Western industrialized nations, see Victor Gruen, *Centers for the Urban Environment: Survival of the Cities*. New York, 1973.

28  Willy Brandt, speech to the *Europäische Forschungsgruppe für Flüchtlingsfragen*, Liechtenstein, August 1956. Quoted in Europäische Forschungsgruppe für Flüchtlingsfragen/Forschungsgesellschaft für das Weltflüchtlingsproblem, *Flüchtlingsprobleme in Berlin*. Liechtenstein, 1956, p. 4.

29  Figures from Senator für Arbeit und Sozialwesen, ed., *Deutsche flüchten zu Deutschen: Der Flüchtlingsstrom aus dem sowjetisch besetzen Gebiet nach Berlin*. Berlin, 1956, p. 15.

30  ibid.

31  Senat von Berlin, *Flüchtlinge überfluten die Insel Berlin*. Berlin, 1953, p. 72.

32  ibid.

33  Senator für Arbeit und Sozialwesen, op. cit., p. 56. See also Senat von Berlin, op. cit., p. 42.

34  Senat von Berlin, op. cit., p. 66.

35  ibid., p. 65.

36  ibid.

37  ibid., p. 66.

38  ibid., p. 65.

39  *Der Abend*, 28 July 1952.

40  *Der Abend*, 12 September 1952.

41  *Der Abend*, 10 October 1952.

42  ibid.

43  *Der Abend*, 28 July 1952.

44  *Der Abend*, 28 July 1952.

45  See for example Christine Buci-Glucksmann, *Walter Benjamin und die Utopie des Weiblichen*. Hamburg, 1984; Susan Saegert, "Masculine cities and feminine suburbs: polarized ideas, contradictory realities," *Signs: Journal of women in culture and society*, 1980, 5 (3: supplt.) S96–111; Siegrid Weigel, " 'Die Städte sind weiblich und nur dem Sieger hold.' Zur Funktion des Weiblichen in Gründungsmythen und Städtedarstellungen." In: Sigrun Anselm and Barbara Beck, eds., *Triumph und Scheitern in der Metropole. Zur Rolle der Weiblichkeit in der Geschichte Berlins*. Berlin, 1987, pp. 207–27.

46  Hans Högg, op. cit., p. 13.

47 Högg (op. cit., p. 7) for example developed the concept of the contemporary city as *Stadtlandschaft* (urban landscape), which he described as "one element in the spiritual quest for an open relationship with nature, for a natural development of the personality, and for an escape from the unnaturalness of the massed crowd and from the mechanism of urban centers."

48 See Klaus Theweleit, *Männerphantasien*, Vol. I, *Frauen, Fluten, Körper, Geschichte*, Frankfurt-am-Main, 1977, esp. pp. 235–310, for a discussion of the flood as threatening femininity. For an account of women's work in the masculine public domain after 1945, see for example Ruth Strege, op. cit.; Annette Kuhn and Doris Schubert, eds., *Frauen in der deutschen Nachkriegszeit*, Vol. I, *Frauenarbeit 1945–1949*. Düsseldorf, 1984, pp. 25–120; and Ingrid Schmidt-Harzbach, ed., *Serie Nachkrieg* I-IV, *Courage*, 1982, (6) 34–40; (7) 47–54; (8) 40–3; (9) 39–47.

49 Senator für Arbeit und Sozialwesen, op. cit., p. 56.

50 Klaus Strohmeyer, *Warenhäuser, Geschichte, Blüte und Untergang im Warenmeer*. Berlin, 1980, p. 166.

# 12

# Gender-Bending in Paradise: Doing "Female" and "Male" in Japan

Jennifer Robertson[1]

*Curiosity builds bridges between women and between the present and the past; judgment builds the power of some over others.*[2]

■ Making It, Theoretically Speaking ■

At the crux of social organization are situation and strategic interactions. Gender and the relationship between sex, gender, and sexuality are sociohistorical constructions: they are products of multiple, competing discourses conducted over the course of both a culture's history and an individual's lifetime.[3] [ ... ] I will explore the production, reproduction, and refraction of representations of gender in twentieth-century Japan, using as my focal context the Takarazuka Revue, an all-female theater founded in 1914.

First, a review of the meanings of several key terms. Regardless of their popular conflation, there is a major difference between *sex roles* and *gender roles*. The former term refers to the various capabilities of female and male genitalia, such as menstruation and seminal ejaculation. The latter terms pertain to sociocultural and historical conventions of deportment and costume attributed to females and males.[4] Sexuality may overlap with sex and gender but remains a separate domain of desire and erotic pleasure.[5] Sex, gender, and sexuality may be related but they are not the same thing. The degree of their relationship, or the lack thereof, is negotiable and negotiated constantly. In Japan, as among Anglo-Americans,[6] a person's gender initially is assigned, and (hetero)sexuality assumed, at birth on the basis of genital type, but this is neither an immutable assignment nor an unproblematic assumption. Although the Japanese apparently recognize two sexes and two genders, "female" gender (femininity) and "male" gender (masculinity) are not ultimately regarded as the exclusive province of anatomical females and males. Sex, gender, and sexuality may be popularly perceived as irreducibly joined, but this remains a situational, and not a permanently fixed, condition.[7]

Linguistic distinctions in Japanese between sex and gender are created through suffixes. Generally speaking, *sei* is used to denote sex, as in *josei* for female and *dansei* for male. Since the *dan* in *dansei* (*dan* may also be read as *otoko*) can refer both to male sex and "male" gender, the suffix *sei*, with its allusions to fundamental parts (e.g., genitalia), is necessary in order to specifically denote sex. Gender is denoted by the suffix *rashii*, with its allusion to appearance or likeness.[8] A female-like or "female" gendered person is *onnarashii*, a malelike person, *otokorashii*. The emphasis here is on the person's proximity to a gender stereotype. When attention is drawn to an individual's resemblance to a particular female or male, the term often used is *joseiteki* (like a/that female) or *danseiteki* (like a/that male). That an individual resembles a particular female or male is precisely because both parties approximate a more generic gender stereotype. The difference between *onnarashii/otokorashii* and *joseiteki/danseiteki* is significant, although the two terms sometimes are used interchangeably in popular discourse. Further complicating matters is the use of the terms *onna* and *otoko* to refer to both sex and gender, the difference evident only in the context used.

The Takarasienne, as the Revue's actors are called (after Parisienne), include *otokoyaku*, who specialize in signifying "male" gender, and *musumeyaku*, who specialize in signifying "female" gender. Upon their acceptance to the Takarazuka Music Academy, they are *assigned* their "secondary" genders, for, as in real life, there are no gender-role auditions. The assignment is based on height, voice, facial shape, personality, and, to a certain extent, personal preference. Secondary gender roles are premised on contrastive gender stereotypes themselves; for example, "males" ideally should be taller than "females," have a lower voice than "females," and exude *kosei* (charisma), which is disparaged in "females." The Takarazuka theater demonstrates that gender ideology, like most ideologies, functions to contain differences or antinomies by *setting up differences*, for the dominant sex/gender (male/"male") "needs constructions of difference in order to signify itself at all."[9]

## ■ Gender and Hierarchy: Now and Then ■

Since its founding in 1918, four years after the Revue itself was established, the Academy has solicited applications from females between 15 and 24 years of age. Today, most of the applicants are 19 years old, and, as required, are either junior high or high school graduates or are enrolled in a high school. Graduation from the two-year Academy marks a Takarasienne's public debut as a gender specialist and enables her to perform on stage as a bona fide member of one of the four troupes comprising the Revue. [ ... ]

The Takarazuka Music Academy presently provides a two-year curriculum of Japanese and Western performing arts training. Of the 734 applicants in 1985, 42 (or one in 17.5) were accepted. The annual tuition averages about 260,000 yen, and the students must purchase from their own funds the school's gray, military-style uniform. (The switch from Japanese- to Western-style outfits was made in 1929.) Most of the students live with one or two roommates in the Sumire (Violet) Dormitories (the violet is the Revue flower), where they are socialized into a life of discipline and vertical (i.e., age- and gender-based) relationships. All of the residents are required to clean the dorms, but the first-year, or junior (*kōhai*), students are also responsible for cleaning the classrooms under the watchful eyes of the second-year, or senior (*senpai*), students. A strict curfew (10:00 p.m.) is maintained, and first-year students are not allowed to venture outside the campus itself. Males are strictly forbidden from the premises with the exception of fathers and brothers, who, like all guests, are limited to the lobbies.[10] [ ... ]

The Takarazuka Revue (Takarazuka Kagekidan) was founded by Kobayashi Ichizô (1873–1957), the Hankyû railroad and department store tycoon. In his autobiography, *Takarazuka manpitsu* (Takarazuka jottings, 1960), Kobayashi notes that he was partly motivated to create an all-female revue as a novel solution to his financial woes. Two years earlier he had opened and then quickly closed a luxury indoor swimming pool in the village of Takarazuka, west of Osaka. The spa, a Victorian-Moorish complex, failed to attract guests for two ostensible reasons. Not only had Kobayashi overlooked the proscription of mixed bathing, but he had neglected to install devices to heat the water. Converting the pool complex into a theater "made good business sense," and the Revue was promoted as "wholesome family entertainment."

Kobayashi also conceived of the all-female Revue as a commercially viable complement to the all-male Kabuki theater. Complementary, perhaps, but not equally privileged or prestigious for reasons related to Japanese paternalism in general and to Kobayashi's choice of nomenclature in particular.

Kabuki *onnagata*, as the name implies, are regarded as exemplary models (*kata*) of "female" (*onna*) gender for females offstage to approximate. Neither *otokoyaku* nor *musumeyaku* are terms used in the Kabuki theater. *Yaku*, unlike *kata*, connotes serviceability and dutifulness. An *otokoyaku* thus showcases the potentiality rather than modeling the supposed actuality of "male" gender. Novelist Nôzaka Akiyuki sums up this nomenclatural disparity: "The Takarazuka *otokoyaku* affects a 'male' guise, while the [Kabuki] *onnagata* acts on his feelings and is completely transformed into a 'female.' Contrarily, as the term *otokoyaku* attests, the female who plays a 'male' role is but performing a duty."[11]

The *otokoyaku*'s rather paradoxical task, then, is to eliminate what is different yet to display as much difference as possible, both as a female performing "male" gender and as the antithesis of *musumeyaku*. She must, through technologies of gender such as clothing, speech, gestures, and ambience, signify "male" gender in such a way as to make it, and her very person, appear uncoded or "natural."[12] However, unlike the *onnagata*, she must not, at the same time, be "completely transformed" into her secondary gender. The parameters of the "naturalization" of "male" gender riveted early twentieth-century discourses on the social ramifications of the Takarazuka Revue.

Kobayashi resorted to the terminology of kinship in naming the Takarazuka "female" gender-specialist *musumeyaku*, or "daughter role," instead of *onnayaku*, or "'female' role." The conflation of gender-and-kinship attribution in the vocabulary of the Takarazuka Revue alludes to the principle that gender and kinship are mutually constructed: "Neither can be treated as analytically prior to the other, because they are realized together in particular cultural, economic and political systems."[13]

Kobayashi's choice of nomenclature was informed by the "good wife, wise mother" (*ryôsai kenbo*) model of female subjectivity and "female" gender codified in the Meiji Civil Code (1898–1947), together with the primacy of the patriarchal, conjugal household. Females acting on their own behalf outside the household were regarded by the state as socially disruptive and dangerously anomalous.[14] The public vocation of the actor, however, reversed the usual association of females with the private domain and, consequently, distinctions between "private" and "public" were neither incumbent upon nor possible for Takarasienne: "One result of this is that although [the actor] is aware of the dominant rules governing the society of which her small dramatic world is a part, her experience permits her to fuse the value-systems, and to bring the naturally secluded private interpersonal sphere of women in the home into the light of public scrutiny."[15]

The fusion was manipulated in a number of ways. Whereas Kobayashi sought to use the actor as a vehicle for introducing the artistry (*geijutsu*) of the theater into the home,[16] some Takarasienne and their fans used the theater as a starting point for an opposing strategy, including the rejection of gender roles associated with the patriarchal household and, as I discuss subsequently, the construction of a style or mode of sexuality.

Kobayashi tempered the revolutionary potential of the actor by relegating the "female" gender specialists to the status of "daughter," with its attendant connotations of filial piety, youthfulness, pedigree, virginity, and unmarried status. These were precisely the characteristics that Kobayashi sought in the young recruits and which marked the makings of a "good wife, wise mother." To clinch the filial and paternal symbolism, he encouraged all Takarasienne to call him "father" (*otôsan*). Gender assignment notwithstanding, all the actors thereby were "daughters." Many Takarasienne and their fans eventually appropriated kinship terminology effectively to subvert the "father's" filial symbolism and assert their own. [ ... ]

The representational inequality between the Kabuki *onnagata* and the Takarazuka *otokoyaku* is paralleled by the inequality between the *otokoyaku* and the *musumeyaku*. The naive and compliant daughter represents not only femininity but also the female subject in a patriarchal society who is excluded from participating in discourses on "female" gender and sexuality. Kobayashi, on the other hand, as the privileged father invested much energy in advocating arranged marriages for retired Takarasienne, in keeping with the state-sanctioned "good wife, wise mother" model of "female" gender.[17] The *otokoyaku*, Kobayashi argued, participates not in the construction of alternative "female" gender roles but in the glorification of "male" gender. He proclaimed that "the *otokoyaku* is not male [sex] but is more suave, more affectionate, more courageous, more charming, more handsome, and more fascinating than a real male."[18] [ ... ]

The *otokoyaku*, according to Kobayashi, was neither a model of alternative "female" gender roles nor a model of "male" gender for males offstage to emulate. Rather, *otokoyaku* ultimately enhanced the "good wife, wise mother" role. Kobayashi theorized that by performing as "males," females learned to understand and appreciate the male/"male" psyche. Consequently, when they eventually retired from the state and married (which he urged them to do), they would be better able to perform as "good wives, wise mothers," knowing exactly what their husbands expected of them.[19] Significantly, even after graduating from the Academy and joining the Revue proper, a Takarasienne is still called "student" (*seitô*), for, as Kobayashi believed, the wedding ceremony marks the start of her real career, whereupon a woman becomes a full-fledged actor and the conjugal household her stage. His theory about *otokoyaku* seems to exploit the "double consciousness" of females (and people in any subordinate position), which "arises from the fact that to survive, one must understand how those who dominate define the world and oneself. One must be able to know what they think and what they expect and what the limits of freedom are."[20]

■ Enter the *Shôjo* ■

A number of Takarasienne nevertheless interpreted and appropriated their secondary genders in such a way as to resist and subvert Kobayashi's designs. In order to show how they did this, it is necessary to review from another angle the origins of the Revue and its popular reception.

Originally called the Takarazuka Choir (Takarazuka Shôkatai), Kobayashi changed the name within five months to the Takarazuka Girl's Opera Training Association (Takarazuka Shôjo Kageki Yôseikai). This name change, specifically with the addition of the term *shôjo*, set the enduring public image of the Takarazuka theater, even though *shôjo* was removed in a final name change in 1940.

Literally speaking, *shôjo* means a "not-quite-female" female. To become a fully female adult in Japan involves marriage and motherhood. *Shôjo*, then, denotes both (ostensibly virgin) females between puberty and marriage and that period of time itself (*shôjoki*).[21] *Shôjo* also implies heterosexual *inexperience* and homosexual *experience*, and, significantly, both male chauvinists and some lesbian feminists have appropriated the term. The former use it to disparage lesbians, convinced that "lesbian" names not a mode of sexuality but a "virgin" ("unadult") female.[22] The latter use the term *chôshôjo*, or "ultra *shôjo*," in reference to adult females who eschew heterosexism and believe in the power of sisterhood.[23]

The state's emphasis on universal – if segregated and sexist – education, together with the notion that a brief stint in the burgeoning industrial and commercial workforce was a desirable thing for females, effectively increased the number of years between puberty and marriage.[24] Tenure in the Takarazuka Revue further lengthened the *shôjo* period, a point made in a newspaper article on a leading Takarasienne which bore the headline: "Still a *shôjo* at 36!"[25] This was not intended as a compliment. Takarasienne by definition were unmarried, but the reporter here was drawing attention to the disturbing lack of correspondence between chronological age and *shôjo* existence.

Occupants of the *shôjo* category of "female" gender included the "new working woman" (*shinshokugyôfujin*) and her jaunty counterpart, the "modern girl" (*modan gâru*, or *moga*), herself the antithesis of the "good wife, wise mother." Whereas the flapperlike *moga* fancied herself an actor whose stage was the street she cruised, the "new working woman" aspired to the revue stage. An article on department store clerks in a series on the "soul of the working woman" published in the *Osaka Mainichi* (May 29, 1923) noted that instead of marriage, clerks expressed a desire to join the Takarazuka Revue, which, moreover, proved to be the most popular form of entertainment for "working women." The large number of teenagers who flocked to Takarazuka soon after its founding attested to the popularity of the Revue and prompted a ban on all junior high school students from attending Takarazuka performances.[26] Throughout the pre- and interwar periods, the Revue continued to attract "rebellious" teens, female and male, who ran away from home to be closer to their idols or who selected Takarazuka as an appropriately romantic setting for their "love suicides" (*shinjū*).[27]

Kobayashi envisioned Takarazuka as a world of "dreams and romance" and named the early theater complex "Paradise" to emphasize symbolically its idealism. He was inspired by a new genre of literature, *shôjo* fiction (*shosetsu*), most tenaciously associated with Yoshiya Nobuko (1904–73), an influential, prolific author and a lesbian. Her widely read stories framed female couples in a dreamy, sweetly erotic light. Unlike her fiction, Yoshiya's own life-style was patently political, even subversive, in that she openly rejected marriage, motherhood, and the compulsory heterosexuality of the Civil Code.[28]

Kobayashi shared Yoshiya's romantic vision but colored it heterosexual: his dream world was one in which gallant males were sustained by adoring females. The irony remains that this idealized vision of heterosexuality was enacted by an all-female cast. (Of course, it is not ironic in the sense that females were regarded as the main vehicles for the representation of masculinity.) It was an irony that, initially at least, was lost on Kobayashi but not on either the performers and their fans or on the critics. Contrary to Kobayashi's original intentions, Takarasienne inverted the image of the *shôjo* and in the process inspired an enduring style for a Japanese lesbian subculture; namely, "butch/femme."

## ■ Refracted Gender Roles ■

My evaluation of the ways in which the Takarazuka Revue served as the medium of resistance to the "good wife, wise mother" role and, for some Takarasienne and their fans, as the style of a lesbian subculture is informed by Adrienne Rich's idea of a lesbian continuum. Rich's continuum spans the wide range of female-identified experience, from resisting the bride-price to choosing a female lover or life partner, and provides a sense of continuity between past and present discourses on sex, gender, and sexuality.[29]

The following expressions were used in reference to female couples in early twentieth-century Japan: the generic *dôseiai*, or "same-sex love," and, more popularly, "Class S" (*kurasu esu*). The "S" stands for sex, sister, or *shôjo*, or all three combined. "Class S" continues to conjure up the image of two schoolgirls, often a junior-senior pair, with a crush on each other, an altogether typical and accepted feature of the *shôjo* period of the female life cycle.[30] Parents and society at large continue to censure casual and premarital heterosexual relations, the prevention of which is the reason for the persistence of Takarazuka's strict females only policy. One Revue director has further proposed that the "presence of males would pollute the very essence of Takarazuka," which he regards as a "sacred site."[31] This unprecedented reversal of the tenacious myth that females are ritually polluted due to their sex roles, primarily menstruation and parturition, alludes to the paradisiacal "otherness" attributed to Takarazuka.

Among Takarasienne, one slang expression used since the 1920s in reference to female couples has been *deben*, from *demae bentô*, or "take-out lunch box." The basic idea is that intimacy between two cloistered females is analogous to a lunch of "rice" (*gohan*) and "dishes eaten along with the rice" (*okazu*).[32] Apparently, the "male" partner is identified with rice, a crop saturated with gendered meaning.[33] Takarasienne and their fans have used the kinship terms "older brother" (*aniki*) and "younger sister" (*imôto*) to denote either a female couple or lesbian sexuality.

The term "lesbian" (*rezubian*) itself was not used to name a politicized female identity (as opposed to sexual practices per se) until the 1970s.[34] As an important aside in this connection, it is important to note that an Anglo-American informed lesbian identity names a subjectivity significantly different from that denoted by the various Japanese terms. The difference is in the configuration of sexual practices conceived and enacted in terms of roles which correspond both to the kinship terms "older brother" and "younger sister" and to the asymmetrical but interdependent relationship between *otokoyaku* and *musumeyaku*. Regarding the latter, the leading *otokoyaku* and *musumeyaku* of each troupe are paired as a "golden combination" (*goruden konbi*) for the duration of their careers. This dyadic structure alludes to the monogamy and fidelity underlying the idealized heterosexual relations promoted by the state since the Meiji period. In addition, the "male" lesbian is referred to in popular parlance as *tachi*, written in the *katakana* syllabary, with the likely meaning of "one who wields the 'sword.'" The corresponding term for the "female" lesbian is *neko*, literally "cat" but also a historical nickname for unlicensed geisha, which "could be written with characters implying the possibility of pussy from these cats." [ ... ]

The erotic potential of the Takarazuka *otokoyaku* was recognized within a decade of the Revue's founding. In his 1921 book on the life-style of the Takarasienne, Kawahara Yomogi included a chapter on love letters from female fans which he regarded as examples of "abnormal psychology" (*hentai seiri*). Eight years later, in 1929, the mass media began to sensationalize the link between the Takarazuka

Revue and lesbian practices. The *Shin Nippô*, a leading daily newspaper, ran a series on Takarazuka called "Abnormal Sensations" (*hentaiteki kankaku*). The male author was alarmed that *otokoyaku* would begin to feel natural doing "male" gender. Their private lives, he fretted, would soon "become an extension of the stage."[35]

His worst fears came true when, less than a year later, the leading dailies exposed the same-sex love affair between Nara Miyako, a leading *otokoyaku*, and Mizutani Yaeko, the leading woman of the *Shinpa* (New School) theater. (Several other same-sex affairs involving Takarasienne were also reported. The *Osaka Nichinichi* publicized on September 11, 1930 the makings of a love affair between the cinema actor Hara Komako and leading Takarasienne Amatsu Otome.) What this and other critics found most alarming was nothing short of a revolutionary change of context; namely, the transformation of the *otokoyaku* from the showcase of "male" gender to the stereotype of the "male" female. What had been presented and perceived as artifice on stage had revealed itself as natural off-stage. Inasmuch as many Takarasienne had applied to the Academy because they were avid fans and wanted to be closer to their idols,[36] or because they wanted to do "male" and in some cases "female" gender, the stage was an extension of their private lives and not the reverse. For Takarasienne and their fans, resistance to prescribed sex and gender roles and compulsory heterosexuality lay precisely in a change of context.[37]

The critics were particularly disturbed by the realization that the Takarazuka *otokoyaku*, like the "modern girl" (*moga*), could effectively undermine a gender role (the "good wife, wise mother") that was premised on the conflation of sex, gender, and sexuality and on women's dependence upon and subordination to men. Consequently Nara, the "male," was pushed into the limelight of damnation. For an anatomical female to assume "male" gender is for her to rise in the gender hierarchy, which is subversive, from a patriarchal point of view. Therefore, Kobayashi, along with media critics and the state, sought to limit the scope of the *otokoyaku*'s "male" behavior to the Takarazuka stage. Mizutani was treated more leniently for the likely reason that, as the "female," she did not appear different enough to be perceived as a heretic.[38] [ . . . ]

The brouhaha that erupted over the Nara-Mizutani affair was part of the larger sociocultural discourse on the problematic relationship between eros and modernism. The review *Parisette*, staged in 1930, ushered in Takarazuka's overtly modern and erotic phase.[39] From this production onward, Takarasienne ceased to apply the traditional stage makeup, *oshiroi* (whiteface). Modernism warranted a transition from denaturalized flesh to its naturalization. The whiteface had disguised the fact that the mask worn by Takarasienne was their gender specialty, which, as it turned out, did not so much hide as reveal their sex, gender, and sexuality.

The naturalization of "male" females continued with *otokoyaku* Kadota Ashiko's sudden decision to cut off her hair in the spring of 1932. As reported in the press, Kadota was irked by the unnaturalness of having to stuff her regulation long hair under every type of headgear except wigs, for the all-male management had deemed that wigs would give *otokoyaku* an overly natural appearance. Takarazuka fans and *moga*, on the other hand, had sported short hair at least a decade ahead of their idols.[40]

Hair is redolent of symbolism throughout Japanese history. Prior to the *moga*, short hair announced a woman's withdrawal from secular and sexual affairs. The "modern girl" turned hair symbolism on its head, and short hair became the hallmark of the extroverted, maverick, and, in the eyes of the state, dangerous woman. *Otokoyaku* gave short hair yet another layer of symbolic meaning: "butch" sexuality. The Takarazuka management eventually sought to divest short hair of its radical symbolism by assuming authority over haircuts. Since at least the postwar period and probably before, a student assigned to "male" gender is required to cut her hair short by the end of her first semester at the Academy. Until ordered to do otherwise, all junior students are required to wear their hair in shoulder-length braids.

So many of Kadota's *otokoyaku* colleagues followed suit that a worried Kobayashi offered them money and "gifts from Tokyo" in exchange for growing out their hair.[41] Critics, meanwhile, had a field day with the new bobbed look. Newspaper articles referred disparagingly to the haircuts as "male heads" (*otoko no atama*) and noted that many *otokoyaku* were also using the term *boku*, a self-referent that signifies "male" gender.

The naturalization of "male" females gathered momentum with leading *otokoyaku* Tachibana Kaoru's proclamation in February 1932 that "I just don't feel 'female'" (*watashi wa onna to iu ki ga shinai*). She went on to dismiss marriage as "the vocation of boxed-in gals" (*hako-iri gâru no shigoto*). One male journalist likened Tachibana to Yoshiya Nobuko, the author of *shôjo* fiction, whom he claimed "lived like a *garçon* (*garuson*)." "Too many females," he concluded angrily, "have forgotten that they are 'female.'" Bemoaned in general was women's loss of *onnarashisa*, or female-likeness, to an epidemic of "abnormal psychology."[42] Critics, using androcentric logic, did not equate a rejection of wifehood and motherhood with a rejection of female subordination but with the desire of women to become more like men.

That the male journalist referred to the lesbian as a "*garçon*," as opposed to an "older brother," is significant, for his remark alludes to the nativist cast of the popular discourses at the time which dwelled on the relationship between Japan and the Euro-American world. Insofar as he and other male critics linked the advent in Japan of lesbianism to Takarazuka, which was inspired by the French revue, they apparently regarded "butch" (*garçon*) sexuality in particular as an "un-Japanese" phenomenon. "Class S" relations apparently were unexceptional in their eyes, but a butch/femme pairing was perceived as alien and consequently unnatural. [ ... ]

## ■ Setting Things Straight ■

All the adverse publicity motivated Kobayashi to remove the now problematic term *shôjo* in the final name change of 1940 for two ostensible reasons: to acknowledge the more eroticized ("adult") content of the modernizing theater and to prepare for the short-lived inclusion of a male chorus. Kobayashi's controversial plan to recruit male vocalists was a strategic move to denaturalize *otokoyaku* style and deflect allegations of lesbian relationships among Takarasienne and their fans. The invisible but audible presence of anatomically correct males would set things straight.

Political factors exacerbated the "moral panic" over "male" females. The late 1930s and early 1940s was a period of intensified militarization and of increasing state control over females' minds and bodies.[43] Pronatal policies and a cult of sanctified motherhood took precedence over the mobilization of female laborers, despite the steady depletion through conscription of the male workforce.[44] Not surprisingly, Takarazuka *otokoyaku* were desanctioned: they were singled out and denounced as the "acme of offensiveness" (*shûaku no kiwami*), and in August 1939, the Osaka Prefectural Government (Public Peace Section) outlawed *otokoyaku* from public performances in that prefecture. Not only were all Takarasienne chastised in the mass media for their "abnormal and ostentatious" life-style but they were ordered by the state to conform to a strict, military-style dress code. The actors were not permitted to answer fan mail, much less socialize with their fans.[45]

The state, colluding with Kobayashi, sought to limit the symbolic cogency and allegorical potential of the Takarasienne to the image of the "good wife, wise mother," an image further reified at that time as *Nippon fujin*, or "Japanese woman." Typical of the musicals staged during this period of militarization and state censorship was *Illustrious Women of Japan* (*Nippon meifu den*, 1941), a nationalistic extravaganza dedicated to heroines, mothers of heroes, and "women of chastity," hardly the stuff of *shôjo* fiction nor inspiration for lesbian style.[46]

## ■ Concluding Remarks: Enter the *Onnayaku* ■

The immediate postwar influence of the United States ramified in manifold directions, including girls' and women's rights, however circumscribed and short-lived that particular ramification.[47] Takarazuka productions, which had been suspended in March 1945, reopened, with SCAP (Supreme Commander for the Allied Powers) permission, in February 1946.

The issue of female subjectivity and self-sufficiency informed revitalized discourses on sex, gender, and sexuality. Enright, writing in the early 1950s, makes note of the "considerable homosexuality" and "considerable lesbianism" in Japan at that time. "The latter," he continues, "strikes the eye; one wonders whether this, and the great popularity of the Girls' Opera, are not a kind of protest against the lingering assumption of male superiority."[48]

Mochizuki, on the other hand, suggests that with the "adoption of coeducation" in postwar Japan, "the homosexual tendency" among schoolgirls and between Takarasienne and their fans "has been rapidly disappearing." Neither Enright nor Mochizuki acknowledge lesbianism as a mode of female sexuality but rather rationalize it either as merely a protest against "lingering male superiority" or a temporary solution to the absence of males. Mochizuki even likens "homosexual tendencies" in young women – specifically Takarasienne and their fans – to "something like the measles, a childhood disorder, which will soon pass away."[49] Usami Tadashi, a Revue historian, makes the similarly queer claim that Takarazuka offers "young women *who aren't yet women*... a safe introduction to the opposite sex."[50] Usami, of course, is referring to *shôjo*, those "not-quite-female" females.

[...]

The history of gender discourses generated by the Takarazuka Revue alone indicates that a lesbian subculture has been not so much absent from Japanese society – although many indigenous forces have sought to eliminate it – as it has been ignored by most (published) Japanologists. Apart from those who fear being stigmatized or ostracized for undertaking serious research on Japanese sexualities, those who do pursue this line of study may encounter, depending on their own sex, gender, and sexuality, a sociohistorically motivated silence surrounding the issue of adult female sexualities in particular. The persistence of the ideology that, *shôjo* notwithstanding, females are objects of male desire and not the subjects of their own desire effectively inhibits both naming that desire and the possibility of open discussion on the topic of lesbian sexuality in Japan.[51]

In the prewar period, *otokoyaku* sought to naturalize and appropriate "male" gender; in the postwar period, *musumeyaku* have sought to make "female" gender more than just a foil for masculine privilege. Significantly, in a fanzine (*Takarazuka Fuan*) published independently and occasionally in those published by the Revue, Takarasienne and their female fans refer to the actor not as *musumeyaku* ("daughter role") but as *onnayaku* ("'female' role"), thereby claiming a nomenclatural parity with the *otokoyaku*. [...] The actors began to stress their female being over their status as daughters and, accordingly, demanded more definitive roles.

The all-male directorship responded to these demands by creating highly visible, dynamic, and often overtly sensuous "female" characters. However, in a move which undercut *musumeyaku* intentions, the directors assigned these new roles to *otokoyaku*. In this way, the construction and performance of "female" gender remained the privilege of both males and "males." *Musumeyaku*, contrarily, never have been reassigned to "male" roles: the transposition of gender is not a reciprocal operation. As several *musumeyaku* have remarked, "Japanese society is a male's world, and Takarazuka is an *otokoyaku's* world."[52]

Many *otokoyaku*, along with disfranchised *musumeyaku*, have protested the directors' gender-switching antics, and many *otokoyaku* claim to have experienced, as a result of playing "female" roles, a sense of conflict or resistance (*teikô*) and a loss of confidence. Gô Chigusa, an *otokoyaku* who retired in 1972, also remarked that on the rare occasion that she was assigned "female" gender, her fans complained bitterly of their resultant dis-ease (*kimochi warui*); that eerie feeling when the familiar suddenly is defamiliarized.[53] Blair's analysis of Euro-American actors is particularly cogent here: "For women whose roles have been directed by men, but who have power to convey new images of women through the media, the conflict between personal autonomy and political organization is experienced as a personal conflict."[54]

Some young women, such as Minakaze Mai, who had enrolled in the Academy specifically to do "male" gender were assigned instead to do "female" gender. Minakaze, or Maimai, as she is called by friends and fans,[55] was assigned to do "female" gender because of her short (160 cm) stature. In order to resolve the conflict between her offstage desires and her onstage role, she has "stopped wearing bluejeans" and is "always exerting [herself] to the fullest to be a *musumeyaku*, even in [her] private life" (*watakushi seikatsu de mo musumeyaku ni narikirô to kyôryoku shite iru*). Minakaze is not alone in originally believing that females encountered less resistance doing "female" gender. She now agrees with several of her colleagues that locating "the 'female' within the female poses a perplexing problem" (*onna no naka no onna'tte muzukashii no yo*). Similarly, after ten years of performing only "male" roles, *otokoyaku* Matsu Akira, who retired in 1982, was unable to perform a "female" role: "Even though I am a female, the thing called 'female' just won't emerge at all" (*Onna de arinagara, zenzen onna to iu mono ga denai*).[56] Whether in terms of resistance or emergence, the Takarasienne have drawn attention to the incompatibility between their experiences as females and the dominant construction of "female" gender.

Kobayashi's assertion that "Takarazuka involves studying the male" (*Takarazuka ga dansei no kyôiku shite-iru*) is only partially correct.[57] "Female" gender is also taught and studied; this, in fact, is the primary objective of the Academy. Takarasienne who are assigned "female" gender contrary to their personal preference represent all Japanese females who are socialized into gender roles not of their own making. Consequently, girls and women are suspended between the depiction and definition of "female" gender and the achievement or approximation of such – ironically, a limbo many young women have sought to avoid by enrolling in the Academy.[58]

Competing discourses on the construction and performance of gender have informed, shaped, and have been shaped by the Takarazuka Revue. However, whatever consciousness the actors have of their political (i.e., feminist) and also subversive (or revolutionary) potential has been compromised, at least publicly, by their need to survive within an organization, a vocation (show business), and a society where male/"male" privilege has been the rule.

The history of the Revue shows that Takarasienne have, and on occasion have exercised, the potential to challenge the sociocultural status quo maintained by compulsory heterosexuality and the "good wife, wise mother" model of "female" gender. 1932 marks their first "rebellion" in the name of self-representation: Kadota Ashiko cut off her hair, and Tachibana Kaoru declared publicly that "marriage was the vocation of boxed-in gals." In response to Kadota, the all-male management eventually assumed authority over haircuts. With respect to Tachibana's assertion, it remains that the majority of Japanese women are boxed into marriage, an institution premised – regardless of the quality of a particular couple's married life – on compulsory heterosexuality and the unequal distribution of power. [ ... ]

Social organization is both a process and product informed by and informing discourses on the relationship of sex, gender, and sexuality. These discourses negotiate and renegotiate the configuration and meaning of social relations within such contexts as kinship, marriage, and work. Theories and methodologies must focus on the differential relations between females and males, as well as among females as a group and males as a group. The consciousness of gender and its technologies generates a mode of apprehension of all social reality. "And from that apprehension, from that ... knowledge of the pervasiveness of gender, there is no going back to the innocence of 'biology'" or to the specious notion of "gender neutrality." As de Lauretis reminds us, "what is becoming more and more clear ... is that all the categories of our social science stand to be reformulated *starting from* the notion of gendered social subjects."[59] What is also clear is that technologies of gender construction utilized in the Takarazuka Revue draw from and inspire social organization(s) offstage: gender, after all, is theatrical, and society offers its actors a stage larger than the Revue's.

## NOTES

Fieldwork and archival research in Japan (Tokyo and Takarazuka) during the summer of 1987 were funded by the following fellowships and grants: Japan Foundation Professional Fellowship, Northeast Asia Council of the Association for Asian Studies Grant, and Social Science Research Council Research Grant. Heartfelt thanks to the late N. Serena Tennekoon for help in preparing this manuscript.

1   See also my later work, particularly "The Politics of Androgyny in Japan: Sexuality and Subversion in the Theater and Beyond," *American Ethnologist* 19(3) (1992): 419–42; and *Takarazuka: Sexual Politics and Popular Culture in Japan* (Berkeley: University of California Press, 1998 [3rd printing 2001]), esp. ch. 2.

2   J. Nestle, "The Fem Question," in *Pleasure and Danger: Exploring Female Sexuality*, ed. C. Vance (Boston: Routledge and Kegan Paul, 1985), p. 234.

3   T. de Lauretis, *Technologies of Gender: Essays on Theory, Film, and Fiction* (Bloomington: Indiana University Press, 1987); R. Firth, *Elements of Social Organization* (Boston: Beacon Press, 1963); M. Foucault, *The History of Sexuality*, vol. 1: *An Introduction* (New York: Vintage Books, 1980); S. Kessler and W. McKenna. *Gender: An Ethnomethodological Approach* (Chicago: University of Chicago Press, 1985); K. Silverman, "Histoire d'O: The Construction of a Female Subject," in *Pleasure and Danger*, ed. Vance; and C. Vance, "Pleasure and Danger: Toward a Politics of Sexuality," in *Pleasure and Danger*, ed. Vance.

4   Kessler and McKenna, *Gender*, pp. 1–12.

5   Vance, "Pleasure and Danger," p. 9.

6   While this method of gender assignment is most typical of but not limited to Anglo-Americans, the lack of specific information on the assignment and assumption of "female" or "male" gender among non-Anglos makes me reluctant to generalize for all Americans. The unrepresentativeness of Anglo gender categories for non-Anglos is addressed cogently by A. M. Alonso and M. T. Koreck in the context of AIDS and the construction of "Hispanic" sexualities ("Silences: 'Hispanics,' AIDS, and Sexual Practices," *Differences* [forthcoming]). To generalize a "Japanese" notion of gender admittedly is problematic given the various ethnic groups comprising that superficially homogeneous society, although "Japanese" arguably is a more inclusive signifier than is "American."

7   There is an ever-expanding ethnographic literature on the situationality and fluidity of the relationship between sex, gender, and sexuality.

8   *Kôjien*, 2nd enlarged ed., 3d printing (Tokyo: Iwanami Shoten, 1978), p. 1214; M. Fukutomi, "*Rashisa*" *no shinrigaku* (The psychology of "gender"), Kodansha gendai shinsho 797 (Tokyo: Kodansha, 1985).

9   J. Williamson, "Woman Is an Island: Femininity and Colonization," in *Studies in Entertainment: Critical Approaches to Mass Culture*, ed. T. Modelski (Bloomington: Indiana University Press), pp. 100–1.

10  Y. Ueda, *Takarazuka ongaku gakkô* (The Takarazuka Music Academy) (Tokyo: Yomiuri Raifu), pp. 118–19.

11  K. Sasaki and S. Tanabe, *Yumei no kashi o tabete – waga itoshi no Takarazuka* (Eat the dream candy – our beloved Takarazuka) (Tokyo: Kodansha, 1984), p. 130.

12  Williamson, "Woman Is an Island," pp. 100–1, 268.

13  J. F. Collier and S. Yanagisako, "Toward a Unified Analysis of Gender and Kinship," in *Gender and Kinship: Essays toward a Unified Analysis*, ed. J. F. Collier and S. Yanagisako (Stanford: Stanford University Press, 1987), p. 7.

14  S. Nolte, "Women, the State, and Repression in Imperial Japan," Working Papers on Women in International Development, no. 33 (Michigan State University), p. 3.

15  J. Blair, "Private Parts in Public Places: The Case of Actresses," in *Women and Space: Ground Rules and Social Maps*, ed. S. Ardener (New York: St. Martin's Press, 1981), p. 205.

16  I. Kobayashi, *Takarazuka manpitsu* (Takarazuka jottings) (Tokyo: Jitsugyo no Nihon-sha), p. 106.

17  Ibid., pp. 27, 29, 34, 91.

18  Ibid., p. 38.

19  Kobayashi, *Takarazuka manpitsu*, pp. 38, 91; Y. Ueda, *Takarazuka sutâ: sono engi to bigaku* (Takarazuka stars: Their acting and aesthetics) (Tokyo: Yomiuri Shinbunsha, 1974), p. 139.

20  K. P. Addelson, "Words and Lives" and A. Ferguson, J. Zita, and K. P. Addelson, "On 'Compulsory Heterosexuality and Lesbian Existence': Defining the Issues," in *Feminist Theory: A Critique of Ideology*, ed. N. Keohane, M. Rosaldo, and B. Gelpi (Chicago: University of Chicago Press, 1982), p. 181.

21  Y. Kawahara, *Takarazuka kageki shôjo no seikatsu* (The life-style of Takarasienne) (Osaka: Ikubunkan Shoten, 1921), p. 112.

22  H. Ôzawa, *Yoshiya Nobuko no genten to natta shôjo shosetsu* (Yoshiya Nobuko's first *shôjo* novel), *Shôjoza* 1 (1985): 25.

23  M. Takano, *Chôshôjo to fueminizumu no kyôhan kankei ni* (The conspiratorial partnership between ultra-*shôjo* and feminism), *Kuriteiiku* 6 (1987): 53–63.

24  N. Murakami, *Taishôki no shokugyôfujin* (Working women of the Taisho period) (Tokyo: Domesu Shuppan, 1983).

25  *Shin Nippô*, April 2, 1940.

26  *Kageki* 1 (1918): 5–6.

27  *Osaka Asahi*, July 17, 1923: *Osaka Mainichi*, July 12, 1932.

28  Y. Komazaka, "Yoshiya Nobuko: onnatachi e no manazashi" (Yoshiya Nobuko: On looking at women), *Shisô No Kagaku* 51, no. 9 (1975); 55–64; Ôzawa, "Yoshiya Nobuko no genten"; S. Tanabe, "Kaisetsu: taoyaka ni yasashiki sebone no hito" (Commentary: The person with soft and graceful mettle), in *Nyonin Yoshiya Nobuko* (The woman Yoshiya Nobuko), ed. T. Yoshitake (Tokyo: Bungei Shunjun, 1986); T. Wada, "Nihon

no senpai rezubiantachi" (Japan's lesbian elders), *Bessatsu Takarajima* 64 (1987): 78–9; Yoshitake, "Nyonin Yoshiya Nobuko."

29 A. Rich, "Compulsory Heterosexuality and Lesbian Existence," in *Powers of Desire: The Politics of Sexuality*, ed. A. Snitow, C. Stansell, and S. Thompson (New York: Monthly Review Press, 1983); Zita, "Historical Amnesia"; Ferguson, Zita, and Addelson, "On 'Compulsory Heterosexuality and Lesbian Existence.'" pp. 166–7.

30 M. Mochizuki, "Cultural Aspects of Japanese Girl's Opera," in *Japanese Popular Culture*, ed. H. Kato (Tokyo: Tuttle, 1959); E. Norbeck and H. Befu, "Informal Fictive Kinship in Japan," *American Anthropologist* 60 (1958): 109.

31 S. Takagi, *Rebyû no ôsama: Shirai Tetsuzô to Takarazuka* (The king of revue: Shirai Tetsuzô and Takarazuka) (Tokyo: Kawade Shobo, 1983), p. 76.

32 M. Kasahara, *Takarazuka episodo 350* (350 Takarazuka episodes) (Tokyo: Rippu Shobo, 1981), p. 44.

33 *Kageki* 44 (1923): 14; see J. Robertson, "Sexy Rice: Plant Gender, Farm Manuals, and Grass-Roots Nativism," *Monumenta Nipponica* 39, no. 3 (1984): 233–60.

34 Y. Hirozawa, *Iseiai chôsei to iu fuashizumu* (The fascism of compulsory heterosexuality), *Shinchihei* 6, no. 150 (1987): 34–9 and "Yûasa Yoshiko hômonki" (An interview with Yûasa Yoshiko), *Bessatsu Takarajima* 64 (1987): 67–73.

35 *Shin Nippô*, March 16, 1929.

36 Kawahara, *Takarazuka kageki shôjo no seikatsu*, p. 16.

37 This change of context obviated the dilemma posed by C. Smith-Rosenberg – that "women's assumption of men's symbolic constructs involved women in a fundamental act of alienation" (*Disorderly Conduct*, p. 266), as Nestle explains with respect to American butch/femme culture ("The Fem Question"):

> Both butches and fems [*sic*] have a history of ingenuity in the creation of personal style, but since the elements of this style – the clothing, the stance – come from the heterosexually defined culture, it is easy to confuse an innovative or resisting style with a mere replica of the prevailing custom. But a butch lesbian wearing men's clothes...was not a man wearing men's clothes; she was a woman who created an original style to signal to other women what she was capable of doing – taking erotic responsibility. (235)

> ...The butch has been labeled too simplistically the masculine partner and the fem her feminine counterpart. This labeling forgets two women who have developed their styles for specific erotic, emotional, and social reasons. Butch-fem relationships...were complex erotic and social statements, not phony heterosexual replicas. They were filled with a deeply lesbian language of stance, dress, gesture, love, courage and autonomy... Butches were known by their appearance, fems by their choices. (232, 233)

38 Cf. ibid., p. 234.

39 *Kyoto Shinbun*, November 20, 1930.

40 *Osaka Asahi*, July 17, 1923.

41 *Nichinichi*, April 24, 1932.

42 *Ôsaka Mainichi*, February 10, 1932; *Nichinichi*, April 18, 24, 1932: *Hôchi*, July 26, 1932.

43 S. Nolte, "Women, the State, and Repression in Imperial Japan" and "The 'New Japanese Woman': The Home Ministry's Redefinition of Public and Private, 1890–1910," in *Recreating Japanese Women, 1600–1945*, ed. G. L. Bernstein (forthcoming).

44 T. Havens, "Women and War in Japan, 1937–45," *American Historical Review* 80, no. 4 (1975): 913–34.

45  *Osaka Asahi*, May 15, August 20, 1939: *Osaka Nichinichi*, August 20, 1939, August 19, 1940; *Kokumin*, September 6, 1940.

46  *Ôsaka Chôhô*, September 7, 1940; *English Mainichi*, February 22, 1941.

47  R. Atsumi, "Dilemmas and Accommodations of Married Japanese Women in White-Collar Employment," *Bulletin of Concerned Asian Scholars* 20, no. 3 (1988): 54–62; S. Pharr, "Soldiers as Feminists: Debate within US Occupations Ranks over Women's Rights Policy in Japan," in *Proceedings of the Tokyo Symposium on Women*, ed. International Group for the Study of Women (Tokyo: International Group for the Study of Women, 1978), pp. 25–35.

48  D. J. Enright, *The World of Dew: Aspects of Living Japan* (London: Secker and Warburg, 1955), p. 123.

49  Mochizuki, "Cultural Aspects," pp. 172, 170.

50  Usami in J. Bailey, "The Never-Never, Chocolate Mousse Land of Takarazuka," *Tokyo Weekender* 17, no. 22 (1986): 1, my italics.

51  See articles in *Bessatsu Takarajima* 64 (1987), *Onna Erosu* 16 (1981), and *Shinchihei* 6 (1987).

52  *Takarazuka Gurafu* 1 (1967): 54.

53  *Takarazuka Gurafu* 1 (1967): 71; 5 (1968): 70–1; 4 (1971): 49; 7 (1974): 68; 7 (1977): 38.

54  Blair, "Private Parts," p. 222.

55  Takarasienne have three names: their legal name, which very few people outside the Revue offices know; their self-selected stage name, which is how they are known publicly; and an endearing nickname coined by and known only to close friends and fans. One significant nomenclatural development since the 1930s has been the actors' virtual rejection of the "female" (i.e., diminutive) suffix *ko* from their stage names. 232 actors out of 394, or 59 percent, in 1937 had names with the *ko* suffix, as opposed to only 25 of 379, or 6.5 percent, in 1977 (Hashimoto, *Takarazuka kageki no 70 nen*, p. 62).

56  *Nihonkai*, April 18, 1987; *Hankyû* 6 (1987); *Takarazuka Gurafu* 7 (1974): 68.

57  I. Kobayashi in *Kageki* 272 (1948), 29.

58  The number of applicants in the postwar period ranges from 579 (57 admitted) in 1946 to 734 (42 admitted) in 1985, with a low of 175 (70 admitted) in 1959, to a high of 1,052 (49 admitted) in 1978 (Ueda. *Takarazuka ongaku gakkô*, p. 25). The 1978 peak reflects the tremendous popularity of the musical *The Rose of Versailles* (1974–6), attended by more than 1.4 million persons (Hashimoto, *Takarazuka kageki no 70 nen*, p. 89). Written by leading cartoonist and *shôjo* fiction writer Ikeda Riyoko, *The Rose of Versailles* focuses on the life and death of Oscar, a female raised as a "male" in order to succeed her father in a patriline of generals, although she dies a "female" female. The popularity of the production, together with the unprecedented number of applicants to the Academy following its two-year run, suggests that aspiring Takarasienne were attracted to the Revue by the notion, exemplified by Oscar, of gender as a costume drama in which clothing as performance undercuts the ideological fixity and essentialism of conventional "female" and "male" gender (A. Kuhn, *The Power of the Image: Essays on Representation and Sexuality* [London: Routledge and Kegan Paul, 1985], p. 53).

59  De Lauretis, *Technologies of Gender*, pp. 20, 139.

# 13

# The Marriage of Feminism and Islamism in Egypt: Selective Repudiation as a Dynamic of Postcolonial Cultural Politics

## Lila Abu-Lughod

## ■ Modernist Visions ■

Many Egyptian secularist liberals and progressives fear that women's rights are now under threat. They see signs of this in the growing popularity in the last two decades of the new forms of dress called Islamic or modest dress and the adoption in particular of the form of head covering called the *hijab*, institutionalized in the reversion to more conservative personal status laws, and publicized in calls made in Parliament, mosques, and the media for women's return to the home and their "traditional" roles.

Among the most influential sites for the articulation of their views are print media and television. Secularists have enjoyed access to these media since the 1950s and 1960s, although they have had to contend with government censors and periodic political repression. Thus one can look to state-controlled forms such as the enormously popular evening dramatic television serials for representations of their views on women – views that do not take the form of polemics and may not be completely conscious, and thus are especially revealing.[1] [ ... ]

The two writers whose productions and views I will examine here are considered progressive and secular, sharing a disdain for the commercial values and productions of recent years, a deep concern about the increasingly conservative social climate in Egypt, and a fundamental belief in television drama as a tool of social education. [ ... ]

Usama Anwar 'Ukasha, for example, widely regarded as the most brilliant writer of television serials, provides a glimpse of this in his most spectacular and complex serial, *Hilmiyya Nights* (*Layali al-Hilmiyya*), aired in the late 1980s and early 1990s. In over a hundred episodes its rich group of characters, people originally from a traditional Cairo neighborhood called Hilmiyya, were taken through the events of modern Egyptian history. [ ... ]

An important theme of *Hilmiyya Nights*, like many of his serials, is how women are to balance work and love, careers and marriage. The intractability of this social problem is dramatized most fully in the story line of the semi-tragic relationship between the young protagonists 'Ali and Zohra. 'Ali and Zohra are in love; they share their dreams and aspirations. Zohra finds in 'Ali the love and support she has never experienced. Others try to thwart the relationship, but it is finally Zohra's apparent dedication to her career that spells its end. In their conversations, Zohra has confided in 'Ali about the importance of an independent career for someone whose life circumstances have forced her to rely on herself. When 'Ali is offered a fellowship to do graduate study abroad, he asks Zohra to marry him and accompany him. Her father resists, and after a while, somewhat mysteriously, she stops pressuring her father. 'Ali gives up his opportunity to go abroad but then gets arrested while attending a political meeting.

It then becomes clear that behind Zohra's growing coldness to 'Ali is the fact that her boss, through flattery about her talents as a journalist and promises to promote her career, is seducing her. She agrees to a secret marriage with him, but when she gets pregnant, her family forces a shotgun public wedding, and then she goes abroad. An innocent 'Ali gets out of prison, discovers that Zohra has betrayed him, and, disillusioned in love and politics, becomes an unscrupulous businessman. He is made to represent in *Hilmiyya Nights* the corrupt and materialistic entrepreneurs who made fortunes under the free-market policies initiated by President Sadat after the death of Nasser.

Despite the negative message about women's career ambitions that this plot line might suggest, consideration of a later stage in 'Ali's and Zohra's lives and other relationships in *Hilmiyya Nights* shows 'Ukasha to be more balanced. The most telling defense of women's rights to careers comes in the marital troubles that develop between 'Ali and Shireen. She is the beautiful, talented, and principled young journalist of modest background 'Ali finally marries. Increasingly he tries to control her activities and to restrict her career. He demands, while he has fled the country to escape prosecution for his business crimes, that she give up her work. As 'Ukasha portrays these events, 'Ali looks like an unreasonable patriarchal bully. He spoils his second chance for happiness in love by treating his wife like a possession in an age, the 1980s. when women's rights to professions have been firmly established. [ ... ]

'Ukasha pushes his viewers by showing that love and marital happiness should not be incompatible with women's work. He does not pretend that the resolution of the tension between the two is easy. He wants to make a distinction, however, the same defensive distinction that most Egyptian modernist reformers from the nineteenth century on have tried to make: between women's rights to work and to develop themselves and the dangerous forms of illicit sexuality that the mixing between the sexes might ignite. Unlike the Islamists to be discussed below, however, ʿUkasha paints his fallen characters like Zohra with sympathy. He shows the social genesis of the human weaknesses that led to their mistakes, rather than blaming the West, or the Devil, as might Islamists.

One of the few women writers of television serials of her generation, Fathiyya al-ʿAssal also uses her serials to present progressive views on social issues. A vivacious woman of 60, mother of grown children, and committed political activist in Hizb al-Tagammuʿ (the leftist party), she is adamant that feminist issues cannot be divorced from general social and political issues. She criticizes fellow Egyptian feminist Nawal El-Saadawi, lionized in the West, for her exclusive focus on women's issues like marital abuse. This focus, she notes, corresponds (too) nicely to the depoliticized agenda of the American-based Ford Foundation, which sponsored El-Saadawi's short-lived feminist organization, the Arab Women's Solidarity Union. As Al-ʿAssal explains, "I'm against men beating their wives and women submitting to being beaten, of course. But that is not the only issue. For me the issue is how women can be liberated economically, politically, and intellectually; then they will be automatically liberated from men."[2]

Literacy and education for women are long-standing interests of Al-ʿAssal's. In fact, she traces her beginnings as a drama writer to her days as a literacy instructor who was frustrated that her students escaped the classroom to sit with the janitor whenever the radio serials were broadcast. She decided to try her hand at radio drama in 1957 and went on to television in 1967. She deplores the fact that people watch television more than they read, and tries to encourage reading in her television serials.

Al-ʿAssal is more uncompromising than ʿUkasha both on the importance of women's work – as a means of fulfillment *and* domestic bliss – and of companionate marriage. She looks to her controversial 1982 serial, *She and the Impossible* (*Hiya wa al-mustahil*) as the best example of her views. In it she combined her perennial push for education and economic independence for women with a strong vision of love as the only proper basis of marriage. The serial, as she described it, was about a man who divorced his illiterate wife once he got educated. After he left her, she persevered and got a job and then went to university while raising her son on her own.

After twelve years, the husband came back and wanted to remarry her because she was no longer uneducated ("ignorant"). As Al-ʿAssal explained,

> She refused and told him that the Zaynab whom he had chosen in the past now rejected him.... The husband then suggested they should return to each other in order to raise their son. She argued that they should get back together only if they loved each other, in which case they could live under one roof and raise the boy together.... My point was to emphasize the value of a home as a home. That is to say, a man and a woman should enter only on the condition that they love one another; otherwise it would be sheer betrayal. These are new values, of course.

[ ... ]

■ Islamists: The Other End of the Spectrum? ■

Those supporting some sort of self-consciously Muslim identity and associated with a range of positions regarding the importance of structuring society and the polity in more Islamic terms now also produce popular forms of public culture. While progressive television writers and other intellectuals have worked through the official state-run instruments of mass media, the Islamists (except a few associated with the state) are forced to disseminate their messages through magazines, books, and booklets sold in bookstores and street stalls, pamphlets distributed in mosques, and sermons and lessons, often recorded on cassettes carrying notices like "Copyright in the name of all Muslims." [ . . . ]

The television writers just discussed define their projects as modernist. They respect aspects of the West and are quite familiar with its literature and culture, but see themselves as nationalists with Egypt's social good at heart. Enlightenment, advancement, and progress are central to their vocabularies, and they share a sense that their most dangerous adversaries on social issues are the Islamists who do not use the lexicon of "modernity" and yet target the same "masses" they try to uplift. For example, Wafiyya Kheiry, a liberal screen-writer, expresses her worries about the direction Egypt is taking by bemoaning the way that the social climate has changed television programming since the progressive 1960s and 1970s. Referring to a serial she had written in 1975 about the difficulties of establishing collegiality between men and women in the workplace, she said, "If I were to write a serial along these lines today, men would simply respond by asserting that women should go back to the home; then all these problems would be avoided. Now the fundamentalists would claim that all these problems are due to the fact that women are going out to work in the first place."[3] [ . . . ]

Al-'Assal, on the other hand, though she has had many run-ins with the censors, reserves her contempt for another group of veiled women involved in media: the so-called repentant artists who have captured the press and the imaginations of many in the past few years. These are a small group of famous actresses, singers, and belly dancers, stars of film and stage, who have given up their careers and taken on the new head covering called the *hijab*. In small booklets the decisions of these born-again stars are explored and marketed, one book sensationalizing the phenomenon by portraying these women as embattled. The blurb on the back cover reads, "After more than twenty actresses and radio personalities had adopted the veil (*hijab*) . . . war was declared on them. . . . Those carrying the banner of this war are 'sex stars' and 'merchants of lust.'"[4]

These actresses have done what an increasing number of urban Egyptian women have done: adopted the new modest Islamic dress as part of what they conceive of as their religious awakening.[5] Because they are such well-known figures, their actions have been publicized and capitalized on by the Islamists to further legitimize the trend toward women's veiling and to support their call for women's return to the home. Secularists and progressives, those opposed to veiling as a sign of "backwardness," suspiciously accuse these actresses of taking fat salaries from the

Islamic groups for hosting study groups at which conservative religious authorities or unqualified women proselytize. Fathiyya al-'Assal sees them as gullible victims of the Islamic groups, who have preyed on their guilt about their genuinely dissolute lives with fiery talk about "Hell, God, and Judgment Day." [ . . . ]

Here I want to point out only one interesting aspect of the reformed actresses' self-presentations. A recurring theme in their narratives, bolstered by the interviews with their husbands that accompany their stories, is how their careers had caused them to neglect their husbands and children. In the book called *Repentant Artists and the Sex Stars!*, Shams al-Barudi, a former film star introduced as someone "associated with seduction roles," is reported as saying, "I now live a happy life in the midst of my family, with my noble husband who stood by me and encouraged me and congratulated me on each step . . . and my three children."[6] Her husband, a former actor and movie director explains, "I had long wished that Shams would retire from acting and live for her household." In talking about how she had changed, he said, "Shams has now become a wife who cares for her husband . . . and a mother who tends her children and lives her life like any other wife . . . she is a mother with a calling [to raise her children in a Muslim way]."[7] In a recent interview where he modifies his position on art and justifies his return to acting, he nevertheless ends with a similar statement: "My wife is the wealth God has bestowed on me. My beloved wife shares my life, for better or worse, and we adore our children, care for them, and show them every concern."[8] [ . . . ]

This call for women's "return" to the roles of wife and mother, also harped on by popular religious authorities such as Shaykh Al-Sha'rawi and the younger Dr. 'Umar 'Abd al-Kafi, who preaches his message on cassettes, is a cornerstone of a program constructed as "Islamic" or authentic. Such figures claim to be radically different from the progressive television writers who see women's work as essential to national development and social progress. Although there are important differences among Islamists that should not be ignored, I would still argue that the Islamists and other conservatives, and especially their women followers, are not as different from the liberals as they might think.[9] In particular, although they may claim to represent a "return" to the culturally authentic, rejecting the emancipation of women as a Western corruption, their positions are no more "traditional" than those of the progressives. They are certainly less positive about women's work than are the progressive television writers whose productions I described above, but on the value of education and conjugal love they hardly disagree.

As is often the case, men, and especially the male religious authorities, seem to be more conservative than the women to whom they preach. Someone like Shaykh al-Sha'rawi is obsessive in his condemnation of Western corruption and his insistence on the importance of women's veiling. He tries to persuade women that their place is in the home, using odd arguments – asserting, for example that Marilyn Monroe herself had wished she had been able to be a housewife.[10] Women's work is problematic for these figures because it involves them in a public world now distinctly separate, as it is in all modern capitalist societies, from the private world of home and family.

There has indeed been a backlash against working women, which many analysts relate to high levels of unemployment for men (exacerbated in Egypt by the dismantling of the public sector after Sadat's open-door policy and by fewer opportunities for migration to the Gulf). Many Islamists argue that women should not work outside the home, God having given them the noblest of occupations – raising His creatures. The reality is, however, that most of the women who have taken on the veil are in fact working or expect to work. Most families aspiring to achieve or maintain middle-class status cannot do without a second income.[11] And Egyptians have become used to women professionals in all areas. As Zuhur puts it, work for the Islamists is one of the "negotiable" issues.[12] Given these realities, at most what figures like Sheikh al-Sha'rawi can do is tell women that if they must work, they should comport themselves properly and have no physical contact with men in work situations.[13] This, of course, is not so different from what 'Ukasha suggests in *Hilmiyya Nights* in showing the sexual perils of working or what Wafiyya Kheiry suggests in showing the difficulties of establishing cross-sex collegiality (although both, it must be stressed, are more positive about professional women's work as an avenue for personal development).

The findings of one of the few serious surveys of veiled university women, reported on by both Leila Ahmed and Mervat Hatem and conducted in the early 1980s by Zaynab Radwan, show that the survey's subjects actually accept many components of what we might consider the modernist feminist project.[14] As Ahmed has noted, Radwan's study, while confirming that unveiled women were more feminist than their veiled counterparts on matters of women's education, work, political participation, and rights in marriage, showed that on most issues the majority of women shared what could be called feminist goals.[15] The margin of difference between the veiled and unveiled groups was often only slight. For example, 99 percent of unveiled women thought work outside the home was acceptable, but so did 88 percent of the veiled students. Badran has argued that in the late 1980s, there has even been a liberalization on gender issues within Islamist ranks. She points to Islamist women like Safinaz Kazim and Hiba Ra'uf who insist on women's rights to the public sphere.[16]

The support for women's education is more consistent. Radwan's 1982 study showed that 98 percent of unveiled women believed that women had the right to pursue the highest level of education possible; the figure for veiled women was 92 percent. And even the most conservative new charismatic religious figures, such as Dr. 'Umar 'Abd al-Kafi, whose daily appearance on a television show during Ramadan 1993 (hosted by Kariman Hamza, the only veiled public broadcaster) made him a media star, barely attacked education for women.[17] He insisted only that women should not go far from home unaccompanied to attend university, and that wives should not work hundreds of miles away from their families.[18]

It is on matters of marriage, however, that one sees the most overlap between the liberal secular and Islamist positions. Although the television writers place more stress on women's equality and dignity in marriage and say little about motherhood, those advocating a "return" to Islam and tradition see conjugal love and the nuclear family as ideal.[19] [ ... ]

Evidence of Islamists' concern with marital love can be found in the articles and advice columns that appear on the women's page of the newspaper published by Al-Azhar, *Al-Luwa' al-Islami*. These articles, on themes like how to achieve marital happiness or a stable and calm marital life, urge husbands and wives to be patient, forgiving, and tolerant of each other.[20] Although those interviewed, like the Islamist thinker Yusuf Qaradawi, outline women's duties as including serving their husbands, raising children, and keeping house – with statements like "virtuous women care only about satisfying, pleasing, and serving their husbands, taking good care of their home and family"[21] – they also urge husbands to be good-natured and to remember their wives' rights to kind words and tender gestures;[22] describe the proper management of household affairs as involving mutual consultation and cooperation rather than the domination of one partner;[23] condemn forced marriage; and, like the progressive writer Al-'Assal, assert that financial considerations should not be paramount in spouse selection.[24]

There is certainly no single Islamist voice on these matters. For example, although Qaradawi and 'Aliyya al-'Asqalani, the woman writer and interviewer responsible for many of the articles on the women's page, characterize marriage as properly based on the emotions of amity (*mawadda*) (described as a higher emotional state than love) and mercy (*rahma*) and meant to produce peace of mind (*sakina*) and serenity (*tamanina*), others, like Muhammad Ibrahim Mabruk, are happy to use the word love (*hubb*). In his recent book, *Islam's Position on Love: A Revolt against the Materialism of Our Age, the Love of Man toward Woman and Woman toward Man*, he denounces forced marriages and declares that Muslims, unlike Westerners, have always agreed about the value of love because they know it is not an illusion but a spiritual matter.[25] [...]

What all these Islamists share is the fact that the framework is religious, marriage being characterized as a spiritual blending (*imtizaj ruhi*) or as a resemblance between lovers' souls (*mushakala bayn nufus al-'ushaq*), and all their positions are justified and supported by reference to Islamic texts, whether the Qur'an or traditions of the Prophet, or to the example of the Prophet. [...]

From a somewhat bizarre television experience comes another kind of confirmation of the importance for Islamists of these "modern" values for marriage. One evening in 1990 there was a fleeting episode of a television serial that was not continued the following day. It began innocently enough, resembling any evening serial, with parents discussing with their grown children's possible marriage partners, an outdoor scene at a club where a meeting had been arranged between a fashionably dressed young couple, and a slight twist on a predictable theme with the parents urging their handsome son to consider the daughter of their wealthy neighbors.

But suddenly all the usual terms of the evening serials were unsettled. The young man went to complain to his grandparents about his parents' materialistic motives. In language rich with pious phrases he revealed his dilemma. Quoting the well-known tradition of the Prophet Muhammad about what qualities to value in a woman, he asserted that he too valued piety above wealth and beauty. He confessed that he already knew who he wanted to marry. She was a pious woman, a veiled woman who was a classmate of his in medical school. This episode pitted arranged marriage against the love match, but it was the secular modern parents who wanted to arrange the match for their son and the Islamist son who wanted the love marriage with his colleague.

Although I was never able to discover the story behind this unusual drama, it was easy to see why it was yanked from the air, apparently after two episodes. Made by a private Islamic production company, it violated the segregation of religious from secular programming in its heavy incorporation of quotations from the Qur'an and the traditions of the Prophet. And it made positive mention of the modern urban religious men and women who, until 1992, were strictly ignored in television drama.[26] Yet what is so revealing about it is its suggestion that for the pious, educated, middle-class youths, the ideals of companionate marriage are just as vital as they are for the progressive secular nationalist feminists like Fathiyya al-'Assal.[27] In fact, sharing the values of a new generation and being, as the Islamist Zaynab al-Ghazali put it, comrades within a movement, should strengthen the bonds of marriage.[28]

## ■ Historical Roots ■

Many characterize the current call by conservatives for women to return to the home as a call for the "retraditionalization" of women's status and roles.[29] And indeed the assertion of the proper role of a woman as wife and mother, with the assumption of a happy nuclear family, husband and wife devoted to each other and to their children, is now – as the comment of the husband of the born-again film star Shams al-Barudi suggests, and the writings of Islamist thinkers indicate – couched in an Islamic religious idiom that gives it a pedigree. The duty of the mother is to raise good Muslim children, and the love between husband and wife is described in terms of emotions with Qur'anic resonances like mercy and amity.

But I would argue that this vision of family and women's proper relation to husband and children is profoundly modern and its sources are entwined with the West as surely as are the negatively perceived public freedoms of women the Islamists denounce. Yet this bourgeois vision of women's domesticity, rooted in a much earlier phase of Western and Egyptian feminist reform, has become so ensconced in upper-, middle-, and even lower-middle-class Egyptian society that none of those arguing for a rejection of Western ways seek to dislocate it. Instead, they assimilate it to "tradition" and try to find Islamic bases for it while vilifying as foreign the other side of what being a Western emancipated woman might mean. This is not to say that the Islamist inflection or translation of the ideals does not change the model in important ways; it is merely to note that the claims to a pure indigenous tradition are spurious.

To understand why I say this, one needs to understand the historical context of contemporary debates and the situation of women. A good place to begin is with a critical examination of the ideas of the most prominent instigator of Egyptian debates on women, the elite reformer Qasim Amin, whose controversial *The Liberation of Women*, was published in 1899 while Egypt was under British occupation. More recently, a reassessment of his contributions has begun, with Timothy Mitchell questioning the colonial roots of his feminism and showing its link to a large-scale modernizing project intended to open up the women's world to the same surveillance and individualized subjection to the state as was imposed on the rest of the population, and to organize the family into a house of discipline for producing a new Egyptian mentality.[30] [...]

For Amin, the principal benefits of Egyptian women's becoming educated and exposed to the world seemed to be two: they would become better mothers, capable of bringing up the kinds of good citizens required by the modern nation; and they would become better marriage companions for the educated modern man, capable of truly loving and understanding him. [...] As Mitchell has pointed out, and Shakry has elaborated, his criticism of Egyptian women's methods of child rearing is shot through with the obsessions with hygiene, rationality, and discipline that characterized the "enlightened" West and were adopted by colonial modernizers, indigenous or foreign.

Here I will be more concerned with his views on marriage. Although defensive throughout his book about his intent to stay within an Islamic framework, giving women only the rights they had according to the true principles of Islam, the Paris-educated Amin is blatant in his admiration for European society. Scathing in his condemnation of contemporary Egyptian women who were, in his words, incapable of truly loving their husbands, and of Islamic scholars who had reduced marriage to a contract by which a man has the right to sleep with a woman, he devotes many pages to painting a romantic picture of the kind of spiritual, mutual love he envisions between husbands and wives. He uses a passage from the Qur'an again to justify this: "He created for you helpmeets from yourselves that ye might find rest in them, and He ordained between you love and mercy." But the sources of this saccharine vision are clearly Western, and he uses the model of intense friendship to characterize it.[31] He dedicated his second book on the subject of women to his fellow nationalist Sa'd Zaghlul, whose friendship, he says, had led him "to consider the value of such a love when shared between a man and his wife" and which he then offers as "the secret of happiness that I declare to the citizens of my country, men or women."[32] [...]

Amin in vivid terms portrayed the dismal state of marriage in his era. He argued that marital unhappiness was the rule, although he believed it was the upper- and middle-class urban men who suffered the most because the gap between themselves and their ignorant (uneducated) women was the greatest. They wanted order and systematically arranged homes; they wanted to share the ideas they cherished, their concerns about the society they served and the country they esteemed, their joys and pain. When they found their wives ignorant, wanting only money or attention from them, they came to despise them and turned away. This made their wives hate them. He concluded, "From then on life is like hell for both of them."[33]

One must wonder at the sources of his strange and negative depiction of marital life and the condition of women in Egypt. The resemblances between his descriptions and those of the missionaries and colonial officials, for example, are striking. Although the missionary women working in the Muslim world blamed the men as well as the system of seclusion, they too described the Muslim family as loveless and described upper-class women as idle. As evidence for the absence of love in marriage, besides numerous anecdotes about miserable marriages, they noted that "there is no word in the Arabic language for home." In a nice circulation of ideas, Annie Van Sommer's introduction to a 1907 collection of missionary women's accounts of their experiences in Muslim lands (*Our Moslem Sisters: A Cry of Need from Lands of Darkness*) cites the "Egyptian gentleman" Qasim Amin as an authority on the lovelessness of Muslim marriage.[34] [ ... ]

He accuses seclusion of being a source of moral corruption because it encourages upper-class women to mix with lower-class and less respectable women, to talk freely to peddlers ("women who are ignorant of their roots, their background, or their condition, and who have not adopted any points of good character"), and to be exposed to prostitutes (dancers) at wedding celebrations. He finds it problematic that "[t]he woman of the house sees no harm in visiting her servant's wife; in fact, she may be entertained by conversing with her and listening to her tales. She gives minimal consideration to the appropriateness or inappropriateness of the topics of conversation."[35] This anxiety over women's talk surfaces elsewhere in his complaint that idle women spend their time talking to their friends: "While with friends and neighbors, her deep sighs ascend with the cigarette smoke and coffee steam as she talks loudly about her private concerns: her relationship with her husband, her husband's relatives and friends, her sadness, her happiness, her anxiety, her joy. She pours out every secret to her friends, even those details associated with private behavior in the bedroom."[36]

Here I would like to suggest that Amin is signaling his desire to undermine the solidarities of a relatively separate women's world, distinguishing an emergent middle class, and dividing women by placing them into separate bourgeois nuclear families. He also seems to want to put an end to the sexually explicit language of that world that is often hostile to men. [ ... ]

Amin's program was for a liberation of women that would make of them good bourgeois wives and mothers in a world where state and class ties would override those of kin, capitalist organization would divide the world into the distinct spheres of private and public, and women would be subjected to husbands and children, cut off from their kin and from other women. His was a project of domesticating women that relied heavily on Western models of the time. Clearly it is this modernist and "feminist" tradition within which the Islamists work, even as they transform some of its elements. They do not gesture toward the sex-segregated world Amin denounced or toward the alternative model with different cultural and political roots that I have described for the contemporary Awlad 'Ali Bedouin in Egypt. As Homi Bhabha has argued for other postcolonial societies, access to any sort of real "tradition" has been made impossible by the historical cultural encounter with the West.[37]

## ■ Conclusion: Beyond the Rhetoric ■

It has been nearly a hundred years since Qasim Amin published his two contro-versial books. As feminist scholars have recently documented, he wrote in a context where women writers were already raising many of the concerns he raised. The struggles for women's rights and the transformation of women's lives were carried forward by a range of women writers and activists and an impressive series of feminist organizations in the early to mid-twentieth century, led by women like Huda Sha 'rawi, Saiza Nabarawi, and later Doria Shafik, who were far more radical than Amin in their demands for education and women's rights to the public sphere.[38]

Mostly tied by class to Europe and Europeans, even as many were anti-imperialist, they adopted not just the "feminist" projects of education and public roles for women but also the ideals of uplifting the lower classes and the key components of a new domesticity – companionate marriage and scientific child rearing. They thus retained and elaborated many of the ideals Amin promoted. Their journals carried dire stories about the tragedies of forced marriage and polygyny, carried information on how to run a proper household, and provided advice about child rearing. In short, as part of their call for awakening women and transforming their lives and possibilities, they encouraged modern bourgeois "ra-tional" modes of housewifery and child rearing, similar to the modes of domesticity being developed and marketed through magazines in Europe and the United States at the time.[39] Most telling, they promoted the ideal of the conjugal couple, arguing against arranged marriage, polygyny, men's rights to easy divorce, and women's lack of access to the same. Their motives were different from Amin's, since they did not put themselves in the place of the modern man looking for a companion or blame women for marital unhappiness. They were more concerned with abuses of women. But they idealized companionate marriage as much as he did.[40]

It was Nasser who in the 1950s and 1960s could be said to have nationalized many of these feminist projects, removing at least from the goals of women's education and employment the taint of foreign influence with his own impeccable nationalist credentials. It was during his presidency that what Hatem calls "state feminism" was introduced, and independent women's organizations were sup-pressed.[41] His policies of mass education and guaranteed employment for gradu-ates, regardless of sex, were based on a conception of woman as worker and citizen whose participation was essential for national development. [ ... ]

Urban women today, of a variety of classes, veiled and unveiled, are generally more radical than Qasim Amin was on issues of education, work, and participation in some aspects of the public sphere, such as politics. If they were informed enough about Egyptian history to know about the early-twentieth-century Egyptian feminists whose activities and views have been so crucial, they would probably denounce them.[42] Yet they are the inheritors of the political gains made for women by these women who took up where Amin left off, as they are the beneficiaries of Nasser's policies of mass education and employment.[43] [ ... ]

For the upwardly mobile lower middle classes, from whom the Islamists draw much of their support, I suspect it is changes in the nature of the economy and social organization that combine with the middle-class images offered as models by television and magazines that underpin this vision. After all, even the progressives' serials, which clearly reinforce the Nasserist legacy of support for women's work and education, take for granted, if they do not glorify, the ideals of the "modern" couple and the companionate marriage. It could well be argued that the religious leaders' stress on the couple arises from a need to accommodate to and appropriate widely shared popular attitudes and demographic realities, not just of the upper and middle classes but increasingly of the lower classes as well.[44]

Just as the *hijab* and the modest dress being adopted around the Middle East are modern forms of dress, representing, despite the rhetoric, not any sort of "return" to cultural traditions but rather a complex reaction to a wide set of modern conditions (including, to be sure, a confrontation with Western consumerism), so the Islamist call for women to return to their roles as wives and mothers does not represent anything resembling what could be considered "traditional." These roles were fundamentally altered in the twentieth century. To "return" to the home after the world has become fundamentally divided between a domestic and public sphere, after wage labor for all has transformed social and economic relations, after kin-based forms of social and economic organization have been attenuated, and after being a wife and mother has come to be thought of by some as a career, is to go to a new place and take on a radically new role.

The enmeshment with the West of an earlier period of such notions about the organization of family and the roles of women, like the colonial roots of many of the socioeconomic transformations that went along with these, are conveniently forgotten by the Islamists. This occlusion enables them to gain the moral high ground by seeming to reject the West, in their fixation on the chimera of sexual or public freedom, while not fundamentally challenging widely held ideals – like conjugal love, the nuclear family, the companionate marriage, and women's education – and economic necessities, like women's work, of late-twentieth-century middle- and lower-middle-class life in Egypt.

Cultures cannot simply displace or undermine each other, as the quotations with which this chapter opened might suggest. The complex processes of borrowing, translating, and creating new mixtures – what some theorists prefer to call cultural hybrids – cannot be subsumed under this sort of dichotomous image.[45] Nor can the ways in which new ideas are given firm bases by social and economic trans-formations as well as ideological familiarization, especially now through powerful forms of mass media. What the case of feminism in Egypt shows, however, is that the elements of borrowed, imported, or imposed "culture" are susceptible to disaggregation for political purposes. Elements that apply to only a tiny minority can be singled out for self-serving vilification as foreign, while those widely accepted, especially by the large middle and lower middle classes, are less likely to find themselves carrying the tainted label, "Made in the West."

It seems to be a common dynamic of postcolonial cultural politics that cultural transplants are selectively and self-consciously made the object of political contest.

As analysts, we need to stand outside these struggles, writing the history of feminism in Egypt with an awareness of its multifaceted nature, historical stages, and complex intertwinement with the West while regarding the claims of the Islamists to cultural authenticity or countermodernity with healthy suspicion.

## NOTES

1 Literacy rates still make newspaper (and book) reading the habit of a minority, while radios are in every home, popularized by Nasser (the first president of postindependence Egypt) in the 1950s and 1960s as a political instrument. Most people have access to television. Among the most widely watched television programs are the evening dramatic serials, which provide the occasion for a good deal of national discussion and debate of major social issues.

2 This and all other quotations are from two interviews with the author on June 27 and 28, 1993.

3 All quotations are from an interview with the author on June 22, 1993.

4 The book was coauthored by ʿImad Nasif and Amal Khodayr and entitled *Fannanat taʾibat wa nijmat al-ithara*! It listed no publisher, but its publication date was 1991 and it was in its eighth printing in January 1993.

5 The phenomenon of "the new veiling" is extremely complex. Among those who have written insightfully on it, showing clearly how the religious motivation for it, stated by many as the reason, needs to be balanced by an understanding of how veiling contributes to greater freedom of movement in public, easier work relations in mixed-sex settings, respectability in the eyes of neighbors and husbands, greater economy, and social conformity, are Leila Ahmed, *Women and Gender in Islam* (New Haven: Yale University Press, 1992); Fadwa El Guindi, "Veiling Infitah with Muslim Ethic" *Social Problems* 28 (1981): 465–85; Mervat Hatem, "Economic and Political Liberalization in Egypt and the Demise of State Feminism," *International Journal of Middle East Studies* 24 (1992): 231–51; Valerie Hoffman-Ladd, "Polemics on the Modesty and Segregation of Women in Contemporary Egypt" *International Journal of Middle East Studies* 19 (1987): 23–50; Arlene MacLeod, *Accommodating Protest: Working Women, the New Veiling, and Change in Cairo* (New York: Columbia University Press, 1991); and Sherifa Zuhur, *Revealing Reveiling: Islamist Gender Ideology in Contemporary Egypt* (Albany: State University of New York Press, 1992). Elizabeth Fernea's documentary film *A Veiled Revolution* is especially good at revealing many meanings of the new modest dress.

6 Nasif and Khodayr, *Fannanat taʾibat*, pp. 49, 61.

7 Ibid., pp. 60–1.

8 Interview of Hasan Yusuf with Amal Surur and ʿUmar Tahir, *Nusf al-dunya*, May 4, 1997, p. 21.

9 See Mervat Hatem, "Egyptian Discourses on Gender and Political Liberalization: Do Secularist and Islamist Views Really Differ?" *Middle East Journal* 48, no. 4 (1994): 661–76, for an important assessment of this convergence.

10 Barbara Stowasser, "Religious Ideology, Women and the Family: The Islamic Paradigm," in her *The Islamic Impulse* (Washington, DC: Center for Contemporary Arab Studies, Georgetown University, 1987), pp. 262–96.

11 See MacLeod, *Accommodating Protest*.

12  Zuhur, *Revealing Reveiling.*

13  Stowasser, "Religious Ideology, Women and the Family," p. 269.

14  Ahmed, *Women and Gender in Islam*, and Hatem, "Economic and Political Liberalization."

15  Ahmed, *Women and Gender in Islam*, pp. 226–7.

16  Margot Badran, "Gender Activism: Feminists and Islamists in Egypt," in *Identity Politics and Women: Cultural Reassertions and Feminisms in International Perspective*, ed. V. M. Moghadam (Boulder, Colo.: Westview Press, 1993), pp. 205, 211–14.

17  For more on this announcer, see Fedwa Malti-Douglas, "A Woman and Her Sûfîs" (Washington, DC: Center for Contemporary Arab Studies Occasional Papers, Georgetown University, 1995).

18  This conservative's views are critically described in two articles by Ibrahim 'Issa, "Mashayikh Kariman Hamza," *Roz al-Yusuf*, March 15, 1993, p. 23, and "D. 'Umar 'Abd al-Kafi shaykh al-nisa'. . . wa al-fitna al-ta'ifiyya," *Roz al-Yusuf*, March 29, 1993, pp. 23–5.

19  One should, perhaps, distinguish more carefully among ideals of marriage, noting the differences between a bourgeois notion of the couple and what could more accurately be called companionate marriage, carrying implications of equality between marital partners. But for the purposes of this argument, I am simply trying to locate the ideal of the couple.

20  Maha 'Umar, "Min ajl hayat zawjiyya mustaqirra wa hadi'a," *Al-Luwa' al-Islami*, August 8, 1996, p. 17. I am grateful to Mervat Hatem and Saba Mahmood for guiding me to this material.

21  "'Indama tarfud al-mar'a khidmat zawjiha wa al-qiyam bi'shu'un al-manzil." *Al-Luwa' al-Islami*, August 8, 1996, p. 16.

22  Yusuf al-Qaradawi, *Fatawa mu'asira li-lmar'a wa al-usra al-muslima* (Cairo: Dar al-Isra', n.d.), p. 65; 'Aliyya al-'Asqalani, "Li kul mushkila hal," *Al-Luwa' al-Islami*, December 21, 1995, p. 17.

23  'Aliyya al-'Asqalani, "Al-Tasallut yudammir al-'alaqa al-zawjiyya: sultat al-rajul fi al-bayt la tu'add istibdadan," *Al-Luwa' al-Islami*, July 6, 1995, p. 16.

24  Al-Qaradawi, *Fatawa mu'asira*, pp. 33–4.

25  Muhammad Ibrahim Mabruk, *Mawqif al-Islam min al-hubb* (Cairo: Al-Nur al-Islami, 1996), p. 19.

26  For more on this exclusion, see my "Finding a Place for Islam: Egyptian Television Serials and the National Interest," *Public Culture* 5, no. 3 (1993): 493–513. See my "Dramatic Reversals," in *Political Islam*, ed. Joel Beinin and Joe Stork (Berkeley and Los Angeles: University of California Press, 1996), for a discussion of how this policy of exclusion shifted such that there is now a media campaign against "extremists."

27  Note also the similarities to the feminist discourse in the Egyptian press in 1930, which Badran summarizes as scorning "marriages made with an eye toward material advance or elevation in status." Margot Badran, *Feminists, Islam, and Nation: Gender and the Making of Modern Egypt* (Princeton: Princeton University Press, 1995), pp. 139–40.

28  See Zuhur, *Revealing Reveiling*, pp. 93–5. Deniz Kandiyoti (personal communication) also notes that marital choice within the circle of activists versus an older generation's attempts to control and arrange marriages on other bases is a classic theme in the political subculture of the Turkish Islamist youth.

29  See for example, Soha Abdel Kader, *Egyptian Women in a Changing Society, 1899–1987* (Boulder, Colo.: Lynne Reinner, 1987), p. 137.

30  Timothy Mitchell, *Colonising Egypt* (Cambridge: Cambridge University Press, 1988), pp. 111–13.

31  Amin. *The Liberation of Women*, p. 20.

32  Qasim Amin. *The New Woman*, trans. Samiha Sidhom Peterson (Cairo: American University in Cairo Press, 1995), p. xi.

33  Amin. *The Liberation of Women*, p. 17.

34  Annie Van Sommer and Samuel M. Zwemmer. *Our Moslem Sisters: A Cry of Need from Lands of Darkness* (New York: Fleming H. Revell Company, 1907), pp. 7 and 28.

35  Amin, *The Liberation of Women*, p. 55.

36  Ibid., p. 33.

37  Homi Bhabha. *The Location of Culture* (London and New York: Routledge, 1994), p. 2.

38  Badran, *Feminists, Islam, and Nation*: Beth Baron, *The Women's Awakening in Egypt* (New Haven: Yale University Press, 1994): Cynthia Nelson, "Biography and Women's History: On Interpreting Doria Shafik," in *Women in Middle Eastern History*, ed. Nikki Keddie and Beth Baron (New Haven: Yale University Press), pp. 310–33. and *Doria Shafik, Egyptian Feminist: A Woman Apart* (Gainseville: University Press of Florida, 1996).

39  Marilyn Booth in "'May Her Likes Be Multiplied': 'Famous Women' Biography and Gendered Prescription in Egypt, 1892–1935." *Signs* 22, no. 4 (1997): 827–90, presents rich detail on the contents of these journals, and particularly the use of biographies of famous women to suggest models for young women of the future.

40  For more on women's campaigns and writing on marriage, see Badran, *Feminists, Islam and Nation*, esp. pp. 135–40, and Beth Baron, "The Making and Breaking of Marital Bonds in Modern Egypt" in Keddie and Baron, *Women in Middle Eastern History*, pp. 275–91, esp. pp. 277–8. Badran notes that the 1930s saw a shift in emphasis from concern with the maternal role to that of the wife.

41  Hatem, "Economic and Political Liberalization."

42  Mervat Hatem's "Egypt's Middle Class in Crisis: The Sexual Division of Labor." *Middle East Journal* 42, no. 3 (1988): 407–22, p. 419, reports that most of the veiled college women surveyed denounced Qasim Amin but so did many of the unveiled women.

43  As a result, like just about everyone else in Egypt, they unthinkingly presume that education is good, despite the facts that the benefits of such a poor quality of education as is available in the overtaxed state system, leading to poorly paid employment at best, are dubious, and that the continuing debt to the West for the development of secular education is easy to see for those who want to. For example, none of those asserting the new Islamic identities complain that in the competitive university faculties where the veiled women are concentrated the influence of the West is most direct: it is there, in the scientific fields of medicine, engineering, and pharmacy that English is even the language of instruction.

44  See Marcia Inhorn, *Infertility and Patriarchy* (Philadelphia: University of Pennsylvania Press, 1996), esp. pp. 148–50. It would be worth exploring demographically the class breakdown of historical shifts from extended to nuclear households. For instance, Judith Tucker, in *Women in Nineteenth Century Egypt* (Cambridge: Cambridge University Press, 1985), p. 100, has argued in her study of the Egyptian peasantry and urban lower classes that even in the nineteenth century "[i]t was the small nuclear family, the husband and wife unit, that formed the basis of much business and property holding, not the large extended family of received wisdom and inheritance law logic."

45  Bhabha, *The Location of Culture*, has pursued this idea furthest.

# 14

# Freeing South Africa: The "Modernization" of Male–Male Sexuality in Soweto

## Donald L. Donham

Identity is formed at the unstable point where the "unspeakable" stories of
subjectivity meet the narratives of history, of a culture.

Stuart Hall, *Minimal Selves*

■ Of Dress and Drag ■

In February 1993, a black man in his mid-thirties named Linda (an ordinary male
name in Zulu) died of AIDS in Soweto, South Africa. Something of an activist,
Linda was a founding member of GLOW, the Gay and Lesbian Organization of
the Witwatersrand. Composed of both blacks and whites, GLOW was and is the
principal gay and lesbian organization in the Johannesburg area. Because Linda
had many friends in the group, GLOW organized a memorial service at a member's
home in Soweto a few days before the funeral.

Linda's father, who belonged to an independent Zionist church, attended and
spoke. He recalled Linda's life and what a good person he had been, how hard he
had worked in the household. But then he went on, in the way that elders
sometimes do, to advise the young men present: "There was just one thing about
my son's life that bothered me," he said. "So let me tell you, if you're a man, wear
men's clothes. If you're colored, act colored. Above all, if you're black, don't wear
Indian clothes. If you do this, how will our ancestors recognize [and protect] you?"
Linda had been something of a drag queen, with a particular penchant for Indian
saris.

To Linda's father and to his church, dress had ritual significance. One might even say that there was an indigenous theory of "drag" among many black Zionist South Africans, albeit one different from that in North America. To assume church dress not only indicated a certain state of personhood, it in some real sense effected that state.[1] Writing on Tswana Zionists, who like the Zulu have been drawn into townships around Johannesburg, Jean Comaroff (1985) asserted, "The power of uniforms in Tshidi perception was both expressive and pragmatic, for the uniform instantiated the ritual practice it represented" (1985: 220).[2]

If dress had one set of associations within Zionist symbolism, it had others for a small group of young black South African activists who saw themselves as "gay." To the members of GLOW present, most of whom were black, Linda's father's comments were insulting. Most particularly, they were seen as homophobic. As the week wore on, GLOW began to organize to make their point and to take over the funeral.

As Saturday neared – nearly all Soweto funerals are held on the weekend – tensions rose. There were rumors that there might be an open confrontation between the family and GLOW. Along with Paul, a member of GLOW from Soweto, I attended, and the following is a description of what transpired, taken from a letter that I wrote home a few days later to my American lover:

[...] When we arrived, Simon Nkoli, one of the first black gay activists in South Africa, was speaking. Simon was dressed in an immaculately white and flowing West African (male) outfit with gold embroidery. He spoke in English, and someone translated simultaneously (into Zulu). His speech was about gay activism in South Africa and the contributions that Linda, his dead friend, had made. At points in his speech, Simon sang out the beginning lines of hymns, at which point the congregation immediately joined in, in the [style] of black South African singing, without instruments and in part-harmony.

After Simon, there were other speeches by the ministers of the church. They emphasized that Linda was a child of the church, that his sins had been forgiven, and that he was in heaven. Diffusing any trace of tension between the church and GLOW, one of the ministers rose and apologized on behalf of Linda's father for offending the group earlier in the week.

Toward the end of the service, the gay people congregated on the front steps outside the community center and began singing in English a song that began with "We are gay and straight together..." When the people came pouring out and finally the coffin was carried out, the GLOW members in their T-shirts took the handles of the casket from the men of the church and placed it in the hearse. The several hundred people present boarded two very large transport buses hired for the occasion and probably 20 private automobiles to go to the cemetery [...]

After the graveside service, GLOW members gathered at one of the member's houses in Soweto and proceeded to get drunk. I had had enough. Driving back to Johannesburg (it's a little over 30 minutes), I almost had an accident. Tired and with my reflexes not working for left-hand-of-the-road driving, I turned into oncoming traffic. By the end of the day, I felt overwhelmed. Another gay man dead – yet another. And his burial had brought together, for me, a mind-numbing juxtaposition of peoples and projects, desires and fears – Zionist Christians and gay activists, the first, moreover, accommodating themselves to and even apologizing to the second. Could anything comparable have happened in the United States? A gay hijacking of a funeral in a church in, say, Atlanta?

## ■ Apartheid and Male Sexuality ■

Although engaged in another research project, in my free time with friends like Paul, I thus stumbled onto a series of questions that began to perplex me: Who was Linda? In the letter quoted above, I had unproblematically identified Linda as "gay." But in *his* context, was he? And if so, how did he come to see himself as so? And I quickly confronted questions of gender as well. Did Linda consider himself as male? And if so, had he always done so?

As issues like these began to pose themselves, I soon realized that for black men in townships around Johannesburg, identifying as gay was both recent and tied up, in unexpectedly complex ways, with a much larger historical transformation: the end of apartheid and the creation of a modern nation; in a phrase, the "freeing" of South Africa.

This story, more than any other, constitutes for most South Africans (certainly black South Africans) what Stuart Hall, in the epigraph at the beginning of this paper, referred to as a "narrative of history." It structures identity, legitimates the present, and organizes the past. There are indeed few places on earth in which modernist narratives of progress and freedom currently appear so compelling. This undoubtedly results, at least in part, because apartheid itself was an antimodernist project that explicitly set itself against most of the rest of the "developed" world.

As Foucault (1980) has argued, current Western views on sexuality and modernity are inextricably intertwined.[3] After Foucault, it would be difficult to interpret the conjugated transitions in South Africa as merely the result of the end of a repressive regime – a denouement that opened up spaces in which black men could, at last, claim their gayness, as if being "gay" were naturally pre-given. But if such a conclusion looks implausible, Foucault's own explanation of the formation of modern notions of sexuality also does not capture the full dynamic of the black South African case.

According to Foucault, current Western notions of homosexuality – that is, the concept of the homosexual as a distinct species of person – developed during the 19th century out of the sexual sciences and the dividing practices of modern states. Foucault's method, what he first called archaeology and later genealogy, was to work "across" time – within the same spatial unit. But what happens when one proceeds across space as well as time?[4] At a minimum, a series of new dynamics come into view – ones involving the transnational flow of persons, signs, commodities, and, I shall argue, narratives that (help) create new subject positions. Of late, communications technologies have accelerated and intensified these flows to create what seem to be qualitatively new cultural phenomena.

So how did Linda become gay? I never met or interviewed Linda, but fortunately, for the purposes of this article, before he died Linda wrote an extraordinarily self-revealing article with Hugh McLean entitled "*Abangibhamayo Bathi Ngimnandi* (Those Who Fuck Me Say I'm Tasty): Gay Sexuality in Reef Townships" (McLean and Ngcobo 1994). The collaboration between Hugh and Linda – both members of GLOW – was itself a part of the transformations I seek to understand: the creation of a black gay identity, Linda's "coming out," and the "freeing" of South Africa.

To begin with, Linda did not always consider himself – to adopt the gender category appropriate at the end of his life – to be "gay." If anything, it was female gender, not sexuality as such, that fit most easily with local disciplinary regimes and that made the most sense to Linda during his teenage years. Indeed, in apartheid-era urban black culture, gender apparently overrode biological sex to such a degree that it is difficult, and perhaps inappropriate, to maintain the distinction between these two analytical concepts.[5]

[ ... ] In black township slang, the actual designation for the effeminate partner in a male same-sex coupling was *stabane* – literally, a hermaphrodite. Instead of sexuality in the Western sense, it was local notions of sexed bodies and gendered identities – what I shall call sex/gender in the black South African sense – that divided and categorized. But these two analytical dimensions, gender and sex, interrelated in complex ways. While she was growing up, Linda thought of herself as a girl. [ ... ]

If an urban black South African boy during the 1960s and 1970s showed signs of effeminacy, then there was only one possibility: she was "really" a woman, or at least some mixed form of woman. Conversely, in any sexual relationship with such a person, the other partner remained, according to most participants, simply a man (and certainly not a "homosexual").[6]

This gendered system of categories was imposed on Linda as she grew up:

> I used to wear girls' clothes at home. My mother dressed me up. In fact, I grew up wearing girls' clothes. And when I first went to school they didn't know how to register me. [quoted in McLean and Ngcobo 1994: 170]

Miller recorded the following impressions:

> Linda didn't strike one as particularly effeminate. He was lanky and graceful, with the body of a dancer. The day we met he was wearing white pants and a white cotton sweater with big, clear-framed glasses and a string of red African beads around his neck. But even as an adult, he was treated like a girl at home by his parents. They expected him to do women's jobs – to be in the kitchen, do the washing and ironing and baking. "You can get me at home almost any morning," he told me. "I'll be cleaning the house." There were girls' shopping days when he, his mother, and his sister would go off to buy underclothes and nighties. Each day, he would plan his mother's and father's wardrobes. As a teenager, Linda began undergoing female-hormone treatments, on the recommendation of a doctor. When he finally decided to halt treatments, his father, a minister of the Twelfth Apostle Church, was disappointed. It seemed he would rather have a son who grew breasts and outwardly

appeared to be a girl than a son who was gay. Even today, Linda sings in the choir at his father's church – in a girl's uniform.

"What part do you sing?" I asked him.

"Soprano, of course," he replied. "What did you think?" [1993: 15]

The fact that Linda wore a girl's uniform in church into the early 1990s offers some insight into his father's remarks that caused such a stir in GLOW. His father was not, it seems, particularly concerned with "cross-dressing." Phrasing the matter this way implies, after all, a naturally given bodily sex that one dresses "across." To Linda's family, he was apparently really a female. What the father was most upset about was dressing "across" race, and the implications that had for ancestral blessings.

In sum, black townships during the apartheid era found it easier to understand gender-deviant boys as girls or as a biologically mixed third sex. By the early 1970s, a network of boys who dressed as girls existed in Soweto, many of whom came to refer to themselves in their own slang as *skesana*.[7] [ ... ]

Skesanas dressed as women and adopted only the receptive role in sexual intercourse. Here is Linda speaking:

> In the township they used to think I was a hermaphrodite. They think I was cursed in life to have two organs. Sometimes you can get a nice *pantsula* [tough, macho guy] and you will find him looking for two organs. You don't give him the freedom to touch you. He might discover that your dick is bigger than his. Then he might be embarrassed, or even worse, he might be attracted to your dick. This is not what a *skesana* needs or wants. So we keep up the mystery. We won't let them touch and we won't disillusion them.... I think it makes you more acceptable if you are a hermaphrodite, and they think your dick is very small. The problem is, the *skesanas* always have the biggest dicks. And I should know.... [quoted in McLean and Ngcobo 1994: 168–9, emphasis in original]

[ ... ] Although the connection would have been anathema to the Puritan planners of apartheid, skesana identity was finally tied up with the structure of apartheid power – particularly with the all-male hostels that dotted Soweto. In these hostels, rural men without the right to reside permanently in Soweto and without their wives lived, supposedly temporarily, in order to provide labor to the white-dominated economy. From the 19th century onward, there is evidence that at least some black men in these all-male environments saw little wrong with taking other, younger workers as "wives." In these relationships, it was age and wealth, not sex, that organized and defined male–male sexual relationships; as boys matured and gained their own resources, they in turn would take "wives." This pattern has been described among gangs of thieves on the Rand in the early 20th century (van Onselen 1982) and among gold mine workers into the 1980s (Moodie 1989).

Certainly, in Soweto in the 1960s, hostels populated by rural men had become notorious sites for same-sex sexual relations. Township parents warned young sons not to go anywhere nearby, that they would be swept inside and smeared with Vaseline and raped (see also Mathabane 1986: 68–74). To urban-raised skesanas like Linda, however, these stories apparently only aroused phantasy and desire. Linda described a "marriage ceremony" in which she took part in one of the hostels, as follows:

> At these marriage ceremonies, called *mkehlo*, all the young *skesanas*... sit on one side and the older ones on the other. Then your mother would be chosen. My mother was MaButhelezi. These things would happen in the hostels those days. They were famous. The older gays [*sic*] would choose you a mother from one of them. Then your mother's affair [partner] would be your father. Then your father is the one who would teach you how to screw. All of them, they would teach you all the positions and how to ride him up and down and sideways.... [quoted in McLean and Ngcobo 1994: 163, emphasis in original]

## ■ Modernity and Sexuality in the "New" South Africa ■

By the early 1990s, a great deal had changed in South Africa and in Linda's life. Nelson Mandela had been released from prison. It was clear to everyone in South Africa that a new society was in process of being born. This clarity had come, however, only after more than a decade and a half of protracted, agonizing, and often violent struggle – a contest for power that upended routines all the way from the structures of the state down to the dynamics of black families in Soweto. As a result, the cultural definitions and social institutions that supported the sex/gender system in which Linda had been raised had been shaken to its roots.

By the 1990s, Linda and his friends no longer felt safe going to the hostels; many rural men's compounds in the Johannesburg region had become sites of violent opposition to the surrounding black townships, the conflict often being phrased in terms of the split between the Inkatha Freedom Party and the ANC. Also, as the end of apartheid neared, rural women began to join their men in the hostels, and the old days of male–male marriages were left behind. Looking back from the 1990s, Linda commented,

> This [male–male marriage] doesn't happen now. You don't have to be taught these things. Now is the free South Africa and the roles are not so strong, they are breaking down. [quoted in McLean and Ngcobo 1994: 164]

I will make explicit what Linda suggested: with the birth of a "free" South Africa, the notion of sexuality was created for some black men, or more precisely, an identity based on sexuality was created. The classificatory grid in the making was different from the old one. Now, *both* partners in a same-sex relationship were potentially classified as the same (male) gender – and as "gay."

Obviously, this new way of looking at the sexual world was not taken up consistently, evenly, or completely. The simultaneous presence of different models of same-sex sexuality in present-day South Africa will be evident by the end of this article. Whatever the overlapping ambiguities, it is interesting to note who took the lead in "modernizing" male–male sexuality in black South Africa: it was precisely formerly female-identified men like Linda and Jabu.[8] [ ... ]

If one sexual paradigm did not fully replace another in black townships, there were nonetheless significant changes by the early 1990s. Three events, perhaps more than others, serve to summarize these changes. First was the founding of a genuinely multiracial gay rights organization in the Johannesburg area in the late 1980s – namely, GLOW. Linda was a founding member. Second, around the same time, the ANC, still in exile, added sexuality to its policy of nondiscrimination. As I shall explain below, the ANC's peculiar international context – its dependence on foreign support in the fight against apartheid – was probably one of the factors that inclined it to support gay rights. According to Gevisser (1994),

> ANC members in exile were being exposed to what the PAC's [Pan-Africanist Congress] Alexander calls "the European Leftist position on the matter." Liberal European notions of gender rights and the political legitimacy of gay rights had immense impact on senior ANC lawyers like Albie Sachs and Kader Asmal, who have hence become gay issues' strongest lobbyists within the ANC. [1994: 75]

Finally, a third event that heralded change was the first gay pride march in Johannesburg in 1990, modeled on those held in places like New York and San Francisco that celebrated the Stonewall riots of 1969. Linda and his friends participated, along with approximately one thousand others. This annual ritual began to do much, through a set of such internationally recognized gay symbols as rainbow flags and pink triangles, to create a sense of transnational connections for gay South Africans.

How was Linda's life affected by these changes? Exactly how did sexuality replace local definitions of sex/gender in her forms of self-identification? According to Linda himself, the black youth uprising against apartheid was the beginning:

> Gays are a lot more confident now in the townships. I think this happened from about 1976. Before that everything was very quiet. 1976 gave people a lot of confidence.... I remember when the time came to go and march and they wanted all the boys and girls to join in. The gays said: We're not accepted by you, so why should we march? But then they said they didn't mind and we should go to march in drag. Even the straight boys would wear drag. You could wear what you like. [quoted in McLean and Ngcobo 1994: 180]

As black youth took up the cause of national liberation and townships became virtual war zones, traditional black generational hierarchies were shaken to the core. Black youth came to occupy a new political space, one relatively more independent of the power of parents. But as such resistance movements have developed in other times and places, gender hierarchies have sometimes been strengthened (Landes 1988; Stacey 1983). In resisting one form of domination, another is reinforced. In the black power movement in the United States during the 1960s, for example, masculinist and heterosexist ideals were sometimes celebrated.[9]

Why did this reaction, with respect to gender, *not* take place in South Africa? One respect in which the South African case differs, certainly compared to the United States in the 1960s, is the extent to which the transnational was involved in the national struggle.[10] Until Mandela was released, the ANC was legally banned in South Africa. Leaders not in prison were based *outside* the country, and there can be no doubt that the ANC could not have accomplished the political transition that it did without international support. In this context, the international left-liberal consensus on human rights – one to which gay people also appealed – probably dampened any tendency to contest local racial domination by strengthening local gender and sexuality hierarchies. Any such move would certainly have alienated antiapartheid groups from Britain to Holland to Canada to the United States.

But the significance of the transnational in the South African struggle was not only material. The imaginations of black South Africans were finally affected – particularly, in the ways in which people located themselves in the world. And it was precisely in the context of transnational antiapartheid connections that some skesanas like Linda, particularly after they were in closer contact with white gay people in Johannesburg, became aware for the first time of a global gay community – an imagined community, to adapt Benedict Anderson's phrase, imaginatively united by "deep horizontal bonds of comradeship" (1991: 7).[11]

How did this occur? Perhaps the incident, more than any other, that catalyzed such associations, that served as a node for exchange, was the arrest of Simon Nkoli.[12] Nkoli, by the 1980s a gay-identified black man, was arrested for treason along with others and tried in one of the most publicized trials of the apartheid era – the so-called Delmas treason trials. After Nkoli's situation become known internationally, he became a symbol for gay people in the anti-apartheid movement across the globe. For example, in December of 1986, while he was in prison, Nkoli was startled to receive more than 150 Christmas cards from gay people and organizations around the world (Nkoli 1994: 255).

According to Gevisser,

> In Nkoli, gay anti-apartheid activists found a ready-made hero. In Canada, the Simon Nkoli Anti-Apartheid Committee became a critical player in both the gay and anti-apartheid movements. Through Nkoli's imprisonment, too, progressive members of the international anti-apartheid movement were able to begin introducing the issue of gay rights to the African National Congress. The highly respectable Anti-Apartheid Movements of both Britain and Holland, for example, took up Nkoli's cause, and this was to exert a major impact on the ANC's later decision to include gay rights on its agenda. [1994: 56]

These cultural connections and others eventually helped to produce changes in the most intimate details of skesanas' lives. To return to Linda, gay identity meant literally a new gender and a new way of relating to his body. In Linda's words,

> Before, all skesanas wanted to have a small cock. Now we can relax, it does not matter too much and people don't discuss cocks as much.... Before, I thought I was a

woman. Now I think I'm a man, but it doesn't worry me anyway. Although it used to cause problems earlier. [quoted in McLean and Ngcobo 1994: 168–9]

In addition to how he viewed his body, Linda began to dress differently:

I wear girl's clothes now sometimes, but not so much. But I sleep in a nightie, and I wear slippers and a gown – no skirts. I like the way a nightie feels in bed. [quoted in McLean and Ngcobo 1994: 170]

Consider the underneath-of-the-iceberg for the intimacies that Linda described: it is difficult to reconstruct the hundreds of micro-encounters, the thousands of messages that must have come from as far away as Amsterdam and New York. Gevisser outlines some of the social underpinnings of this reordering:

The current township gay scene has its roots in a generalised youth rebellion that found expression first in 1976 and then in the mid-1980s. And, once a white gay organisation took root in the 1980s and a collapse of rigid racial boundaries allowed greater interaction between township and city gay people, ideas of gay community filtered into the already-existent township gay networks. A few gay men and lesbians, like Nkoli, moved into Hillbrow. As the neighborhood started deracialising, they began patronising the gay bars and thus hooking into the urban gay subculture – despite this subculture's patent racism. GLOW's kwaThema chapter was founded, for example, when a group of residents returned from the Skyline Bar with a copy of *Exit* [the local gay publication]: "When we saw the publicity about this new non-racial group," explains Manku Madux, a woman who, with Sgxabai, founded the chapter, "we decided to get in touch with them to join." [1994: 69]

[ . . . ]

## ▪ Foucault in a Transnational World ▪

One of the distinctive features of modernity is an increasing interconnection between the two "extremes" of extensionality and intentionality: globalising influences on the one hand and personal dispositions on the other.

Anthony Giddens, *Modernity and Self-Identity*

In the West so relentlessly analyzed by Foucault, sexual identity was produced by a long, internal process of disciplining and dividing. Visiting airline stewards were not part of the story. What is striking about black South Africa is the transparency with which the transnational is implicated in and imbricated with gay identity formation. When asked to date the beginning of the gay movement in Soweto, some young black men answered that it commenced when a gay character appeared on *Dynasty* on local South African television (McLean and Ngcobo 1994: 180).

It goes without saying that the category of gay people that this process has produced in South Africa is hardly homogeneous, nor is it the same as in Western countries. Being black and gay and poor in South Africa is hardly the same as being black and gay and middle-class, which is again hardly the same as being white and gay and middle-class, whether in South Africa or in North America. Despite these differences, there is still in the background a wider imagined community of gay people with which all of these persons are familiar and, at least in certain contexts, with which they identify. How this imagined community becomes "available" for persons variously situated across the globe is a major analytical question.

In Paul Gilroy's (1993) analysis of the black diaspora, he writes suggestively of the role of sailors, of ships, and of recordings of black music in making a transnational black community imaginatively real. As black identity has been formed and reformed in the context of transnational connections, black families have typically played some role – complex to be sure – in reproducing black identity. Gay identity is different to the degree that it does not rely upon the family for its anchoring; indeed, if anything, it has continually to liberate itself from the effects of family socialization.[13]

This means, ipso facto, that identifying as gay is peculiarly dependent upon and bound up with modern media, with ways of communicatively linking people across space and time. In North America, how many "coming out" stories tell about trips to the public library, furtive searches through dictionaries, or secret readings of novels that explore lesbian and gay topics (Newton 1984)? A certain communicative density is probably a prerequisite for people to identify as gay at all, and it is not improbable that as media density increases, so will the number of gay people.[14]

In less-developed societies of the world today, then, transnational flows become particularly relevant in understanding the formation of sexual communities. Sustained analysis of these connections has hardly begun, but I would suggest that we start not with ships but with airplanes, not with sailors (although they undoubtedly played their role here as well, particularly in port cities) but, in the South African case, with tourists, exiled antiapartheid activists, and visiting anthropologists; and finally not with music, but with images, typically erotic images – first drawings, then photographs, and now videos, most especially of the male body.

Given the composition of the global gay community, most of these images are of the *white* male body. For black men, then, identifying as gay must carry with it a certain complexity absent for most white South Africans. Also, the fact that international gay images are overwhelmingly *male* probably also affects the way that lesbian identity is imagined and appropriated by South African women, black and white. In any case, it could be argued that these kinds of contradictory identifications are not exceptional under late capitalism; they are the stuff of most people's lives. And lately the flow of images has been greatly accelerated; South African gays with access to a modern and a computer – admittedly, a tiny minority so far – can now download material from San Francisco, New York, or Amsterdam.

Each niche in this flow has its own characteristics. For North Americans, the national struggle was separated by two centuries from the gay struggle.[15] In South Africa, these two occurred more-or-less simultaneously, at least for black people. The resulting unevenness of the global-in-the-local disrupts ordinary notions of political "progress." In relation to economic development, Trotsky emphasized long ago that previously "backward" areas can leapfrog ahead of "advanced" ones. At present, the constitution in South Africa prohibits discrimination on the basis of sexual orientation. Who could imagine anything similar happening in the United States?

The overlapping of the national and gay questions means that gay identity in South Africa reverberates – in a way that it cannot in the United States – with a proud, new national identity. Let me quote the reaction of one of the *white* gays present at Linda's funeral:

> As I stood in Phiri Hall behind the black gay mourners behind the hymn-singing congregants, I felt a proud commonality with Linda's black friends around, despite our differences; *we were all gay, all South African.* [Gevisser 1994: 17, emphasis added]

In conclusion, let me suggest that a fuller understanding of sexual identity, in South Africa and elsewhere, requires a revitalized attention to ethnography. Foucault's work remains in many ways foundational in this enterprise, but it also presents serious limitations. Even for the "West," Foucault overstressed what Sedgwick (1990: 44–8) has called a unidirectional narrative of supersession. In fact, cultural change tends to be more various, more fractured, more incomplete. What I am calling the "modernization" of male–male sexuality involves, then, not so much the replacement of one cultural system by another, but the addition of a new cultural model to older ones – with a certain splintering, a certain weighting of new schemas in the lives of at least a few particularly visible actors. [ ... ]

Finally, and most important for the case at hand, Foucault did not problematize the role of cultural exchange across space, of transnational connections that bring, at ever quickening speeds, "unspeakable" stories of subjectivity into relationship with narratives of history. Ethnography is required to meet this goal, an ethnography that traces the global in the local, that analyzes the interplay between globally circulating narratives that persuasively cast past sufferings and offer future liberations, on the one hand, and the local technologies of communication that help conjure up the imagined communities that will enact those liberations, on the other.

But let me give Linda the last say. Here he uses sexuality as a point of self-identification, but in a way that is not unrelated to her previous notions of gender and sexuality:

> The thing that has done most for gays in the township are the marches we have had for gay and lesbian rights. These have been very important and I hope that we will be legalised with an ANC government. Then maybe we can even get married in Regina Mundi [one of Soweto's principal churches, one particularly associated with the struggle against apartheid] and they won't be throwing in the teargas. [quoted in McLean and Ngcobo 1994:181]

## NOTES

*Acknowledgments.* I would like to thank Mark Auslander, Jacqueline Nassey Brown, Carla Freeman, Bruce Knauft, Esther Newton, and Luise White for their comments and suggestions on earlier versions of this article, as well as the editor and reviewers for *Cultural Anthropology.* As I make clear below, this essay could not have been written without Gevisser and Cameron 1994, and most particularly, without the article by McLean and Ngcobo therein. See also Krouse 1993.

1  This notion of what might be called the production of personhood – that who one is can be transformed and worked upon by dress – appears to mirror, in important ways, local concepts of sex/gender. That is, notions of sex and gender are not understood as being simply given by nature. Rather, sex/gender is created, in part, through dress, gesture, and demeanor.
2  The classic studies on Zulu Zionists are Sundkler 1961 and 1976.
3  Parts of Foucault's argument were prefigured in McIntosh 1968 and developed more-or-less independently in Weeks 1977.
4  Stoler (1995) has posed this question in a different way, one focused more precisely upon race and colonialism.
5  For an early statement of the position that the distinction between sex and gender may reflect Western culture rather than a useful analytical device, see Collier and Yanagisako 1987: 14–50.
6  That a special label existed (at least by the 1980s, although the timing of this development is not clear) for *injonga*, men who sexually penetrated other men, indicates that at another level, matters were more complex. According to McLean and Ngcobo (1994), "The man who calls himself an *injonga* is someone who consciously adopts the role of a man who has sex with men. He is different from the 'accidental' homosexual, the *pantsula* (macho township guy) who sleeps with what he believes to be a hermaphrodite or with someone who pretends, and who he pretends, is female" (1994: 166, emphasis in original). Again, according McLean and Ngcobo, "Many *injongas* were *skesanas* once" (1994: 166, emphasis in original). *Skesana*, as I shall explain below, is a slang term for men who are women, men who are penetrated by other men. Such age-related progression through sexual roles recalls the arrangements of rural black South African migrant workers described in Moodie's classic article (1989).
7  According to Linda, "A *skesana* is a boy who likes to be fucked" (quoted in McLean and Ngcobo 1994: 164).
8  For a moment when female-identified men took the lead in gay identity politics in the United States, consider the Stonewall rebellion in New York City during 1969. See Duberman 1993.
9  See Eldridge Cleaver's reaction to James Baldwin (1968: 97–111). At the same time, it is important to remember that there were other voices in the black resistance movement. Black Panther Huey P. Newton, before the 1970 Revolutionary People's Constitutional Convention in Philadelphia, called for an alliance with the gay liberation movement. See Stein n.d.
10  Perhaps the most interesting case to which to compare South Africa would be Israel. There also, politics is peculiarly transnationalized, with many local political actors

anxious to be seen as "progressive." And there also, gays and lesbians enjoy relative legal protection, for example, the opportunity to serve openly in the Israeli military. I thank Esther Newton for calling my attention to the Israeli case.

11  The link between Anderson's work and sexual identity has been made by Parker, Russo, Sommer, and Yaeger 1992.

12  Trials often seem to serve a notable role in making "public" what is ordinarily kept "private," in circulating images of same-sex sexuality. See in particular Duggan 1993.

13  Whether heterosexually-based families must necessarily inculcate homophobic norms is an interesting question. Clearly, individual families can create non-homophobic environments. But to date, I am unaware of any society that accomplishes such an ideal across the board.

14  Historians have emphasized the urban connections of gay culture for some time; see Boswell 1980 and D'Emilio 1992: 3–16.

15  This does not mean that the connections between the gay movement in the United States and previous political currents of the 1960s can be neglected. The link with the women's and black civil rights movements is obviously crucial.

## REFERENCES

Anderson, Benedict 1991 *Imagined Communities: Reflections on the Origin and Spread of Nationalism.* Revised ed. London: Verso.

Boswell, John 1980 *Christianity, Social Tolerance, and Homosexuality.* Chicago: University of Chicago Press.

Chauncey, George Jr. 1985 Christian Brotherhood or Sexual Perversion? Homosexual Identities and the Construction of Sexual Boundaries in the World War I Era. *Journal of Social History* 19: 189–212.

Cleaver, Eldridge 1968 *Soul on Ice.* New York: McGraw-Hill.

Collier, Jane, and Sylvia Yanagisako, eds. 1987 *Gender and Kinship: Essays Toward a Unified Analysis.* Stanford, CA: Stanford University Press.

Comaroff, Jean 1985 *Body of Power Spirit of Resistance.* Chicago: University of Chicago Press.

D'Emilio, John 1992 Capitalism and Gay Identity. *In Making Trouble: Essays on Gay History, Politics, and the University.* New York: Routledge.

Duberman, Martin 1993 *Stonewall.* New York: Plume.

Duggan, Lisa 1993 The Trials of Alice Mitchell: Sensationalism, Sexology, and the Lesbian Subject in Turn-of-the-Century America. *Signs* 18: 791–814.

Foucault, Michel 1980[1976] *An Introduction, vol. 1. The History of Sexuality.* Robert Hurley, trans. New York: Vintage Books.

Gevisser, Mark 1994 A Different Fight for Freedom: A History of South African Lesbian and Gay Organisation – the 1950s to the 1990s. *In Defiant Desire: Gay and Lesbian Lives in South Africa.* Mark Gevisser and Edwin Cameron, eds. Pp. 14–88. Johannesburg: Ravan Press.

Gevisser, Mark, and Edwin Cameron, eds. 1994 *Defiant Desire: Gay and Lesbian Lives in South Africa.* Johannesburg: Ravan Press.

Gilroy, Paul 1993 *The Black Atlantic: Modernity and Double Consciousness.* Cambridge, MA: Harvard University Press.

Krouse, Matthew, ed. 1993 *The Invisible Ghetto: Lesbian and Gay Writing from South Africa.* Johannesburg: COSAW Publishing.

Landes, Joan B. 1988 *Women and the Public Sphere in the Age of the French Revolution.* Ithaca, NY: Cornell University Press.

McIntosh, Mary 1968 The Homosexual Role. *Social Problems* 16: 182–92.

McLean, Hugh, and Linda Ngcobo 1994 Abangibhamayo Bathi Ngimnandi (Those Who Fuck Me Say I'm Tasty): Gay Sexuality in Reef Townships. In *Defiant Desire: Gay and Lesbian Lives in South Africa.* Mark Gevisser and Edwin Cameron, eds. Pp. 158–85. Johannesburg: Ravan Press.

Miller, Neil 1993 *Out In The World: Gay and Lesbian Life from Buenos Aires to Bangkok.* New York: Vintage Books.

Mathabane, Mark 1986 *Kaffir Boy: The True Story of a Black Youth's Coming of Age in Apartheid South Africa.* New York: Macmillan.

Moodie, T. Dunbar, with Vivien Ndatshe and British Sibuyi 1989 Migrancy and Male Sexuality on the South African Gold Mines. In *Hidden From History: Reclaiming the Gay and Lesbian Past.* Martin Bauml Duberman, Martha Vicinus, and George Chauncey Jr., eds. Pp. 411–25. New York: New American Library.

Newton, Esther 1984 The Mythic Mannish Lesbian: Radclyffe Hall and the New Woman. *Signs* 4: 557–75.

Nkoli, Simon 1994 Wardrobes: Coming Out as a Black Gay Activist in South Africa. In *Defiant Desire: Gay and Lesbian Lives in South Africa.* Mark Gevisser and Edwin Cameron, eds. Pp. 249–57. Johannesburg: Ravan Press.

Parker, Andrew, Mary Russo, Doris Sommer, and Patricia Yaeger, eds. 1992 *Nationalisms and Sexualities.* New York: Routledge.

Sedgwick, Eve 1990 *The Epistemology of the Closet.* Berkeley: University of California Press.

Stacey, Judith 1983 *Patriarchy and Socialist Revolution in China.* Berkeley: University of California Press.

Stein, Marc n.d. "Birthplace of the Nation": Imagining Lesbian and Gay Communities in Philadelphia. Unpublished MS.

Stoler, Ann 1995 *Race and The Education of Desire: Foucault's History of Sexuality and the Colonial Order of Things.* Durham, NC: Duke University Press.

Sundkler, Bengt G. M. 1961 *Bantu Prophets in South Africa.* London: Oxford University Press.

—— 1976 *Zulu Zion and Some Swazi Zionists.* Oxford, England: Oxford University Press.

van Onselen, Charles 1982 *Studies in the Social and Economic History of the Witwatersrand, 1886–1914, vol. 2. The Regiment of the Hills-Umkosi Wezintaba: The Witwatersrand's Lumpenproletarian Army, 1890–1920.* London: Longman.

Weeks, Jeffrey 1977 *Coming Out: Homosexual Politics in Britain.* New York: Quartet Books.

# 15

## Very Close to *yinfu* and *ënu*, Or How Prefaces Matter for *JPM* (1695) and *Enu Shu* (Taipei, 1995)

## Naifei Ding

I have previously tried to claim, in an essay on Zhang Zhupo and his *Jin Ping Mei* (*JPM*), to find a "heterosexual male desire" in the strategies of reading whereby both textual object (*yinfu*) and reading subject (a virtual virtuous male reader) are constructed, simultaneously and reciprocally.[1] After presenting that essay two years ago, I remember a friend saying to me afterwards that she couldn't agree with the use of "heterosexual" in the context of a late Ming, early Qing *JPM* (or something to that effect). I was too busy worrying about how to prove the blatant "narrative misogyny" with which Zhang Zhupo's commentaries so clearly colluded, and which certainly (it seemed to me) his commentaried edition had helped to crystallize as part of the *JPM* mythology. It is only in thinking this chapter, and attempting to rethink one line in Zhang Zhupo's *dufa*, that I now begin to understand anew my friend's reservation about the notion of a "heterosexual" male desire in a late Ming and early Qing context.

*JPM* is undoubtedly "about" a polygamous household, and crucially "about" the sexual relations between the head of that household (Ximen Qing) and mostly the women, but also some boys in that household. Significantly, the latter, whether women or boys, are all ritually, symbolically, and in ways familial-social and politico-economic inferior to Ximen Qing. Such an "inferiority" no longer resounds with the weight and meanings it would have had in the time–space wherein the narrative was produced and mostly read, until about a century ago. To non-problematically "name" the modality of desire both as represented in the narrative, and between the "virtual" reader that is the commentator, and the text filled with his interjections, a "heterosexual" male desire, is to assume a seamless continuity between representations of male–female desire and sexual relations in the late Ming/early Qing and the present. This is not even to bring up the complexities of translation and transposition of ideas and practices concerning and surrounding gender and sexuality in the present moment between, say, English and different regions/gradations of "Chineseness." If "heterosexual" has been in at least some fields (I am thinking of gay and lesbian studies, feminist and queer theories) deeply problematized and deconstructed, returned as it were to history and the social, then I must rethink the relations of desire and sex on at least two levels: at the level of the representation of sexual relations within the narrative, and in the space between the narrative and at least two of its "virtual" reader(s), who may be said to engage in relations of desire with the text and its representations. I continue to hold that the *JPM*, especially in its Zhang Zhupo version, is a deeply misogynist narrative, but I can no longer think it so in a total way without any leaks or let-ups (which perhaps will take time and changes in our conditions to misapprehend and apprehend in turn). I am interested in reformulating the Zhang Zhupo commentaries' relation of desire to their host text. I shall try to show how one line in his 108 *Dufa* items might be read as a stray thread that could well undo any attempt (even or especially my own) to stabilize and cohere any one sexualized proclivity on the part of its virtual reader, be it desire and fear or nondesire.

I would like to use this reformulation of Zhang Zhupo's (and my own) shifting relation to a desired object-text to reflect for the moment on another problematic text that appeared in Taiwan a few years ago. This is a short-story collection entitled *Enu Shu* (the Book of Bad Women; "bad" as in evil, malignant, degenerate, licentious, immoral, etc.), written by Chen Xue and published by Huang Guan, a popular press in Taiwan in 1995. The book appeared as part of three books in a new series called *xin ganguan xiaoshuo*, that is, "new sensual narratives" or "new erotica." All three writers were, at the time of publication, first-time, young, self-proclaimed queer authors. The book appeared with the first wave of lesbian and gay groups in several universities in Taiwan, and following upon the international success of Li An's *Wedding Banquet*. (*The Wedding Banquet* was so successful abroad, that the president of Taiwan decided to see it with his entire family. A "Taiwanese" father's acceptance of his son's gay marriage in New York had become an international and local hit, a film for family viewing.) Of the three "new erotica" books, however, Chen Xue's was the only one sold in a plastic cover, usually reserved for "pornographic" materials such as *Penthouse* and *Playboy*, with an additional stamp forbidding all those under 18 from purchasing the book. The material inside was deemed unsafe for the consumption of the young and innocent. All three books came with prefaces by well-known Taiwan cultural critics and/or writers. But only Chen Xue's preface came with a caveat: a warning to the author, and explanation to all potential readers. The warning defined "how to write" properly literary rather than merely escapist writing, while the explanation belabored "how to read" insufficiently self-affirming narratives of unclassifiable but highly suspect female homoerotic desires.

## ▦ Becoming Licentious Women[2] ▦

The author of the *Jin Ping Mei* must have experienced danger, difficulty, poverty, and sorrow and must have been thoroughly acquainted with the ways of the world in order to be able to depict the inner spirit of his characters with such verisimilitude [*moshen*]. (59)[3]

However, if the author had felt it necessary to have personally experienced every-thing he describes in order to produce this book, the *Chin P'ing Mei* could never have been written. Why is this? *The various licentious women in the book engage in illicit relations with men in a variety of different ways.* If the author had to have personally experienced all of these things in order to understand them, how could he have done it? Thus, it is apparent that there is nothing a genius [*caizi*] cannot apprehend if he concentrates his mind upon it. (60)

For Zhang Zhupo, who is more often than not identified with the purported writer of *JPM*, the question raised here is an urgent one – what in the writer's practical experiences can possibly explain the verisimilar narrative effect in the casting of all these licentious women and their variegated illicit sexual engagements? What is simultaneously affirmed in this question, is the "truth-effect" of these representa-tions as well as the genius of their identifiably virtuous male literati writer. Zhang Zhupo's answer, however, seems a bit *ad hoc*, the repeating of a quasi-Buddhist cliché: anything can be apprehended to the concentrated force of the heart–mind that is one (not scattered, not dispersed). As if he too felt this insufficient, Zhang goes on to elaborate in item 61,

Once his concentration has enabled him to apprehend what he needs to know about a character, the author [writer] must be able to become that character himself [*xian-shen*] before he can speak for him. *Thus, he has actually become the various licentious women whom he describes, and he is able to expound his lesson through them.* (61; my emphasis)

Apprehension, presented as the ability of the one to partake of all and any, is not enough to speak for each of these diverse characters. In order to successfully ventriloquize such varied figures, the writer must fantasmatically become each, so as to speak for/as if (in the virtual corporeality of) each (*shi you zhenge xianshen ifan fang shuode ifan*). Thus, it is in the writing process (*xie zhu yinfu*) that the writer actualizes the becoming of each licentious woman in the representation of her personhood (*zhen nai ge xian yinfu ren shen*), so as to speak his (the writer's) lessons (*fa*) to all. Through the process of writing, it is as if the writer becomes one licentious woman after another, the better to speak in their (immoral feminine) voice *his* (moral and masculine) lessons for his readers. Yet, in using this quasi-Buddhist rhetoric as a trope for how the writer could have written in such detail of what was surely not beyond but rather *beneath* his (gender and sexual) experiential knowledge, Zhang Zhupo inadvertently skews certain axes of the writable and readable for one in his (and the writer's putative) position. A quasi-Buddhist rhetoric (*i xin*; *xian shen shuo fa*) facilitates and masks this skewing and its potentially queer consequences. The latter, of course, is only anachronistically excavatable. Let me now try to detail how in proposing the becoming various *yinfu* on the part of the genius writer in order the better to present his lessons to the reader, this particular process and trope may be seen to skewer narrative "truth" (the register of the verisimilar), aesthetic pleasure (the register of affect), and moral-lesson (the register of an ethics of learning). Skewer, as in rendering askew, but also as in forcibly stringing and weaving the three together.

How then can we understand Zhang Zhupo's particular and, on second and third readings, increasingly defamiliarizing use of *xianshen shuofa*, a by now clichéd Buddhist trope? What does this Buddhist trope do to Zhang Zhupo's elucidation of, first, the writer's intentions, and second, the seemingly improper objects of that intention – the many *yinfu* of *JPM*, and finally, the virtual reader's reading of those objects, and through the latter, his apprehension of the writer's lessons (as actualized intentions)?

For one thing, the trope metaphorically renders the writer as a Buddha-like teacher who in order to convincingly speak his teachings, speaks in the guise of the (partial and encompassed) object of these teachings. Thus, *yinfu* as representation is an illusion (fiction) whose sole verity ("truth" effect) lies in the writer's intentions or moral-lessons, and in the reader's retrieval of the latter by reading through illusion to lesson. To some extent, the reader must invert the process of writing, and go from each particular *yinfu* and her illicit sexual engagement, to the lesson that speaks in *yinfu* form, to the writer ventriloquist whose voice and lesson must be carefully discerned despite, or even because of, its being – in drag?

If not in drag, the lesson is as it were embodied and elucidated in the form of a problematic, indeed a devalued and profane object, a clearly "bad" object, if only in terms of this object's distance from the projected writer's and the virtual reader's positions – whether morally, or in terms of gender, status (*shenfen*) and sexual practices. Clearly, such an object *necessitates* the presence and explanations of a virtual reader who knows the trick to a correct and purgative reading. At the same time, the explanation given, that the writer has had to *ge xian yinfu renshen*, that is, to become each and every one of these awful debased women, so as to speak their particular evil truths in the dual tonal register that will resonate with his more "general" voice and lesson, is at the very least, a strange (*qi*) explanation. Strange in the imagery of a writer (and virtual reader) whose ultimately women-fearing and desire-devaluing voice and teachings are embodied in precisely the negative bodily forms (apparitions of course) that is their object of opprobrium. Where does the one start and the other begin, how are we to discern the two levels of voices, the one dissolute the other stern and lecturing? It would have been discursively so much more consistent and less paradoxical to align one's virtuous languages and selves to virtuous widows and filial *guixiou* feminine practices.[4] The purported writer of *JPM* and the virtual reader that is Zhang Zhupo in this case face a much more arduous task. To dress up as bad objects and enact virtuous teachings is dangerous. Unless one is Buddha-like, devoid of desires. Otherwise, at what point and in what guise, might some stray desiring thoughts (of identificatory pleasures, even if relayed and twice removed as in the case of Zhang Zhupo) *not* seep into, leak out of, this long process of writing and reading that constitutes *ge xian yinfu renshen*. This is why I have anachronistically chosen to over-read this particular usage of Zhang Zhupo as a moment of a possibly relayed identificatory pleasure taken with *yinfu* (he – the writer has become *yinfu*; I become him, and through him, *yinfu*). For if sexual desire *for* women is evil and to be eradicated, then perhaps one (leaky) way out for an unspeakable, not-writable desire on the part of a virtuous male (and female) reading position is through sexual desire *as bad objects*.

But to recapitulate on the signifying process involved in Zhang Zhupo's use of *xianshen shuofa*, a residual Buddhist ideology in Zhang's considered use (specifically to explain the inexplainable: how, without experiential knowledge, a genius male writer could write *yinfu* into such verisimilar forms and contortions) would seem to establish the differential value and ontological status of each. The writer and virtual reader are in the position of the subject as either enunciator/writer of (eternal) truths, or reader-retriever of gems (truth, meaning, etc.) amidst dross (flotsam, illusory waste material); this is the order of the upright, the superior, the weightier. Whereas the many licentious women and their illicit sexual engagements are of another and lesser, encompassed order of things, bad and ephemeral objects, whose negative value and illusory (fictive) status serve to *embody* another subject, a higher other's teaching.

To push this line of thinking a bit further, one could then say *yinfu* are by definition fake, insofar as they are illusory fiction, written and read as such in the service of human(e) mankind's realization of the equally illusory nature of his desires (*for* bad objects). Paradoxically, this realization and its attendant purge or attenuation of sexual desire relies on the *degree* of verisimilitude achieved by the representation in question. Bad objects notwithstanding, these have to be bad *enough* to call forth and transfix the (male) desire that will then wither in its root when it encounters the lesson that inheres within these seductive forms. The greater the verisimilitude, the more invested the reader, and the more effective the lesson and process of a purgative cure.[5]

At the same time, the greater the verisimilitude, the more totalizing the momentary strategic transposition whereby writer becomes *yinfu* – albeit working toward the purgation of the virtual reader. Yes, Zhang Zhupo seems to be conceding, having cornered himself by referring to the experiential knowledge necessary for a narrative aesthetic and ethical verisimilitude, the writer had to virtually become *yinfu*, and that is why we can take a pleasure in reading (even in reading *yinfu*) that is not, ultimately, an *immoral* pleasure. For it is in the process of reading, as an inversion of the process of writing, that we may realize or penetrate to the moral bone-teachings of these ephemeral seductive body-figures.

But what if this moral pleasure is leavened, slightly bloated (or gloating or ecstatic-hysteric) and more ambivalent than it needs to be, by the fantasized merger, the becoming two in one, of writer-subject and *yinfu*-object? What if this fantasized transformation of gender and ontological status were one aspect of the imaginative and desiring effects of a Buddhist trope?[6] Just imagine becoming bad bondmaid-concubine for even just a second!

I think one might consider the possibility of Zhang Zhupo as having strategically deployed an available Buddhist figure of speech in order to resolve a knot in his ethico-aesthetics of the *JPM*. It would be precisely such a strategy that would then allow Zhang Zhupo to construct between two ethically polarized but aesthetically parallel effects of writing (the projected writer/virtual reader; the object of writing-reading), a linkage forged in Buddhist transformational thinking, yet limned in a gender-skewing status-inverting desire.[7]

## ■ Queer Subjects, Straitened Readings ■

> The lesbian sentiment [*nutongxinglian ganqing*] that we read in *Enu Shu* are almost all intentionally extracted from social context, and yet the more it [lesbian sentiment?] wishes to escape society's interventions the more it will express that part of it which is society's slave.
>
> In Chen Xue's writing, every passage of lesbian erotics is filled with guilt (*zuië gan*). But what guilt need the lesbian have? What guilt need women's erotics have? Why is it necessary to place lesbian erotics at a great distance from everyday situations? Does not Chen Xue's persistent "escape by way of exoticism" (*yizhi taobi*) precisely reflect the overarching shadow of society's restrictions?[8]

This is the blurb on the back cover of Chen Xue's collection of short stories, *Enu Shu*, published in 1995 (Taipei). It is taken from the preface to the collection, a preface written by one of Taiwan's foremost fiction writers and critics, Yang Zhao, for the generation now under 40.[9] Yang interprets Chen's title and the collection's various evilwomen (*ënu*) as suffering from guilt, a guilt which he deems both source and proof of (continued) enslavement to social repression and restrictions. The proof of guilt, according to Yang, lies in the author's *intentional* extraction of lesbian sentiment and thematics from any recognizable social context that nevertheless succeeds in extending its shadowy influence through the very forms used to escape it. These forms must then be seen as enslaved to the very social mechanisms they would seem to deny.

For Yang Zhao, the three forms that indict Chen Xue's lesbian subjects as "guilty" of continued enslavement to a sexually repressive social regime are (1) a first-person narrator that evinces what Yang considers to be "false consciousness" (in English in parentheses in the original), (2) the projection of lesbian sentiment onto mother–daughter (incestuous) relations, or onto the transfigurations of a narcissistic narrator, and (3) the situating of her stories in an "alien" space (*yizhi kongjian*), an "exotic place" (*yi jie*). On the latter, Yang writes that Chen Xue has "borrowed from the magic realism of South America," and what with "a teeny bit of Mo Yan and Han Shaogong [PRC modernist writers] added in, has created an exotic place" (15). What Yang is implying of course (and the patronizing tone is not an addition in my translation) is that there is nothing new here. Nothing, that is, apart from the "lesbian subject" that in any case is dealt with altogether problematically. Thus, he concludes, "Why must lesbian erotics be situated at such a great distance from *the everyday*? Chen Xue's persistent 'escape by exoticism' precisely serves to reflect the immense shadow cast by society's restrictions" (15). Chen Xue escapes through a reactive extraction of the narrative self from the recognizably "everyday" (the latter is rendered exotic and alien), which everydayness constitutes the specific restrictions of this particular society towards female homoerotics and homosexuality. In short, Chen Xue's fictional topography is insufficiently "everyday-taiwan," just as her fictional erotics are not "Lesbianism per se."

But an even greater problem, besides the shadows cast upon a situatedness that cannot therefore somehow sufficiently concretize (in Yang's reading), is a homoerotics that is likewise insufficiently *sure of itself*, and therefore projected onto and dependent upon modalities of desire that are *not* lesbian but defective (how is not made clear), perhaps even heterosexist.

> Although Chen Xue focuses her writing on lesbians, yet the homo-erotics of women in her stories are lacking in the legitimacy of an assertive existential mode [*lizhi qizhuang cunzai de hefaxing*]. She will habitually write homosexuality as a fictive projection of a [daughter's] mother-complex (as in "Seeking the Angel's Lost Wing"), or as the myriad transformations of a narcissistic desiring formation (as in "Labyrinth of the Night"). Having written a whole book of/about/filled with lesbians (*yi zhengben de nutongxinglian*), paradoxically, Chen Xue is actually denying "Lesbianism *per se*" (*nutongxinglian qingyu de shizhi zishen*; or, the actual substance of a female homoerotics). (14–15)

"Habitually" (*xiguan xingde*) again registers a devaluation. As if, for Yang, the author had slipped up here, had fallen back into modes of thinking, writing, and desiring that *cannot be lesbian*, since they are so patently something else, something recognizable and categorizable to this particular reader (Yang Zhao) as a "mother-complex" or an extreme case of "narcissism" and autoerotic transformations. This leads Yang to state categorically that the central paradox of Chen Xue's book is its *denial* (*foren*) of what he terms "Lesbianism per se," which in a book "filled with/about lesbians" can only be seen as a denial of its own "subject."

This denial, according to Yang, is exemplified at the level of narration, and in the voice–person of the narrator.

> Moreover, in terms of form, these four short stories uniformly use the first person confessional mode, without other experimentation in narrative form. Chen Xue's confessional mode is a superficial one, with the narrator detailing her thoughts and actions as if these were actual, with the effect of a seeming sincerity, as if she were telling the truth. Yet reading on to the end, we clearly feel a huge tension in the text, and this tension arises from the conflict and struggle between the narrator's consciousness and subconsciousness. What the narrator self-consciously presents as a sincere confession is actually none other than a "false consciousness" [*huanjia yishi*], and [her] true feelings and thoughts are repressed, distorted, and hidden between the lines. The source of this repression is of course not personal but social. (14)

The crux of the problem with Chen Xue's collection, for Yang Zhao, is simply this: the author and all the first-person narrators of her stories are afflicted with a "false consciousness" of which they are insufficiently aware, and this then would explain not just the "surface" or "superficial" quality of the first-person narrations, but also the thematic representation of pseudo-lesbian relations (mother–daughter eroticism; narcissistic auto-eroticism), and the formal recourse to "alien" or "exotic" places and situations. Further, this "false consciousness" is diagnosed as one shared by both author (Chen Xue) and her narrators, as evidenced in Yang Zhao's noting Chen Xue's "intentionality" in thematic and formal choices. But it is her use of a "sincere" first-person narrator that is finally most damning.

It is important to restate that Yang Zhao's preface is both typical and atypical in its relation to the text it is prefacing. On the one hand, it is typical in its "assessment" of the new author upon first publication and therefore constituting a sort of "stamp of approval" pending a newcomer's entrance into the field of fiction and literature. It is atypical in the relative sternness or even harshness of its judgment, and in the fact that the commercial press in question did not ask the author to agree to this particular writer-critic for her preface.[10] Yang Zhao's preface pronounced the book in *literary* terms adequate but barely so. Literature is, declares Yang Zhao, "simultaneously deeply embedded in the network that is society, yet at the same time transcends and even leads society" (11). Insofar as Chen Xue's stories *inadvertently, despite their author's intentions,* "reflect the overarching shadow of society's restrictions" (15), they must be seen as lacking in literary inventiveness, and of positive value only in the extent to which they (passively) reflect social embeddedness. In short, they cannot help being flawed, and that is exactly how they may still be read as socially illuminating (of the "false consciousness" with which they are ridden). And yet, without this preface, or what in effect amounts to a "how to read Chen Xue's first novel," the "unknowing" reader might never have quite defined literature in this way, nor read Chen Xue in this particular light (as failed contender for lesbian literariness) and context.

But what precisely is the context provided by this prefacer who can so off-handedly define Literature, judge what counts and what doesn't, and finally, as an aside, decide who and what and how is "Lesbianism, per se"?

The context or continuum in which Chen Xue's collection is placed, measured, and found lacking, is an interesting one. Yang Zhao begins his preface by outlining two works, one written in 1891, on biological differences between the sexes by Harry Campbell, and the other a recent analysis of Western phallocentrism's feminine idols of perversity by Bram Dijkstra. For Yang Zhao, the preceding century in the West is marked by male anxiety over the "discovery" of female sexuality. "What if women have desires? What would be the difference between the desires of women and that of men? More importantly, *what would be the influence, the effects, of women's desires on men*?" (7). The "discovery" of women and women's sexual desires and its attendant male anxiety produced a flurry of works which "superficially idolized the newly discovered female sexual desire, but actually deeply and in the harshest way condemned it, equating female sexual desire to the evil power that seduces people to criminality, and this is what those European males did, at the end of the last century" (8).

A hundred years later, a new question arises. It is now the age of "men discovering men, and women discovering women," says Yang Zhao. If the heterosexual romance has been overwritten, then it is now possible to enter into a new field, "a barren field awaiting tilling" – that is, the erotic adventures of women with women, and the erotic seductions of men and men.

If "at the end of the nineteenth century, men were horrified by the newly discovered potentials of female sexual desires, and thereupon created a whole spectrum of evil figures representing desiring women, then, *in the same way*, at the end of the twentieth century, *when women find out about other women's internal desires*, they will also panic and fear and feel unused to such desires, and therefore take measures in writing that hedge with, escape, and justify these ambivalent feelings" (13). This then is how Yang Zhao understands and situates Chen Xue's work. Chen Xue is *analogous* to the men who hated and idolized women's sexuality at the turn of the last century. Her work both escapes from and seeks to justify a perverted lesbian erotics in ways parallel to what European men tried to do with European women's sexuality 100 years ago. The implicit accusation is that Chen Xue and her narrators are too guilt-ridden to adequately represent (in writing, as representative voice and "identity") a sufficiently contextualized Taiwanese "Lesbianism, per se."

Chen Xue is twice boxed in. The larger encasement is the context of a discourse of (European) male discovery and fear of women's sexuality; the second box is a 1990s Taiwanese literary field (11–15). The first establishes the reactive modality of her representations of female homoeroticism; the second shows up the extent to which her first error (fear of women who desire woman; lack of an in-your-face *lizhi qizhuang* attitude) extends to become a second more serious failure, that is, the ability to "represent" a local, locatable in a readable everyday "Lesbianism, per se." Chen Xue is therefore twice inauthentic. Her fear approximates that of *European* men who fear and fantasize about women's sexuality. Her writings reproduce a homoerotics that mimics what it ought not to mimic, and ensconces that mimicry in a mystifying alien surrounding. As if that could save its inauthenticity from being detected.

But is not inauthenticity an effect, rather than cause, of the boxes envisaged in this here? What is this *lizhi qizhuang*, this rationally self-affirming in-your-face lesbian representation embedded in an everyday (Taiwanese) sociohistoric that would measure up to Yang Zhao's expectations? How would it be configured and marked to ensure its "immediate" legibility to "anyone"? Where and how would such an "authentic" and "authenticating" discourse and its enunciating positions exist? Might there not be a specifically Taiwanese sociohistoric, but also economic and cultural conditions for it's apparent non-existence, its invisibility and nonlegible practices, *excepting in forms and in places hardly recognizable as such, that is, ascertainably "Lesbian" and certifiably "Taiwanese"?*[11]

## ■ Embodiments of *ënu*? ■

Let me now juxtapose to Yang Zhao's reading two anecdotes and one hypothesis that will serve to encircle my question: what are some of the situations and contradictions that might reciprocally constitute a taiwanese lesbian representation and discourse as diffuse, one among many, easily unnoticed and unrecognized, but never completely unlinked?

The first story is of one Taiwanese lesbian telling a queer female friend of the difficulty amongst the former's circle of friends in getting their hands on Chen Xue's book. This book has sold like wildfire. They've sold out in many of the larger bookstores. It's become *the* bedside book – yes, of course. Silence, and knowing smiles.

The second story is of a large family gathering at one of those typical festivities in Taiwan where the patriline must be emotionally and sociopolitically reaffirmed, and when all manner of sexual rebels and emotional escapees sometimes find themselves stranded in rather straitened circumstances. One nunnish aunt finds not so unexpectedly in her tomboyish niece's bedroom, a copy of Chen Xue's book. The niece's "best friend"/lover is also unexpectedly present at the familial gathering, and though not a stray word passes between the three, the year will be a better one for all three, the aunt decides, when burning incense and kowtowing to the now amiable ancestors.

I am not sure what to make of such stories. They abound nowadays among not many women in Taiwan, some out, most not, and all queer in some degree, though not all recognizably or consistently so, and are passed around with relish. They attest to "other" readings of and around Chen Xue's book as well as female homoerotic uses of Chen Xue's stories, that displace and make somewhat irrelevant "serious" critical judgment, especially when these come in the guise of such as Yang Zhao's preface. But my essay also wishes to seriously address this very "irrelevance." How has this "irrelevance" come about if not through just the kind of "invisibility effect" that Yang Zhao ironically attributes to Chen Xue, thus *producing* it as an effect of her textual "denial" and "false consciousness."?

To frame Chen Xue's stories and narrators as *analogous* to that of panicked European males of a previous turn of a century in the face of their "discovery" of female sexuality (no less imaginary and fantasmatic than their previous unknowing of female sexuality) would have been disingenuous, had it not been so revelatory of the preface's particular labor of unknowing and the erotics of that ignorance. Chen Xue's "denial" and "false consciousness" must be aligned to that of *European* male phantasies of the last turn of the century, just as the erotics of her stories are seen to slavishly reproduce certain hegemonic (hetero)social sexual taboos and clichés. The missing mediating subject here of course is the geopolitically situated and gendered reader who couples these together. One is almost tempted to read, in the place of *European*, an authoritative voice of the Taiwan literary establishment, and in the instance of taboos and clichés, the "straight mind" retracing its own laws. Denial and false consciousness revert back to its mediating subject, and a slavish (hetero)erotics stalls and sputters in the closed circuit that constitutes a "straight" (correct, *lizhiqizhuang*) literary and mental field of reading.

Now for the hypothesis. Yang Zhao has glossed the semantics of *ënu* as guilt-ridden. I have said that in thus reading *ënu* and its varied embodiments in Chen Xue's stories, he is inscribing guilt as a cover-up for a reticent shamelessness (*wuci*) in representation and in practice.[12] In reading *ënu* as shameless homoerotic female figures in Chen Xue's fiction, I would like to suggest their emotional and erotic affiliations with the various types of *feinu*, or "nonfemales" produced in a medico-hygienic discourse of the late Ming. These were women who were deemed deficient solely due to their being incapable of sexual reproduction.[13] On the other hand, *ënu* etymologically recalls the undesirables of sexual-hygienic manuals of that same (and earlier) periods, women whose physical attributes and aggressive sexual practices signaled their malignant qualities for men. If *ënu* used to circulate as "objects to avoid" in sex manuals for male readers, then Chen Xue's *ënu* now circulate as objects of desire amongst lesbians, female readers of homoerotic tendencies, and queers.

## ■ Reading "Very Close to"... *yinfu* and *ënu* ■

Prefaces matter. Their matter is the stuff of literary capital (its accumulation or depletion or exchange from the currency of nearby fields, such as the political or the academic), just as it is the stuff of market salesmanship. Prefaces have since the book markets of the late Ming Jiangnan region helped to ensure the place, price, and circulation of their books. But great differences obtain since the time when non-entities could make a lasting literary (*wenren* at large) name for themselves by putting out their own editions of popular, infamous, or renowned fictional works or poetry anthologies (I am thinking of Jin Shengtan, for one example). Whereas in today's literary market in Taiwan, nobodies must find famous names to preface their first publication and/or win a major literary prize as mark of literary worth. Yet, surprisingly, narratives of female sexuality, then considered dangerously licentious and now seen as problematically homoerotic, continue to *demand* prefacing, commentaries, interpretation. As if the labor of a preliminary and preparatory knowing and telling would divert whatever damage was believed would follow upon an uninitiated reading. How else to explain the urgency and seriousness of a Zhang Zhupo and a Yang Zhao's "how to read"?

But here too there are telling differences. A "Zhang Zhupo" had no doubt that these were "verisimilar *yinfu*" he was reading, nor was he worried that other readers would fail to recognize such finely brushed up lascivious and seductive *yinfu* and their sexual acts. (He could thus of course be "accused" of producing the very "yinfu" he was reading/writing.) The only thing Zhang was worried about was that the particular products of this talent for fictional verisimilitude would be held against their genius writer. Thus, Zhang devises two strategies for reading. One, read in the place of the writer, as if you were the writer, or at least as if in the place of the virtual reader (i.e. the place of Zhang's pre-*hui* and interlinear commentaries):

"You must read it as though it were your own work in order not to be deceived by it ... Only if you start out with the assumption that you will have to work out every detail for yourself in order to avoid being deceived will you avoid being deceived" (Roy, p. 224). And two, read all these *yinfu* and their sexual escapades recitatively, *out loud* (*dui ren du*), as if the writer (and you the complicit reader) were reciting (performing?) *yinfu* for their exposure and his/your purgative cure. "Nowadays, if a scholar (*du shu zhe*) reads the *JPM* his parents and teachers are sure to forbid it, and they themselves do not dare to read it openly (*dui ren du*). People do not understand that only a true scholar is able to read the *JPM* properly. *Anyone who reads it on the sly is really reading an obscene book*" (Roy, p. 232). The answer (and secret) to not falling for illusory, licentious, base women is simply to "become" licentious *yinfu* for the duration of an acting out, a purge and a reading (out loud).

As for *Enu Shu*, we could well repeat Zhang Zhupo only changing the value and accent on "obscene": "anyone who reads it on the sly is really reading an obscene book." Even those who read it to each other, out loud, may well be reading obscenely, an obscene book. Therefore the need for a plastic cover, an age limit, and a censorious preface. Censorious not as in "how to read pleasurably yet not fall prey to the pleasures of this text," but rather as in "how to read and *police* whatever desires, however unknowable, misrecognizable, in this text and in reading." The 1990s in Taiwan are not, at least not in a totalizing way, a place where multifarious sexual pleasures and desires may be written and read only in the name of an eventual (confucian-buddhist?) enlightenment and/or (buddhist-daoist?) purgation. Yet, other techniques of management and control have set in and begun their work, quietly and effectively. This, together with recent state policy's accelerated bringing of all informal and illegal economies (sexual and otherwise) to legal light and regulation (e.g. the police harassment of gays on Chang De Road just outside of what is now no longer called the New Park; the "abolishing" of legal prostitution in Taipei as part of an anti-obscenity and antipornography campaign and policy). Yang Zhao's reading of Chen Xue's *ënu* figures and female homoerotics accomplishes the policing of several boundaries at once. One line is the "90s Taiwan literature" (p. 11) that Chen Xue remains just this side of, not firmly inside, but not quite out for good either (a borderline case). Then there is the line of fictional representation of, and the book's implied representativeness as a particular "Lesbianism, per se" (p. 15), which again Chen Xue falls short of, due to the "escapism" in her representation of situatedness (is this anywhere in Taiwan? not really says the preface), and the "incest" topoi of her narratives (how can this be a "proper" lesbianism?).

Against and in response to the increasingly imperious demand for readings that either police or incarcerate in "representative" positionalities, I should like to, stealing from Gayatri Spivak's quotation,[14] recite a passage written to enjoin readings and writings that neither occupy the place of, nor seek to speak authoritatively on, but rather hover *very close to* ...

> Don't claim to "speak for" or, worse, to "speak on," barely speaking next to, and if possible *very close to*: these are the first of the solidarities to be taken on by the few Arabic women who obtain or acquire freedom of movement, of body and of mind.[15]

Let me reiterate that for those who continue to find (some part of) themselves for one unspeakable/illegible reason or another residing in the space and time of base (*jian*, considered inferior and immoral, incorrect, perverted, queer, homosexual, transsexual, or all of the above) modes of sexual practices and familial-social personhood. It is imperative that those parts/persons that have acquired "freedom" from this encompassed order stay centrifugally, counterintuitively, not falling in with the weightier side of the watermelon, very close to, so as to struggle alongside of penumbra social movements and aggregations in the fight.

## NOTES

1  See Naifei Ding, *Obscene Things: Sexual Politics in Jin Ping Mei* (Durham, NC: Duke University Press, 2002).

2  I have followed David Roy's translation (in "How to Read the Chin P'ing Mei" in *How to Read the Chinese Novel* [Princeton, NJ: Princeton University Press, 1990]) of *xianshen* as "becoming." The use of this translation here might also retrieve two instances in English (also translated) of literary transpositions and theoretical transversality: Gustave Flaubert's "I am Madame Bovary" and Félix Guattari's "Becoming a Woman," in *Molecular Revolution: Psychiatry and Politics* (Penguin: 1972, 1977, 1984).

3  The numbers following this and subsequent quotations from Zhang Zhupo's *Dufa* indicate their item number in both the Chinese and Roy's translation of "How to Read the Chin P'ing Mei," in *How to Read the Chinese Novel*.

4  See Katherine Carlitz, "Desire, Danger and the Body: Stories of Women's Virtue in Late Ming China," in *Engendering China: Women, Culture and the State*, eds. Christina Gilmartin et al. (Stanford, CA: Stanford University Press, 1994), 34–67. Also Patricia Sieber, "Corporeality and Canonicity: A Study of Technologies of Reading in Early Modern *Zaju* Drama," in *Graven Images: Culture, Law, and the Sacred* 2; and Kimberly Besio, "On the Borders of the Han: Gender, Cultural Identity and Canon Formation in Early Modern Drama," unpublished manuscript.

5  See Peter Rushton, "The Daoist's Mirror: Reflections on the Neo-Confucian Reader and the Rhetoric of *Jin Ping Mei*" (in *CLEAR* 8, nos. 1–2, July 1986), on *JPM*'s purgative effect, though his conclusion differs from mine in this and previous chapters. I have also used "virtual reader" in this essay in a way consonant with his use of "virtual" for Zhang Zhupo's position in the text.

6  I have used the following texts in reading this Buddhist trope: Kenneth K. S. Ch'en, *Buddhism in China* (Princeton, NJ: Princeton University Press, 1964); *The Buddhist Tradition in India, China and Japan*, ed. W. T. de Bary (New York: Vintage Books, 1972); Diana Y. Paul, *Women in Buddhism* (Berkeley: University of California Press, 1979, 1985); a facsimile copy of the *Foxue Dacidian* (Taipei, 1985). See especially Paul's introduction to and translation of sutras in the chapter entitled "The Bodhisattvas with Sexual Transformation."

7  "More generally, then, every 'dissident' organization of the libido necessarily makes common cause with the feminine body in its becoming, as an escape route from the repressive social structure, as a possible route to a 'minimum' of sexual becoming, and as the last life-buoy to cling to for safety from the established order. I stress this point particularly, because the becoming of the female body must not be confused with the category of woman as considered in marriage, the family and so on. This kind of

category can only exist within the particular social field that defines it, in any case. Women as such does not exist at all.... Conversely, anything that infringes the norms, that breaks with the established order, is in some way related to animal becoming, feminine becoming and the rest. *Wherever there is a semiotic system being broken down, there is also a sexualization being broken down.* We should not, it seems to me, discuss the problem of homosexual writers, but rather try to discover the homosexual element in every great writer, even one who is heterosexual in other respects." Félix Guattari in "Becoming a Woman" (pp. 234–5). Zhang Zhupo was perhaps "intending" the reverse of Guattari's proposal: that is, to gloss and read a dissipated, overfeminized text in such a way as to enable its reinsertion into the literary patriline. The market achieved what he tried to do, without however mitigating the paradox of his attempt. In Zhang's moral overreadings lie the flickerings of a dissident libidinal charge.

8   Chen Xue, *Enu Shu* (Taipei: Huangguan, 1995). The page numbers following all subsequent quotations of Yang Zhao's preface to *Enu Shu* will refer to this edition.

9   This is from the blurb for Yang Zhao's new collection of essays.

10   Personal communication.

11   Both "Lesbian" and "Taiwanese" may be considered hotly contested discursive terrains at this moment (early 1997) in Taiwan. Of course, there is a huge discrepancy in the stakes and size and location of these terrains. Whereas the former is debated primarily within one sector of the cultural field, plus a segment of the internet, the other is in ascending and cumulative construction nationwide, at all levels and in all domains. I will use the small case "lesbian" and "taiwanese" for an alternative and nondominant (nonstatist) sense of these two nouns.

12   For the reticent shamelessness of Chen Xue's writing, see forthcoming paper by Amie Parry, "Anti-Realism, Anti-Reticence: Chen Xue's Reality/Dream Dialectic." Trans. into Chinese by Jonathan Yeh. *Working Papers in Gender/Sexuality Studies 2000.* Special Issue: "The Cultural Construction of Female Subjectivity: Alternative Approaches to Female Sexualities." Chungli, Taiwan: Center for the Study of Sexualities, National Central University.

13   See Charlotte Furth, "Androgynous Males and Deficient Females," *Late Imperial China* 9(2) (1988): 1–31.

14   In a panel discussion with Assia Djebar at University of California, Berkeley in the summer of 1995.

15   Assia Djebar, "Overture," *Women of Algiers in Their Apartment* (Charlottesville, VA: University of Virginia Press, 1992), p. 2.

# Part IV

## Media Production and Consumption

# Introduction

## Toby Miller

■ The State of Play ■

The current production and consumption orthodoxies of media, communication, and Cultural Studies form a contradictory hybrid that has at best only minimal dialogue between its five components: (a) use of certain theories of subject-formation, as per Marxism or psychoanalysis, to account for the ideological positioning of audiences by texts; (b) textual analysis by critics whose interpretations stand for other audiences, subjectivities, cultures, and occasions of viewing; (c) political-economic accounts of ownership and control; (d) counting of like and unlike signs of textual content without significant regard for context or genre; and (e) ongoing laboratory and classroom studies into the effects of the media on violence and education. The first two categories characterize humanities approaches, while the last three characterize social-science approaches. The first three categories represent significant trends within Cultural Studies and progressive academia in general, whereas the last two categories relate more closely to "normal science" work. Each approach is dominated by US and Western European histories, locations, and authors. Is this state of play acceptable to the project of an internationalist Cultural Studies?

Cultural studies is animated by subjectivity and power – how human subjects are formed, and how they experience cultural and social space. Cultural studies' continuities come from a shared concern and method: the concern is the reproduction of culture through structural determinations on subjects versus their own agency, and the method is historical materialism. The media are clearly central to such processes. Most popular and significant media texts (websites, films, newspapers, television, radio, and electronic games) are commodities whose key appeal lies in their meanings. Critical political economy and sociopolitical theory are natural allies of textual analysis and audience ethnography in understanding them. But a certain tendency has maintained that these approaches are mutually exclusive, on the grounds that one is concerned with structures of the economy and polity, and the other with structures of signification and interpretation. This need not be the case. Historically, the best critical political economy, sociopolitical theory, textual analysis, and ethnography have worked through the imbrication of power and signification at all points on the cultural continuum. Ideally, blending the approaches can heal divisions between fact and interpretation and between the social sciences and the humanities, under the sign of a principled approach to cultural democracy. That requires a focus on the contradictions of organizational structures, their articulations with everyday living and textuality, and their intrication with the polity and economy, refusing any bifurcation that opposes the study of production and consumption, or fails to address axes of social stratification.

Cultural studies has been crucially concerned with debates over whether media audiences are primarily passive or active in their viewing habits: do they simply accept the products of the commercial media on the terms presented to them, or do they produce meaning and engage in resistance under their own cognizance? One hundred and fifty years ago, it was taken as read that audiences were active, given their unruly and overtly engaged conduct at cultural events. But the emergence of public education in the West in the nineteenth century, allied to the disciplines of literary criticism and psychology and the decline in importance of "live" performance, shifted critical rhetoric about audiences. Since the advent of the mass media, especially television, much energy has been devoted to evaluating the active versus passive sides to media audiences. Media use symbolizes time, and the alleged misuse of time has become integral to the desire to police everyday media consumption. As a consequence, the audience has engaged intellectuals and social movements in various guises: as a group of consumers, students, felons, voters, and idiots. Sometimes the criticisms made of audiences are about the presumed impact of particular genres (TV wrestling is degrading, infotainment is commercial, and talk TV trivializes current affairs – by contrast, "real" sports bind the nation, and "real" journalism informs the electorate) as much as they are to do with categories of people and their practices.

Cultural studies has defended audiences against these charges of inactivity, arguing that "the people" engage in resistive readings of media texts that reference their own social struggles rather than adhering to producers' preferred responses. This defense of the audience emerged during the 1960s, when Harold Garfinkel developed the notion of the "cultural dope" to explain the condescending views about audiences to the popular media that were prevalent at the time. The "dope" is a mythic figure "who produces the stable features of the society by acting in compliance with pre-established and legitimate alternatives of action that the common culture provides." Garfinkel argued that the "common sense rationalities ... of here and now situations" used by ordinary people were obscured by this demeaning categorization (1992: 68). It remains the case, by and large, that when the audience is invoked as a category by the industry, critics, and regulators, it becomes such a "dope."

Cultural studies rightly reacts strongly against this stereotype, preferring as a working assumption that subordinate groups adopt and adapt signs and objects of the dominant culture, thereby reorganizing them to manufacture new meanings. By looking at how culture is used and transformed by "ordinary" and "marginal" social groups, Cultural Studies sees people not simply as consumers, but as potential producers of new social values and cultural languages. In this sense, it is vitally connected to issues of collective self-determination – how social movements gain control over the means of their existence. Consumption is thought to be the epicenter of such subcultures. Paradoxically, then, the practice of consumption reverses members' status as consumers. They become producers of new texts "in use" that inscribe their sense of alienation, difference, and powerlessness. (The decline of the British economy and state across the 1970s was said to be exemplified by punk's use of rubbish as an adornment: bag-liners, lavatory appliances, and ripped and torn clothing.) But then commodified fashion and convention take over, as capitalism appropriates the appropriator. For example, even as the UK media announced in the 1970s that punks were folk devils, and set in train various moral panics about them, the fashion and music industries were sending out spies in search of new trends to market. An awareness of this double-edged investment in commodities, that they may be appropriated by subcultures as acts of resistance, then recommodified, with rebellious connotations resignified as gimmicks, illustrates the need to bracket production and consumption via political economy and textual and audience analysis.

## ■ A Call for Change ■

The existing agenda of media, communication, and Cultural Studies has undervalued political-economic-sociological-anthropological approaches. In its stead, we should acknowledge the policy, distributional, promotional, and exhibitionary protocols of the media as much as their textual ones. Enough talk of "economic reductionism" without also problematizing "textual reductionism." Enough valorization of close reading and armchair accounts of human interiority without regard for the conditions of global cultural labor and the significance of work, texts, and subjectivities within social movements and demographic cohorts. Enough analysis of animation, for instance, without reference to the international political economy that sees an episode of *The Simpsons* decrying globalization, when the program has itself been made by non-union animators in southeast Asia.

We must avoid reproducing a thing called, for example, "cinema," "TV," or "new media" (urggh) studies, and instead do work that studies media texts and contexts, *regardless of its intellectual provenance*. Cultural labor, industry frameworks, audience experiences, and cultural policy should be integral. Institutions do not have to be arid areas of study, and the links to everyday life are real. The remarkable international actions of young people against globalization these past three years shows that they can be energized around such topics, notably the world division of labor – so let the media part of Cultural Studies "get" real, too, and perhaps even diminish the provincialism of positivistic content analysis and effects studies done within communication studies at the proverbial "large university in the [North American] mid-West."

Second, as a set of basic agenda items, we must ask some tough questions: Are the media really giving the people of the world what they want, or do they operate via a brutal form of monopoly-capitalist business practice? And is state-supported or -controlled media culture expanding the vision and availability of the good life to include the ability of a people to control its representation? Or is that culture merely a free ride for fractions of a comprador, cosmopolitan, or social-movement *bourgeoisie*? To what extent do "their" media engage national populations – for example, do the latter spend more time consuming imports than their "own" texts? The political audit we make of an audiovisual space should consider its openness, both on-camera and off, to the demographics of those inhabiting it. For example, no national medium that claims resistance to the US is worthy of endorsement if it does not attend to the needs and stories of sexual and racial minorities and women, along with class politics.

We need to view the media through twin theoretical prisms. On the one hand, they can be understood as the newest component of sovereignty, a twentieth-century addition to ideas of patrimony and rights that sits alongside such traditional topics as territory, language, history, and schooling. On the other hand, the media are a cluster of culture industries, structured in dominance by capital, the state, and the North. As such, they are subject to exactly the rent-seeking practices and exclusionary representational protocols that characterize such liaisons. In this analysis, we must keep in mind Cultural Studies' guiding maxims, of subjectivity and power.

The methods of the literary and library historian Roger Chartier are helpful guides for locating the meaning of media texts: (a) a reconstruction of "the diversity of older readings from their sparse and multiple traces"; (b) a focus on "the text itself, the object that conveys it, and the act that grasps it"; and (c) an identification of "the strategies by which authors and publishers tried to impose an orthodoxy or a prescribed reading on the text" (1989: 157, 161–3, 166). This grid from the new cultural history (a) turns away from reflectionism, which argues that a text's key meaning lies in its overt or covert capacity to capture the *Zeitgeist*; (b) rejects formalism's claim that a close reading of content can secure a definitive meaning; and (c) eschews amateur-hour humanities psychoanalysis or rat-catching sadism (a.k.a. psychology) to unlock what is inside people's heads. Instead, Chartier directs us to consider the passage of texts through space and time, noting how they accrete and attenuate meanings on their travels, as they rub up against, trope, and are themselves troped by other fictional and social texts.

To this end, the five selections contained here traverse questions of production, consumption, policy, and politics, in an international frame: (i) US–Palestinian *littérateur* Jenine Abboushi Dallal evaluates the contemporary Israeli–Palestinian conflict on the Web, a crucible of cultural and political sovereignty;

(ii) Italian semiotician Umberto Eco shows how meaning is made and transformed at all points along the circuit of television production, in a paper originally produced for a public-broadcasting consultancy in the 1960s; (iii) Canadian activist video artist Richard Fung foregrounds his Caribbean-Chinese-gay subjectivity in an account of porn; (iv) Mexican-Argentinian anthropologist Néstor García-Canclini looks at the contemporary global interplay of citizenship and consumption in media culture; and (v) US ethnographer Faye Ginsburg investigates the conditions of existence for indigenous media within "Northern" societies. This combination of the micro- and macro-, illustrating how and where meaning is made and remade, points a way forward in the project of media democracy. An internationalist Cultural Studies should require nothing less.

REFERENCES

Chartier, Roger (1989). "Texts, Printing, Readings." In *The New Cultural History*, ed. Lynn Hunt. Berkeley: University of California Press, 154–75.
Garfinkel, Harold (1992). *Studies in Ethnomethodology*. Cambridge: Polity Press.

# 16

## Hizballah's Virtual Civil Society

### Jenine Abboushi Dallal

Israel lost its protracted war in south Lebanon after 22 years of brutal occupation, from Israel's "Operation Litani" in March 1978 to its withdrawal in May 2000 (Israel continues to occupy the Shebaá farms, which Hizballah vows to liberate). Of course, it is largely the success of the resistance movement's armed struggle in south Lebanon, led by Hizballah, that inflicted cumulative loses on a scale so critical as to lead to Israeli withdrawal. Yet in the final months of occupation, south Lebanon was brought to world attention following a series of remarkable events played out in the international media. The media images displayed around the world of Birzeit University students pelting the French prime minister Lionel Jospin with stones (26 February 2000) in retaliation for calling Hizballah "terrorists" and the students' chants announcing more than solidarity ("from Birzeit to south Lebanon, one people who will not die!") were followed by declarations in Lebanon and around the Arab world that "we are all Hizballah," including that of Yousef Chahine (the famous Egyptian filmmaker), who announced in print his fervent support for Hizballah, save ideology. The lionizing of Hizballah in the Arab world also emanates from the movement's success, particularly since the late 1980s, in developing its profile as a Lebanese and Arab nationalist movement, with a Mao-esque social policy and program for social justice, and as a movement bent on political intervention and participation (in party politics). This has been achieved through increasingly sophisticated and compelling uses of the new media and information technologies.

What is new and striking is Hizballah's innovative uses of new media in adapting and inventing rhetorics, that is, images and video to address conflicting constituencies both local and international. Hizballah's multimedia spread includes *al-Ahd* newspaper as well as al-Manar television station and Nour radio station, both broadcasting from south Lebanon; but the targeting of conflicting audiences is most clear in the movement's internet presentations. Hizballah's internet strategies in particular must be thought of in terms of presentation and performance and not communication, representation, or dialogue. There are two reasons for this: first, the audiences that Hizballah solicits are no longer limited to potential supporters or sympathizers, local and international (however large this audience is, and it is large). At this point, Hizballah also addresses imagined audiences of nonrecruitable subjects: Western publics and governments, the Israelis and Israeli government, and Arabs and Lebanese with non-Muslim and non-Islamist political and religious affiliations. (Recruitable subjects are those who might support the resistance in the south, either through military participation, political support, campaigning during Lebanese parliamentary elections, or monetary contributions.)

In this sense, Hizballah's discourses, information, and images are recorded and presented but not necessarily communicated or received by targeted audiences. (In other words, it is not always clear whether there's someone on the other end of the phone line.) The second reason is that Hizballah's purpose seems not to render its movement, program, and activities more palatable for hostile or Western audiences. Rather, it seeks to stake its ground in international media as a kind of counterinformation system, which it has done from the beginning, and more recently, to present itself as a vital political player to be reckoned with. As such, Hizballah's media presentation is compelling to the extent that it circumvents the terms of collaboration by addressing Israeli and Western audiences without directly servicing their range of conventions, expectations, and values. Instead, Hizballah presents itself as the liberationist, "social radical" force that it is (the epigraph on its web page, prior to its destruction 7 October 2000 by pro-Israeli hackers, was "Hizballah – social radicals," meaning a movement for social justice) and to which spectators must largely accommodate (so the burden of political accommodation implicitly comes from the other side). In terms of straightforward dialogue, communication, or collaboration, the secretary general of the movement, Hassan Nasrallah, says of possible contacts with the United States, "We do not communicate with the Americans."

Indeed, Hizballah's web site developed into a dynamic presentation that contradicts the implicit contracts of conventional communication, in which addresser and addressee are in dialogue and in affiliation at some level. The transformation I describe in Hizballah's modes of address is evident in its complex political uses of the internet. When the web page was first constructed, it featured a revolving globe titled "Allah's world" and grisly images, such as one depicting Israeli soldiers carrying a bloody, decapitated child victim of an Israeli air raid. The new site (www.hizbollah.org and www.hizballah.org, crashed by pro-Israeli hackers last October), in contrast, is interactive and user-friendly, not defiant but confident, inventive, and bold. The home page displays a set of images and links to a selection of video clips of Hizballah's guerilla operations (and a link to a free download of RealMedia to enable visitors to readily access the clips). Another still is of Nadia al-Hussain, the anchorwoman of al-Manar (Hizballah's television station), a link to a video clip of a news report. But the first is of Nasrallah himself, a handsome still of him looking charismatic, modestly self-assured, and relaxed in front of an enormous and flamboyant floral arrangement. The web site bears out the figure Nasrallah strikes of worldly sophistication and provides links to what seems like every kind of account written about Hizballah, both hostile and balanced (there is no straightforward or crude propaganda: no need for this, it seems). Links to a host of sites with information about Hizballah, Israeli government agencies and ministries, the US State Department, *Time*, the *International Herald Tribune*, and the *Christian Science Monitor*, for example, are quickly blocked and moved, only to be hijacked again by Hizballah from another location. Another link provides an entire master's thesis on Hizballah from the University of Stockholm, with each footnote featured as a link.

This kind of openness and these confident, rogue internet exploits aim not to strictly control information, media images, and representations but instead to demonstrate the significance of Hizballah's vision and activities – military, political, and social. The aim is also to put on display the apparent frenzied Western media and governmental attempts to control representations of the resistance movement and Israeli occupation and to thwart Hizballah's project to amass, catalog, and publicize wide-ranging perspectives and information. Its web site is essentially a performance site that makes visible the terms of a media and ideological battle, an extension of the battle against Israeli occupation on the ground in south Lebanon for 22 years – the details of which largely remain hidden from view by Western media, governments, and military censors.

The mélange of discourses in Hizballah's web site has a rather extraordinary effect, with voices, images, opinions, and information coming from conflicting directions. The opening blurb defining the movement, for example, refers to Hizballah in the third person and strangely employs the (not hijacked but adapted) discourses of Western reportage and scholarship. All together, the rhetorical context seems almost too wide in this interactive web site, as if distant targeted audiences are more estimated and imagined than known. The gaps between addresser and addressee open up imaginative spaces of aesthetic, discursive, and technological innovation and, at times, strangeness and incoherency. As such, Hizballah's internet exploits amount to a new kind of media performance, one that does not and cannot aspire to the terms of conventional communication.

Hizballah has developed transnational media forms that do not conform to nor are in dialogue with dominant global cultural forms. Its virtual performance space interrupts not only national boundaries but also assumed fault lines of ideological, cultural, and political affiliations. Most recently and dramatically, Hizballah's internet ventures extended to a sophisticated cyberwar, after its site was attacked in October 2000, in support of the current Palestinian Intifada against the Israeli occupation. Since then, Hizballah developed a new internet spread on a much larger scale, with a constellation of sites, each with specific functions. The official site (www.hizballah.org) is rather flat, and the current sites that most resemble the pre-October one are the Manar television site (www.almanar.com) and the site for the Islamic Resistance Support Association (www.moqawama.net). The Manar site includes reportage clips, programming links (e.g., to children's programs), and even *anashid* (resistance songs), many recast from the Palestine Liberation

Organization days (such as Marcel Khalifeh's "Unadikum," with lyrics by the Palestinian poet Tawfiq Zayyad). These are accompanied by video clips that interchange episodes from Hizballah's struggle with prayer scenes from al-Aqsa mosque in Jerusalem and footage of Israeli repression in the occupied territories (the demolition of Palestinian homes, shot Palestinian demonstrators being carried off, etc.). The *moqawama* (resistance) site includes links to a large and diverse list of articles in Arabic, English, and French about the movement, Israel, Zionism, and the occupation. For example, the articles include excerpts from Western media, an old British Orientalist text about Zionism and the Bible, articles by leftist Israeli writers (such as Israel Shahak), and Palestinian and Lebanese historians and commentators.

But Hizballah's real virtual energy and creativity, after October 2000, is clearly directed to its ongoing cyber assaults on Israeli sites and, to a lesser extent, US sites and others. The pro-Palestinian attacks far exceed the pro-Israeli ones in number, sophistication, and damage inflicted (particularly in the commercial sector). The most spectacular were attacks on the sites of the Bank of Israel, Israeli Foreign Ministry, Tel Aviv Stock Exchange, and Israeli Knesset, all on 26 October, and the 1 November attack on the American Israeli Public Affairs Committee (the pro-Israel lobby).[1] The site was compromised by pro-Palestinian messages and the posting of credit card numbers of thousands of financial supporters of Aipac. Pro-Israeli hackers, in addition to successfully forcing down Hizballah sites, created decoy sites that mock Hizballah's occasional want of suave English prose. One such site reads, "We are sorry to say that Israel was write. The land of Israel belongs to the people of Israel" (www.hizballa.com). More adolescent pranks include a decoy club site featuring inverted Lebanese flags (with upside-down cedar trees) and a "No Coca-Cola" logo in stylized script, which is then reversed and altered to appear to read "No Muhammad, No Mecca" in Arabic and urges Muslims to boycott this *kafir* (blasphemous) soft drink (http://clubs.yahoo.com/clubs/hizballah?s).

It is important to emphasize that these new forms of transnational discourse and virtual creation grew out of the specific political context of south Lebanon, a territory relentlessly marginalized both nationally and internationally. For most of the 22-year Israeli occupation (1978–2000) and resistance to it, Western media decontextualized and dehistoricized south Lebanon, when representing it at all, and otherwise actively obscured it from view. I wish to suggest that certain geopolitical and cultural locales, such as the south Lebanon of Hizballah, present unyielding problems of representation – problems that Hizballah has confronted and successfully transformed in very interesting and effective ways. Instead of thinking of the new transnationalism in implicit terms of Western locales and models of postnational subjects as Third World exiles and emigrés in the West, I wish to foreground south Lebanon as a transnational and liminal space that has presented almost insurmountable challenges of representation.

To recognize and understand new modes of global media that are set in opposition to dominant forms of global culture (and their implicit political agendas), we must shift the location of the transnational – a counter-intuitive notion, and yet concepts of globalism and global culture all have implicit centers.

We must think of the transnational in terms of spaces like south Lebanon – a Third World hinterland long concealed from international view – and not First World metropolitan spaces (e.g., in the United States, as the anthropologist Arjun Appadurai finally encourages us to imagine in *Modernity at Large*) or subjects (not usually modeled after, say, migrant workers, but rather the comparatively privileged members of Third World intelligensia). Most important, we cannot understand opposition to dominant forms of global culture simply in terms of local resistance (the global/local binary). As Hizballah's new media informs us, our understanding of global culture must include new genres, discourses, and political trajectories. These new forms and multilingual discourses are staged from locales and by movements resistant to Western economic and political exploitation and, in terms of their political and cultural agendas, can be imagined to move on a south by south axis.

NOTE

1   See *Israeli-Palestinian Cyber Conflict* Report v2.OPR, 3 Jan. 2001, iDEFENSE.

# 17

# Towards a Semiotic Inquiry into the Television Message

## Umberto Eco

*The text which follows was a paper given at 'The Study Group for the setting-up of an interdisciplinary research model on the television audience relationship', held in Perugia by the Italian Centre for Mass Communication Studies of Perugia and by the Department of Ethnology and Cultural Anthropology of the University of Perugia (23–24 October, 1965). The text was part of an 'outline draft' proposed by the author, by Paolo Fabbri, Pierpaolo Giglioli, Franco Lumachi, Tullio Seppilli and Gilberto Tinacci-Mannelli. The text owes much to their contributions.*

*This research proposal first appeared – as we have already said – in 1965. Since then, the author has developed more fully his perspective on methodology in* La Struttura Assente, *Milano Bompiani, 1968 (cf. the revised edition* La Structure Absente, *Paris, Mercure de France, 1972, and the forthcoming* The Semiotic Threshold, *The Hague, Mouton).*

## ■ I  Introduction ■

To understand the extent of the influence of the television message on the audience, it is not enough to carry out a market research survey on the preferences of the viewers.

What we consider urgent is to understand, not: (a) what the audience likes (a piece of research which would no doubt be very useful, but totally inadequate as guidelines for an organization which is concerned with the promotion of culture rather than with commercial aims); but rather (b) **what in fact the audience gets**, both through the programmes it likes and through those it dislikes.

Issue (b) implies that a given television programme is analysed as a message in relation to which we single out: (1) the intentions of the sender; (2) the objective structure of the message (3) the reactions of the addressee to items 1 and 2.

It is clear that such research is concerned with the television outputs as **a system of signs**. As is true of every system of signs, signs and their correlations are to be seen in relation to a **sender** and an **addressee**; based on a **code** supposed to be common to both; emitted in a **context** of communication which determines the meaning of the three previous terms.

As we shall see, research on the television outputs as a system of signs does not have as its sole object the clarification of the formal aspects of the process of communication. Some definitions which follow will help us to understand how, when considering the various levels of a message, the so-called **content levels** must also be brought into consideration. In other words, **a system of signs is not only a system of sign vehicles but also a system of meanings**.

We emphasize however that we do not intend to restrict all potential research on television programmes to semiotic research. If, as we shall see, the analysis of the public comes in necessarily as a second 'checking' phase of the semiotic research, and the two are closely linked, none the less there exist enormous areas for different kinds of sociological research (for example the real influence of television on the public behaviour of a community).

Semiotic research is therefore only one aspect of research: but it is essential for answering a question which, in plain words, could be put this way: 'When I send a message, what do different individuals in different environments actually receive? Do they receive the same message? A similar one? A totally different one?'

Questions of this kind are common to all research in human communication; but they are particularly pressing in the field of mass communication.

In the past, the author of a communicative act, such as for instance the artist of the palace of Knossos in Crete, produced a message (for example the coloured stucco relief of the Prince of the Lilies) for a well defined community of receivers. Such a community would have had the same reading code as the artist: it knew for instance that the stick held in the left hand stood for a sceptre, that the flowers which appeared on the necklace, on the diadem and in the background were lilies; that the yellow-brown colour of the face meant youth; and so forth. The fact that this work could be looked at in a completely different way by the Achaean conquerors, who had different attributes to express royalty, was purely accidental to the communication itself. It was an **aberrant decoding** which the artist would never have thought of.

There were different kinds of such aberrant decodings:

(a)  first of all for foreign people **who didn't know that particular code** (as is the case for us with the Etruscan language);

(b)  for future generations, or people from a different culture who would super-impose a different code on the message; (this is what happened in the first centuries of Christianity, and even after, when a pagan image was interpreted as a holy one; the same thing would happen today to an Oriental who knew nothing about Christian iconography and so could mistake an image of St. Paul for a warrior, since by convention he carries a sword);

(c)   for different hermeneutic traditions: (the romantic interpretation of a sonnet of the Stilnovo school which would understand as erotic images what the poet conceived of as philosophical allegories);

(d)   for different cultural traditions, which understand the message as if it were based on their code rather than on that in which it was originally cast: (thus the Sixteenth Century scholar could take as a mistake in perspective the picture by a primitive conforming to the conventions of 'herring-bone' perspective rather than to Brunelleschi's rules).

We could give other examples. But, in each case, the aberrant decoding was the unexpected exception, not the rule. It was the task of philologists in the later, and more sharply critical, epochs, more discerning of historical and ethnological differences, to guarantee the correct decoding.

Things are completely different when we consider a message transmitted to an undifferentiated mass of receivers and channelled through the mass media. In this case the transmitter of the message works within a communicative code which he knows *a priori* is not shared by all the receivers. We need only read a book like *New Lives for Old* by Margaret Mead to observe how the natives of the island of Manus (Melanesia) would interpret the American films shown to them by the occupation troops. These stories of American characters, situated in a different ethical, social and psychological context, were seen in the light of the natives' own frame of reference; the consequence of all this was the birth of new type ethics which was no longer either native or western.

An example of such a situation can be given by the pun well-known to schoolchildren: /I Vitelli dei romani sono belli/. If we refer the sentence to the Italian language code, it means: 'The Roman calves are beautiful'; if we refer it to the Latin language code, it means: 'Go, Vitellus, to the war cry of the Roman god'.

This is an extreme example of something which occurs quite normally in most transmissions in the field of the mass media. The aberrant decoding (which was a mere accident with regard to the message which the Renaissance painter actually addressed to his patron and his fellow-citizens, living in an identical cultural context) **is the rule in the mass media**.


■ II   Phases of the Research ■


1.   (a)   The research will therefore, first of all, define terms such as 'code' 'message', 'levels of meaning';

(b)   It will then make a distinction between the codes of the transmitting organization and the codes of the specific technical operators (producers-authors working within the organization); analyse some messages, establishing the codes they refer to and all the references the addressees are supposed to have. This constitutes the first phase of the semiotic analysis of the message.

2.   In a second phase it will have to check, by means of field research, how the messages, previously analysed, have in fact been received in selected sample situations – and this constitutes the main contribution to research in this field.

3.   Thirdly, all the data on how they were received having been collected, these will have to be compared to the analysis previously carried out on the messages themselves to see: (a) if all the different cases of reception were justified; (b) if some receptions had shown levels of meaning in the message which had escaped notice of both our analysis and the sender; (c) if some receptions proved that given messages could be interpreted totally differently from what was intended for the communication, though none the less consistently; (d) if, in given situations, the users project freely on the message, whatever it is, the meanings they would want to find there. And so forth.

The research could lead to conclusions of different kinds. We could discover that certain messages, supposed to be especially full and penetrating for a given meaning, prove to be the least communicative.

We could discover that the community of the users has such freedom in decoding as to make the influencing power of the organization much weaker than one could have thought. Or just the opposite.

We might have to conclude that those political or cultural organizations which work towards modifying the attitudes of the sending organization, should instead concentrate on the receiving end (audience education) because this is where the battle of the meanings, of the freedom or the passivity of reception, etc, actually takes place.

We could discover that the redundancy load necessary for the unequivocal reception of a message is such that it is totally useless to carry on political or cultural struggles to put middle-length messages into programmes, while it would be better to bring a wide range of pressures to bear for the production of a few messages with a high redundancy load and, of necessity, greater length.

This research therefore develops out of the belief that what the researcher sees on the video is not necessarily what the common viewer sees. And that there is a gap between the image which appears on the video – as it has been conceived by the transmitting organization – and the images received by the viewers in many and different situations, a gap which can be filled (or possibly enlarged) only through a deeper knowledge of the mechanisms of communication.

This research derives from the persuasion that the problem of communication is an ideological problem and not merely a technical matter.

The pages which follow are concerned with the phase of semiotic research referred to as phase 1 [ (a) and (b) ] of the research as a whole. As can easily be understood, phase 2 (audience research) requires the practical application of the theoretical propositions of phase 1, that is of some sociological field work. Only after this will it be possible to pass on to phase 3 where possibly we'll arrive at some theoretical conclusions.

## ■ III Preliminary Definitions ■

### The message

We are not concerned here with the television message as an ideal content of communication, an appeal, or a group of abstract meanings.

First of all a message is a **sign object** in which the first impact is made up of sign vehicles as relations among luminous impulses on the video. The relations among these impulses could cover the whole idea of message from the purely quantitative point of view of a 'theory of information'. On the contrary, from the point of view of a 'theory of communication', the message is the objective complex of sign vehicles built on the basis of one or more codes to transmit certain meanings, and interpreted and interpretable on the basis of the same or other codes.

A message can have different **levels of meaning**: a road sign showing a child held by the hand by one of his parents, means, first of all to the layman, 'child accompanied by a parent'; but to the road user who knows a certain 'code', it means: 'with care, schoolchildren'. The same sign copied or put on canvas by a pop artist, automatically acquires more levels of meaning.

It is possible to decode each level of meaning, referring it to a specific reference table. So far we have been referring to these reference tables by the generic name of 'code'. We'll try now to define this concept better and to analyse it.

### The code

By code we mean a system of communicative conventions **paradigmatically** coupling term to term, a series of sign-vehicles to a series of semantic units (or 'meanings'), and establishing the structural organization of both systems: each of them being governed by combinatorial rules, establishing the way in which the elements (sign-vehicles and semantic units) are syntagmatically concatenated.

We mean by code, for instance, a verbal language such as English, Italian or German; visual systems, such as traffic signals, road signals, card games, etc; and so on. Verbal languages or road signal languages are mixed and complex codes, in so far as they: (a) entail two planes, the plane of expression (sign-vehicles) and the plane of content (semantic units); and (b) they allow either a paradigmatic or selective choice or a syntagmatic (combinatorial) enchainement.

Musical codes (if we assume that music does not carry any meaning – which remains to be demonstrated) have only (a) an expression plane which allows both the paradigmatic and syntagmatic possibility. So they are complex but not mixed.

Morse code has both the expression and the content plane, but allows only a paradigmatic possibility, in so far as its dots and dashes, expressing the letter of the alphabet, are to be combined according to the combinatorial rules of the verbal and written language. So it is mixed, but only paradigmatic or selective; whereas the traffic-lights code is mixed and complex because it prescribes combinatorial rules between elements endowed with meaning.

After these definitions, let us restrict the concept of code to the basic conventional systems; it is in fact with these elements that it is possible to then work out 'secondary codes' or 'sub-codes', more or less systematized, which furnish new **lexical** elements or give a different connotation to lexical elements contained in the basic code.

The word /disegno/ (design) and the word /leggi/ (law) have definite meanings in Italian: but the combination /disegno di leggi/ (design for a law; bill) – which is a metaphor in itself – is not understandable by making reference to the meanings of the two nouns; to be understood it must be referred to a specialised jargon which gives to this syntagm a specific meaning. This jargon, which works in relation to the language-code, becomes then a specific subcode. A listener can have the code but not the subcode. A recent inquiry carried out by the RAI [*RADIO TELEVISIONE ITALIANA* (Italian Radio-Television State Network)] on the reception of the News has brought to light a situation of this kind.

In the reception of a message, the singling out of the right code and lexicon is made easier through the **communication context** in which the message is sent. The context, 'parliamentary news' makes easier the singling out of the right lexicon to decode the syntagm 'design for a law'.

We must emphasize that the concepts of code and subcode do not make reference only to linguistic conventions but to every possible field of conventional references: the conventions at the basis of gastronomic choices (conventions of palate-taste) form a code, more or less systematised, which can vary in every culture.

The statement /Pork steaks are good and nourishing, so they must be eaten, provided they belong to us/, uttered in the context of the present western culture, has one meaning if interpreted according to the English language code; and if it is then referred to: (a) the most accepted system of medical-sanitary-dietetic rules; (b) the system of social rules known as the 'criminal code'. If it is uttered in the context of a Muslim country, where pork is considered impure and is forbidden, the statement, even if it did not mean something different, would nevertheless be interpreted as an instigation to crime rather than an obvious statement. Its semantic-syntactic dimension would not change, but its **pragmatic dimension** would.

The various codes and subcodes, on which the various levels of meaning of a given message are based, can be differentially systematic and flexible. The conventional system of palate-taste is rather rigid (you can't mix sugar and salt). The conventional system of aesthetic-erotic-taste is more flexible: two different feminine ideals such as Audrey Hepburn and Jayne Mansfield can be both equally desirable and beautiful, by convention.

The use of a subcode generally transforms the process of **denotation** into a process of **connotation**. The expression /winged-boy/, in a poetic-erotic context, must be referred to a mythological reference table (mythological subcode), where it not only **denotes** a winged child but **connotes** 'Eros'. The context, without the form of the message being altered, requires for its decoding the use of a supplementary lexicon which gives the message another level of significance. The man without the mythological lexicon, or who doesn't understand from the context that he needs it, will interpret the message as the indication of a paradoxical situation. Or he might use the wrong subcode (the Biblical one, for example) and decode the message in an aberrant way, as if it were a seraph. (We would like to make clear that such examples are not theoretical, but have their exact equivalents in the reception of television messages).

Having given these definitions, let's try and single out a series of codes and subcodes which occur in the production and in the interpretation of a television message and on which different levels of meaning of the messages are based.

## ■ IV   The System of Codes and Subcodes which Occur in the Definition of a Television Message ■

The television message, in as much as it is formed of images, musical sounds or noises, and verbal emissions, can be considered as based on three basic codes from which then derive dependent subcodes:

1. **The Iconic Code**, which includes also:
    A.   iconologic subcode
    B.   aesthetic subcode
    C.   erotic subcode (these three at the level of selection of the images)
    D.   montage subcode (at the level of combination of the images)
2. **The Linguistic Code**, which includes also:
    A.   emotional subcodes
    B.   syntagms with an acquired stylistic value
    C.   syntagms with a conventional value

Let us now describe in detail these various codes and subcodes.

## ■ 1.   The Iconic Code ■

This is based on the processes of visual perception (which are in turn based on a code if perception is, as we here assume, not the photographic recording of a preconstructed presumed reality, but an interaction between the stimuli of a given field and the perceptual schemes, learned and imposed by the subject).

Once it has been perceived on the video, according to the usual perceptual process, a shape can be taken either as **denoting itself** (and this is the case of a circular or triangular shape; of a black line against a white background, etc.) or as **denoting another shape** which the receiver recognizes as an element of his physical and cultural reality (a tree, a letter of the alphabet). To this second type of denotation we can refer back the first, in as much as the perception on the video of a circular shape can be understood as the denotation of a shape of a 'circle'. In this sense the code is always **figurative** or **iconic**; I perceive certain shapes on the video as images of other already known shapes, if the first ones have structural elements similar to the second ones, and if these are enough to be considered their 'reduced model'. It can happen that the receiver sees on the video images of unknown realities (a native who sees for the first time the image of an aircraft). In this case he will perceive the image not on the basis of the figurative code, but on the basis of the common perceptual code, as a form in itself which denotes itself and no more (in the same way in which the same native, hearing the English word /house/ and not having the code to decipher it, takes it merely in the form of sound). You can on the contrary have the case that the receiver, perceiving a form without a meaning, and guessing from the context that it should have one, is able to deduce the code from the message itself. Thus, if I see the image of a strange unknown piece of machinery, I understand that it is the sign vehicle of something, and I include this something in the framework of my knowledge; from that moment onwards I apply the correspondence expected from the code. As the iconic sign has many peculiarities in common with the object it denotes (unlike the linguistic sign which is conventional), communication through images proves more valid and immediate than that through words because it allows the receiver to refer at once to the unknown referent. Such a process can only take place if the whole context of images helps me to fill the gap: I can recognize the image of a chain of molecules if the context of the other images, or a verbal hint do not help me to decode it (in this case decoding becomes more like crypto-analysis, as in reading messages in an unknown code).

Let us leave out of the discussion the possible existence of a code of the collective subconscious. If it exists, in as much as it is subconscious, it escapes the characteristics of conventionality typical of any code. We are interested in it only if it comes out empirically at the level of the decoding analysis (the receivers experience certain forms as a stimulus sufficient for a series of projections, identifications, etc). It will be studied under a different aspect when considering item 1.A (iconological subcode).

## A.  The iconological subcode

Certain images connote something else by tradition. A little old man bent and smiling, and a happy child running towards him with outstretched arms **connotes** a 'grandfather'. A flag perceived as white, red and green (or guessed as such in a black and white context, with for example a 'bersagliere' near it) denotes 'Italian flag' according to a specific international subcode, and in some contexts it could denote 'Italian spirit'. A geometrical form which reproduces a Greek temple on a reduced scale can connote 'harmonious beauty, Hellenism'.

Certain images can be included in this section, which by convention connote something on the basis of unconscious tendencies which have in turn determined the iconological choice: for example, the image of water connotes 'tranquillity' by convention. But in the process of connotation there intervene also unconscious elements which the iconological tradition has accepted and legitimated at the cultural level (in such cases the image could work at the unconscious level even for those who would not be aware of its conventional connotation).

## B.   The aesthetic subcode

Determined by the tradition of taste. A certain representation is 'beautiful' by tradition. A certain **topos** acquires a certain meaning according to aesthetic conventions (for example the end-shot of a lone man walking off down a road into the distance, seen after Chaplin, has a definite connotation).

## C.   The erotic subcode

Brigitte Bardot is beautiful and desirable. A fat woman is not. These two value judgements are based upon conventions, that is upon a historical-sociological sedimentation of taste, accepted by the whole community. This subcode can mingle under many of its aspects with the aesthetic code: a certain type of woman is ridiculous if considered in terms of a comic tradition. A man wearing a black patch on one eye becomes erotically interesting if considered in the iconological subcode which connotes him as a 'pirate', and in an aesthetic subcode which connotes the pirate as 'romantic'.

## D.   The montage subcode

Whereas the preceding subcodes offered a paradigm of available images, this one provides a series of ready-made syntagms. It sets combinatory rules for the images in accordance with the cinematographic and television rules, both in the composition of the shots and in their sequence. The native who is not used to film language will not understand the fact that the person who appears in a reverse shot is the same as the person he has seen before. In the same way he will not understand the connecting function of a 'fondu'. For example, with the help of the montage subcode, it is possible to understand by means of a succession of isolated shots the **meeting** between a child and an old man, while with the help of the iconological subcode it is possible to understand the **grandfather–grandchild relationship**.

## ■ 2.   The Linguistic Code ■

This is the code of the language which is used. All the verbal formulations of a transmission make reference to it. It may not be known in its available totality and its combinatorial complexity. Certain rural communities may have it in a reduced form. Its subcodes are:

## A. *Specialised jargons*

(an enormous range, which includes scientific, political, legal, professional, etc. jargons). The above mentioned RAI inquiry on the reception and comprehension of the News referred to this level of messages. They are mostly lexical patrimonies.

## B. *Stylistic syntagms*

They are equivalent to the aesthetic subcodes at the level of the iconic code. They connote social class, artistic attitude, etc. They include the figures of speech. The various emotional connotations (irony, fear, suspicion, etc.) must make reference to them. One ascertains in relation to them whether a message offends the basic linguistic code, by mistake or intentionally. Other typological connotations related to the linguistic style are included in this code.

# ■ 3. The Sound Code ■

This includes all the sounds of the musical range and the combinatory rules of the tonal grammar; it includes the noises as well, in as much as they are distinct from the sounds and relatable iconically to already known noises. Whereas sounds denote only themselves (they have no semantic weight) noises can have imitative value (imitation of already known noises). Timbres can also have imitative value (bell timbre, drum timbre). In this case noises and timbres are sound images which denote noises and timbres already heard in reality.

## A. *Emotional subcodes*

(for example, 'thriller' music is such by convention).

## B. *Stylistic syntagms*

There is a musical typology in accordance with which a melody is 'country', 'classic', 'wild', etc. Also different types of connotations occur, often with either an emotional or an ideological value. Music linked to definite ideologies.

## C. *Syntagms with a conventional value*

'Attention!', 'To the mess', 'Charge!' Silence. The Drums. They have acquired other connotative values: the charge as 'fatherland, war, valour, etc.'.

### *The framework of cultural reference*

Codes and subcodes are applied to the message in the light of a general framework of cultural references, which constitutes the receiver's patrimony of knowledge: his ideological, ethical, religious standpoints, his psychological attitudes, his tastes, his value systems, etc.

Likewise, the transmitting organization and the technical interpreter codify the message on the basis of their own framework of cultural reference: they select the meanings they want to communicate, why, for whom, and how they should be arranged by means of the different levels of the message.

In this way, both the organization and the technical interpreter take for granted in the receiver a framework of cultural references. They can believe it to be similar to their own, or different; and in this case they will adjust the message according to the gap, or even try to fill it up, stimulating by means of the message a modification of the receiver's framework of cultural references.

This framework, which we could call ideology (using the word in its broadest sense), constitutes a system of assumptions and expectations which interacts with the message and determines the selection of the codes with which to read it.

For example the statement /he is a rebel/ is immediately understood in its denotation value in the light of the language code; but it will acquire, in the first place, a specific connotation if it is uttered in a communication context which relates it to a child or to an irregular fighter – or to someone who challenges the established order; secondly, it acquires more connotations if, in the case of the child, either the ideology of the sender or that of the addressee provides an authoritarian or a liberal pedagogy; or if, in the second case, the ideology of the sender or that of the addressee considers as positive either conforming to the established order or else resisting power.

Likewise, the iconological topos /negro beaten up by white man/ connotes normally 'colonialism', while the topos /black man rapes white woman/ connotes 'racism'; but the two messages can only appear repulsive or thrilling when related to the ideological framework either of the emitter or of the receiver, and only then connote 'a praiseworthy act' or 'a shameful act'. It can happen that a message supposed to connote a 'shameful act' is received as connoting a 'praiseworthy act'.

The cultural reference framework, allows us, therefore to single out the codes and subcodes. A boy wearing a 'blouson noir' can connote 'an antisocial person' in one iconological subcode, 'an unconventional hero' in another. The choice of criterion is always guided by the ideological framework.

We have then an **ideological** system (system of meanings pre-existent to the message) interacting with a system of **rhetorical** devices (codes and subcodes) which regulates the relationship of sign vehicles to meanings in the message. These elements together can be defined as a **significance system**.

The semiological analysis of the message must therefore, delineate the 'significance system' which the message as a whole connotes, and provides the definition of:

(a)   the significance system of the transmitting organization and the significance system that it assumes in the addressee.

(b)   the significance system of the technical interpreter (which can be different from that of the organization) and the significance system that he assumes in the addressee.

What the semiotic analysis cannot define is the actual system of every single addressee. This can only be discovered through field research on the audience.

Thus the semiotic inquiry is only one aspect of research into the process of communication. It can make clear the intentions of the emitter, but not the way the message has been received.


## ■ V   The Message ■

In the finished message, codes and subcodes interact with the receiver's framework of reference and make the different kinds of meaning reverberate one upon another. In as much as the message, at the level of the sign vehicles and meanings, proves to be harmoniously composed and appropriate at all other levels, it acquires artistic quality and comes to have an aesthetic function.

The aesthetic function of a message occurs when the message makes evident, first of all, its own structure as its primary meaning; in other words it is **self-focusing** (that is, when it is organized not only to communicate something but it is 'formed to form').

In the course of the semiotic inquiry one will therefore distinguish:

(a)   messages with an aesthetic quality, where the sign vehicles and the meanings are closely related to each other.
(b)   'non-articulated' messages which enable the message to be analysed separately at each level.
(c)   messages which are supposed to perform a function different from the aesthetic function (according to the following table) and which therefore appear coordinated enough for that purpose, but are not self-focusing.

Likewise, in the course of the analysis of the audience one will distinguish:

(a)   types of reception in which the message is considered as a purely aesthetic object and is understood to have been so intended.
(b)   types of reception in which the message is considered as performing other functions and is understood to have been so intended.

Accepting this, let us examine the six different functions of a message proposed by Roman Jakobson. These functions seldom appear separately; generally they all exist at one time in one message but with one predominating:

## 1. Referential function

The message 'points to' something. It occurs in all the normal processes of denotation and connotation, even if the intended reference tends to restrict to the minimum the semantic field which exists around a sign and to focus the receiver's attention on one single referent.

## 2. Emotive function

The message tends to stimulate emotions (association of ideas, projections, identifications, etc.).

## 3. Imperative function

The message aims to command something, to persuade to an action.

## 4. Phatic function, or contact function

The message aims at establishing a psychological contact with the receiver (the most common form is the expression of greeting).

## 5. Metalinguistic function

The message speaks about another message or about itself.

## 6. Aesthetic function

The message, even if it performs other functions, aims primarily to be considered as such, as a system harmonious at all levels and for all functions.

Each time these different functions are performed, different levels of meaning are stressed. An advertising message can denote 'man, woman, children around a table with a saucepan and a box of X cubes', secondly it can connote 'happiness and serenity' – and in this it performs the **reference, emotional, and imperative functions together** (it could also perform an **aesthetic** function). As a matter of fact, it is very likely for the addressee to interpret it in the light of the first three functions and to leave the fourth one out of consideration. But a more guarded and sensitive addressee could be not persuaded that he must buy X cubes and yet appreciate the technical perfection of the shot and of the characterization.

## The structure of the message

Performing some functions and involving various levels of meaning, the various messages structure themselves in different ways (from a maximum of coherence to a maximum of disarticulation) bringing about a communication dialectic between

**probability** and **improbability** (that is between **the obvious** and **the new** – and ultimately, in a more technical phraseology, between **meaning** and **information**).

The more a message **conforms** to the rules of the significance system which it is based on, the more probable and obvious it is.

The more a message **contravenes** the rules of the significance system which it is based on, the more improbable and new it becomes.

An obvious message communicates a definite meaning which everybody can understand (it communicates what I already know).

An improbable message communicates a load of information (what I do not yet know) which, beyond certain bounds of improbability, becomes mere disorder and 'noise'.

In the message therefore it is necessary to establish **a dialectic between the obvious and the new**.

The message can prove obvious or improbable either in relation to the codes and subcodes which it is based on, or in relation to the receiver's framework of cultural references.

A message like /I say you must love your mother/ conforms both to the rules of the English language code, and to the ethical rules of the reference table of most of the addressees. A message like /I say you must hate your mother/ conforms to the rules of the English language code, but contravenes the ethical dictates of the cultural framework of the addressees and in this it carries a high rate of information with it. As everybody can see, the information, or the improbability, is connected to an element of unexpectedness which upsets the system of expectations of the addressees. The message can simply upset the system of linguistic expectations (in relation to the language code and the stylistic code). If you advertise: /Me like soops!/ (in a sort of Dogpatch dialect) instead of /I prefer this brand of canned soup . . . / you violate the system of linguistic expectations. You do not violate the system of ideological expectations, because the addressee expects during a commercial, that the products will be praised. Thus a message like /Me hate soop!/would be very improbable both in relation to the ideological and to the linguistic framework.

It is useful to note how a message like this has proved informative only the first time it has been received; afterwards an element of repetition has come into it, rendering it obvious. This repetitive element is a sort of **redundance** which is concerned with the iteration over time. The most common form of redundance, on the contrary, acts within a single message, and is used to wrap up the meaning in repetitions so as to make it more and more acceptable. For example: /I say that this brand of canned soup is really good, that is palatable and nutritious/. The message is new and improbable as long as it is based on a minimum of redundance. However, a high rate of improbability runs the risk of not being received and therefore the message must be tempered in small degree with conventionalities, commonplaces, and must be reiterated through a redundance form over time.

One of the problems in message-coding is the balance between the obvious and the new. How few conventionalities are necessary to communicate a piece of information (as a new thing?): this is a problem which both the semiological analysis of the message and the audience survey must come to terms with. Only field surveys of the public will establish whether there is a good enough balance in the television message.

The problem of the relationship between the new and the obvious is only formal in as much as probability and improbability are values which leave out of consideration what is actually communicated and are concerned with the formal structuring of the message. But because they are values which are concerned also with the cultural framework, their efficacy goes beyond the technical aspects of the communication sphere and reaches the more comprehensive sphere of the television communication as ideological matter.

An element of information, in so far as it goes against the accepted rules of a general system of significance, puts the addressee in a state of autonomy, enables him to make an effort of interpretation and obliges him to reconsider his codes and reference tables. Even a piece of political news (which in so far as it is unexpected, is 'informative') such as /The President of the USA has visited Moscow/ obliges the addressee to modify his own experience of American foreign policy. A complex message, such as the TV serial *The Captain's Daughter*, if it presents in a completely new way the character of the rebel Cossack, obliges the receiver (whose cultural framework would persuade him that he who rebels against power is wicked) to modify his own system of ethico-psychological expectations. Information and the improbable are therefore **creative**, in different degrees. Commonplaces, conventionalities, probabilities, on the contrary, work to confirm the reference tables and codes of the receiver.

## ■ VI  Conclusions ■

What is the redundance load below which the 'new' cannot be received, and beyond which it shades into the 'obvious'?

How much does 'novelty' at the level of the sign vehicles imply 'novelty' at the level of the meanings? How much can a message, highly conventional in its conformity to the codes, channel new meanings, able to modify the reference tables of the receivers?

To these and other problems semiotic analysis can provide answers, working out a wider typology of codes and of reference tables; analysing certain messages and delineating their levels and communication structure, in terms of a dialectic between probability and improbability, at the level of the codes as well as of the reference tables. It will be the task of audience research to establish how wide is the gap between the intentions of the emitter and the interpretation of the addressee.

Only at this point will it be possible for us to understand something of the homogeneity of the significance systems of the emitter and of the addressee and therefore something about the real communication effectiveness of the television message in a given social context.

This higher awareness can be of concern to those who have the problem of sender, as well as to those who have an interest in the addressees as a community to be organized and made conscious.

Should this awareness be lacking, the television message will remain an abstract hypothesis of communication, the intention of which one could perhaps guess, but never know in the final reality. In this case the political and cultural operations carried out **on** (or **against**) the organization and **on** the user would also remain abstract.

**translation by Paola Splendore**

## POST-SCRIPTUM 1972

This Report was presented at a time when Italian Radiotelevision's 'Servizio Opinioni' (Audience Survey) – and, indeed, sociological research in general – were more concerned with a sort of Trendex-like polls which aimed to test how many people followed and appreciated a given programme. In the last few years, however (partly as a consequence of the impact of our Report), RAI has begun to test, in a more complex way, not only what the audience likes, but what it understands, comparing the message transmitted with the message received. At present, I am directing a research programme, sponsored by the 'Servizio Programmi Sperimentali' of the RAI which will try to discover how much the **temporal structure** of the discourse of a television programme (presence or absence of flashbacks, high or low stress in causal connections, etc.) determines the 'fit' between the emitted and the received message. In my *La Struttura Assente*, I proposed, also, the possibility of a 'semiotic guerilla warfare'; the gap between the transmitted and the received message is not only an aberration, which needs to be reduced – it also can be developed so as to broaden the receiver's freedom. In political activity it is not indispensable to change a given message: it would be enough (or, perhaps better) to change the attitude of the audience, so as to induce a different decoding of the message – or in order to isolate the intentions of the transmitter and thus to criticize them. In this sense, semiotics becomes not only a cognitive discipline, which enables us to understand how communication works, but also a pragmatic activity, intended to transform communication processes. Methodologically speaking, this project imposes another reading of (from the semiotic point of view) the sociological hypothesis put forward by Merton and Lazarsfeld about the function of group leaders and the face-to-face reinforcement of the mass media message. **U.E.**

# 18

# Looking for My Penis:
# The Eroticized Asian in Gay
# Video Porn

## Richard Fung

Several scientists have begun to examine the relation between personality and human reproductive behaviour from a gene-based evolutionary perspective.... In this vein we reported a study of racial difference in sexual restraint such that Orientals > whites > blacks. Restraint was indexed in numerous ways, having in common a lowered allocation of bodily energy to sexual functioning. We found the same racial pattern occurred on gamete production (dizygotic birthing frequency per 100: Mongoloids, 4; Caucasoids, 8; Negroids, 16), intercourse frequencies (premarital, marital, extramarital), developmental precocity (age at first intercourse, age at first pregnancy, number of pregnancies), primary sexual characteristics (size of penis, vagina, testis, ovaries), secondary sexual characteristics (salient voice, muscularity, buttocks, breasts), and biologic control of behaviour (periodicity of sexual response, predictability of life history from onset of puberty), as well as in androgen levels and sexual attitudes.[1]

This passage from the *Journal of Research in Personality* was written by University of Western Ontario psychologist Philippe Rushton, who enjoys considerable controversy in Canadian academic circles and in the popular media. His thesis, articulated throughout his work, appropriates biological studies of the continuum of reproductive strategies of oysters through to chimpanzees and posits that degree of "sexuality" – interpreted as penis and vagina size, frequency of intercourse, buttock and lip size – correlates positively with criminality and sociopathic behavior and inversely with intelligence, health, and longevity. Rushton sees race as *the* determining factor and places East Asians (Rushton uses the word *Orientals*) on one end of the spectrum and blacks on the other. Since whites fall squarely in the middle, the position of perfect balance, there is no need for analysis, and they remain free of scrutiny.

Notwithstanding its profound scientific shortcomings, Rushton's work serves as an excellent articulation of a dominant discourse on race and sexuality in Western society – a system of ideas and reciprocal practices that originated in Europe simultaneously with (some argue as a conscious justification for[2]) colonial expansion and slavery. In the nineteenth century these ideas took on a scientific gloss with social Darwinism and eugenics. Now they reappear, somewhat altered, in psychology journals from the likes of Rushton. It is important to add that these ideas have also permeated the global popular consciousness. Anyone who has been exposed to Western television or advertising images, which is much of the world, will have absorbed this particular constellation of stereotyping and racial hierarchy. In Trinidad in the 1960s, on the outer reaches of the empire, everyone in my schoolyard was thoroughly versed in these "truths" about the races.

Historically, most organizing against racism has concentrated on fighting discrimination that stems from the intelligence–social behavior variable assumed by Rushton's scale. Discrimination based on perceived intellectual ability does, after all, have direct ramifications in terms of education and employment, and therefore for survival. Until recently, issues of gender and sexuality remained a low priority for those who claimed to speak for the communities.[3] But antiracist strategies that fail to subvert the race–gender status quo are of seriously limited value. Racism cannot be narrowly defined in terms of race hatred. Race is a factor in even our most intimate relationships.

The contemporary construction of race and sex as exemplified by Rushton has endowed black people, both men and women, with a threatening hypersexuality. Asians, on the other hand, are collectively seen as undersexed.[4] But here I want to make some crucial distinctions. First, in North America, stereotyping has focused almost exclusively on what recent colonial language designates as "Orientals" – that is East and Southeast Asian peoples – as opposed to the "Orientalism" discussed by Edward Said, which concerns the Middle East. This current, popular usage is based more on a perception of similar physical features – black hair, "slanted" eyes, high cheek bones, and so on – than through a reference to common cultural traits. South Asians, people whose backgrounds are in the Indian subcontinent and Sri Lanka, hardly figure at all in North American popular representations, and those few images are ostensibly devoid of sexual connotation.[5]

Second, within the totalizing stereotype of the "Oriental," there are competing and sometimes contradictory sexual associations based on nationality. So, for example, a person could be seen as Japanese and somewhat kinky, or Filipino and "available." The very same person could also be seen as "Oriental" and therefore sexless. In addition, the racial hierarchy revamped by Rushton is itself in tension with an earlier and only partially eclipsed depiction of *all* Asians as having an undisciplined and dangerous libido. I am referring to the writings of the early European explorers and missionaries, but also to antimiscegenation laws and such specific legislation as the 1912 Saskatchewan law that barred white women from employment in Chinese-owned businesses.

Finally, East Asian women figure differently from men both in reality and in representation. In "Lotus Blossoms Don't Bleed," Renee Tajima points out that in Hollywood films:

> There are two basic types: the Lotus Blossom Baby (a.k.a. China Doll, Geisha Girl, shy Polynesian beauty, et al.) and the Dragon Lady (Fu Manchu's various female relations, prostitutes, devious madames). . . . Asian women in film are, for the most part, passive figures who exist to serve men – as love interests for white men (re: Lotus Blossoms) or as partners in crime for men of their own kind (re: Dragon Ladies).[6]

Further:

> Dutiful creatures that they are, Asian women are often assigned the task of expendability in a situation of illicit love. . . . Noticeably lacking is the portrayal of love relationships between Asian women and Asian men, particularly as lead characters.[7]

Because of their supposed passivity and sexual compliance, Asian women have been fetishized in dominant representation, and there is a large and growing body of literature by Asian women on the oppressiveness of these images. Asian men, however – at least since Sessue Hayakawa, who made a Hollywood career in the 1920s of representing the Asian man as sexual threat[8] – have been consigned to one of two categories: the egghead/wimp, or – in what may be analogous to the lotus blossom–dragon lady dichotomy – the kung fu master/ninja/samurai. He is sometimes dangerous, sometimes friendly, but almost always characterized by a desexualized Zen asceticism. So whereas, as Fanon tells us, "the Negro is eclipsed. He is turned into a penis. He *is* a penis,"[9] the Asian man is defined by a striking absence down there. And if Asian men have no sexuality, how can we have homosexuality?

Even as recently as the early 1980s, I remember having to prove my queer credentials before being admitted with other Asian men into a Toronto gay club. I do not believe it was a question of a color barrier. Rather, my friends and I felt that the doorman was genuinely unsure about our sexual orientation. We also felt that had we been white and dressed similarly, our entrance would have been automatic.[10]

Although a motto for the lesbian and gay movements has been "we are everywhere," Asians are largely absent from the images produced by both the political and the commercial sectors of the mainstream gay and lesbian communities. From the earliest articulation of the Asian gay and lesbian movements, a principal concern has therefore been visibility. In political organizing, the demand for a voice, or rather the demand to be heard, has largely been responded to by the problematic practice of "minority" representation on panels and boards.[11] But since racism is a question of power and not of numbers, this strategy has often led to a dead-end tokenistic integration, failing to address the real imbalances.

Creating a space for Asian gay and lesbian representation has meant, among other things, deepening an understanding of what is at stake for Asians in coming out publicly.[12] As is the case for many other people of color and especially immigrants, our families and our ethnic communities are a rare source of affirmation in a racist society. In coming out, we risk (or feel that we risk) losing this support, though the ever-growing organizations of lesbian and gay Asians have worked against this process of cultural exile. In my own experience, the existence of a gay Asian community broke down the cultural schizophrenia in which I related on the one hand to a heterosexual family that affirmed my ethnic culture and, on the other, to a gay community that was predominantly white. Knowing that there was support also helped me come out to my family and further bridge the gap.

If we look at commercial gay sexual representation, it appears that the antiracist movements have had little impact: the images of men and male beauty are still of *white* men and *white* male beauty. These are the standards against which we compare both ourselves and often our brothers – Asian, black, native, and Latino.[13] Although other people's rejection (or fetishization) of us according to the established racial hierarchies may be experienced as oppressive, we are not necessarily moved to scrutinize our own desire and its relationship to the hegemonic image of the white man.[14]

In my lifelong vocation of looking for my penis, trying to fill in the visual void, I have come across only a handful of primary and secondary references to Asian male sexuality in North American representation. Even in my own video work, the stress has been on deconstructing sexual representation and only marginally on creating erotica. So I was very excited at the discovery of a Vietnamese American working in gay porn.

Having acted in six videotapes, Sum Yung Mahn is perhaps the only Asian to qualify as a gay porn "star." Variously known as Brad Troung or Sam or Sum Yung Mahn, he has worked for a number of different production studios. All of the tapes in which he appears are distributed through International Wavelength, a San Francisco-based mail order company whose catalog entries feature Asians in American, Thai, and Japanese productions. According to the owner of International Wavelength, about 90 percent of the Asian tapes are bought by white men, and the remaining 10 percent are purchased by Asians. But the number of Asian buyers is growing.

In examining Sum Yung Mahn's work, it is important to recognize the different strategies used for fitting an Asian actor into the traditionally white world of gay porn and how the terms of entry are determined by the perceived demands of an intended audience. Three tapes, each geared toward a specific erotic interest, illustrate these strategies.

**Below the Belt** (1985, directed by Philip St. John, California Dream Machine Productions), like most porn tapes, has an episodic structure. All the sequences involve the students and *sensei* of an all-male karate *dojo*. The authenticity of the setting is proclaimed with the opening shots of a gym full of *gi*-clad, serious-faced young men going through their weapons exercises. Each of the main actors is introduced in turn; with the exception of the teacher, who has dark hair, all fit into the current porn conventions of Aryan, blond, shaved, good looks.[15] Moreover, since Sum Yung Mahn is not even listed in the opening credits, we can surmise that this tape is not targeted to an audience with any particular erotic interest in Asian men. Most gay video porn exclusively uses white actors; those tapes having the least bit of racial integration are pitched to the speciality market through outlets such as International Wavelength.[16] This visual apartheid stems, I assume, from an erroneous perception that the sexual appetites of gay men are exclusive and unchangeable.

A Karate dojo offers a rich opportunity to introduce Asian actors. One might imagine it as the gay Orientalist's dream project. But given the intended audience for this video, the erotic appeal of the dojo, except for the costumes and a few misplaced props (Taiwanese and Korean flags for a Japanese art form?) are completely appropriated into a white world.

The tape's action occurs in a gym, in the students' apartments, and in a garden. The one scene with Sum Yung Mahn is a dream sequence. Two students, Robbie and Stevie, are sitting in a locker room. Robbie confesses that he has been having strange dreams about Greg, their teacher. Cut to the dream sequence, which is coded by clouds of green smoke. Robbie is wearing a red headband with black markings suggesting script (if indeed they belong to an Asian language, they are not the Japanese or Chinese characters that one would expect). He is trapped in an elaborate snare. Enter a character in a black *ninja* mask, wielding a *nanchaku*. Robbie narrates: "I knew this evil samurai would kill me." The masked figure is menacingly running the nanchaku chain under Robbie's genitals when Greg, the teacher, appears and disposes of him. Robbie explains to Stevie in the locker room: "I knew that I owed him my life, and I knew I had to please him [long pause] in any way that he wanted." During that pause we cut back to the dream. Amid more puffs of smoke, Greg, carrying a man in his arms, approaches a low platform. Although Greg's back is toward the camera, we can see that the man is wearing the red headband that identifies him as Robbie. As Greg lays him down, we see that Robbie has "turned Japanese"! It's Sum Yung Mahn.

Greg fucks Sum Yung Mahn, who is always face down. The scene constructs anal intercourse for the Asian Robbie as an act of submission, not of pleasure: unlike other scenes of anal intercourse in the tape, for example, there is no dubbed dialogue on the order of "Oh yeah...fuck me harder!" but merely ambiguous groans. Without coming, Greg leaves. A group of (white) men wearing Japanese outfits encircle the platform, and Asian Robbie, or "the Oriental boy," as he is listed in the final credits, turns to lie on his back. He sucks a cock, licks someone's balls. The other men come all over his body; he comes. The final shot of the sequence zooms in to a close-up of Sum Yung Mahn's headband, which dissolves to a similar close-up of Robbie wearing the same headband, emphasizing that the two actors represent one character.

We now cut back to the locker room. Robbie's story has made Stevie horny. He reaches into Robbie's pants, pulls out his penis, and sex follows. In his Asian manifestation, Robbie is fucked and sucks others off (Greek passive/French active/bottom). His passivity is pronounced, and he is never shown other than prone. As a white man, his role is completely reversed: he is at first sucked off by Stevie, and then he fucks him (Greek active/French passive/top). Neither of Robbie's manifestations veers from his prescribed role.

To a greater extent than most other gay porn tapes, *Below the Belt* is directly about power. The hierarchical dojo setting is milked for its evocation of dominance and submission. With the exception of one very romantic sequence midway through the tape, most of the actors stick to their defined roles of top or bottom. Sex, especially anal sex, as punishment is a recurrent image. In this genre of gay pornography, the role-playing in the dream sequence is perfectly apt. What is significant, however, is how race figures into the equation. In a tape that appropriates emblems of Asian power (karate), the only place for a real Asian actor is as a caricature of passivity. Sum Yung Mahn does not portray an Asian, but rather the literalization of a metaphor, so that by being passive. Robbie actually becomes "Oriental." At a more practical level, the device of the dream also allows the producers to introduce an element of the mysterious, the exotic, without disrupting the racial status quo of the rest of the tape. Even in the dream sequence, Sum Yung Mahn is at the center of the frame as spectacle, having minimal physical involvement with the men around him. Although the sequence ends with his climax, he exists for the pleasure of others.

Richard Dyer, writing about gay porn, states that

> although the pleasure of anal sex (that is, of being anally fucked) is represented, the narrative is never organized around the desire to be fucked, but around the desire to ejaculate (whether or not following from anal intercourse). Thus, although at a level of public representation gay men may be thought of as deviant and disruptive of masculine norms because we assert the pleasure of being fucked and the eroticism of the anus, in our pornography this takes a back seat.[17]

Although Tom Waugh's amendment to this argument – that anal pleasure is represented in individual sequences[18] – also holds true for *Below the Belt*, as a whole the power of the penis and the pleasure of ejaculation are clearly the narrative's organizing principles. As with the vast majority of North American tapes featuring Asians, the problem is not the representation of anal pleasure per se, but rather that the narratives privilege the penis while always assigning the Asian the role of bottom; Asian and anus are conflated. In the case of Sum Yung Mahn, being fucked may well be his personal sexual preference. But the fact remains that there are very few occasions in North American video porn in which an Asian fucks a white man, so few, in fact, that International Wavelength promotes the tape *Studio X* (1986) with the blurb "Sum Yung Mahn makes history as the first Asian who fucks a non-Asian."[19]

Although I agree with Waugh that in gay as opposed to straight porn "the spectator's positions in relation to the representations are open and in flux,"[20] this observation applies only when all the participants are white. Race introduces another dimension that may serve to close down some of this mobility. This is not to suggest that the experience of gay men of color with this kind of sexual representation is the same as that of heterosexual women with regard to the gendered gaze of straight porn. For one thing, Asian gay men are men. We can therefore physically experience the pleasures depicted on the screen, since we too have erections and ejaculations and can experience anal penetration. A shifting identification may occur despite the racially defined roles, and most gay Asian men in North America are used to obtaining pleasure from all-white pornography. This, of course, goes hand in hand with many problems of self-image and sexual identity. Still, I have been struck by the unanimity with which gay Asian men I have met, from all over this continent as well as from Asia, immediately identify and resist these representations. Whenever I mention the topic of Asian actors in American porn, the first question I am asked is whether the Asian is simply shown getting fucked.

**Asian Knights** (1985, directed by Ed Sung, William Richhe Productions), the second tape I want to consider, has an Asian producer-director and a predominantly Asian cast. In its first scenario, two Asian men, Brad and Rick, are seeing a white psychiatrist because they are unable to have sex with each other:

> RICK: We never have sex with other Asians. We usually have sex with Caucasian guys.
> COUNSELOR: Have you had the opportunity to have sex together?
> RICK: Yes, a coupla times, but we never get going.

Homophobia, like other forms of oppression, is seldom dealt with in gay video porn. With the exception of safe sex tapes that attempt a rare blend of the pedagogical with the pornographic, social or political issues are not generally associated with the erotic. It is therefore unusual to see one of the favored discussion topics for gay Asian consciousness-raising groups employed as a sex fantasy in *Asian Knights*. The desexualized image of Asian men that I have described has seriously affected our relationships with one another, and often gay Asian men find it difficult to see each other beyond the terms of platonic friendship or competition, to consider other Asian men as lovers.

True to the conventions of porn, minimal counseling from the psychiatrist convinces Rick and Brad to shed their clothes. Immediately sprouting erections, they proceed to have sex. But what appears to be an assertion of gay Asian desire is quickly derailed. As Brad and Rick make love on the couch, the camera cross-cuts to the psychiatrist looking on from an armchair. The rhetoric of the editing suggests that we are observing the two Asian men from his point of view. Soon the white man takes off his clothes and joins in. He immediately takes up a position at the center of the action – and at the center of the frame. What appeared to be a "conversion fantasy" for gay Asian desire was merely a ruse. Brad and Rick's temporary mutual absorption really occurs to establish the superior sexual draw of the white psychiatrist, a stand-in for the white male viewer, who is the real sexual subject of the tape. And the question of Asian–Asian desire, though presented as the main narrative force of the sequence, is deflected, or rather reframed from a white perspective.

Sex between the two Asian men in this sequence can be related somewhat to heterosexual sex in some gay porn films, such as those produced by the Gage brothers. In *Heatstroke* (1982), for example, sex with a woman is used to establish the authenticity of the straight man who is about to be seduced into gay sex. It dramatizes the significance of the conversion from the sanctioned object of desire, underscoring the power of the gay man to incite desire in his socially defined superior. It is also tied up with the fantasies of (female) virginity and conquest in Judeo-Christian and other patriarchal societies. The therapy-session sequence of *Asian Knights* also suggests parallels to representations of lesbians in straight porn, representations that are not meant to eroticize women loving women, but rather to titillate and empower the sexual ego of the heterosexual male viewer.

*Asian Knights* is organized to sell representations of Asians to white men. Unlike Sum Yung Mahn in *Below the Belt*, the actors are therefore more expressive and sexually assertive, as often the seducers as the seduced. But though the roles shift during the predominantly oral sex, the Asians remain passive in anal intercourse, except that they are now shown to want it! How much this assertion of agency represents a step forward remains a question.

Even in the one sequence of *Asian Knights* in which the Asian actor fucks the white man, the scenario privileges the pleasure of the white man over that of the Asian. The sequence begins with the Asian reading a magazine. When the white man (played by porn star Eric Stryker) returns home from a hard day at the office, the waiting Asian asks how his day went, undresses him (even taking off his socks), and proceeds to massage his back.[21] The Asian man acts the role of the mythologized geisha or "the good wife" as fantasized in the mail-order bride business. And, in fact, the "house boy" is one of the most persistent white fantasies about Asian men. The fantasy is also a reality in many Asian countries where economic imperialism gives foreigners, whatever their race, the pick of handsome men in financial need. The accompanying cultural imperialism grants status to those Asians with white lovers. White men who for various reasons, especially age, are deemed unattractive in their own countries, suddenly find themselves elevated and desired.

From the opening shot of painted lotus blossoms on a screen to the shot of a Japanese garden that separates the episodes, from the Chinese pop music to the chinoiserie in the apartment, there is a conscious attempt in *Asian Knights* to evoke a particular atmosphere.[22] Self-conscious "Oriental" signifiers are part and parcel of a colonial fantasy – and reality – that empowers one kind of gay man over another. Though I have known Asian men in dependent relations with older, wealthier white men, as an erotic fantasy the house boy scenario tends to work one way. I know of no scenarios of Asian men and white house boys. It is not the representation of the fantasy that offends, or even the fantasy itself, rather the uniformity with which these narratives reappear and the uncomfortable relationship they have to real social conditions.

**International Skin** (1985, directed by William Richhe, N'wayvo Richhe Productions), as its name suggests, features a Latino, a black man, Sum Yung Mahn, and a number of white actors. Unlike the other tapes I have discussed, there are no "Oriental" devices. And although Sum Yung Mahn and all the men of color are inevitably fucked (without reciprocating), there is mutual sexual engagement between the white and nonwhite characters.

In this tape Sum Yung Mahn is Brad, a film student making a movie for his class. Brad is the narrator, and the film begins with a self-reflexive "head and shoulders" shot of Sum Yung Mahn explaining the scenario. The film we are watching supposedly represents Brad's point of view. But here again the tape is not targeted to black, Asian, or Latino men; though Brad introduces all of these men as his friends, no two men of color ever meet on screen. Men of color are not invited to participate in the internationlism that is being sold, except through identification with white characters. This tape illustrates how an agenda of integration becomes problematic if it frames the issue solely in terms of black–white, Asian–white mixing: it perpetuates a system of white-centeredness.

The gay Asian viewer is not constructed as sexual subject in any of this work – not on the screen, not as a viewer. I may find Sum Yung Mahn attractive, I may desire his body, but I am always aware that he is not meant for me. I may lust after Eric Stryker and imagine myself as the Asian who is having sex with him, but the role the Asian plays in the scene with him is demeaning. It is not that there is anything wrong with the image of servitude per se, but rather that it is one of the few fantasy scenarios in which we figure, and we are always in the role of servant.

Are there then no pleasures for an Asian viewer? The answer to this question is extremely complex. There is first of all no essential Asian viewer. The race of the person viewing says nothing about how race figures in his or her own desires. Uniracial white representations in porn may not in themselves present a problem in addressing many gay Asian men's desires. But the issue is not simply that porn may deny pleasures to some gay Asian men. We also need to examine what role the pleasure of porn plays in securing a consensus about race and desirability that ultimately works to our disadvantage.

Though the sequences I have focused on in the preceding examples are those in which the discourses about Asian sexuality are most clearly articulated, they do not define the totality of depiction in these tapes. Much of the time the actors merely reproduce or attempt to reproduce the conventions of pornography. The fact that, with the exception of Sum Yung Mahn, they rarely succeed – because of their body type, because Midwestern-cowboy-porn dialect with Vietnamese intonation is just a bit incongruous, because they groan or gyrate just a bit too much – more than anything brings home the relative rigidity of the genre's codes. There is little seamlessness here. There are times, however, when the actors appear neither as simulated whites nor as symbolic others. There are several moments in *International Skin*, for example, in which the focus shifts from the genitals to hands caressing a body; these moments feel to me more "genuine." I do not mean this in the sense of an essential Asian sexuality, but rather a moment is captured in which the actor stops pretending. He does not stop acting, but he stops pretending to be a white porn star. I find myself focusing on moments like these, in which the racist ideology of the text seems to be temporarily suspended or rather eclipsed by the erotic power of the moment.

In "Pornography and the Doubleness of Sex for Women," Joanna Russ writes

Sex is ecstatic, autonomous and lovely for women. Sex is violent, dangerous and unpleasant for women. I don't mean a dichotomy (i.e., two kinds of women or even two kinds of sex) but rather a continuum in which no one's experience is wholly positive or negative.[23]

Gay Asian men are men and therefore not normally victims of the rape, incest, or other sexual harassment to which Russ is referring. However, there is a kind of doubleness, of ambivalence, in the way that Asian men experience contemporary North American gay communities. The "ghetto," the mainstream gay movement, can be a place of freedom and sexual identity. But it is also a site of racial, cultural, *and* sexual alienation sometimes more pronounced than that in straight society. For me sex is a source of pleasure, but also a site of humiliation and pain. Released from the social constraints against expressing overt racism in public, the intimacy of sex can provide my (non-Asian) partner an opening for letting me know my place – sometimes literally, as when after we come, he turns over and asks where I come from.[24] Most gay Asian men I know have similar experiences.

This is just one reality that differentiates the experiences and therefore the political priorities of gay Asians and, I think, other gay men of color from those of white men. For one thing we cannot afford to take a libertarian approach. Porn can be an active agent in representing *and* reproducing a sex–race status quo. We cannot attain a healthy alliance without coming to terms with these differences.

The barriers that impede pornography from providing representations of Asian men that are erotic and politically palatable (as opposed to correct) are similar to those that inhibit the Asian documentary, the Asian feature, the Asian experimental film and videotape. We are seen as too peripheral, not commercially viable – not the general audience. *Looking for Langston* (1988),[25] which is the first film I have seen that affirms rather than appropriates the sexuality of black gay men, was produced under exceptional economic circumstances that freed it from the constraints of the marketplace.[26] Should we call for an independent gay Asian pornography? Perhaps I am, in a utopian sort of way, though I feel that the problems in North America's porn conventions are manifold and go beyond the question of race. There is such a limited vision of what constitutes the erotic.

In Canada, the major debate about race and representation has shifted from an emphasis on the image to a discussion of appropriation and control of production and distribution – who gets to produce the work. But as we have seen in the case of *Asian Knights*, the race of the producer is no automatic guarantee of "consciousness" about these issues or of a different product. Much depends on who is constructed as the audience for the work. In any case, it is not surprising that under capitalism, finding my penis may ultimately be a matter of dollars and cents.

ACKNOWLEDGMENTS

I would like to thank Tim McCaskell and Helen Lee for their ongoing criticism and comments, as well as Jeff Nunokawa and Douglas Crimp for their invaluable suggestions in converting the original spoken presentation into a written text. Finally, I would like to extend my gratitude to Bad Object-Choices for inviting me to participate in "How Do I Look?"

# NOTES

1   J. Philippe Rushton and Anthony F. Bogaert, University of Western Ontario, "Race versus Social Class Difference in Sexual Behaviour: A Follow-up Test of the r/K Dimension," *Journal of Research in Personality* 22 (1988), 259.

2   See Eric Williams, *Capitalism and Slavery* (New York: Capricorn, 1966).

3   Feminists of color have long pointed out that racism is phrased differently for men and women. Nevertheless, since it is usually heterosexual (and often middle-class) males whose voices are validated by the power structure, it is their interests that are taken up as "representing" the communities. See Barbara Smith, "Toward a Black Feminist Criticism," in *All the Women Are White, All the Blacks Are Men, But Some of Us Are Brave: Black Women's Studies* (Old Westbury, NY: The Feminist Press, 1982), 162.

4   The mainstream "leadership" within Asian communities often colludes with the myth of the model minority and the reassuring desexualization of Asian people.

5   In Britain, however, more race–sex stereotypes of South Asians exist. Led by artists such as Pratibha Parmar, Sunil Gupta, and Hanif Kureishi, there is also a growing and already significant body of work by South Asians themselves which takes up questions of sexuality.

6   Renee Tajima, "Lotus Blossoms Don't Bleed: Images of Asian Women," *Anthologies of Asian American Film and Video* (New York: A distribution project of Third World Newsreel, 1984), 28.

7   Ibid., 29.

8   See Stephen Gong, "Zen Warrior of the Celluloid (Silent) Years: The Art of Sessue Hayakawa," *Bridge* 8, no. 2 (Winter 1982–3), 37–41.

9   Frantz Fanon, *Black Skin White Masks* (London: Paladin, 1970), 120. For a reconsideration of this statement in the light of contemporary black gay issues, see Kobena Mercer, "Imaging the Black Man's Sex," in *Photography/Politics: Two*, ed. Pat Holland, Jo Spence, and Simon Watney (London: Comedia/Methuen, 1987); reprinted in *Male Order: Unwrapping Masculinity*, ed. Rowena Chapman and Jonathan Rutherford (London: Lawrence and Wishart, 1988), 141.

10  I do not think that this could happen in today's Toronto, which now has the second largest Chinese community on the continent. Perhaps it would not have happened in San Francisco. But I still believe that there is an onus on gay Asians and other gay people of color to prove our homosexuality.

11  The term *minority* is misleading. Racism is not a matter of numbers but of power. This is especially clear in situations where people of color constitute actual majorities, as in most former European colonies. At the same time, I feel that none of the current terms are really satisfactory and that too much time spent on the politics of "naming" can in the end be diversionary.

12  To organize effectively with lesbian and gay Asians, we must reject self-righteous condemnation of "closetedness" and see coming out more as a process or a goal, rather than as a prerequisite for participation in the movement.

13  Racism is available to be used by anyone. The conclusion that – because racism = power + prejudice – only white people can be racist is Eurocentric and simply wrong. Individuals have varying degrees and different sources of power, depending on the given moment in a shifting context. This does not contradict the fact that, in contemporary North American society, racism is generally organized around white supremacy.

14  From simple observation, I feel safe in saying that most gay Asian men in North America hold white men as their idealized sexual partners. However, I am not trying to construct an argument for determinism, and there are a number of outstanding problems that are not easily answered by current analyses of power. What of the experience of Asians who are attracted to men of color, including other Asians? What about white men who prefer Asians sexually? How and to what extent is desire articulated in terms of race as opposed to body type or other attributes? To what extent is sexual attraction exclusive and/or changeable, and can it be consciously programmed? These questions are all politically loaded, as they parallel and impact the debates between essentialists and social constructionists on the nature of homosexuality itself. They are also emotionally charged, in that sexual choice involving race has been a basis for moral judgment.

15  See Richard Dyer, *Heavenly Bodies: Film Stars and Society* (New York: St. Martin's Press, 1986). In his chapter on Marilyn Monroe, Dyer writes extensively on the relationship between blondness, whiteness, and desirability.

16  Print porn is somewhat more racially integrated, as are the new safe sex tapes – by the Gay Men's Health Crisis, for example – produced in a political and pedagogical rather than a commercial context.

17  Richard Dyer, "Coming to Terms," *Jump Cut*, no. 30 (March 1985), 28.

18  Tom Waugh, "Men's Pornography, Gay vs. Straight," *Jump Cut*, no. 30 (March 1985), 31.

19  *International Wavelength News* 2, no. 1 (January 1991).

20  Tom Waugh, "Men's Pornography, Gay vs. Straight," 33.

21  It seems to me that the undressing here is organized around the pleasure of the white man in being served. This is in contrast to the undressing scenes in, say, James Bond films, in which the narrative is organized around undressing as an act of revealing the woman's body, an indicator of sexual conquest.

22  Interestingly, the gay video porn from Japan and Thailand that I have seen has none of this Oriental coding. Asianness is not taken up as a sign but is taken for granted as a setting for the narrative.

23  Joanna Russ, "Pornography and the Doubleness of Sex for Women," *Jump Cut*, no. 32 (April 1986), 39.

24  Though this is a common enough question in our postcolonial, urban environments, when asked of Asians it often reveals two agendas: first, the assumption that all Asians are newly arrived immigrants and, second, a fascination with difference and sameness. Although we (Asians) all supposedly look alike, there are specific characteristics and stereotypes associated with each particular ethnic group. The inability to tell us apart underlies the inscrutability attributed to Asians. This "inscrutability" took on sadly ridiculous proportions when during World War II the Chinese were issued badges so that white Canadians could distinguish them from "the enemy."

25  Isaac Julien (director), *Looking for Langston* (United Kingdom: Sankofa Film and Video, 1988).

26  For more on the origins of the black film and video workshops in Britain, see Jim Pines, "The Cultural Context of Black British Cinema," in *Blackframes: Critical Perspectives on Black Independent Cinema*, ed. Mybe B. Cham and Claire Andrade-Watkins (Cambridge, Mass.: MIT Press, 1988), 26.

# 19

# From the Public to the Private: The "Americanization" of Spectators

## Néstor García-Canclini

The future of multiculturality depends not only on policies of national and international integration. The habits and tastes of consumers condition their capacity to become citizens. Their exercise of citizenship is shaped in relation to artistic and communicational referents, and to their preferred entertainment and forms of information. Let's examine how cultural practices and preferences are being restructured in relation to the transformations taking place in the film, television, and video industries.

The crises of the film industry have almost always been related to technological changes. The appearance of the talkies, cinemascope, and competition from television were some of the innovations that cast doubt on the cinematographic industry and language. In the past decade, the questions about the continued existence of cinema are really about diminishing audiences.

Thousands of movie houses have shut down in all Latin American countries, as in other continents. Movie theaters have become video game parlors, evangelical churches, or parking lots in Montevideo, São Paulo, Bogotá, and Mexico City. In a country such as Argentina, with a strong cinematographic tradition, seven provinces no longer have movie houses.[1]

Nevertheless, more films are seen now than in any prior period. But they are watched at home, on television, or on video. Of 16 million Mexican homes, more than 13 million have a television set and more than 5 million own a video player. There are 9,589 video clubs distributed throughout the country, including popular areas and small peasant villages.

The dissemination of video and the growth of its profits are the greatest in the United States. Income from the rental and sale of videos went from $3.6 million in

1985 to $10.3 million in 1991. It is not usual for a cultural industry to triple its earnings in six years. These figures increased in the same period in which audiences vacated movie houses. In 1989, these constituted 80 percent of film revenues; currently they provide barely 25 percent.

In what ways is it different to view film when it passes from the movie house to home projection? This chapter, which synthesizes several research findings in four Mexican cities,[2] highlights four transformations:

1. A new relation between the real and the imaginary.
2. A different positioning of the phenomenon of film between the public (urban cultural consumption) and the private (reception of entertainment at home).
3. A reorientation of cinema in relation to national and transnational culture.
4. The emergence of multimedia spectators, who relate to film in various ways – in movie houses, or via television, video, and entertainment magazines – and who consider it part of a broad and diversified system of audiovisual programs.

## ■ Intimacy in a Crowd ■

The film viewer is an invention of the twentieth century. We can trace its origins in Robertson's camera obscura, in nineteenth-century experiments with photography and X-rays, and, of course, in Lumière's, Félix Mesquich's, and others' first projections, when people still did not know how to look at those "animated scenes," and the public, on seeing the locomotive approaching on the screen, frantically rushed out.[3]

Only with the construction of permanent movie theaters, from 1905 on, did there begin to emerge habits of perception and attendance, a new distinction between the real and the imaginary, another sense of verisimilitude, of solitude and collective ritual. People learned to be film viewers, to go to dark auditoriums periodically, to choose to sit at the proper distance from the screen, to enjoy movies by themselves or in the company of others, to pass from the intimacy of the projection to the exchange of impressions and gregarious celebration of the stars. Films thus came to be selected by the names of the actors or the directors, to be situated in film history or among the ads in culture and entertainment sections.

What remains of all this when movies are viewed on television, in one's illuminated living room, interrupted by ads, the telephone, or other members of the family? What becomes of cinema when we no longer go to the movie house but to the video club, or when we watch whatever appears on television?

Video is appealing above all because it costs more or less the same to rent as to buy a movie ticket. Moreover, each video is watched by several people, and viewing it at home eliminates extra expenses (carfare, food), the dangers of the city, the lines, and other inconveniences. Older moviegoers, accustomed to the theaters, may lament the loss of the spectacle and the poor quality of the television screen, but video viewers welcome the possibility of operating the projection themselves, stopping it, going back over scenes, and above all not having to put up with commercial breaks.[4] It is logical for broad sectors of the viewing public to prefer home entertainment instead of having to travel throughout the city. But for film – a traditional stimulus for going out and using the city, where urban themes are generated – to become a reason for staying in the privacy of the home means that a radical change has taken place in the relations between cinema and public life.

Film widened its communicative action thanks to television and video. But this expansion transformed the productive process and the ways of viewing films. Instead of going to the theater to seek, in Carlos Monsiváis's words, "intimacy in a crowd," a devoted community gathered in the dark silence in front of the screen, television and video encourage the restricted sociability of the couple or the family and a diminished attention to the film. They permit distractions and even enable other activities while one follows the story line. Also changed are the ways of getting information on what to watch, on how to develop tastes and locate them within the history of film and the history of the nation.

## ■ From the National to the Transnational ■

The success of what is known as Mexican cinema's "golden age" – approximately 1940 to 1954 – was due to the creativity of several filmmakers (Emilio Fernández, Luis Buñuel, Ismael Rodríguez) and the presence of actors capable of becoming idols (Pedro Infante, Jorge Negrete, María Félix, and Dolores del Río, among others). Also important was the convergence of entrepreneurs and state support, and a distribution system that reached almost all of Latin America. These factors combined with the capacity of the cinematic narratives and characters to represent Mexican national culture and contribute to the sentimental education of the masses who migrated to the cities in those years.

The mass media contributed to the formation of cultural citizenship. Through radio and cinema, Carlos Monsiváis says, Mexicans learned to recognize themselves within an integrated whole, above ethnic and regional divisions. Ways of acting and speaking, tastes and codes of customs, disconnected or in conflict in the past, were brought together in the language with which films represented the emergence of the masses, legitimizing their styles of feeling and thinking.[5] The continental expansion of Mexican cinema, like that of Argentine cinema, during World War II and subsequent years was aided by Hollywood's abandonment of the Latin American market as it concentrated on producing propaganda films for US troops stationed in Europe. "We had a privileged position," observes Ignacio Durán Loera, "because we had greater access to raw materials – acetate and celluloid – which in Argentina were very difficult to obtain in time of war."[6]

This favorable international situation was key for the success of Mexican cinema. But its contribution to the modernization and massification of national culture was also a key factor in the development of this art industry. Cinema was not merely a prosperous commercial activity; it became that because it also played a major, imaginative role in the renewal and growth of society.

Mexican cinema's role in shaping a mass audiovisual culture and a symbolic language to express social process lost its effectiveness because of a combination of factors. The most important were the reduction of state support; the closing off of the Cuban market with the revolution and the contraction of South American markets due to economic difficulties; the rapid expansion of television as a new agent of entertainment and conditioner of the social imaginary; competition from US cinema, which, revamped thematically and formally and strengthened by large investments and greater effectivity in distribution, gained control of international markets.[7]

To these processes one should also add the changes in the relation between film and national culture when its principal means of diffusion are television and video. On the one hand, these new means enable a more balanced distribution throughout the national territory of what is shown in Mexico City. In contrast with the situation in museums, libraries, and theaters, most of which are concentrated in the capital, the dissemination of TV channels and video clubs throughout the country, with homogeneous programming designed by monopolies, makes it possible for viewers in large and small cities to have access to almost the same cinematographic repertoire. This "egalitarian democratization" is heightened by the designers of television programming and video club catalogs who cater to tastes based on the premise that everybody in the country resembles one another.

But such a "national unification" achieved by the mass distribution of cinema is, in a way, paradoxical. In contrast to education and cultural policies that throughout this century sought to construct a common Mexican identity on the basis of national symbols, of actors, objects, and customs issued from the nation, almost 80 percent of the films available on video are of US origin. European cultures with which Mexico has long had relations, particularly the Spanish, as well as Latin American cultures, with which we share a common language, history, and political projects, are represented in less than 10 percent of available film on television and video. Mexican film available in video clubs also fails to reach 10 percent of the total and the inventory virtually excludes films that document contemporary conflicts. When we consider all this together with the preponderance of North American film, it is logical, as Déborah Holtz observes, that video viewers should relate to cinema with the assumption that "reality resides elsewhere."[8]

The predominance of one foreign film industry can be even more disconcerting on taking into account that corporations linked to US capital, Multivisión and Blockbuster, control minority stakes in television and video markets. The hegemonic role of Televisa in these media suggests that the unilateral audiovisual repertoire is solely of its own making and conforms to its cultural objectives. Televisa's interests in Spanish, Latin American, and US Hispanic markets are evident in only a few entertainment programs (*Siempre en domingo*), news magazines (*Eco*), and short-lived series of Mexican films or spectacles (*Cadena de las Américas*). We can assume that most viewers' preferences for US pictures and the overriding popularity of North American stars (Kevin Costner, Arnold Schwarzenegger, Tom Cruise, Sylvester Stallone, Mel Gibson), confirmed by a survey we conducted in Mexico, are determined in part by the bias of the repertoire and the near absence of other national cinemas.

What do video viewers think of Mexican cinema? They see it through the comparative framework established by US film. This is borne out not only by the predominance of US movies and actors mentioned in surveys, but also by development of aesthetic taste, the value placed on spectacle and types of stars, and of course on the skewed proportion of programming. US film is thought of as the norm precisely because US product has a 60–85 percent market share in all venues: movie houses, television, and video. Blockbuster video outlets make a glaring classificatory slip that bears this out. The majority of their racks are classified by "genre" (action, suspense, comedy, children, etc.), represented almost exclusively by US films, with a few Mexican exceptions. In a corner, we find a few dozen European, Latin American, and perhaps a couple of Asian films, all united under the category "foreign film." US film does not appear in this section. Is it therefore not a national cinema? Is it then film pure and simple?

There is a significant difference between male and female viewers of national and US cinemas. Majorities of both genders prefer US film, but because men are most attracted to action films (thrillers, adventure, and espionage films), their answers on surveys show a higher preference for North American movies. Women, on the other hand, show a preference for "sentimental" and "family" dramas, which leans them more toward Mexican cinema. In any case, for both men and women the relation between the national and the North American is negotiated symbolically through action and social violence, while Mexican cinema – where these modes are less prevalent – provides scenarios for the portrayal of sentimental and family conflicts.

That Mexican film occupies such a low standing in movie theaters and video clubs does not mean, at least so far as our data indicate, that there is an equally low interest in and value placed on it by film, TV, and video viewers throughout the country. A considerable percentage of those interviewed, when asked what they did not find in video clubs, mentioned Mexican films. Although it is clear that the majority prefer US films, it is not the case that all sectors judge Mexican film in the same way, nor show preference for the same films. The 25 to 40 age group showed greater interest in some new national films such as *La tarea* and *Like Water for Chocolate*. Others that can be included in this category, *Danzón*, *Rojo amanecer*, and *La mujer de Benjamín*, on the other hand, sparked the interest of those in the 45 to 60 age group, because of the greater correspondence between the events presented and the age of the protagonists (e.g., those who lived through the student demonstrations of 1968). The percentage of new films mentioned in our question regarding the most recently rented video, also indicates that national cinema is not neglected by the majority. Nor is this interest limited to the golden age of Mexican cinema. What is evident from the declared preferences is that there is not only *one* national film public. Diverse eras, genres, styles, with different proportions of entertainment and artistic pursuit, find faithful or recently interested publics. The question that arises here is whether current cinematographic policies, in which the aesthetic dimension of films is subordinated to ratings, can take into consideration this multicultural diversity of publics.

## ■ Film, Television, and Radio: Multimedia Spectators ■

Up to 20 years ago, films could recoup their cost through national and international movie-theater chains. As we noted in the preceding chapter, now they have to venture into many other venues to attempt to make good on their investment: national television and that of other countries, cable, parabolic antenna, and video broadcasts. In Mexico and other countries, these latter circuits are usually under the control of transnational corporations. As cinema becomes more dependent on new technologies, it is increasingly difficult to produce film and video in Latin American countries, where investment in these areas has fallen off in recent years, as a result of reductions in public spending and the lack of interest in providing incentives for innovation in cutting-edge technologies.

Video has become, in less than a decade, the most diffused venue for viewing films. Those who go to movie theaters once a week or every two weeks rent two or three films on video per week. Add to them those who have lost the custom of going to movie theaters, or who shrink from traversing the city to a theater showing the film they want to see, and the masses who never had the custom to go to movie theaters and nevertheless see from two to four films per week on video or television.

The study we carried out in Mexico City provides a profile of these new spectators. Sixty percent of video club clients are less than 30 years old. Only those who grew up watching video have a "natural" relation to the television screen and are less bothered by it than those who go to movie theaters. Video, however, is popular not only among the young. More video viewers have children than those who go to the movies, which implies that they stay at home because of family obligations. Many of those who watch videos at home also go to the movies, but for them the family promenade or friendly gathering is as important as the choice of film. People go out not only to enjoy the film but also for the rituals before and after the showing.

The moviegoer, that invention of the beginning of the century, has been changing in the past decade. Surveys that ask about moviegoers' and video viewers' knowledge of film history show that the majority of both groups do not know the names of the directors. Almost all moviegoers leave the theater before the credits. In video clubs, arrangement of films by genre, with little or no information about the directors, contrasts with the saliency of actors' names and "intense" (dramatic, sexual, violent) scenes represented on the box covers. This suggests that these businesses have no interest in locating the films in cinema history or in relation to their "authors." Whereas access to the movie house is usually guided by consulting newspaper listings and one's own viewing history, which often involves having to go to other parts of the city, video viewers go to rental clubs near their home without making prior decisions.

One of the most notable differences between cinephiles and videophiles is that the relation of the latter with film takes place in a present without memory. Video clubs in Mexico City consider films older than 18 months to be of no interest, and for them to remain on exhibition that long they must turn a good profit. Video renters' dissatisfaction almost never refers to the lack of films from other periods or from countries other than the United States, but rather to the lack of sufficient copies of films that have recently premiered. What is important is not the film itself, nor the director, but the most recent film available, especially if it is an "action-adventure," the most requested genre in video clubs.

> Immediacy and the value of the instantaneous are reflected in what young videophiles seek. The number of images that succeed each other by fractions of a second are the beginning of a challenge to time that does not correspond to time. It is the illusion of a transgression emanating from the rhythm that this fictitious reality imposes. The pleasure of expectation thus modifies the way of seeing. This survey confirms that the new image consumers are addicted to rhythm more than they are to plots. (Déborah Holtz).

The proliferation of video clubs throughout the city and the uniformity of available repertoires make it possible for consumption to be a neighborhood activity. Everyone has all the available titles near their home. In the Federal District there is one movie theater for every 62,868 inhabitants, and some districts have fewer than five theaters. There is, on the other hand, one video club for every 4,500 inhabitants (Déborah Holtz).

If the passage from movie houses to video clubs means fewer trips throughout the city, the selection of films to view on television, as is well known, is even more passive. Pay-per-view is available only for the smallest minorities, and almost all TV viewers have their options limited by the four or six films that the channels air during the evening. People do not see what they prefer, but they prefer what they are offered.[9]

## ■ Diversification of Tastes and Citizenship ■

Let me review two of the conclusions pertinent to the analysis of cultural policy that ensue from our research on viewers' aesthetics: on the one hand, the preponderance of spectacular action over other dramatic and narrative modalities; on the other, the possibility that national cinemas can subsist in the midst of the transnational and multimedia reorganization of audiovisual production and markets.

1. It is thought-provoking that cinematographic and televisual repertoires, as well as audience tastes, should give precedence to an aesthetics of action in an age that has seen the demise of the heroic phase of political movements. Politics has often put a premium on action: the antitheoretical pragmatism or "militance" of political parties, the exaltation of everyday heroism and of "what-can-be-demonstrated-in-concrete-practice" in social movements, and, of course, the extreme subordination of politics in guerrilla hyperactivism. The failure of many armed groups, the decline of militant cadre in political parties, the displacement of political *action* by *acting* in the media, and the institutionalization of social movements all led to a shift from radical heroism to negotiation and other mediated forms of resolving power struggles.

Of all these changes, the transference of political staging to the electronic media is the process that best preserves in a depoliticized mode what there is of action in politics. After all, we are speaking of theatrical action. Let's not forget that politics, from solemn parliamentary speeches to everyday rituals in which hierarchies are acknowledged, has always had a theatrical side. But televisual spectacularization accentuates it, and thus modifies political action.

Fernando Collor, Carlos Menem, and Alberto Fujimori are some of the leaders who in recent years have cultivated this change. Their publicity campaigns, both preelectorally and while in power, cast them in the role of sports figures and thus constructed their public images. Menem has sought to display his omnipotence by playing soccer and tennis, piloting airplanes, driving race cars, and going out with exuberant models all in the same day. Renato Janine Ribeiro has said that Collor's image crafters transmitted "an impression of efficiency, energy and youth, suggesting to public opinion that through his physical energy and will the president could conquer the problems of Brazil, from inflation to underdevelopment.[10]" It is not political action itself (an even less reasoned argument) that is offered to resolve social problems, but rather, brute force. The mass-media political hero bases himself more on brute force than on his intelligence or ability. Of all the examples of this semantic shift in what can be understood as political action – or its convergence with media action – there is none better than George Bush's welcoming of Brazil's president at the White House with the sobriquet "Indiana Collor." Ribeiro recalls Bush's curious interpretation of the *Indiana Jones* films:

> Spielberg's character is, above all, an archaeologist, an intellectual. The filmmaker's strategy to make him likable, even if he is in the service of knowledge (a cause that generally makes characters hateful to mass audiences), was to have him carry out his quest with the utmost energy, giving him a kind of second existence. Neither Bush nor Collor, however, showed any interest in research, or in Indiana's knowledge-producing dimension. Moreover, the "heroic" phase of Collor's presidency was marked by a strong and explicit aversion to the academic, scientific, and cultural sphere. In sum: *Indiana Jones* is, in Bush's universe of references, a hero of force rather than knowledge.[11]

The denouement of the transubstantiation of political action into communicational action is not always so felicitous as in the impeachment of Collor in Brazil. Ribeiro concludes his analysis by arguing that the destruction of the public sphere provoked by these heroic presidents can boomerang on them when citizens and media ally to restore the dignity of the public. However, Latin America's recent history suggests that there are numerous situations in which societies accept the transubstantiation and prefer a political scene in which political heroes resemble those of film and television.

The majority consensus held on to by the governments of Menem and Fujimori seems to be based on the complacency with their omnipotent exhibitionism and their capacity to confirm it through financial stability. If we take into consideration the signs of productive stagnation, the increase in unemployment and poverty, one cannot but think that the overwhelming vote for these figures is not due to their power to transform their countries and generate well-being, but to that more modest power that consists of overcoming the panic produced in periods of hyperinflation and instability. Correlatively, the recent electoral failures of opposition parties are interpreted in Argentina, Peru, Mexico, and other countries as an expression of fear of what might be lost if there are changes, if the economy is destabilized, if inflation returns, and it is not possible to continue enjoying certain commodities. The fact that these interpretations are linked to worries about consumption shows the degree to which it is operative in shaping citizen opinions. Consequently, it is not so surprising that the media should play an important role in generating consensus or that the frivolous actions that politicians use to demonstrate their power should take on a positive meaning.

The consensus achieved among majorities by politicians who act against their interests has been explained by reference to the evasive effects of the media, whose model is the preponderance of alienating entertainment over consciousness-raising information in North American culture industries. I prefer another hypothesis: the correspondence (rather than mechanical determination) of, on the one hand, narrative structures, the rise of spectacular action, and the fascination with a memoryless present in film and television, and, on the other, an anecdotal rather than argumentative vision in political discourse, as well as a media-constructed political heroism that enables leaders to show their power not through their intervention in the structural changes of history but in the mininarration of feats of virtuosity linked to corporal ability and consumption. In this same vein, we can correlate the declining attendance at places of public cultural consumption (movie houses, theaters) and the retreat to the home for electronic entertainment with declining public forms for the exercise of citizenship.

2. I should like to explore whether it is possible for national cinemas, as integral parts of the cultures of each country, to survive under the current conditions in audiovisual markets. To answer this question implies knowing what possibilities there are for Latin American cinemas to reformulate their projects so as to insert themselves in the new relations among financing sources, producers, directors, distributors, promoters, and, of course, the diverse types of audiences, some of whom go to movie theaters, but most of whom devote their evenings and weekends to video rentals and their television screens.

Nevertheless, we can report that audience surveys do not condemn movie theaters to the ash can of history. Although surveys show that the youngest, the unmarried, and those over 50 prefer to see films there, movie theaters continue to be attractive for all ages and social strata. The desire to see films in movie houses surpasses 50 percent of viewers in the four Mexican cities studied, but the percentage of those who actually attend theaters does not rise higher than 36 percent. Practice would be closer to desire, the surveyed explain, if movie-house projections were of better quality, if they were more diversified, if the theaters were cleaned and renovated periodically, and if complementary services (parking, drinks, etc.) made attendance more pleasant.

The mass success of some Mexican pictures, such as *Sólo con tu pareja*, that deal with topics of interest to youth, or of films that relate national history to everyday intimacy, as, for example, *Like Water for Chocolate, Rojo amanecer*, and other similar films, indicates that Mexican pictures that transcend the stereotypes of commercial success can find an audience. Our research confirmed that quality films can attract a relatively broad, albeit selective, public predisposed to relate to demanding films and capable of establishing a more complex relation with them than mere entertainment. A good example are the Muestras Internacionales de Cine [International Film Festivals] in Mexico City, which have an excellent public resonance.

Nevertheless, the most salient feature in the restructuring of markets is the segmentation of publics. On the one hand, we have an elite with knowledge of film history who attends the Cineteca, annual festivals, cine clubs, and views television film showings with few commercial breaks (channels 11 and 22); on the other, an enormous audience that is not even aware that there are options other than Televisa and video clubs.

It may be possible to construct intermediate circuits. This is beginning to take place in large and medium-size cities where small "art cinemas" with daily multiple programming have been established. In some cases, commercial television, and not only the "cultural channels," carries out this function. Surveys at movie theaters and video clubs on what people want to see on television and video show that mass audiences are more diversified and complex than is assumed by those who divide them into the educated and the entertained.

The system of video clubs seems condemned to being the most monotonous circuit in terms of repertoire. This is due to its speedy economic success as a purveyor almost exclusively of US-made entertainment. In Mexico, as in other countries, this aesthetic unilateralism is more the result of the pragmatic criteria of business than a careful attention to the interests and preferences of viewers. In a way, the "neglect" of the internal differences in the mass of videophiles corresponds to a depersonalized form of consumption: videophiles are less inclined to ritual than moviegoers, and have not made prior choices about what to see. The vast majority of video viewers declared in our surveys that they go to the clubs without knowing what they will rent.

Nevertheless, a minority of viewers are beginning to inform themselves in newspaper sections on what's new in video and in other media that provide brief reviews. Moreover, there are enough examples of Latin American countries with better equipped video clubs, as regards quality and international representation (Argentina, Brazil, Colombia). They also make good profits, which suggests that including Jim Jarmusch, Derek Jarman, and the best of Latin American cinema will not sink similarly stocked businesses in Mexico. Some examples of the new Mexican cinema lead us to such optimistic predictions. *Danzón*, which sold 25,000 cassettes, is not the only example. On this view, neither television nor video are substitutes for movie houses; there is, rather, an interdependence between the three media that can contribute to the revitalization of cinematographic production, which is what happened in European countries.

It is reasonable to think that the integration of the audiovisual field is based not only on the complementarity of cinema, television, and video as regards production and distribution. When we observe changes in audience habits, we have grounds for surmising that viewers might propose solutions for the combination of cinema with repertoires available in movie houses and on television and video. Movies today are a multimedia process, followed by multimedia spectators.

Perhaps this integrated vision of the various distribution circuits for film and the greater attention to the cultural diversities of publics will liberate us from the spectacular uniformity with which the crisis of the audience is currently being addressed. World cinema does not seem to be the only way to intensify the connections of film and publics, nor to give a shot in the arm to sagging national cinemas. Even Spielberg's films and those of other astute market multiculturalists can backfire from too much of a good thing: the obsession to chock their films with attractive ingredients from everywhere. No need to even mention what happens in the hands of less expert filmmakers who kill a story's verisimilitude to satisfy the demands of international coproducers, who must have or get rid of this or that actor. When it seemed that Raúl de la Torre's *Funes, un gran amor* was going to receive US financing, the owner of the whorehouse was cast as a North American. When the money came, it was Italian, so Gian María Volonté was chosen to play that role.

> Such a circumstance brings into existence a new category of characters: the foreigners. In many recent Argentine films, curious characters wend their way through the plot without the slightest idea of what they are doing there; sometimes they even admit it. The most obvious example is Volonté's *Funes...*, who meanders through the film muttering unintelligible utterances and who finally flees terrified, at the same time as the whorehouse disappears, this whorehouse of the fictive narrative, of the absurd story of the film and the grotesque project that he was bamboozled into.[12]

The large demand for films that deal with historical themes or contemporary social problems is evidence that light entertainment is not the only reason why people continue to see films. For large numbers, which are even higher among the youngest viewers or the most educated, the problematic treatment of current issues, close to everyday life, as well as intercultural matters and artistic innovations, is the motivation for watching movies. The diversification of tastes might have something to do with the cultural formation of a democratic citizenship.

The question is to what extent this variety of interests will be considered in policies for the production and distribution of films, even when they are not the most profitable. Without a more active role on the part of public power in the definition of the rules of use and circulation of film, seeking, for example, greater financing in the television and video sectors, it is unlikely that a quality cinema can be promoted, one that will also serve to fill movie houses and help increase profits. Will we have film for publics or for corporate executives? Are these mutually exclusive options?

## NOTES

1   Information from the Argentine Subsecretariat of Culture.

2   The study *Los nuevos espectadores. Cine, televisión y video en México* (Mexico City: Imcine-CNCA, 1994) was edited by Néstor García Canclini and carried out with the participation of Déborah Holtz, Javier Lozano Espinosa, María Eugenia Módena, Ella Fany Quintal, Guadalupe Reyes Domínguez, Ana Rosas Mantecón, Enrique Sánchez Ruiz, and José Manuel Valenzuela. It is based on surveys of film and video spectators in Mexico City, Tijuana, and Mérida between 1990 and 1993.

3   This is how Félix Mesquich tells the story of the 1896 projection of *L'Arivée d'un train en gare de La Ciotat* in his *Tour de manivelle. Souvenirs d'un chasseur d'images* (Paris: Grasset, 1933), 5–6; quoted in André Gaudreault and Germain Lacasse, "Premier regard, les 'néo-spectateurs' du Canada Français," *Vertigo* 10 (Paris: 1993): 19.

4   Ana Rosas Mantecón, "Los públicos de cine," in García Canclini, *Los nuevos espectadores.*

5   Carlos Monsiváis, "Notas sobre el Estado, la cultura nacional y las culturas populares," *Cuadernos politicos* 30 (Mexico City, 1984).

6   Ignacio Durán Loera, "El cine mexicano y sus perspectivas, *Intermedios* 4 (October 1992). See also Emilio García Riera, *Historia documental del cine mexicano* (Guadalajara: CNCA, Gobierno de Jalisco, Imcine, 1992), especially vol. 3.

7   See, for example, García Riera, *Historia documental del cine mexicano*, vols. 4 and 5; and Hugo Vargas, "El cine mexicano: la eterna crisis y la nueva generación," *La Jornada Semanal* 87 (29 February 1991).

8   Déborah Holtz, "Los públicos de video," in García Canclini, *Los nuevos espectadores.*

9   Ella Fany Quintal and Guadalupe Reyes Domínguez, "Mérida: ver cine en una ciudad de provincia," in García Canclini, *Los nuevos espectadores.*

10  Renato Janine Ribeiro, "A política como espetáculo," in Evelina Dagnino, ed., *Anos 90. Politica e sociedade no Brasil.* (São Paulo: Editora Brasiliense, 1994).

11  Ibid.

12  Raúl Becerro, "El cine por venir," *Punto de vista* 47 (Buenos Aires, December 1993): 8.

# 20

# Embedded Aesthetics: Creating a Discursive Space for Indigenous Media

## Faye Ginsburg

The closing years of the twentieth century are witnessing a radical re-orientation of thought in the human sciences which defies conventional disciplinary boundaries and demands a new 'turning': away from the rationalising modes of modernity and towards a different grasp of the nature of knowing itself.... The power of visual media as a means of knowledge-creation is only hesitantly grasped by many in public life.... But, from the viewpoint of the emergent visual-aural culture of the twenty-first century, "what's on" creates the context for what is known and hence finally for what "is."

Annette Hamilton

Since the late 1970s, Aboriginal Australians (and other indigenous people) have been engaged in developing new visual media forms by adapting the technologies of video, film, and television to a range of expressive and political purposes. Their efforts to develop new forms of indigenous media are motivated by a desire to envision and strengthen a "cultural future" (Michaels 1987a) for themselves in their own communities and in the dominant society. Aboriginal cultures, of course, are extremely diverse, as Aboriginal cultural critic and anthropologist Marcia Langton has pointed out in her recent book on indigenous media production. "There is no one kind of Aboriginal person or community," she writes:

There are [two] regions which can be characterised, however, with reference to history, politics, culture and demography....

> The first region is "settled" Australia...where most provincial towns and all the major cities and institutions are located, and where a myriad of small Aboriginal communities and populations reside with a range of histories and cultures....
>
> The second region is "remote" Australia where most of the tradition-oriented Aboriginal cultures are located. They likewise have responded to particular frontiers and now contend with various types of Australian settlement. [Langton 1993: 12–13]

Aboriginal media productions are as various as Aboriginal life itself, ranging from low-budget videos made by community-based media associations for both traditional people in remote settlements and groups in urban centers; to regional television and radio programming for Aboriginal groups throughout Central Australia made by organizations such as the Central Australian Aboriginal Media Association (CAAMA); to legal or instructional videos (often quite creative) made by land councils as well as health and other service groups; to documentaries and current affairs for national broadcasting; to independent features directed by cosmopolitan Aboriginal artists such as Tracey Moffatt whose first feature film, *Bedevil*, premiered at Cannes in 1993. Such works are inherently complex cultural objects, as they cross multiple cultural boundaries in their production, distribution, and consumption. For example, Aboriginal producers often collaborate with non-Aboriginal media workers, be they media advisers to remote settlements or staff at Australia's national television stations. Works themselves are often hybrid, combining traditional ritual knowledge and/or performance with MTV-style special effects. In terms of circulation and reception, these productions are seen by multiple audiences, including other Aboriginal and non-Aboriginal viewers in Australia, via circulation of video letters as well as local, regional, or national broadcasts, or by diverse overseas audiences through film festivals and conferences.

With an interest in enlarging analyses of film texts to account for broader contexts of social relations,[1] I have found it helpful to think of Aboriginal media as part of a *mediascape*, a term created by Arjun Appadurai to account for the different kinds of global cultural flows created by new media technologies and the images created with them in the late 20th century. Appadurai argues for situated analyses that take account of the interdependence of media practices with the local, national, and transnational circumstances that surround them (Appadurai 1990: 7). Using such a model for indigenous media helps to establish a more generative discursive space for this work which breaks what one might call the fetishizing of the local, without losing a sense of the specific situatedness of any production. The complex mediascape of Aboriginal media, for example, must account for a range of circumstances, beginning with the perspectives of Aboriginal producers, for whom new media forms are seen as a powerful means of (collective) self-expression that can have a culturally revitalizing effect. Their vision coexists uneasily, however, with the fact that their work is also a product of relations with governing bodies that are responsible for the dire political circumstances that often motivated the Aboriginal mastery of new communication forms as a means of cultural intervention.[2] Such contradictions are inherent to the ongoing social construction of *Aboriginality*. Cultural critic

Fiona Nicoll offers a helpful explication of the term that has been the subject of considerable debate.[3] As she writes:

> "Aboriginality"... [is] a colonial field of power relations within which Aborigines struggle with the dominant settler culture over the representation of things such as "identity," "history," "land," and "culture." In contrast to the category "Aboriginal culture," which is always defined in opposition to a dominant "non-Aboriginal culture," the concept of "Aboriginality" must be thought in *relation* to "non-Aboriginality." For it was the white settlers who lumped the various indigenous peoples under the homogenizing name of "Aborigines," then brought into being the categories of "Aboriginal history," "Aboriginal culture," "Aboriginal experience" and "Aboriginal conditions." [1993: 709]

Thus, not only are Aboriginal film and video important to Aboriginal Australians, but they cannot be understood apart from the contemporary construction of Aboriginality. As nation-states like Australia increasingly constitute their "imagined communities" (Anderson 1983) through the circulation of televisual and cinematic images of the people they govern, Aboriginal media have become part of the mediascape of the Australian *national imaginary*.[4] Put in concrete terms:

> "Aboriginality" arises from the subjective experience of both Aboriginal people and non-Aboriginal people who engage in any intercultural dialogue, whether in actual lived experience or through a mediated experience such as a white person watching a program about Aboriginal people on television or reading a book. [Langton 1993: 31]

## ■ Discursive Spaces/Social Action ■

This essay is an extension of a larger effort initiated by Aboriginal cultural activists to develop a "discursive practice" – both for Aboriginal makers and for others who make and study media – that respects and understands this work in terms relevant to contemporary indigenous people living in a variety of settings (Langton 1993). Specifically, it examines how Aboriginal media makers understand their own work. How, one might ask, do people understand indigenous media works as they move through the complex circuits sketched above? What are the aesthetic standards – the discourses and practices of evaluation – that are applied to indigenous productions as they are positioned differently in various exhibition contexts? Are Aboriginal ideas about their "beauty/value" able to cross over cultural borders? I am concerned in particular with how notions of the value of indigenous media are being negotiated at different levels of Aboriginal media production.[5] While there are multiple arenas of Aboriginal production (local, regional, urban, etc.), in this essay I will focus on three sites of Aboriginal media work: remote communities; national television; and transnational networks of indigenous media producers that form around events such as film festivals or coproductions.

In these different arenas, Aboriginal producers from very different backgrounds use a language of evaluation that stresses the *activities* of the production and circulation of such work in specific communities as the basis for judging its value. In communities where traditional Aboriginal cultural practices are still relatively intact, such evaluation is culturally very specific, corresponding to notions of appropriate social and formal organization of performance in ceremonial or ritual domains. In her analysis of Aboriginal media production, Marcia Langton argues that such media from remote areas are "community-authored" (1993: 13). Summarizing studies in the 1980s of the organization of video production at the remote Warlpiri settlement of Yuendumu (Michaels and Kelly 1984), Langton writes that "the camera and camera person are attributed with the ritual role of *kurdungurlu* (ritual managers) ... because they are witnesses to events and affirm their truth," while those in front of the camera are *kirda* (ritual owners) with acknowledged rights and obligations to tell and perform certain stories and ceremonies (1993: 65). Based on my own contact with Yuendumu in 1992, it is unclear whether these specific arrangements still endure in the 1990s. However, the general principle of kin-based rights to tell certain kinds of stories and ceremonial knowledge continue to shape production practices. More generally, then, "[t]here are rules, which are somewhat flexible, for the production, distribution and ownership of any image, just as there are under traditional law for sacred designs which ... refer to ancestors and ancestral mythology" (Langton 1993: 65).

In ways that are both similar and different, urban Aboriginal mediamakers are also concerned with their media productions as a form of social action. While their works are more typically understood as authored by individuals (Langton 1993: 13), many urban Aboriginal producers nonetheless see themselves as responsible to a community of origin (for example kin and friends in the urban neighborhood of Redfern in Sydney), although it is a sense of community less bound by specific cultural rules than that of people in remote settlements. This is especially true of those working for Australian state television who shoulder the specific burden of creating an "authentic" Aboriginal presence in the mass media and, more broadly, in Australia's national imaginary.[6] This tendency to evaluate work in terms of social action is striking to an observer schooled in Western aesthetics. With few exceptions, questions of narrative or visual form are not primary issues for discussion per se, despite the obvious concern for it in individual works. Rather, for many Aboriginal producers, the quality of work is judged by its capacity to embody, sustain, and even revive or create certain social relations, although the social bases for coming to this position may be very different for remote and urban people.[7] For the sake of discussion, I will call this orientation *embedded aesthetics*, to draw attention to a system of evaluation that refuses a separation of textual production and circulation from broader arenas of social relations.[8] For example, Eric Michaels, an American researcher who helped develop Aboriginal media production with Warlpiri people at Yuendumu in Central Australia, noted that for the people he worked with:

> [Aboriginal] art or video objects become difficult to isolate for analysis because the producer's intention is the opposite. Warlpiri artists demonstrate their own invisi-

bility in order to assert the work's authority and continuity with tradition. They do not draw attention to themselves or to their creativity. [Michaels 1987a: 34]

My argument, then, is that this new and complex object – Aboriginal media – is understood by its producers to be operating in multiple domains as an extension of their collective (vs. individual) self-production. However, it is important to recognize that Aboriginal producers from various locales and backgrounds – remote, urban, rural – come to their positions through quite different cultural and social processes. In the case of urban Aboriginal mediamakers, their embrace of *embedded aesthetics* may be an extremely self-conscious choice, produced out of contact with a variety of discourses. In the cases below, I will sketch the multiple ways that this kind of positioning of indigenous media emerges from very different social bases for the understanding of Aboriginality and its representation, especially as it passes across cultural and national borders.

## ■ Remote Control: Media in Traditional Communities ■

My first examples are drawn from two successful community-based Aboriginal media associations developed at relatively traditional remote settlements in the Central Desert area of Australia. The first is Ernabella on Pitjantjatjarra lands in South Australia, just south of Uluru (Ayers Rock). The second settlement is Yuendumu on Warlpiri lands in Central Australia, northwest of Alice Springs, home to the Warlpiri Media Association since 1982. Both are Aboriginal settlements with highly mobile populations that can vary from 500 to 1,500 over the course of a year. Founded by missionaries in the 1940s, they became self-governing by the 1970s and retain infrastructures consisting of a community store, a town office, a police station, a primary school, a health clinic, a church, an art association, and local broadcast facilities (Langton 1993).

In 1983, people at Ernabella began producing video programs with the encouragement of white schoolteachers and advisers, in particular Neil Turner, who settled in the community, learned the language, and facilitated the development of Ernabella Video Televison (EVTV) from its inception to the present. Established in 1985, EVTV operates from a small video production, editing, and playback facility and an inexpensive satellite dish that provides local broadcasts of work produced by EVTV as well as items selected from national television feeds. Determined to be as independent as possible from government subsidies, EVTV has supported itself successfully through a self-imposed tax on cold drinks in the community store, the sales of EVTV videos, and occasional public and private grants (Batty 1993; Molnar 1989; N. Turner 1990).

Over the first decade of its existence, EVTV has produced over 80 edited pieces as well as thousands of hours of community television under the direction of a respected couple, Simon and Pantiji Tjiyangu, and a local media committee made up of male and female elders. Their concerns range from monitoring the content of work shown – so that images are not circulated that violate cultural rules regulating what can be seen (e.g. tapes of women's sacred ceremonies are not edited and are only accessible to appropriate senior women) – and the timing of viewing so that television transmission, whether locally produced or the national satellite feed, does not interfere with other cultural activities.

Perhaps because the supervision of EVTV is largely in the hands of elders, the video work of Ernabella is distinguished by its emphasis on ceremonies, in particular the stories, dances, and sand designs that are associated with the Kungkarangkalpa (Seven Sisters Dreaming) (which explains the origins of the Pleiades constellation). In adapting such forms to video, EVTV producers include in their tapes the production process itself, which can involve the whole community, including children, dancers, storytellers, and video crew. For example, in tapes such as *Seven Sisters Dreaming: Tjukurpa Kungkarangkalpa Tjara* (made in 1985) one sees not just a performance as we understand it in the West. Dances and enactments of the story of the Seven Sisters are preceded by extensive preparation and participation by those members of the Pitjantjatjara community who are responsible for ritual knowledge and ceremony. This aspect of Pitjantjatjara ritual performance has been reconfigured to accommodate video production: the tape includes not only ritual preparation but also other participants offering their comments on the ritual as they sit at night by the campfire to view the day's rushes (Leigh 1992: 3). Such reflexivity is not a Brechtian innovation; rather, it authorizes the reconfiguring of traditional practices for video as "true" and properly done.

In addition to such framing of the production process, the value or beauty of such videos for the Pitjantjatjara videomakers is extratextual, created by the cultural and social processes they mediate, embody, create, and extend. The tapes underscore the cosmological power of ceremonies to invigorate sacred aspects of the landscape; they reinforce the social relations that are fundamental to ritual production; and they enhance the place of Pitjantjatjara among Aboriginal groups in the area, as well as for the dominant Australian regional culture. Over the last decade, people from Ernabella frequently have been invited to "perform" in nearby cultural centers such as Adelaide. Knowledge of these issues is important to understanding the value of EVTV tapes as texts that cross over cultural borders, reaching other Aboriginal and non-Aboriginal audiences. As media activist Philip Batty commented:

> the work of EVTV had the effect of engendering a kind of local renaissance in traditional dance, performance and singing. The various video programmes depicting the actual land where the dreaming lines were located gave renewed strength to traditional beliefs and values within the communities. [Batty 1993: 113]

As another example of indigenous media work emerging from remote Aboriginal settlements, the Warlpiri Media Association (WMA) began producing tapes in 1982 and established their own unlicensed local television station similar to that of EVTV, in April 1985. Frances Juppurrurla Kelly, a young Warlpiri man, became a key videomaker and central figure in developing WMA. Much of what has been written about that group for outsiders came out of the work of Eric Michaels, for the (then) Australian Institute of Aboriginal Studies, which commissioned him to research the impact of Western media on traditional Aboriginal people in Central Australia. When he arrived at Yuendumu, he discovered that:

> [t]here was, in the early 1980s, a considerable creative interest among Aborigines in the new entertainment technology becoming available to remote communities. There was equally a motivated, articulate, and general concern about the possible unwanted consequences of television, especially among senior Aborigines and local indigenous educators. In particular, the absence of local Aboriginal languages from any proposed service was a major issue. [Michaels 1987a: 11]

As a result, Michaels also brought an interventionist approach to his research, encouraging people to produce their own videos without imposing Western conventions of shooting and editing. The broader concern that Michaels shared with Yuendumu videomakers was that, if people could make videos based on Aboriginal concerns, they might escape the more deleterious effects of broadcast television by substituting their own work for mainstream satellite television signals. While they had not tried video production before, Yuendumu residents were familiar with mainstream cinema, as well as the active production of Aboriginal popular music, as well as radio programs in Central Australia.[9] Since 1982, Warlpiri videomakers have produced hundreds of hours of tapes, on a range of subjects including sports events, health issues, traditional rituals, and their own history, as in *Coniston Story*, a tape in which the Aboriginal descendants of a revenge massacre of Warlpiri people by whites go to the site of the tragedy and tell their version of this "killing time." In an analysis of *Coniston Story*, Michaels notes that "one is struck by the recurrent camera movement, [and] the subtle shifts in focus and attention during the otherwise even, long pans across the landscape," shifts that Western interpreters might see as 'naive' camerawork (1987a: 51). Rather, Frances Jupurrurla Kelly (the Warlpiri producer/director and camera operator) explains that the camera is following

> the movement . . . of unseen characters – both Dreamtime [ancestral] and historical – which converge on this landscape. . . . Shifts in focus and interruptions in panning pick out important things in the landscape, like a tree where spirits live or a flower with symbolic value. [Cited in Michaels 1987a: 52]

Jupurrurla's explanation suggests that in developing a new mode of telling Warlpiri history through video, his concerns were consistent with traditional Aboriginal cosmology in which the particular geographic features of the areas they inhabit (and the kin-based rights and responsibilities attached to them) are central to authorizing myths and ceremonies. Michaels argued that this emphasis on the meaning of landscape is apparent in many Warlpiri tapes and accounts for the value and beauty of such sequences for Warlpiri viewers (Michaels 1987b).

What is not immediately visible in the tapes themselves is that people organize themselves around media production in terms of the responsibilities of specific groups for knowledge and practices associated with certain geographic areas, similar to the case of Ernabella discussed above. In other words, the ways in which tapes are made and used reflect Warlpiri understandings of kin-based obligations for ceremonial production and control of traditional knowledge, as these index cosmological relationships to particular features in regional geography (Michaels and Kelly 1984). "The credibility of the resulting tape for the Warlpiri audience is dependent upon knowing that these people were all participating in the event, even though the taped record provides no direct evidence of their presence" (Michaels 1987a: 46). Thus, for Warlpiri videomakers, cultural production – if it is of any value – is understood as part of a broader effort of collective self-production always associated with the *jukurrpa*, the ontological system of kin- and land-based ritual knowledge, translated into English originally as "the dreaming" (Stanner 1956) and now also as "the law." Notions of value embedded in jukurrpa run contrary to Western notions of the social relations of aesthetic production that emphasize the creative "self-expression" of individuals who are assigned responsibility as authors. Rather:

> stories are always true, and invention even when it requires an individual agent to "dream" or "receive" a text, remains social in a complex and important sense that assures truth. Rights to receive, know, perform, or teach a story (through dance, song, narrative, and graphic design) are determined by any identified individual's structural position and social/ritual history within an elaborately reckoned system of kin. Novelty can only enter this system as a social, not an individual invention. Not only is one's right to invent ultimately constrained, it is particularly constrained with respect to the kinship role for it is the genealogy of an item – not its individual creation – which authorises it. [Michaels 1987b: 65]

These principles through which some Aboriginal videos from remote settlements are mediated within and across cultural borders are consistent with the evaluative processes used for other "hybrid" Aboriginal media such as acrylic painting. As Fred Myers writes regarding the evaluations Pintupi painters from the Central Desert area make of their work, "the painters themselves have been unforthcoming about such aesthetic considerations." (Myers 1994: 15). Indeed

> The[ir] principal discourse...emphasizes their works as vehicles of self-production and collective empowerment...these are not necessarily interpretations that are outside the processes of representation themselves. [Myers 1994: 35]

In addition to providing a means for enhancing forms such as ritual performance, Aboriginal film and video offer innovative possibilities for collective self-production. As novel forms, these media provide sites for the re-visioning of social relations with the encompassing society, an exploration that more traditional indigenous forms cannot so easily accommodate. In media production, Aboriginal skills at constituting both individual and group identities through narrative and ritual are engaged in innovative ways that are often simultaneously indigenous and intercultural, from production to reception. For example, Yuendumu residents have produced a series of children's programs designed to teach literacy in

Warlpiri. The series was invented by elders and schoolteachers, both white and Aboriginal. With grants written with the help of a media adviser, they received funding from the Australian government and hired a local Anglo-Australian film-maker, David Batty (with whom they had worked before), to create the series *Manyu Wana* ("Just for Fun"). The result has been an ongoing series of collaborative community-based productions where kids, teachers, and filmmaker work together to improvise and then enact humorous short sketches to illustrate both written and spoken Warlpiri words in ways that seem to engage multiple audiences. Immensely popular in Yuendumu and neighboring Aboriginal communities, *Manyu Wana*, despite its very local origin and monolingual use of local language, has also been seen and appreciated all over the world.

## ■ National Imaginaries ■

Since the early 1980s, the demand for more Aboriginal participation and visibility in the Australian mediascape has been increasing, not only for local access to video in remote areas, but also for more Aboriginal representation on mainstream national television. This concern is not simply about equal access but a recognition that distortion and/or invisibility of Aboriginal realities for the wider Australian public can have a direct effect on political culture. Continuing exclusion of work by Aboriginal people from Australia's media institutions has sharpened Aboriginal awareness of the connections between political enfranchisement and the need to control their own images in the public sphere.

Aboriginal people – in terms of content and staffing – are still virtually absent from Australia's three commercial television networks (Langton 1993: 21).[10] However, two important efforts to increase an Aboriginal presence on public television were initiated in 1989. These were (1) the Aboriginal Programs Unit (APU) of the Australian Broadcasting Corporation (ABC), the stateowned national television station that reaches all of Australia; and (2) the Aboriginal Television Unit of the Special Broadcast Service (SBS),[11] Australia's state-funded station set up to provide culturally and linguistically appropriate programming, both imported as well as locally produced, for Australia's many ethnic communities.

In April 1989, the Special Broadcast Service initiated a 13-part television series devoted to Aboriginal issues, called *First in Line*, the first prime-time current affairs show in Australia to be hosted by two Aboriginal people. This was a border crossing of considerable significance to Aboriginal cultural activists.[12] The producers and crew were primarily Aboriginal, and they consulted with communities throughout Australia for items stressing the positive achievements of Aborigines (Molnar 1989: 38–9). Eventually, *First in Line* was discontinued, and an Aboriginal unit was established with Rachel Perkins at the head, a young Aboriginal woman who had trained at the Central Australian Aboriginal Media Association (CAAMA). She has been creating programming through the use of work such as *Manyu Wana* from regional and local Aboriginal media associations. In 1992, she commissioned and produced a series, *Blood Brothers*, comprised of four documentaries on different aspects of Aboriginal history and culture (Rachel Perkins, interview, May 2, 1992). While these efforts are important, the SBS has a relatively small audience and budget.

By contrast, the state-controlled and -funded Australian Broadcasting Corporation (ABC) has a much greater resource base and reaches a national audience. In 1987, the ABC set up the Aboriginal Programs Unit (APU),[13] but it was not until 1989 that their first Aboriginally produced and presented program, *Blackout*, began broadcasting on a Friday-evening time slot. This series, a weekly magazine show on Aboriginal issues, is still being produced. (In 1992, it was awarded the United Nations Human Rights Media Award). Additionally, APU programs occasional series such as *The First Australians*, an 8-part series of independent documentaries on Aboriginal topics broadcast on Thursday nights in 1992.[14]

Unlike the producers from remote settlements, Aboriginal producers at APU grew up in urban or "settled" areas, are bicultural, often hold university degrees, and are sophisticated about the ins and outs of national television vis-à-vis their interests as indigenous makers. People like Frances Peters and Rachel Perkins are new kinds of cultural activists who are regular *border crossers*, a position they occupy as part of their own background (from Aboriginal families educated in the dominant culture's pedagogical system) and out of a recognition that they must speak effectively to (at least) two kinds of Australians. Like the more remote-living Aboriginal mediamakers discussed above, they are concerned with their work as part of a range of activities engaged in cultural revival, identity formation, and political assertion. Through their work in televisual media production, they have been able to assert the multiple realities of contemporary urban Aboriginal life, not just for their own communities but also in the national public culture where Aboriginal activism and political claims are generally effaced from the official histories.

For example, in 1991, Peters worked with fellow APU producer David Sandy to produce the first documentary special of APU for broadcast in 1992. The title, *Tent Embassy*, refers to the event that galvanized the beginning of what some have called the "Aboriginal civil rights movement." On Australia Day (January 26) 1972, four young Aboriginal men erected a small tent on the lawns of the Parliament House in Canberra and declared themselves a sovereign nation. The action succinctly dramatized the issue of Aboriginal land rights in the Australian imagination and helped catalyze a broader social movement. The return, in 1992, of some of the original activists, now in their forties, to the site of the original protest to reassert their claims and to occupy Parliament House as well becomes the occasion for the film to explore the last 20 years of Aboriginal politics. The history moves from the confrontational activism of the Aboriginal Black Power and the Black Panther movements in the 1970s, to the establishment in the 1980s of the Aboriginal and Torres Straits Islanders Commission (ATSIC), a five-billion-dollar bureaucracy that has been criticized by some activists as co-opting Aboriginal political power. *Tent Embassy* is built out of the stories of key activists – lawyer Paul Coe, scholar and activist Roberta Sykes, public figure Charles Perkins – as we see them in archival footage, in extended contemporary interviews. It opens with a wonderfully humorous dramatic recreation that suggests the spontaneous origins of the first protest and holds fast to the principle of making people primary over issues. Other events are tracked through archival footage, not only of the embassy protest, but also of crucial events leading up to it, such as the discovery of bauxite on Aboriginal lands in the 1960s, which helped put land claims on the national political agenda.

For productions like *Tent Embassy* to be effective in reaching large, mixed audiences, they require aesthetic considerations that negotiate multiple cultural perspectives. The challenge for producers is to create visions of Aboriginal culture and history that simultaneously address the realities of Aboriginal communities and intervene in representations of Australian national histories in ways that will attract both Aboriginal and non-Aboriginal audiences. Frances Peters (and a number of other Aboriginal producers) are exploring how to reposition cultural authority in their works by using satire, humor, and drama. These provide complex commentaries on their own identities and on their relationships with the dominant society, without simplifying or reducing the Aboriginal experience for what are still predominantly white audiences. In Peter's words:

> Aboriginal people in Australia are not one nation; the differences are there, but we're all Aboriginal....I [am] trying to break a lot of image stereotypes. I think those stereotoypes may have something to do with why many indigenous artists are moving away from documentary and into fiction or drama films. We are sick of the documentary format; we've seen so many of them about us...so unfortunately what we've done is associate documentary with just another form of stereotyping. We've got the opportunity as aboriginal filmmakers to change that. [Peters 1993: 102]

Producers at APU are engaged in more than the creation of media images of themselves that alter their place in the world of representations. In considering this kind of work in relation to questions of indigenous aesthetics, one must recognize the value they place on media production as a form of social action. Frances Peters articulated this position clearly to me in discussing her position as an Aboriginal producer:

> Unlike you, we can't remove ourselves from the programs we're making because they're about us as well. And because they are about us, we always have that responsibility to our Aboriginal culture and country...we can't walk away and just make a program on a different theme next time.... Ultimately you're not really answerable to a hell of a lot of people.... But with us, with every program that we make, we are ultimately responsible to a larger Aboriginal community. And we can't remove ourselves from that responsibility. [Frances Peters, interview, April 30, 1992]

Peter's comments speak to the complex and embedded sense that indigenous producers bring to their work, never seeing it as existing apart from the mediation of social relationships, especially with communities of origin, whether urban or remote. However, *community* is not, for her, some romantic notion of a unified social position. It is, rather, a complex and unstable social construct, implicated in the changing understandings of Aboriginality in Australia today, as bureaucratic structures for the administration of Aboriginal funding and policies have proliferated. As much as she feels accountable to a broader Aboriginal world, she queries the concept:

> Which community? Our communities have become bureaucratized and class-stratified. Accountability is riddled with fear of being made to feel guilty, or that you aren't Aboriginal enough. [Peters 1993: 105]

Her positioning (along with that of other producers) intersects and is influenced by emerging Western theoretical discourses in the arts, built on frameworks of multiculturalism, which emphasize "cultural diversity as a basis for challenging, revising, and relativizing basic notions and principles common to dominant and minority cultures alike, so as to construct a more vital, open, and democratic common culture" (T. Turner 1993: 413). In the world of Aboriginal media making, an approach built out of contemporary identity politics (which has influenced many urban-based Aboriginal producers) intersects with concerns that shape the work of more traditional Aboriginal producers from remote communities, thereby creating a sense (or even illusion) of coherence in the ways that a broad range of Aboriginal makers evaluate their work. Regardless of this outcome, it is important to recognize that urban Aboriginal producers working in bicultural settings have embraced an *embedded aesthetic* as a strategic *choice*. Their efforts to develop an alternative approach to their work, while emerging from their experiences as Aboriginal Australians, are nonetheless self-conscious; the Western aesthetic conventions of the dominant society are culturally available to them as well. This sense of self-conscious positioning is evident in Frances Peters's description of coming to consciousness in her days as a student and Aboriginal radio producer:

> So, I was going to university, getting a formal education, and then spending my Saturday afternoons having great fun at an Aboriginal radio station [Radio Redfern], breaking all the rules. We were creating our own sounds, basically, we were promoting our music, and we were telling our own news in ways and forms that we chose. All that raised a lot of questions for me about the media and how I was going to see myself working in it. It was hard; it was a battle, and I used to fight in every one of those classes at University. [Peters 1993: 99]

## ▪ Transnational Mediations ▪

For most producers, their sense of community is very local. However, new and more expanded communities of identity are emerging through collaborative activities that transcend the boundaries of the nation-states that encompass them. Over the last five years, indigenous media productions have increasingly become part of *global cultural flows*. Connections are being built by indigenous producers who have been organizing a transnational indigenous network via film festivals and conferences, as well as joint productions such as the Pac Rim initiative, a documentary series being made jointly by indigenous filmmakers from Australia, New

Zealand, the United States, and Canada. These events are becoming the basis for constituting an emergent organization of indigenous media producers. For example, the First Nations Film and Video Makers World Alliance (FNFVWA) was formed at the September 1992 Dreamspeakers Festival in Edmonton, Canada, itself the first indigenously organized international Aboriginal film and video festival. In such exhibition venues organized by and for indigenous people, media workers frame their work with a discourse of self-determination, clearly placing collective and political interests over those of individual expression. Such positioning is evident, for example, in the following statement of aims of the FNFVWA drawn up in 1992:

a. to raise awareness of First Nations issues
b. to establish a film and video communication network
c. to ensure that traditional lands, language, and culture are protected
d. to implement work and training exchanges
e. to establish a world conference
f. to ensure environmental protection and management
g. to promote our teachings of history and culture
h. to distribute and market our own films.

A major concern of all those indigenous filmmakers who attended Dreamspeakers was the need for our works to be distributed amongst other indigenous groups in other countries, that we are our own international market. The problem we felt was that our works are almost always received [more positively] by overseas audiences than by those in our own countries.

This statement of principles developed by a group of indigenous attendees (and the weeklong Dreamspeakers Festival itself) was striking in the lack of discussion of themselves as artists concerned primarily with formal issues or even freedom of expression. The indigenous media makers in the alliance, who came from all over the world, were all engaged in asserting the relationship of their work to broader arenas of social action. Such positions complicate structures of distribution and public culture in which the (media) artist's position is valued as being outside or critical of society, as in Adorno's view of art as an "intrinsic movement against society," a social realm set apart from the means-end rationality of daily bourgeois existence (Adorno 1970: 336, quoted in Bürger 1984: 10).

Recent shows of indigenous film/video that have been organized by dominant cultural institutions situate them as new forms of aesthetic/political production yet continue to look for aesthetic innovation in the text itself, rather than in the relations of production and reception that shape the evaluation and mediation of the text in unexpected ways. Mainstream showcases, for example, continue to focus on "individual makers" in places associated with "auteurship" in the arts, such as programs of the Museum of Modern Art (1990, 1993), the New Museum (1990), or the Walter Reade Theater at Lincoln Center (1992), all sites of exhibition of indigenous media in New York City. In such venues, indigenous work is in tension with Western discourses that valorize the individual as a political or artistic agent in opposition to a broader polity. Although this has been changing as the broader zeitgeist in the West embraces multicultural and identity-based politics as frames for the exhibition of various expressive media, the structures for showing work in most cases still put forward "the artist," repressing the embeddedness of individual artistic production in broader social and political processes. For the most part, indigenous producers reject this dominant model of the media text as the expression of an individuated self and continue to stress their work as on a continuum of social action authorizing Aboriginal cultural empowerment.

In conclusion, I want to emphasize that the social relations built out of indigenous media practices are helping to develop support and sensibilities for indigenous actions for self-determination. Self-representation in media is seen as a crucial part of this process. Indigenous media productions and the activities around them are rendering visible indigenous cultural and historical realities to themselves and the broader societies that have stereotyped or denied them. The transnational social relations built out of these media practices are creating new arenas of cooperation, locally, nationally, and internationally. Like the indigenous producers themselves, I suggest a model that stresses not only the text but also the *activities* and social organization of media work as arenas of cultural production. Only by understanding indigenous media work as part of a broader mediascape of social relations can we appreciate them fully as complex cultural objects. In the imaginative, narrative, social, and political spaces opened up by film, video, and television lie possibilities for Aboriginal mediamakers and their communities to reenvision their current realities and possible futures, from the revival of local cultural practices, to the insertion of their histories into national imaginaries, to the creation of new transnational arenas that link indigenous makers around the globe in a common effort to make their concerns visible to the world.

## NOTES

*Acknowledgements.* For editorial comments on this and earlier drafts, I thank Debbora Battaglia, Paul Brodwin, Susan Harding, Toby Miller, and Fred Myers. Fieldwork on which this work is based could not have been done without the help of Fred Myers in 1988 and Françoise Dussart in 1992, in the logistics and languages of Aboriginal research in the field and out; I am deeply grateful to both of them. In addition, I want to thank the following people in Australia who shared their time and insights with me: Philip Batty, Freda Glynn, Annette Hamilton, Francis Jupurrurla Kelly, Ned Lander, Marcia Langton, Mary Laughren, Michael Leigh, Judith and David MacDougall, Michael Niblett, Rachel Perkins, Frances Peters, Nick Peterson, Tim Rowse, David Sandy, Neil Turner, and Peter Toyne. For research support, I am grateful to the Research Challenge Fund of New York University (1988) and the John Simon Guggenheim Foundation (1991–2). Portions of this piece were drawn from two essays (Ginsburg 1993b and 1994b). The Annette Hamilton quote used as the epigraph is from Hamilton 1993: 5.

1  For a fuller development of this position, see Ginsburg 1994a.

2   These contradictions, some have argued, are typical of liberal welfare states and their
    indigenous populations, a system that Jeremy Beckett calls welfare colonialism (1988).

3   For examples of debates on Aboriginality, see Beckett 1988, Thiele 1991, Lattas 1991,
    and others in a special issue of *The Australian Journal of Anthropology* entitled Recon-
    sidering Aboriginality.

4   I follow Annette Hamilton's use of the term *national imaginary*. Drawing on ideas from
    Benedict Anderson, Edward Said, and Jacques Lacan, Hamilton uses the term to
    describe how contemporary nation-states use visual mass media to constitute *imagined
    communities*. She uses Lacan's idea of the imaginary as the mirror-phase in human
    development when the child sees its own reflection as an "other": "Imaginary relations
    at the social, collective level can thus be seen as ourselves looking at ourselves while we
    think we are seeing others" (Hamilton 1990: 17). As examples, she cites the current
    popularity of Aboriginal art and popular music, as well as films such as *Crocodile
    Dundee*, in which the outback and Aboriginal knowledge play a critical role, as if
    Australian appropriation of Aboriginal culture can justify "the settler presence in the
    country, and indeed...the presence of Australia as part of a world cultural scene"
    (Hamilton 1990: 18). Given current world conditions, representations of the Austra-
    lian nation must take account of what Hamilton calls an increasingly "international-
    ised image-environment," in which images of indigenous peoples now carry a heavy
    semiotic load (1990). Aboriginal media have become implicated in the circulation of
    commodified images of Aboriginality, including "hi-tech primitives" engaged in their
    own televisual production. For a fuller discussion of this position, see Ginsburg 1993a.

5   For a discussion of the origins and use of the term *indigenous media*, see Ginsburg
    1993a.

6   While the opportunities of such positions are obvious, there is some concern on the
    part of Aboriginal filmmakers that they are expected to confine their work to conven-
    tional or romanticized representations of Aboriginality, what Haitian anthropologist
    Michel-Rolph Trouillot calls "the savage slot" (Trouillot 1991).

7   Urban-based filmmakers such as Tracey Moffatt may be more oriented toward formal
    issues, although they, too, often couch their interests in terms of their social possibil-
    ities as *interventions* into dominant conventions of representation regarding Aboriginal
    men and women in popular culture, as was the case with both *Night Cries* (1990) and
    *Nice Coloured Girls* (1987). In the case of makers such as Moffatt, this language may be
    less a product of Aboriginal categories and more a reworking of available discourses in
    the independent cinema movement, of which she is a part.

8   For an interesting discussion of similar issues in relation to Aboriginal writing, see
    Muecke 1992.

9   For a fuller discussion of the development of Australian Aboriginal media in different
    locales, see Batty 1993, Ginsburg 1991 and 1993a, Michaels 1987a, Molnar 1989, and
    O'Regan 1993.

10  Langton notes:

> One network was even broadcasting a drama series featuring a European acting in place
> of the original Aboriginal Character, Bony, from the novels of Arthur Upfield...A new
> and welcome twist...was the appointment of Stan Grant, an Aboriginal journalist, to the
> position of anchor on *Real Life* [a nightly current affairs program]. [1993: 21]

11  In 1978, the government established a separate Special Broadcast Service (SBS) initially
    to serve immigrant minorities. By the mid-1980s, the SBS altered its policy to include
    the presentation of Aboriginal radio and television programs and to take as its

mandate the correction of popular misconceptions about Aboriginal history and culture.

12  Michael Johnson and Rhoda Roberts were the hosts for 38 programs that aired Tuesday nights at 7:30.

13  While the state-controlled and -funded Australian Broadcasting Corporation (ABC) had been training Aborigines since 1980, by 1987 only seven Aborigines were employed there. That same year, the prime minister established the Aboriginal Employment and Development Policy (AEDP), which requires all industries to have 2 percent Aboriginal employment by 1991 (Molnar 1989: 36–8).

14  As of 1993, APU had six Aboriginal staff who produce *Blackout*, a weekly late-night program on Aboriginal affairs, as well as occasional documentaries and dramatic works. As such, it is a precedent-setting model for including indigenous people and their concerns in the imaginary of the nation-state and beyond.

## REFERENCES

Adorno, Theodor W. 1970 *Ästhetische Theorie. Gesammelte Schriften*, 7. Frankfurt: Suhrkamp.

Anderson, Benedict 1983 *Imagined Communities*. Verso: London.

Appadurai, Arjun 1990 Disjuncture and Difference in the Global Cultural Economy. *Public Culture* 2(2): 1–24.

Batty, Philip 1993 Singing the Electric: Aboriginal Television in Australia. In *Channels of Resistance*. Tony Downmunt, ed. Pp. 106–25. London: British Film Institute.

Beckett, Jeremy 1988 The Past in the Present; The Present in the Past: Constructing a National Aboriginality. In *Past and Present: The Construction of Aboriginality*. Jeremy Beckett, ed. Pp. 191–217. Canberra: Aboriginal Studies Press.

Bürger, Peter 1984 *Theory of the Avant-Garde*. Theory and History of Literature, 4. Minneapolis: University of Minnesota Press.

Dutchak, Philip 1992 Black Screens. *Cinema Papers* (March–April) 87: 48–52.

Ginsburg, Faye 1991 Indigenous Media: Faustian Contract or Global Village? *Cultural Anthropology* 6(1): 92–112.

—— 1993a Aboriginal Media and the Aboriginal Imaginary. *Public Culture* 5(3): 557–78.

—— 1993b Station Identification: The Aboriginal Programs Unit of the Australian Broadcasting Corporation. In *Visual Anthropology Review* 9(2): 92–6.

—— 1994a Culture and Media: A (Mild) Polemic. *Anthropology Today* (April): 5–15.

—— 1994b Production Values: Indigenous Media and the Rhetoric of Self-Determination. In *Rhetorics of Self-Making*. Debbora Battaglia, ed. Berkeley: University of California Press.

Hamilton, Annette 1990 Fear and Desire: Aborigines, Asians, and the National Imaginary. *Australian Cultural History* 9: 14–35.

—— 1993 Foreword. In *Well, I Heard It on the Radio and I Saw It on the Television*. By Marcia Langton. Pp. 5–7. Sydney: Australian Film Commission.

Langton, Marcia 1993 *Well, I Heard It on the Radio and I Saw It on the Television*. Sydney: Australian Film Commission.

Lattas, Andrew 1991 Nationalism, Aesthetic Redemption, and Aboriginality. *The Australian Journal of Anthropology* 2(2): 307–24.

Leigh, Michael 1992 Fade to Black: An Introductory Essay. In *Cultural Focus, Cultural Futures.* (Film festival catologue.) Pp. 1–3. Canberra: Department of Foreign Affairs and Trade.

Michaels, Eric 1986 Hollywood Iconography: A Warlpiri Reading. Paper presented at the International Television Studies Conference, British Film Institute, London.

—— 1987a *For a Cultural Future: Francis Jupurrurla Makes TV at Yuendumu.* Melbourne: Art and Criticism Monograph Series.

—— 1987b Aboriginal Content: Who's Got It—Who Needs It? *Art and Text* 23–4: 58–79.

—— 1988 Bad Aboriginal Art. *Art and Text* 28 (March–May): 59–73.

Michaels, Eric, and Francis Jupurrurla Kelly 1984 The Social Organization of an Aboriginal Video Workplace. *Australian Aboriginal Studies* 1: 26–34.

Molnar, Helen 1989 Aboriginal Broadcasting in Australia: Challenges and Promises. Paper presented at the International Communication Association Conference, March.

Muecke, Steven 1992 *Textual Spaces: Aboriginality and Cultural Studies.* Kensington: New South Wales University Press.

Myers, Fred 1994 Beyond the Intentional Fallacy: Art Criticism and the Ethnography of Aboriginal Acrylic Painting. *Visual Anthropology Review* 10(1): 10–43.

Nicoll, Fiona 1993 The Art of Reconciliation: Art, Aboriginality and the State. *Meanjin* 52(4): 705–18.

O'Regan, Tom (with Philip Batty) 1993 An Aboriginal Television Culture: Issues, Strategies, Politics. In *Australian Television Culture.* Pp. 169–92. St. Leonards, Australia: Allen and Unwin.

Peters, Frances 1993 Breaking All the Rules. (Interview with Jacqueline Urla). *Visual Anthropology Review* 9(2): 98–106.

Stanner, W. E. H. 1956 The Dreaming. In *Australian Signpost.* T. A. G. Hungerford, ed. Pp. 51–65. Melbourne: F. W. Cheshire.

Thiele, Steve 1991 Taking a Sociological Approach to Europeanness (Whiteness) and Aboriginality (Blackness). *The Australian Journal of Anthropology* 2(2): 179–201.

Trouillot, Michel-Rolph 1991 Anthropology and the Savage Slot: The Poetics and Politics of Otherness. In *Recapturing Anthropology.* Richard Fox, ed. Pp. 17–44. Santa Fe: School of American Research Press.

Turner, Neil 1990 Pitchat and Beyond. *Artlink* 10(1–2): 43–5.

Turner, Terence 1993 Anthropology and Multiculturalism: What Is Anthropology That Multiculturalists Should Be Mindful of It? *Cultural Anthropology* 8(4): 411–29.

# Part V

## Popular Practices

# Introduction

## John Nguyet Erni

In places gripped by colonial and neocolonial state power, all three words – *popular, culture, practices* – are likely to be entangled with the imposed hardship of survival, of making do under adverse circumstances. That popular cultural practices in so many places outside the North Atlantic contexts are embroiled in tangible and specific struggles over democracy, political repression, and the threat of historical amnesia, should haunt North Atlantic Cultural Studies and suggest its continued banality. I am determined to place this little comma in between "popular" and "culture," so as to insinuate a reminder that the routine conjoinment of the two into a reified site and theory of celebration in so many North Atlantic Cultural Studies, has occluded a radically different politics of struggle in other places, where each of the two concepts enunciates its own disputed and ambiguous relations and logics with the sovereign state. As for the concept of practice, the politics of the popular that you'll find in post- and neo-colonial places tend to be, on the one hand, more about the dispersal of tactics than about the deployment of strategies, and on the other hand, more about mutual appropriation between state actors and the masses than about a simplistic sense of resistance by the latter.

An understanding of popular practices in non-North Atlantic contexts, thus, entails seeing them as struggles likely to be found in ordinary people's yearning for a decolonization of everyday life. Those who engage in popular practices must invent localized ways of using what is made available to effect a disruption of the status quo. Meanwhile, such practices may be circumscribed by the state's effort to reappropriate the people's energies and tactics, rendering the "popular" an un-stable political frontier and thus echoing Stuart Hall's theory of politics "without guarantee." In a way, then, the state and the people wheedle each other into a contingent kind of popular existence.

Before I go on to say a bit more about the nature of popular practices found in coordinates other than the North Atlantic ones, let us not be amnesiac about the specificity out of which the whole question of popular culture/popular practice landed in the yards of British and American based Cultural Studies in the first place. Knowing this specific historical and theoretical trajectory can help to connect its tendencies with the other formations of popular practices found elsewhere.

Shaped by the general cultural upheaval of the 1960s and the formation of the New Left, British Cultural Studies practitioners witnessed – firsthand in many cases – how the terrain of popular culture became an important site of political and social conflict. Among leftist teachers and scholars, the attention to "mass media effects" would be quickly shifted to this broader, more politicized terrain of popular culture. More specifically, as Colin MacCabe (1986) and many others have pointed out, it was a shift toward a formal engagement with the high culture versus low culture debate. As early as 1964, Stuart Hall and Paddy Whannel argued in *The Popular Arts* that "the struggle between what is good and worthwhile and what is shoddy and debased is not a struggle *against* the modern forms of communication, but a conflict *within* these media" (1964: 15). The distinction between the tasteful and the disdained was marked internally in popular television programs, rock music, or comic books. This was not only because of competing textual codes at play, but also of the contradictory tastes of the audiences: the British or American working class. Through a (privileged) equation between popular culture and working-class culture, British and US Cultural Studies in the 1970s and early 1980s maintained that understanding the political motivation that marginalized the "popular class" and the "debased culture" they consumed was a key aspect of a repoliticized media studies.

At some level, this repoliticizing impulse spurred a nostalgic idealization of the (precommercial) lost past thought to have formerly belonged to an "authentic" working-class culture. Tony Bennett (1986) calls this a "walking backward into the future" (18), whereby any form of communication consumed by the working class, such as community newspapers and radio, is assumed to prefigure revolution! Integrating Gramsci's treatment of the "national-popular," Iain Chambers (1980) proposes a corrective by leaving open the possibility of articulation between popular culture and working-class culture in a larger political context (especially in England), where the "popular" can be (and has been) actively appropriated to serve the purposes of hegemonic nationalism. In this respect, the whole subculture debate in England surrounding working-class youth's relation with popular culture in the 1970s, represented a highly specific moment of theorizing within the visible group of Cultural Studies writers (Hall, Hebdige, Willis, McRobbie, etc.) over the complex relations between working-class struggle and the formation of nationalism. We may say this was British Cultural Studies' version of struggle over the "decolonization of everyday life."

Regrettably, and I hope this is a tolerable generalization, the subsequent history of the popular culture studies that traveled across the US from the 1980s onward had lost much of this specificity. In an important sense, what has been lost was any kind of sustained conceptualization of the relations between popular culture and

US nationalism (and its many forms of internal colonization that go well beyond the subjugation of youth and the working class). I will not belabor this point, nor do I wish to ignore those Cultural Studies works found in the US that do concern themselves with the "national-popular" question (e.g. the works of Kobena Mercer, bell hooks, Ella Shohat, Gloria Anzaldúa, and so on). But I will conjecture that some uneasiness with Cultural Studies (founded or unfounded) may be registered at the level where so many popular culture studies over the years are perceived to be silent about how "the popular" comprises, and is constituted by, the questions of nationalist formations, domination, repression, and violence. In many contexts outside the North Atlantic, especially in the South, the emancipative promises of popular cultural practices and movements tend to be recognized alongside an acute sense of uncertainty about their utopian potentials. In other words, the struggle with state power through popular practices and movements can be fraught with risks and contradictions.

Several major books produced in the 1990s concerning popular cultures in the South have indeed illuminated this contestative nature of "the popular." Rowe and Schelling's *Memory and Modernity: Popular Culture in Latin America* (1992), John Lent's *Caribbean Popular Culture* (1990) and *Asian Popular Culture* (1995), and Karin Barber's *Readings in African Popular Culture* (1997), all share the aim of divesting popular culture studies of their normative Euro-American milieux. But in so doing, these books also stumble onto a common ground: a shared confrontation with western modernity. Modernity is thus a kind of inevitability, since places that bear such putatively unifying signifiers as "Latin America," "Caribbean," "Asia," and "Africa" have all experienced degrees of industrialization and social and economic massification. Moreover, since "modernity" often means a set of political and economic calculations by the states, this shared confrontation with modernity found in popular cultures will necessarily confront the states. Given these inevitable encounters, is it any wonder that directly or implicitly all these books contain a discussion of "hybridity"?

In the first chapter of Rowe and Schelling's volume on popular culture in Latin America, we find a discussion of how the cultural life of both the peasant class and the urban class in Latin America interacting with European culture has undergone varying degrees of what they call "mestizaje" in different areas over time. According to Rowe and Schelling, mestizaje assumes a synthesis of European and Latin American cultures, where neither is eradicated by the other. The idea of mestizaje is further explored in literary texts and the electronic media. In another part of the book, there is an analysis of the state consolidation of power in Mexico. Rowe and Schelling suggest that Mexican political leaders after the revolution of 1910 were determined to build a "populist" regime by actively promoting (a) Mexican intellectuals' elaboration of the idea of cultural identity and (b) popular education to gain the allegiance of the popular classes. In an important sense, then, the consolidation of state power was attempted through a synthesis of the elite and popular classes. Therefore, hybridity in Latin American popular culture is not only about cultural synthesis, it could simultaneously be a state-sanctioned agenda!

It is easy to take hybridity as a feature of mass commercial culture, especially as globalization has habitually become a framework in studies of popular culture in capitalist states across Asia, Latin America, etc. John Lent's effort to compile studies of popular cultures in the Caribbean and across Asia in two different volumes, represents this view of hybridity-as-mass-culture. The essays found in both volumes enact a kind of academic flea market displaying a broad range of mass culture analyses: carnival music in Trinidad, sports in Jamaica, musicians in Singapore, cartoon magazines in Sri Lanka, so on and so forth. We may call it a "flat" view of hybridity – a kind of mirror image of the potpourri-style popular culture studies found in the North Atlantic that I critiqued earlier.

But, cultural plurality can be taken more seriously. Karin Barber's *Readings in African Popular Culture*, too, evokes the trope of hybridity in her introductory remarks: "There is a vast domain of cultural production which cannot be classified as either 'traditional' or 'elite,' as 'oral' or 'literate,' as 'indigenous' or 'Western' in inspiration because it straddles and dissolves these distinctions" (Barber, 1997: 1–2). The book is devoted to studies of this "vast domain." It includes essays that range from a macro-anthropological perspective on the world system on conversation between cultures" (e.g. Ulf Hannerz's "The World of Creolization"), through historical documents of how significant popular cultural work battles with state ideologies (e.g. Ngugi wa Thiong'o's "Women in Cultural Work: The Fate of Kamiriithu People's Theatre in Kenya"), to micro-realist analysis of everyday popular practices as forms of self-consciousness and self-understanding (Olatunde Bayo Lawuyi's "The World of the Yoruba Taxi Driver: An Interpretative Approach to Vehicle Slogans" – selected in this section). Throughout, one gets a sense that cultural plurality is not reducible to crude forms of mass culture, but is instead linked to multiple levels of struggles with the many faces and consequences of modernity – as world system, or state ideologies, or social class stratification.

To sum up, let me outline, in a simplistic manner, some of the dominant tendencies in studies of popular cultures, practices, and movements originating from many settings outside of the North Atlantic:

1 *Context-sensitivity*: Studies are rich in historical, political, and cultural specificities, even when they are still invested in the dichotomy of dominance vs. resistance.

2 *Multiple fronts of engagement with the cultural elites*: Critical research uncovers popular sensitivies in order to mount multiple dissenting discourses against cultural chauvinism and conservatism espoused by the state and other political elites.

3 *Concern with, and struggle over, the problem of "hybridity"*: The popular classes and their practices confront the problem of hybridity in various ways – temporally, with historical continuities and discontinuities of popular cultural life; conceptually, with the tradition/modernity conjuncture embedded in popular works; politically, with the situation of mutual appropriation between the state and the masses.

4   *Self-consciousness*: The decolonization of everyday life through popular prac-
    tices and consciousness, has tended to engender self-reflexivity, which takes
    "popular struggles" as a barometer to assess serious questions of nationalism,
    historical memory, cultural identity, violence, and survival. Further, the same
    self-reflexivity is sometimes used to provide metacritiques of local academic
    practices and debates in Cultural Studies there.

It is to this set of tendencies that the selection in this section is dedicated. The
idea that the popular is embedded in the tactics of everyday maneuver is shown in
South African anthropologist Olatunde Bayo Lawuyi's study of vehicle slogans
found in taxis driven by the Yoruba people in southwestern Nigeria. Expressions
of social mobility – upward and downward – displayed prominently in the slogans,
Lawuyi finds out, represent the taxi drivers' tortured negotiations with state
ideologies and economic policies. They also represent the taxi drivers' competitive-
ness toward each other over their recycled heroic tales of triumph over hardship. In
the end, such kind of popular practice becomes an alternative way of talking about
social stratification among the Yoruba, but more in terms of their mixed beliefs
about destiny and divinity than in terms of their economic status. The fact that
social stratification can be reworked – reimagined – through popular practices so
as to confront one's own socio-economic disenfranchisement is also found in
young school boys and girls in Hong Kong, who struggle with their boredom in
the imposed and alienating English learning environment in their schools. Chinese
sociolinguist and critical educationist Angel Lin's essay draws on Paul Willis's
classic study of "symbolic creativity" among working-class British youth in her
ethnographic research with primary-school English-language classrooms in Hong
Kong. In her study, she finds a wealth of parodic, laughter-producing mispronun-
ciations made by the students. Lin does not romanticize such practices, since the
study also reveals a sense of despair among the students, whose future they
themselves perceive to be bleak in a city where their working-class background,
and implied lack of "international skills" such as a command of English, is
discriminated against by future employers. Here, economic imperatives mix with
ideologies about upward mobility in a place long ruled by colonialists, producing a
context where the young students know the only way to fight their boredom in
learning English is to, in a sense, dismantle it through verbal play.

Language and literacy are no doubt common sites of struggle for self-
understanding and self-worth in colonial and postcolonial places. Deliberate
distortion of formal literacy, as performed by Lin's subjects, can be used to
challenge the state's educational agenda. For the Cantonese-speaking students in
Hong Kong, the verbal play becomes an elaborate "private" communication used
to irritate their English teachers, but more importantly, to mock the colonialism of
its imposed hegemony. Private literacy, as it were, is also the subject of South
African historian Keith Breckenridge's essay on migrant mineworkers' love-letter
writing. Breckenridge dispels the myths that these migrant workers in the early
period of the twentieth century were illiterate. Yet they did rely on skilled amanuenses to help write the letters. Love letters not only served as a heterosexual

romantic vehicle for these workers and their lovers in the city, they also outlined a very interesting "private sphere." Breckenridge suggests that this particular form of private literacy has been a very important part of African popular culture and, more significantly, has implications for the notion of cultural citizenship in the township and its democratic future. Like the Yoruba taxi drivers and the school students in Hong Kong, the mineworkers' popular practice plows a new ground for self-legitimacy under contradictory circumstances. In the end, then, no one can guarantee self-satisfaction.

A similar kind of fuzziness is also found in the private struggle for self-legitimacy among Japanese gay men, as Australian Cultural Studies scholar Mark McLelland's essay shows. McLelland looks at the role of a popular gay advice column in the formation of a private sphere among closeted gay men in Japan, and finds that this popular practice evinces all kinds of blurred discursive boundaries typified by the problem of the closet. He suggests that the famous pair of Japanese gay liberationists who reply to their online gay male audience about private struggles over family, marriage, secrecy, etc., are caught between western sexual ideologies calling for expressiveness and openness and pervasive Japanese social ideologies calling for discreetness in sexual matters and respect for family-centeredness. As a popular practice, this online advice column has "no sense of place," dangling over the space between advocacy of self-satisfaction and that of self-sacrifice for collective social stability. Ultimately, public advice column writing as a popular practice gives the whole problem of the "closet" a public shape, and thus can be taken as a telltale benchmark for seeing the repression in Japan's ongoing maintenance of nationhood.

The last selection in this section is also about nation-building, but less through repression than through explicit reworking of domestic – and thus gendered – ideologies. Africanist Cultural Studies scholar Igor Cusack's essay on the creation of cuisine and cookbooks in Equatorial Guinea lets us see the process by which the "popular" can pass from local tactics belonging to ordinary households into systematic strategies of colonial reinscription of power appropriated by the ruling elites. By examining cookbooks, Cusack suggests how the very notion of a cuisine embodies ethnic and colonial histories. The African cuisine he examines, in particular, embodies the colonial hybrid: geography mixes with colonial history, which blends with intercultural gender norms, which then muddles up with cross-Atlantic desires for "pan-Africanism" when consumed and promoted by African Americans. Imperialism, capitalism, and nationalism are reflected in the cookbooks, which in turn permeate into popular dissemination across the oceans.

In a sense, the popular is the signifier for the politics of ambivalence, for the marginal class as it is for the elites. The qualitative differences, however, must be marked between each side's relationship with the popular, even though it may be a floating mark. In many non-North Atlantic contexts, popular practices are more likely to be noticeable via the use of tactics on the part of the victims of nationalist repression or dismissal, and via the use of strategies on the part of the state apparatus trying to win over popular hegemony. As a result, each insinuates the other into a field of contingent relations, which may otherwise be known as everyday life.

## REFERENCES

Barber, Karin (ed.) (1997). *Readings in African Popular Culture*. Bloomington & Indianapolis: Indiana University Press.

Bennett, Tony (1986). "The politics of 'the popular' and popular culture," in T. Bennett et al. (eds.), *Popular Culture and Social Relations*. Milton Keynes: Open University Press, 6–21.

Chambers, Iain (1980). "Rethinking 'popular culture'," *Screen Education* 36: 113–17.

Hall, Stuart and Whannel, Paddy (1964). *The Popular Arts*. New York: Pantheon Books.

Lent, John A. (ed.) (1990). *Caribbean Popular Culture*. Bowling Green, OH: Bowling Green State University Press.

Lent, John A. (ed.) (1995). *Asian Popular Culture*. Boulder, CO: Westview Press.

MacCabe, Colin (ed.) (1986). *High Theory/Low Culture: Analyzing Popular Television and Film*. Manchester: Manchester University Press.

Rowe, William and Schelling, Vivian (1992). *Memory and Modernity: Popular Culture in Latin America*. London: Verso.

# 21

# The World of the Yoruba Taxi Driver: An Interpretative Approach to Vehicle Slogans

## Olatunde Bayo Lawuyi

The purpose of this paper is to analyse the slogans which are so prominent and ubiquitous on motor vehicles as expressions of social stratification among the Yoruba of southwestern Nigeria.[1] I interpret the slogans in the context of the taxi owners' and drivers' social interactions, not just as disembodied expressions of a total Yoruba world view. In studying the slogans I pay particular attention to processes of accumulation of wealth, status mobility and the way these are affected by cultural values. It is argued that the vehicle owners make different claims at different stages of their careers. Their fears and hopes at each stage must be understood in the light of the contemporary Christian and traditional mix of beliefs about destiny, the world and God.

Of major interest to the present inquiry is the subjective dimension of Yoruba social stratification. There is no doubt that much information is available on status criteria, but the scope of questions asked and the relevance of the answers to the analysis of Yoruba world views are limited. Traditional social stratification is typically linked to lineage, wealth and rank (Bascom, 1942, 1951; Lloyd, 1954, 1966). Yet processes of change, first initiated by colonial rule, have brought about fundamental changes in these criteria. Many recent studies have tended to explain events within the Yoruba sphere such as the Agbekoya movement (1968–70) as reflections of the general Nigerian socio-political structure (Joseph, 1978; Gutkind, 1973, 1975; Williams, 1976, 1980; Peace, 1974, 1975, 1979).

Recent studies have been based on the notion that there are two competing social groups, the rich and the poor, with irreconcilable differences. These differences may be worked out in terms of the opposition between poor peasants and urban elites or the opposed interests of the rural and the urban poor. The attention given the urban poor is due to the fact that they stand in the front line of confrontation because most of Africa's wealth is located in the cities (Gugler and Flanagan, 1978). Colonial rule is often blamed for this lopsided economic structure (Ake, 1976) because it set up new industrial centres and created new patterns of competition and mobilization (Sandbrook and Cohen, 1975). And in so far as inequality seems to exist among the various social strata of modern and traditional structures, political consciousness has derived from oppression, control, exploit-ation and paternalism. The resultant contradictions became a key element in political activism (Fallers, 1973; Anifowose, 1973; Gutkind, 1975).

These kinds of arguments display little insight into the complexity underlying Yoruba social mobility. The mobility can be upwards or downwards, although the latter has received less attention. Exploitation also occurs, both within and between classes. What the authors in general have failed to highlight is the relevance of indigenous ideas and beliefs to historical action; there is little or no treatment of the complex resonances of allusion and metaphor. The fluid and vertiginous densities of symbolic constructs are often left unanalysed. As McCaskie (1983) has noted in a critique of previous literature on African economic history, the scanty attention to world views results in conclusions unrelated to both the explicit and the implicit representations of people's ideas.

The data for the present study are derived from the observation of inscriptions (i.e. vehicle slogans) on taxis and interviews with taxi drivers, taxi owners, taxi conductors (agbero) and sign writers. Sixty people were interviewed informally at various times, at the motor parks and in their homes. They comprised twenty taxi drivers, twenty taxi owners, ten sign writers and ten agbero.[2] Questions were designed to elicit responses on life histories and careers, the structure of transport, and the beliefs and ethical values which underlay the identity constructions in economic relationships. Most of the interviews were conducted in Ile-Ife.

## ■ The Social Relations of Transport in Ile-Ife ■

Ile-Ife is 200 kilometres from Lagos.[3] It is situated in the semi-forest belt and in 1976 had an estimated population of 350,000. Although reputed to be the cradle of Yoruba civilization founded by Oduduwa, it is one of several major Yoruba urban centres with an estimated growth rate of 3 per cent. The city has many schools, several hospitals, a university and numerous entrepreneurial projects. The majority of people are cash-crop farmers; most of them have cocoa plantations. Apart from farming, small businesses are on the increase and are dominated by migrants who have come to work in schools, hospitals and the university. Included in the small-scale projects are supermarkets, boutiques and mechanic shops.

Taxi driving and owning is a lucrative small business. The taxis operate within the city and more widely within Oyo State; several of them are also involved in interstate journeys. The taxis are mostly Peugeot cars, though other vehicles of Japanese make, such as Toyota and Datsun, are also common. For those involved in the transport business taxi driving is work. The work is performed in morning and afternoon shifts for taxis operating within the Ile-Ife limits. However, when a taxi is on a long-distance journey, it has one permanent driver.

The received wisdom is that work, class and power relationships are essentially material transactions, social relations being treated as aspects of economic realities. But social relationships, even in the sphere of production, are affected by history and a specific cultural context (Akeredolu-Ale, 1973, 1975). The taxi driver can shift between his person and affect-oriented performance on one hand and his time and efficiency-oriented driver culture on the other (Jordan, 1978). The type of behaviour exhibited determines the nature of relations with the taxi owner and the passengers, and the success made of the transport business. Success encourages hard work. Both the taxi driver and the owner stand to benefit from any economic success. Whereas the driver may get a fatter paypacket, the owner's social prestige may grow because of his entrepreneurial ability. However, a driver's ambition to better himself may lead him to acts of dishonesty, which may not only damage the business but bring about a status reversal. This also happens when the driver makes money from the business, becomes self-employed and gains in social prestige. The owner's status invariably changes if the taxi business is his main source of livelihood.

Competition among transporters is keen because transport's contribution to the gross domestic product is quite low (Falola and Olanrewaju, 1986). A study conducted by Olanrewaju (1977) shows figures ranging from 3.1 per cent to 18.3 per cent between 1964 and 1972 for various African countries. Yet in Nigeria, after trading operations and real estate, the most lucrative business is transport (Joseph, 1978). The major objective of those who invest their resources in a transport business is to become self-employed. This is because government jobs are not considered adequately rewarding and, as the recent mass retrenchment of workers has shown (Adu, 1965; Sanda, 1982), they can be rather insecure. To be self-employed, people use political leverage to secure low-interest loans from banks and government agencies to buy vehicles or build houses. Though not all of them prove to be reliable in keeping to their loan agreements, the loans nevertheless allow them to set up businesses which respond to the great demand for road transportation and the consequent opportunities to make money which exist in Nigeria.

There are three types of transport vehicles: trailers, buses and taxis. The trailers are used for haulage of heavy materials, mainly on interstate journeys. Unlike buses, trailers rarely carry passengers. The buses, in fact, carry more passengers than taxis, which, in the case of Peugeot station wagons, take up to seven passengers.

A newly bought taxi is usually taken to a sign writer to have slogans painted on it. There is an independent, highly flourishing and lucrative business of sign writing in most Yoruba towns. In Ile-Ife these businesses can be found in and around the local markets and in the centre as well as the outskirts of the town. Often sign writers are to be found near panel beaters, who work with the roadside mechanics in repairing damaged vehicles. My survey of Ile-Ife sign writers shows that their average age is thirty-five, with typically at least a primary school leaving certificate, and they have worked on average ten years in their trade.

Taxi owners are not necessarily taxi drivers, but most of the taxi owners had at one time or the other been taxi drivers. A business may be built up by an owner-driver, but as he acquires a fleet of taxis he needs drivers, who aim to become independent operators themselves. My survey showed 100 per cent ($n = 20$) of drivers to be men. Driving, like other mechanical jobs, is supposed to be 'rough' and, in the Yoruba world view, to be outside a woman's competence; the rigour and energy which it needs are deemed incompatible with a woman's commitment to her family. Men, on the other hand, can easily rationalize prolonged absence from home as a form of work ethic.

With respect to taxi ownership, however, female involvement is on the increase. Ten per cent of my sample of owners ($n = 20$) who have taxis on the road were women, but I was made to understand that there may be many more women involved.[4] The two women in the sample appeared competent to supervise vehicles on intercity and interstate routes, yet their taxis plied only the intra-city routes. In this way, they reasoned, they could stay at home and take care of their families while relying on relatives and co-drivers to check the movements of their drivers.

It is people in the age range twenty-one to forty (70 per cent of owners) who have most of the taxis on the road. This is because those in the upper age bracket have diversified their economic interests and have gone into the retail trade, car dealership and other small businesses. Sixty per cent of the taxi drivers revealed that they have been driving for over ten years. The religious affiliations of drivers were 50 per cent Christian, 45 per cent Muslim and 5 per cent traditionalists, a distribution which does not differ significantly from that in the Ife population at large. It is therefore not surprising that those interviewed did not think that religion has influenced their occupational choice. Rather, religion is used to create a certain morale: there is a feeling that religion helps to improve the chances of success in a hazardous and unpredictable activity.

In addition to their own managerial ability, transporters look to the intervention of superior spiritual forces to prevent accidents, attract passengers and keep policemen – who demand bribes – off the road. Consequently I found signs of juju in most of the vehicles. All traditional religious adherents, 80 per cent of Muslims and 60 per cent of Christians, used juju, the Christians showing most ambivalence towards the practice. Many think it is un-Christian but nevertheless feel it is unavoidable in a milieu where life and property are so insecure.

The presence of juju in vehicles is a resort to symbolic action in the face of uncertainties. In Nigeria armed robbers may attack and steal the vehicles. The roadside mechanic may have mistakenly connected two wires that could ignite and burn the vehicle. Nobody can predict when accidents will occur, as drivers in a hurry overtake dangerously. The juju in the vehicle serve to remind the drivers of their power to escape from any danger. They can be in the form of feathers or in the shape of a lock or a comb. To these symbols, hidden under the dashboard, displayed on the windscreen or put under the driver's seat, are ascribed the power to make drivers disappear into thin air when accidents occur. Alternatively they may prevent accidents. They also bring wealth by attracting passengers. Through their mystifications the juju make it possible for the individual to survive the disruptive processes created by national and international tensions which affect economic processes (Cohen, 1976). The juju themselves are not mechanical reflections of power relations, but are autonomous entities which can act on the power order and modify it.

For instance, most of those involved in the transport business are in dire need of some power in order to boost their morale. Most taxi drivers are not Ile-Ife indigenes, but immigrants from other Yoruba towns and villages attracted initially by the prospect of getting a job in one of the few industrial enterprises or in the university. Most of them had at least a primary school certificate. Usually, when they could not secure a bureaucratic job but did not want to return to their home town (cf. Plotnicov, 1965), they took to taxi driving after obtaining a taxi licence. Many of those employed in transport are thus semi-skilled workers.

The unskilled workers are mostly the *agbero*, who stay in the vehicles, especially the buses, and assist the drivers in collecting fares, controlling passengers, and monitoring the traffic to the rear. As noted by Onoghoete (1980), the *agbero* has an important function when, as is the case on many Nigerian roads, the traffic is highly congested. In such instances one cannot imagine

> the number of accidents that would occur per day... if these professionals [i.e. *agbero*] called 'pilots' and 'captains' were nonexistent and not in a position to say to the drivers 'O wọ ọ' ('It has entered the line'), 'Jadẹ' (Move out), 'Jadẹ dìẹ' ('Move out slightly'), 'Jadẹ tan' (Move out completely)... Also unimaginable is the confusion that could result were the drivers to drive the *danfo* (cab) vehicle, collect fares and give change to their passengers during trip. [Onoghoete, 1980: 6]

While undoubtedly the activities of the *agbero* may ease the drivers' task, their instructions, issued at once and sometimes in contradiction, may also help to confuse them. Many of the *agbero*, in fact, can be seen hanging on to the vehicles' tailboards, especially when the vehicles are full of passengers. The risk to their lives notwithstanding, the thought of having no job at all constrains them to accept their situation.

Not all the taxis on Ile-Ife roads are roadworthy. The exhaust pipes of some of them are conduits for the escape of poisonous carbon monoxide fumes due to incomplete combustion of petrol. The treads on the tyres have become unrecognizable because of wear. Neither the passengers, the *agbero* nor the drivers appear to be so worried about the condition of the vehicles as to want to disboard. Of course, the vehicles may be the only form of public transport to the passengers' destinations. But even if they cared, they are exhorted to tolerate the situation by slogans like 'No moless' and 'Play cool', which are inscribed on the inside and outside of the vehicles.

Alternatively, the slogan may read '*Tiẹ dà?*' ('Where is yours?'). This is to signify that the vehicle owners have special powers which, however unroadworthy their vehicles are, make them better off than those without. Indeed, success, no matter the degree, is worth some respect. The slogan 'Where is yours?' locates the power in a social relationship in which control over labour and product (or any other resource) is not a primary issue. Rather, the travellers themselves know that, if angered, the driver may refuse to take them to their destination, for a certain power inheres in the driver's or owner's control of the vehicle and in a sense makes him a privileged citizen.

> The association of trucks with power has affected the driving habits of the Nigerian populace. The unwritten rule seems to be that everything and every one must give way to trucks. Groups of women walking to market scramble for the roadside ditches, as these unruly vehicles career along at reckless speeds through intersections. [Pritchett, 1979: 31]

The social power of the driver is quite different from his economic power, which is ultimately maintained by reward and deprivation. The vehicle owner pays the taxi driver for his services. This usually amounts to one third of the daily income. The *agbero* gets less. However, as the amount received may be insufficient to feed and clothe the *agbero* and his family, the driver may collude with the *agbero* to defraud the vehicle owner. Because many of the vehicle owners have themselves been drivers, they are aware of the possibility of being defrauded and usually take steps to prevent it, such as changing drivers and *agbero* at the same or at different times. My survey shows that a taxi driver hardly stays longer than four years before being replaced. But even before they are laid off, many drivers accumulate enough capital to buy their own vehicles.

A profound insight into the Yoruba concept of work and its social and economic consequences is provided in the aphorism 'E ṣe nidi pẹpẹ a jẹ nidi pẹpẹ ('Whoever works at the altar must eat at the altar'). That is, you make your wealth from your place of work. And as soon as you become wealthy (invariably by diverting resources to your own use) there may be no more work to do as services may have become paralysed. This relationship to work might help explain the suspicion between the owner and driver on one hand and the driver and *agbero* on the other. The driver is responsible for reporting income to the owner. But the *agbero* collects the fares from the passengers and passes them on to the driver. Any driver or *agbero* has the opportunity to misappropriate the collected fares. The vehicle may wear out from use, but the driver or *agbero* makes sure that, as soon as it does, he is about to start another job.

A delicate relationship exists between the individual and work. Because work must be available in order that people may be employed, it is necessary that something remains on the altar for everybody to be satisfied. Yet, as a vehicle slogan suggests, 'Work is the medicine for poverty' ('Iṣẹ ni oogun iṣẹ'). But linking work with medicine brings a contradiction, in that if work solves the problem of poverty – or cures that 'illness' – then there ought to be no need for juju, which is also commonly used as medicine. Juju would seem to do what work itself can do, unless we are to take the statement as an ironical comment on the uselessness of such charms compared to work itself.

Further analysis of Yoruba world views, however, indicates that, in actual fact, work and juju complement each other. Work is a physical activity; the charms do not deal directly with labour but are suggestive of the power that inheres in social relationships. The juju or charms do not encourage greater energy input into the working situation. Indeed, they are not meant as medicine for tiredness. Rather, they are used to facilitate profit and protect the individual and property in a competitive environment. The Yoruba belief is that one must work hard to succeed ('*Ninu ikoko dudu ni ẹko funfun ti nwa*' – 'It's from a black pot that white porridge comes'). But, as they also say, work brings about the destruction of the labourer: 'A brave soldier perishes in battle at last; so too a skillful swimmer often ends his life by drowning in water. What we relish most kills us.' The value of work is further strengthened by a fear of an uncertain future ('*Ko si ẹda to mọ ọla*' – 'No mortal creature can know tomorrow'), the suspicion of a social situation which is open to any possibility. The uncertainties make it important that work must end with the accumulation of wealth or property. Through this accumulation one gains in power and social prestige (Lloyd, 1966), which are then protected by juju.

Nevertheless it must be stressed that there is in the Yoruba world view a distinction between labour and its appropriation. Those who appropriate labour do not work hard and do not suffer as much as the labourer: '*Oṣiṣe wa l'orun, ẹni maa jẹ wa ni iboji*' ('The worker is under the full heat of the sun but one will eat in a quiet, restful place'); that is, the consumers are often ignorant of the worker's condition and, by implication, do not often work within the existing system to win reform for working people. The individual who accepts this point must also accept the legitimacy of work as 'medicine for poverty'; that is, poverty is removed only by the underprivileged working for their own survival. Their commitment is not to work itself but to survival and social mobility. Work is but a means to an end, a self-fulfilling end which originates in the perception of work as an organizing forum for an individual/collective relationship with economic or political opportunities (Adejare and Afolayan, 1981).

Not everyone can make a success of work because this requires identifying opportunities and selecting people who, through their encouragement, link the individuals to the opportunities. Those who failed to use the situation of work to advance their social mobility are said to have *ori buruku* – bad head or destiny (Falola, 1982). Before their *ori* becomes better, they have to realize that work is necessary to become wealthy, and that wealth is important for the control it gives over others (Bascom, 1951; Eades, 1980). To be successful, work must be complemented by destiny, character and the avoidance of mystical attack by others (Horton, 1961; Bascom, 1969; Falola, 1982). If these other factors do not operate in one's favour, no matter the energy input into work, there will be no economic success.

## ■ The Driver's Career and the Struggle Against *Aiye* ■

Some of the concerns of the entrepreneur – the avoidance of mystical attack, the desire to become wealthy, the care not to overstep the delicate balance of authority relationships, the complicated issues over the use of one's power – express the personal continuities and discontinuities experienced by individuals in their life histories (Neugarten, 1975). The experiences of the drivers and owners can be taken as an important index of their specific personality or character. They remember, according to their social background, their encounters with policemen and armed robbers, the numbers of accidents they have had and their new statuses. Those who feel their status has improved significantly since entering the transport business tend to minimize the pestilence of the police. To them, names, titles and other status symbols are embedded in and are reflections of the associations which they have entered into in the course of business and self-development. For example, a middle-aged man and a chief said: 'Everybody around here knows me. I know every part of the country. When I was young, I will take the taxi down to Kaduna. I can be gone for days. No accident. The police know me. They call me by my nickname. Everybody loves me. Driving is hazardous but I like it. You know many don't want to leave their homes. Driving is fun. My brother... you see, we drivers know many people, from all walks of life.'

Basically, taking into consideration the life histories of the transport entrepreneurs, we identified three stages of self/business growth. The diversity of experience is largely a consequence of the entrepreneurs' maturity. The young ones, who optimistically say in slogans 'The young shall grow' and 'I am still young', are less than thirty years old, are mostly driver-owners, are more aggressive and much more easily disappointed by failure – they especially fear accidents or poor profits.

Older driver-owners, those over the age of thirty, are much more hopeful of a better tomorrow. They are familiar with the transport business and can take some of the shock of failure. In spite of their familiarity with the transport business, however, they are still troubled by the competition for passengers and by unfilled expectations. They often experience a mid-life crisis created by family demands – the responsibility for their wife's trade or their children's schooling. Reflecting their socio-psychological dispositions are such slogans as 'The struggle continues', 'Unlimited promotion', 'Aiye le' ('The world is hard'), 'Wọn fi oju jọ ọrẹ', ('They pretend to be friends'). The slogan 'When there is life there is hope' is also frequently adopted, expressing hope for future wealth, enough money to buy several new taxis and put up buildings. Said a thirty-five-year-old informant: 'I sometimes think I can make it. My father never did much before he died. He was not popular. He was poor. My mother it was that took care of my needs. We are a poor family struggling to survive. My taxis might bring a lot of money today. Tomorrow, [I am told] all may be lost to the policemen or to repair of mechanical damage. If only I had the money, I wouldn't care. But I need to have a roof over my head and my extended family. If you saw Mr X this time five years ago, he was like me. Now he owns a big shop in Ibadan... A big man in Ife.'

Wealth brings political power. It is therefore not surprising to find that successful transporters are politically powerful in Yoruba society. The more money the transporters make, the greater their ability to afford luxury goods like colour televisions, video sets and rugs to decorate the house. One transporter even boasted of having used his money to marry a graduate whom university professors were interested in. Wealth enables a man to extend his sphere of influence by projecting an image of being a public figure. While some people under the age of forty are public figures, most members of the elites are older. They have become wealthy by diversifying their assets into more stable sources of income such as estate construction and small businesses. As public figures they donate huge sums of money at ceremonies and are honoured with special seats at public and private functions. These individuals are expected to 'declare surplus', meaning that there must be public occasions at which some of the accumulated goods and symbolic resources percolate down to the poor, to the members of the extended family and to loyal party members and attendants. Their success is more appropriately conveyed in slogans such as 'Adelebare' ('I met honour/wealth at home') and 'Ọmu iya dun' ('Mother's breast is sweet').

But downwards mobility too is not uncommon. Properties are lost to fire, armed robbers or accidents. Life becomes difficult. To survive individuals seek out old friends and relatives to whom they have acted as benefactors. Some friends may help; others may not. Friends who refuse help although they have the resources to do so become labelled as *aiye*. The term *aiye* is a subtle, complex notion for events ('Aiye d'aiye oyinbo' – 'The world is now governed by the whites'), time ('L'aiye Babalola' – 'In Babalola's time') and morality ('Aiye daru' – 'The world has no order, no sense of morality'). That time and space are so blurred in it indicates, I believe, its metaphysical significance.

To the struggling transport entrepreneur, 'Aiye le ('The world is hard'). This is a philosophical statement about human existence, in particular its vagaries. When property is lost and friendship fails, it is time to ponder not only on human frailty but also on the dynamics of social mobility as embodied in the slogan 'No condition is permanent'. Although a few transport entrepreneurs do manage to recover their position after a hope-shattering experience, there are some who abandon the transport business altogether. One of them, a man of forty-five, said: 'I bought my first taxi when I was young. It plied the intercity routes because I thought I could make money fast doing so. All went well for a while. One day the driver had an accident with it. There were casualties. It became a police case. They [the police] dilly-dallied on the matter until I spent all my savings. But, by my mother-in-law's grace, I got another taxi on the road. I insisted it must ply intra-city routes. You see, the driver went out of the way and crashed the car again. I was downfall [demoralized]. No money. Nothing to feed my wife and children. I became a beggar. I, who used to give people money. I am now looking for another business.'

The Yoruba believe that 'Ti ọna kan ko ba di, ọna mi ko le la' ('Failure creates alternative means for self-development'). Personal norms and expectations, operating to stimulate or restrain behaviour, can turn failure to success and success to failure. The individual is considered to have an *ori* ('destiny') which can affect achievement positively or negatively; in addition to the role of *ori*, fortunes can be changed by a man's character and appropriate ritual sacrifices (Idowu, 1962). If the rituals function as intended they serve to regularize or stabilize psychological dispositions in a highly dynamic, continuously changing social situation (Cohen, 1976). Their symbols, the juju, stand conspicuously for beliefs, sentiments and emotions which are evoked by the need for a sense of security.

When fortune changes it challenges the fundamental Yoruba belief that individuals are spiritually endowed with capacity for success. In the Yoruba world view, *ori*, or destiny, is naturally good unless otherwise changed by laziness, by *aiye*, by a man's character or by Orunmila, the god of divination. Hence any failure in business transactions or in life must be attributed to sources other than God, the creator of human destiny.

Negative social mobility or change in fortune is frequently attributed to the influence of *aiye*. Whenever, 'the world' is used in slogans, it invokes reactions which range from fear to appreciation of an immense, malignant power, '*Aiye toto*' ('What an extraordinarily unimaginable development or event!'). *Aiye* is a power, a superior that must be begged ('*Aiye e ma binu wa*' – 'World, don't be angry with us') lest personal fate be altered ('*Aiye ẹ ma pa kadara wa da*' – 'World, don't change our fate'). The concept of *aiye* has several other meanings. In the aphorism '*Ẹyin aiye*' ('You of the world') individuals are labelled as cunning, dubious and unpredictable in their social relationships. 'The world is a market, heaven is home' ('*Aiye l'o ja, ọrun n'ilẹ*') is clearly stated in another aphorism. *Aiye*, then as an objectification of the world, speaks of a social setting where, as in the marketplace, individuals voluntarily interact and negotiate to produce a certain balance of power relations (Lawuyi, 1986). More generally for the Yoruba, *aiye* serves as a key to a value system, conveying those self-conceptions, motivations and understandings by which the individual relates to society. Indeed, with appropriate linguistic modifiers it means pretence, time, tribal territory, the dominion of a political leader, a market, the whole world, the evil ones, witches and sorcerers, unformed and dangerous characters, spiritual forces and a point on a journey. It represents the good and negative aspects of human development:

> *Aiye mo juba.*
> I respect the world.
> *Aiye nreti eleya.*
> The world awaits a failure.
> *Aiye a kamara.*
> A world of intrigues.

The inherent dichotomy of 'I' and 'the world' is one of moral exclusiveness. 'I', unless strengthened by spiritual forces – which is why there are juju in most of the taxis – is never equal to but is opposite and complementary to *aiye*. The more one is emphasized, the less is heard of the potentials of the other. There is no 'I', which is symbolized by *ori*, without *aiye*, as there is no action without a context. Similarly, there is no *aiye* without *ori*, no theatre without actors and actresses. *Ori* connotes action potentiality:

> *Ori sun mi bare.*
> *Ori* led me to wealth.
> *Ori lo ni iṣe.*
> *Ori* is the doer/performer.

Thus the references to *ori* encourage people to become conscious of their own power and of their natural right to participate in all that is best in the society.

To this end, social identity must be carefully organized. Parents, employers, friends and kinsfolk who have been benefactors are remembered in slogans such as '*Ọla iya*' ('Mother's benevolence'), '*Ọla ọrẹ*' ('Friend's benevolence'), '*Ọla ẹgbọn*' ('Brother's benevolence'), '*Ọrẹ meji*' ('Two friends') and '*Ọla papa*' ('Father's benevolence'). Benevolent mothers are praised more often than fathers because, according to those interviewed, mothers part with their resources more easily than fathers do. In the Yoruba world view, '*Iya ni wura baba ni jingi*' ('Mothers are gold, fathers are mirrors'). Yoruba society is patrilineal and polygynous. Consequently a son will find his father a mirror because he will hope to be like him, to replace him in the social structure (e.g. *joye baba rẹ*); but because his father has many wives whose various children are rivals, it is to his mother that a man must look for unstinted support (i.e. *wura*, 'gold').

Several slogans also mention God as a symbol of positive identification and trustworthy authority. God in Yoruba belief is a creator, a king, an all-wise, all-knowing, all-seeing, omnipotent and benevolent being (Idowu, 1962). Thus, as a symbol of knowledge and creativity, God is emblematic of a situation in which the individual can manipulate existing symbols or create new ones to enhance his chances of success.

> *Abanise ni Oluwa.*
> God is a doer/performer.
> *Oluwa ni agbara mi.*
> God is my strength.
> *Nipa ife Olugbala ki y'o si nkan.*
> Through the Saviour's love, there will be no danger.

The power attributed to God (or His representative) is superior to that of *aiye*, and so He enables an individual to transcend any limitations in the course of his business pursuits.

## ■ Conclusion ■

The main argument of this article is that much can be learned about the production and usage of vehicle slogans if the elements are analysed in terms of their implications for social interaction. Basically, the creation and diffusion of the slogans is the consequence of their being a form of language that makes social life meaningful and consequently provides the reader with a vital key for understanding the experiences of an important sector of Nigerian society. In this article, the focus has been on the interactions between the vehicle owners, the drivers and the *agbero*. Members of these groups struggle to accumulate capital and to develop businesses of their own as means of achieving personal independence and enhanced social status. Their struggles for upward social mobility are shaped by cultural traditions which condition the manner in which they pursue their goals and select their identities.

## NOTES

1 The author acknowledges with thanks the contributions of the anonymous reviewers whose comments have shaped the orientation of this article. Appreciation is also extended to Toyin Falola, Leke Atewologun and my wife, Toyin Lawuyi, for their help in formulating this essay. An earlier draft of this article was read at a Social Sciences Faculty Seminar of Obafemi Awolowo University, Ile-Ife.

2 The interviews were conducted from February to April 1986. The analysis of vehicle slogans is a continuing interest.

3 There are nineteen states and the federal capital territory, Abuja, in Nigeria. The taxis for each state are marked in different colours. Those of Oyo state (including those in Ile-Ife) are painted yellow and deep red. Statistics on the population of Ile-Ife were supplied by the Department of Demography and Statistics of Obafemi Awolowo University.

4 Conservative estimates put the figure at 10 per cent. Those interviewed are of the opinion that the present figure is about 20 per cent up on estimates for the previous year.

## REFERENCES

Adejare, O. and Afolayan, A. (1981) 'Semiotics: the unexplored level of variation in second language use', paper read at SEAMEO Seminar, Singapore, 19–23 April.

Adu, A. L. (1965) *The Civil Service in New African States.* London: Allen & Unwin.

Ake, C. (1976) 'Explanatory notes on the political economy of Africa', *Journal of Modern African Studies* 14 (1), 1–23.

Akeredolu-Ale, E. O. (1973) 'A socio-historical study of the development of entrepreneurship among the Ijebu of western Nigeria', *African Studies Review* 16 (3), 347–64.

——(1975) *The Underdevelopment of Indigenous Entrepreneurship in Nigeria.* Ibadan: Ibadan University Press.

Anifowose, F. O. (1973) 'The Politics of Violence in Nigeria: a case study of the Tiv and Yoruba areas', PhD thesis, Manchester University.

Bascom, W. R. (1942) 'The principle of seniority in the social structure of the Yoruba', *American Anthropologist* 44 (1), 37–46.

——(1951) 'Social status, wealth and individual differences among the Yoruba', *American Anthropologist* 53 (4), 490–505.

——(1969) *The Yoruba of Southwestern Nigeria.* New York: Holt, Rinehart & Winston.

Cohen, A. (1976) *Two-Dimensional Man.* Berkeley: University of California Press.

Eades, J. S. (1980) *The Yoruba Today.* Cambridge: Cambridge University Press.

Fallers, L. A. (1973) *Inequality: social stratification reconsidered.* Chicago: University of Chicago Press.

Falola, T. (1982) 'Religion, rituals and the Yoruba pre-colonial domestic economy: myth and reality', *Ife Journal of Religions* 2, 27–37.

—— and Olanrewaju, S. A. (1986) *Transport Systems in Nigeria*. New York: Syracuse University.

Gugler, J. and Flanagan, W. G. (1978) *Urbanization and Social Change in West Africa*. Cambridge: Cambridge University Press.

Gutkind, P. C. W. (1973) 'From the energy of despair to the anger of despair', *Canadian Journal of African Studies* 7 (2), 179–98.

—— (1975) 'The view from below: political consciousness among the urban poor in Ibadan', *Cahiers d'études africaines* 57 (1), 5–35.

Horton, R. (1961) 'Destiny and the unconscious in West Africa', *Africa* 31, 110–16.

Idowu, E. B. (1962) *Olodumare: god in Yoruba belief*. London: Longman.

Jordan, J. W. (1978) 'Role segregation for fun and profit: the daily behaviour of the West African lorry driver', *Africa* 48 (1), 30–46.

Joseph, R. A. (1978) 'Affluence and underdevelopment: the Nigerian experience', *Journal of Modern African Studies* 16 (2), 221–39.

Lawuyi, O. B. (1986) 'Reality and meaning: a review of the Yoruba concept of esu', *Afrika und Ubersee* 69 (2), 299–311.

Lloyd, P. C. (1954) 'The traditional political system of the Yoruba', *Southwestern Journal of Anthropology* 101, 366–84.

—— (1966) 'Class consciousness among the Yoruba', in *The New Elites of Tropical Africa*, ed. P. C. Lloyd, London: Oxford University Press for the International African Institute.

McCaskie, T. (1983) 'Accumulation, wealth and belief in Asante history', *Africa* 53 (1), 23–43.

Neugarten, B. L. (1975) 'Continuities and discontinuities of psychological issues into adult life', in *Life: the Continuous Process*, ed. F. Rebelsky, New York: Alfred A. Knopf.

Olanrewaju, S. A. (1977) 'The role of transport in African economic development', *African Development Studies* 1 (2), 40–50.

Onoghoete, G. M. (1980) 'The Danfo *Agbero*-Bus Conductor Occupational Group in a Metropolitan Centre', BSc dissertation, University of Ife, Ile-Ife.

Peace, A. (1974) 'Industrial protest in Nigeria', in *Sociology and Development*, eds. E. de Kadt and G. P. Williams, London: Tavistock.

—— (1975) 'The Lagos proletariat: labour aristocrats or populist militants?' in *The Development of an African Working Class*, eds. R. Sandbrook and R. Cohen, London: Longman.

—— (1979) *Choice, Class and Conflict: a study of Southern Nigerian factory workers*. Brighton: Harvester Press.

Plotnicov, U. (1965) 'Nigerians: the dream is unfulfilled', *Trans-Action* 3, 18–22.

Pritchett, J. (1979) 'Nigerian truck art', *African Arts* 12 (2), 27–31.

Sanda, A. O. (1982) 'Premature Retirement as Avenues of Losing Revenue', paper presented at the National Conference on Alternative Sources of Government Revenue, organized by NISER, University of Ibadan, 6–10 December.

Sandbrook, R. and Cohen, R. (1975) 'Workers and progressive change in underdeveloped countries', in *The Development of an African Working Class*, eds. R. Sandbrook and R. Cohen, London: Longman.

Williams, G. (1976) *Nigeria: Economy and Society*. London: Rex Collings.

—— (1980) *State and Society in Nigeria*. Idanre: Afrografika Publishers.

# 22

# Doing Verbal Play: Creative Work of Cantonese Working-Class Schoolboys in Hong Kong

## Angel M. Y. Lin

You want to know why I don't pay attention in English lessons? You really want to know? Okay, here's the reason: NO INTEREST!! It's so boring and difficult and I can never master it. But society wants you to learn English! If you're no good in English, you're no good at finding a job!

14-year-old schoolboy, informal interview (from Lin, 1999: 407; original in Cantonese)

the major drama of resistance in schools is an effort on the part of students to bring their street-corner culture into the classroom.... it is a fight against the erasure of their street-corner identities.... students resist turning themselves into worker commodities in which their potential is evaluated only as future members of the labor force. At the same time, however, the images of success manufactured by the dominant culture seem out of reach for most of them.

McLaren, 1998: 191

## ▪ 1. Introduction ▪

Despite Hong Kong's international cosmopolitan appearance, the majority of its population is ethnic Chinese, and Cantonese is the mother tongue of the majority. The British were a minority that had, however, constituted the privileged class of the society until July 1, 1997, when Hong Kong's sovereignty was returned to China and Hong Kong became a Special Administrative Region (SAR) of China.

The English-conversant bilingual Chinese middle class has, however, remained the socio-economically dominant group in Hong Kong, and English is still the most important language of social mobility even in the post-1997, post-British-rule era. For instance, a 1998 survey on business corporations in Hong Kong found that the majority of business corporations said they would prefer employees with a good command of English to employees with a good command of Chinese (*Sing Tao Jih Pao*, May 21, 1998). Besides, English continues to be the medium of instruction in most universities and professional training programs in Hong Kong.

The domination of English has gained renewed legitimacy in the post-British-rule era when any possible postcolonial critique of English dominance can be powerfully neutralized by the hegemonic discourses of global capitalism. The Hong Kong schoolchild is now expected by the official authorities to emerge from the school with fluency in both English and Putonghua (the national standard Chinese language, which is linguistically related to but quite different from Cantonese, the native tongue of the majority of Hong Kong children). For instance, the most recent language education policy document released by the Hong Kong government ("Action Plan to Raise Language Standards in Hong Kong," January 2003) draws heavily on the hegemonic discourses of global capitalism. In this language education policy document, English is highlighted side by side with "Chinese," which is taken to mean the standard national Chinese language rather than the local people's native language, Cantonese. There is a double domination faced by the local people and schoolchildren. Cantonese, the local tongue, can never be expected to be valued, not in education, nor in society, albeit always with an invisible taken-for-granted existence in the background. The global language of English and the national language of standard Chinese are placed at the top of the linguistic hierarchy constructed and legitimized mainly through the global capitalist discourses (e.g., Hong Kong serving as a bridge between China and the West in the global economy). Elsewhere in the policy document, employers' demands are cited as the driving force for improving schoolchildren's "language standards," which refer to proficiencies in English and Putonghua. A labor production model of education is explicitly highlighted. The document also calls on universities to ensure the enforcement of a high English-language requirement for university admission: Grade C or above in the GCE O-Level English examination or Band 6 in the International English Language Testing System (IELTS).

Yet, for the majority of working-class children in Hong Kong, English remains something beyond their reach. Unlike their middle-class counterparts, they typically live in a lifeworld where few will (and can) speak or use English for any authentic communicative or sociocultural purposes. To most of them, English is little more than a difficult and boring school subject which, nonetheless, will have important consequences on their life chances. Many of them have an ambivalent, want–hate relationship with English. While they accept the socio-economic fact that English is very important for their future prospects, they also readily believe that they are no good in English; for instance, in the words of a working-class adolescent girl (G) to the ethnographic fieldworker (F) in Candlin, Lin and Lo's study (2000: 33, original in Cantonese):

F: Yes, yes, and you, do you have any aspiration, what do you want to do?
G: I want to be a teacher.
F: Teacher {chuckling}, Miss Chan {playfully addressing the girl as a teacher}, it's good to be a teacher, it suits you well. At this moment it seems to suit you.
G: Don't know if it will change in the future.
F: You have to be patient, you have to proceed gradually.
G: I have to meet the requirement, my English is poor.

The above exchange shows the working-class adolescent girl's lack of confidence in fulfilling her dream of becoming a teacher in the future because of her own self-image as someone with "poor English." Her resigned acceptance of both the importance of English for her future and her poor status in terms of her English ability led to her indication of a lack of confidence in fulfilling her aspiration despite the fieldworker's encouraging remarks. Such low self-esteem as a result of their sense of failure in mastering English makes English a subject highly imbued with working-class students' want–hate desires. The English classroom often becomes a site for their local struggles and oppositional practices (for detailed analysis of the societal and schooling contexts of their resistance practices, see Lin, 1996a, 1996b, 1997a, 1997b, 1997c, 1999, 2000).

The extreme boredom accompanying the often meaning-deprived, mechanical practices that are typical of an English classroom in a working-class school (e.g., Classrooms B and C in the ethnographic study by Lin, 1999) adds to the need for the active creative work of students in their attempt to make life more bearable. Their recurrent remark to the researcher is that the lessons are so boring that they have to do something to "gaau-siu" (literally: "stir up laughter") or else they will be bored to death (Lin, 1996b). Similar to the observation made by Paul Willis of working-class youths in Britain, there seems to be "work, even desperate work, in their play" (Willis, 1990: 2). Cantonese verbal play seems to be a kind of folk symbolic creative work and implicit ideological critique through mocking laughter and parodic language (Bakhtin, 1981) that these seemingly poorly literate children are constantly engaged in. Often simply dismissed as vulgar, uncooperative behavior by teachers and educators, their verbal creativity has to date received little serious attention from mainstream educational studies and Cultural Studies in Hong Kong. It is the purpose of this paper to bring to the fore samples of the kind of creative work that these children are engaged in. The purpose is to show how they seem to work at being human, in an often alienating schooling institution, where it seems only through some meaning creation and human control in a grounded aesthetic (Willis, 1990) of verbal play can they re/find their creative capacities and identities as living, acting beings. In the following sections, we shall first briefly discuss the methodology used, and then we shall look at some samples of the creative work of some working-class schoolboys. The data has been taken from a larger ethnographic study of 8 classrooms in 7 schools (Lin, 1996b). The techniques of conversation analysis are used in the analysis of youth talk in the examples.

## ■ 2. Understanding Youth Cultures through Conversation Analysis of Youth Talk ■

Conversation analysis (Sacks, 1992; Psathas, 1995; Silverman, 1998; ten Have, 1999) as a branch of discourse analysis has been famous for its fine-grained analysis of everyday talk in both ordinary and institutional settings. As an offshoot of the linguistic turn in the humanities and social sciences, conversation analysis has its theoretical roots in Heidegger's phenomenology and Wittgenstein's ordinary-language philosophy. It emphasizes the need to understand social action and human culture as co-constructed in the everyday, mundane, local interactions of social actors. It stresses the need to analyze the details of talk to uncover the co-construction of implicit interactional procedures through which social actors make sense of and to one another. Conversation analysis has been used to analyze media discourse, gender discourse, youth talk, youth subcultures and construction of identities (e.g., Shotter, 1993; Eder, 1995; Bell and Garrett, 1998; Grahame and Jardine, 1990; Antaki and Widdicombe, 1998; Widdicombe and Wooffitt, 1995). In the next section, the analytical techniques of conversation analysis will be drawn upon to conduct a fine-grained analysis of Cantonese working-class students' talk in an English classroom in Hong Kong. The transcripts of the talk have, however, not followed the strict transcription conventions of conversation analysis, so as to render them more readable to the general reader.

## ■ 3. Doing Verbal Play in a Boring English Lesson ■

Data examples in this section are taken from Mr. Chan's[1] class at the beginning of an English reading lesson. The school is located in a working-class residential area. The reading passage is a story titled, "Tin Hau, Queen of Heaven," in the storybook *Chinese Myths*, which the class uses for English reading. In the immediately preceding period, the students have just finished a dictation test. Many students are chatting and laughing with one another in their seats and do not quiet down until turn [459] in the transcript:

*Example 1: The pre-reading phase*

(English translations of Cantonese utterances are placed in < >.)

> T:   Alright let's take a break...then we'll do:: (1.5 seconds)
> BOY1:   GWU JAI SYU:: <STORYBOOK::>! {spoken in Anglicized tone}
> T:   (aah) story book...
> BOY2:   Gwu jai syu <Storybook>! {spoken in Anglicized tone}
> BOY3:   Gwu-jai-syu <Storybook>.

T:   Read…storybook. SHH:::! {Ss have now quieted down} Laah…mh-hou king-gai aa <Okay…don't chat>! SHH::! King-gai yiu faht-chaau gaa haa, faht-keih <Chatting will be punished by copying, standing>. (2 seconds) Yau-sik mh fan-jung laa <Let's take a break of five minutes>. Break. SHH!! (6 seconds) Ngoh aai neih jihng aa <I ask you to be quiet>!

## i.   A preliminary description

The teacher first announces that they will take a break and then something interesting happens: he continues to say, "then we'll do::" which is followed by a pause of 1.5 seconds. This is ambiguous: it can be at that moment hearable as a lapse of memory or as an invitation for a response from the students, i.e., leaving a blank for the students to fill in with what they are going to do. A boy (Boy1) grabs the chance to complete the teacher's sentence (which has been afforded by the fill-in-the-blank-type pause) and what he shouts out in a funny English tone from his seat (without raising his hand to self-nominate first, and without standing up while he shouts out his contribution) is even more interesting: "GWU JAI SYU!" (meaning "storybook"). "Storybook" is an English word that this boy may know well as this is not the first time they have had a "storybook" lesson. One can believe that it is well within his English vocabulary to have said "storybook" instead of "gwu jai syu." However, the boy's rendering of "gwu jai syu" seems to be a mocking way of speaking. It seems to mock the laughable stereotypical way in which an English-speaking person, or "Gwai-Lou" (a Cantonese slang word for foreigners) speaks Cantonese. This way of mocking and joking about Gwai-Lou's stereotypical accented way of speaking Cantonese has been common in popular Cantonese movies and television dramas in Hong Kong.

However, nobody is heard to laugh after that remark by the boy; the lesson videotape shows that most other students have all the time been chatting with their neighbors and few seem to have paid any attention to the teacher or the boy. It is the teacher who seems to be responding to the boy's utterance by an acknowledgment particle "aah" and a reformulation of the boy's contribution into standard English: "storybook."

The camcorder microphone placed at a back corner of the classroom has picked up the voices of two boys following suit after the first boy's "GWU JAI SYU" remark and the teacher's reformulation. One boy (Boy2) uses the same Anglicized accent while the other (Boy3) uses the normal Cantonese tone.

These voices probably are not available to the teacher as the walkman-recorder carried by the teacher has not picked up any of these two echoing remarks of the two boys (Boy2 and Boy3). The teacher goes on to ask the students to be quiet, and they do quiet down for a short time.

## ii.   Points of interest

First of all, the teacher explicitly announces that they are going to "do storybook" or "read storybook." He orients his students towards a clear recognition of what they are going to do: "doing, reading storybook," right from the beginning of the lesson. The next thing he does after announcing this lesson agenda is to write out 10 reading comprehension questions on the blackboard. Then he asks the students to open the book and to turn to the right unit, and announces the title of the text. The reading task is made very conspicuous right at the beginning of the reading lesson. The students therefore should be oriented towards "doing and reading storybook."

However, the data seems to speak to the contrary. While the above discussion has shown that both the teacher and students in Mr. Chan's class explicitly recognize their lesson activity as "doing and reading storybook," most of the students are actually oriented towards talking about things of their own! The lesson video- and audio-tapes show that the majority of students in Mr. Chan's class are not attentive to the teacher at all. Most of the time, most students (e.g., those sitting in the middle to back rows) are chatting with neighbors, producing a low white noise that is broken only for very short periods of time, e.g., after the teacher has asked them to be quiet or to stop talking. There is no unified participation framework in the classroom. Instead, the students are split into numerous more or less separate, simultaneous, small informal conversation groups, with the teacher and a small number of students near the teacher interacting on the front, public stage.

While secondary school students are officially supposed to speak in English in English-language lessons in Hong Kong, the students in Mr. Chan's class always speak in Cantonese, whether privately or publicly, except when reading out from the English textbook, and when they read, they read haltingly, showing great difficulties in pronouncing many English words in the text. It seems that many students in Mr. Chan's class are neither willing nor linguistically able to engage in a public, English dialogue with the teacher. When some students are willing to participate in a public dialogue with the teacher, they do so in very unique ways.

For instance, the boy (Boy1) who shouts out "GWU JAI SYU" provides us with evidence that at least some students are willing to take the initiative to engage in a public dialogue with the teacher. It has been discussed above that we have reason to believe the boy has the ability to say the English word "storybook," which is officially normal and appropriate to say in this situation, but he chooses instead to formulate his public contribution in an off-beat way. He has self-selected and grabbed the public discourse slot (afforded by the teacher's 1.5 second pause) as an opportunity to slip in an utterance of his own choice, which does not entirely conform to the teacher's expectations. Although the teacher acknowledges it, he immediately reformulates it into an officially acceptable English word.

There are at least three different options from which the boy (Boy1) could have chosen: gwu-jai-syu, storybook, and "gwu jai syu." The first is the Cantonese word for "storybook" spoken in normal Cantonese accent. This is an officially unacceptable and inappropriate choice (because this is an English lesson): using it publicly would render him hearable as being blatantly uncooperative with the teacher and unwilling to speak English. However, this may render him hearable to other like-minded students as being "one of us." This may be seen as indicative of an insulated Cantonese sociocultural island that is opposed to the Chinese–English bilingual middle-class "Mainland." On the other hand, a Cantonese word does not seem to be the most suitable material to complete an English utterance.

The second option, "storybook," is officially the most acceptable one. Besides, it seems to be the most suitable material to complete an English utterance. However, using it would render the boy hearable to other students as too cooperative with the teacher and the official lesson agenda.[2]

The third option (actually, this is the option created by the boy himself), "gwu jai syu," a Cantonese word spoken in a stereotypical "Gwai-Lou-speaking-Cantonese" accent, seems to have the merits of both of the above options but not their shortcomings. Using it renders the boy hearable to the teacher not as blatantly uncooperative as the first option would. After all, "Tin Hau" (an Anglicized name of the Chinese Heaven-Queen, a word that both their teacher and English story-book use) is an entirely acceptable "English" word. The Anglicized intonation used by the boy when he speaks "gwu jai syu" also fits with the English intonation of the teacher's utterance and so can serve as an admissible candidate to seamlessly complete the teacher's English utterance.

On the other hand, he would not be hearable by other students as brown-nosing the teacher or being too cooperative with the lesson's official English-learning agenda because, after all, it is a Cantonese word: it seems that he is not really speaking Gwai-Lou's English; rather, he's mocking Gwai-Lou's Cantonese! This has the additional double effect of being funny and "turning the tables," that is, reasserting the centrality of Cantonese in relation to English. (Lombardi [1996] has observed a similar phenomenon in Brazil: Portuguese-speaking Brazilians, who are not comfortable with the socio-economic need to learn English, mock the poor Portuguese of English-speaking North Americans by playing on Brazilian pronunciations of English words.) A similar playful mocking practice is commonly found in many of the popular Cantonese movies in the 1990s in Hong Kong, especially those by the famous comedy movie star Stephen Chow. Typically playing a working-class underdog who is nevertheless streetwise, witty, and verbally creative, Stephen Chow often engages in such mocking verbal play, creating verbal spectacles with comical effects that especially appeal to Cantonese working-class audiences.

The reading text itself seems to have provided the boy with a source of creative discourse resources: the reading text is about a Chinese legend with Chinese characters. Normally these students talk about Chinese things in Cantonese, but this strange occasion has required them to talk about Chinese things in English, like a Gwai-Lou talking about Chinese things in their Anglicized Cantonese, e.g., using the Anglicized name "Tin Hau" for the Chinese Heaven-Queen. This seems to be a good context to do a playful mocking of Gwai-Lou's poor Cantonese.

The absurdity of this situation is also something that may prompt a mocking. These students' English is limited and there is evidence that they do not know many of the words in the text. And yet, the content of the story is so boringly familiar that they feel that they do not really need to read the story to know what the story is about (there is some evidence of this in the later phases of the lesson). Some natural questions that they may ask in such a situation seem to be: Why on

earth do I need to go through all this pain to read a story that I already know?!
What is the point of reading a Chinese story in English? It may make some sense
only if I were a Gwai-Lou learning about Chinese things, and gee, I might just as
well get some fun out of this boring and difficult situation by mocking the Gwai-
Lou's way of speaking Cantonese! Another instance of this is seen in Boy2's
utterance: another boy seemingly following the example of the first boy (Boy2)
by echoing it shortly after him. There are two other similar instances found in the
lesson.

It appears that some other students are engaged in a different kind of playful
mocking. Before we can discuss some examples of this, we need to examine the
kind of Initiation–Response–Feedback (IRF) discourse format (Sinclair and
Coulthard, 1975; Heap, 1988) in Mr. Chan's class that has allowed students to do
this different kind of verbal play (cf. Grahame and Jardine, 1990). Based on analysis
of the larger data corpus from Mr. Chan's class (Lin, 1996b), we can characterize
the typical IRF format used in Mr. Chan's class as having the expanded structural
sequence shown below:

a.   Teacher-Initiation [first in English, then translated into Cantonese]
b.   Student-Response [in Cantonese]
c.   Teacher-Feedback [in Cantonese and then in English]

Now, what is interesting is how some students make use of this IRF format to slip
in their Cantonese verbal play (c.f. Grahame and Jardine, 1990). Let us look at the
following example taken later on from the answer-checking phase in the same
lesson.

*Example 2: The answer-checking phase*

Having given students 10 minutes to read the text silently, Mr. Chan begins to
engage the students in a process of co-constructing a certified lesson knowledge
corpus. This process is carried out through the use of the IRF format (see above
and Lin, 1996a), in very much the same way it has been used in the pre-reading
phase (see Example 1 above). However, in this phase the questions to be asked by
the teacher in the initiation slots are already known as a pregiven list, and the
answers to be provided by the students in the response slots are also supposed to
be preformulated (or pre-marked-out by students in their storybooks). So, it is not
so much a discussion or "talking about" the storybook as it is "checking answers"
to the pregiven questions. This is actually a recurrent practice in other lessons of
this class and in many working classrooms in Hong Kong (e.g., checking answers to
grammar exercises, vocabulary exercises, etc.).

Throughout this phase, the teacher highlights the need *to base one's answer on
relevant parts in the text* by asking students where in the text they can find the
answer to his question. The need to base one's answer (or to "find the answer") in
the text is a recurrent concern of the teacher, voiced in his recurrent prompts and
follow-up questions, such as "Where can you find it?," "Does the book really say

so?," "Look at paragraph X, line Y," etc. However, there are times when a bookish answer is very boring, especially when these students feel that this story of the Chinese Heaven-Queen is so familiar (some evidence of this found in other parts of the transcript). And the pregiven set of factual questions has left so little room for imagination for these lively 13/14-year-old boys. In the following excerpt from the same answer-checking phase, we find the creativity of the schoolboys bursting out in a niche that they exploit and capitalize on in an otherwise probably uninteresting IRF discourse sequence (to make the transcript easier to read, the original Cantonese utterances are omitted and only their English translations in are provided in < >; S's refer to students; S1, S2, S3 refer to Student1, Student2, Student3):

> T: <What happened>?...Leih-Lohn-Mihng[3] (2 seconds) <when she answered her mum> (1 second) <her mum called her name, and when she answered her mum, what happened>?
> LEIH: <Her old-man fell off to the (ground)>. {chuckling towards the end of his sentence}
> s's: Haha! haha! haha! hahahaha! {other S's laughing hilariously}
> T: <What>?! (2 seconds) <louder>! {speaking against a background of S's' laughter}
> CHAN: <Her old-man fell off to the street>! {chuckling}
> s1: Hihihihik!! {laughing}
> s2: <(Is there) a street>?
> T: <Is there a street>? {T speaking in an amused tone; some students laugh}
> LEIH: <fell into the sea>
> T: <Where did he fall into>? {quite amusingly}
> LEIH: <Sea that is>.
> T: <Yes...fell into the sea>.
> s1: <fell off to the street> hahaha!
> s2: <Her old-man fell off to the street>.
> T: Right? (1 second) Her father dropped into the SEA!
> s3: Hekhek! {laughing}
> T: Right? (2 seconds) <in that manner died>...SHH! (1 second) <okay>... <finally>...SHH! number ten...

The teacher's question has been asked in English earlier, but no student response has been forthcoming, and the teacher is asking it again in Cantonese, and also specifically directs it to a student (Leih-Lohn-Mihng), ensuring that someone is going to answer it. Now, something interesting happens. Leih says something (the Cantonese word "louh-dauh" literally means "old-bean" and is a common colloquial, not very respectful word for "father") which rouses other students to hilarious laughter.

The boy (Leih) has exploited the Response slot to do something playful, to slip in a contribution that will turn the whole story into a comic-strip type of story, which they enjoy reading outside the classroom (based on what they told me when I chatted with them after school, and on their responses to questions about the kinds of extracurricular reading they do in a questionnaire I gave them). In their most favorite comic strips, which have been translated into Cantonese-style Chinese from Japanese, the characters usually do funny, impossible things – e.g. a boy changes into a girl when he falls into cold water and changes back to a boy when he's showered with hot water; or, the father of the boy changes into a big black bear when coming into contact with hot water, etc. – and amusement and enjoyment come from the superimposing of impossible and unpredictable fantasy with the familiar, predictable, and boring mundane world. It seems that the boy (Leih) who provides this funny answer is a skillful storyteller with a ready audience, and this is reflected in the overwhelmingly positive response from his fellow students (i.e., their hilarious laughter, showing their great amusement derived from this twist of the story effected by his answer: her father fell off into the street [from a merchant ship amidst a stormy ocean])! His change in the plot would make a very funny and imaginative comic-strip type story. Besides, the boy seems also to be skillfully slipping in a euphemistic version of a taboo slang Cantonese word "puk-gaai!" (literally meaning "drop to the street"), which is used to curse others (it can be translated as "drop dead!" or "go to hell!"). His fellow students' hilarious laughter seems to have also arisen from this implicit version of a taboo slang word being offered as an answer to the teacher's formal question.

The teacher cannot hide his own amusement but insists on the reading text as the authoritative basis for students' answers to the question. He challenges, "Go douh yauh gaai me?" (Is there a street?), and goes on to demand that the student give him a text-based answer, which he can acknowledge, reformulate into English, affirm and certify. Throughout the lesson the teacher has been demonstrating to his students that reading a storybook means extracting information from the text to answer a set of pregiven questions, and it seems there is little more you can do or play around with while reading a story text.

## ■ 4. Creative Work in an Alienating World ■

The organization of the above reading lesson is not an isolated example. Similar examples can be found in other classes in my larger corpus of classroom data (Lin, 1996b). The point of English reading lessons in many working-class schools seems to be primarily one of practice in extracting prescribed information from texts. This seems to have followed naturally from the pragmatic emphasis of the school English curriculum and the way English reading comprehension is assessed in public examinations. English seems to be conceived as mainly for academic and job-related purposes in Hong Kong. The information-extraction approach to reading seems to dominate most English reading practices in school, even when the texts being read are stories and not a type of technical, academic or job-related manuals which might more typically require information extraction in many contexts. The schools thus seem to serve as training grounds to churn out graduates skilled in extracting specific information from English texts to accomplish prescribed tasks.

School children, however, might seize whatever opportunities they can find in the classroom to negotiate their own sense of the text – for instance, text not as an information-holder but as a source of enjoyment. When the prescribed school text proves to be unimaginative or unengaging, they exercise their own creativity to recreate a new plot, to negotiate a comic type of story, which suits their taste. It seems that they are negotiating their own kind of creative literacy, in spite of its illegitimacy in the school context. There is lots of creative work in their verbal play.

While their verbal play seems to get them nowhere in terms of gaining the necessary linguistic capital to get a good job in the future, it does point to their creative, active response to an alienating, dehumanizing institution in which they find themselves trapped. While a typical mainstream adult comment on their behavior is likely to be that of disapproval (e.g., "These students have given up on themselves; see how they waste their precious learning time to talk about nonsense!"), their response is far from that of passive self-abandonment. There seems to be an acute insight (albeit often an implicit one) on the part of these schoolboys: they seem to fully recognize their lack of any chances to fully master English (unlike their middle-class counterparts who have all kinds of familial support to learn English) and to get any high-level jobs in the future; they seem to have a thorough sense of the kind of low-paying jobs that they will probably end up with after studying in their school (which, like many other schools located in working-class areas in Hong Kong, is labeled and stigmatized as "low-banding"). They seem to want to make the best out of a no-win situation. They want to have fun, and be creative beings, despite all the gloomy prospects implicitly built into their social position; it is as if they want to forget as best as they can through their active, creative verbal play. This radical transformation of reality is fun and tension-releasing, at least for the moment, and reflects an attempt to focus on the present, when the future is too gloomy to think of. In my informal chats with these schoolboys, they struck me with an immense cynicism about the adult world and a refusal to talk about their future. One of their recurrent remarks is: it's so boring; we have to make fun ("gaau-siu")! There is work, even desperate work, in their fun-making. It is as if they were shouting this to us: "Hey, we're gonna live with dignity and fun no matter what!"

NOTES

1   All personal names are pseudonyms and all identifying details of the school and participants have been replaced.
2   This interpretation is based on my understanding of the students' culture through my informal contact and chatting with them. A common phrase they use to describe a fellow student suspected of doing brown-nosing is "bok mat aa!?," meaning "to gain what!?" The phrase is usually spoken disapprovingly to describe a fellow student who takes the initiative to speak English in class.
3   This is the name of a student. The original name has been changed into a pseudonym.

## REFERENCES

Antaki, C. and Widdicombe, S. (1998). *Identities in Talk*. London: Sage.

Bakhtin, M. M. (1981). *The Dialogic Imagination: Four Essays*. Austin, TX: University of Texas Press.

Bell, A. and Garett, P. (eds.) (1998). *Approaches to Media Discourse*. Oxford: Blackwell.

Candlin, C. N., Lin, A. M. Y., and Lo, T.-W. (2000). *The Discourse of Adolescents in Hong Kong*. Final Project Report (City University of Hong Kong Strategic Research Grant: #7000707). Department of English and Communication, City University of Hong Kong, Hong Kong.

Eder, D. (1995). *School Talk: Gender and Adolescent Culture*. New Brunswick, NJ: Rutgers University Press.

Grahame, P. R. and Jardine, D. W. (1990). Deviance, resistance, and play: A study in the communicative organization of trouble in class. *Curriculum Inquiry* 20(3), 283–304.

Heap, J. L. (1985). Discourse in the production of classroom knowledge: Reading lessons. *Curriculum Inquiry* 15(3), 245–79.

Heap, J. L. (1988). On task in classroom discourse. *Linguistics and Education* 1, 177–98.

Lin, A. M. Y. (1996a). Bilingualism or linguistic segregation? Symbolic domination, resistance, and code-switching in Hong Kong schools. *Linguistics and Education* 8(1), 49–84.

Lin, A. M. Y. (1996b). *Doing English Lessons in Secondary Schools in Hong Kong: A Sociocultural and Discourse Analytic Study*. Unpublished doctoral dissertation, University of Toronto, Canada.

Lin, A. M. Y. (1997a). Hong Kong Children's rights to a culturally compatible English curriculum. *Hong Kong Journal of Applied Linguistics* 2(2).

Lin, A. M. Y. (1997b). Bilingual education in Hong Kong. In Cummins, J. and Corson, D. (eds.), *Encyclopedia of Language and Education, Volume 5: Bilingual Education* (pp. 281–9). Dordrecht: Kluwer Academic Publishers.

Lin, A. M. Y. (1997c). Analyzing the "language problem" discourses in Hong Kong: How official, academic, and media discourses construct and perpetuate dominant models of language, learning, and education. *Journal of Pragmatics* 28, 427–40.

Lin, A. M. Y. (1999). Doing-English-lessons in the reproduction or transformation of social worlds? *TESOL Quarterly* 33(3), 393–412.

Lin, A. M. Y. (2000). Lively children trapped in an island of disadvantage: Verbal play of Cantonese working-class schoolboys in Hong Kong. *International Journal of the Sociology of Language* 143, 63–83.

Lombardi, J. (1996, Jan. 5). *Mocking English and Spanish in Brazil*. E-mail message sent to the Language-Culture Electronic Discussion Network, University of Chicago.

McLaren, P. (1998). *Life in Schools: An Introduction to Critical Pedagogy in the Foundations of Education*. New York: Longman.

Psathas, G. (1995). *Conversation Analysis: The Study of Talk-in-Interaction*. Thousand Oaks, CA: Sage.

Sacks, H. (1992). *Lectures in Conversation*. Oxford: Blackwell.

Shotter, J. (1993). *Conversation Realities: Constructing Life Through Language*. London: Sage.

Silverman, D. (1998). *Harvey Sacks: Social Science and Conversation Analysis*. Cambridge: Polity Press.

Sinclair, J. and Coulthard, M. (1975). *Towards an Analysis of Discourse*. London: Oxford University Press.

*Sing Tao Jih Pao* (1998). English important for job promotion: Blow to mother-tongue education [in Chinese]. *Sing Tao Jih Pao*, May 21.

ten Have, P. (1999). *Doing Conversation Analysis: A Practical Guide*. London: Sage.

Widdicombe, S. and Wooffitt, R. (1995). *The Language of Youth Subcultures: Social Identity in Action*. New York: Harvester Wheatsheaf.

Willis, P. (1990). *Common Culture: Symbolic Work at Play in the Everyday Cultures of the Young*. Buckingham, UK: Open University Press.

# 23

## Love Letters and Amanuenses: Beginning the Cultural History of the Working Class Private Sphere in Southern Africa, 1900–1933

### Keith Breckenridge

■ Introduction ■

This chapter is an effort to begin to answer two related questions. Was there a private sphere amongst the southern African rural poor before apartheid? And, if so, what were its characteristics? The answers develop along the following lines. I start by examining some of the rich contradictions of literacy on the mines. First, migrants made (and continue to make) extensive use of letters to communicate across the gap between town and countryside. This reliance on the written word was true from the very establishment of the mining industry. It was true despite the overwhelming illiteracy of working people in southern Africa. Here I want to make a corollary point that the popular conception of widespread 'functional illiteracy' as a national failure misconceives the character of household communication and family politics.[1] On the contrary, migrant heads of households have actively and deliberately cultivated a radically constrained form of literacy specifically organized around the writing of the vernacular letter.

A related problem emerges from the consideration of the authoring and content of the letters. I have argued elsewhere that explicitly political letters were very important in the shaping of events on the Witwatersrand, at least before 1933. But they were always very small in number.[2] The vast majority of the letters written to and from the mines were concerned with matters more personal. Often the most personal forms of affection between men and women were expressed in stylized love letters. These intensely affectionate messages, especially between courting couples, stood in pronounced opposition to the ubiquitous emotional conservatism of *hlonipha* – the etiquette for respectful demeanor between genders and generations. Letters, as Schapera observed in 1933, constituted the private sphere[3] of migrant life. But here lurks another paradox. For these deeply affectionate letters – which Habermas has described as the 'purely human relations' of the European private sphere and which surely qualify for the adjective 'private' – were usually authored by skilled amanuenses and commonly read aloud. Letter writing in southern Africa, even within the household, was intrinsically indirect and collaborative.[4]

Which brings us to the character of the private sphere in southern Africa. There is a wealth of evidence from Europe and the United States that the epistolary novel, and private letters, helped construct both new kinds of bourgeois individuals, and new relations of affection between them in the eighteenth and nineteenth centuries.[5] In the nineteenth century South Africa, mission-educated young people enthusiastically used letters for different reasons, but with some similar effects. At the outset, then, we can observe a fairly straightforward confrontation between marriage shaped by the concerns of kinship and the public negotiations of the extended family, and courtship organized by individual desire and the private love-letter. 'How,' to restate Justice Nhlapo's question, 'do you command your daughter to marry a man of your choice when a missionary education has exposed her to reading and writing, and courtship by letter – not to mention financial independence through wage labour?'[6] But this straightforward dichotomy between communalism and individualism masks more than it reveals. Outside the ranks of the most enthusiastic and literary converts, letters did not, in fact, conjure emotionally individualized selves amidst the blurred ranks of the lineage. Precisely because South African patriarchs sought to limit the domestic consequences of literacy, and because the state exercised a national educational policy of malign neglect, the literary domain of courtship has necessarily remained collaborative. The amanuensis has constructed the private sphere in South Africa, either from within the family or networks of peers. Working class South Africans have constructed private lives, and individual selves, out of an unusual combination of literary affect and collaborative authorship (and reading).

The domain of 'popular culture' in South Africa is usually understood as essentially oral and intensely performative. The combination of David Coplan's two excellent monographs – one on black urban cultural performance and the other on Basotho migrants' *lifela* – captures very clearly the extent to which literacy has been written out of the field of popular culture. As one of the informants in David Coplan's recent study of the migrants' 'auriture' explained: 'If you want to understand my song, mister, just listen to the music.'[7] Without losing the insights we can derive from these and other works, I want to suggest here that a particular form of literacy has been a very important part of African popular culture. Roger Chartier has suggested that popular forms of reading and writing that differed markedly from the radical solitude of the silent bourgeois reader began to dissolve 'the macroscopic opposition between "popular" [oral] and "high" [literate] culture' in the course of the seventeenth and eighteenth centuries in Europe.[8] Something very similar was happening in South Africa after the 1890s. In the process, these new documents and the new acts of reading and writing associated with them began to constitute new forms of privacy.

But what does the character of the African private sphere have to do with democracy? In short, a great deal. For the character of the private sphere (or private life, if you prefer) determines the very character of political individuals. Every major political philosopher after the French Revolution, from Hegel to Proudhon (with the notable exceptions of Marx and Engels) argued that the family – defined as a private domain in opposition to the public – provided the foundation of political ethics.[9] The modern notion of citizenship is premised on what Taylor describes as 'free, self-determining subjects' constituted and constrained by the affective and economic interests of the family.[10] 'The Bourgeois individual,' Chakrabarty observes, 'is not born until one discovers the pleasures of privacy.'[11] In part, then, this is an attempt to ask questions about the relationship between selfhood and democracy in southern Africa that have been answered in very interesting and provocative ways for India.[12] 'Nationalist thought was premised precisely on the assumed universality of the project of becoming individuals, on the assumption that "individual rights" and abstract "equality" were universals that could find a home anywhere in the world, that one could be both an "Indian" and a "citizen" at the same time.'[13] The stakes here are high. If the failure of the nationalist project in India (and by sleight of hand, the Third World) follows from its incomplete grasp of the form of selfhood, and the power of private life organized by 'tradition', then the presence and character of privacy in southern Africa determines the very viability of the liberal democratic revolution in South Africa in particular, and the movement away from what Mamdani has described as 'rural despotism' in general.[14] I maintain that there are grounds for believing that the form of the private sphere is recognizably modern in South Africa, but in order to discover them we must begin the investigation.

### ■ Of Letters ■

The public history of literacy – from the first transcription of isiXhosa in 1799 to the first publication of *Imvo Zabantsundu* almost a century later – is well documented.[15] Opland, for example, has recently remarked on the ambivalence of the idea of the book in isiXhosa praise poems reflecting, perhaps, the dramatic technological advantages gained from fixed long distance communication and the devastating political mischief associated with writing. His general point that despite the rapid spread of literacy, schooling and publishing in the Eastern Cape between 1860 and 1900, the isiXhosa *izibongo* 'have proved remarkably resilient and persistent ... heedless of the technology of print and unaffected by it' confirms the peculiarly constrained quality of literacy in South Africa.[16] Opland's commentary also confirms the symbolic importance isiXhosa speakers attached to personal and official letters (and books, for the word *iincwadi* does not distinguish between them).

Occasionally real evidence of the workings of the lettered private sphere does make its way into the files of the archives. In 1897, for example, James Scott, the rector of the Empolweni mission near Greytown complained to the Postmaster-General of Natal that 'for some time the native girls attending our training Institution have been pestered with filthy abominable letters forwarded unstamped.' He attached, as an example, a letter from a young man working in Durban. This long missive, written in beautiful hand in isiZulu, on lined paper apparently torn from a pass office register, contains a litany of complaints against Mntyali, 'the favourite of the missionary'. Far from being a 'filthy abominable' proposal of love, the letter is a study of the complexities of courtship by letter writing on the mission.

At its heart was a furious complaint against Mntyali's censorship of love letters:

> Cease this which you do of taking our letters which we write to the children and reading them, they say truly that you suck position at the cost of people, what do you think. I have heard something bad it seems that you take the letters of the boys of your people at beer drinks and give them to the girls of the College notwithstanding you take our letters and read them, why, then, you court for the boys of your people.[17]

The image of the nineteenth century schools that emerges from the Rector's appeal for official intervention, and the detailed description offered here, is certainly far from the staid scholarly atmosphere presented by the missionaries. Sexual play was clearly a very important new use for literacy. 'I was ringleader in fruit-stealing from the orchard, taking sugar from the mission kitchen and sending love messages to girls,' Gilbert Coka relates of his time at the Swedish Mission boarding school at Dundee in the 1920s. 'All three tasks required dexterity.'[18]

That writing, and especially the composition of love-letters, was enthusiastically adopted by the converts on the missions seems clear. An obvious analytical question emerges from this prolific correspondence: Did writing define a new class, separated and alienated from the broader mass of peasants in the nineteenth century? Putting aside, for the moment, the implications of the Mayers' work on the distinction between 'Red' and 'School' ideologies amongst the isiXhosa speaking people, there are very good grounds for seeing writing as a definitive marker of class. Ngilambi Sohlathi, who was born soon after the turn of the century, made a very clear distinction between the manual jobs underground which all 'cause damage to one's blood' and the work of the clerks, the *amabhalana*, literally the ones who cause writing. 'The clerks are the better ones, because they work sitting down like this here.' In an effort to get his aged uncle to differentiate forms of work underground, Jones Mzayifani (who attended three years of school) responded: 'Educated people can't be like us, the uneducated people, who don't know anything.'[19] No one has expressed the sense of alienation that writing can prompt amongst uneducated migrants more clearly than the informant called Johannes Rantoa by Guy and Thabane. 'You know as for me I did not study,' Rantoa related, 'I just see blackness on these things.'[20]

Yet the migrants wrote. As early as the first decade of this century, A.M. Mostert, an independent recruiter for the mines on the West Rand, provided paper, envelopes and postage to the workers in his compounds. 'I find that the boys are very fond of writing these letters,' he told the committee drafting the 1912 Native

Labour Regulation Bill, 'and write more than 4,000 a month.' (His compounds housed about 8,000 workers.) He was also careful to take advantage of the free advertising that travelled with each letter. On the back of the envelopes he provided was printed the name of the mine, and across the front the slogan, '*I stokwe sa kwa Mostert*'. The literal translation of this Zulu phrase was 'A tobacco-roll at Mostert's place', but – taking its meaning from an earlier understanding of the value of labor – it also meant 'Piece-work with Mostert'.

The letters that built the twentieth century private sphere in South Africa tended not to end up in the archives of the state or the Chamber of Mines. Nor are they easily found in private collections today. But there can be little doubt that almost all of the '4,000 envelopes a month' dispatched by Mostert contained such letters.

Certainly by the time Isaac Schapera completed his fieldwork in Bechuanaland in the early 1930s, 'letter-writing [had] developed into one of the most useful agencies for keeping the town Native in touch with his relatives and friends at home'.[21] Some of the best examples of the letters that built friendships and families across the gulf of migrancy in this period can be found in Schapera's *Married Life in an African Tribe*.

The letters are inadequate in some respects. Schapera had strong ideas about the usefulness of vernacular quotation, believing it 'more annoying than helpful, especially where it serves no obvious purpose other than to lend an air of greater authority to what is said', and he obviously had little interest in the semantic or idiomatic analysis, which would be possible for fluent Tswana readers. He also sought to protect his informants by erasing their identities completely.[22] The result is a disembodied corpus of letters, which resist intense sociological or literary scrutiny. It is difficult not to echo Malinowski's prim comment: 'There is such a thing in social science as documentation, that is, the presentation of data really at first hand'.[23] We are forced to rely (and this was probably Schapera's intention) on the ethnographer's interpretation.

But they do allow us to answer a number of important questions. Was letter writing an elite form of correspondence restricted to clerical workers? What was the relationship between interest and emotion in the constitution and management of migrant households? What was the character of affection for migrant men and their wives and children? If there was an African private sphere, how was it defined? These letters, as Schapera explained, give us 'among the most valuable evidence of what the people feel and say to one another in private'.[24]

Schapera conducted his fieldwork in British Bechuanaland between 1929 and 1934. He was, as far as I know, the only ethnographer working in southern Africa who collected letters from his informants. (Aside from noting the 'courtesy of their recipients' he is mysteriously silent about the ways in which he came into possession of the letters.)[25] Nonetheless, what is clear is that letter writing, whilst clearly associated with those who had attended some school, was not an elite activity in Bechuanaland in the early 1930s. 'The writers were in most cases not classed as "educated" even by the Natives themselves', Schapera explained in 1933, 'they had acquired just sufficient learning in the village schools to be able to read and write.'[26] We can see here the same imperative towards a strictly limited literacy, a mastery of writing determined in the final analysis by the capacity to read and write the vernacular letter.

For its time Schapera's ethnography is astonishingly open-minded. And much of the refreshingly direct, and romantic, discussion he offers of sexual life in Bechuanaland is presented by means of the love letters of migrants and their partners. One of the most eloquent was written by a young man in Johannesburg:

> I still think of how we loved each other; I think of how you behaved to me, my wife; I did not lack anything that belonged to you. All things I did not buy, but I just got them, together with your body; you were too good for me, and you were very, very sweet, more than any sweet things that I have ever had. We fitted each other beautifully. There was nothing wrong; you carried me well; I was not too heavy for you, nor too light, just as you were not too heavy for me nor too light; and our 'bloods' liked each other so much in our bodies.[27]

Schapera's informants offer metaphysical celebrations of love and commodity fetishism that echo and perhaps surpass John Donne. Letters were not always celebrations of love. Some dealt with the intense pain of betrayal and abandonment made only more intense by the prolonged absences of migrant employment. Almost all of the letters combine a detailed consideration with the micro-economics of household reproduction with an affective interest in personal relations with kin and lovers.

Of course, some of the letters that Schapera quotes were not written to or by mine workers. Tswana men who went to the Witwatersrand often tried to find work away from the dangers of the mines.[28] But there are sets of letters here that explicitly dealt with the predicament of workers on the mines in the Depression years. One such set was composed by a man at Crown Mines to his wife in the Kgatla Reserve. They are remarkable for their preoccupation with the calculus of household management. Here is one fairly typical example:

> First receive my letter. I greet you and ask how you are. I have got a sore shoulder, I don't use its hand. All this time I have not been writing to you because I heard you say that you were going to the cattle-post. Now just lately R——came here and told me that you are still at home. I let you know that I sent a shawl with S——when he left here to go home; I don't know whether he has given it to you. I have heard your word when you say that a plough is also needed. My wife, there you have spoken the truth; but I don't know whether we can manage in one year all the things that we lack, for I am still thinking that when I come home I must bring with me some shillings with which we can help ourselves. And now the winter is coming, and it is going to be cold; there are no good blankets for the night. I will try to send you a blanket, because I have stopped using one of the blankets, the white which was already getting old.[29]

Amidst their careful discussions of how to make a tiny wage cover many pressing needs, we can see the banal force of the state's documentary regime, and their attempts to use their own letters to circumvent it:

> I also let you know that I always forget about my tax-receipt. You must ask M——
> (her brother) to send it. If you can go to Mosanteng (where he formerly lived in

Mochudi), get me a little yellow paper, it is (a pass) for work, it is in the big yellow book, and put into your letter. I want to get this paper because I want to show it to people when I look for work. As I haven't bought anything for myself I shall come home in summer. Greet all your people and my children.[30]

Collected during the famine of the Depression years, these letters speak of bitter poverty, and the complete dependence of parents, wives and children on the wage earners in the city. A widowed mother writing to her son working in Johannesburg revealed the interior of financial extremity, the humiliation of betrayal by some children and a searing demand for empathy.

> I greet you and ask how you are living. I am sick, my child, I have nothing to say except starvation. You have left me in loneliness. The starvation is very, very serious. I beg you to send me just one bag of corn, so that I can help my child who is at the cattle-post.... The whole day, my child, we sit at the store hoping to get a little corn (as relief rations) but we come back empty. I don't know what to do, but you must know that I depend upon you, and put all my hopes in you. You must 'carry' us, as you usually do. Other men are striving for themselves, but M——does not care for anything; he looks to me, but I have nothing for him. Do not let the eyes of the people look at me (with scorn). You complain that I do not write to you, but you know that I have nothing with which to buy stamps. That is all I can tell you. Many greetings, my child.[31]

The letters that Schapera includes in *Married Life* reveal more directly than almost any other source the terrible ordeal that migrant families faced in the Depression years. Note, for example, in this extract the overlaying of loneliness and starvation, humiliation and idleness. Partly because of the emotional insights these letters offer I have sought for many years to collect personal letters from migrant informants, with spectacularly little success.

It is, I think, an indication of the intensely private character of letters that so few have ended up in the hands of social historians. Perhaps the most famous cache of personal letters, the 'black plastic bag containing five hundred or more pieces of paper which Kas Maine had been careful to preserve' was only delivered to Charles van Onselen after the old man's death – seven years after the oral research project was initiated, and several years after researchers began asking for personal papers.[32] My own informants will happily discuss the writing of letters but they are politely but resolutely reticent in the face of my badgering – the letters were burnt on the male migrant's final return home.

Jones Mzayifani, my friend, informant and guide, attempted to explain the absence of letters and diffuse my scepticism with the following story.

> She says, 'I am staying with a wife at the Place of Gold'. And she writes: 'Tata I hear that you're staying with a wife at the Place of Gold'. Then I refute that, and after some time she discovers that indeed I have a wife at the Place of Gold. So when I return these letters must be burnt so that we can talk about a problem which is not there, finish. For if we keep these letters she will say all right let us open these letters. Then I will find that the problem that she wrote about in the letters is there. So the letters must be burnt. So that we can talk about something that is not there.[33]

He means, of course, 'so that we *cannot* talk about something that *is* there'. There is an important element of truth in this account; it does seem likely that women would have been more likely to make use of archived letters in conflicts over resources within the household. For the moment, however, I must simply acknowledge that I do not know what has become of this correspondence. It may serve as something more than rationalization to note that the very extensive studies of the influence of reading on the emergence European private life have had similar difficulties tracing personal letters, relying instead on books – the form and content of libraries, guidebooks, memoirs, and diaries.[34]

## ■ The Politics of the Amanuensis ■

While it is important, and I hope interesting, to examine the lettered activities of workers on the Witwatersrand in the early years of this century, we must not lose sight of the essentially limited character of literacy in southern Africa even into the present.[35] The evidence is clear that African literacy in this region was constrained in two fundamental ways. The first and most obvious of these constraints was regional. The development of particular mission churches was in every instance as complex as regional politics, but it still seems fair to suggest that the 'School' people of the eastern Cape, the *Amakholwa* of Natal and the converts of the GammaNgwato kingdom in northeastern Botswana were important exceptions to the general rule of the rejection of Christianity, and literate education. The centralized states of Zululand, Pondoland, Sekhuhkhuneland, and even Lesotho, were very hostile to the establishment of mission stations prior to conquest, and the expansion of Zionist churches in the twentieth century suggests that these regions have remained resistant to lettered Christianity.[36]

The kings usually motivated this resistance to the spread of Christianity, but it is also clear that an important constraint on the development of literacy operated at the level of the household. There can be little doubt that African patriarchs – in a pattern that mimicked the political stance of the monarchs – sought to control the spread of Christian education amongst their children. In 1957, an unnamed informant presented what is almost a stereotypical account of rural education in southern Africa in this century: 'All that my father wanted,' the informant explained to Philip and Iona Mayer, 'was that I should be able to read and write a Xhosa letter. One of the reasons was that when he received a letter from anywhere he had to take it to an educated man to read it for him. He disliked this, because the contents might be strictly private family matters.'[37]

One way to think about this limited literacy would be to describe it as utilitarian or functional. It surely was that. Rural African households at least before World War II sought to have some control over the most common, and the most powerful, elements of the documentary world – letters, forms, signatures, tax receipts, invoices – whilst preventing children from entering the domain of the thoroughly literate. In this world, the figure of the amanuensis took on particular significance.

A constrained form of letter writing has been an essential element of migrant labour in southern Africa from the outset. The evidence from recruiters is unequivocal on this question. Migrants expected them to pay for, read and write letters and to handle the repatriation of money. Charles Green, one of J.S. Marwick's recruiters in southern Natal in 1897, complained bitterly about this literally thankless task.

> I have so far written and received more than 100 letters which I have hitherto acted for them as amanuensis and beyond pens ink and paper have I shd think affixed quite 40/-worth of stamps "postage". Which is a dead loss besides the continual bother of reading and writing their letters. Which however amusing or affording an insight into Native ideas the continued reiteration of the same thing has become dull stale and unprofitable.[38]

(In a puzzling effort to stop the Ixopo workers from using Green as an interpreter, Marwick posted a letter on the notice-board of his Johannesburg compound explaining that he would, in future, levy a 10 per cent surcharge on any cheques cashed.) In the years after the emergence of the Native Recruiting Corporation, recruiters and shopkeepers were formally charged with the task of the amanuensis. They had little choice but to endure the 'dull, stale and unprofitable' task.

The cultural division between 'Red' and 'School', traditionalist and progressive, is real in the lives of rural people even into the present. But the relationship, as the Mayers pointed out, is not fixed and the technology of letter writing in fact encouraged a kind of mutual interdependence. 'School' people in the countryside were called upon to act as amanuenses for unlettered relatives or neighbours.[39] On the Witwatersrand, and especially in the compounds, the distribution of political power encouraged literate workers to act as amanuenses for the much more powerful networks of migrant homeboys. 'These tough guys respected me,' Beinart's informant M explained about his association with the Mpondo *Izitshozi* gangs in the 1930s, 'because I used to write letters and read papers.'[40]

For some time, and perhaps for several decades, the role of the amanuensis in southern Africa has been domesticated. Almost all letters from partially or completely illiterate rural correspondents are written and sometimes read by members of an extended household tasked with that responsibility. (Thabo Mbeki) 'Some of the workers interviewed read and wrote their own letters,' Catherine Kell reports from her research into literacy education in the contemporary Western Cape, 'others drew on a person "well-known to them" to do it for them, either as children within the family, or as adults upon entering the migrant labour system.'[41]

The general point here is that migrant workers have achieved a partial mastery of literacy that is sufficient for their particular needs. They have sought a mastery of the technology of writing whilst remaining free of the regime of ongoing technological transformation, standing back from the cascading remaking of individual subjectivity that has driven so much cultural change in this century. A more specific claim, however, is that the very idea of authorship amongst southern African migrant workers runs counter to the intensely private and individualized concept of writing that emerged in Europe in the eighteenth century. While the amanuensis has been a fairly common feature of almost all partially literate societies, in southern Africa, even the intensely affective 'private' domain of courtship seems to have been shaped by a pattern of displaced, and collective, authorship.

In the 1930s, the compounds of the gold mines housed approximately 300,000 young African men, many of them single and in search of appropriate wives. Older migrants remember a distinct practice of collective authorship on the mines. Lahlekile Mphephandaku worked briefly on the mines in the later 1930s, and then spent most of his adult life working for Reef municipalities. To his own and general hilarity he related to Vukile Khumalo and myself the art of writing love letters in the compounds.

> During Sundays and Saturdays we used to go out of our rooms and lie down on the lawn. Then we would write letters to the girls at home, yes. A person would mention his girlfriend – and others would follow, and others would be sitting and writing letters [here]. After that we would say; 'on Monday these letters must go to the Post Office', yes. It must be clear when November comes whether this girl rejects us or not.
>
> VK: I see.
>
> *Lahlekile Mphephanduku:* Then we would stay and wait for the letter [he] had sent. When the letter arrives we would gather again to hear what the girl says. Awu! she rejects [us], she says; she wants to see [us] face to face.
>
> VK: Ha! then what do you do?
>
> *Lahlekile Mphephanduku:* [but] The one who is fortunate [among us] receives good news, the girl accepts his request. Then we would go home.

Whilst we should interpret this joint authorship as a kind of play, it does also bear the distinct imprint of Mpondo peer organizations. For the girls receiving the letters at home would also 'write together' in response to the love letters from the mines.[42]

The point here is not simply that migrants made use of collective authorship because of their illiteracy. They appear, on the contrary, to have chosen to make use of skilled letter writers, even where they were able to write themselves. David Sogoni, for example, is a well-educated man by the standards of his peers, and he certainly spent enough time at school to write a letter comfortably. At the mines, however, he stayed with his older brothers in 'one room at the mine' and the process of courting by letter he describes seems to have required the skills of more than a single individual. 'Yes,' he answered in reply to the question of whether or not he wrote letters,

> we talked with a lady at home. We would call someone who was able to write, and come together to share opinions. And talked to a lady there. Each one of us would come with a plan... Ha! Once the lady responds favourably you would leave your job and go home to your new girlfriend.[43]

The very form of eloquence described here seems to have demanded the efforts of more than a single individual. In a similar fashion, Vukile Khumalo has observed that amongst the community of letter writers that developed around the Colenso's Ekukhanyeni Mission station it was a common practice to call upon those, like Magema Fuze, who were recognized as skilled writers to 'look for good or beautiful words'.[44]


## ■ Conclusion ■

Modern letter writing in South Africa seems to have broken completely free from its Protestant moorings. Under the combined influence of state neglect and the deliberate efforts of homestead heads, literacy, whilst ubiquitous, was radically constrained and necessarily collaborative. Literacy on the mines – and therefore in the subcontinent more generally – was never the intensely private activity that formed the core of protestant Christianity. For the non-conformist missions, the Comaroffs have suggested, the act of reading itself was central to the idea of 'self improvement', the fulcrum of the epistemological revolution the missions brought to southern Africa in the nineteenth century. 'In addressing the written word,' they have argued, 'readers internalised it, reflected upon it in the deepest recesses of their being, and entered into silent conversation.'[45] The movement towards silent, individualized reading – which Chartier has shown had extraordinary cultural significance – has been much more limited than was the case in the most literate regions of early modern Europe and north America.[46] Indeed, whilst writing and reading letters helped constitute the private sphere, reading was not private. Letters, and letter writing were, as Barber has observed for a very different literary form, 'about the individual self, but not about interiority'.[47]

The practice of letter writing helped constitute new kinds of individualized subjects substantially made from the overlap of economic and emotional interests. In the first instance, workers were shaped by, and preoccupied with, an array of personal economic constraints and requirements. We can see this quite clearly from the content of the letters examined here. From the mournful complaints of the abandoned mother that 'other men are striving for themselves' to the intimate domestic arithmetic between husband and wives, letters provided a medium for (and insight into) the development of a new kind of *homo economicus*. In a similar way, the letters between young male migrants and their lovers reveal forms of desire and romantic love at a great remove from the imperatives of lineage and the idioms of *hlonipha*.

Was there an African private sphere in South Africa prior to the rise of the apartheid state? Yes, certainly. Even this very small sample suggests that migrants adopted the literary technology of the colonial state to construct a new individualized and affective domain. But the evidence is also clear that the working class private sphere was simultaneously personal and collaborative. Did the working class private sphere in South Africa produce autonomous individuals free to articulate their rights and expectations of the state independent of the communal demands of their families, villages and chiefs? I don't know, yet.

## NOTES

1 'Illiteracy: South Africa's Economic Time-bomb', *Mail and Guardian*, 7 March 1997, http://web.sn.apc.org/wmail/issues/970307/BUS40.html 30/08/99 10:49:25.

2 K. Breckenridge, 'An Age of Consent: Law, Discipline and Violence on the South African Gold Mines, 1900–1933', PhD Dissertation, Northwestern University, 1995.

3 By the term 'private sphere', I mean an overlapping set of concerns focussed on the economic and affective management of the household, explicitly conceived in opposition to the 'public sphere'.

4 J. Habermas, *The Structural Transformation of the Public Sphere*, T. Burger and F. Lawrence (Trans.) (Cambridge, MA, MIT Press, 1989), p. 48.

5 E. Fox-Genovese, 'Women and the Enlightenment,' in R. Bridenthal, C. Koonz and S. Stuard (eds), *Becoming Visible: Women in European History* (Boston, Houghton Mifflin, 1987), p. 259. G. Rudé, *Europe in the Eighteenth Century: Aristocracy and the Bourgeois Challenge* (London, Weidenfeld and Nicolson, 1972), p. 150. J. Lewis, *The Pursuit of Happiness: Family and Values in Jefferson's Virginia* (Cambridge, Cambridge University Press, 1983), pp. 179–87.

6 T. Nhlapo, 'Women's Rights and the Family in Traditional and Customary Law', in S. Bazilli (ed), *Putting Women on the Agenda* (Johannesburg, Ravan Press, 1991), p. 121.

7 D. Coplan, *In Township Tonight: South Africa's Black City Music and Theatre* (Johannesburg, 1985); *In the Time of Cannibals: the Word Music of South Africa's Basotho Migrants* (Chicago, University of Chicago Press, 1994), p. 9.

8 R. Chartier, 'Texts, Printings, Readings', in Lynn Hunt (ed), *The New Cultural History* (Berkeley, University of California Press, 1989), p. 170 and *A History of Private Life: Passions of the Renaissance*, R. Chartier (ed), A. Goldhammer (Trans.) (Cambridge, MA, Harvard University Press, 1989), p. 157.

9 M. Perrot, 'The Family Triumphant', in M. Perrot (ed), A. Goldhammer (Trans.), *A History of Private Life: volume IV, From the Fires of Revolution to the Great War* (Cambridge, MA, Harvard University Press, 1990), pp. 99–113.

10 C. Taylor, *Sources of the Self: the Making of the Modern Identity* (Cambridge, MA, Harvard University Press, 1989), p. 395.

11 D. Chakrabarty, 'Postcoloniality and the Artifice of History: Who Speaks for 'Indian' Pasts?', *Representations*, 37 (1992), p. 9.

12 Chakrabarty, 'Postcoloniality'; P. Chatterjee, *The Nation and its Fragments: Colonial and Postcolonial Histories* (Princeton, Princeton University Press, 1993).

13 Chakrabarty, 'Postcoloniality', p. 9.

14 M. Mamdani, *Citizen and Subject: Contemporary Africa and the Legacy of Late Colonialism* (Cape Town, James Currey, 1996).

15 J. Guy, 'Making Words Visible: Aspects of Orality, Literacy, Illiteracy and History in Southern Africa', *South African Historical Journal*, 31 (November 1994), pp. 3–27; A. Jordan, *Towards an African Literature: the Emergence of Literary Form in Xhosa* (Berkeley, University of California Press, 1973), pp. 37–102; J. Opland, *Xhosa Oral Poetry: Aspects of a Black South African Tradition* (Johannesburg, Ravan Press, 1983), pp. 1–19; L. Switzer, *Power and Resistance in an African Society: the Ciskei Xhosa and the Making of South Africa* (Madison, University of Wisconsin Press, 1993), pp. 113–33.

16   J. Opland, 'The Image of the Book in Xhosa Praise Poetry', *Current Writing*, 7, 2 (October 1995), p. 44.

17   Natal Archives Depot (hereafter NAD) PMG 46, GPO3/1895 Obscene letter sent through post to native of Impolweni Mission station complaint from Reverend J. A. S. Scott, 1895, 15 December 1897.

18   G. Coka, 'The Story of Gilbert Coka', in M. Perham (ed), *Ten Africans* (Evanston, Northwestern University Press, 1963), p. 276.

19   Interview, Ngilambi Sohlathi by J. Mzayifani and K. Breckenridge, 17 October 1992.

20   J. Guy, 'Making Words Visible', p. 16.

21   I. Schapera, 'The Native as Letter Writer', *The Critic: A South African Quarterly Journal*, 2, 1 (September 1933), p. 20.

22   I. Schapera, *Married Life in an African Tribe* (New York, Sheridan House, 1941), p. 9.

23   *Ibid.* Malinowski goes on. 'Indeed, it would have been probably better if the author had given us a brief appendix including a native glossary with its English equivalents, and maybe even a few characteristic texts in native which illumine and document the tribesman's ideas on procreation, kinship, legitimacy, and other typical Bantu aspects of sex, marriage, and family.'

24   Ibid.

25   Jean and John Comaroff asked Schapera directly about the 'ethnographic basis of *Married Life in an African Tribe*'. His answer mentioned written survey responses from female informants but makes no reference to the letters. J. Comaroff and J. Comaroff. 'On The Founding Fathers, Fieldwork And Functionalism: a Conversation With Isaac Schapera.', *American Ethnologist*, 15, 3 (1988). pp. 559–60.

26   Schapera. 'The Native as Letter Writer', p. 21.

27   Schapera, *Married Life*, p. 46. An extended version of the same letter, although edited, was published in 'The Native as Letter Writer', p. 24.

28   Schapera, *Married Life*, p. 147.

29   Schapera, *Married Life*, p. 145.

30   Schapera, *Married Life*, p. 144.

31   Schapera, *Married Life*, p. 152.

32   C. van Onselen, 'The Reconstruction of a Rural Life from Oral Testimony: Critical Notes on the Methodology Employed in the Study of a Black South African Sharecropper', *Journal of Peasant Studies*, (April 1993).

33   Discussion with Jones Mzayifani, Vukile Khumalo and Keith Breckenridge, Isiyaya 19/10/1996. See also the instructions for disposal on the exquisite love letter above: 'These letters have got secret matters, you mustn't lose them, if you don't want to keep them burn them all in the fire'. Schapera, 'The Native as Letter Writer', p. 24.

34   Chartier (ed), *A History of Private Life*, pp. 111–59, 327–61, 363–95. (A final, somewhat parenthetical, point on this subject of the missing letters. In the course of my very brief stays in the village of Isiyaya, I was on several occasions witness to the writing of letters – about the fining of delinquent children and the negotiation of marriage. In each case, a school-going child took down the letter. More importantly, the same families that are currently involved in an elaborate set of correspondences make every effort to protect their archived letters, if indeed any exist, from my prying social scientist search for source material.)

35   J. Guy, 'Making Words Visible', p. 13. Guy reports that the National Union of Mineworkers estimated that 62 per cent of its members were 'functionally illiterate' in 1994.

36   P. Landau, *The Realm of the Word: Language, Gender and Power in a Southern African Kingdom* (Cape Town, David Philip, 1995), p. 96; N. Etherington, *Preachers Peasants and Politics in Southeast Africa, 1835–1880* (London, Royal Historical Society, 1978), pp. 71–86; P. Delius, *Land Belongs to Us: the Pedi Polity, the Boers and the British in the Nineteenth Century Transvaal* (Johannesburg, Ravan Press, 1983), pp. 120–3, 169–78; E. Eldredge, *A South African Kingdom: the Pursuit of Security in Nineteenth Century Lesotho* (Cambridge, Cambridge University Press, 1993), p. 95.

37   P. and I. Mayer, *Townsmen and Tribesmen: Conservatism and the Process of Urbanization in a South African City* (Cape Town, Oxford University Press, 1961), p. 28. See also C. van Onselen, *The Seed is Mine: the Life of Kas Maine A South African Sharecropper, 1894–1985* (Cape Town, David Philip, 1996), for an extended account of the constraints on the expansion of literacy amongst rural South Africans.

38   NAD, SNA I/1/241, 574/1897; Chas Green: Refuses to read letters or receive moneys for natives from their friends and relatives in Johannesburg, 1897, 26 March 1897.

39   P. and I. Mayer, *Townsmen or Tribesmen*, p. 35. On the Highveld the definition of distinct 'School' and 'Traditionalist' communities seems to have been much more fluid, in large part, probably, because of the relative weakness of mission activity. See, for example, Kas Maine's manoeuvring for amanuenses in C. van Onselen, *The Seed is Mine*, pp. 75–6, 138, 178, 202, 269, 279.

40   W. Beinart, 'Worker Consciousnes, Ethnic Particularism and Nationalism: the Experiences of a South African Migrant, 1930–1960', in S. Marks and S. Trapido (eds), *The Politics of Race, Class and Nationalism in Twentieth Century South Africa* (London, Longman, 1987).

41   C. Kell, 'Teaching Letters: the Recontextualisation of Letter-Writing Practices in Literacy Classes for unschooled Adults in South Africa', Unpublished paper, Cape Town, 1998, p. 7, and see p. 8 for informant's account.

42   Interview, Lahlekile Mphephanduku by V. Khumalo and K. Breckenridge, Isiyaya, 19 October 1996. We can see a similar collective project of translation in Kell's research of contemporary practices of reading letters amongst isiXhosa speakers in the western Cape. Here too the economy of letter writing amongst the migrant population encourages the collectivization of the private sphere. 'I used to be tactful, skip the bad message until I call other people there', one of her informants described the difficult task of relating bad news, 'then tell, that is if you know something is not well, then you read it as is in front of people who can help me to ease the situation.' C. Kell, 'Teaching Letters', p. 8.

43   Interview with David Sogoni by V. Khumalo and K. Breckenridge, Isiyaya, 19 October 1996.

44   Twala cited in V. Khumalo, 'Ekukhanyeni Letter-writers: Notes Towards a Social History of Letter Writing in KwaZulu-Natal, 1890–1900', Unpublished paper, Ann Arbor, 1999, p. 13.

45   J. and J. Comaroff, *Of Revelation and Revolution: Christianity, Colonialism and Consciousness in South Africa*, vol. 1 (Chicago, University of Chicago Press, 1991), p. 34.

46   R. Chartier (ed), *A History of Private Life: Passions of the Renaissance*, vol. III, A. Goldhammer (Trans.) (Cambridge, MA, 1989), pp. 124–44.

47   K. Barber, 'Reasons for Writing: Autonomy, Self-realisation and the Public in the Yoruba Intermediate Classes', Unpublished paper, Birmingham, 1995, p. 7.

# 24

# Live Life More Selfishly: An On-line Gay Advice Column in Japan

## Mark McLelland

■ Gay Life in Japan ■

> Somehow, even with my gay friends I'm not able to discuss questions like 'What do
> you think about being gay?' or 'How are you going to live as a gay from now on?'
> I have no idea what other Japanese gays think about these things. (McLelland, 2000a,
> p. 233)

The adoption of an openly 'gay lifestyle' that is possible in major urban centres of
the Western world is problematic in contemporary Japan. Marriage and the family
system are firmly entrenched in Japanese society (Edwards, 1989; Brinton, 1992)
and living one's life without the support offered by the family is difficult. The
Japanese state, through tax benefits and other means, proactively supports the
narrowly defined heterosexual family unit while simultaneously penalizing unmarried couples and unmarried mothers (Chalmers, in press). Reproductive heterosexuality within the context of the marital family is so normative in Japan that it is
understood to be a requirement for adult status (*ichininmae ni naru*). As Chalmers
(in press) points out 'the act of heterosex (within the private sphere) is reduced to
the singular function of human reproduction within a particular family type. The
result of judging this representation as the "norm" is that all other forms of
"familying" and household structures are virtually ignored.' This means that to
be an unmarried adult in Japan can in itself be considered 'queer', as James
Valentine points out: 'to be unmarried is a form of disability. Not to be paired
up is clearly odd' (1997, p. 99). There are therefore many disadvantages for both
men and women in adopting a 'gay identity' that would exclude them from the

social benefits available only through conforming to a lifestyle organized around the heterosexual family unit.

Yet, paradoxically, although the institutions framing the lives of most Japanese men and women seem inflexible when compared with the more varied lifestyles available in some Western societies, Japanese popular culture tolerates a wide variety of non-normative sexual representations and narratives (Buruma, 1984; Bornoff, 1991; Buckley, 1991; McLelland, 2000a) as well as a vast and largely unregulated sex industry (Constantine, 1993; Morrison, 1998; Altbooks, 1998). As Chalmers (cited above) points out, it is only 'within the private sphere' that sexuality is reduced to reproduction. A wide variety of non-marital sexual expression is available for men and, albeit in much more limited circumstances, for women too (Kelsky, in press). Although the age of consent for women for heterosexual intercourse is 13, this does not apply to boys and no age of consent is mentioned in Japanese law for male participation in either heterosexual or homosexual sex. Likewise, the law is equally silent on female–female sexual practice (see my discussion in McLelland, 2000a, pp. 37–41). As Jennifer Robertson points out, 'As long as an individual's sexual practices do not interfere with or challenge the legitimacy of the twinned institutions of marriage and household, Japanese society accommodates – and in the case of males, even indulges – a diversity of sexual behaviors' (1998, p. 145). However, the strong association of non-marital sexual behaviour with the entertainment sphere means that sexual activity is difficult to politicize in Japan. As one man who writes into gay activist Ito Satoru's homepage argues: 'If you're gay [*gei datte*] you can do anything you want with regard to love and sex, so is it really necessary to go on about gay lib [*gei ribu*]?'

Furthermore, information about Japan's gay male subculture (less so for the lesbian scene) is easy to come by. Throughout the 1970s and 1980s information about Japan's gay scene was available in the gay male press. Japan's first gay magazine, *Barazoku*, was published in 1972 and was followed by *Za Gei*, *Sabu* and *Samson* published in the early 1980s and *Badi* and *G-Men* published in the early 1990s (McLelland, 2000a, p. 128). These magazines were aimed at readers who appreciated a certain 'type' (*taipu*) of sexual partner and contained a great deal of information on clubs, bars and cruise spots where these types were known to hang out. In the early 1990s, mainstream media in Japan experienced a 'gay boom' (Lunsing, 1997; McLelland, 2000a, pp. 32–7) in which popular magazines and journals, and to a lesser extent TV and film, began to take an interest in Japan's gay subculture, making information about gay meeting places and lifestyles more widely available. This more open climate enabled gay men and lesbians to publish their own coming out narratives. These included Fushimi Noriaki's *Private Gay Life* (1991), Kakefuda Hiroko's (1992) *On Being 'Lesbian'* and Ito Satoru's (1992) *Two Men Living Together: My Gay Pride Declaration*. As terms such as 'gay' (*gei*), 'lesbian' (*rezubian*) and 'gay pride' (*gei puraido*) in the titles alone show, all these authors are familiar with Western constructs of homosexual identity. Indeed, Ito Satoru, whose Website is discussed below, is now well known in the West as a Japanese gay activist following the inclusion of his brief biography in Summerhawk et al.'s 1998 book *Queer Japan* and the publication in English of his book *Coming*

*Out in Japan* by Transpacific Press in 2000. A variety of English terms associated with lesbian and gay sexuality such as *homofobia* (homophobia), *kamu auto* (coming out) and *gei puraido* (gay pride) have now entered Japanese as loanwords. However, despite the proliferation in the 1990s of a whole range of new sexual terminology borrowed from English, the entertainment-oriented gay press has remained largely unaffected. All of Japan's six major gay magazines are aimed exclusively at gay men and focus on entertainment, not politics; even issues such as AIDS and safe sex which occupy a great deal of space in Western gay media are hardly mentioned.

Unfortunately, despite the increased attention paid to Japan's homosexual sub-cultures throughout the 1990s, the media have tended to rehearse a familiar range of stereotypes rather than seriously portray the lives of gay men and lesbians. Many activists are sceptical of the increased media visibility achieved during the 'gay boom', branding the attention 'voyeuristic' (Ishino and Wakabayashi, 1996, p. 100); Ito Satoru, in particular, has accused the media of sensationalism since 'to feature homosexuals whose daily lives are really no different from heterosexuals does not make interesting programming' (cited in Summerhawk et al., 1998, p. 90). Depending on the context, gay men tend to be represented as woman-like com-edians, beautiful ideal lovers or sex maniacs (McLelland 1999a, b) and, as the life stories of gay men gathered by Yajima (1997) show, it has been difficult for men growing up with same-sex desires to discover positive role models for their expression.

Despite these difficulties, Japanese society turns a blind eye to discrete sexual practice on the part of men and few gay men face restrictions on meeting and forming casual or more long-term relationships with other men. All medium-sized and larger cities have numerous gay bars, saunas, hotels and cruising spots, as well as callboy outfits that offer 'home delivery' services. These are well advertised on the Internet (McLelland, 2000b) and also in the back of the gay magazines which feature up to 300 pages (about a third of each issue) of ads (McLelland, 2000a, pp. 127–34). However, opportunities for 'living as a gay' (*gei toshite ikiru*) outside the entertain-ment world are seriously circumscribed by the close connection made between marriage, child rearing and career, all of which are necessary to become a fully adult and responsible person. As the opening quotation illustrates, gay men in Japan have few resources for imagining what a 'gay lifestyle' might be and it is difficult to find discussion about gay lifestyles on Japan's gay scene or in the gay media.

However, one place in which such discussion is common is *Sukotan* http://www.sukotan.com, Japan's most visited Internet site dealing with gay issues run by activists Ito Satoru and Yanase Ryuta, who also happen to be Japan's most famous 'gay couple' (*gei kappuru*). They attracted mainstream media attention in Japan in 1992 and again in 1994 after publication of the books *Two Men Living Together: My Gay Pride Declaration* and *Love Notes of Men who Love Men: a Partnership of Love, Cohabitation and Work*. Ito and Yanase's Internet site brings together a wide variety of information about homosexuality in Japan (concerned with 'sexuality' rather than 'sex'), which would otherwise be difficult to access, and serves as a forum for them to express their own attitudes and opinions on a wide

MCLELLAND: LIVE LIFE MORE SELFISHLY

variety of topics. For instance, they review books and films relating to gay life, criticize media portrayals of lesbians and gays, comment on national and international gay events and also run a problem page. The page is entitled *[These Are the Things that] We Are All Troubled By: [Through Discussing them] Let's Grow Strong*[1] and, as far as I have been able to ascertain, it is the only Internet gay advice column where the identity of the advisers is known. In their responses to the problems posted, Ito and Yanase act as a 'gay couple', they demonstrate their feelings for each other, draw examples from their shared life together and try to sort out the problems of others as they sort out their own through dialogue.

The advantage of using the *Sukotan* sample is that Ito and Yanase, as Japan's most high-profile gay couple, are public figures who have between them given countless interviews and published a number of books and pamphlets and whose ideas and attitudes are clearly stated. The emphasis of this paper is therefore not so much on the problems experienced by the men who write into the page but on the advice that is given. As discussed below, research on advice columns in Japan has shown that they tend to support the status quo and throw the problem back on to the writer, encouraging him or her to develop the inner resources necessary to solve the problem or conflict. Ito and Yanase, however, firmly believe that with regard to many of the problems faced by gay men in Japan, it is society that is at fault. They are happy to criticize authority figures such as parents, teachers and bosses as well as friends and colleagues whose homophobic attitudes hinder the expression of gay men's 'individuality' (*jibunrashisa*).[2] Despite the fact that Japan has a long tradition of 'woman's liberation' (*uumanzu ribu*) where a small but very vocal minority of women have complained bitterly about the narrow gender roles and life paths available for women in Japan (Iwao, 1993; Buckley, 1994), it is only recently that Japanese men have begun to voice similar complaints. Ito, along with other gay liberationists such as Fushimi Noriaki,[3] is a key figure in this discourse and is involved in building bridges between gay and feminist activists.[4] Ito recently published the transcription of his dialogue with feminist Ochiai Keiko entitled *Live Like Yourself: Homosexuality and Feminism* in which the importance of 'being true to oneself' is highlighted for both gay men and feminist women (Ito and Oohiai, 1998).

'Being true to oneself' may seem a rather obvious and clichéd response to people expressing dissatisfaction with the constraining effects of their social environment yet, in Japan, this is quite a new and radical position for an 'expert' functioning in the role of adviser to take. Japan, like other East Asian societies that have come under strong Confucian influence, fits the 'collectivistic' model outlined by Sanitioso (1999, p. 71) as opposed to the more 'individualistic' societies of the West.[5] The common-sense position adopted by many Westerners would be that happiness is to be achieved through the expression of purely personal desires and aspirations that are seen as authentic expressions of selfhood. However, in Japan, as Lebra (1976) points out, a sense of 'belongingness' is central to many Japanese people's sense of wellbeing and they are prepared to pay a high price in terms of fulfilling 'obligations' (*gimu*) in order to ensure group membership and protection. As the advice literature discussed below illustrates, an individual is unlikely to be encouraged to take risks, instead being encouraged to realize his or her self worth through performing an appropriate role in the family and community.

## ■ Japanese Advice Columns ■

The most extensive discussion of Japanese advice columns in English is McKinstry and McKinstry's (1991) analysis of the popular *Jinsei annai* (life's guide) column which appears in the *Yomiuri*, one of Japan's top-selling newspapers. They note that this column and others like it are rather different in tone from English-language equivalents such as Ann Landers in that both the letters themselves and their replies are 'completely serious – really almost somber' (1991, p. 11). Whereas American advice columnists express their personality in their responses, often in an entertaining or amusing manner, in the case of *Jinsei annai*, the team of staff writers are deadly serious and seldom make reference to their own lives. However, the most striking feature of the advice given is its somewhat harsh tone. Letter writers looking for sympathy, a shoulder to cry on or simply for a forum to vent their frustration, are unlikely to be satisfied by the replies they receive which tend to throw the problem back at the writer. For instance, despite the fact that nearly one-quarter of all letters came from wives who were dissatisfied with their husbands' behaviour, divorce was never raised as a possibility unless the writer herself had already mentioned it in the body of her letter (1991, p. 65). In fact, as McKinstry and McKinstry point out, 'throughout this project we did not encounter any replies giving the slightest encouragement to any kind of unconventional behavior' (1991, p. 28). Also, they discovered that 'quite often distraught wives [were] blamed by respondents for the very complaint they have made against their husbands' (1991, p. 50). McKinstry and McKinstry provide a wide selection of letters and responses. The hectoring tone of the latter is indicative of 'the ingrained Japanese distaste for people who fail to take responsibility for their own shortcomings' (1991, p. 50) and 'the strongly held belief that emotional problems, unless a physical causation can be demonstrated, are rooted in self-centredness' (1991, p. 73). Time and again, the complaining women are told to reflect on how they themselves might be the cause of the problem they perceive in their husband or children and to *gaman suru* (strive) to rectify the problem through their own efforts.

This attitude is not restricted to newspaper advice columns but is apparent throughout popular media. An episode of *Life Consultancy Special*[6] that I viewed in 1998 featured a panel of advisers including Nomura Sachiyo, the wife of one of Japan's top baseball coaches and author of a number of advice books including *Can You Judge Men? Here Are 17 Checkpoints,*[7] who was particularly harsh with the women she was meant to advise. For instance, a young wife with two small children complained that she had lost her identity since marriage and now only existed in the eyes of the world as 'Yu's mother or Mr Yamanaka's wife.' She complained that she felt lonely since her husband was always at work and her children spent most of their time sleeping. She would like to take up a hobby or do voluntary work to meet more people but had neither time nor money. Finally, she asks 'Is this all that my life amounts to?' Nomura Sachiyo (herself a career woman with a wide variety of interests) expressed little sympathy for this woman's situation, telling her directly that she should look for satisfaction inside the home, not outside it. The other (all female) panellists agreed, finding it amusing that she should complain that her children spend most of their time sleeping, calling her 'lucky'. She was told that instead of complaining, she should reflect on her good fortune, after all 'with a loving husband and two beautiful children, there really is no reason for you to feel lonely'. The housewife, now in tears, thanked the panellists politely for their advice.

The conformist nature of this advice may be read in terms of the 'collectivistic' nature of Japanese society, but it should be remembered that much of the advice given by American columnists prior to the 1970s was similarly conformist. As Hays (1984, p. 12) points out in her analysis of three decades of Ann Landers' columns 'in 1970, Ann Landers still sounded very much the conservative', and it was not until the 1980s that Hays detects what she calls a 'quantum leap' into a 'do your own thing' system of values (1984, p.13). Smith and Levin (1974) in their analysis of advice columns also noticed a change over time in the way blame was attributed in cross-sexual relations from the period 1947–1951 which 'yielded more frequent support for the position "male right/female wrong" (57%)' to the period 1967–1971 in which women were blamed for the problem in only 41 per cent of cases.

Despite indications that younger Japanese people, especially women, are growing increasingly dissatisfied with the comparatively narrow life paths available to them (Ishii-Kunz, 1989; McLelland, 1999b; Kelsky, in press), the quantum leap into the 'do your own thing' system of values that has come to typify Western societies has yet to take place in Japan. As will be described below, it is in gay liberation and feminist discourse that this position is most likely to be articulated. On their advice page, Ito and Yanase invert the relationship between (potentially) progressive complainer and conservative adviser and, instead, are more likely to criticize the writer for his narrow-minded views and support for outmoded social values.


## ■ The *Sukotan* Problem Page ■

The analysis that follows focuses not so much upon the problem letters themselves but upon Ito and Yanase's advice which, unlike that offered in conventional advice columns, often contradicts what Lunsing calls the 'commonsense' (*jooshiki*)[8] that he regards as 'an important organising principle in Japan' (in press). As marriage and the family in Japan are central to common-sense notions of how an individual should structure his or her life, in this article I have concentrated on three letters directly concerning problems relating to marriage.[9] However, my point is not to oppose the 'good' advice given by Ito and Yanase with the 'bad' advice to be found in more conventional media but to point out that both worldviews, the 'individualist' as well as the 'conformist', are equally bounded by taken-for-granted assumptions about the individual and his or her responsibilities, and each has its own drawbacks.

As discussed above, the traditional understanding of the self in Japan stressed its socially constructed nature: an individual only became fully adult or complete (*ichininmae ni naru*) by entering into the social relations that conferred that status. For women this involves getting married 'on schedule' (Brinton, 1992), giving birth to and raising children as full-time homemakers. Men, too, must get married, vigorously pursue their career and be seen to provide a stable home for their wife and children. Thus, adult status was not granted chronologically but largely achieved by entering into a set of clearly defined social relationships. The new ideology professed by Ito and Yanase, however, is more atomistic, stressing that self-identity must come from the inside as an expression of pre-existent, essential 'truths' about the person. In this system, accepting inalienable facts about the self such as sexual orientation and openly proclaiming them is the way in which 'selfhood' (*jibunrashisa*) is to be achieved. These basic truths about the person take priority over socially imposed roles and expectations. In the *Basic Information about Homosexuality* section of their Internet site, they write:

> You may be troubled or pained by the fact that you are a homosexual [*dooseiaisha*][10] and may even wish that you could change into a heterosexual [*iseiaisha*]. But whatever the time, wherever the place, homosexuals [*dooseiaisha*] are a fixed percentage of the population. If you can truly accept this you will gain in confidence and take the first step towards living your life as a homosexual [*dooseiaisha toshite ikiru*].

It is no surprise, then, that they regard a gay lifestyle as necessarily in conflict with the way Japanese society is currently organized around the reproductive demands of the family system. However, although they are able to give convincing reasons why the common-sense understanding of marriage is inadequate for many people, they are less able to articulate what a 'gay lifestyle' might be. Consequently, despite their own pioneering role as an out gay couple, they can offer little advice on how to negotiate a place for a homosexual identity within the family and workplace.

Before looking at the problem letters it is necessary to consider further the meaning of marriage in contemporary Japan since it is the importance placed upon marriage as the final step towards becoming a fully adult and responsible person, rather than any legal or moral restrictions, that inhibits the development of a 'gay identity'. Kirsten Refsing says that in Japan 'marriage has been perceived as a practical arrangement in which two *outwardly compatible* persons with unambiguous role definitions enter into the socially well defined project of establishing a family' (1995, p. 345, my emphasis). The emphasis upon 'outward compatibility' as opposed to 'romantic love' has meant that men-loving men and women-loving women do not necessarily assume that they cannot or should not get married to a member of the opposite sex. Indeed, gay activist Fushimi Noriaki does not rule out marriage for gay men, describing it simply as a 'mutual reproduction project' (*saiseisan purojekuto*) (1991, p. 17). Eroticism is generally down-played in Japanese conceptions of marriage and for Japanese men 'masculinity' is not predicated on successfully performing the role of lover but 'is often equated with men's ability to provide financially' (Ishii-Kunz, 1993, p. 57) which means a husband's role is defined more in terms of breadwinner than lover. Ishii-Kunz suggests that 'to be masculine in Japan...men accede to work demands that require physical distance from their families' (1993, p. 57). The absence of a clearly defined 'couple culture' (Ueno, 1987, p. 82, n. 15) in Japan means that a man's lack of desire for his wife is largely irrelevant to his successful performance of the role of husband.

Marriage is such an important life event that it is taken for granted that people in an individual's group should take an interest in his or her marriage prospects, often serving as intermediaries in getting suitable individuals together for *o-miai* (marriage introduction meetings). It is thought natural that parents, in particular, should have a say in the suitability of a prospective spouse. For instance, one letter cited by McKinstry and McKinstry in their analysis of the *Jinsei annai* advice column is about the problems that arise when one parent is not satisfied with the spouse chosen by the child. Entitled 'Husband desperately against son's marriage even though young couple committed to marriage after two-year relationship', the letter describes the conflict that a son's choice of marriage partner is creating between the mother who supports the choice and the father who does not. As the mother (who wrote the letter) comments 'I think we should trust our son's judgement since he has known her for two years.' However, the father, who does not consider the girl to be 'good enough' has threatened to turn his wife out of the house if she continues to support the marriage. The response to the mother's problem is conciliatory, commenting 'maybe you should try to find out what it is that your husband objects to so much...do not forget that she will be a member of your family. It is reasonable to find out more about her background.' The advice is to postpone the marriage while the mother can investigate the girl's background thoroughly and, if nothing 'unfavourable' comes to light, this will give the mother more 'ammunition' to persuade the father. McKinstry and McKinstry conclude on the basis of this and other similar problem letters that 'parents in Japan still believe that they are within their rights to pass judgement on the social standing of the opposing family any time marriage is proposed' (1991, p. 165). It is in the above context, where marriage is seen as a family and at times a community affair, that Ito and Yanase's advice given to gay men troubled by marital concerns should be read.

The three men who write into the *Sukotan* problem page expressing concerns over marriage are all troubled by the 'commonsense' view of marriage outlined above. For instance, a 31-year-old man writes:

> My biggest worry is the marriage problem. No matter how many times my parents bring up the idea of a marriage introduction [*o-miai*] I always reply that 'I'll find [a bride] myself'. But as my parents take me at my word, I feel my behaviour is unforgiveable...if there is a good way of dealing with one's parents please let me know.

In response, Yanase asks 'For whose sake do you get married? It isn't for your parents, it's for yourself isn't it?' Ito adds 'Whether you get married or not won't alter your difficulties and if you think about the unhappiness of the woman you don't love, I think it's better not to marry.' Yanase then picks up the theme of responsibility (*sekinin*), commenting that it is the individual, not his parents, who has final responsibility for his own life and, as a result, 'You should live more selfishly' (*moto wagamama ni ikiyoo*). The choice of the term 'responsibility' (*sekinin*) here is significant as it is usually used in relation to the obligations (*gimu*) that an individual has to others in his or her 'in group' (*uchi*). The common-sense view would be that a son (who in the Confucian belief system has the obligation to carry on the family name) has a responsibility to wed and produce descendants not simply for his own sake but for that of his parents and grandparents. Here Yanase asserts that the final responsibility is not to others but to the self, an attitude that in common-sense terms would seem selfish. He pre-empts this criticism by exhorting the man to 'live more selfishly', a position unlikely to be endorsed by those in the writer's 'in group'.

Ito agrees with Yanase's point, adding that 'If you constantly think "This is unforgivable for my parents" or "I mustn't worry my parents,"...won't your own life disappear?' He mentions his own experience of hiding his homosexuality from his parents until he was 39 at which point he confessed to his mother. Her response was not to accept his sexuality but to accept his decision to live his own life. As she said at the time 'You have to let people live as they wish.' Ito believes that if parents really love their children then they will respect the life choices they make. Yanase, however, is less optimistic, referring to Ito's mother (with whom they live) as 'amazing'. He comments that 'Don't you think it's exceedingly difficult to live for your own sake in Japanese society?' After all, he says, fathers work for the sake of their companies until they drop, mothers spend all their energy caring for the household and children exhaust themselves trying to get into a good university for the sake of their parents. It is therefore difficult to think in such a way that puts the individual first.

Despite these points of agreement, Yanase and Ito do differ in the advice they offer the concerned man. Yanase feels that he should first communicate to his parents that he has no desire to marry, whereas Ito says that this will not work unless he 'comes out' (*kamu auto*) as gay. Ito argues that he wasted years unable to separate himself from his parents and that he was therefore unable to 'cut out' his own lifestyle. Yet Yanase comments that 'It's easy to say that [he] should come out but if you think about [his] situation for a minute, you'd realise this would be terrible...[he] has no confidence in himself as gay...there is no-one to support him and he would end up being hurt.' Ito says if that is the case, then he should make some gay friends with whom to share his problems with his parents. Yanase agrees, saying that this would be one small step on the path [towards self-acceptance] adding 'people can change so don't give up.'

Ito and Yanase's responses outlined above contradict conventional wisdom in several ways. Most apparent is their insistence that the individual's primary responsibility is to himself and not to his parents and that marriage is not a 'cure' for homosexual feelings but will simply compound the problems gay men experience. However, Yanase's individualism is less relentless than Ito's in that he thinks the writer should simply communicate to his parents that he is not interested in marriage whereas Ito believes this can only be done by 'coming out' as gay. By the end of the exchange, it seems that Ito, too, is less sure that this is the best strategy, agreeing that the man should first build up a support group of gay friends before making any statements about his sexuality.

Another 31-year-old man writes:

> There's a girl that I've been going out with who doesn't know that I am gay... When we have sex it feels good but I always imagine I'm doing it with a guy... Since I am already in my 30s, my parents and my superiors in the workplace are asking me 'When are you going to marry your girl-friend?'... Should I lie about my feelings and get married or should I live life as a gay [gei toshite jinsei wo ikiru beki na no ka]?

In response to the second man's similar letter, Ito and Yanase acknowledge that it is a problem faced by a large number of gay men. They lament that despite the fact that the number of single people is growing 'Those who decide not to marry are subject to various pressures.' Ito points out the relentless nature of people's expectation that men over a certain age will be married, with shopkeepers, neighbours and colleagues all asking about one's wife. However, even when you make it clear that you are single, the response is not to respect that choice but to say 'You'd better hurry up and get married.' He acknowledges that some men may give in and get married just to escape the pressure. Yet Ito counters this social pressure to get married by pointing out the different pressures that a gay man who marries a woman will be subject to. Firstly, he mentions that he should visualize the lack of freedom and problems that being married will create: he will have to have sex with someone he is not attracted to and will have to share his life with a partner with whom he cannot get along. Moreover, he will not be able to express 'the most important thing inside yourself: your fascination for the same sex'. However, both Ito and Yanase do acknowledge that because getting married is considered the natural thing to do, it is easier for a gay man to visualize what his life will be like after marriage than it is to imagine other ways of living. For those men who choose not to marry and prefer to 'live as gay' (gei toshite ikiru) there is the problem that information about how to do so 'is exceedingly small'. They encourage the writer to search the Internet, read books and ask gay friends in order to find out about what lifestyles are possible before making a decision.

The concerns of the 27-year-old man whose posting appears below are slightly different:

> I like men... I'm not sexually interested in women... but in the environment in which I've been brought up it's understood to be natural and the best thing for men and women to get married, set up a household and rear children... I'm afraid that solely on the basis of my sexual orientation I won't be able to get married and will have to live alone... Isn't marriage a wonderful thing? Isn't it great to have a family? But when I think I cannot have this I feel sad... and yet I don't want to give up on the chance for marriage.

This man does not want to avoid marriage but is, instead, troubled by the fact that he may be excluded from getting married 'solely on the basis of [his] sexual attraction'. The man's praise for the institution of marriage and the household, as opposed to 'love' for a particular female partner, illustrates the extent to which 'marriage' as an adult individual's definitive life event is considered in the abstract, separate from feelings held for any particular partner.

Ito and Yanase's response to this letter is, again, characterized by an attack on the taken-for-granted centrality of marriage. Ito states that all the advantages that married couples experience: helping each other out, sharing problems, spending a happy time together, are not necessarily limited to 'a man/woman family'. He points out how Yanase and himself have been sharing their lives for the past four years. Ito also criticizes the man's seemingly naïve assumption that families are always happy, pointing out that relations between family members are often spiteful and harmful. Yanase agrees, commenting that he fails to understand the 'yearning' (*akogare*) that the writer feels for marriage. For gay men, he says that marriage means giving up a lot including masturbation, gay magazines, personal space and privacy. Just as the workplace is a closet (*kuroozetto*), after marriage the home also becomes a closet.

Ito returns to the idea that the positive characteristics of the family are something that can only be experienced by a male/female couple. He points out that the same kinds of feelings and support that can be experienced in a marriage can also be felt between friends or between a same-sex couple, adding that people only assume marriage to be the ultimate path to happiness because that is the only story fed to them by the media. Yanase also laments the lack of 'couple role models' (*kappuru no rooru moderu*) for gay men. Finally, they advise the writer, as in the above two cases, to use the Internet to search for the homepages of 'gay couples' (*gei no kappuru*) in search of role models.

The above responses to the 'marriage problem' (*kekkon mondai*) experienced by many Japanese gay men are significant in that both Ito and Yanase encourage the writers to be more 'individual' and to take personal responsibility for their life choices rather than just conform to society's expectations. Yet the most striking omission in this advice is a description of what an alternative, non-family-oriented lifestyle might be or how it might be achieved. Although they encourage the writers to make gay friends, search the Internet and read books in search of 'resources to think about a gay life', given the strength of common-sense views of how a man should live his life, it is doubtful just how useful this advice can be to men who are already established in their careers.

However, one letter from a 21-year-old university student about to graduate asks for Ito and Yanase's advice on how to choose appropriate employment. This gives them a chance to say more about what a gay lifestyle might be; not surprisingly, it seems to involve rejecting the common-sense criteria of a good career. The student writes:

> I am a fourth year University student. Sooner or later I need to decide on what kind of work I will do. Of course, I don't want to come out and I would feel insecure about working as a gay. How should I go about choosing a company?

Ito begins by rejecting the common-sense life path that most Japanese would endorse. He says 'You had better give up the idea of getting married, forming a stable family, advancing in your career and accumulating savings.' He particularly rejects employment in Japan's finance industry because even heterosexuals feel constrained to marry against their wishes in these occupations, pressure being put upon male employees to marry in order to ensure their promotion. He points out that working in such industries will use up a lot of energy just in resisting pressure from others to conform.

Yanase agrees with Ito, commenting that during his time working at an electronics firm he was extremely stressed out by the pressure to conform exerted by his straight colleagues and by his own internalized homophobia. He was even unable to participate in workplace conversations about female pop stars because he felt unable to say 'I have absolutely no feelings for women.' Ito suggests that taking a job in which it is not necessary to mix much with one's colleagues is attractive to many gay men. Computing work, for example, would be suitable because it involves sitting at one's own computer all day without having to interact with other employees. Another possibility is to give up on regular salaried employment and work freelance (*furiitaa*) instead. Ito concludes by cautioning the writer to think very carefully before committing himself to becoming a 'company man' (*kaisha ningen*),[11] since he will be bound both body and soul to the company for life.

The advice on employment strategies given here once more strikes at the commonsense understanding of how a man should plan his career. Traditionally, sons have felt pressured to work hard at school in order to enter elite universities that are the only gateways to the best jobs in the civil service, finance or in top manufacturing companies. Known as the 'escalator system',[12] once a man succeeds in stepping on to this career path he is carried along through serial promotions all the way to retirement largely independent of any demonstrated ability. The advantage of the escalator system is that it provides job security and facilitates the arrangement of home-loans that are often organised by elite companies on employees' behalf. To reject the escalator system outright, particularly for the life of a freelancer who is excluded from the benefits accruing to permanent company employees, is again unlikely to be endorsed by the writer's 'in group' of friends and family.

To appreciate just how radical Ito and Yanase's attack on the career system would seem to many Japanese, it is helpful to consider the response to a letter reproduced in McKinstry and McKinstry (1991, pp. 193–4) in which a young man complains about the boring, restrictive job he has at an office machine company. This 23-year-old man complains that he has to work so much overtime he has no time for other activities, asking 'What good is money if you don't have time to spend it?' He would like to join a company that offers recreational facilities and encourages activities other than work. The response, typical of the *Jinsei annai* columnists is 'anything is what you make it' and the man is encouraged to stick with the job he has. This points to the inflexibility of the Japanese career system where even a man as young as 23 is considered to have irreversibly committed himself to working for the same company. Not surprisingly, the man's aspirations are hardly encouraged by his family; he says in the letter that his father criticizes him since 'a person cannot be happy if he is always thinking only about himself'.

Ito and Yanase's insistence on personal choice, freedom and the right of the individual to 'cut out' his own life path independent of his family or social expectations seems unremarkable in terms of the 'individualistic' model of self-realization characteristic of most Western societies. However, as the contrast with the more mainstream advice offered by the *Jinsei annai* columnists shows, it is clearly at variance with many people's common-sense notions about how life should be lived in Japan.

## ■ Conclusion ■

The large number of English loan words used in their responses such as 'gay couple', 'coming out', 'homophobia', 'closet' and 'role model', and the highlighting of characteristically Western notions of selfhood such as 'individuality' (*jibunra-shisa*) and 'lifestyle' (*ikikata*), suggest that Ito and Yanase understand 'living as a gay' (*gei toshite ikiru*) very much through Western models. Through their Internet site, lectures, publications and interviews, Ito and Yanase have been key players in introducing Western models of homosexuality to the Japanese public as well as explaining the situation facing many gay men in Japan to people in the West. Some Western commentators like Barbara Summerhawk et al. (1998) in their book *Queer Japan* accept at face value the opinions of activists such as Ito that Japan is somehow 'behind' the West in terms of acknowledging diversity in sexual identity. For instance, they cite Ito's claim that Japanese men experience 'difficulties in *the* "identity-development process"' (1998, p. 11, my emphasis). Summerhawk et al.'s use of the singular here is problematic when it is considered that research in developed 'gay communities' such as Sydney has failed to discover a homogeneous 'gay identity' or a singular identity-development process, leading Gary Dowsett to speak of 'the impossibility of identity' (1996, p. 274) in relation to men who experience homosexual desire.

As Dennis Altman points out, 'In Japan despite both extensive American influence and a considerable commercial world it does not appear that a large open community [of lesbians and gays] is developing' (1995, p. 133). Ito and Yanase would seem to agree when they point out that the major difficulty confronting gay men is the total absence in Japanese society of alternative life paths that do not require the individual to get married 'on schedule' and ride the escalator employment system towards retirement, producing and rearing a couple of children on the way. Many gay men find it easier to imagine placing themselves within the family system, despite the difficulties that they realize this will cause, rather than creating a lifestyle that would better suit their sensibilities. To reject both marriage and the career system in favour of 'living as a gay' is to reject the key institutions that, for men, mark the entry to full personhood and carries a sense of selfishness and irresponsibility. As one 26-year-old man writes into the problem page:

> Regarding my parents, I just can't get rid of the idea that being born gay is unforgive-able. Although I have recently come to realise that homosexuality isn't acquired... I

feel bad because I cannot show my parents the faces of their grandchildren and because, if they knew I was gay, they would feel sad. Since they have raised me up till now I am indebted to them [*giri ga aru*] . . . and I can't get it out of my head that I am behaving badly towards my parents.

It is striking that Ito and Yanase have very little to offer in their advice to such men other than to encourage the writers to be more individual, more selfish and more self-reliant. It is doubtful that simply making a few gay friends, surfing through 'gay couple' Internet sites or working through the *Sukotan* reading list is going to help the men who write in to Ito and Yanase's page 'live as gay' in their everyday lives, since 'living as gay' is clearly not a straightforward project in modern Japan.

The absence in Japanese society of culturally endorsed alternative lifestyles characterized by flexibility with regard to sexual relationships and employment helps to explain the somewhat harsh tone taken by conventional advice columnists. Perhaps they feel, like some gay men, that the consequences of opting out of the key institutions of Japanese society are much worse than the personal costs involved in conforming to them. So far, it is only in gay, lesbian and feminist circles that common-sense views about lifestyle have been challenged. Unfortunately, as Ito and Yanase acknowledge, it is not easy in Japanese society to forge a lifestyle for oneself independent of established patterns. The fact that they themselves have done so, does, however, offer a role model for younger gay men who have not yet committed themselves to social institutions such as marriage and career from which it will be difficult to extricate themselves (should they want to) at a later date. Yet, whether young gay men in Japan will put aside common-sense notions about how they should live their lives and take up Ito and Yanase's call to 'live life more selfishly' remains to be seen. Indeed, as the vagueness of Ito and Yanase's advice shows, it is not at all clear what it might mean to 'live as gay' in contemporary Japan.

## NOTES

1 *Minna de nayande ookikunaroo.*
2 *Jibunrashisa*, a Sino-Japanese compound, means 'like-oneself-ness' and is often used in gay and feminist literature to express a sense of 'individuality'. The more abstract term for 'individuality' is *kosei*, the Chinese-character translation of 'individuality' introduced into Japan along with other Western philosophical notions at the end of the nineteenth century.
3 Fushimi Noriaki has written a number of books, including the pioneering *Private Gay Life* (1991) and *The Art of Pleasure* with bisexual author Saito Ayako (1997).
4 Lesbians tend to be overlooked by both gay and feminist groups in Japan (McLelland, 2000a, pp. 32–4).
5 For a discussion of collectivism versus individualism in Japanese society see Ishii-Kunz (1989).
6 *Jinsei soodan supesharu*, TBS, 22 December 1998, 8.00 pm.

7   *Anata: otoko no kantei dekimasuka? Chiekkupointo wa 17kashoo,* Tokyo: Kuresutosha, 1995. Nomura's advice on how to find out if a man is gay involves 'checking out' his appearance for designer clothes and perfumed handkerchiefs, his apartment for 'womanish things' such as chandeliers and lace curtains and his cooking-style which will appear 'womanlike'.

8   Lunsing glosses *jooshiki* as 'a word many informants used to explain what they had to deal with when relating to people who are not familiar with lifestyles and ideas other than "normal"' (in press).

9   A total of 34 questions and responses were posted between 1 May 1997 and 4 May 2000. They can be loosely divided into categories dealing with gay relationships, coming out, marriage, gay identity, social interaction, sexual problems and miscellaneous.

10  *Dooseiaisha* (literally same-sex-love-person) and *iseiaisha* (literally other-sex-love-person) are the Chinese character translations of the English terms 'homosexual' and 'heterosexual' and were popularized at the beginning of the twentieth century in sexological literature translated from European languages. *Dooseiaisha* has a somewhat medical nuance and is thus avoided by other gay rights activists such as Fushimi Noriaki who considers it to be pathological. He prefers, instead, the loan-word *gei* ('gay') because of its connection with the American Civil Rights Movement. See McLelland (2000a, pp. 7–12) for a discussion of Japanese terminology relating to homosexuality.

11  For a description of how company men are 'crafted' by a variety of induction procedures, see Dasgupta (2000).

12  This description refers to Japan prior to the bursting of the bubble economy in the late 1980s. Nakane (1972), in her chapter on 'Characteristics and value orientation of Japanese man' (note the singular) accepts the escalator system as the paradigmatic lifecourse for *all* men despite the fact that it was only ever available to the top 30 per cent of men who graduated from elite universities. Nevertheless, it was and is still widely aspired to. For a discussion of the anxieties caused by the gradual breakdown of this system, see Dasgupta (2000).

## REFERENCES

Altbooks (1998) *SEX no arukikata: Tookyoo fuuzoku kanzen gaido (How to Find Your Way Around Sex: the Complete Guide to Tokyo's Sex Scene).* Tokyo: Mediawaakusu.

Altman, Dennis (1995) The new world of 'Gay Asia', special edition of *Meridian*, pp. 121–38.

Bornoff, Nicholas (1991) *Pink Samurai: the Pursuit of Politics and Sex in Japan.* London: Grafton Books.

Brinton, Mary (1992) Christmas cakes and wedding cakes: the social organisation of Japanese women's life course, in T. S. Lebra (ed.), *Japanese Social Organization.* Honolulu: University of Hawaii Press.

Buckley, Sandra (1991) Penguin in bondage: a tale of Japanese comic books, in C. Penley and A. Ross (eds), *Technoculture.* Minneapolis: University of Minnesota Press.

Buckley, Sandra (1994) A short history of the feminist movement in Japan, in J. Gelb and M. Lief Palley (eds), *Women of Japan and Korea: Continuity and Change.* Philadelphia: Temple University Press.

Buruma, Ian (1984) *Behind the Mask: On Sexual Demons, Sacred Mothers, Transvestites, Gangsters and other Japanese Cultural Heroes.* New York: Meridian.

Chalmers, Sharon (in press) Lesbian (in)visibility and social policy in Japanese society, in V. Mackie (ed.), *Gender and Public Policy in Japan.* London: Routledge.

Constantine, Peter (1993) *Japan's Sex Trade: a Journey through Japan's Erotic Subcultures.* Tokyo: Charles Tuttle.

Dasgupta, Romit (2000) Performing masculinities? The 'salaryman' at work and play, *Japanese Studies* 20 (2), pp. 189–200.

Dowsett, Gary (1996) *Practicing Desire: Homosexual Sex in the Era of AIDS.* Stanford: Stanford University Press.

Edwards, Walter (1989) *Modern Japan through its Weddings: Gender, Person and Society in Ritual Portrayal.* Stanford: Stanford University Press.

Fushimi, Noriaki (1991) *Puraibeeto gei raifu (Private Gay Life).* Tokyo: Gakuyoo shoboo.

Fushimi, Noriaki and Saito Ayako (1997) *Kairaku no gijutsu (The Art of Pleasure).* Tokyo: Kawade bunkoo.

Hays, Charlotte (1984) The evolution of Ann Landers: From prim to progressive, *Public Opinion* (December/January), pp. 11–13.

Ishii-Kunz, Masako (1989) Collectivism or individualism? Changing patterns of Japanese attitudes, *Sociology and Social Research* 73 (4), pp. 174–8.

Ishii-Kunz, Masako (1993) Japanese fathers: work demands and family roles, in Jane C. Hood (ed.), *Men, Work and Family.* London: Sage.

Ishino, Sachiko and Naoko Wakabayashi (1996) Japan, in R. Rosenbloom (ed.), *Unspoken Rules: Sexual Orientation and Women's Human Rights.* London and New York: Cassell.

Ito, Satoru (1992) *Otoko futarigarashi: boku no gei puraido sengen (Two Men Living Together: My Gay Pride Declaration).* Tokyo: Taroojiroosha.

Ito, Satoru and Ochiai Keiko (1998) *Jibunrashiku ikiru: dooseiai to feminizumu (Live More Like Onself: Homosexuality and Feminism).* Tokyo: Kamogawa booklet.

Ito, Satoru and Yanase Ryuta (1994) *Otoko to otoko no ren'ai nooto: ai to kurashi to shigoto no paatonashipp u (Love Notes of Men who Love Men: a Partnership of Love, Living Together and Work).* Tokyo: Taroojiroosha.

Ito, Satoru and Yanase Ryuta (2000) *Coming Out in Japan,* F. Conlan (trans.). Melbourne: Transpacific Press.

Iwao, Sumiko (1993) *The Japanese Woman: Traditional Image and Changing Reality.* New York: The Free Press.

Kakefuda, Hiroko (1992) *Rezubian de aru to iu koto (On Being 'Lesbian').* Tokyo: Kawade Soboo shinsha.

Kelsky, Karen (in press) *Women on the Edge: Gender, Race and the Erotics of the International in Japan.* Durham: Duke University Press.

Lebra, Takie Sugiyama (1976) *Japanese Patterns of Behavior.* Honolulu: University of Hawaii Press.

Lunsing, Wim (1997) 'Gay boom' in Japan: changing views of homosexuality?, *Thamyris* 4 (2), pp. 267–93.

Lunsing, Wim (in press) *Beyond Common Sense: Negotiating Constructions of Sexuality and Gender in Contemporary Japan.* London: Kegan Paul International.

McKinstry, John and Asako Nakajima McKinstry (1991) *Jinsei Annai: 'Life's Guide' Glimpses of Japan through a Popular Advice Column.* New York: M. E. Sharpe.

McLelland, Mark (1999a) How to be a nice gay: the stereotyping of gay men in Japanese media, *New Zealand Journal of Asian Studies* 1 (1), pp. 42–59.

McLelland, Mark (1999b) Gay men as women's ideal partners in Japanese popular culture: are gay men really a girl's best friends?, *U.S.–Japan Women's Journal* (English supplement), 17, pp. 77–110.

McLelland, Mark (2000a) *Male Homosexuality in Modern Japan: Cultural Myths and Social Realities.* Richmond: Curzon Press.

McLelland, Mark (2000b) Out and about on Japan's gay net, *Convergence* 6 (3), pp. 16–33.

Morrison, Andrew (1998) Teen prostitution in Japan: regulation of telephone clubs, *Vanderbilt Journal of Transnational Law* 31 (2), pp. 457–97.

Nakane, Chie (1972) *Japanese Society.* Berkeley: University of California Press.

Refsing, Kirsten (1995) The discourse of cultural differences in Danish–Japanese marriages, in S. Clausen, R. Starrs and A. Waddell-Wedellsborg (eds), *Cultural Encounters: China, Japan and the West.* Aarhaus: Aarhaus University Press.

Robertson, Jennifer (1998) *Takarazuka: Sexual Politics and Popular Culture in Modern Japan.* Berkeley: University of California Press.

Sanitioso, Rasyid (1999) A social psychological perspective on HIV/AIDS and gay or homosexually active Asian men, in Peter Jackson and Gerald Sullivan (eds), *Multicultural Queer: Australian Narratives.* New York: Haworth Press.

Smith, Terry and Jack Levin (1974) Social change in sex roles: an analysis of advice columns, *Journalism Quarterly* 51, pp. 525–7.

Summerhawk, Barbara et al. (eds) (1998) *Queer Japan: Personal Stories of Japanese Lesbians, Gays, Transsexuals, and Bisexuals.* Norwich: New Victoria Publishers.

Ueno, Chizuko (1987) The position of Japanese women reconsidered, *Current Anthropology* (supplement), 28 (4), pp. S75–S82.

Valentine, James (1997) Pots and pans: identification of queer Japanese in terms of discrimination, in A. Livia and K. Hall (eds), *Queerly Phrased: Language, Gender and Sexuality.* Oxford: Oxford University Press.

Yajima, Masami (1997) *Dansei dooseiaisha no raifuhisutori (Homosexual Men's Life Histories).* Tokyo: Gakubunsha.

# 25

# African Cuisines: Recipes for Nation-Building?

## Igor Cusack

## ■ 1.   Introduction ■

Thomas Sankara, the former President of Burkina Faso, once wrote, '[S]o, do you not know where imperialism is to be found? . . . just look at your plate!' (Barrot 1994: 26).[1] Cuisines, whether national, regional, or 'ethnic,' should not be considered as neutral, innocent concoctions. Like most of material culture, they are clearly products of dominant ideologies and related power structures, and this paper suggests that African cuisines are nurtured by such ideologies as imperialism, capitalism and nationalism. Most emerging African national cuisines – and what people actually eat in Africa, not necessarily quite the same – clearly reflect the colonial encounter and the subsequent dependent relationship with the West, as well as indigenous ethnic culinary practices.

Catherine Palmer has pointed out that food, along with landscape and the body, is an aspect of the modern material world that is important to both individual and collective identities (1998: 183). There is no doubt that food, and the way various ingredients are combined and cooked, is an important element of a national cultural identity. In this paper, I want to examine the development of African cuisines in relation to the nation-building project. Although conclusions must be tentative, it is suggested that over recent years national cuisines are being established and national dishes are being identified.

As illustrated below, a number of actors of varying importance are involved in this building work: states and their ruling élites, various government bodies belonging to the old colonial powers, publishers and writers on 'ethnic' cuisines and travel guides based in the United States and Europe, Afro-American writers, African Studies academics, expatriates and settlers, returning members of diasporas, and perhaps even designers of web-pages advising African embassies in the

United States. Nationalist ideology is far more omnipresent amongst all the significant actors than is usually recognised. As might be expected, the African consumer may also play a crucial role in deciding what items to include in the national culinary corpus.

In considering what to include on national web-sites, governments have to abstract what they believe to be the essential components of their national identities and cultures. These web-sites are therefore good places to start when looking for what the ruling élites consider to be the important facets of national culture and how important cuisine is to that culture. Any nation-building project in a complex multi-ethnic state in Africa will be difficult and will resemble the process of assembling a collage made of different materials from diverse sources. A national cuisine is a useful part of building a national culture, a 'prop' in the process, as Benedict Anderson describes it, of imagining the nation (1991: 5–7). As a crucial step in the establishment of national cuisines 'cookery books' or 'cookbooks' (US usage) are being published both in Africa and the West as 'authentic' recipes are assembled, collated and adapted. Appadurai claims that '[c]ookbooks...belong to the humble literature of complex civilizations...They reflect the boundaries of edibility...and the structure of domestic ideologies' (1988: 3). Nationalism is one of these domestic ideologies, being internalized as the dominant ideology of the international system of states.

These cookery books come in a great variety of guises, and it is important to ask who is expected to read the book and who is to do the cooking. Is a book for 'an American kitchen' or for an African village, or even both? Clearly those books aimed at the 'American kitchen' are not directly helping to construct a nation in Africa, but they are perhaps reinforcing the globally held view that every nation must have its own cuisine. Recipes and cookery books are also produced with a specific readership or readerships in mind (Barthes 1973: 73–8).[2] In this article, I will focus on cookery books. However, it is worth noting that most Africans have not learnt how to cook from written recipes but orally from mothers and grandmothers. African cuisine is largely an oral cuisine. Cookery books assume a literate population, as do recipes published in newspapers. However, radio and television cookery programmes are also important for the illiterate.[3]

I will first look at the notion of 'a national cuisine' before examining African cuisines as viewed and promoted in the West and then as developed or not in Lusophone, Anglophone and Francophone Africa. I will present a more detailed study of the first signs of a national cuisine emerging in Equatorial Guinea, as this illustrates well the range of actors implicated in the promotion of national cuisines. Finally, I will ask how these developments of a national cuisine might be implicated in building a gendered concept of the African nation.

In this discussion, the usual problems related to the very diversity of Africa arise. It is difficult to avoid generalisations that may be inappropriate for large sections of the continent. I do not set out to investigate thoroughly any particular culinary history, although I do look in some detail at the case of Equatorial Guinea. I do not explore the complexities of 'culinary taboos,' nor examine in detail how particular cuisines are actually practised in the field. Perhaps these national cuisines are just conceits of a westernised élite supported by the international system of states, and of little importance when one comes to consider what is actually eaten. But if so, this is not crucial to the argument presented here, as it is the constructed edifice of the national cuisine, whatever it is, that contributes to the nation-building project. The paper's aims are modest: to ask some questions about whether and how national cuisines in Africa have emerged, or are emerging, and about who is nurturing their development.

## ▪ 2.  National Cuisines ▪

In the developed world it is taken for granted that every nation has its own cuisine. Stephen Mennell has even claimed that 'the emergence of recognisably "national" cuisines coincided with the formation of nation-states in the fifteenth century,' while Reay Tannahill argues that 'culturally defined food choices and patterns of eating came to be seen as "characteristic" of a people and country' (Palmer 1998: 187). Philippe Couderc has recently written of 'the dishes that have made France' (1995), and it is clear that cuisine is a significant factor in the maintenance of a French national identity. Each nation has its own cuisine, although the globalisation of culinary culture has added complexity to the relationship between food and nation (Cook and Crang 1996: 131–54). Thus the roast beef of old England is being replaced by chicken tikka masala.

Palmer (1998) also shows how foods may contribute towards the quiet flagging of the nation. Food may function as an example of what Michael Billig has called 'banal nationalism': everyday, unnoticed nationalism. Billig uses the term 'banal nationalism' to explain how 'the established nations of the West are reproduced ... nationalism, far from being an intermittent mood in established nations is an endemic condition' (Billig 1995: 6–8). In all sorts of minor ways, people are 'reminded of their national place in the world of nations' (ibid. 8). Billig's analysis is concerned with the 'established nations' such as Britain and the Unites States, and perhaps he underplays the extent of overt nationalism in Britain. However, this 'banal' flagging of the nation also appears in the recently established nations. How does banal nationalism become involved in national cuisines? The development of a national cuisine will involve the summoning of a variety of dishes into the ambit of the discourse of the nation, and the very mention then of some national dish will quietly flag the nation. Thus, for example, the serving of *Doro Wat*, a dish of stewed chicken garnished with hard-boiled eggs, one of the national dishes of Ethiopia, will gently remind the Ethiopian diner of the nation – assuming, of course, that he or she is aware of this particular discourse of nationhood.

Any national cuisine will have complex and multiple origins. Jeffrey M. Pilcher, discussing the emergence of Mexican national cuisine, has shown how a complex culinary history has contributed to a range of Mexican national identities where the 'most common culinary metaphor for the Mexican nation was *mole poblano*' (turkey in deep-brown sauce) and how various 'struggles of class, gender, ethnicity, and region [have] helped forge this national [culinary] culture' (1996: 193). Arjun Appadurai has also argued that contemporary Indian national cuisine fostered by the production of recipe books by middle-class Indian women has blurred both ethnic and caste boundaries (1988: 3–24). It is clear that similar complex culinary histories could be mapped in Africa.

## ■ 3.   African Cuisines and What Africans Eat ■

Culinary history is complex and evolving, and it is likely that any contemporary African cuisine will have been built on pre-colonial, colonial and these more recent globalising influences. Hundreds of different plants and many animals were and are gathered by Bantu groups for consumption in the Equatorial rain forests (Vansina 1990: 89), and many of these will eventually contribute to a national cuisine. Many food items in Africa have origins in Asia and in the Americas, with some of those from the East appearing long before the colonial encounter – the banana and plantain, of South East Asian or Indian origins, are thought to have appeared and spread through Africa in the first millennium AD (ibid.: 89). The Portuguese brought a great variety of food items both from the New World and Asia after their appearance on the coasts of Africa in the 15th century, including the groundnut from Brazil, now so common a feature in West African cooking. Cornmeal, again a basic part of African cuisine, was a New World product. Any culinary history of Africa will necessarily reflect these complex origins, although the colonial imprint would be expected to be important even if the only residual influence were to be the boundary of the colonial state within which the traditional ethnic dishes are collated.

The colonial legacy has clearly been a major contributor to contemporary African cuisines. For instance, rice is an essential part of Senegalese cuisine, and Senegal is now a major importer of rice from Indochina. Why? From about 1870, the French began growing ground nuts, so that by the 1930s over half of the agricultural land in Senegal was allocated to this crop. Meanwhile, in Indochina the French were producing rice, so that importing rice to Africa made sense. As a result, the government of independent Senegal is burdened with an enormous rice import bill and wants to boost the consumption of local grains such as millet and sorghum. However, rice is easy to cook, while the local grains need more complex preparation (Seye et al. 1994: 93–4). The colonial culinary inheritance has been crucial here.

The colonial legacy has also resulted in Africans being enthusiastic consumers of bread. Indeed, Okello Oculi writes of 'the wheat invasion and promotion of African stomachs into colonised silos for bread made from American wheat' (Oculi 2000: 60). However, to import wheat to central Africa is very expensive. Acting on the advice of the 'International Centre for Potatoes' based in Peru, bread made with one third sweet potato and wheat has been produced in Burundi. As Burundi is one of the biggest producers of sweet potato in Africa, this presents a considerable savings in import bills. In Casamance (Senegal), some maize tortillas based on Mexican experience have been introduced with considerable success (Barrot and Hakizimana 1994: 114; Lepaideur et al. 1994: 118).

Since the independence of the African states, the West has remained a dominant influence. When the EU had a major surplus of milk, cheap milk powder was sent to Africa. This resulted in the setting up of a number of factories where this powder was turned back into milk, with disastrous consequences for indigenous milk producers in the Sahel. This is put more colourfully by Oculi when he points out that 'German companies would, by the 1980s, dry up the milk in udders in Nigerian nomadic cattle by flooding Nigerian urban throats with chemical German milk' (Oculi 2000: 55). Vast quantities of the poorer cuts of beef were also sent by the EU, this time resulting in the collapse of beef exports from the Sahel countries to places like Côte d' Ivoire. The rapid growth of African towns and cities has also profoundly changed the eating habits of many Africans, and it is here that imports such as rice and EU surpluses will be concentrated. Like ideas, food travels very quickly. Thus foods and recipes are able to move rapidly from one African state to another: troubles in Gabon in the early 1990s resulted in a move away from rice to the importation from Cameroon of one its 'national dishes,' *foufou*, made from manioc flour (Ndoutoum and Zongo 1994: 36–9). More recently and on a smaller scale, *alloco*, fried plantain cubes, that were first sold in Côte d' Ivoire in the allocodrome in Abidjan have now spread to many parts of Francophone Africa (ibid.: 35–7).

Many attempts by Western governments and NGOs to introduce more nutritious combinations of cereals and new food items have ended in failure, often in farce, and have often greatly distorted existing indigenous food production due to low cost of the subsidised surpluses or rejection by African societies. However, some interesting examples of Latin and Central American experience in food provision in the tropics have transferred well to Africa, such as the sweet potato bread discussed above. Cow's milk is a difficult product to preserve in the tropics, and in addition, local cattle in the Sahel region have poor yields and are scattered over vast areas. As mentioned above, reconstituted powdered surplus milk from the EU has been the major source of milk in many African cities. However, Brazil has had a very successful programme of producing and supplying soya milk and has successfully reduced malnutrition in some children. In Nigeria, an Indian entrepreneur has introduced soya milk sold in sachets into Lagos with success, and now other factories produce soya milk in Burundi and Côte d' Ivoire (Kiabou et al. 1994: 68–70).

If a national cuisine is just a symbol of national identity, like a national anthem or flag, then all it requires is collating and labelling as such. Who might label it for a start? Clearly when 'Hippocrene International Cookbooks' publish *A Taste of Eritrea: Recipes from one of Africa's Most Interesting Little Countries*, then an Eritrean cuisine has been defined, labelled and collated, at least for North American purchasers of cookery books and for those carrying out internet searches on African cuisine (Warren 2000). However, it is not just Western cooks who recognise an Eritrean cuisine. The Government of Eritrea's official web-pages, currently under construction, contain a small section headed 'Eritrean Cuisine' (Eritrea: official web-site: 3–4). As in most African countries, those foods eaten by the urban rich, including items such as spaghetti and rice, differ to those eaten in rural areas where cereals such as taff, maize, sorghum and millet predominate.[4] Eritrea is an excellent choice for the assembling of a national cuisine, as 'Eritrea's cuisine includes fruits and vegetables brought by the Italians, chilli peppers from the Turks, European-style beer from the British, a traditional bean stew from the Egyptians, and many staples from Ethiopian cuisine,' all of which seems rich material from which to build a national cuisine (ws: Foodbooks: 3).[5]

This is excellent material for packaging an Eritrean cuisine into a Western cookery book and for allowing the Eritrean national entrepreneurs to add another section to their presentations of Eritrean culture. Another factor may be at work here, although it may be complicated in this instance because of the recent secession of Eritrea from Ethiopia. Many members of African diasporas living in the big cities of the West will frequent or at least know of restaurants serving dishes from their national cuisine. Here, that national cuisine is neatly confined and summarised within a printed menu. Ethiopian and some Eritrean restaurants can be found in many cities. For example, in Harlem in New York, 'a taste of Ethiopia' can be found at the confusingly named Asmara Restaurant, and a visit might also be made to the Massawa Ethiopian and Eritrean Restaurant. Other restaurants specialise in Senegalese dishes, in food from Ghana, Nigeria, Ivory Coast, Guinea and Sierra-Leone (ws: Dining in Harlem). A comprehensive list of 65 pages of African Restaurants is available on line (ws: African Restaurants). Any member of an African diaspora returning home to one of these countries having spent some time in Harlem, or in London or Paris, will be very much aware that African countries are supposed to have their own cuisine and may have had their own cuisine redefined by these restaurants in foreign lands. A visitor to Berne in Switzerland, for example, would be able to visit the Ekabo restaurant and on certain nights have a Nigerian or a Kenyan or a Congolese buffet (ws: Ekabo). With some quarter of a million African professionals living out of Africa (Saul and Leys 1999: 26), a fair proportion of the intelligentsia, the scope for such influence is great. In addition, in most African capitals and big towns it is possible to eat at a range of restaurants presenting a range of national cuisines: Chinese, Vietnamese, Italian, and Indian restaurants stand alongside English and Irish pubs. All this will reinforce the notion that all nations have national cuisines.


## ■ 4.   African Cookery Books for the Western Kitchen ■

In the US, Europe and elsewhere, there is clearly a considerable and growing interest in African cooking, and a great number of cookery books can be found with a range of recipes taken and adapted from all over Africa. For example, in the UK a popular Channel Four television programme spawned a book entitled *A Taste of Africa* (Hafner 1993).[6] This book is clearly aimed at the Western cook in the Western kitchen. Here a Ghanaian, Dorinda Hafner, presents recipes which include many from parts of the Americas: Brazil, Jamaica, Cuba, New Orleans, Trinidad and Tobago and Martinique and Guadeloupe, as well as from 10 African countries. This inclusion of the New World mimics a long-standing interest in 'African cooking' by African-Americans. For instance, the Food Heritage Press web-site lists 'African-American Cookbooks to Feed the Soul,' and alongside many titles such as *Mama Dip's Kitchen* and *The African-American Heritage Cookbook* are books of purely African Continental cooking such as *The African Cookbook: Menus and Recipes from Eleven African Countries and the Island of Zanzibar* and *Tastes of North Africa* (Council 1999; Quick Tillery 1996; Sandler 1997). Harva Hachten's *Best of Regional African Cooking*, originally published in 1970, was one of the first African cookbooks designed for 'the American kitchen' and, along with a few other books such as Tebereh Inquai's *A Taste of Africa* (1998), does not include New World recipes. Other books aimed at the Western kitchen include recipes gathered from certain African regions such as West Africa (Jackson 1999). Books on African cuisine for the Western kitchen have also been published in Australia (Hultman 1986).

In France, in recent years, similar collections of African recipes have been published (Villers and Delaroziere 1995; Chalendar 1993; Ben Yahmed 1999). Again, some of these include African-American recipes and, for example, recipes from Brazil and Martinique are presented in the special edition of *Revue Noire* (1996/7) on African cuisine. The French are less squeamish than their Anglo-Saxon counterparts and include recipes for animals such as monkeys, although it is not made clear, for example, where dried monkey or indeed a '*bon Marcassin*' can be obtained in France by one wishing to present a dish of *Singe au Kôkô* (Villers and Delarozieres 1995: 176). In Spain, a number of cookery books on African cuisine have also appeared both in Spanish or Castellano (Olá Puye et al. 1998; *Departamento de la Mujer* 1997) and in Catalan (Agboton 1989).

Thus we have a range of cookery books published in the West, mainly aimed at the cook in a Western kitchen. They either look at Africa as a whole, or at regions such as West or East Africa, although recipes are usually allocated to a specific country such as 'Zambian groundnut soup' (Hatchen 1997: 212–13) or placed in country-specific sections such as 'Madagascar Cuisine' (Ngozi 1998: 184–90). Unusually, Elizabeth A. Jackson in *South of the Sahara* divides her recipes into sections by ethnic groups such as the Dogon of Mali or the Mossi (1999: 114, 164).

Diane M. Spivey (1999) has recently produced a curious cookbook/culinary history looking at 'the global migration of African cuisine.' This is a very detailed work which attempts to establish the influence of African cooking on, for example, Indian (Tamil/Dravidian), Kampuchean, Mexican (Olmec), or even French cooking. However, the absence of footnotes (although there is an enormous bibliography) means claims such as America's having been discovered by Africans long before Columbus, or peanuts having originated outside the Americas, fail to convince. William Beinart presents a more balanced view when he points out that '...Africa was perhaps not blessed with the most promising domesticable food plants or animals... [and] ...notable in the [African] growing crop repertoire were American domesticates such as maize, cassava or manioc, tomatoes, many beans, chili, potato, tobacco, cocoa, prickly pear, agave and avocado' (Beinart 2000: 286).

Country-specific books such as the Eritrean example mentioned above are also published in the West, although most of these books cover North African or South African cooking. A Tanzanian cookery book written by workers on an AIDS prevention programme has been published in the United States (Greene and Hunter: 1995). This contains some 238 recipes which were collected from 'the country's finest hotels and restaurants' and 'has become very popular in Tanzania.'[7] A Peace Corps volunteer who had worked in Gabon has also organised or written *The Congo Cookbook*, available on the internet (ws: Congo Cookbook). A short book on Ghanaian cookery has also recently been published in the UK, and at least one other in the United States (Fuller 1998; Otoo 1997). Laura Edet has assembled some five hundred recipes for her *Classic Nigerian Cookbook* published in the UK (Edet 1996). We are told in the first lines of the introduction that 'through centuries of conquering armies and internecine conflicts, Nigeria has retained a distinct and sophisticated identity with her own culture, language, folklore and above all, cuisine.' However the author does acknowledge that the assembled recipes come from many of the ethnic groups of Nigeria, thus recognising the diverse origins of Nigerian cooking (ibid.: 8–9). These books are generally aimed at the Western cook, but perhaps also at African nationals living in the West.

## ■ 5.   African National Cuisines ■

What, then, is the position in Africa itself? Is there evidence, for example, of a national cuisine developing in Namibia, one of Africa's other recent independent states? Does a characteristic Namibian cuisine exist in the country, and has it been recognised or even labelled as such? The only Namibian cookery book identified so far is *Das Südwester Kochbuch*, a collection of recipes in German. Walter Hendricks, a chef/lecturer at the Polytechnic of Namibia has confirmed that unfortunately there is no other book published on Namibian cuisine and that he personally uses a web-site based at the University of Pennsylvania.[8] Here 'the academy' itself is implicated in the collation of a national cuisine. There is a considerable German influence in the cuisine of Namibia, and travellers are told that 'Schwartzwald-Torte with whipped cream . . . runs deep throughout this nation's culinary highways and byways' (Camerapix 1994: 302). In addition, all local beers adhere to the German purity laws laid down in 1516 by Duke William IV of Bavaria, and samples of 'Windhoek Lager' are sent several times a year to the Beer institute in Munich to ensure that standards are met (ibid.: 303). The ingredients exist for a unique African cuisine, but apparently it has yet to be claimed as such by the vigorous builders of the nation who are promoting other elements of Namibian national identity such as 'reconciliation' and an annual Celebration of Heroes Day (Fosse 1997: 427–50).

This is not the case for Cape Verde. Books which discuss Cape Verdean culture include, for example, music and literature, but also cuisine. Recipes are published in newspapers and some Crioulo cookbooks are available (Lobban 1995; Romano 1970). The Cape Verdean embassy in the United States hosts the Cape Verdean national web-site, and under the heading 'Cultural Aspects: Cuisine' we are told that 'Cape Verdians express their uniqueness in their cuisine. Immediately we think of the *catchupa*, cooked for lunch and stewed next day.' Catchupa, a mash of beans and maize, often with sausage and meat, is the national dish, often eaten at breakfast. Thus any mention of catchupa will quietly 'flag' the nation. Other actors involved in the promotion of a Cape Verdean cuisine include the old colonial power, Portugal, which produces a web-site on Lusophone gastronomy – Os Sabores Lusófonos. This gives example of recipes from Portugal's former African colonies, as well as East Timor and Brazil (ws: Sabores Lusófonos). Maria Odette Cortes Valente (1989), in perhaps a final neocolonialist flourish, claims that all Lusophone cooking in Africa, Brazil, Goa, Macao and East Timor was the discovery of the Portuguese. Perhaps because of this continued concern by the old imperial power, Lusophone African countries clearly consider a national cuisine as an important part of the national culture. The Angolan government web-site, under the heading, 'Art and Culture', includes 'the cuisine of Angola'. Here a number of recipes are presented, including what is probably the national dish of Angola, chicken muamba (ws: Angola). Onions, tomatoes and garlic have perhaps infiltrated into Angolan and other Lusophone cooking from the old metropole and the Mediterranean. For instance, river fish with onions and tomato (*peixinios de cebola e tomate*) is a typical dish of São Tomé and Principe, with the palm oil adding the African flavour (Cortes Valente 1989: 53).

The cuisine of Anglophone Africa certainly reflects the colonial heritage of British cooking. Alongside Nigerian recipes for *efo* (vegetable soup) and *obe ata* (pepper soup) appear Scotch eggs and sausage rolls (ws: Motherland Nigeria/ Recipes: 1–21). *Nyama Na Irio*, in Kenya, according to the 'African Studies' cookbook, is prepared by blending instant mashed potato, tinned peas and kernel corn, and forming this into a smooth green volcano shape on a plate and filling the crater with steak served in a sauce of tinned onion soup (ws: Kenya: African Studies: 4–5). The *Tanzania Cookbook* begins with how to make tea and includes such items as bread and jam fritters. Here, however, is a comprehensive cookery book that is addressed to an African audience, including new cooks, 'mothers and health workers' (Pendaeli-Sarakikya 1978: 4, 145). It also provides advice on substitute ingredients that has become necessary, so we are told, because of the rise in the cost of living in Tanzania (ibid.: vii).

European settlers have also been involved in assembling cookery books. *A Zimbabwean Cookery Book* was clearly once *A Rhodesian Cookery Book*, as there is not quite enough room for the insertion of 'Zimbabwean' for 'Rhodesian' in the text of a recent edition, which otherwise remains the same as in 1967. 'Haddock fish Pie' and 'Welsh Rarebit' and most of the other recipes are 1950s British ones – with a few South African additions – despite a claim to a 'distinct Zimbabwean flavour.' However, the recipes are to be shared with 'the women of the country' and the ingredients, so it is claimed, 'can be found in any home or purchased in any grocery shop in Zimbabwe' (Hayward 1967: Foreword). *The Kenya Cookery Book and Household Guide*, written by members of St. Andrew's Church Women's Guild, Nairobi, claims to be the oldest Kenyan cookery book and was first published in 1928: it is still recommended 'for every Kenyan kitchen' and contains innumerable recipes for biscuits, cakes and puddings (1994: back cover). The contributors to *Karibu, Welcome to the Cooking of Kenya* are a more multicultural group: Kenyans,

Indians, Pakistanis, Kenyan-born Europeans, and various expatriates. The cooks who are expected to use these recipes are probably the same expatriates and the Kenyan élite; the eclectic mixture of recipes includes 'Christmas pudding' and 'minted peas' as well as 'a blend of Asian and African food' and Japanese dishes (Gardner 1992).

In Anglophone Africa a considerable number of cookery books have been published: in Malawi, Liberia, Ghana, Nigeria, and especially in Kenya.[9] Once recipes from a particular nation have been packaged together under the heading 'Nigerian' or 'Kenyan,' then a start has been made to defining a national cuisine, at least among the literate élites who may purchase them.

What about Francophone Africa? Apart from North African cuisines, which are well represented in both cookery books and restaurants in France and North America, there is less evidence of attempts to build national cuisines in sub-Saharan Francophone Africa than in, say, Lusophone Africa. It is possible that the very strength of the idea of French cuisine and the assimilation of African élites into French culture has stifled any desires to build independent national cuisines. The publication of books on African cuisine in France is very recent when compared with the United States, although one book on African gastronomy did appear in 1930 (Isnard). Francophone African national web-sites have other concerns: in Mauritania, for example, poetry, music, 'intellectual knowledge' and architecture are listed under cultural heritage, with no mention of cuisine (ws: Mauritania: 3).

*Le Grand Livre de la Cuisine Camerounaise* is a comprehensive survey of ingredients and recipes used by the different ethnic groups and the regions of Cameroon. The book has a certain ethnographic, scientific approach which, for example, gives botanical details for the plants and animals used in Latin, French and local languages. The recipes are certainly not for the 'American kitchen' and include very basic methods of cooking such items as plantains or manioc but also, for example, a number of recipes for dog – and we are told cat is cooked in the same way (Grimaldi and Bikia 1985: 124–9). It is not clear who might actually use the recipes in this book. Its publication was supported by French aid in the same way as the Spanish aid agency was involved in a similar book produced for Equatorial Guinea, discussed below.

Senegal has a number of national dishes including *le thiéboudiene* (rice and fish) and *Poulet Yassa*, from the Casamance region. Côte d'Ivoire has *poulet kédjénou* cooked in special large earthenware pots known as *canari* (Villers and Delaroziere 1995: 159). Smoked beef feet – *pattes de boeuf fumeés* – has become a characteristic product from Ouagadougou in Burkina Faso and is exported to many of the neighbouring countries. It is used for making a beef *consommé* for breakfast, eaten with bread, which is supposed to 'fix you up' if you have drunk too much beer (Ndoutoum and Zongo 1994: 38). 'Air Madagascar' proclaims that Koba, a mixture of rice, banana and peanut, is the national snack of Madagascar and suggests you 'prepare a mouthwatering Madagascar meal [Akoyo sy voanio] in the convenience of your own home' (ws: Air Madagascar). Despite the emergence of these national dishes, there seems little evidence of summoning of national cuisines to the nation-building project by the state over most of Francophone Africa.

The main driving force for the creation of national cuisines in Africa appears to come from the West, and in particular from African-Americans. There is considerable interest in African cuisine often treating the continent as a whole or in regions, a Pan-African cuisine. In parts of Lusophone and Anglophone Africa, as well as generally North Africa from Ethiopia to Morocco, and perhaps in Senegal, a national cuisine is well recognised as being part of the national culture. As certain dishes become 'national dishes,' the very mention of these will reinforce any sense of national identity.

In the next section the development of an Equatoguinean cuisine will be discussed illustrating, in particular, the emergence of a new 'national cuisine' and also the range of actors who are complicit in the process of construction of such national cuisines.

## ■ 6.   Equatorial Guinea: A Newly Emerging National Cuisine? ■

Equatorial Guinea is the only Spanish-speaking state in sub-Saharan Africa. Since independence from Spain in 1968, this multi-ethnic state has been ruled by two 'Nguemist' dictators. Francisco Macías Nguema, one of the few tyrants of post-colonial Africa, was installed after free elections in 1968 and was then overthrown and executed in 1979 by his nephew, Teodoro Obiang Nguema, who remains in power today.

The importance of food to a person's identity is well illustrated by one vital component of Spanish colonial rule: the system of emancipation. A 'native' or *indigéna* had to be a Christian to become an *emancipado* and would then be excluded, for example, from having to do compulsory work in the cacao plantations. It was easy for the Patronato, the Church-dominated body which controlled 'native affairs,' to exclude anybody who might cause trouble. Once an individual obtained a *carta de emancipación* he (always he) was allowed to set himself up like a European. He became an honorary Spaniard, pure enough to partake of the bread and wine of the Catholic faith. The *emancipado* was also allowed to buy and consume olive oil and bread and take alcoholic drinks in the same bars as the whites (Ndongo Bidyogo 1977: 57). Food and drink were an important part of the coloniser's identity and when the colonised were admitted as honorary Europeans they were deemed pure enough to partake of the same imported food.

So, has an effort been made to establish an Equatoguinean cuisine in the years following independence? Certainly Mari Cruz Nchama Evuna, an administrative attaché at the Equatoguinean Embassy in Washington, is adamant that 'we have our own cuisine, not a Spanish one.'[10] Nchama Evuna is the daughter of Alejandro Evuna Owono Asangano, who is part of the ruling clique in Equatorial Guinea, the Clan de Mongomo (Liniger-Goumaz 1993: 217). In the official Republic of Equatorial Guinea web-site, based at the embassy in Washington, one of the most detailed sections is entitled 'National Cuisine,' providing details of

'Equatorial Guinea's Popular Dishes' (ws: Equatorial Guinea). We are told that 'Equatorial Guinea's national cuisine is simple and tasty' and that, for example, 'a dish that is enjoyed by all ethnic groups is "pepe soup".' Lists of the favourite meals of the different ethnic groups are also included: *djomba*, a Combe dish; *mendjaa*, a Fang dish; and *bitalif* soup, a Bubi one. Here the national élite are assembling the favourite foods of different ethnic groups and repackaging them as part of the Equatoguinean national cuisine.

What about educational material or cookery books in the independent state? The *Enciclopedia Guinea Ecuatorial*, is a book prepared for use in schools in Equatorial Guinea by Catholic religious orders in Spain but with major contributions from Equatoguinean authors. Here, lists are provided showing the country's main cooking ingredients, including, for example, plantains, sweet potato, bread fruit, yam, *malanga*, ground-nuts and snails (Sánchez Buján and Lopoha Obiamo 1993: 358). There are two different plants called *malanga*, the *malanga cubana* and the *malanga bubi*: for both plants, the tubers and the leaves can be eaten and they form an important part of Equatoguinean cuisine (Colectivo Helio 1997: 35). The presence of the *malanga cubana* on the island of Bioko shows the Cuban influence which can be traced clearly back to the settlement of freed slaves and political prisoners from Cuba in the mid 19th century. Inclusion of this 'regional' ingredient from the island of Bioko in the national cuisine of Equatorial Guinea appropriates it for the nation. A number of recipes are also included in the *Enciclopedia* – one, for example, for *sopa de pescado con cacahuete*, a ground nut soup with fish, onions and tomato, typical of West Africa (Sánchez Buján and Lopoha Obiamo 1993: 366).

Many more detailed recipes are given in a publication supported by the Spanish Ministry of Health and Consumer Affairs called *La alimentación y la cocina en Guinea Ecuatorial* (The provision of food and cooking in Equatorial Guinea). Here the emphasis is on traditional cooking and methods of hunting and fishing, with antelopes, anteaters, monkeys and various fish and birds included (Sánchez Zarzosa and Domingo Bodelón 1991). This book was based on a short course held in a hospital at Evinayong, in the 'Continental' part of the country[11] in 1985, but included recipes from other parts of the state. In the introduction, the authors affirm that '[e]very village, every region, every country has its own characteristic way of procuring food and drink and of feeding itself, and which forms a defining part of its culture' (ibid.: 13).[12] The book is clearly aimed at a readership in the villages and towns of the Equatorial Guinea as it explains, for example, how to cook food wrapped in leaves over an open fire or in a cooking pot filled with sand. Perhaps curious recipes such as that for *Lomandoha*, containing young *malanga* leaves, fish and homemade chocolate will one day become a national dish (ibid.: 33–4). By collecting the traditional recipes in a book entitled *La alimentación y la cocina en Guinea Ecuatorial*, the authors have appropriated them for the nation, and anyone using the book will be reminded of their membership in that nation. Juan Chema Mijero, the director of the national library of Equatorial Guinea from 1962 to 1982 has written a poem called *El Caracol* ('The Snail') containing some of these African and Equatoguinean ingredients:

| Caracolito, caracolito | Little snail, little snail |
| enséame dónde está tu madre | tell me where your mother is |
| y dónde está tu padre | and your father too |
| si no quieres | if you do not want |
| que te coma | to be eaten |
| con hojas de malanga | with leaves of *malanga* |
| y aceite | and oil. |

(Chema Mijera, 1984:65)

Even though visitors to Equatorial Guinea are more likely to eat in a Spanish or Lebanese restaurant, they are also able to obtain the food *de País*, that is, 'of the country.' Various recipes for both Spanish and Equatoguinean regional or ethnic group dishes have recently been published in a magazine published in Malabo (the capital of Equatorial Guinea) called *El Patio*. There is no regular press in Equatorial Guinea, so *El Patio*, published by the Centro Cultural Hispano-Guineano, and directly funded by the Spanish Overseas Aid Agency (AECI), is the most widely read printed matter in the country.[13] With a print run of 2,500, and with each copy being widely circulated, *El Patio* is likely to be read by a large proportion of the literate Equatoguinean population.[14] In a recent edition, alongside a recipe (under the heading *Cocina Espaola*) for *gazpacho andaluz* is one for *mbombi muadjakasi*, fish cooked with lemon and pepper in banana leaves (*El Patio*, Oct. 1999: 63). The reader can use an oven or a fire, and it can be surmised that the cook envisaged here is not just a member of the westernised élite but an ordinary member of the Equatoguinean public.

From this brief review of Equatoguinean cuisine it can be seen that the Spanish government, both the Aid Agency and the Ministry of Health and Consumer Affairs, and Spanish religious orders as well as the Equatoguinean ruling élite have so far been implicated in the building of a national cuisine.

## ◼ 7. Gendered Recipes for Building the Nation? ◼

Nira Yuval Davies points out how 'constructions of nationhood involve specific notions of both "manhood" and "womanhood"' (1997:1). There are a number of ways in which nationalist projects can be gendered. Nation-building based on emphasising a common cultural heritage may be differently gendered, for example, than a process built on ideas of shared citizenship. In addition, the gendered nature of nationhood will vary as societies evolve and change. Some theorists of nationalism, the 'primordialists,' certainly see nations as extensions of kinship relations. Others, like Etienne Balibar, write of the nation being a retrospective 'fictive ethnicity' and argue that there is a need for a principle of exclusion or closure which cannot be provided, for example, by a language community, but which can be by the belief in belonging to a common 'race' (Balibar 1991: 96–9). Clearly women play a central role in the building of such a national community, and 'women, sexuality and family [are significant as] symbols in the reproduction of a

◼ 373 ◼

nation and its boundaries' (Steans 1998: 65). Nations are the natural extensions of family relationships where, as Cynthia Enloe paints it, the men protect the 'womanandchildren' and where the key role for women is to be mothers of patriots, their sons (Yuval-Davis 1997: 15). How might cuisine be implicated in such processes?

Most national symbols such as flags, shields and emblems, as well as national war memorials, are clearly gendered and will often be associated with male security forces, perhaps seen as marching together to the future of the nation. These symbols of national identity adorn national web-sites that often contain national anthems which can be downloaded, as for instance from Gabon's official home page (ws: Gabon). These symbols are perhaps the forward-looking, modernising aspect of the Janus-face of nationalism (Nairn 1997: 67, 71–2; McClintock 1993: 61–80; T. Cusack 2000).

Women in Africa, and elsewhere, on the other hand, are often seen as the guardians of tradition. For example, Dogon Yaro, from Niamey in Niger, who writes in Sahel Dimanche, complains that modern wives are no longer able to cook properly, unlike their mothers or grandmothers. So instead of returning home after work to the 'culinary platitudes' (such as a mush of millet) produced by wife or wives, the men prefer to go to the Gargotières, small street food stalls, run by foreign Yao women from the coast. Traditional culture is being lost and it is the 'Modern African Woman' who is to blame (Barrot 1994: 23–7).

Pilcher has shown how, in the evolution of contemporary Mexican cuisine, females played a crucial role in the assembling of colonial and Pre-Columbian recipe books and suggests that women were perhaps less concerned with the social stigma associated with the Pre-Columbian dishes. Male chefs, in turn, were the main proponents of the French influence on Mexican cuisine (Pilcher 1996: 211–14). So if cuisine is a crucial part of Mexican national identity, that cuisine has at least been partially built by women. In Africa, women are perhaps also more willing than men to assemble recipes from different ethnic groups, as women are less implicated in the power structures inherent in the maintenance of these groups. Perhaps this is the case in the Equatoguinean cookery book discussed above. Indeed, from the brief review of African cuisine above it is clear that it is mostly women, whether in the West or in Africa, who are collecting and collating recipes into a national corpus.

The public appropriation of a national cuisine results in the creation of just another symbol of the nation, especially if certain dishes are proclaimed national ones. However the assembling of a national cuisine blends various regional and ethnic traditions together, summoning some from the past, like the roast beef of old England that has been celebrated as a national dish. Women, then, might be viewed as assistants to the dominant male ruling élites, who are very willing to present the national cuisine alongside the flags and anthems that symbolise the nation they wish to construct. It might therefore be argued that while women are collating recipes and looking to the past, men are appropriating the resulting national cuisine and looking to the future.

How gender enters notions of nationhood can also be derived from the debates concerning the private/public domain. Feminist writers are surely correct in pointing out the intrusion, in the 'liberal' West, of the 'public' into the 'private' space which patriarchal societies might wish to maintain. It is interesting to note that even if the notion of all societies being patriarchal might be challenged, a large part of Africa lies in what has been termed 'the patriarchal belt' which stretches across Northern Africa, through the Middle East to India and parts of China (Yuval-Davis 1997: 7). However, in élite circles at least, it is clear that women's domestic role, confined to the home, is more widespread than this limited geographical area would suggest.

Colonial, settler and post-colonial cookery books are sharply focused on the housewife. For example, in choosing meat 'the housewife herself must visit the butcher's shop and be guided by the butcher as he is the expert' (Members of St. Andrews Church 1994: 69). In *Mary Ominde's Cookery* book, a Kenyan housewife is shown on the front cover cheerfully assembling the next meal with her young son smilingly looking on. The author declares: 'The book attempts to remind the housewife of the importance of a balanced diet when planning the family menu, especially where there are children. This in itself is a contribution to the development of nation building...' (1975: introduction). It is clear for whom the nation is being built here, presumably the grinning son. Elsewhere in the 'African Studies' cookbook we are told 'how a dinner is served in Kenya': 'the hostess opens the door dressed in a bright floor-length skirt and a striking bandanna wound loosely about her head. She stands there, hands outstretched, to bid you welcome... Our hostess returns to the kitchen to pound the groundnuts...' (ws: Kenya, Menus and Recipes). Pendaeli-Sarakikya, in her *Tanzania Cookbook*, seems to be writing for the 'intelligent cook [who] can select recipes and alter them to meet her immediate needs' (1977: vii). Certainly in the illustrations in Equatorial Guinea's first cookery book there is no doubt as to who is sitting at the cooking pot, and in the foreword to *Authentic African Cuisine from Ghana* we are told that 'part of becoming a women in Ghana culture is learning to cook these flavourful foods' (Sánchez Zarzosa and Domingo Bodelón 1991: 14; Otoo 1997: v). Everywhere a similar pattern emerges. During the hour long 'coffee ceremony' held in Eritrea, 'a woman' has to prepare the coffee and we are told 'it is shameful to let the coffee boil over' (ws: Mebrat Tzehaie: 2). If women are confined to the private sphere they will have little role in the public development of the nation, while at the same time that part of the nation-building project which appeals to tradition, which looks to the past, envisages woman in a role confined to that private domain, in the house or hut or in the bounded yard.

However, perhaps the whole idea of a private sphere is not one that should be applied as a general rule in sub-Saharan Africa. Gwendolyn Mikell argues that the domestic-public dichotomy takes some unique forms in sub-Saharan traditional cultures and that 'the domestic–public dichotomy has no "universal" form. Although the association of women with the domestic realm... is common to many societies... there is considerable variation in gender roles' (1997: 6–10). In some traditional African groups women, for example, still have their own method of fishing (Vansina 1990: 91). Mikell also argues that African models emphasise the communal or corporate group as opposed to the individual, so that there may be an overlap between the domestic and the public/political spheres and that women play a wider range of roles in Africa than many places elsewhere (1997: 8). Oyérónké Oyêwùmí also argues that Western gender discourses have been imposed on Yorùbá cultures. In the particular Yorùbá society she examines, the category 'woman' does not exist as a category for organising society. She argues that 'the body was not the basis of social roles, inclusions, or exclusion: it was not the foundation of social thought and identity' (Oyêwùmí 1997: x). However, this study is specific to one section of the Yorùbá, and she accepts that Western gender discourses have now infiltrated even this specific Yorùbá culture.

In many societies, it is only when cooking takes place in the public sphere, say in a restaurant or in the open air – whether at an Australian barbecue or a Provençal *ailloli* that men 'man' the stoves. However, it is nearly always women who serve grilled fish and plantain in the stalls along Garden Street in Limbé in Cameroon, or 'delicious salads' at the Grand Marché in Lomé or in the 'allocodrome' in Abidjan. Indeed, in most of sub-Saharan Africa, women emerge from the private sphere to sell at markets and serve 'street eats,' an essential and indeed vital part of public life.

So what conclusion might one reach about the contribution of an African national cuisine to the gendering of the African nation? Men have generally played a dominant part in every aspect of political and cultural life in Africa, so that a national cuisine collated by women at least gives women a part in the shaping of the national cultural identity, even if their role here fits into the usual pattern of ethno-cultural nationalism, with women associated with tradition and the nation's fictive past. It is not clear whether the more complex gender relationships seen in traditional African societies can impinge upon the nation-building project. Because the nation-building project itself is very much a product of the westernised élites, it is likely that any gendering of the nation will follow Western patterns.

## ■ 8.   Conclusions ■

The aims of this chapter have been modest: to ask some questions about the emergence of national cuisines in Africa, about what is happening and who is involved. It is clear from this brief discussion that the West is deeply implicated in this process. This should come as no surprise, since, after all, the nation-building efforts are taking place within Western constructions resulting from the 19th century 'scramble for Africa'. Spain and Portugal seem to be the most enthusiastic of the former colonial powers in nurturing cuisines in their old colonies. Britain and France have also clearly left their imprint on the emerging African cuisines, but for probably different reasons (indifference and arrogance?) appear to have little interest in what is happening today. African-Americans have, however, generated interest in African-American cooking and hence African cooking and the large African populations in the West have provided a focus for this interest. The process of appropriation of the nation's cuisines by the ruling élites in sub-Sahara Africa has only just begun, and the next few years will provide a clearer view as to what role national cuisines are to play in the project of nation-building and what contribution to the gendering of the nation this might make. Once these national cuisines are established, however, national dishes will unobtrusively flag the nation and thus help maintain that nation without recourse to overt nationalist rhetoric and flag-waving.

## NOTES

1 *'Vous ne savez pas ožest l'impérialisme?...Regardez dans votre assiette!'*
2 Dishes pictured in the magazine *Elle* are smoothly coated, ornamented, accompanied by 'mythical economics' and aimed at the 'small-income' reader. The real problems, such as actually obtaining and paying, for example, for a golden partridge decorated with cherries, are ignored. On the other hand, in *L'Express*, which has middle-class and more affluent readers, the cookery 'is real and not magical.'
3 Television programmes showing, for example, the preparation of groundnut stew were broadcast in Nigeria as early as the 1960s.
4 This is similar to a point made by the Somali author, Nuruddin Farah, who has one of his characters writing, '[Y]ou can sit in Mogadiscio of comforts, eat a mountainful of spaghetti while my peers in the Ogaden starve to death...' (1986: 19).
5 'ws': see web-site references listed below.
6 A recent research project funded by the Department of International Development (DfID) had shown how cookery programmes, unlike much other TV coverage, present 'positive images' of the Developing World. See ws: DfID news; summary document, p. 13.
7 See MSU Tuesday Bulletin (3), 01/30/1996 as on http://www.sas.upenn.edu/African_Studies/Newsletters/tues_13096.html
8 Personal communication, 14 March 2000. A Namibian-published book on seafood has also reportedly been produced for the Lisbon World Exhibition.
9 A number of these have been included in the references below.
10 Telephone conversation with the author, 30 August 1996.
11 Equatorial Guinea consists of two islands, Bioko (former Fernando Poo) and Annobon, along with Rio Muni, a rectangular territory on the continent of Africa.
12 *'Cada pueblo, cada región, cada país, tiene una forma propia y característica de procurarse los alimentos y de alimentarse, lo cuál constituye una parte definitoria de su cultura.'*
13 Spain has concentrated on fostering educational and cultural links with its former colony, while France, trying to extend its influence in the region, has been more concerned with the economy (I. Cusack 1997). Two newspapers, *La Opinión* and *El Tiempo, G.E.*, have very recently been launched in Malabo (*El Patio* April–May 2000, 69: 6).
14 The total population of Equatorial Guinea is probably still less than half a million.

## REFERENCES

Anderson, Benedict. 1991. *Imagined Communites*. Revised Edition. London: Verso.
Agboton, Agnès. 1989. *La Cuina Africana*. Barcelona: Columna.

Appadurai, Arjun. 1988. How to make a national cuisine: cookbooks in contemporary India. *Comparative Studies in Society and History* 30(1): 3–24.

Balibar, Etienne. 1991. The nation form: history and ideology. In *Race, Nation, Class*, ed. by Etienne Balibar and Immanuel Wallerstein, pp. 86–106. London: Verso.

Barrot, Pierre. 1994. Les platitudes culinaires de ma femme.... In *L'Afrique, côté cuisines*, compiled by P. Barrot for SYFIA, pp. 23–27. Paris: Syros.

—— and André Hakizimana. 1994. Du pain à tout prix. In ibid., pp. 111–14. Paris: Syros.

Barthes, Roland. 1973. *Mythologies*. London: Paladin.

Beinart, William. 2000. African history and environmental history. *African Affairs* 99 (395): 269–302.

Ben Yahmed, Danielle. 1999. *Les Merveilles de la Cuisine Africaine*. France: Du Jaguar.

Billig, Michael. 1995. *Banal Nationalism*. London: Sage.

Camerapix (comp/ed). 1994. *Spectrum Guide to Namibia*. Boston: Spectrum.

Chalendar, Pierrette. 1993. *La Cuisine Africaine*. France: SAEP.

Chema Mijero, Juan. 1984. El caracol. In *Antología de la literatura Guineana*, ed. by Donato Ndongo-Bidyogo, pp. 65–6. Madrid: Editora Nacional.

Colectivo Helio. 1997. *La encrucijada de Guinea Ecuatorial*. Madrid: Incipit.

Collective. *Das Südwester Kockbuch*. Windhoek, Namibia.

Cook, Ian and Philip Crang. 1996. The world on a plate: culinary culture, displacement and geographical knowledges. *Journal of Material Culture* 1 (1): 131–54.

Cortes Valente, Maria Odette. 1989. *A Cozinha Descoberta pelos Portugueses*. Portugal: Gradiva.

Couderc, Philippe. 1995. *Les Plats qui ont fait la France*. Paris: Editions Julliard.

Council, Mildred. 1999. *Mama Dip's Kitchen*. North Carolina: University of North Carolina Press.

Cusack, Igor. 1997. *Equatorial Guinea: the inculcation and maintenance of Hispanic culture*. (Occasional Papers Series No. 20). Department of Hispanic, Portuguese and Latin American Studies, University of Bristol.

—— 1999. Hispanic and Bantu inheritance, trauma, dispersal and return: some contributions to a sense of national identity in Equatorial Guinea. *Nations and Nationalism* 5(2): 207–36.

Cusack, Tricia. 2000. Janus and gender: women and the nation's backward look. *Nations and Nationalism* 6 (4): 541–61.

Dede, Alice. 1969. *Ghanaian Favourite Dishes*. Accra: Anowuo Educational Publications.

Departamento de la Mujer. 1997. *Sabor africano*. Bilbao: Afro Vasca, Departamento de la Mujer.

De Witt, Dave, Mary Jane Wilan and Melissa J. Stock. 1998. *Flavors of Africa Cookbook*. Rocklin, California: Prima.

Dike, Phiner, 1993. *Nigerian Cooking*. Shaker Heights, Ohio: Phiner's International Cuisine.

Edet, Laura. 1996. *Classic Nigerian Cook Book*. London: Divine Grace Publishers.

Eldon, Kathy and Eamon Mullan. 1981. *Tastes of Kenya*. Nairobi: Kenway.

Farah, Nuruddin. 1986. *Maps*. London: Pan.

Fosse, Leif John. 1997. Negotiating the nation: ethnicity, nationalism and nation-building in independent Namibia. *Nations and Nationalism* 3 (3): 427–50.

Fuller, B. G. 1998. *Ghanaian Cookery*. London: New Millennium.

Gabon: Ministere de la Culture, des Arts et l'Education Populaire. 1985. *Cuisine Africaine*. Toulouse: Editions Universelles.

Gardner, Ann. 1992. *Karibu, Welcome to the Cooking of Kenya*. Nairobi: Kenway.

Grant, Rosamund. 1995. *Taste of Africa*. London: Lorenz Books.

Greene, Arlin E. and Susan S. Hunter. 1995. *Tropical Appetites: Fine Cooking and Dining in Tanzania*. New York: Gecko Publishing.

Grimaldi, Jean and Alexandrine Bikia. 1985. *Le Grand Livre de la Cuisine Camerounaise*. Yaoundé (Cameroon): Sopecam.

Hachten, Harva. 1997. *Best of Regional African Cooking*. New York: Hippocrene Books.

Hafner, Dorinda. 1993. *A Taste of Africa*. London: Headline.

Hayward, Yvonne (ed). 1967. Reprinted 1973, 1978, 1980, 1987, 1990, 1993. *A Zimbabwean Cookery Book*. Gweru (Zimbabwe): Mambo Press.

Hoffman, Selena. 1989. *African Recipes: Liberian Cooking*. Petersburg, Virginia: Ebonics Publications Internationale.

Hultman, Tami (ed). 1986. *The Africa News Cookbook: African Cooking for Western Kitchens*. Australia: Penguin Australia.

Hyder, Samira. 1976. *Recipes from the Kenya Coast*. Nairobi: Longhorn Kenya Ltd.

Inquai, Tebereh. 1998. *A Taste of Africa: An African Cookbook*. Trenton, New Jersey and Asmara, Eritrea: Africa World Press.

Isnard, Leon. 1930. *La Gastronomie Africaine*. Paris: Albin Michel.

Jackson, Elizabeth A. 1999. *South of the Sahara: Traditional Cooking from the Lands of West Africa*. Hollis, New Hampshire: Fantail.

Karimbux, Adil. 1998. *A Taste of Kenyan Cooking*. Nairobi: Kenway.

Kiabou, Bamba et al. 1994. Le lait: poudre blanche et dépendance. In *L'Afrique, côté cuisines*, compiled by P. Barrot for SYFIA, pp. 65–70. Paris: Syros.

Kimenye, Barbara. 1997. *The Modern African Vegetable Cookbook*. Nairobi: Kenway.

Lee, H. Amala (ed). 1995. *African Cuisine: Liberian Cooking*. Liberia: African Consultant Service.

Leplaideur, Marie-Agnès, Madieng Seck and Souleymane Ouattara. 1994. Le Sahel contre-attaque. In *L'Afrique, côté cuisines*, compiled by P. Barrot for SYFIA, pp. 115–19. Paris: Syros.

Lobban, Richard A. Jr. 1995. *Cape Verde: Crioulo Colony to Independent Nation*. Boulder, Colorado: Westview Press.

*Malawi's traditional and modern cooking*. N.p. (Malawi): 1992.

Max Liniger-Goumaz. 1993. *Who's Who de la dictature de Guinée Equatoriale*. Geneva: Les Editions du Temps.

McClintock, Anne. 1993. Family feud: gender, nationalism and the family. *Feminist Review* 44: 61–80.

Members of St. Andrew's Church Women's Guild, Nairobi. 1994 (first edition 1928). *The Kenya Cookery Book and Household Guide*. Nairobi: Kenway.

Mennel, Stephen. 1985. *All Manners of Food*. Oxford: Blackwell.

Mikell, Gwendolyn (ed). 1997. *African Feminism: the Politics of Survival in Sub-Saharan Africa*. Philadelphia: University of Pennsylvania Press.

Nairn, Tom. 1997. *Faces of Nationalism: Janus Revisited*. London: Verso.

Ndongo Bidyogo, Donato. 1977. *Historia y Tragedia de Guinea Ecuatorial*. Madrid: Editorial Cambio 16.

Ndoutoum, Jean-de Dieu and Ibrahim Zongo. 1994. L'Afrique aux Africains. In *L'Afrique, côté cuisines*, compiled by P. Barrot for SYFIA, pp. 35–9. Paris: Syros.

Ngozi Kachikwu, Princess. 1998. *The Dishes of Africa*. Atlanta: Cross-Cultures.

Nyaho, E., E. Amarteifio and J. Asare. 1970. *Ghana Recipe Book*. Accra: Ghana Publishing Corp.

Oculi, Okello. 2000. *Discourses on African Affairs*. Trenton, New Jersey and Asmara, Eritrea: African World Press.

Olá Puye, Mercedes et al. 1998. *Cocina Africana*. Barcelona: Icaria.

Ominde, Mary. 1975. *African Cookery Book*. Nairobi, Kampala, Dar es Salaam: Kenway.

Otoo, David and Tamminay. 1997. *Authentic African Cuisine from Ghana*. Colorado Springs: Sankofa.

Oyêwùmí, Oyérónké. 1997. *The Invention of Women: Making an African Sense of Western Gender Discourses*. Minneapolis: University of Minnesota Press.

Palmer, Catherine. 1998. From theory to practice: experiencing the nation in everyday life. *Journal of Material Culture* 3 (2): 175–99.

Pendaeli-Sarakikya, Eva. 1978. *Tanzania Cookbook*. Dar es Salaam: Tanzania Publishing House.

Pilcher, Jeffrey M. 1996. Tamales or timbales: cuisine and the formation of Mexican national identity, 1821–1911. *The Americas* 53(2): 193–216.

Quick Tillery, Carolyn. 1996. *The African-American Heritage Cookbook: Traditional Recipes and Fond Remembrances from Alabama's Renowned Tuskegee Institute*. Secaucus, New Jersey: Birch Lane Press.

*Revue Noir*. 1996/1997. Special edition on African Cuisine, No. 23.

Romano, Luis. 1970. *Cabo-Verde-Renascenço de uma Civilização no Atlântico Meádio*. Lisbon: Edição da Revista *Ocidente*.

Sánchez Buján, Paulina and Margarita Lopoha Obiamo. 1993. Cocina. In *Enciclopedia Guinea Ecuatorial*, ed. by Manuel Fernández Magaz. Madrid: FERE.

Sánchez Zarzosa, Ignacio and Antonio Domingo Bodelón. 1991. *La alimentación y la cocina en Guinea Ecuatorial*. Madrid: Ministerio de Sanidad y Consumo.

Sandler, Bea. 1997 (first edition 1970). *The African Cookbook*. New York: Carol Publishing Group.

Saul, John S. and Colin Leys. 1999. Sub-Saharan Africa in global capitalism. *Monthly Review* (July–August): 13–20.

Seye, Cherif, et al. 1994. Riz contre mil. In *L'Afrique, côté cuisines*, compiled by P. Barrot for SYFIA, pp. 35–9. Paris: Syros.

Spivey, Diane M. 1999. *The Peppers, Cracklings, and Knots of Wool Cookbook: the Global Migration of African Cuisine*. New York: State University of New York Press.

Steans, Jill. 1998. *Gender and International Relations*. Cambridge: Polity Press.

Tannahill, Reay. 1975. *Food in History*. St. Albans: Paladin.

Van der Post, Laurens. 1970. *African Cooking*. New York: Time-Life Books

Vansina, Jan. 1990. *Paths in the Rainforests*. Madison: University of Wisconsin.

Villers, Anne and Marie-Françoise Delaroziere. 1995. *Cuisines d'Afrique*. Aix-en-Provence: Edisud.

Warren, Olivia. 2000. *Taste of Eritrea: Recipes from one of Africa's Most Interesting Little Countries*. New York: Hippocrene.

Yuval-Davis, Nira. 1997. *Gender and Nation*. London: Sage.

WEB-SITES (correct at time of writing)

Air Madagascar: http://www.air-mad.com/cuisine.htm

African Studies Cookbook: http://www.sas.upen.edu/African_Studies/Cookbook/about_cb_wh.html

Angola. (Official web-site, food section): http://www.angola.org/culture/foodind.html

Cape Verde (Official web-site): http://www.capeverdeusembassy.org/cuisine.html

Congo Cookbook: http://www.geocities.com/congocookbook/

DfID news: http://www.gov.uk/public/news/pr27july00.html

Dining in Harlem: http://harlem-ontime.com/tour/african

Ekabo (Berne): http://www.harrier.ch/harrier/likkmm/Ekabo.html as at 4 April 2000.

Equatorial Guinea (Official web-site): http://www.equatorialguinea.org

Eritrea (Official web-site): http://www.eritrea.org

Foodbooks: http://www.foodbooks.com/africam.htm

Gabon (Official web-site): http://www.alderan.fr/presidence-gabon/index

Kenya: Menus & Recipes from Africa at http://cygnus.sas.upenn.edu/African_Studies/ Cookbook/Kenya.html

List of African Restaurants: http://www.sas.upenn.edu/African_Studies/Miscellany/African_ Restaurants.html

Mauritania (Official web-site, culture): http://mauritania.mr/Francais/aper_hist_cult_fr.htm

Mebrat Tzehaie. Eritrean Cuisine: http://home.wxs.nl/~hans.mebrat/CUIS.HTM

Motherland Nigeria. Recipes (By Boomie O.): http://www.motherlandnigeria.com/recipes. html

Portugal em linha. Sabores Lusófonos: http://www.portugal-linha.pt/sabores/index.html

Sally's place: http://sallys-place.com/food/ethnic_cusine/africa.htm [sic]

Senegal. Sample Menu & Recipes: http://sas.upenn.edu/African_Studies/Cookbook/cb_ spot.html

# Part VI

## Race, Ethnicity, and Nation

# Introduction

## Wimal Dissanayake

Race, ethnicity and nation have assumed the status of privileged categories of analysis in contemporary cultural redescription. They are frequently deployed as if they are unproblematic categories with determinate referents. However, the ineluctable fact is that they are contested concepts that possess many archives; they generate pluralities of meaning. They index the fact that citizens live at the crossroads of manifold trajectories of subjecthood. Each of them is simultaneously constitutive and disruptive of the other. Indeed, they constitute agonistic sites where identity, cultural memory, power, ideology, and politics intersect. At the same time, they also can become zones of consensus. Moreover, these concepts have complex ancestries and they are inflected and reinflected by the discursive imperatives and validations of modernity. They, in many ways, present an uneasy conjunction: race, ethnicity, and nation feed into each other as they reinforce and unsettle each other. The interarticulations between localism and globalism that characterize the contemporary world invest these concepts with evolving layers and densities of meaning. Race and ethnicity also tend to forge alternative alliances and promote the participation in different configurations of belonging within the nation-state. Race, ethnicity, and nation foreground the fraught issues of belonging and unbelonging in vivid and acute ways. The idea of difference is central to them; indeed it is constitutive of their ontology. However, we need to keep in mind the fact that difference does not always have to promote division; it can also form the basis of solidarities. These general statements can prove to be useful in reading the five essays gathered in this section.

In exploring the discursive complexities of race, ethnicity, and nation, it is important that we focus on situated critical analyses rather than universalized abstract categorizations which very often take on the appearance of natural divisions. Etienne Balibar's concept of "complete understanding" which he advances in discussing nationhood, is particularly relevant in this regard. He observes, "complete understanding will only be achieved through the study of the historical situatedness, starting from the specificity of their contradictions and the constraints imposed on them by global structures to which they belong."

When we subject the intersecting concepts of race, ethnicity, and nation and the complex trafficking among them to the kind of complete understanding that Balibar advocates, we begin to observe the conceptually ambivalent spaces that they inhabit. The performative syntax of belonging and unbelonging that each of these categories promotes and legitimates is inscribed and circumscribed by ambiguity. Jean-Luc Nancy's notion of "being-in-common" that he formulates in his remarkably perceptive observations on the discursive formations of community is particularly serviceable in this regard. By the locution "being-in-common" he does not refer to the fact of having something in common, but rather to the fact of being exposed to others in a web of relationship of sharing. What is interesting about these relationships is that the limits on individual members that they impose are neither stable nor elusive.

What is needed, then, in discussing the ideas of race, ethnicity, and nation is to displace these onto alternate spaces of conceptual analysis and critical redescription. One useful way of doing this is to move away from the mainstream Anglo-American and European conceptualizations towards the culturally grounded self-understandings and frames of intelligibility of the rest of the world. The papers collected in this section, and indeed in the whole volume, are a first step in that direction.

The concept of race has generated much discussion in recent times, at times heated and acrimonious. Over the years it has been glossed in diverse ways, seeking to capture its elusive nature. Initially, the focus was on biology – the biological basis of race with its valorizations of the white race. This was followed by a greater attention being given to questions of psychology, the focus of interest being the moral and ethical attitudes associated with race, social superiority and inferiority. Here the emphasis was largely on the individual. In the following phase, race was studied as a complex collectivity and the concomitant economic and social bases of race were explored. Today, one perceives a greater interest on the discursive formations, problematics of representation, and cultural politics. In the essay included in this section, Cornel West refers to it as "genealogy," obviously drawing on Foucault. These stages do not follow neatly, as I have indicated, and some of the earlier formulations still possess swaying power. Questions of self-representation, cultural politics, ideological interpellations, power enter into the analytics of race in a way that was absent in earlier formulations. Although there is a danger in this approach of confining race merely to textuality and discursivity, the more discerning of the analysts have sought to bring in the vital issues of material provenance and historical formations as well. While it is important to recognize race as a discursive construct, it is equally important to regard it as vitally tethered to social and material realities.

What is important for us to examine is how race is lived, experienced, and challenged in contemporary societies. It is a space from which one looks at oneself, one looks at others, and at the socius in general. It is also important to relate questions of race to questions of class and gender. It is only this tripartite configuration of race, class, and gender that allows us to investigate the tensions and contradictions of race more cogently. Ethnicity and nationhood, like race, are vitally linked to theoretical articulations of difference. It is through these articulations of difference that we would be in a position to fashion new vocabularies of analysis, new ways of mapping and unmapping the difficult terrain of race. Race and racism are not external to us; they are discourses that constantly inflect our day-to-day life and our self-images. The diverse modalities of cultural identification and discursive addresses demand close and sustained attention, keeping in mind the fact that self-identification appears as the troubling aporia in the discourses of race, ethnicity, and nation.

The evolving explorations into race have resulted in the formulation of a number of useful concepts such as "double consciousness" (W. E. B. Du Bois), "racialization" (Frantz Fanon), "institutional racism" (Stokely Carmichael and Charles V. Hamilton), "racial antagonism" (Oliver Cromwell Cox), "articulation" (Stuart Hall), and "genealogy" (West). For theorists such as Kwame Anthony Appiah and Henry Louis Gates, "race" constitutes an arbitrary signifier, without any determinate referent. In his *Race, Writing, and Difference* (1986), Gates remarks that "Race is the ultimate trope of difference because it is so very arbitrary in its application." This approach has been severely criticized by others like Joyce Ann Joyce, who argues that this deconstructive move is tantamount to abdicating African-American culture.

In this section, we have chosen to include three important essays on race. The first is by Anthony Appiah, and seeks to examine race from a fresh viewpoint. He draws important distinctions between racism and racialism and intrinsic racism and extrinsic racism. It is Appiah's intention to deconstruct each of these socially constructed forms of racism. The second essay is by Cornel West, and here the author seeks to map the existing theories and concepts of race and to clear a theoretical space for his genealogical approach. Both these writers work within, against, and upon Western formulations and understandings of race. In the third essay, Paul Gilroy offers a useful critique of antiracism by urging us to relocate it in a wider discursive and material domain. He underlines the need to create a radical and democratic civil society by linking the immediate local concerns associated with antiracism with larger globalizing forces. His discussion of antiracism focuses on the complexities of racism.

Ethnicity, like race, is a contested concept. It is overdetermined, hence indeterminate, and aims to move in several directions at once. It is deeply embedded in the psyche of people, stirring deep passions, and promoting precipitate action. One has only to look at the African subcontinent or south Asia to realize the truth of this statement. Ethnicity, as generally understood, rests on the notion that people can be grouped on the basis of physical or cultural differences. In the voluminous literature on ethnicity, one can identify two main camps: primordialists, and instrumentalists or circumstantialists. Primordialists like Edward Shils and Clifford Geertz have sought to underline the importance of fundamental affiliations like location, language, kinship, religion, etc. Circumstantialists, on the other hand, emphasize historical variables and social and political determinants, and focus on questions of political economy and power relations. These two approaches compliment and subvert each other. In more recent times, certain scholars have sought to move beyond these two camps by making use of Pierre Bourdieu's notion of the habitus as a way of transcending the binarism of primordialism and instrumentalism.

More and more, scholars of ethnicity are coming round to the view that ethnicity is not something given but constructed historically, politically, and culturally. Questions of cultural politics, subordinating exigencies of modernity, agonistic fantasies of representation assume an increased burden of meaning. Scholars like Stuart Hall point out the provisional and discourse-bound nature of ethnicity. In modern societies there is a constant tension between the demands of the nation-state and the hopes of ethnicity, resulting in ethnicity moving from a quietist, culturalist register to a more proactive political register. This tension occurs at different locations in the national imaginary. Some attempt to challenge the unitary and hegemonic metanarrative of the nation-state; others seek to undo the mono-ethnicism perpetuated by states, for example in the Pacific Islands.

Ethnicity is a form of collective belonging that is processual. It is a process of collective becoming rather than collective being in the Heideggerian sense. Hence the forms of intelligibility associated with the constitution and understanding of ethnicity are provisional and contingent. Indeed it is a form of self-identification that is on the move. Scholars such as Stuart Hall have written illuminatingly on this aspect of blood and belonging. Unfortunately, due to problems of space we cannot include an essay by him in this section.

The third topic of this section is nation. Nationhood, as with most other forms of identity, revolves around the question of difference – how the uniqueness of one nation differs from another. It is located at the point of intersection of a multiplicity of discourses related to history, geography, politics, culture, identity, religion, economics, etc. Many important thinkers have attempted to define nationhood from their distinct optics. Elie Kedourie says that the idea of nationhood is an essentially European product. Ernest Gellner examines nationality in terms of industrialism and modernity. Hobsbawm advances the view that nationhood displays a certain cunningness in that it serves to keep intact the endangered ways of life of the privileged by appealing to the past for historical validation, while Balibar sees nationhood in terms of the production of people, and Homi Bhabha stresses the idea of narrativity. The exposition of nationhood that has generated the greatest amount of interest in recent times is that of Benedict Anderson, who defines it as an imagined community, both inherently limited and sovereign.

It is against this backdrop of thinking that we have to consider the two essays by two eminent Indian social scientists included in this section. The first, "Whose Imagined Community," by Partha Chatterjee, is a critique of Anderson's celebrated formulation. While his analysis advanced our knowledge, he failed to take into consideration the plight of the peripheralized within the nation. The second essay, by Arjun Appadurai, stresses the importance of thinking beyond the nation at a time of greater migration, displacement, and transnationalization of economies, and how patriotism is played out within the space of transnations. A point about nationhood is that it is under siege. With the intensification of globalization, multinational corporations, post-Fordist flexible accumulation, the nation, it is claimed, is under siege. At the same time, subnationalities comprising ethnic groups are beginning to play an ever more important role. However, we must not rush to write the obituary of the nation; it is still, in many ways, the inescapable reference point for discussions of communal belonging.

The conjunction between race, ethnicity, and nation demands sustained analysis. These are sites of circulation that urge us to question the ways in which racial and ethnic self-recognitions are assimilated into the national narrative. The coercive ideological ambitions of the nation-state, and its concomitant valorization of homogeneity, are constantly challenged by the articulations of race and ethnicity. To understand the full force of this dynamic, the discursive objects of race, ethnicity, and nation have to be freed from their Anglo-American and European mainstream focalizations, and related to the idiom of self-understanding, the lived experiences, frames of intelligibility, and metacodes of self-awareness of the nonwestern peoples. It is only then that we would be able to understand the complex ways in which race, ethnicity, and nation are produced and reproduced in nonwestern societies, and how they refocus on contradictory social subjectivities within the performative discourses of race, ethnicity, and nation. To map these complex configurations, we need to unmap the hegemonic formulations of western imaginings. The promise and premise of the five essays gathered in this section is to open up a space of alterity in which newer theoretical positions could be productively pursued.

# 26

# Racisms

## Kwame Anthony Appiah

### ■ Extrinsic and Intrinsic Racism ■

It is not always clear whether someone's theoretical racism is intrinsic or extrinsic, and there is certainly no reason why we should expect to be able to settle the question. Since the issue probably never occurs to most people in these terms, we cannot suppose that they must have an answer. In fact, given the definition of the terms I offer, there is nothing barring someone from being both an intrinsic and an extrinsic racist, holding both that the bare fact of race provides a basis for treating members of his or her own race differently from others and that there are morally relevant characteristics that are differentially distributed among the races. Indeed, for reasons I shall discuss in a moment, *most* intrinsic racists are likely to express extrinsic racist beliefs, so that we should not be surprised that many people seem, in fact, to be committed to both forms of racism.

The Holocaust made unreservedly clear the threat that racism poses to human decency. But it also blurred our thinking because in focusing our attention on the racist character of the Nazi atrocities, it obscured their character as atrocities. What is appalling about Nazi racism is not just that it presupposes, as all racism does, false (racialist) beliefs – not simply that it involves a moral incapacity (the inability to extend our moral sentiments to all our fellow creatures) and a moral failing (the making of moral distinctions without moral differences) – but that it leads, first, to oppression and then to mass slaughter. In recent years, South African racism has had a similar distorting effect. For although South African racism has not led to killings on the scale of the Holocaust – even if it has both left South Africa judicially executing more (mostly black) people per head of population than most other countries and led to massive differences between the life chances of white and nonwhite South Africans – it *has* led to the systematic oppression and economic exploitation of people who are not classified as "white," and to the infliction of suffering on citizens of all racial classifications, not least by the police state that is required to maintain that exploitation and oppression.

Part of our resistance, therefore, to calling the racial ideas of those, such as the Black Nationalists of the 1960s, who advocate racial solidarity, by the same term that we use to describe the attitudes of Nazis or of members of the South African Nationalist party, surely resides in the fact that they largely did not contemplate using race as a basis for inflicting harm. Indeed, it seems to me that there is a significant pattern in the modern rhetoric of race, such that the discourse of racial solidarity is usually expressed through the language of *intrinsic* racism, while those who have used race as the basis for oppression and hatred have appealed to *extrinsic* racist ideas. This point is important for understanding the character of contemporary racial attitudes.

The two major uses of race as a basis for moral solidarity that are most familiar in the West are varieties of Pan-Africanism and Zionism. In each case it is presupposed that a "people," Negroes or Jews, has the basis for shared political life in the fact of being of the same race. There are varieties of each form of "nationalism" that make the basis lie in shared traditions; but however plausible this may be in the case of Zionism, which has in Judaism, the religion, a realistic candidate for a common and nonracial focus for nationality, the peoples of Africa have a good deal less in common culturally than is usually assumed. I discuss this issue at length in *In My Father's House: Essays in the Philosophy of African Culture*, but let me say here that I believe the central fact is this: what blacks in the West, like secularized Jews, have mostly in common is that they are perceived – both by themselves and by others – as belonging to the same race, and that this common race is used by others as the basis for discriminating against them. "If you ever forget you're a Jew, a goy will remind you." The Black Nationalists, like some Zionists, responded to their experience of racial discrimination by accepting the racialism it presupposed.[1]

Although race is indeed at the heart of Black Nationalism, however, it seems that it is the fact of a shared race, not the fact of a shared racial character, that provides the basis for solidarity. Where racism is implicated in the basis for national solidarity, it is intrinsic, not (or not only) extrinsic. It is this that makes the idea of fraternity one that is naturally applied in nationalist discourse. For, as I have already observed, the moral status of close family members is not normally thought of in most cultures as depending on qualities of character; we are supposed to love our brothers and sisters in spite of their faults and not because of their virtues. Alexander Crummell, one of the founding fathers of Black Nationalism, literalizes the metaphor of family in these startling words:

> Races, like families, are the organisms and ordinances of God; and race feeling, like family feeling, is of divine origin. The extinction of race feeling is just as possible as the extinction of family feeling. Indeed, a race *is* a family.[2]

It is the assimilation of "race feeling" to "family feeling" that makes intrinsic racism seem so much less objectionable than extrinsic racism. For this metaphorical identification reflects the fact that, in the modern world (unlike the nineteenth century), intrinsic racism is acknowledged almost exclusively as the basis of feelings of community. We can surely, then, share a sense of what Crummell's friend and co-worker Edward Blyden called "the poetry of politics," that is, "the feeling of race," the feeling of "people with whom we are connected."[3] The racism here is the basis of acts of supererogation, the treatment of others better than we otherwise might, better than moral duty demands of us.

This is a contingent fact. There is no logical impossibility in the idea of racialists whose moral beliefs lead them to feelings of hatred for other races while leaving no room for love of members of their own. Nevertheless most racial hatred is in fact expressed through extrinsic racism: most people who have used race as the basis for causing harm to others have felt the need to see the others as independently morally flawed. It is one thing to espouse fraternity without claiming that your brothers and sisters have any special qualities that deserve recognition, and another to espouse hatred of others who have done nothing to deserve it.[4]

Many Afrikaners – like many in the American South until recently – have a long list of extrinsic racist answers to the question why blacks should not have full civil rights. Extrinsic racism has usually been the basis for treating people worse than we otherwise might, for giving them less than their humanity entitles them to. But this too is a contingent fact. Indeed, Crummell's guarded respect for white people derived from a belief in the superior moral qualities of the Anglo–Saxon race.

Intrinsic racism is, in my view, a moral error. Even if racialism were correct, the bare fact that someone was of another race would be no reason to treat them worse – or better – than someone of my race. In our public lives, people are owed treatment independently of their biological characters: if they are to be differently treated there must be some morally relevant difference between them. In our private lives, we are morally free to have aesthetic preferences between people, but once our treatment of people raises moral issues, we may not make arbitrary distinctions. Using race in itself as a morally relevant distinction strikes most of us as obviously arbitrary. Without associated moral characteristics, why should race provide a better basis than hair color or height or timbre of voice? And if two people share all the properties morally relevant to some action we ought to do, it will be an error – a failure to apply the Kantian injunction to universalize our moral judgments – to use the bare facts of race as the basis for treating them differently. No one should deny that a common ancestry might, in particular cases, account for similarities in moral character. But then it would be the moral similarities that justified the different treatment.

It is presumably because most people – outside the South African Nationalist party and the Ku Klux Klan – share the sense that intrinsic racism requires arbitrary distinctions that they are largely unwilling to express it in situations that invite moral criticism. But I do not know how I would argue with someone who was willing to announce an intrinsic racism as a basic moral idea; the best one can do, perhaps, is to provide objections to possible lines of defense of it.

## ■ De Gustibus ■

It might be thought that intrinsic racism should be regarded not so much as an adherence to a (moral) proposition as the expression of a taste, analogous, say, to the food prejudice that makes most English people unwilling to eat horse meat, and most Westerners unwilling to eat the insect grubs that the !Kung people find so appetizing. The analogy does at least this much for us, namely, to provide a model of the way that *extrinsic* racist propositions can be a reflection of an underlying prejudice. For, of course, in most cultures food prejudices are rationalized: we say insects are unhygienic and cats taste horrible. Yet a cooked insect is no more health-threatening than a cooked carrot, and the unpleasant taste of cat meat, far from justifying our prejudice against it, probably derives from that prejudice.

But there the usefulness of the analogy ends. For intrinsic racism, as I have defined it, is not simply a taste for the company of one's "own kind," but a moral doctrine, one that is supposed to underlie differences in the treatment of people in contexts where moral evaluation is appropriate. And for moral distinctions we cannot accept that "de gustibus non est disputandum." We do not need the full apparatus of Kantian ethics to require that public morality be constrained by reason.

A proper analogy would be with someone who thought that we could continue to kill cattle for beef, even if cattle exercised all the complex cultural skills of human beings. I think it is obvious that creatures that shared our capacity for understanding as well as our capacity for pain should not be treated the way we actually treat cattle – that "intrinsic speciesism" would be as wrong as racism. And the fact that most people think it is worse to be cruel to chimpanzees than to frogs suggests that they may agree with me. The distinction in attitudes surely reflects a belief in the greater richness of the mental life of chimps. Still, I do not know how I would *argue* against someone who could not see this; someone who continued to act on the contrary belief might, in the end, simply have to be locked up.

## ■ The Family Model ■

I have suggested that intrinsic racism is, at least sometimes, a metaphorical extension of the moral priority of one's family; it might, therefore, be suggested that a defense of intrinsic racism could proceed along the same lines as a defense of the family as a center of moral interest. The possibility of a defense of family relations as morally relevant – or, more precisely, of the claim that one may be morally entitled (or even obliged) to make distinctions between two otherwise morally indistinguishable people because one is related to one and not to the other – is theoretically important for the prospects of a philosophical defense of intrinsic racism. This is because such a defense of the family involves – like intrinsic racism – a denial of the basic claim, expressed so clearly by Kant, that from the perspective of morality, it is as rational agents *simpliciter* that we are to assess and be assessed.

For anyone who follows Kant in this, what matters, as we might say, is not who you are but how you try to live. Intrinsic racism denies this fundamental claim also. And, in so doing, as I have argued elsewhere, it runs against the mainstream of the history of Western moral theory.[5]

The importance of drawing attention to the similarities between the defense of the family and the defense of the race, then, is not merely that the metaphor of family is often invoked by racism; it is that each of them offers the same general challenge to the Kantian stream of our moral thought. And the parallel with the defense of the family should be especially appealing to an intrinsic racist, since many of us who have little time for racism would hope that the family is susceptible to some such defense.

The problem in generalizing the defense of the family, however, is that such defenses standardly begin at a point that makes the argument for intrinsic racism immediately implausible: namely, with the family as the unit through which we live what is most intimate, as the center of private life. If we distinguish, with Bernard Williams, between ethical thought, which takes seriously "the demands, needs, claims, desires, and generally, the lives of other people,"[6] and morality, which focuses more narrowly on obligation, it may well be that private life matters to us precisely because it is altogether unsuited to the universalizing tendencies of morality.

The functioning family unit has contracted substantially with industrialization, the disappearance of the family as the unit of production, and the increasing mobility of labor, but there remains that irreducible minimum: the parent or parents with the child or children. In this "nuclear" family, there is, of course, a substantial body of shared experience, shared attitudes, shared knowledge and beliefs; and the mutual psychological investment that exists within this group is, for most of us, one of the things that gives meaning to our lives. It is a natural enough confusion – which we find again and again in discussions of adoption in the popular media – that identifies the relevant group with the biological unit of *genitor*, *genetrix*, and *offspring* rather than with the social unit of those who share a common domestic life.

The relations of parents and their biological children are of moral importance, of course, in part because children are standardly the product of behavior voluntarily undertaken by their biological parents. But the moral relations between biological siblings and half-siblings cannot, as I have already pointed out, be accounted for in such terms. A rational defense of the family ought to appeal to the causal responsibility of the biological parent and the common life of the domestic unit, and not to the brute fact of biological relatedness, even if the former pair of considerations defines groups that are often coextensive with the groups generated by the latter. For brute biological relatedness bears no necessary connection to the sorts of human purposes that seem likely to be relevant at the most basic level of ethical thought.

An argument that such a central group is bound to be crucially important in the lives of most human beings in societies like ours is not, of course, an argument for any specific mode of organization of the "family": feminism and the gay liberation movement have offered candidate groups that could (and sometimes do) occupy the same sort of role in the lives of those whose sexualities or whose dispositions otherwise make the nuclear family uncongenial; and these candidates have been offered specifically in the course of defenses of a move toward societies that are agreeably beyond patriarchy and homophobia. The central thought of these feminist and gay critiques of the nuclear family is that we cannot continue to view any one organization of private life as "natural," once we have seen even the broadest outlines of the archaeology of the family concept.

If that is right, then the argument for the family must be an argument for a mode of organization of life and feeling that subserves certain positive functions; and however the details of such an argument would proceed it is highly unlikely that the same functions could be served by groups on the scale of races, simply because, as I say, the family is attractive in part exactly for reasons of its personal scale.

I need hardly say that rational defenses of intrinsic racism along the lines I have been considering are not easily found. In the absence of detailed defenses to consider, I can only offer these general reasons for doubting that they can succeed: the generally Kantian tenor of much of our moral thought threatens the project from the start; and the essentially unintimate nature of relations within "races" suggests that there is little prospect that the defense of the family – which seems an attractive and plausible project that extends ethical life beyond the narrow range of a universalizing morality – can be applied to a defense of races.

## ■ Conclusions ■

I have suggested that what we call "racism" involves both propositions and dispositions.

The propositions were, first, that there are races (this was *racialism*) and, second, that these races are morally significant either (a) because they are contingently correlated with morally relevant properties (this was *extrinsic racism*) or (b) because they are intrinsically morally significant (this was *intrinsic racism*).

The disposition was a tendency to assent to false propositions, both moral and theoretical, about races – propositions that support policies or beliefs that are to the disadvantage of some race (or races) as opposed to others, and to do so even in the face of evidence and argument that should appropriately lead to giving those propositions up. This disposition I called "racial prejudice."

I suggested that intrinsic racism had tended in our own time to be the natural expression of feelings of community, and this is, of course, one of the reasons why we are not inclined to call it racist. For, to the extent that a theoretical position is not associated with irrationally held beliefs that tend to the *dis*advantage of some group, it fails to display the *directedness* of the distortions of rationality characteristic of racial prejudice. Intrinsic racism may be as irrationally held as any other view, but it does not *have* to be directed *against* anyone.

So far as theory is concerned I believe racialism to be false: since theoretical racism of both kinds presupposes racialism, I could not logically support racism of either variety. But even if racialism were true, both forms of theoretical racism would be incorrect. Extrinsic racism is false because the genes that account for the gross morphological differences that underlie our standard racial categories are not linked to those genes that determine, to whatever degree such matters are determined genetically, our moral and intellectual characters. Intrinsic racism is mistaken because it breaches the Kantian imperative to make moral distinctions only on morally relevant grounds – granted that there is no reason to believe that race, *in se*, is morally relevant, and also no reason to suppose that races are like families in providing a sphere of ethical life that legitimately escapes the demands of a universalizing morality.

## NOTES

1   As I argued in "The Uncompleted Argument: Du Bois and the Illusion of Race," *Critical Inquiry*, 12 (Autumn 1985); reprinted in Henry Louis Gates (ed.), *"Race," Writing and Difference* (Chicago: University of Chicago Press, 1986), pp. 21–37. The reactive (or dialectical) character of this move explains why Sartre calls its manifestations in Négritude an "antiracist racism"; see "Orphée Noir," his preface to Senghor's *Anthologie de la nouvelle poésie nègre et malagache de langue française* (Paris: PUF, 1948). Sartre believed, of course, that the synthesis of this dialectic would be the transcendence of racism; and it was his view of it as a stage – the antithesis – in that process that allowed him to see it as a positive advance over the original "thesis" of European racism. I suspect that the reactive character of antiracist racism accounts for the tolerance that is regularly extended to it in liberal circles; but this tolerance is surely hard to justify unless one shares Sartre's optimistic interpretation of it as a stage in a process that leads to the end of all racisms. (And unless your view of this dialectic is deterministic, you should in any case want to play an argumentative role in moving to this next stage.)

   For a similar Zionist response see Horace Kallen's "The Ethics of Zionism," *Maccabaean*, August 1906.
2   "The Race Problem in America," in Brotz's *Negro Social and Political Thought* (New York: Basic Books, 1966), p. 184.
3   *Christianity, Islam and the Negro Race* (1887; reprinted Edinburgh: Edinburgh University Press, 1967), p. 197.
4   This is in part a reflection of an important asymmetry: loathing, unlike love, needs justifying; and this, I would argue, is because loathing usually leads to acts that are *in se* undesirable, whereas love leads to acts that are largely *in se* desirable – indeed, supererogatorily so.
5   See my "Racism and Moral Pollution," *Philosophical Forum*, 18 (Winter–Spring 1986–7), pp. 185–202.
6   *Ethics and the Limits of Philosophy* (Cambridge, Mass.: Harvard University Press, 1985), p. 12. I do not, as is obvious, share William's skepticism about morality.

# 27

# Race and Social Theory

## Cornel West

■ Toward a Genealogical Materialist Analysis ■

In this section, I shall set forth a schematic outline of a new conception of African American oppression that tries to bring together the best of recent Marxist theory and the invaluable insights of neo-Freudians (Ranke, Becker, and Kovel) about the changing forms of immortality quests and perceptions of dirt and death in the modern West, along with the formulations of the poststructuralists (Derrida, de Man, Foucault, Said) on the role of difference, otherness and marginality in discursive operations and extradiscursive formations.

My perspective can be characterized as a genealogical materialist analysis, that is, an analysis that replaces Marxist conceptions of history with Nietzschean notions of genealogy, yet preserves the materiality of multifaceted structured social practices. My understanding of genealogy derives neither from mere deconstructions of the duplicitous and deceptive character of rhetorical strategies of logocentric discourses, nor from simple investigations into the operations of power of such discourses. Unlike Derrida and de Man, genealogical materialism does not rest content with a horizon of language. In contrast to Foucault and Said, I take the challenge of historical materialism with great seriousness. The aspects of Nietzsche that interest me are neither his perennial playfulness nor his vague notions of power. What I find seductive and persuasive about Nietzsche is his deep historical consciousness, a consciousness so deep that he must reject prevailing ideas of history in the name of genealogy. It seems to me that in these postmodern times, the principles of historical specificity and the materiality of structured social practices – the very founding principles of Marx's own discourse – now require us to be genealogical materialists. We must become more radically historical than is envisioned by the Marxist tradition. By becoming more "radically historical"

I mean confronting more candidly the myriad effects and consequences (intended and unintended, conscious and unconscious) of power-laden and conflict-ridden social practices – for instance, the complex confluence of human bodies, traditions and institutions. This candor takes the form of a more theoretical open-endedness and analytical dexterity than Marxist notions of history permit – without ruling out Marxist explanations a priori.

Furthermore, a genealogical materialist conception of social practices should be more materialist than that of the Marxist tradition, to the extent that the privileged material mode of production is not necessarily located in the economic sphere. Instead, decisive material modes of production at a given moment may be located in the cultural, political or even the psychic sphere. Since these spheres are interlocked and interlinked, each always has some weight in an adequate social and historical explanation. My view neither promotes a post-Marxist idealism (for it locates acceptable genealogical accounts in material social practices), nor supports an explanatory nihilism (in that it posits some contingent yet weighted set of material social practices as decisive factors to explain a given genealogical configuration, that is, set of events). More pointedly, my position appropriates the implicit pragmatism of Nietzsche for the purposes of a deeper, and less dogmatic, historical materialist analysis. In this regard, the genealogical materialist view is both continuous and discontinuous with the Marxist tradition. One cannot be a genealogical materialist without (taking seriously) the Marxist tradition, yet allegiance to the methodological principles of the Marxist tradition forces one to be a genealogical materialist. Marxist theory still may provide the best explanatory account for certain phenomena, but it also may remain inadequate to account for other phenomena – notably here, the complex phenomenon of racism in the modern West.

My basic disagreement with Marxist theory is twofold. First, I hold that many social practices, such as racism, are best understood and explained not only or primarily by locating them within modes of production, but also by situating them within the cultural traditions of civilizations. This permits us to highlight the specificity of those practices that traverse or cut across different modes of production, for example, racism, religion, patriarchy, homophobia. Focusing on racist practices or white-supremacist logics operative in premodern, modern and postmodern Western civilization yields both racial continuity and discontinuity. Even Marxist theory can be shown to be both critical of and captive to a Eurocentrism that can justify racist practices. And though Marxist theory remains indispensable, it also obscures and hides the ways in which secular ideologies – especially modern ideologies of scientism, racism and sexual hedonism (Marxist theory does much better with nationalism, professionalism and consumerism) – are linked to larger civilizational ways of life and struggle.

Second, I claim that the Marxist obsession with the economic sphere as the major explanatory factor is itself a reflection of the emergence of Marxist discourse in the midst of an industrial capitalism preoccupied with economic production; and, more important, this Marxist obsession is itself a symptom of a particular Western version of the will to truth and style of rationality that valorizes control, mastery and domination of nature and history. I neither fully reject this will to truth, nor downplay the crucial role of the economic sphere in social and historical explanation. But one is constrained to acknowledge the methodological point about the degree to which Marxist theory remains inscribed within the very problematic of the unfreedom and domination it attempts to overcome.

Genealogical materialist analysis of racism consists of three methodological moments that serve as guides for detailed historical and social analyses:

1. A *genealogical* inquiry into the discursive and extradiscursive conditions for the possibility of racist practices, that is, a radically historical investigation into the emergence, development and sustenance of white-supremacist logics operative in various epochs in the modern Western (Eastern or African) civilization.
2. A *microinstitutional* (or localized) analysis of the mechanisms that promote and contest these logics in the everyday lives of people, including the ways in which self-images and self-identities are shaped and the impact of alien, degrading cultural styles, aesthetic ideals, psychosexual sensibilities and linguistic gestures upon peoples of color.
3. A *macrostructural* approach that accents modes of overdetermined class exploitation, state repression and bureaucratic domination, including resistance against these modes, in the lives of peoples of color.

The first moment would, for example, attempt to locate racist discourses within the larger Western conceptions of death and dirt, that is, in the predominant ways in which Western peoples have come to terms with their fears of "extinction with insignificance," of existential alienation, isolation and separation in the face of the inevitable end of which they are conscious. This moment would examine how these peoples have conceptualized and mythologized their sentiments of impurity at the visual, tactile, auditory and, most important, olfactory levels of experience and social practice.

Three white-supremacist logics – the battery of concepts, tropes, and metaphors constituting discourses that degrade and devalue people of color – operative in the modern West may shed some light on these issues. The *Judeo-Christian racist logic*, which emanates from the biblical account of Ham looking upon and failing to cover his father Noah's nakedness, thereby provoking divine punishment in the form of blackening his progeny, links racist practices to notions of disrespect for and rejection of authority, to ideas of unruly behavior and chaotic rebellion. The *"scientific" racist logic*, which promotes the observing, measuring, ordering and comparing of visible physical characteristics of human bodies in light of Greco-Roman aesthetic standards, associates racist practices with bodily ugliness, cultural deficiency and intellectual inferiority. And the *psychosexual racist logic* endows black people with sexual prowess, views them as either cruel, revengeful fathers, frivolous, carefree children, or passive, long-suffering mothers. This logic – rooted in Western sexual discourses about feces and odious smells – relates racist practices to bodily defecation, violation, and subordination, thereby relegating black people to walking abstractions, lustful creatures, or invisible objects. All three white-supremacist logics view black people, like death and dirt, as Other and Alien.

An important task of genealogical inquiry is to disclose in historically concrete and sociologically specific ways the discursive operations that view Africans as excluded, marginal and other and to reveal how racist logics are guided (or contested) by various hegemonic Western philosophies of identity and universality that suppress difference, heterogeneity and diversity. Otto Ranke and Ernest Becker would play an interesting role here, since their conception of societies as codified hero-systems or as symbolic-action systems that produce, distribute, and circulate statuses and customs in order to cope with human fears of death or extreme otherness may cast light on modern Western racist practices. For example, with the lessening of religious influence in the modern West, human immortality quests were channeled into secular ideologies of science, art, nation, profession, race, sexuality and consumption. The deep human desire for existential belonging and for self-esteem – what I call the need for and consumption of *existential capital* – results in a profound, even gut-level, commitment to some of the illusions of the present epoch. None of us escapes. And many Western peoples get much existential capital from racist illusions, from ideologies of race. The growing presence of Caribbean and Indian peoples in Britain, Africans in Russia, Arabs in France, and black soldiers in Germany is producing escalating black/white hatred, sexual jealousy and intraclass antagonisms. This suggests that the means of acquiring existential capital from ideologies of race is in no way peculiar to the two exemplary racist Western countries, the United States and South Africa. It also reminds us that racist perceptions and practices are deeply rooted in Western cultures and become readily potent in periods of crisis, be that crisis cultural, political or economic.

The second moment, the microinstitutional or localized analysis, examines the elaboration of white-supremacist logics within the everyday lives of people. Noteworthy here is the conflict-ridden process of identity formation and self-image production by peoples of color. The work of Goffman and Garfinkel on role-playing and self-masking, the insights of Althusser, Kristeva, and Foucault on the contradictions shot through the process of turning individual bodies into ideological subjects (for instance, "colored," "Negro," "black" subjects) and the painful struggle of accepting and rejecting internalized negative and disenabling self-conceptions (for instance, pervasive lack of self-confidence in certain activities, deep insecurities regarding one's capacities) among people of color, as highlighted in Memmi and Fanon, are quite useful to this analysis.

The third (and last) moment, the macrostructural analysis, deepens the historical materialist analyses of Genovese, Hall, and Patterson, with the proviso that the economic sphere may, in certain cases, not be the ultimate factor in explaining racist practices. As I noted earlier, there is little doubt that it remains a crucial factor in every case.

# 28

# The End of Antiracism

## Paul Gilroy

■ Racial Justice and Civil Society ■

I think it is important to concede that what we can loosely call the anti-antiracist position associated with sections of the new right and with populist politics has fed on crucial ambiguities in antiracist and multicultural initiatives.

The definition of racism as the sum of prejudice and power can be used to illustrate these problems. Power is a relation between social groups not a possession to be worn like a garment or flaunted like an antiracist badge. Prejudice suggests conscious action if not actual choice. Is this an appropriate formula? The most elementary lessons involved in studying ideas and consciousness seem to have been forgotten. Racism, like capitalism as a whole, rests on the mystification of social relations – the necessary illusions that secure the order of public authority.

There are other aspects of what has become a multiculturalist or antiracist orthodoxy which can be shown to replicate in many ways the *volkish* new right sense of the relationship between race, nation and culture – kin blood and ethnic identity. I have already mentioned how the left and right distinction has begun to evaporate as formally opposed groups have come to share a sense of what race is. These problems are even more severe when elements of the black community have themselves endorsed this understanding. Here I am thinking of the definition of race exclusively in terms of culture and identity which ties certain strands in antiracism to the position of some of the new right ideologues.

By emphasizing this convergence I am not saying that culture and identity are unimportant, but challenging the routine reduction of race to them alone which obscures the inherently political character of the term. The way in which culture is itself understood provides the key to grasping the extraordinary convergence between left and right, antiracist and avowedly racist over precisely what race and racism add up to.

At the end of the day, an absolute commitment to cultural insiderism is as bad as an absolute commitment to biological insiderism. I think we need to be theoretically and politically clear that no single culture is hermetically sealed off from others. There can be no neat and tidy pluralistic separation of racial groups in this country. It is time to dispute with those positions which, when taken to their conclusions, say 'there is no possibility of shared history and no human empathy'. We must beware of the use of ethnicity to wrap a spurious cloak of legitimacy around the speaker who invokes it. Culture, even the culture which defines the groups we know as races, is never fixed, finished or final. It is fluid, it is actively and continually made and re-made. In our multicultural schools the sound of the steel pan may evoke Caribbean ethnicity, tradition and authenticity, yet they originate in the oil drums of the Standard Oil Company rather than the mysterious knowledge of ancient African griots.

These theoretical problems are most visible and at their most intractable in the area of fostering and adoption policy. Here, the inflated rhetoric and culturalist orthodoxies of antiracism have borne some peculiar fruit. The critique of the pathological views of black family life that were so prevalent in Social Services during the late seventies and early eighties has led directly to an extraordinary idealization of black family forms. Antiracist orthodoxy now sees them as the only effective repositories of authentic black culture and as a guaranteed means to transmit all the essential skills that black children will need if they are to 'survive' in a racist society without psychological damage. 'Same-race' adoption and fostering for 'minority ethnics' is presented as an unchallenged and seemingly unchallengeable benefit for all concerned. It is hotly defended with the same fervour that denounces white demands for 'same race' schooling as a repellent manifestation of racism. What is most alarming about this is not its inappropriate survivalist tone, the crudity with which racial identity is conceived nor even the sad inability to see beyond the conservation of racial identities to the possibility of their transcendence. It is the extraordinary manner in which the pathological imagery has simply been inverted so that it forms the basis of a pastoral view which asserts the strength and durability of black family life and, in present circumstances, retreats from confronting the difficult issues which result in black children arriving in care in the first place. The contents of the racist pathology and the material circumstances to which it can be made to correspond are thus left untouched. The tentacles of racism are everywhere, except in the safe haven which a nurturing black family provides for delicate, fledgling racial identities.

### ■ The Forces of Antiracism ■

I want to turn now to the forces which have grouped around the antiracist project and to the question of class. There is a problem here in that much of the certainty and confidence with which the term has been used have collapsed along with the secure life-time employment which characterized industrial capitalism. Today, for example, I think it means next to nothing to simply state that blacks are working class when we are likely to be unemployed and may not recognize our experience and history in those areas of political life where an appeal to class is most prominent. Class politics do not, in any case, enjoy a monopoly of political radicalism. Obviously people still belong to classes, but belief in the decisive universal agency of the dwindling proletariat is something which must be dismissed as an idealist fantasy. Class is an indispensable instrument in analysing capitalism, but it contains no ready-made plan for its overcoming. We must learn to live without a theological faith in the working class as either a revolutionary or an antiracist agent.

There is a major issue here, but I want to note it and move on to consider a different aspect of how race and class intersect. A more significant task for class analysis is comprehending the emergence of a proto-middle class grouping narrowly constituted around the toeholds which some blacks have been able to acquire in the professions, mostly those related directly to the welfare state itself – social work, teaching, and now antiracist bureaucracies. A Marxist writer would probably identify this group as the first stirrings of a black petit bourgeoisie. I do not think this grouping or grouplet is yet a class either in itself or for itself and it may never become one. For one thing it is too small; for another it is too directly dependent on the state institutions which pay its wages. But it is with this group that antiracism can be most readily identified and we need to examine it on its own terms and in its relationship to other more easily identifiable class groupings. It is obviously in an uncomfortably contradictory position – squeezed between the expectations of the bureaucracies on which it relies and its political affiliation to the struggles of the mass of blacks which it is called upon to mediate, translate and sometimes police. It is caught between the demands of bureaucratic professionalism and the emotive pull of ethnic identification.

This not-yet-class plays a key role in organizing the political forces of antiracism centred on local authorities. It involves three opposed tendencies which have evolved an uneasy symbiosis. They are not wholly discrete. The campaign for autonomous Black Sections in the Labour Party, for example, involves elements of each of them. First, there is the equal opportunities strand, which has its roots in the social democratic 'race' interventions of the 1960s. It has also borrowed heavily from the experience of Afro-America's shift into electoral politics – the black mayors' movement and so on. This tendency is proud and secure in its bureaucratic status and it identifies equality (antiracism) with efficiency and good management practice. Policy questions dominate political ones and antiracism emerges from the production of general blueprints which can be universally applied. Of course, equal opportunities afford an important interface between struggles around race and gender and they can be a locus of possible alliances. However, in the context of local authorities these initiatives can also host a competition between different political forces over which of them is going to take immediate priority. We should therefore be wary of collapsing antiracism let alone black emancipation into equal opportunities.

The second tendency is what used to be called Black nationalism but is now fragmented into multiple varieties, each with its own claim to ethnic particularity. It is now emphatically culturalist rather than political, each ethnic or national group arguing for cultural relativism in the strongest form. Very often, these mutually unintelligible and exclusive ethnic cultures just happen to be the same as the groups which common sense tells us are 'races'. Perversely and ironically, this tendency has happily co-existed with old-style Labourism for which ethnic absolutism and cultural relativism have provided an obvious means to rationalize and balance its funding practices.

The third tendency is the most complex. It unendingly reiterates the idea that class is race, race is class and is both black and white. Its spokespeople have sought refuge from inter-ethnic conflict in some of the more anachronistic formulae of socialist class politics. For them class is the thing which will unify the diverse and end the polyphonic ethno-babble in the new municipal Tower of Babel. Class remains synonymous with organized labour, regardless of the fact that in the context of local authorities organized labour is not always very radical. This tendency overlooks the role which the bureaucratic hierarchy plays in coercing the actually existing working class into antirace line. So far its class-based line has been almost exclusively animated by a critique of race awareness training – a practical strategy which has been thrown up in the grating between the first two tendencies. This is an important issue, but it is nonetheless the most gestural and superficial aspect of deeper problems, namely culturalism and ethnic absolutism. This tendency has mistaken the particular for the general – racism awareness training is a symptom, not a cause in its own right.

Apart from their conceit, these diverse yet inter-dependent groupings share a statist conception of antiracism. In making the local state the main vehicle for advancing antiracist politics they have actively confused and confounded the black community's capacity for autonomous self-organization. Here, we must make an assessment of the politics of funding community organizations and the dependency which that creates.

There is every likelihood that the versions of antiracism I have criticized will wither away as the local state structures on which they have relied are destroyed by the conflict with central government. But antiracist activities encapsulate one final problem which may outlive them. This is the disastrous way in which they have trivialized the rich complexity of black life by reducing it to nothing more than a response to racism. More than any other issue this operation reveals the extent of the antiracists' conceptual trading with the racists and the results of embracing their culturalist assumptions. Seeing in black life nothing more than an answer to racism means moving on to the ideological circuit which makes us visible in two complementary roles – the problem and the victim.

Antiracism seems very comfortable with this idea of blacks as victims. I remember one simplistic piece of Greater London Council propaganda which said 'We are all either the victims or the perpetrators of racism'. Why should this be so? Suffering confers no virtue on the victim; yesterday's victims are tomorrow's executioners. I propose that we reject the central image of ourselves as victims and install instead an alternative conception which sees us as an active force working in many different ways for our freedom from racial subordination. The plural is important here for there can be no single or homogeneous strategy against racism because racism itself is never homogeneous. It varies, it changes and it is *always* uneven. The recent history of our struggles has shown how people can shrink the world to the size of their communities and act politically on that basis, expressing their dissent in the symbolism of disorderly protest while demanding control over their immediate conditions. However you feel about the useless violence of these eruptions, it was the riotous protests of 1981 which created the space in which political antiracism became an option.

We must accept that for the years immediately ahead these struggles will be essentially defensive and probably unable to make the transition to more stable, totalizing forms of politics. But the challenge we face is the task of linking these immediate local concerns together across the international division of labour, transcending national boundaries, turning our back on the state and using all the means at our disposal to build a radical, democratic movement of civil society. This kind of activity could be called the micro-politics of race, though in practice, as where we align ourselves with the struggles of our brothers and sisters in South Africa, it is more likely to prove the micro-politics of race's overcoming.

## REFERENCES

Gilroy, P. (1987) *There Ain't No Black in the Union Jack*, London, Hutchinson.
Honeyford, R. (1988) *Integration or Disintegration*, London, Claridge Press.
Lewis, R. (1988) *Anti-Racism: A Mania Exposed*, London, Quartet.
Miles, R. (1989) *Racism*, London, Routledge & Kegan Paul.
Palmer, F. (1987) *Antiracism: An Assault on Education and Value*, London, Sherwood Press.

# 29

# Whose Imagined Community?

## Partha Chatterjee

Benedict Anderson demonstrated with much subtlety and originality that nations were not the determinate products of given sociological conditions such as language or race or religion; they had been, in Europe and everywhere else in the world, imagined into existence.[1] He also described some of the major institutional forms through which this imagined community came to acquire concrete shape, especially the institutions of what he so ingeniously called "print-capitalism." He then argued that the historical experience of nationalism in Western Europe, in the Americas, and in Russia had supplied for all subsequent nationalisms a set of modular forms from which nationalist elites in Asia and Africa had chosen the ones they liked.

Anderson's book has been, I think, the most influential in the last few years in generating new theoretical ideas on nationalism, an influence that of course, it is needless to add, is confined almost exclusively to academic writings. Contrary to the largely uninformed exoticization of nationalism in the popular media in the West, the theoretical tendency represented by Anderson certainly attempts to treat the phenomenon as part of the universal history of the modern world.

I have one central objection to Anderson's argument. If nationalisms in the rest of the world have to choose their imagined community from certain "modular" forms already made available to them by Europe and the Americas, what do they have left to imagine? History, it would seem, has decreed that we in the post-colonial world shall only be perpetual consumers of modernity. Europe and the Americas, the only true subjects of history, have thought out on our behalf not only the script of colonial enlightenment and exploitation, but also that of our anticolonial resistance and postcolonial misery. Even our imaginations must remain forever colonized.

I object to this argument not for any sentimental reason. I object because I cannot reconcile it with the evidence on anticolonial nationalism. The most powerful as well as the most creative results of the nationalist imagination in Asia and Africa are posited not on an identity but rather on a *difference* with the "modular" forms of the national society propagated by the modern West. How can we ignore this without reducing the experience of anticolonial nationalism to a caricature of itself?

To be fair to Anderson, it must be said that he is not alone to blame. The difficulty, I am now convinced, arises because we have all taken the claims of nationalism to be a *political* movement much too literally and much too seriously.

In India, for instance, any standard nationalist history will tell us that nationalism proper began in 1885 with the formation of the Indian National Congress. It might also tell us that the decade preceding this was a period of preparation, when several provincial political associations were formed. Prior to that, from the 1820s to the 1870s, was the period of "social reform," when colonial enlightenment was beginning to "modernize" the customs and institutions of a traditional society and the political spirit was still very much that of collaboration with the colonial regime: nationalism had still not emerged.

This history, when submitted to a sophisticated sociological analysis, cannot but converge with Anderson's formulations. In fact, since it seeks to replicate in its own history the history of the modern state in Europe, nationalism's self-representation will inevitably corroborate Anderson's decoding of the nationalist myth. I think, however, that as history, nationalism's autobiography is fundamentally flawed.

By my reading, anticolonial nationalism creates its own domain of sovereignty within colonial society well before it begins its political battle with the imperial power. It does this by dividing the world of social institutions and practices into two domains – the material and the spiritual. The material is the domain of the "outside," of the economy and of statecraft, of science and technology, a domain where the West had proved its superiority and the East had succumbed. In this domain, then, Western superiority had to be acknowledged and its accomplishments carefully studied and replicated. The spiritual, on the other hand, is an "inner" domain bearing the "essential" marks of cultural identity. The greater one's success in imitating Western skills in the material domain, therefore, the greater the need to preserve the distinctness of one's spiritual culture. This formula is, I think, a fundamental feature of anticolonial nationalisms in Asia and Africa.[2]

There are several implications. First, nationalism declares the domain of the spiritual its sovereign territory and refuses to allow the colonial power to intervene in that domain. If I may return to the Indian example, the period of "social reform" was actually made up of two distinct phases. In the earlier phase, Indian reformers looked to the colonial authorities to bring about by state action the reform of traditional institutions and customs. In the latter phase, although the need for change was not disputed, there was a strong resistance to allowing the colonial state to intervene in matters affecting "national culture." The second phase, in my argument, was already the period of nationalism.

The colonial state, in other words, is kept out of the "inner" domain of national culture; but it is not as though this so-called spiritual domain is left unchanged. In fact, here nationalism launches its most powerful, creative, and historically significant project: to fashion a "modern" national culture that is nevertheless not Western. If the nation is an imagined community, then this is where it is brought into being. In this, its true and essential domain, the nation is already sovereign, even when the state is in the hands of the colonial power. The dynamics of this historical project is completely missed in conventional histories in which the story of nationalism begins with the contest for political power.

In order to define the main argument of this book, let me anticipate a few points that will be discussed more elaborately later. I wish to highlight here several areas within the so-called spiritual domain that nationalism transforms in the course of its journey. I will confine my illustrations to Bengal, with whose history I am most familiar.

The first such area is that of language. Anderson is entirely correct in his suggestion that it is "print-capitalism" which provides the new institutional space for the development of the modern "national" language.[3] However, the specificities of the colonial situation do not allow a simple transposition of European patterns of development. In Bengal, for instance, it is at the initiative of the East India Company and the European missionaries that the first printed books are produced in Bengali at the end of the eighteenth century and the first narrative prose compositions commissioned at the beginning of the nineteenth. At the same time, the first half of the nineteenth century is when English completely displaces Persian as the language of bureaucracy and emerges as the most powerful vehicle of intellectual influence on a new Bengali elite. The crucial moment in the development of the modern Bengali language comes, however, in midcentury, when this bilingual elite makes it a cultural project to provide its mother tongue with the necessary linguistic equipment to enable it to become an adequate language for "modern" culture. An entire institutional network of printing presses, publishing houses, newspapers, magazines, and literary societies is created around this time, *outside* the purview of the state and the European missionaries, through which the new language, modern and standardized, is given shape. The bilingual intelligentsia came to think of its own language as belonging to that inner domain of cultural identity, from which the colonial intruder had to be kept out; language therefore became a zone over which the nation first had to declare its sovereignty and then had to transform in order to make it adequate for the modern world.

Here the modular influences of modern European languages and literatures did not necessarily produce similar consequences. In the case of the new literary genres and aesthetic conventions, for instance, whereas European influences undoubtedly shaped explicit critical discourse, it was also widely believed that European conventions were inappropriate and misleading in judging literary productions in modern Bengali. To this day there is a clear hiatus in this area between the terms of academic criticism and those of literary practice. To give an example, let me briefly discuss Bengali drama.

Drama is the one modern literary genre that is the least commended on aesthetic grounds by critics of Bengali literature. Yet it is the form in which the bilingual elite has found its largest audience. When it appeared in its modern form in the middle of the nineteenth century, the new Bengali drama had two models available to it: one, the modern European drama as it had developed since Shakespeare and Molière, and two, the virtually forgotten corpus of Sanskrit drama, now restored to a reputation of classical excellence because of the praises showered on it by Orientalist scholars from Europe. The literary criteria that would presumably direct the new drama into the privileged domain of a modern national culture were therefore clearly set by modular forms provided by Europe. But the performative practices of the new institution of the public theater made it impossible for those criteria to be applied to plays written for the theater. The conventions that would enable a play to succeed on the Calcutta stage were very different from the conventions approved by critics schooled in the traditions of European drama. The tensions have not been resolved to this day. What thrives as mainstream public theater in West Bengal or Bangladesh today is modern urban theater, national and clearly distinguishable from "folk theater." It is produced and largely patronized by the literate urban middle classes. Yet their aesthetic conventions fail to meet the standards set by the modular literary forms adopted from Europe.

Even in the case of the novel, that celebrated artifice of the nationalist imagination in which the community is made to live and love in "homogeneous time,"[4] the modular forms do not necessarily have an easy passage. The novel was a principal form through which the bilingual elite in Bengal fashioned a new narrative prose. In the devising of this prose, the influence of the two available models – modern English and classical Sanskrit – was obvious. And yet, as the practice of the form gained greater popularity, it was remarkable how frequently in the course of their narrative Bengali novelists shifted from the disciplined forms of authorial prose to the direct recording of living speech. Looking at the pages of some of the most popular novels in Bengali, it is often difficult to tell whether one is reading a novel or a play. Having created a modern prose language in the fashion of the approved modular forms, the literati, in its search for artistic truthfulness, apparently found it necessary to escape as often as possible the rigidities of that prose.

The desire to construct an aesthetic form that was modern and national, and yet recognizably different from the Western, was shown in perhaps its most exaggerated shape in the efforts in the early twentieth century of the so-called Bengal school of art. It was through these efforts that, on the one hand, an institutional space was created for the modern professional artist in India, as distinct from the traditional craftsman, for the dissemination through exhibition and print of the products of art and for the creation of a public schooled in the new aesthetic norms. Yet this agenda for the construction of a modernized artistic space was accompanied, on the other hand, by a fervent ideological program for an art that was distinctly "Indian," that is, different from the "Western."[5] Although the specific style developed by the Bengal school for a new Indian art failed to hold its ground for very long, the fundamental agenda posed by its efforts continues to be pursued to this day, namely, to develop an art that would be modern and at the same time recognizably Indian.

Alongside the institutions of print-capitalism was created a new network of secondary schools. Once again, nationalism sought to bring this area under its jurisdiction long before the domain of the state had become a matter of contention. In Bengal, from the second half of the nineteenth century, it was the new elite that took the lead in mobilizing a "national" effort to start schools in every part of the province and then to produce a suitable educational literature. Coupled with print-capitalism, the institutions of secondary education provided the space where the new language and literature were both generalized and normalized – outside the domain of the state. It was only when this space was opened up, outside the influence of both the colonial state and the European missionaries, that it became legitimate for women, for instance, to be sent to school. It was also in this period, from around the turn of the century, that the University of Calcutta was turned from an institution of colonial education to a distinctly national institution, in its curriculum, its faculty, and its sources of funding.[6]

Another area in that inner domain of national culture was the family. The assertion here of autonomy and difference was perhaps the most dramatic. The European criticism of Indian "tradition" as barbaric had focused to a large extent on religious beliefs and practices, especially those relating to the treatment of women. The early phase of "social reform" through the agency of the colonial power had also concentrated on the same issues. In that early phase, therefore, this area had been identified as essential to "Indian tradition." The nationalist move began by disputing the choice of agency. Unlike the early reformers, nationalists were not prepared to allow the colonial state to legislate the reform of "traditional" society. They asserted that only the nation itself could have the right to intervene in such an essential aspect of its cultural identity.

As it happened, the domain of the family and the position of women underwent considerable change in the world of the nationalist middle class. It was undoubtedly a new patriarchy that was brought into existence, different from the "traditional" order but also explicitly claiming to be different from the "Western" family. The "new woman" was to be modern, but she would also have to display the signs of national tradition and therefore would be essentially different from the "Western" woman.

The history of nationalism as a political movement tends to focus primarily on its contest with the colonial power in the domain of the outside, that is, the material domain of the state. This is a different history from the one I have outlined. It is also a history in which nationalism has no option but to choose its forms from the gallery of "models" offered by European and American nation-states: "difference" is not a viable criterion in the domain of the material.

In this outer domain, nationalism begins its journey (after, let us remember, it has already proclaimed its sovereignty in the inner domain) by inserting itself into a new public sphere constituted by the processes and forms of the modern (in this case, colonial) state. In the beginning, nationalism's task is to overcome the subordination of the colonized middle class, that is, to challenge the "rule of colonial difference" in the domain of the state. The colonial state, we must remember, was not just the agency that brought the modular forms of the modern state to the colonies; it was also an agency that was destined never to fulfill the normalizing mission of the modern state because the premise of its power was a rule of colonial difference, namely, the preservation of the alienness of the ruling group.

As the institutions of the modern state were elaborated in the colony, especially in the second half of the nineteenth century, the ruling European groups found it necessary to lay down – in lawmaking, in the bureaucracy, in the administration of justice, and in the recognition by the state of a legitimate domain of public opinion – the precise difference between the rulers and the ruled. If Indians had to be admitted into the judiciary, could they be allowed to try Europeans? Was it right that Indians should enter the civil service by taking the same examinations as British graduates? If European newspapers in India were given the right of free speech, could the same apply to native newspapers? Ironically, it became the historical task of nationalism, which insisted on its own marks of cultural difference with the West, to demand that there be no rule of difference in the domain of the state.

In time, with the growing strength of nationalist politics, this domain became more extensive and internally differentiated and finally took on the form of the national, that is, postcolonial, state. The dominant elements of its self-definition, at least in postcolonial India, were drawn from the ideology of the modern liberal-democratic state.

In accordance with liberal ideology, the public was now distinguished from the domain of the private. The state was required to protect the inviolability of the private self in relation to other private selves. The legitimacy of the state in carrying out this function was to be guaranteed by its indifference to concrete differences between private selves – differences, that is, of race, language, religion, class, caste, and so forth.

The trouble was that the moral-intellectual leadership of the nationalist elite operated in a field constituted by a very different set of distinctions – those between the spiritual and the material, the inner and the outer, the essential and the inessential. That contested field over which nationalism had proclaimed its sovereignty and where it had imagined its true community was neither coextensive with nor coincidental to the field constituted by the public/private distinction. In the former field, the hegemonic project of nationalism could hardly make the distinctions of language, religion, caste, or class a matter of indifference to itself. The project was that of cultural "normalization," like, as Anderson suggests, bourgeois hegemonic projects everywhere, but with the all-important difference that it had to choose its site of autonomy from a position of subordination to a colonial regime that had on its side the most universalist justificatory resources produced by post-Enlightenment social thought.

The result is that autonomous forms of imagination of the community were, and continue to be, overwhelmed and swamped by the history of the postcolonial state. Here lies the root of our postcolonial misery: not in our inability to think out new forms of the modern community but in our surrender to the old forms of the modern state. If the nation is an imagined community and if nations must also take the form of states, then our theoretical language must allow us to talk about community and state at the same time. I do not think our present theoretical language allows us to do this.

## NOTES

1 Benedict Anderson, *Imagined Communities: Reflections on the Origin and Spread of Nationalism* (London: Verso, 1983).
2 This is a central argument of my book *Nationalist Thought and the Colonial World: A Derivative Discourse?* (London: Zed Books, 1986).
3 Anderson, *Imagined Communities*, pp. 17–49.
4 Ibid., pp. 28–40.
5 The history of this artistic movement has been recently studied in detail by Tapati Guha-Thakurta, *The Making of a New "Indian" Art: Artists, Aesthetics and Nationalism in Bengal, 1850–1920* (Cambridge: Cambridge University Press, 1992).
6 See Anilchandra Banerjee, "Years of Consolidation: 1883–1904"; Tripurari Chakravarti, "The University and the Government: 1904–24"; and Pramathanath Banerjee, "Reform and Reorganization: 1904–24," in Niharranjan Ray and Pratulchandra Gupta, eds., *Hundred Years of the University of Calcutta* (Calcutta: University of Calcutta, 1957), pp. 129–78, 179–210, and 211–318.

# 30

# Patriotism and Its Futures

## Arjun Appadurai

■ The Form of the Transnation ■

The formula of hyphenation (as in Italian-Americans, Asian-Americans, and African-Americans) is reaching the point of saturation, and the right-hand side of the hyphen can barely contain the unruliness of the left-hand side. Even as the legitimacy of nation-states in their own territorial contexts is increasingly under threat, the idea of the nation flourishes transnationally. Safe from the depredations of their home states, diasporic communities become doubly loyal to their nations of origin and thus ambivalent about their loyalties to America. The politics of ethnic identity in the United States is inseparably linked to the global spread of originally local national identities. For every nation-state that has exported significant numbers of its populations to the United States as refugees, tourists, or students, there is now a delocalized *transnation*, which retains a special ideological link to a putative place of origin but is otherwise a thoroughly diasporic collectivity.[1] No existing conception of Americanness can contain this large variety of transnations.

In this scenario, the hyphenated American might have to be twice hyphenated (Asian-American-Japanese or Native-American-Seneca or African-American-Jamaican or Hispanic-American-Bolivian) as diasporic identities stay mobile and grow more protean. Or perhaps the sides of the hyphen will have to be reversed, and we can become a federation of diasporas: American-Italians, American-Haitians, American-Irish, American-Africans. Dual citizenships might increase if the societies from which we came remain or become more open. We might recognize that diasporic diversity actually puts loyalty to a nonterritorial transnation first, while recognizing that there is a special American way to connect to these global diasporas. America, as a cultural space, will not need to compete with a host of global identities and diasporic loyalties. It might come to be seen as a model of how to arrange one territorial locus (among others) for a cross-hatching of diasporic communities. In this regard, the American problem resembles those of other wealthy industrial democracies (such as Sweden, Germany, Holland, and France), all of which face the challenge of squaring Enlightenment universalisms and diasporic pluralism.

The question is, can a postnational politics be built around this cultural fact? Many societies now face influxes of immigrants and refugees, wanted and unwanted. Others are pushing out groups in acts of ethnic cleansing intended to produce the very people whose preexistence the nation was supposed to ratify. But America may be alone in having organized itself around a modern political ideology in which pluralism is central to the conduct of democratic life. Out of a different strand of its experience, this society has also generated a powerful fable of itself as a land of immigrants. In today's postnational, diasporic world, America is being invited to weld these two doctrines together, to confront the needs of pluralism *and* of immigration, to construct a society *around* diasporic diversity.

But such images as the mosaic, the rainbow, the quilt, and other tropes of complexity-in-diversity cannot supply the imaginative resources for this task, especially as fears of tribalism multiply. Tribes do not make quilts, although they sometimes make confederacies. Whether in debates over immigration, bilingual education, the academic canon, or the underclass, these liberal images have sought to contain the tension between the centripetal pull of Americanness and the centrifugal pull of diasporic diversity in American life. The battles over affirmative action, quotas, welfare, and abortion in America today suggest that the metaphor of the mosaic cannot contain the contradiction between group identities, which Americans will tolerate (up to a point) in cultural life, and individual identities, which are still the nonnegotiable principle behind American ideas of achievement, mobility, and justice.

What is to be done? There could be a special place for America in the new, postnational order, and one that does not rely on either isolationism or global domination as its alternative basis. The United States is eminently suited to be a sort of cultural laboratory and a free-trade zone for the generation, circulation, importation, and testing of the materials for a world organized around diasporic diversity. In a sense, this experiment is already under way. The United States is already a huge, fascinating garage sale for the rest of the world. It provides golf vacations and real estate for the Japanese; business-management ideologies and techniques for Europe and India; soap-opera ideas for Brazil and the Middle East; prime ministers for Yugoslavia; supply-side economics for Poland, Russia, and whoever else will try; Christian fundamentalism for Korea; and postmodern architecture for Hong Kong. By also providing a set of images – Rambo in Afghanistan, "We Are the World," George Bernard Shaw in Baghdad, Coke goes to Barcelona, Perot goes to Washington – that link human rights, consumer style, antistatism, and media glitz, it might be said that the United States is partly accountable for the idiosyncrasies that attend struggles for self-determination in otherwise very different parts of the world. This is why a University of Iowa sweatshirt is not just a silly symbol in the jungles of Mozambique or on the barricades of Beirut. It captures the free-floating yearning for American style, even in the most intense contexts of opposition to the United States. The cultural politics of queer nationality is an example of this contradictory yearning in the United States (Berlant and Freeman 1992). The rest of this yearning is provoked by authoritarian state policies, massive arms industries, the insistently hungry eye of the electronic media, and the despair of bankrupt economies.

Of course, these products and ideas are not the immaculate conceptions of some mysterious American know-how but are precisely the result of a complex environment in which ideas and intellectuals meet in a variety of special settings (such as labs, libraries, classrooms, music studios, business seminars, and political campaigns) to generate, reformulate, and recirculate cultural forms that are fundamentally postnational and diasporic. The role of American musicians, studios, and record companies in the creation of world beat is an excellent example of this sort of down-home but offshore entrepreneurial mentality. Americans are loathe to admit the piecemeal, pragmatic, haphazard, flexible, and opportunistic ways in which these American products and reproducts circulate around the world. Americans like to think that the Chinese have simply bought the virtues of free enterprise; the Poles, the supply side; the Haitians and Filipinos, democracy; and everyone, human rights. We rarely pay attention to the complicated terms, traditions, and cultural styles into which these ideas are folded and thus transformed beyond our recognition. Thus, during the historic events of Tiananmen Square in 1989, when it seemed as if the Chinese people had become democratic overnight, there was considerable evidence that the ways in which different groups in China understood their problems were both internally varied and tied to various specificities of China's history and cultural style.

When Americans see transformations and cultural complications of their democratic vocabulary and style, if they notice them at all, they are annoyed and dismayed. In this misreading of how others handle what we still see as *our* national recipe for success, Americans perform a further act of narcissistic distortion: we imagine that these peculiarly American inventions (democracy, capitalism, free enterprise, human rights) are automatically and inherently interconnected and that our national saga holds the key to the combination. In the migration of our words, we see the victory of our myths. We are believers in terminal conversion.

The American "victory" in the Cold War need not necessarily turn pyrrhic. The fact is that the United States, from a cultural point of view, is already a vast free-trade zone, full of ideas, technologies, styles, and idioms (from McDonald's and the Harvard Business School to the Dream Team and reverse mortgages) that the rest of the world finds fascinating. This free-trade zone rests on a volatile economy; the major cities of the American borderland (Los Angeles, Miami, New York, Detroit) are now heavily militarized. But these facts are of little relevance to those who come, either briefly or for more extended stays, to this free-trade zone. Some, fleeing vastly greater urban violence, state persecution, and economic hardship, come as permanent migrants, legal or illegal. Others are short-term shoppers for clothes, entertainment, loans, armaments, or quick lessons in free-market economics or civil-society politics. The very unruliness, the rank unpredictability, the quirky inventiveness, the sheer cultural vitality of this free-trade zone are what attract all sorts of diasporas to the United States.

For the United States, to play a major role in the cultural politics of a postnational world has very complex domestic entailments. It may mean making room for the legitimacy of cultural rights, rights to the pursuit of cultural difference under public protections and guarantees. It may mean a painful break from a fundamentally Fordist, manufacture-centered conception of the American economy, as we learn to be global information brokers, service providers, style doctors. It may mean embracing as part of our livelihood what we have so far confined to the world of Broadway, Hollywood, and Disneyland: the import of experiments, the production of fantasies, the fabrication of identities, the export of styles, the hammering out of pluralities. It may mean distinguishing our attachment to America from our willingness to die for the United States. This suggestion converges with the following proposal by Lauren Berlant:

> The subject who wants to avoid the melancholy insanity of the self-abstraction that is citizenship, and to resist the lure of self-overcoming the material political context in which she lives, must develop tactics for refusing the interarticulation, now four hundred years old, between the United States and America, the nation and utopia. (1991, 217)

That is, it may be time to rethink monopatriotism, patriotism directed exclusively to the hyphen between nation and state, and to allow the material problems we face – the deficit, the environment, abortion, race, drugs, and jobs – to define those social groups and ideas for which we would be willing to live, and die. The queer nation may only be the first of a series of new patriotisms, in which others could be the retired, the unemployed, and the disabled, as well as scientists, women, and Hispanics. Some of us may still want to live – and die – for the United States. But many of these new sovereignties are inherently postnational. Surely, they represent more humane motives for affiliation than statehood or party affiliation and more interesting bases for debate and crosscutting alliances. Ross Perot's volunteers in 1992 give us a brief, intense glimpse of the powers of patriotism totally divorced from party, government, or state. America may yet construct another narrative of enduring significance, a narrative about the uses of loyalty after the end of the nation-state. In this narrative, bounded territories could give way to diasporic networks, nations to transnations, and patriotism itself could become plural, serial, contextual, and mobile. Here lies one direction for the future of patriotism in a postcolonial world. Patriotism – like history – is unlikely to end, but its objects may be susceptible to transformation, in theory and in practice.

It remains now to ask what transnations and transnationalism have to do with postnationality and its prospects. This relationship requires detailed engagement in its own right, but a few observations are in order. As populations become deterritorialized and incompletely nationalized, as nations splinter and recombine, as states face intractable difficulties in the task of producing "the people," transnations are the most important social sites in which the crises of patriotism are played out.

The results are surely contradictory. Displacement and exile, migration and terror create powerful attachments to ideas of homeland that seem more deeply territorial than ever. But it is also possible to detect in many of these transnations (some ethnic, some religious, some philanthropic, some militaristic) the elements of a postnational imaginary. These elements for those who wish to hasten the demise of the nation-state, for all their contradictions, require both nurture and critique. In this way, transnational social forms may generate not only postnational yearnings but also actually existing postnational movements, organizations, and spaces. In these postnational spaces, the incapacity of the nation-state to tolerate diversity (as it seeks the homogeneity of its citizens, the simultaneity of its presence, the consensuality of its narrative, and the stability of its citizens) may, perhaps, be overcome.

## NOTE

1   I am grateful to Philip Scher, who introduced me to the term *transnation*.

## REFERENCES

Berlant, L. (1991) *The Anatomy of National Fantasy: Hawthorne, Utopia, and Everyday Life.* Chicago: University of Chicago Press.
Berlant, L. and Freeman, E. (1992) Queer Nationality. *Boundary 2* 19(1): 149–80.

# Part VII

# Visual Cultures

# Introduction

## Dominic Pettman

I was checking the mailbox in the lobby of my apartment building, when the Chinese man living downstairs, "Roland," pointed at the small design on the front of my T-shirt. This was a moment in itself, because he had never said a word to me in two years of living in Geneva. Roland said (in English), "I have that picture on my wall." The picture in question is from an ancient Chinese scroll, depicting two people peering down into what appears to be a kind of cooking plate, and which happens to be the feature design of a T-shirt I bought from the gift shop of the National Palace Museum in Taipei, Taiwan. I bought it simply because I liked the picture.

Roland was very excited to recognize this cultural icon on one of his fellow (non-Asian) tenants, and ushered me upstairs to his apartment to see the "original" (which was, of course, a mass-produced copy, but maintained something of the aura of the original in contrast to my T-shirt). Inside Roland's apartment I was surprised to encounter at least five other people, all Chinese youths, whom I had never seen before, jammed into this one-bedroom apartment. This was most certainly illegal, but not necessarily sinister, as they looked more bored than exploited, playing video games and deferring passively to their "uncle." We talked a little about the picture, and I asked if Roland was from Taiwan. "No," he replied. "Mainland China...Taiwan stole our treasure." The students laughed a little: an in-joke which could be fleetingly shared with me, a fellow Pacific Rimmer (i.e., expat Australian).

I suppose it would help if I knew the name of this painting, and at one point I was tempted to find it out, in order to seem all the more worldly and knowledge-able in my capacity as section editor of an anthology of international Cultural

Studies. However, my ignorance of the name of the image in question, worn next to my heart at least once a week, seemed too symptomatic of the state of what we might call "international visual culture" to deny, so that I now feel it only fair to confess my ignorance.

The "sign pollution" of modern life flows across political borders, both erasing and reinforcing the social geography which informs the atlases in our minds, and the ways in which we either feverishly redraw, or stubbornly retrace, these boundaries. By the time we know how to talk, the sighted majority are adept semioticians, constantly – *visually* – reading the signs of "our own" culture, or the culture within which we happen to find ourselves. Of course, in these pomo-globo-poco times, the notion of one homogenous and coherent culture inhabiting one clearly delineated space is beginning to dissolve, as the diasporic and the deracinated saturate different social fabrics. Which is why we voraciously *read* the signs around us, cognitively mapping and navigating our way through daily life. For instance, we can be reasonably sure that a small building adorned with Arabic writing, and displaying various vegetables, is a Middle-Eastern grocery store; just as we can almost bet our life savings that a young dreadlocked male wearing a necklace with a copper marijuana leaf also indulges in the signified itself. Appearances, however (we are constantly reminded), can be deceiving.

Which is to say that the notion of "visual culture" is almost tautological, in that we can hardly conceive of *culture* outside of an inherent optical element, as many have repeatedly affirmed (Walter Benjamin, Martin Jay, and Jonathon Crary, amongst a multitude of others).[1] That primal scene of the Western *polis*, Plato's *Republic*, begins with a feast for the eye, emphasizing novelty and difference:

> I went down yesterday to the Piraeus with Glaucon the son of Ariston, that I might offer up my prayers to the goddess; and also because I wanted to see in what manner they would celebrate the festival, which was a new thing. I was delighted with the procession of the inhabitants; but that of the Thracians was equally, if not more, beautiful. When we had finished our prayers and viewed the spectacle, we turned in the direction of the city. (1)

Further on, the same text ponders the visual violence which can be visited on the eye when switching between different spectacular modes: from shadows and other simulacra to sunlight. Indeed, what Michel de Certeau called "a cancerous growth of vision" (1984: xxi) – and what some refer to as scopophilia – is one of the defining aspects of our age, if not our species, so that we have now reached the point described by Jean Baudrillard whereby "the virtual camera is in our heads. No need of a medium to reflect our problems in real time: every existence is telepresent to itself (1996: 26).

One thing to remember, however, especially in the context and purpose of this anthology, is that "we" is never fixed, never easily identified, and sometimes even illegible to the point of invisibility: ("al-Qaeda" being the most recent and – ironically – "spectacular" instance of a community which is both everywhere and nowhere; delineated only by traces). Moreover, the flood of patriotic, digitally manipulated photographs of Osama Bin Laden after the September 11 attacks speaks volumes about the transitional stage we are witness to, whereby new technologies act as the conduits for age-old intercultural reflexes and conflicts.[2] Similarly, albeit on a far less ominous register, we could point to the gallery of Photoshopped pictures of the French football team, after their humiliating exit from the 2002 World Cup, as an interesting (and practically *instantaneous*) development in visual culture. Those with the access and the skills now seem to express themselves through this new art-form, inflicting global *charivaris* on the dupes or demons of the day, and diffusing them through the internet for a potentially global audience.

Such an unprecedented scenario suggests that the demands on our reading skills are only increasing, despite any alleged "decline in literacy." Now we must read between the pixels, as well as the lines; recognizing that a picture can indeed be worth a thousand words (unless it is a *.tif* file, in which case it is worth half a billion words – at least in terms of storage space). Thus we (there's that "we" again), internalize the parallel transition, the change in cultural emphasis, from Derrida's *logos* to Naomi Klein's logos, from script to icon.

Many, if not most, cultural forms are "visual," and yet "culture itself" is stubbornly difficult to represent: that is, holistically, through images alone. Heidegger's depiction of the "world picture" amounts to a compulsion to visualize, map, grid, and – above all – represent something as elusive as *the world*. As such, globalistic discourses are often reduced to a jigsaw puzzle, with no guiding master-picture and less than half the pieces. "Seeing seems to be a rather calculating business, and all this makes one wonder whether one can ever 'see' something of which one has had no previous knowledge."[3] And to complicate things further, we must contend with the realization that much of what we call culture can only be captured negatively, like those distant planets identified by astronomers via their silhouettes and shadows. Perhaps we are less what we show than what we *refuse* to show (which is not always the same thing as hiding).

Benjamin warns of the potential loss of critical distance when confronted with the power of the image – particularly the moving image – and the distracting capacities of the spectacle. Indeed, this somatic confusion is captured by none other than Marge Simpson, who admits to her children that watching a St. Patrick's parade releases a whole flood of emotions within her, "joy, excitement... *looking*." Others, however, relish the critical semiotic challenges which contemporary visual culture may throw in all directions. Today's Afghan carpets are just as likely to include helicopters and other symbols of war, as simple "apolitical" designs, and this tells us something (just as it tells "them" something, most probably, radically different). Tamil Tigers, now thankfully finding themselves in a time of relative calm, are busy churning out low-budget war movies, using the actual detritus of the recent struggles. This too tells us something worth telling ourselves and each other.

Which brings us to the contributions for this section, all responses to this continuous avalanche of visual material,[4] in very different ways, and utilizing very different sites, signs, and texts. Simon During unpacks his own concept of the "global popular" in an edited version of an influential essay "Toward the Global Popular," which is often cited but no longer available.[5] Focusing on the spectacularized genealogy of Arnold Schwarzenegger, During explores the cultural translation of this "diffuse phenomenon," paying particular attention to the economic and aesthetic shifts which compel us to think through methodology as much as a passing moment in recent history. While it does not explicitly thematize visual culture, this piece – via cinema and its antecedents – both accounts for, and utilizes, a rigorously heterogeneous model of techno-optic globalization.

In a complementary and contrasting piece, "Sex Machine: Global Hypermasculinity and Images of the Asian Woman in Modernity," Lili Ling discusses the parallel media constructions of a "global hyperfeminity." Beginning with three versions of globalization which currently dominate the *popular* imagination – "the West is best," "the West vs. the rest," and "Jihad vs. McWorld" – Ling focuses on East Asia and the "culture wars" waged between discursive categories such as tradition and modernity, East and West, young and old, hip and unhip, masculine and feminine. She then rallies against certain critical perspectives, including liberalism, Marxism, and institutionalism, which reify globalization as a cultural force emanating purely from the West.

The contribution by Rachel Hughes, "The Abject Artefacts of Memory," also explores the relationship between hypervisibility, bodies, intercultural framing, and visual culture, however in a far more sinister register (itself reinforcing the frighteningly smooth transition between the spectacular blockbusters of Hollywood and TV advertising, and the "atrocity exhibitions" associated with a century of diligent genocides). Hughes discusses the politics of representation around a 1997 exhibition of Cambodian photographs which were produced by Khmer Rouge perpetrators during the period 1975–9. Focusing particularly on the responses of visitors and curators to the photographs, displayed at the Museum of Modern Art in New York, Hughes argues that the "contemporary propensity to memorialize" hampers attempts to specify and politicize the past violence of states and peoples.

Ella Shohat and Robert Stam's contribution addresses questions of Eurocentrism, postcolonialism, and transnationalism, particularly as they impact on the place of visual culture within Cultural Studies. And rounding off the contributions, Sudeep Dasgupta's "Visual Culture and the Place of Identity" argues that "culture" is far more embedded in material and mediamatic practices than many contemporary critics are willing to admit. Dasgupta emphasizes the interconnection of discourses of history, tradition, economic change, and contemporary *realpolitik*.

Of course, it remains to be seen if "visual culture," as a general interdisciplinary field, is circumscribed enough to keep the necessary coherence needed to continue as such, but for the moment its very flexibility seems to be fostering an interesting dialogue between vocabularies as varied as anthropology, art history, phenomenology, cinema studies, human geography, cognitive theory, architecture, industrial and graphic design. (And who knows, perhaps ophthalmologists may have something to say about the matter, as the bibliography generated by this area develops further.)[6]

The prominent practitioner W. J. T. Mitchell believes that "this unnecessary thing" – visual culture – acts as a "dangerous supplement" to the classic pincer movements of art history and aesthetic theory. Moreover, he believes that as a quasi-field or pseudo-discipline, visual culture has the potential to fold certain questions back onto other related domains, so that it becomes possible to "make seeing show itself" (an important contribution to an area only beginning to come to grips with the realization that "scopic regimes can be overturned repeatedly without any visible effect on either visual or political culture") (2002: 175).

One thing, however, is for certain. Western models of optical perception have changed dramatically since the Middle Ages, when vision was considered to be completely passive; the image imprinted on the brain in the manner of a seal onto a wax tablet.[7] Today researchers are realizing that vision is a far more active process, and that an enormous amount of what we see – or what we *think* we see – is actually "filled in" by the brain, in order to minimize processing power (according to the same logic as virtual memory in a computer). As a consequence of these findings, some scientists are already claiming that the brain "secretes reality," and thus the eyes are in fact two-way organs: absorbing photons as previously thought, but also emitting them, like human headlights.[8]

Vision, then, becomes the fountainhead of the individual (who in turn is an extension of the culture they happen to emerge from). Thus, almost all visions – from the sublime to the banal – are *ecstatic*, in that they occur largely outside of ourselves. Indeed everything we classify as art, language, and literature is the result of the attempt to both comprehend and communicate these visions.

Visions which always already originate from elsewhere.

## NOTES

1  The nonsighted minority "see" in other ways, as discussed at more length in Kenneth J. Gergen's *The Saturated Self*, and captured beautifully by Alfred Bester in his astonishing science fiction novel *The Stars My Destination*.

2  For a more detailed discussion of this phenomenon see my article, "From the 7-11 to September 11: Popular Propaganda and the Internet's War on Terrorism," available at www.blackjelly.com/Mag3/features/osama.pdf.

3  Otto Lowenstein, *The Senses*, quoted in McLuhan, Fiore, and Agel, *War and Peace in the Global Village* (San Francisco: Hardwired, 1997 [1968]), p.10.

4  Images, of course, are often embedded within or framed by sound; an aspect that should not be forgotten when fetishizing the pictorial over the aural.

5  In this volume, Cindy Patton refers to the "simultaneous habitation" of certain practices and discourses, reminding us that "visual culture" can also be "popular," and/or "technological," despite the practical necessities of dividing anthologies into autonomous categories.

6 Even the inaugural issue of the *Journal of Visual Culture*, first published in 2002, prudently sidesteps any attempt to delineate the field as such, preferring to leave it up to the articles themselves to trace possible disciplinary borders, rather than ask them to explicitly address a pre-established core of concerns. I would take this opportunity also to remind the reader of those all-too-familiar limitations of space and time, without which I would have included pieces from each of the above areas. One of the stated purposes of this present volume, however, is to foster more activity on the crossroads between such domains and approaches, to which I hope this section contributes as much in terms of general inspiration and momentum, as specific areas of writing and research.

7 See Giorgio Agamben's exemplary chapter "Eros at the Mirror" in his book *Stanzas* (Minneapolis: University of Minnesota Press, 1993).

8 BBC, *The Brain Story*, part 3/6: *The Mind's Eye*, 2001. Presented by Susan Greenfield.

## REFERENCES

Baudrillard, J. (1996). *Cool Memories II*. Trans. C. Turner. Cambridge: Polity Press, 1996.

de Certeau, M. (1984). *The Practice of Everyday Life*. Trans. S. Rendall. Berkeley: University of California Press, 1984.

Mitchell, W. J. T. (2002). "Showing and Seeing: A Critique of Visual Culture." *Journal of Visual Culture* 1(2): 165–81.

# 31

# Visual Culture and the Place of Modernity

## Sudeep Dasgupta

> The spectacle is not a collection of images; rather, it is a social relationship between people that is mediated by images.
>
> Guy Debord, *The Society of the Spectacle*

Within contemporary Cultural Studies, the establishment of space as both a central focus of study and a crucial dimension for theorizing identity is evidenced in analyses including that of diaspora, architecture, cultural identity, and postcolonial politics.[1] Visual culture is one prime location where the question of space and globalization come together. At one level, the shifts in technological transmission have reduced the pedagogical relationship between the nation-state and the citizens confined within its territory. For example, the state control of television in India collapsed with the rise of satellite broadcasting. At another level, the movements of people beyond the borders of the nation-state entailed a corresponding targeting by global media of different groups who "shared a culture" that was problematic-ally seen as "national" in character. The complex spatial character of much visual culture, however, tends to be seen at the level of the "spectacle," in Debord's terms, that is, a focus on culture in relative isolation to questions of politics, economics, and the distribution of power. Part of the burden of this chapter is to map the complex spatial configurations of visual culture across the chains of value-coding; value here being understood in cultural and economic terms. The necessity of such a focus is crucial if international Cultural Studies is not to remain cordoned off simply at the level of the "cultural," whereby globalization is narrowly conceived in terms of expansion, rather than the unevenness and inequality through which the global cultural economy is discernible in visual culture.

Often the use of the concept of "space" has been confusing given that it either collapses or ignores the different valences that attach to such a notion. Thus, we have the "space of the imagination," the "space of the nation," the "spacing in the text," the "space of subjectivity." My brief here is not to investigate this complex phenomenon; rather, I will argue for situating the debates around space through an analysis of global media including the internet, television, and films, and the role they play in constructing particular notions of "place," whether these be concrete and lived, affective or representational in form. In particular, I want to locate the dimensions of contemporary mass-mediated constructions of identity around the Indian nation, as a form of dialectical decoding and recoding of capitalism in its complex, economic, social, and political relations. The spatial turn in relation to globalization can be adduced from Deleuze and Guattari's argument that the abstract form of contemporary capitalism continually deterritorializes and reterritorializes the complex of power relations within which politics becomes possible. For our present concerns, global media such as satellite television and the internet overflow the logic of the nation-state and its public (citizens), and in a certain sense, the national territory becomes increasingly part of a larger planetary space for the circulation and consumption of media. While calling attention to these deterritorializations, I will argue, through a discussion of nationalism, that contemporary forms of politics mediated by global communication networks are involved in a complex dialectic between space as an evanescent and fleeting dimension of social reality and "place" as the contingent and fabricated ground through which politics is being played out.

For example: D. N. Rodowick, in his latest impressive contribution to media studies, argues for the centrality of a spatial understanding of meaning and signification in relation to philosophy and new media.[2] He is inspired primarily by that most postmodern of media, MTV. Through a reading of Jean-François Lyotard's now classic *Discours, figure* Rodowick argues that spatiality consistently undermines the possibility of fixed meaning, of signification itself. The "order of discourse," argues Rodowick, is partly undermined by that nonlinguistic, *visual* space in the text of discourse which cannot be subsumed within the paradigm of oppositions of structuralist linguistics. The visual (hence MTV) provides one of the conditions of possibility for thinking the spacing in the text of written discourse that opens up to a condition of becoming, of potentialities and of expressibility rather than signification (of a prior referent). That is, the specifically visual becomes a warrant for the claim that spatiality disrupts any possibility of signifying a referent, and realism itself. Similarly, Jacques Derrida's insistence on the spacing in the text that marks the impossible fit between signifier and signified opens up a space of undecidability which Homi Bhabha has called "Third Space" and which provides the ground for thinking a politics of minoritization that refuses both the identitarian logic of the Cartesian subject and the pedagogic project of the nation-state.[3] Here "space" is extended from its strictly literary and philosophical domain to that of subject formation and the nation-state. Interrogating the politics of contemporary Hindu Nationalism in its particular transnational dimensions and the role of media in this process might be one way of interrogating the critical purchase of such a postmodernist focus on space in authors like Rodowick and Bhabha.

"Social space is a social product," argues Henri Lefebvre in *The Production of Space*.[4] In this useful materialist reading of space, he differentiates between spatial practices, representational spaces, and the spaces of representation. This tripartite division can be understood in terms of the lived, the perceived, and the conceived. Spatial practice within particular social relations at a given moment in history comprises what Lefebvre calls spatial practice. The ongoing lived negotiation of movement and confinement, the channeling of mobility through the dialectic of access and prohibition, itself generated by the organization of spatial relations of power, are the focus of this dimension. Representations of space such as architecture, urban planning, and – for our purposes – the circuits for the production, distribution, and consumptions of goods and services, are embedded in a particular logic of contemporary capitalism. I stress "contemporary," for globalization is hardly a new phenomenon, and it takes on particular historical forms. Needless to say, then, a critical engagement with discourses of space must entail not just questions of place, but also history. Representational spaces are directly lived by dominated groups yet mediated by symbolic forms and cultural repertoires, and the importance of the visual cannot be underestimated in this context. Social relations of power, aesthetic practices of visuality, and physical constructions of spatial relations, provide a differentiated and differential framework for understanding the constitution of space – not as an empty dimension to be filled nor a quasi-transcendental alibi for collapsing philosophy and social reality. Further, these dimensions cannot be understood outside of the question of history, which in the guise of "time" has been superseded in the postmodernist fascination with space. The logic of that refusal is itself suspect, for it is based on a simplification that asserts that since time has been understood as linear, teleological, and therefore totalitarian, space must become the prime signifier and instrument for understanding postmodernity. That is, the ghost of Hegel can now be laid to rest, it is claimed, given that dialectical thinking has been surpassed by the discourse of difference and deference. Operating in the background of this chapter, then, is a call for revisiting the question of temporality whose complexity was elaborated, for example, in the work of the Frankfurt School, Walter Benjamin, and their reading of Marx and Hegel. Besides history, the importance of practice and of product are crucial; that is, space is understood as the historically specific result of a complex ensemble of social practices. Read in this way, space cannot be figured, like Rodowick and Bhabha argue, as a kind of enabling condition of possibility. That is, a motor for a nonsignifying and non-essentialist identity politics, given that it has no ontological Being that must always exist within any act of signification (Rodowick) or enunciation (Bhabha). In the following section I will explore the historical and geographical dimensions of the spatial politics of Hindu nationalism and the role of media in order to elaborate on a visual-materialist reading of space as "place."

Needless to say, my argument is not that once one attends to history or institutions one supplements or adds onto the philosophical and conceptual arguments of space; rather, I am insisting that to collapse the conceptual into the historical and the social is to engage in a sort of conceptual megalomania which Theodor Adorno called "onto-theology."[5] If there is indeed a gap between the concept and the referent, assuming the irrelevance of mediation between the two results in certain fault-lines developing in the argument. This conceptual overinflation is one mark of the discourse of postmodern space. The other fastens on the sheer suffusion of the social by media imagery: the unmooring of the image from the space of the nation such that the transnational suffusion of images leads to a focus on spatial dislocation in which contemporary subjectivity is unable to ground itself. In the first section, I will locate the historical situation of the media scene – in particular, television – and map out the spatial overlap between India and the developed West in political and popular discourse on media. I will also situate this overlap in relation to the collapse between the "Indian" space of religious nationalism and the western focus on consumerism. In the second section, I will elaborate on the construction of place through the spatially dissonant use of the internet as well as through the representational form of film.

## ▓ India's Place in Capitalist Modernity ▓

When television was introduced in India after initial reservations by its first Prime Minister, it was perceived as a state organ whose function was to educate and inform a developing country along the trajectory to modernization and progress. The role of commercial interests was severely curtailed until the paradoxical success of a pedagogically conceived soap opera, *Hum Log*, whose message of family planning and harmony was drowned out by the success of the sale of its sponsor's product, instant soup. As the control of the state unraveled through the 1980s and the early 1990s, a major technological change in broadband broadcasting elsewhere was to have a lasting impact on the nation's mode of imagining itself to itself and to the rest of the world – and that was satellite television. Suddenly exposed to global networks, particularly CNN, middle-class urban audiences lapped up the images of war and destruction (the "televised" Gulf war in 1990) fed to them via cable and satellite, as well as the panoply of consumerist lifestyles and commodities on offer in the imaginary, perceptual field of the visible and the aural. *Santa Barbara*, *The Bold and the Beautiful*, *MTV Asia*, and other programming offered a media landscape that was to have a profound effect on the production of space in all its forms within the country. For at the very same time, the country was forced to open up to the world market at the behest of the IMF and the World Bank, and the middle-classes were to reap the benefit of the accelerated consumption potential that their rising incomes made possible within a growing market for luxury goods. The nexus between advanced forms of capital accumulation (primarily finance capital) and technologically enabled spatial extension of the social world of images and things had a profound impact on many different dimensions of everyday life.[6]

It is at this particular conjuncture that visual culture provides a crucial index for understanding what the "international" might mean in Cultural Studies. For the images that suffuse what Yuri Lottman calls the "semiosphere" are not just signifiers of some flattened notion of contemporary power relations under globalization. Rather, viewed from the vantage-point of a particular, differentiated audience of Indian mass media, the images of "global culture" provide an eloquent index of the place of the local as a shifting locus of power relations within the spatial organization (and representation) of the global. For example, in the very structure of the soap opera *Hum Log*, as well as the character of the imagery, the clear shift from a discourse of pedagogy to one of consumerism can be identified. This visual resignification of the place of the "nation" in the context of globalization is much more evident in the contemporary moment where satellite television has become a mainstay in the cultural sphere of mass consumption.

For example, in Channel [V]'s music show, *Cabaret*, clips of famous cabaret songs from films of the days gone by are re-presented by its hostess, "Raspberry Dolly." When we see German-born Helen, one of the most popular stars of the big screen in the 1970s, performing her risqué cabaret numbers in shimmering gowns one is immediately confronted with another image of the Indian nation – as one where popular culture was not the preserve of some "traditional Indianness," but already global in certain ways, crossing some of the boundaries that traditional patriarchal discourses of the character of the Indian nation were repeating. At this level already, then, the visual culture of the present cannot be seen as the "re-presentation" of some "national tradition" of sobriety and culture, but one which is already drawing the tradition/modernity division into question. In the guise of *Cabaret*, though, a mise-en-abyme structure is set into motion, since the songs from old films are introduced by Raspberry Dolly, herself clad in her crimson off-shoulder gown, a shimmering boa draped around her naked shoulders. However, as presenter, her dress and style of speaking (a combination of Hindi and English) is a marker of a very contemporary moment in Indian mass culture. That is to say, it would have been unthinkable prior to the economic and cultural globalization of the Indian nation-state to have had such presenters, addressing their audiences in this language, and dressed in such daringly "Western" ways. However, this kind of presentation of the effects of cultural globalization is grounded firstly in a notion of the Indian past that is not exactly "traditional." This double movement, grounding a contemporary visual text in something specifically resonant with Indian film culture, while simultaneously choosing that aspect of the past which is hardly "traditional" ( this is not "folk dances from the Northeast," for example) emblematizes the particular discursive flexibility of a certain form of cultural nationalism in India at the contemporary moment. If the example above highlights the problematic status of the past ("tradition" as the ground for Indian culture) and marks the contemporary moment as one which provides the conditions of possibility for the style of presentation (Raspberry Dolly), a further example will highlight the contradictory and conflictual character that marks "global culture."

Take the singer Baba Sehgal, and his hit song "Ab Mein Vengaboy" ("Now I'm a Vengaboy"). This megastar, whose songs have an almost revolving airtime on MTV India, Channel [V], and other channels, provides one instance of a kind of hybrid articulation: one in which articulating one's identity is located neither in a primal scene of Indian tradition, nor a wholehearted appropriation of western pop. This "lonely boy from Bhatinda," sporting a crew-cut, fur coat, stars-and-stripes boxing pants, and heavy Indian silver jewelry, emblematizes a particular form of identity which through these visual markers constructs an affective notion of belonging to a place – a place which does not disavow a constructed "indianness," while at the same time embracing those images of global culture which were vigorously rejected in the preglobalized cultural space of India. It is an identity that circulates especially widely on satellite TV networks in a slew of different strategies, including Indian film music programming, fashion shows, talk shows, soap operas, and the like. The mode of address is very street-cred Hindi slang, the kind of "lingo" western observers mistakenly characterized as postmodern in their reading of Salman Rushdie, yet sprinkled with generous doses of English, this amalgam commonly called "Hinglish" in marketese. This is not the anglicized, colonial English which young people in private schools still learn, but the vernacularized version. According to Sehgal's songs, one can play the *dhol* (Indian drum) but rap can also add some extra spice. Further, identity is understood here in the easy consumption and sporting of various identities: "Kabi I look like Jackie Chan, Kabi Like Amitabh Bachchan [Sometimes I look like Jackie Chan, Sometimes like Amitabh Bachchan]. I am coming in Autorickshaw. My favorite comic Laurel and Hardy. Very Infectious, I have a Lexus." The smooth shuffling between expensive cars and autorickshaws, rap and Punjabi songs provides an accurate articulation of the present complex notions of belonging, the habitus through which a certain form of urban middle-class youth culture roots itself in the idiolect of Indian everyday life, as well as the aspirations and assumptions of certain western lifestyles under contemporary globalization.

This form of articulating contemporary Indian identity might be problematically called "hybrid," but it is one which is expressed in terms of a strongly consumerist discourse of a commodity culture that is accessible to a certain section of the petit-bourgeoisie in India; a class of the population whose power has grown exponentially in economic terms and which finds this power addressed repeatedly in the mass media. Music television, for example, has been addressing the youth market in India with particular enthusiasm, and here, at the level of institutional analysis, one can trace the power-lines of inclusion and exclusion which a flattened notion of hybridity fails to capture. The MTV and Brand Equity Youth Marketing Forum in 1998 in Bombay provided the platform for MTV to "humanize" itself as a channel with a social purpose, while simultaneously delivering the trendy set in person to advertisers and marketeers. In February 1999, the channel announced for the second year running it would host the forum. As Arun Arora, CEO of *The Economic Times*, put it, "This is an opportunity for the industry to share with each other our collective understanding of the largest consumer segment in the world."[7] The popularity of the channel stems precisely from this convergence of its middle-class urban youth audience and its extensive capacity, through programming and organizing campaigns within civil society, to deliver them to consumer good corporations. Sunil Lulla, MTV General Manager, paraphrases its strategy as that of "Indianize, Humanize, and Humourize."[8] In this example, the relationship between visual images as signifiers of the contemporary "global" discourse of a fabricated local nationalism on the one hand, and the institutional discourses and practices of consumerism and "humanism" on the other, enable a more complex, differential, and sedimented understanding of the "international" in Cultural Studies – as an uneven dynamic, that constructs specifically directed discourses of the "local" within the context of capitalist globalization.

A recent MTV station ID figures this complex relationship in condensed fashion to great effect. Its handheld-camera aesthetic follows two middle-aged, kurta-clad men who stuff *paan* (betel leaf), stamped with the MTV logo, into their mouth. In the next shot, a close-up of the MTV logo in white against a white wall, is splattered with jets of *paan* juice, presumably from the men. As the juice drips down, the voice-over states "MTV India." The resonance of such an address, sedimented in the mundane experience of chewing *paan*, the blood-red stained walls of buildings combined with the simultaneously appreciative and denigratory gesture of flashing the MTV logo and covering it in spit, condenses in a few seconds the attitude of most viewers to the channel. Spitting on something is hardly a mark of warmth or affection. But when the object spat on (the logo of MTV) is presented by MTV itself, this self-abasing gesture functions precisely as a seduction. What could be more flattering than the symbol of global media power (MTV) abasing itself in front of the mighty Indian viewer? Just another example of hybrid "global culture," or a clever mode of self-presentation through obeisance to the empowered subject of global India?

Is this then yet another example of the localization of global symbolic imagery into the idiom of some "native" dialect? Obviously not, for the simple reason that what is local here is hardly confined to the nation and its culture. Even the spit ejaculated on the symbol of MTV is a sort of baptism, a contorted sign of welcome to the brotherhood of the global citizen/consumer. It confers a legitimacy (the stain of the "nation"?) on a symbol of what would have been termed "western materialism and corruption" in an older Indian discourse of nonalignment. And, after all, it is an advertisement for MTV on MTV, a signifier ensconced within the bosom of the institution it so ambivalently represents. To call this "hybridity" would be too easy, for hybridity as a concept tends to flatten out the structurally existing lines of force which mark what elements combine to produce the hybrid. In much visual culture, for example, the resonances that particular far-flung imagery possess are the result of decision-making processes which concretize questions of interest, access, and power. Hybrid realities such as those of fisherwomen forced into prostitution in cities because fishing rights have been sold to multinationals, will always remain virtual – not finding their way to our television screens as easily as the glamorous mish-mash of fashion styles where the West discovers India, for example, and themes an entire year on its high streets, in its movie theatres and music stores.

## ■ Spatial Practices and the Representation of Indian Identity ■

Much attention within contemporary Cultural Studies has rightly sought to high-light the ideological and exclusionary dimensions of the discourse of the "local" (in the nation, for example) by highlighting the production of locality, rather than assuming its fixed, already-existing objecthood. But what might it look like to shift the perspective from the invented character of the "local" to that of the global? For instance, in the case of a country like India, integrated now to a large extent within capitalist globalization, how does the "world out there" get represented in visual culture? Do such images point just to the production of locality ("Indian culture" in its global avatar), or might they not also provide a visual repertoire for imagining the "global" world out there that the Indian nation so desires? My question here thus seeks to shift the emphasis of the question away from the fabrication of the local within globalization, to the fabrication of the global within the context of discourses of the local – here, a certain form of "Indian" identity.

In this section I shall look at the production of space through the *use* of media such as the internet, as well as the *formal* and *substantive* characteristics of representational practice, through an example of film, in the production of na-tional and affective space under capitalism. This practice is mediated through the consumption of films, television, and increasingly the internet, as well as the representational spaces that Lefebvre identifies, including aesthetic practices within such media. The internet has proven one such medium for recoding the deterri-torializing consequences of global capitalism. While much is made of the post-Fordist character of "our" postmodern economic landscape, and the catalytic role of miniaturization and electronic technology, the internet is able to harness and lubricate some of the most fundamentally identitarian logics of subject formation. These shifts are, of course, not reminiscent of some Cartesian subject; a return of the repressed of tradition, but actively engage with the complex spatial dimensions of our contemporary reality.[9] For example, diasporic groups primarily in the overdeveloped West are at the forefront of using the internet in fabricating notions of Hindu identity that span the ages and must be protected against the onslaught of Muslims. A collection of websites under the umbrella of the Global Hindu Elec-tronic Network (GHEN) provides one such virtual location where the concrete lived spaces of the diaspora are linked not only to each other but to temples in India, to the redrawing of Indian identity and its physical and symbolic borders. (Such virtual locations are also crucial in funding political organizations back home.) The local temple in the suburb of Monroeville outside Pittsburgh, which I visited often, for example, was the nodal point for Indian Hindus across the US and Canada, while actual temples in India can be "visited" and prayers offered online, right down to the breaking of coconuts. Moreover, the cyber-mall on this one site (www.eprarthana.com) offers designer Ganesha clocks on sale with your credit card. Here, the electronically mediated spatial dispersal of "postmodernity" is mediated by marble, concrete, and stone temples, by highways and cyberspace, by the movements of people and money; and the space thus constructed is a complex product of physical, affective, and social space where aesthetic representation, discursive spatial practice, and the spatial practice of the social all form a complex ensemble of productive practices.

In the Rajkumar Santoshi's controversial film *Lajja* (2002), we glimpse the spatial recording of identity in its transnational dimension to great effect. Ostensibly a film about the degraded status of women in India, in which the four main characters – all named after different forms of the Goddess Sita – undergo different trials, the film could be easily read as an example of postmodern space in aesthetic practice, what Lefebvre calls the "nonverbal" – that is, visual aspects of representational practice. The stunning opening scene is comprised by dramatic aerial shots of the Manhattan skyline over which floats a red *saree*, accompanied by the soundtrack of women's screams and the Budapest Philharmonic Orchestra. The immorality of the West, here embodied by the Indian husband who has no qualms about partner-swapping, is matched by the sorry state of women in India, where rape, bride-burning, and female infanticide mark their everyday lives. The film moves between these two continents, whose immorality is couched in consumerist excess and visual spectacle (the opulence of the West is highlighted by nightclubs, cityscapes, huge mansions) and physical and material deprivation (caste slavery, poverty, dowry, rape).[10] The spatial dislocation and figural excess (in Rodowick's terms) is nevertheless grounded in one particular symbol – the *Bharatiya Nari*, or chaste Hindu woman, whose status becomes the signifier of the nation's honor and civilization. In its melodramatically staged attack on the Indian state, Hinduism (in particular on Ram, the leading figure in the Hindu Nationalist pantheon), as well as the Indian nation, the film harnesses and resignifies the complex spatial dimensions of the symbolic and material space of the nation. An indication of this complex dialectic between spatial mobility and grounded embodiment were the attacks on the film and its maker by the Shiv Sena in India, whose outrage was aimed not at wife-swapping and the Manhattan urban nightlife, but at the implication that the various avatars of Sita might question the central discourses of Hinduism on the status of women.

The film functioned as a fulcrum on which were balanced a range of different aims: an assault on the status of Indian women across the globe, both in the materialistic and immoral West as well as within the repressive religious idioms of India; a fantasmagoric spectacle of conspicuous consumption that offered a feast to the eye, whether in the elaborate portrayal of a Hindu wedding or the sexualised landscape of a New York nightclub; a range of sexualized imagery from the explicit and provocative dance performances in the West to the melodramatic visual and aural depictions of rape and physical abuse. The director received a government exemption on tax for peppering the film with public-service announcements about the status of women, female infanticide, and dowry, while reaping enormous profits from the presence of a star cast, elaborate dance sequences, and a representation of the glitzy life of the West. All these dimensions lock into and work through different spatial dimensions of contemporary life, including the affective space of nostalgia of the diaspora, and the consumerist discourses of upward and outward mobility of India's middle classes. It circulated within the physical spaces of theaters throughout the world, the private homes of diasporic audiences through video, global reviews, and through the numerous websites spawned to discuss films, including its own official online address. Here the representational spaces of global postmodernity become articulated to specific concerns that are grounded in the question of national identity and the status of women. Simultaneously, national identity and the status of women are increasingly addressed not through the delimited territorial space of the nation-state or the symbolic space of "Indian" society, but circulate through audiences and imagery that take in the West and the Rest. This sort of "nomadism" seems to have a particular field of legibility that is confined by a nationalist discourse. The film begins with a dramatic and seemingly rhetorical question by the director: "After all, isn't the measure of a nation's greatness measured by the status of its women?" The universalist implications of this question can only be answered in the idiom of a religious nationalist discourse on the Indian woman.

## ■ Conclusion ■

Lefebvre's intervention in the intellectual discourse on space and postmodernity was at least twofold: first, he distinguishes between different forms of spatial practice in order to prevent the sort of conceptual conflation that results in contemporary critical discourse; second, he highlights the role of capitalism in the current fracturing of the spatial coordinates of lived reality. This latter point is argued by first volatilizing and historicizing capitalism as a complex ensemble of multiple forms of capitalist relations, some industrial and commercial, others financial and speculative, that do not share either the same structure of temporality nor the same spatial dimensions. This point must also be understood in the context of Raymond Williams's important reminder that the "base" in the architectural metaphor of base–superstructure in Marxism implied both historical change and contradiction, as well as a processual understanding of social relations and not an object or thing.[11] All these arguments frame my discussion of media, postmodernism, and place above. The profound shifts in the ecology of media imagery that circulates through the globe are channeled by highly capitalized institutions whose interests are not purely cultural. The spaces they move through are linked to the scattering of people who have complex affective links to the imaginary of the Indian nation, whether nostalgia for home among the diaspora or anticipatory voyeurism for those left out of the global cultural marketplace. Secondly, this dizzying array of imagery that is graspable in the aesthetics of fragmentation, disjuncture, and difference does not exemplify the absolute character of the floating signifier, unmoored from all possibility of meaning and signification. *Contra* Rodowick, then, the visual does ground itself in history, in specific networks of spatial relations where meaning is constructed in complex ways, and articulated to a politics of location. "Hindu" India is indeed a geographical and affective space, and it is through the supposedly "postmodern" fragmentation of space that it is continually made and remade. Here the question of form and aesthetic representation is crucial, appealing to the desire for empowerment through consumption, nostalgic longing, and moral superiority, as well as celebrating the global membership of the Indian nation in planetary space. These relate to the specific forms of immigration, the classes with the possibility of mobility, the mobility of different forms of capital, and the consequent redrawing of lived space.

Further, if the complex, temporally differential and spatially dynamic dimensions of the multiple forms of capitalism mark globalization, then surely it must be taken seriously given that it is in the context of globalization that media are seen as prime signifiers of postmodernity.[12] I have argued that here the commodity form of value finds itself concretized in the representational aesthetic of contemporary mass-mediated global visual culture. This too has important spatial implications for how the political space of the nation, the economic spaces of globalization, and the affective spaces of nationalism are harnessed in different ways. Indeed, we do find a proliferation of different forms of representation from the old black-and-white films of the sixties, contemporary MTV montage, transnationally located cinema – and each have their own peculiar temporality and space within both the media scene and within history. To view this plurality as pure difference and postmodern pastiche is to fail to recognize that each are concretely linked to different logics of cultural, economic, and political space. The proliferation of styles is not thus a dizzying descent into the postmodern abyss of nonmeaning, but can be understood as the *channeled* access to representational forms and spaces and linked to spatial practices themselves.

The descent into space in contemporary theories of postmodernity can be critiqued by attending to the historically differential dimensions of social space as the contingent product of particular practices. These need not mean that space as absolute contingency and nonbelonging must be replaced by traditionalist notions of pure place with clearly marked boundaries. It has been the burden of this chapter precisely to argue the opposite – that spatial practices and representational spaces cross the "pure borders" of identity, nation, and territory, but they do become grounded, and do reterritorialize space into place as a practiced, embodied, and lived reality. The dialectic between space and place under contemporary forms of modernity can be collapsed into the discourse of sheer difference only at the cost of an ignorance that social space and cultural politics are mediated by practice.

## NOTES

1   Paul Gilroy, *The Black Atlantic* (Harvard University Press: Cambridge, MA, 1995); Stuart Hall, "Introduction: Who Needs Identity," in Stuart Hall and Paul du Gay, eds., *Questions of Cultural Identity* (Sage: London, 1996); Homi Bhabha, *The Location of Culture* (Routledge: London, 1994). In the context of the historical-materialist attacks by theorists on the poststructuralist reading of the postcolonial condition, it is striking that Hall's rebuttal, routed through Bhabha, is that of space. In particular, he turns to Derrida's poststructuralist critique of metaphysics, and spatial metaphors of "thinking

at the limit," "decentring," "cultural fragmentation" and the like abound. Both the collapse of philosophical critique into historico-political analysis, and the emphasis of spatial disjuncture over emplaced closure in his essay are the target of my critique below. See Stuart Hall, "When was 'the Postcolonial'? Thinking at the Limit," in I. Chambers and L. Curti, eds., *The Postcolonial Question: Common Skies, Divided Horizons* (Routledge: London and New York, 1996): 242–60.

2  D. N. Rodowick, *Reading the Figural, or, Philosophy after the New Media* (Duke University: London and Durham, 2001), esp. ch. 1. See also Jean-François Lyotard, *Discours, figure* (Klinksieck: Paris, 1971).

3  Bhabha links this notion of "Third Space" to the question of the postmodern. See *The Location of Culture*.

4  Henri Lefebvre, *The Production of Space*, trans. Donald Nicholson Smith (Blackwell: Oxford, 1992).

5  Theodor Adorno, *Negative Dialectics*, trans. E. B. Ashton (Continuum: New York, 2000 [first published 1973]).

6  I do not have the space to trace the complex shifts in television in terms of financing, technology, and changes in function. For an analysis of the role of national programming, see Arvind Rajagopal, "The Rise of National Programming: The Case of Indian Television," *Media, Culture and Society* 15 (1993): 91–111.

7  "Brand Equity, MTV Will Host Youth Marketing Meet," *TOI*, Feb. 26, 1999: 1.

8  "MTV ENJOY!," *Screen*, Aug. 21,1998: 20

9  On the other side of the "East/West" divide, Slavoj Žižek locates a similar phenomenon in the use of cyberspace and its articulation in postmodern theorizing to hybridity, liminality, and the cyborg. For Žižek, this virtual space affords an engagement with spatial disjuncture and identity-as-process through the safe ground of an unquestioned comfort-factor in being located within the realms of privilege and wealth of Western modernity. See *On Belief* (Routledge: London, 2001), particularly ch. 1, "Against the Digital Heresy."

10 See Fredric Jameson, "The Brick and the Balloon: Architecture, Idealism and Land Speculation," in his *The Cultural Turn: Selected Writings on the Postmodern, 1983–1998* (Verso: London, 1998): 162–90, for a closely argued reading of the relationship between urban space, speculative capitalism, and cultural critique.

11 Raymond Williams, *Marxism and Literature* (Oxford University Press: Oxford, 1985).

12 For the relationship between globalization and economic and cultural change, see Sudeep Dasgupta, "Topologies of Nationalism: Constructing the Native Between the Local and the Global," in J. N. Brown and P. M. Sant, eds., *Indigeneity: Construction and Re/Presentation* (Nova Science Publishers: Commack, NY, 1999).

# 32

# Popular Culture on a Global Scale: A Challenge for Cultural Studies?

## Simon During

In what is probably the most wide-reaching transformation of the humanities since literary criticism's rise to power over half a century ago, popular culture has become an important object of academic attention. This shift has helped throw up a new discipline, or at any rate interdisciplinary mix, Cultural Studies, and although the preconditions of popular culture's academicization remain largely unexamined one thing seems clear: it is related, albeit indirectly, to a larger formation – the globalization of the popular. Or to put it more carefully, the recent academic interest in popular cultures forms part of a larger process in which popular-cultural technologies, genres, and works are increasingly moving and interacting across national and cultural borders. Actually, except in quite specific instances, "globalization" is a misnomer, "transnationalization" being a more accurate term. But it is one of these exceptional instances which interests me in this essay. Since the 1980s some cultural products are indeed globally popular and intentionally so; they are distributed and apparently enjoyed everywhere, at any rate wherever electricity is on-line or generators and batteries can be transported and where they are not successfully banned. They belong to what I will call (without any Gramscian resonances) the "global popular."

As we shall see, the global popular is a category which challenges (though it does not overturn) current Cultural Studies, especially their welcome to "difference," "hybridity," and "subversion." This chapter takes up this challenge: it attempts to think the global popular affirmatively at the same time as it explores, self-reflexively, interactions between cultural globalization and the new *visibility* of academic Cultural Studies. I want to argue that to produce academic knowledge of the global popular – its theory, its history – involves a set of new problems and topics (which, perhaps surprisingly, push us to considering strong male bodies, special effects, and other elements which could be collected within the net of "visual culture"). I'll address these issues by referring to Arnold Schwarzenegger, focusing first on his 1990 star-vehicle, Paul Verhoeven's *Total Recall*, and then on (the history of) bodybuilding and magic. Why Schwarzenegger? However much his career may be stalling, he remains a unique phenomenon. Worldwide, he was the most popular movie star during the period in which the contemporary global popular emerged. At least those who have most at stake in such matters think so; looking back at the 1980s, the international film exhibitors' trade show honored him as "International Star of the Decade."

It should already be apparent that the global popular is not to be identified with cultural globalization (or transnationalization) *tout court*. Cultural globalization takes many forms and has many different effects, some of which work in the opposite direction to the global popular. Globalized cultural technologies and networks of production and distribution have, paradoxically enough, generated more and more locally produced and consumed works from news shows to soaps (by the logic of what Japanese marketeers apparently sometimes call "glocalization"). Such cultural technologies have also produced new transnational audiences bounded by language or religion, for instance.[1] Some "glocalized" cultural products appeal to mysteriously disjunct audiences worldwide – how to account for the way that the world's largest producer of *telenovas*, Protele, has been successful in the Swiss and French markets (as well as in Mexico, Turkey, South Korea, and Russia, for example) but a relative failure elsewhere in Europe; how to account for the way that Bombay movies are popular in Greece but not elsewhere in Europe? Situated answers to such a question must take into account the economic flows which result in such metacultural categories as "world music" and "world literature." For instance, Japanese money is beginning to be put into Hollywood and European art cinema for which there is an increasing audience in Japan as well as in the Indian subcontinent and some southeast Asian nations. *The Crying Game*, *Howard's End*, and David Cronenburg's *Naked Lunch*, for instance, were all part-financed by Nikkon Film Development and Finance which is in turn part-owned by Japan's largest distribution house, Nippon Herald. Last in this partial itemization of globalized culture, geosynchronous broadcasting, whether of "mega-events" like the Olympics or of day-by-day transmissions like that transmitted by CNN, also belong to the category, even though such broadcasting mainly reaches only elite groups outside of those (relatively few) countries where cabled television sets or satellite dishes are widely distributed.

No doubt this list could be extended, but I wish to stress that none of these forms of cultural globalization themselves constitute the global popular which, today, only comes into being when a particular product or star is a hit in many markets. Yet it is impossible simply to sever the global popular from other forms of cultural globalization. The reason is not just that together they form a single, if very loose, globalizing system, but that relations between the various kinds of cultural globalization as well as more localized forms of cultural production are constantly changing and transacting.

Cultural globalization is an element in much larger forces and institutions of globalization. Let us make a relatively simple distinction between economic, financial, and cultural globalization.[2] Economic globalization refers to the transnational decentralization of production and services in a process by which low-added-value labor is exported from rich countries, or at least the rich regions of rich countries, to create the (misnamed) "international division of labor."[3] This routinely touches cultural production: *Total Recall*, for instance, was shot in Mexico City to take advantage of low costs, with the highly trained workforce traveling down from California. In the film, the brutalist skyscrapers which embody Earth's interplanetary imperialism are in fact monuments to Mexico City's compradors. Next, financial globalization denotes capital's increased capacity to flow across national borders. This, too, enables the financing of mega-budget movies, as we shall see in more detail, but it connects with cultural globalization in at least two other important ways. Financial globalization helps some non-Western nations and markets become richer and more competitive in relation to the West, and so extends the reach of ethico-political judgments based on the once culture-specific assumption that peoples have a right (and a desire) to become comparatively affluent as well as extending the reach of cultural markets and the state institutions which secure those markets. This process, along with certain anxieties and resistances which flow from it, are often, if indirectly, thematized in globally popular works. All the more so because global-ization also exerts pressure on all national economies, especially weak ones, to compete in export markets and avoid flights of capital. This draws both rich and poor countries towards social policies regulated by neoclassical economic assumptions and methods (sometimes called the "new political economy"), policies relatively sensitive to the needs, including the cultural needs, of new export markets.

To understand cultural globalization's conditions of existence we need to make a detour into entertainment-industry economics more widely. The crucial fact about contemporary cultural markets is the degree to which they are dominated by a single piece of hardware: the television set. In the US, the average household spends 2,500 hours per year watching television and probably less than 10 percent of that time pursuing other recreational cultural activities.[4] This figure is high in inter-national terms, but leisure, the world over, is still increasingly dominated by television viewing. More than cinema, television, often connected to a VCR, is the technology that drives contemporary globalization of audiovisual product. In the US, home-video market revenues overtook worldwide theatrical-release rev-enues in the late 1980s, although in some markets (notably in Asia) the construc-tion of cinemas is also proceeding apace.[5] One crucial fall-out of the move from domestic cinema into video (and cable) is that movie audiences have become increasingly segmented into niche categories, a process also helped by the develop-ment of multiplex cinemas. In the 1970s, new youth markets appeared for a variety of genres and combinations of genres, of which the most successful were teen, horror/slasher, sci-fi, and action movies. This segmentation of the market, as we shall see, fed into globalization.

It is important to recognize that television software is less globalized than its hardware. Certainly product export-flows are not symmetrical; in 1988 only about 2 percent of all US programming (excluding Hispanic and "multicultural" programming) came from abroad, whereas Hollywood – as producer of TV shows as well as films – seems set to become the US's single biggest export industry. Currently a star can only be established globally by Hollywood cinema. Although some global product comes from elsewhere – films picked up on an ad hoc basis by US distributors, such as Cannon or Goldcrest films in the 1980s, or occasional shows or films created from more localized industries like the Hong Kong film or Brazilian and Mexican television industries or by small Canadian and Australian production houses aimed at international television markets (whose most successful players are increasingly located in the States anyway) – only Hollywood produces systematically for worldwide export. This does not mean, of course, that all Hollywood product is equally globalizable.

Although cultural globalization cannot be thought about simply as local culture's enemy (far from it), and although foreign product may be resisted (China's ban on the private ownership of satellite dishes, as well as severe restrictions on internet access and activity, being a good recent example), still the globalization of VCRs, geosynchronous broadcasting, and the emergence of world stars has attenuated many national cultural industries. Thus US television programs like *Dynasty* and *Santa Barbara* beamed into India on Rupert Murdoch's Star TV have proved popular enough for Doordarshan, the Indian public broadcaster, to buy and transmit more US product. This process has been the more marked because cultural industries are being deregulated worldwide under the influence of the new political economy. In Asia, two of the largest film industries, the Indian and the Indonesian, are losing ground – the Indonesian industry which produced about 80 feature films annually in the 1980s is currently producing less than 10 because of lack of government support for the local industry. On the other hand, there has been a transnationalization of US studio ownership, with, most famously, some studios being bought by Japanese hardware manufacturers. Thus *Total Recall* was distributed by Tri Star, part of Columbia, bought by Sony in 1989. And the conglomerates we call "studios" are increasingly entering into off-shore partnerships. AOL-Time Warner, for instance, started a rush in 1990 when, using the satellite PanAmSat (whose footprint covers the Western hemisphere), they joined forces with Omnivisión Latin Entertainment, a Venezuelan company, and formed HBO-Olé to gain access to South American markets broadcasting in Spanish and Portuguese, a project in which Time Warner and its partners were later joined by Sony Pictures Entertainment.[6] Time Warner are also building multiplexes in Japan (where theatrical attendance, dominated by young women, is in decline) with a Japanese supermarket chain, Nichii.[7] In China, Paramount has entered into deals with a Hong Kong company (controlled by members of the mainland politician, Chen Yun's, family) and a Malaysian company (owned by sons of the Malaysian Prime Minister) to multiplex the nation.[8] Hollywood also calls on capital which flows in from a variety of overseas sources: *Total Recall* was produced by Carolco, a now defunct independent, whose investors have included the privately owned

French pay-television group, Canal Plus; Italy's video distributor and media consortium Rizzoli/Corriere della Sera (RCS); the Japanese hardware manufacturer, Pioneer (itself part of the Matsushita empire); and the ubiquitous, state-owned French bank, Crédit Lyonnaise.

It is worth noting as an aside that in 1993 a big share of Carolco was bought by TCI, the largest cable operator in the US and a pioneer in fiber-optic technology, partly on the strength of Carolco's library – which includes the *Terminator* movies and *Basic Instinct* as well as *Total Recall* – and partly on the promise of another Verhoeven/Schwarzenegger megaproduction, *Crusade*.[9] TCI intended to use Carolco to introduce a shift in local distribution which would have had major implications for audiovisual culture globally. They wished to make certain films available on pay-per-view TV in the US simultaneously with their theatrical release. Here we see what will become a familiar theme in this chapter: the muscled male body – in this case, Schwarzenegger's – being used to hinge old forms of cultural production and distribution to new and untried ones.

Nonetheless, the ownership of production (or distribution) houses is not a ground for cultural globalization, not least because production is a localized if diffuse and competitive business, scattered across the talent agencies, the craft unions, the special-effects shops, the costume-hire firms, the CAD (computer assisted design) studios, picture and sound libraries, location-search teams, the domestic space of script-writers, musicians, and so on – a plethora of individuals and small or large, autonomous or semi-autonomous businesses, which come together in particular productions through a surprisingly informal system of networking, extraordinarily responsive to global market shifts, centered in Los Angeles.

It is important to grasp the financial, economic, and technological underpinnings of cultural globalization but, of course, Cultural Studies is more interested in the kinds of questions that come next: what is a global culture going to look like? What are its effects? What wants does it fulfill? In answering such questions, the information that I have just outlined helps us move beyond the generalizations of commentators like Jean Baudrillard, for whom cultural globalization simply means the mutation of previously self-governing agents into signifiers of a commodified, homogeneous, self-enclosed world-imaginary. But, precisely because the global popular crosses so many cultures, these questions resist easy settlement. We can say, however, that answers will not be found where the West once thought they would be, that is, in those Eurocentric dreams of hegemony traditionally embodied in two forms of universalization, one sacred, the other secular. In particular, the global popular makes it harder than ever for us to imagine a unified world-culture under the sway of enlightened universals considered to end irrationality and spread autonomous individuality.

In fact, cultural globalization is occurring along another, much more restricted track – via show-business. It is true that one commonly canvassed reason for the transcultural success of video and other global media like satellite broadcasting is the ease with which such means of transmission allow consumers to bypass local state restrictions and control – an explanation that fits liberal and universalist models of the media.[10] Yet convergences in leisure consumption across many communities do not entail convergences in familial relations or religious practices, for instance – at that level there is little evidence for a large "global homogenization of culture" thesis.[11] Indeed, I will argue that the appeal of the audiovisual global popular is finally to be read in terms of the limited capacities of particular media to provide for individuals' needs and desires, especially male needs and desires, across the various territories which constitute the world image-market. It is just possible to take films that are globally popular and read from them a set of elements that are universal, in the weak sense that they are culturally translatable to the maximum degree. Even then, given the global-cultural system's constant transformations, it does not follow that these will provide the constituents of a yet-to-be-fully-realized global popular.

As the dominant world star at that moment when nondomestic sales began to become more important than domestic sales in the blockbuster sector of the US film industry, Arnold Schwarzenegger belongs to the global popular. He has been, if anything, more popular in Japan, Indonesia, Eastern Europe (the old "second world"), and the Arab countries than in Europe or the Americas. To take just one instance, in Russia, Schwarzy (as the French call him) is, along with Stalin and Hitler, an icon of the fascist People's Socialist Party. His worldwide popularity has increased as his movie career progressed through subcultural films into sword and sorcery movies, to the first *Terminator* and thence into *Total Recall*, then into comedies (*Twins* being one of the first comedies to do well in world markets) and, the beginning of the end perhaps, into (relatively unsuccessful, self-conscious) comedy–action hybrids.[12] *Total Recall*, the pivotal movie in this sequence because it was directly controlled by the star, cost US$60 million and grossed $300 million of which $180 million came from non-US markets against a then-industry average of a 40/60 domestic/foreign revenue split, while about half the domestic revenue ($63 million) came from rentals.[13] But, crucially, information about international consumption is, as Momar Kebe N'Dirgue puts it, "fragmentary, incomplete and sometimes contradictory" because, outside OECD nations, and despite ever more powerful threats from US government and industry agencies, as well as pressure from the GATT, dubbing and "clandestine" markets abound (*The Terminator*, in particular, being notorious for the number of pirated tapes in circulation around the world).[14] Again, to take just two other examples, Bombay has 8,000 unauthorized cable systems using satellite dishes to grab whatever programming they can; and in Taiwan, where a million households are plugged into unlicensed cables, revenues sometimes estimated in the hundreds of millions are lost to Hollywood annually because of so-called "piracy."[15] This is not a "third-world problem": Italy heads the international video-piracy table.

In general, we know that world markets welcome the intensities attached to what I'll call a cinema of action-attractions.[16] It's a cinema heavily dependent on special effects and stunts, particularly the presentation of highly stylized, acrobatic violence which revolves around slashing, guns, and hand-to-hand combat, often borrowing from the visual grammar of non-Western martial arts. These effects are welded into narratives for which violence is a solution to exploitation. In this, globally popular movies extend generic conventions developed in Western youth-markets. In order to acquire more grounded knowledge about what this means, we would need to look towards the situations in which preferences for this kind of movie are enacted. In particular, I would suggest, we should look at how the power to make choices in various local viewing situations is shared between genders, all the more so because outside the core economies, video is not mainly viewed on privately owned VCRs, but in video cafés and, as in rural Papua New Guinea, in mobile video trucks which travel from village to village. In the case of Indian video-cafés, Rami Vasudevan has argued that masculinist violence is attractive in part because it helps exclude women from public space – an argument which might well be extendable to other contexts. And it is clear from many sources that video-viewing can reinforce extended family socialization in countries where it has been threatened by cinema and other public entertainments. Certainly it is strange that, although romances are popular in many cultures, there is not yet a centralized, globally popular women's cinema based on romance[17] (as there has been, in a relatively restricted mode, for the novel), although the *telenova* often dominates primetime broadcasting in countries where women have considerable power over domestic space. Because information about global consumption and its causes is so thin, it is necessary, however, to fall back on interpretation to uncover the cross-culturally translatable wants that globally popular films fulfill. Obviously, this turn to interpretation and speculation runs the risk of substituting our own for other intelligences and feelings. Nonetheless, mindful of that warning, let me analyze in a little more detail two of the crucial features that characterize mainstream contemporary global cinema: male bodies and special effects.

This cinema is marked by a preference for a particular kind of trained male body, not just Schwarzenegger's but many others including Sylvester Stallone's and, for instance, Claude van Damme's. These bodies are culturally specific: Schwarzenegger's body, despite his unprecedented mass, the definition of his cuts (to use bodybuilders' lingo), and his V-shape (one that became popular in bodybuilding in the 1940s), is still modeled on a classical Greek ideal. In his films, his body is a resource available when everything else – guns, money, status, power – run out. It's the stuff of survival, there to be identified with by men whose clout is corporeal. Thus it grounds his appeal across the international division of labor.

But this is a little too easy. Unlike most bodies formed in the unconsidered entanglement between heredity, lifeways, and work, Schwarzenegger's body is more alien than "natural," the product of a rigorous regime of self-government as well as, so he admits, in the past, steroids. More specifically, training incorporates certain relations that are also embedded in screen spectatorship. As it aims to transform bodies, training requires constant self-inspection – touching, looking, imagining – centered on mirrors. These techniques and their desired outcome – self-specularization and bodily transformation – echo the relation between the viewer and the filmed bodies of actors. These relations flow in two directions. Not only does the training eye see the training body in the mirror somewhat as the spectator sees bodies on screen, but the spectator can also identify or take pleasure in trained bodies on the screen all the more intensely because they are the result of transformative routines based on, and aimed at, being seen. What training does, though, is bring these relations closer to everyday life and the private sphere (into the world of houses and gyms) than they can ever be on screen. And it seems to me that, even for those who do not train, trained bodies carry with them the *idea* of training and the routinization of body-transformation and self-specularization.

It is in the join and disjunction between the body as what nature supplies to all and the body as constructed, visualized object that the Schwarzenegger globally popular effect begins to be generated. All the more so, because training requires little capital, cultural or otherwise, but does demand work. Training workouts mime and personalize labor, especially the kind of (Fordist) labor which is exported in the global economy. Movies like *The Terminator* and *Total Recall* intensify this hinging of the constructed, labored-over body to the body-as-resource by presenting stories about, and images of, bodies that are products as well as controllers of technology. In sum, we can read such films as allegorizing the condition of those for whom the body is, first, a ground to be worked upon; second, a source of labor-power for processes of production; and, third, a locus of an undervalued presence in the world but one potentially open to reconstruction and the (learned) pleasures of self-viewing. While it is important to recognize that many lives, especially male lives, meet at least the first of these conditions (from rich white men in expensive gyms to PNG raskals), they bear most pressingly on those with least clout.

Next, special effects. In the cinema of action-attraction, special effects are generally used to construct magical worlds which exceed everyday causal constraints; indeed their techniques go back to the artisanal knowledge of conjurers (traditionally amongst the most cross-culturally peripatetic of popular entertainers). In the context of an analysis of global film's popularity, it is important not to revivify the old ethnographical problem as to whether or not non-Western ontologies and "magical" ritual actions were "rational," as if non-Western audiences tended to be inherently more superstitious than Western ones, and as if the attraction of special effects were a sign that such irrationalities linger.[18] One of the global popular's promises is that it helps us break with that problematic. In fact, we can say that special effects, especially as linked to violence and psychic communication, construct characters who can engage the world, not just outside of the laws of physics, but outside of messy negotiations with the more powerful – negotiations which are likely to require fewer crippling trade-offs to the degree that one has clout, is educated, and so on. In this sense, the movies can be read as operating within psychic economies so as to compensate for disadvantage.

I want, therefore, to explore *Total Recall* in a little more historical depth. Of the various histories at work in the movie, one stands out: the history of the spectacularized, strong body, especially in relation to magic and special effects. After all, this is the distinguishing feature that, more than anything, seems to enable the movie's passage across cultures.

■ II ■

So, a microhistory of exhibited muscle. Spectacles of the strong body have three main tracks back into the past. The first (which will not concern me further here) is the history of representations of big and strong male bodies like that of the mythical hero, Hercules. These reach back into antiquity and retained ritualistic connotations into the early modern period in Europe. Hercules, for instance, retained a function as Florence's pagan guardian into the Christian era, a cultural memory called upon when his naked body, painted by Antonio Pollaiuolo under Medici patronage, became what was probably the first Classical, large-scale image to be depicted in the Antique manner during the Renaissance. In the context of my argument concerning the global popular, it is hardly surprising that a strongman image provides a shunting-point between pre-Christian traditions and the era of modern painting, as it loosely binds culturally different audiences today.

The second track into the past is the long tradition of strongmen and women who performed and continue to perform feats of strength in popular theaters, circuses, and fairs in Europe and elsewhere. And the last is the history of physical training which emerged in the gymnastics developed to maximize health and agility, originally for the conscripted armies of the post-Napoleonic period and then in schools, gyms, and houses. From about 1850 onwards, in the US and Britain, the second of these histories (exhibition) and the third (training) intersect in a variety of ways. Early on, in the late 1850s, a Massachusetts doctor named George Winship, known as the "Roxbury Hercules," displayed his developed body to advertise his "patent graduating dumb-bell" and gym. Winship's self-advertisement belonged to a domain then called "physical culture" – an ensemble made up of competing ideas, values, and techniques all aimed at developing the body in order to maximize health and moral agency. Some of the more important of physical culture's various components are worth noting: muscular Christianity; the *Turnvereine* or gymnastic societies which, established by 1848 revolutionary exiles in the US, specialized in exercises performed *en masse*; a proto-eugenicist, racist movement aimed at producing what Thomas Wentworth Higginson called "the type of individual who would ensure that the American nation would fulfill its destiny"; the new science of anthropometrics, which gave us the sense (and the anxieties that flow from it) that our bodies have quantifiable sizes measurable against norms; and finally a rapidly expanding market for training gear.[19] It almost goes without saying that, from its moment of emergence, humanist intellectuals (notably, Friedrich Schiller in his essay "On the Sublime") singled out and downgraded physical culture because it did not belong to the realms of the spirit, freedom, and the aesthetic.

Until about 1900, physical culture was tied to physical education, but one of its most effective means of dissemination was the circulation of images of developed, especially male, bodies. "Before" and "after" exercise photographs were common from about 1860 and provided guidelines and encouragement for the techniques of self-inspection necessary for training. Both physical culture and physical education were relatively gender-neutral. In fact, in Britain, women dominated physical education until the 1930s, and, in the US, physical culturalists popularized the movement for women's clothing reform and cross-gender sex education, as well as for a "natural" and "healthy" woman's body as against a more conventionally gendered one. Around 1890, however, images and exhibitions of such bodies, which approached nudity, themselves were presented in a new way. Semi-naked bodies showing the effects of scientific training began to appear in traditional and new showbiz sites – in artists' modeling studios, in wrestling and weight-lifting contests and strongman displays like the famous Eugene Sandow's (he specialized in posing as Hercules, Ajax, Samson, etc.), and, last, on film. The athletic half-naked body, clothed without drapery, would itself enter everyday life decisively, leaving behind the gym, the static vitality of the "after" exercise photo, or the eroticized staginess of the Victorian *tableaux vivants* when the one-piece bathing suit for women was popularized in the US by the Australian diver, swimmer, author, film personality, and physical culturalist, Annette Kellerman.

One of Edison's very earliest reels presented members of a *Turnverein* and, tellingly, Sandow's act was the first star performance ever to be filmed – here again, a strongman helps provide a junction between one cultural form and another. The first bodybuilding contest proper was probably held in London in 1899 – organized by Sandow to find the "best-developed" body among those who used his training system. In 1904, Bernarr Macfadden, publisher of the movement's flagship journal *Physical Culture* and an exhibitor of his own muscle, organized "Physical Culture Exhibitions" at Madison Square Gardens, events more directly in the genealogy of both the contemporary bathing-beauty and bodybuilding show. Here, an older discourse of health, grace, and strength merges with one that emphasizes the sexual advantages of being and looking muscled – for both genders – and of wearing fewer and fewer clothes. Such shows antagonized powerful interests – Macfadden was prosecuted by the Society for the Suppression of Vice. By this time, the physical culturalists, who had been allied to the broader health movement, were also in combat with the medical establishment. The movement was defiantly on the side of self-management as against governmental pastoral agencies and the professions, and had become, in effect, a working-class and petit-bourgeois force, committed to unofficial knowledges and styles of self-formation. Magic reappears here: the journal *Physical Culture* made much of its money by advertising quick-fix remedies like the famous peniscope (advertising revenues for non-orthodox remedies having been, of course, a major source of capital for the publishing and media industries since at least the seventeenth century). By the 1920s, Charles Atlas's advertising agency linked muscularity to specifically male aggression and self-esteem, and, around 1927, developed muscles were being advertised as a good in themselves rather than as aids to health and success. By this time, the physical culture movement had ceased to be a coherent and popular movement.

Bodybuilding would stay ghettoized in Western countries until Schwarzenegger, helped by Butler and Gaines and the entrepreneur Joe Wieder, reintroduced it into bourgeois life-patterns and fitness programs. The recent repopularizing of bodybuilding is a complex event which involved, among much else, the sheer presence of Schwarzenegger's photographed body; his descriptions of pumping as autoerotic and a form of self-sculpting (which led to his starring both in a Whitney Museum symposium on "Articulate Muscle: The Male Body in Art" in 1976 and the movie *Pumping Iron*, the latter partly financed by a new sector of the body-culture industry, the waterbed business); his image as a womanizer, which helped drag the sport more securely into the ambit of masculinist heterosexuality (without reducing its appeal to certain queer gazes); as well as perceptions of increasing security breakdown in urban centers; and, of course, the development of youth audiovisual markets and the global popular itself.

In relation to my chapter's argument, I would like to zoom in on two moments in this history. The first belongs to the period before training and gymnastics were formalized and before popular show business or the health industries were developed enough for successful strongmen or women to acquire capital. The circuit for professional strong acts extended beyond Europe, one of its centers being Constantinople, where in 1815 Giovanni Belzoni, a professional strongman, conjurer, and showman of optical illusions whose stage-name had been the "Patagonian Strongman" or (once more) "Patagonian Hercules," hoped to perform along with his wife, who helped in his act as a strongwoman. ("Patagonian" because, into the early nineteenth century, the inhabitants of Patagonia were popularly thought of as giants.)[20] On his way, almost penniless, Belzoni detoured to Egypt where he expected to use skills developed in hydraulic displays and theatrical special effects to irrigate the Nile. Although that project failed, he was hired by the British consul at Cairo to excavate and transport antiquities back to the British Museum. On his return to London, he and his wife wrote accounts of their exploits and organized a very successful exhibition based on their discoveries.

Belzoni's ability to bring off his remarkable acts of pillage (he was generally considered the most successful of all Egyptian antiquity-hunters, the original raider of the lost ark, and the subject of several inspiratory Victorian popular biographies) was linked to his physical presence, which awed the locals as it had done Europeans in a showbiz context, as well as to his knowledge of theatrical effects. For instance, at Abu Simbel, where he made some of his most famous finds, there was no cash economy. How to introduce the locals to paid labor? Belzoni taught them the value of money by using a confederate, a technique common to the conjurers of the time. The locals could not see how a small coin could be worth working for, and to endow it with exchange value, Belzoni dramatically presented a prospective worker with a piastre to exchange for corn. This worked, magically, because he had tipped off an aide to make the exchange for three days' rations. Conversely, when Belzoni used hoists to lift his colossus, some Egyptians thought it was done by magic – which Belzoni seems not to have denied.[21] Here, a strong body, special-effects skills, and a profane ontology work directly to extend the global economy. They also work to place Europe at the center of world history – possessing and exhibiting Egyptian monuments in London signaled British appropriation of a world-historical past. When Belzoni explained to the locals why he wanted the antiquities that they considered worthless, the reason he gave was that they would help him learn about his own ancestors, in effect laying claim to the locals' genealogies. In the face of exploitation by his upper-class employers, resistance by the locals, and competition from the French, as imperialist rivals, Belzoni did not just excavate colossal monuments, he identified with them. Their hugeness could interpenetrate his own, pumping him up in acts of defiance: "Had I not determined to stand, like a pyramid defying the wind, against all their numerous attacks, which poured on me like a torrent, I should not have been able to proceed, even from the commencement."[22] *Total Recall* draws upon these uses for, these emotional flows within, the Egyptological quest-narrative: the mines at Mars are called the "Pyramid" mines and there Schwarzenegger, like Belzoni, by virtue of his strength, uncovers and revivifies a vast lost technology in defiance of a world which he exploits and in which he is exploited.

I have focused on Belzoni because, like Schwarzenegger, he uses special effects, physical strength, and enlightened conjuring tricks to extend globalization. But let me point to one important difference: Schwarzenegger, who plays fictional characters, is available to audiences for their own purposes; Belzoni (though he attacked the upper-class men who misused him) could only enter the public sphere more simply as an agent of Eurocentric power in his autobiographical accounts of his exploits and as an exhibition-organizer. This piece of history helps us see how old the alliance of show business and globalization is, but it also allows us to mark out fictional entertainment as a space for freedom available to contemporary audiences, without which the global popular would be impossible.

The second moment I want to focus on belongs to the period in which bodybuilding was central to a vital, antimedical physical-culture movement. By then, of course, it was no longer necessary or even possible for a strongman to masquerade as a Patagonian in order to exhibit his unclothed body. Indeed, by then, "Patagonians" had gained access to international show business: they were participants in the "Anthropology Day" at the Louisiana Purchase Exposition, St. Louis, in 1904, organized to promote the Olympic Games that were being held simultaneously and intended to introduce training to so-called "primitive" peoples. Indeed, the trained body was becoming internationalized more generally. In Australia, for instance, around 1900, the champion wrestlers were Indians; showmen like Sandow toured internationally, and soon bodybuilding was more popular in Islamic than in Christian countries. But it is in the US around 1920 that we see clearest signs of how complex and far-reaching physical culture's attraction for its followers could be. As proprietor of the magazine *Physical Culture*, Macfadden found himself receiving detailed confessional letters from women who had fallen out of conventional morality, especially sexual morality. Believing these letters had a bigger market than the physical culturalists, Macfadden's wife Mary (whom he had met as the winner of one of his contests, and who performed in his act) encouraged him to establish the journal *True Stories Magazine*, to publish them. Confessional writing flooded in from women who wanted to exhibit and narrativize their trials or successes in print for an anonymous and distant audience. *True Stories* became the largest-circulation journal of its time. With the capital that he acquired from the magazine, Macfadden established the New York tabloid the *Daily Graphic*, much despised by the respectable middle-classes. It provided room for its readers to write stories and reviews, introduced the lonely-hearts column, and developed a showbiz gossip column (by Walter Winchell) which represented the stars with unprecedented casualness and intimacy. In the late 1920s and 1930s, the Macfadden organization pioneered a similar trajectory in radio. Beginning with physical culture and calisthenics programs, they went on to develop "human interest" formats like "True Story Court of Human Relations" on CBS radio or, in 1937, the "Good Will Show" (with its intro line, "What's your problem?") – forerunners of talk shows like Oprah Winfrey's. These spin-offs of physical culturalism are important: they show how a formation, heavily dependent on images of muscular bodies and unambiguously pitched against the most powerful professional and governmental agencies of the time, triggered forms of self-display and self-ethnographization.

We can see a familiar logic at work here: training the body appeals powerfully to those whose bodies are their main resource and for whom spectacularization and confession/testimony across a distance provide means for self-articulation. This supports and extends my reading of why globalization works – and helps us affirm the contemporary global popular. In addition, when, in the physical culture moment, body-centeredness unleashes a capacity to step into the light of publicity, to disseminate personal stories as a form of popular knowledge, we return to a basis of what we can call the supplemental relation between Cultural Studies and the cultural markets. Contemporary Cultural Studies, too, encourages forms of confessional ethnography and self-ethnography in its desire to avoid speaking for or speculating about others. It, too, is staked to the conditions within which the exhibition of lives and their vicissitudes helps constitute knowledge and consumable culture simultaneously. If today, in many Anglophone countries, this self-ethnographization is as likely to be expressed in cultural-studies classrooms and journals as on the pages of *True Stories*, then that is a side-effect of globalization. After all, it is globalization that demands that nations train and certify their citizens in ways that turn both everyday life and show business into resources for academic knowledge.

## NOTES

I would like to acknowledge all those who helped me think through this essay (often by disagreeing with it) – not least Homi Bhabha, David Bennett, John Frow, and Lisa O'Connell.

1  See Armand Mattelart, Xavier Delcourt, and Michèle Mattelart, *International Image Markets: In Search of an Alternative Perspective*, trans. David Buxton (London: Commedia, 1984) and Anthony Smith, "Towards a Global Culture?" in *Global Culture*:

*Nationalism, Globalization and Modernity* (London: Sage, 1990): 171–91, for a discussion of these issues.

2   See Arjun Appadurai, "Disjuncture and Difference in the Global Cultural Economy," *Public Culture* 2(2) (Spring 1990): 1–24.

3   My sense of how what I am calling "economic globalization" works owes much to my reading of Saskia Sassen's *The Global City* (Princeton, NJ: Princeton University Press, 1991).

4   Harold L. Vogel, *Entertainment Industry Economics: A Guide For Financial Analysis* (Cambridge: Cambridge University Press, 1990), p. 53.

5   See Don Groves, "Hollywood Wows World Wickets," *Variety Weekly*, Feb. 22, 1993, p. 85, for information on cinema construction in South Korea, Singapore, Malaysia, Indonesia, and Taiwan.

6   See John Sinclair, "The Decentring of Cultural Imperialism: Televisa-ion and Globoization in the Latin World," in *Continental Shift: Globalization and Culture*, ed. Elizabeth Jacka (Sydney: Local Consumption Publications, 1992), pp. 99–117.

7   For HBO-Olé, see Peter Besas, "Yanks Seek TV El Dorado," *Variety Weekly*, April 12, 1993, p. 24. For the Japanese exhibition deal, see Garth Alexander, "Warner Bros Plexes Japan," *Variety Weekly*, April 19, 1993, p. 36.

8   Don Groves, "Modern Multiplexes to Make China Smile," *Variety Weekly*, April 4, 1994, p. 12.

9   See Matt Rothman and Judy Brennan, "TCI's Film Surprise," *Variety Weekly*, April 26, 1993, pp. 85–6. [This megaproduction, like much "vapor-ware," never came to fruition – D.P.]

10  See, for instance, Douglas A. Boyd, Joseph C. Straubhaar, and John A. Lent, *Videocassette Recorders in the Third World* (New York and London: Longmans, 1989).

11  See John Tomlinson, *Cultural Imperialism* (London: Pinter Publishers, 1990), for a good discussion of these issues and a review of the literature.

12  Nicholas Kent, *Naked Hollywood: Money, Power and the Movies* (London: BBC Books, 1991), p. 109. [In 2003, Arnold Schwarzenegger's final hopes seem to rest with *Terminator 3*, and/or a career in US politics – D.P.]

13  Vogel, *Entertainment Industry Economics*, p. 43.

14  For the "fragmentary" comment, see Momar Kebe N'Dirgue, "West Africa," in *Video Worldwide: An International Study*, ed. Manuel Alvarado (London: John Libbey, 1988), p. 235.

15  Mark Lewis, "Taiwan Struggles With Piracy," *Variety Weekly*, Feb. 22, 1993, p. 92; and "Taiwan Buyers Seek Toons 'n' Tough Guys," *Variety Weekly*, April 5, 1993, p. 91.

16  For "cinema of attraction," see Tom Gunning, "The Cinema of Attractions: Early Film, Its Spectator and the Avant-Garde," in *Early Cinema: Space, Frame, Narrative*, ed. Thomas Elsaesser with Adam Barker (London: BFI, 1990), pp. 56–62.

17  [The global success of James Cameron's *Titanic* could point toward a possible paradigm for just such a genre – D.P.]

18  For a discussion of this tradition, see Stanley Jeyaraja Tambiah, *Magic, Science, Religion and the Scope of Rationality* (Cambridge: Cambridge University Press, 1990).

19  The phrase from Higginson is cited in Roberta J. Park, "Educational Views of Exercise and Athletics in Nineteenth-Century America," in *Fitness in American Culture: Images of Health, Sport and the Body, 1830–1940*, ed. Kathryn Grover (Amherst: University of Massachusetts Press, 1986), p. 147.

20 For an account of the slow disappearance of the false belief that the Patagonians were giants, see Bernard Smith, *European Vision and the South Pacific, 1768–1850* (Oxford: Oxford University Press, 1960), pp. 20–1. The best account of Belzoni's career is to be found in Stanley Mayes, *The Great Belzoni* (London: Putman, 1959).

21 Giovanni Belzoni, *Narrative of the Operations and Recent Discoveries Within the Pyramids, Temples, Tombs, and Excavations in Egypt and Nubia* (London: John Murray, 1820), p. 45.

22 Ibid. pp. 112–13.

# 33

# The Abject Artefacts of Memory: The 1997 Museum of Modern Art New York Exhibition of Photographs from Cambodia's Genocide

## Rachel Hughes

The mass political violence which occurred between 1975 and 1979 in Pol Pot's Cambodia, then known as Democratic Kampuchea, has been variously memorialized both inside and outside of Cambodia. This chapter interrogates a 1997 exhibition of portrait photographs held in New York and widely received as a memorialization of the Cambodian genocide. These photographs were originally produced by Pol Pot's secret police in the largest prison of Democratic Kampuchea, known as "S-21."

The 1997 exhibition at New York's Museum of Modern Art (hereafter MoMA), titled *Photographs from S-21: 1975–1979*, generated significant debate both in published reviews and in the unpublished visitor comment books installed in the exhibition space. For the purposes of this chapter I principally examine published reviews, academic analyses, visitor book responses, and public statements of the co-instigators of the exhibition (the Photo Archive Group and the MoMA Department of Photography).[1] In addition, I draw on observations made in Cambodia, and comments by Cambodian and non-Cambodian key-players associated with the Tuol Sleng Museum of Genocide in Cambodia, the home institution of the S-21 prisoner portrait negatives.[2] By examining the formal and informal responses to a specific visual medium – a Western art-museum exhibition – I raise various questions about the politics of ownership and curatorship of objects.

## ■ Memory and Sovereignty ■

Located in the depopulated city-shell of Phnom Penh, "S-21" was the largest detention and interrogation facility in Democratic Kampuchea. Between 1975 and 1979, some 14,000 to 16,000 individuals were detained at S-21. All save 7 individuals were subsequently killed. The prison's "documentation subunit" was responsible for photographing each individual on their arrival at S-21. The portrait photographs were used to identify prisoners within the facility, and also formed proof of an individual's extermination. A prisoner's photograph was routinely attached to his or her confession document. Confessions were extracted under torture in the pursuit of networks of traitors (*khsae kbot*) which Pol Pot's leadership believed threatened the entire revolutionary state (Chandler, 1999: 6).

After the toppling of Pol Pot by Vietnamese and Cambodian (anti-Khmer Rouge) forces in 1979, the S-21 site was rapidly reconfigured as a "museum of genocide." Thousands of documents including confessions, internal memos, and photographic materials, were subsequently maintained in an archive within the new Tuol Sleng Museum of genocide. The installation of the prisoner portrait photographs in the museum and archive marked the beginning of their consideration, and narrativization, as evidence of a genocide. The museum drew Cambodian and non-Cambodian audiences from far afield. The long-term national and international legitimacy of the new state, the People's Republic of Kampuchea, hinged on the exposure of the violent excesses of Pol Pot. Tuol Sleng Museum provided a coherent, albeit depoliticized, memory of the past; that is, of liberation and reconstruction at the hands of Vietnam, a benevolent fraternal state (see Ledgerwood, 1997; Hughes, forthcoming).[3]

The Tuol Sleng archive was also, at this time, key to history and memory work in Cambodia.[4] During the People's Republic of Kampuchea period the archive was held by various non-Cambodian groups to indicate the general political openness (or otherwise) of the government and, importantly, its willingness to investigate and memorialize the past. This brings me to a crucial point about the archival status of the portrait photographs I am discussing here. They are at once images (supposedly unproblematic, particular mementos of a real person) and also objects (physical things that have survived actual events as evidence, although they cannot directly "show" those events). I want to refer to this doubleness of the S-21 photographs as "artefactual"; such an artefact is both image and object, with all the contradictions that this implies. In the subsequent fate of the S-21 prisoner portrait photographs, it is possible to see how this inherent contradiction has determined the varied uses to which they have been put.

## ■ Intervention and Evacuation: The Politics of Dislocation ■

[I]f there is no archive without consignation in an external place which assures the possibility of memorization, of repetition, of reproduction, or of reimpression, then

> we must remember that repetition itself, the logic of repetition, [remains] indissoci-
> able from the death drive.... Consequence: right on that which permits and condi-
> tions archivization, we will never find anything other than that which exposes to
> destruction, and in truth menaces with destruction, introducing a priori, a forgetful-
> ness and the archiviolithic into the heart of the monument. (Derrida, 1996: 11–12)

In 1993, two North American photojournalists, Douglas Niven and Christopher Riley, visited the Tuol Sleng Museum and its archive. On viewing the photographic materials in the archive, Niven and Riley conceived of a specific photographic archive project for Tuol Sleng. The Cambodian government gave permission for the cleaning, cataloguing, and printing of the S-21 photographs proposed by Niven and Riley.[5] The original *Project Proposal* document of Niven and Riley's Photo Archive Group stated that the photographic archive was "threatened by a volatile political situation, years of neglect, a lack of resources and the absence of trained staff." The project sought to "rescue an endangered photographic archive" while also providing an "opportunity to train Cambodians in archive preservation and advanced photographic techniques" (Photo Archive Group, *Project Proposal*, 1993). The conservation of some 6,000 original photographic negatives commenced in 1994. One hundred of the 6,000 negatives assisted by the project were finally selected for six 100-print editions. Negatives were chosen for "photographic quality, historical value and to present an accurate cross-section of Tuol Sleng's victims" (Photo Archive Group, *Project Summary*, n.d.). Two of the six 100-print editions produced by the project remained in Cambodia, and the remaining four editions were "brought out of the country for safekeeping" (Photo Archive Group, *Project Summary*, n.d.). The desire to "safekeep" the photos is in part attributable to the political uncertainty that followed the UN-sponsored Cambodian national election of May and June of 1993. The *Project Proposal* document also reports talk by various political factions of closing Tuol Sleng, though no substantiation of such talk is given. Further justifications for safekeeping of the photographs may have been made in light of reports that S-21 photographs had gone missing early in the life of the museum.[6] Aside from these disappearances, the negatives lay in the archive for some 13 years before being seen by Niven and Riley.

The *Project Proposal* also notes the Photo Archive Group's "rare and timely opportunity to preserve and present to the world a lasting record of genocide." Further statements in the Proposal argue that "it is impossible to forget the victims' faces" and that "[i]t is in humanity's interest that they be preserved and seen by as wide an audience as possible" (Photo Archive Group, *Project Proposal*, 1993). Lindsay French attests that the primary motivation of Niven and Riley was to draw viewers "closer to their [photographed] subjects," and motivate people to "become aware of the things that happened in Cambodia, and educate themselves about what is going on there now" (French, 2002). It is clear that, from the outset of the project, Niven and Riley's aims were twofold: the revival of the S-21 photographs *in situ*; and the circulation of the S-21 prisoner portraits through various media outside of the Cambodian context. The former intention, to revive the negatives as nationally significant visual records within the museum, displays all the hallmarks of a contemporary humanitarian aid project: an urgent response involving local skilling and empowerment (the training of Cambodians in safeguarding cultural artefacts for the future). The second intention – to go global with exhibitions and a publication, and gain copyright on the photographs – necessarily involved the photographs circulating in international news and visual arts media. French reports that, in exchange for their work, Niven and Riley were "given the rights to 100 images" (French, 2002). This granting of rights to the images is not noted in the Photo Archive Group's own *Project Proposal* or *Project Summary* documents. Neither was any formal arrangement of rights noted in Phnom Penh press reports (see for example Peters, 1994).

Publicity for the Photo Archive Group intensified in late 1994 and 1995 when the group's work was featured in various print media reports: *Time Magazine, Photographers' International, The New York Times, See* magazine, *American Photo, The Daily Telegraph* (UK), *The Age* (Australia), and Associated Press reports.[7] In 1996, photography publisher Twin Palms released *The Killing Fields*, a 9-by 12-inch, casebound text which reproduced 78 individual portrait photographs from the Photo Archive Group's collection. The S-21 prisoner portrait photographs also began to be exhibited in institutional locations worldwide. The generation of sympathy for, and interest in, Cambodia's past and present has undoubtedly been fuelled by the global exposure of the photographs. Crucial questions regarding this exposure, however, remain underexplored. What sort of recognition and interest has been facilitated by the images' repeated exhibition? What representational politics are involved in the continued circulation of these images? In whose memory are these images of deceased persons displayed?

The portrait photographs herald a recent materialization of the "memory" of Cambodia under Pol Pot. Kerwin Lee Klein has recently characterized the contemporary academic and popular concern with memory as a discourse in which "memory" is an essentialized super-category. Klein argues that, despite claims to the contrary, the study of memory covertly restabilizes the postmodern and poststructuralist destabilization of History (Klein, 2000). In the context of Klein's critique of the comprehensive trend toward the materialization of memory – "to identify memory as a collection of practices or material artefacts" – it is possible to further identify the Cambodian archive and photographs as "dramatically imperfect piece[s] of material culture" that are "imbued with pathos":

> Such memorial tropes have emerged as one of the common features of our new cultural history where in monograph after monograph, readers confront the abject object: photographs are torn, mementos faded, toys broken. (Klein, 2000: 135–6)

The disintegrating archive and the S-21 portraits, gazed upon by scholars, photographers, readers, viewers, and visitors, are just such abject materials. I will here note only three key occurrences of the "dramatically imperfect" identity photograph in representations of Democratic Kampuchea.

The first occurs in the 1984 film *The Killing Fields*, which first popularized the Democratic Kampuchea period for mass non-Cambodian audiences.[8] In an early section of the film, American journalist Sydney Schanberg and others attempt to have their Cambodian counterpart, Dith Pran, included in the 1975 evacuation from Democratic Kampuchea. They forge a foreign passport for Dith Pran, for which a portrait photograph is taken. Standard chemicals for the development of the photographic negative are, however, unavailable. One after another, the portraits fade to overexposed pieces of photographic card. The fading photograph symbolizes the foreigners' inability to safeguard their Cambodian colleague. The blank photograph forewarns of Pran's impending subjection to the obliterating demands of the new Khmer Rouge state.

Second, a subset of the S-21 prisoner portraits appear in Niven and Riley's exhibitions and photo print book *The Killing Fields* (1996). They are damaged, scratched, and water-marked portraits chosen for the Photo Archive Group editions. Ghostly shapes and presences appear in these plates, blotting out the side of a face, coiling around the edge of an image, or strewing a strange starry wash of lights across an otherwise underexposed image. These images often receive specific attention from audiences, who welcome the atmospheric effects as relief from the intentional, technically perfect image.

A final portrait is discussed – but not reproduced – in Niven and Riley's book. In an essay following the book's portrait plates, S-21 survivor Vann Nath testifies to the physical and psychological brutality of his incarceration at S-21, and his escape from certain death on account of his artistic skills. Shifted from prisoner to prison-worker, Vann Nath was first employed to paint portraits of Pol Pot, apparently as part of the leader's plan for a personality cult. For this task, Vann Nath worked from a portrait photograph of Pol Pot. Vann Nath has commented of this photo: "Pol Pot's face looked smooth and calm. But the feeling in my heart was that he was very savage and evil" (Vann Nath quoted in Niven & Riley, 1996: 100; see also Vann Nath, 1998: 59). It is Pol Pot's actions and intentions that, for Vann Nath, were not apparent in the photograph.

So it is possible to trace, across these various representations of Cambodia's recent past, a motif of a disappearing portrait, or the portrait which *disappears something*. The drama of this motif evidences a transnational trade in abject portraits from the once-peripheral past. This is a trade facilitated by a "revival of primordialism" (Klein, 2000: 144) – continuing Western designations of susceptibility, singularity, and lack (of "history" and "memory") in the non-West. Knowledge of the photographs is inextricably linked to the activities of the Photo Archive Group; the "history" of the S-21 photographs is narrowed to those details emerging from the Photo Archive Group.

News media reports often assert that Niven and Riley *discovered* the negatives in Cambodia in 1993. In fact, copies of the photographic materials were already in existence at the time of the Photo Archive Project. American human rights activist David Hawk had copied the negatives in the course of his research in the archive in the early 1980s. Hawk later donated these copies to Cornell Library (Ledgerwood, personal communication, 2002). The framing of Niven and Riley's contact with the photographs as a "discovery" dismisses prior curatorial handling. This narrative of discovery lends a certain heroism to Niven and Riley's actions, which contrasts dramatically with the antiheroism and victimhood of the S-21 prisoners.

Niven and Riley's own *Project Proposal* constructs Cambodia as "threatened" by political volatility, as "neglected" and "endangered." The *Project Proposal* promises a techno-bureaucratic transformation of the current archive's chaos into order, an arrest of decay, and the production of a permanent set of clean, archived copies to be located in Cambodia and, importantly, elsewhere. While the root cause of the violence is considered endemic to Cambodia or "Cambodian-ness," the instructive value of evidence of a genocide to other audiences is seen to transcend local (Cambodian) institutional concerns. As such, artefacts like the S-21 portraits, which are both representations and residues of bare life, develop a curious status as heritage artefacts of global interest and of "cultural memory" by a distant few.

In Cambodia, the Tuol Sleng photo archive project is considered by some as having wrongly wrested control of the artefacts (and their use) from Cambodians. One prominent Cambodian researcher, Youk Chhang, has expressed his frustration about the generic nature of the work of the Photo Archive Group. He argues that the initial, specific focus of the project – to assist in the preservation of a national archive of Cambodia – has been overtaken by other priorities: "This is the photograph of Tuol Sleng, it is the history of Cambodia, and everyone should have access equally" (Youk Chhang, personal communication, 2000). An alternative scenario for the use of the S-21 photographs was recently provided by Phnom Penh-based artist Ly Daravuth, with assistance from Youk Chhang. Ly's installation, *Messengers*, was shown as part of a group show he co-curated in January 2000 in Phnom Penh, titled "The Legacy of Absence: A Cambodian Story." The work comprised numerous photographic portraits of young, solemn, black-clothed Cambodians. These are portraits of children taken during the Democratic Kampuchea period, but those depicted were not prisoners of S-21. These are portraits of children who were used to run messages between various local cadres for the regime, known as *angkar* (the organization). Interspersed with these photographs are photographs of children living in present-day Cambodia, whose portraits were taken by Ly. These photographs were composed and doctored so as to mimic the appearance of the S-21 photographs. *Messengers* questions the truth-claims made about victim photographs and documents from the Democratic Kampuchea period in contemporary Cambodia. In a cultural context in which images of S-21 victims are well known and charged with considerable emotion, Ly seeks to interrupt the immediate recognition of victimhood. In addition to this work, Ly and Muan (2000) note work by other contemporary Cambodian artists in which *refusing to testify* is offered up as a way of living with the past. Little such space is opened for such memorializing stratagems – the refusal of victimhood, the refusal to testify, or the active questioning of the truth-artefact – in the MoMA exhibition.

## ■ MoMA and Zones of Affect ■

Twenty-two S-21 prisoner portraits went on public display at the Museum of Modern Art (MoMA) in New York in May 1997. The exhibition, titled *Photographs from S-21: 1975–1979*, was curated by the MoMA Department of Photography. It was mounted in Gallery Three, a smaller gallery configured as "a place where visitors may pause to sit and read, to rest and reflect" (MoMA, internal document, *Gallery Three*).[9] The exhibition's wall text provided a brief history of Cambodia 1975–9 and an outline of Niven and Riley's role in bringing the photos to "a wider audience." It read:

> When the Communist party, the Khmer Rouge, seized power in April 1975, Cambodia had just concluded five years of a disastrous civil war. Between 1975 and 1979, more than 14,000 Cambodians were held captive in S-21, a former high school in the Phnom Penh district of Tuol Sleng. (MoMA, wall text and press release, May 1997, *Photographs from S-21*)

The text confirmed that prisoners had been photographed on arrival at S-21, and that all except 7 had met with "brutal execution." Many visitors and reviewers were prompted to view the MoMA exhibition in light of events coincidently unfolding in Cambodia, and reported worldwide. In July 1997, Cambodia's coalition government led by First Prime Minister Prince Norodom Ranariddh, and Second Prime Minister Hun Sen, collapsed into fighting between the partners. A few weeks later global news media screened extraordinary video footage of Pol Pot himself, alive in western Cambodia.[10] In the context of speculation about a trial of Pol Pot under international law, the S-21 photographs at MoMA were not only tragic reminders of a peripheral past but also contemporary, crucial evidence.

The exhibition space for *Photographs from S-21* was, in the words of one visitor, evocative of "a memorial [and] a sacred place." One reviewer experienced the "small squarish room, carpeted, enclosed" as being "like a vault, a crypt" (Nahas, 1997). Another wrote of the exhibition as a space in which it felt as if "a memorial service [wa]s taking place" (O'Sullivan, 1997). These references, made only in passing, belie an important consideration of earlier functions of the collections of cultural artefacts in private mausoleum-museums. As Clifford (1997: 197) argues, the long history of "exotic" displays in the West provides a context of enduring power imbalance within and against which the contact work of travel, exhibition, and interpretation occurs. Such museum "traditions" (see also Elsner, 1994; Stewart, 1994; and Kirshenblatt-Gimblett, 1998) urge consideration of the MoMA exhibition as a "contact zone" in which the museum's "organizing structure as a collection becomes an ongoing historical, political, moral *relationship*" (Clifford, 1997: 192). Like colonial spoils, the photographs from S-21 are of "exotic" temporal and geographical origin ("year zero" Cambodia, the Cambodian genocide), and their authorship and exact function relatively obscure. Their removal from Cambodia and appearance at MoMA was primarily due to the actions of two individual, expert collectors.

In addition to news of events in Cambodia in mid-1997, the exhibition itself generated heated debate in New York's arts-critique circles. Guy Trebay's review in *Village Voice* criticized the exhibition by asking:

> Who are the people in the Tuol Sleng photos? Who are their families? What is the role of our own amnesiac culture in the atrocities that took place in a former public high school and beyond it in the killing fields? (Trebay, 1997: 34)

It is true that *Photographs from S-21* failed to recall the interconnectedness of Cambodia's modern history and that of the United States.[11] It was not, however, MoMA's intention to provide visitors with a political history of southeast Asia within which to couch their interpretations of the S-21 photos. The curators wished to present the S-21 photographs as an unmediated exhibition of nonmainstream works, and argued that there were clear precedents for such a curatorial approach.[12] In the view of MoMA's senior curator of photography, Susan Kismaric, the presentation of *Photographs from S-21* involved "bearing witness to violations of civility and human rights" (Kismaric, personal communication, 2001). Kismaric considered the controversy around *Photographs from S-21* to be an effect of showing "vernacular photography" in an institution where audiences might more commonly expect to view work from aesthetic, photographic-arts traditions (Kismaric, personal communication, 2001; Kismaric quoted in Trebay, 1997). The assistant curator in the Department of Photography with principal responsibility for *Photographs from S-21*, Adrienne Williams, expressed her personal view of the photographs as "inviting," "sorrowful," and "very striking," and believed they "belong[ed] in a museum" (Williams, 1997; Williams, 1998).

Many visitors to the exhibition were moved to record impassioned, personal comments in the visitor books provided. Visitors debated historical events and individual and state actions, and specific notions of justice, memory, and moral responsibility.[13] Most visitors considered the photographs to be more than documentary evidence. People wrote of the images as providing a way of "seeing" an otherwise unseen history. Many termed the photographs "art" in a wholly positive sense, as enabling greater consideration and understanding of events, thoughts and emotions not experienced firsthand. Like Trebay, however, other responses questioned the appropriateness of *Photographs from S-21*. For some, the exhibition was inappropriate because it was insufficient in its contextualization of the images. Such comments were often confrontational in tone, decrying the exhibition as exploitative:

> I don't believe MoMA had the intention to completely objectify these terrible images, but this mute and "neutral" exhibition does that in the coldest possible way.... As a child of Holocaust survivors, I feel that this kind of behavior is at best indicative of a smugness and an intellectual laziness – AT WORST IT IS INHUMANE.

Others considered the photographs as worthy of exhibition but felt that MoMA, as a bastion of modernist art traditions, was an inappropriate location for such an exhibition. One visitor suggested that the exhibit would be best shown at the offices of the UN, or "at the site where these atrocities took place." MoMA invited a somber consideration of the S-21 photographs as examples of vernacular photography, showing photography as a medium capable of participating in political repression and violations. Controversy arose when MoMA was perceived to have violated the already-fraught contact relationship by narrowing the "history" and the characterization (as simply members of a "vernacular" body of art) of the photographs. As a result the curators were accused of a lapse in morality and a violation of the dead.

It is clear from the multiple characterizations, consistencies, and inconsistencies in the visitor comments, that the photographs produced an *affective excess*. Four major themes may be noted: the presence of the sacred or mystical (unspeakable, ineluctable, inexplicable); a sense of the aesthetic (as [not] art, innocent, tragic, beautiful); a sense of a lack of knowledge (more information needed to contextualize the images, more knowledge needed generally); and an explicitly political response (more care should have been taken, or less interference made, by the museum, or the exhibition as being symptomatic of an apolitical condition at home in the USA/the West or in Cambodia/the "Third World"). One review considered *Photographs from S-21* "one of the year's most moving exhibitions," "a heartbreaking triumph" (Nahas, 1997). Cultural stereotyping and sensationalized reportage flourished in response to *Photographs from S-21*; one writer claiming the exhibition staged "the neutral gaze of the camera meet[ing] the blank stare of a benighted humanity" (Griffin, 1997). The horror of knowing that each photographed individual had been brutally executed is displaced onto minor, visible ruptures of bodily integrity seen in the photographs. One quite fantastic response to the exhibition was the writing of a draft screenplay titled "Photographs from S-21" which was forwarded to MoMA's Department of Photography along with a request for the material assistance from the Museum. The opening scene of the screenplay is set in a gallery space hung with the S-21 portraits. After gallery closing time the room's television monitor "CLICKS on. Without explanation." The portraits spontaneously reappear, in rapid succession, on the television monitor, until a portrait of a young woman

> ... freezes [and] becomes larger/ And larger until just/ Her EYES then/ The WHITE background of her photograph fill [sic] the screen/ Then suddenly everything bursts into WHITE/ ... The framed black and white portraits seem to float in a sea of whiteness. (Soluri and Nolletti Productions, 1999, capitalization in original)

Seeing the gallery as a space haunted by the ghosts of those captured in the photographs was echoed in some visitor comment-book responses: "It's hard to sit here comfortably with all these dead eyes staring."

In his review of *Photographs from S-21*, the *New York Times* critic Michael Kimmelman wrote: "We expect somehow to find in these mug-shots, as in any portrait, something true and essential about the subjects," and also argued that "even mug-shots, notwithstanding their basic function as simple ID's, have roots in artistic conventions as old as the renaissance" (Kimmelman, 1997: C12). Kimmelman remarks upon the flattery and trickery in portraiture, but he stops short of suggesting that the S-21 photographs are aligned with such trickery. Instead he comments that the S-21 portraits are "tricky to judge" and "mute." In his attempt to link portrait traditions and mug-shot photography Kimmelman misses crucial differences between the two. Unlike portraiture, whose involvement in the technologies of the modern state is irregular and relatively minor (although portraits of heads of state can certainly serve a number of functions), mug-shots and colonial anthropometric portraiture are explicit technologies of intervention and control over both subject-citizens and those from whom all political rights have been stripped (see for example Jackson, 1999). A mug-shot does not attempt to show what is "true and essential"; rather it attempts to fix a subjects' individuality *as* criminality. At the other end of the scale, the iconic portraits of Mao, Stalin, Lenin, etc., attempt to fix the leader's image as *the* image of sovereign transcendence (see for example Dickerman, 2001).

With historical hindsight, and from behind the curatorial lens of MoMA and the Photo Archive Group, the photographs now function as reverse mug-shots, for it is the authority behind the lens we now consider the criminal. In the place of the photographed "criminal" (or traitor), now appear innocent victims who died violent deaths. We can be confident only that these images were, from the first, and like all deliberate photographic "identification" images, dissatisfactory and thoroughly *unlike* images of these individuals. As Jean-Luc Nancy asks:

> Why is it that an "identification" photo is most often poorer, duller, and less "lifelike" than any other photo?...When does someone resemble *himself* [in a photo]? Only when a photo shows something of him, or her, something more than what is identical, more than the "face," the "image," the "traits" or the "portrait," something more than the copy of the diacritical signs of an "identity." (Nancy, 2000: 157)

Many audience members, like Kimmelman, remarked on the "muteness" of the S-21 photographs: that the photographic medium prevents the deceased subject from speaking, or the medium as mirroring an incapacity of the subject to have spoken in the moment in which they were being photographed. Reviewer Dominique Nahas observed a "mute dignity" in the photographs. A consideration of photography as "an art of non-intervention" whereby "the person who intervenes cannot record [and] the person who is recording cannot intervene" (Sontag, 1973: 11–12) is being extended in such comments. For viewers of the photographs, it impossible to intervene (while moral orders suggest it should not be possible to *not* intervene). But visitors also transfer this sense of incapacity to the photographed individual, seeing them as incapable of intervening (escaping, resisting, or bearing witness) in a fateful progression of past, present, or future. Barbie Zelizer, writing of the difficulties of viewing photographs of Nazi atrocities, argues that "photography may function most directly to achieve what it ought to have stifled – atrocity's normalization" (Zelizer, 1998: 212).

The curators at MoMA could not have communicated (and presumably would not have wished to communicate) directly with the original Khmer Rouge photographer/s. Nevertheless, the authorship and ownership of the photographs (and to a lesser extent the identity of the 22 victims) were issues that dogged the MoMA exhibition. In the same months that *Photographs from S-21* was showing in New York, a man claiming to have been the chief photographer at S-21, Nhem En, gave a series of interviews to international journalists in Phnom Penh (McDowell, 1997; Smith, 1997). In Cambodia, Nhem En returned to the S-21 site, and viewed the portrait photos now displayed in the Tuol Sleng Museum. The MoMA curators sought clarification of Nhem En's authorship of the photographs by contacting Peter Maguire, one of the historians with whom Niven and Riley had previously collaborated. Nhem En has subsequently been interviewed by historians David Chandler and Peter Maguire, and Photo Archive Group co-founder Doug Niven (Chandler, 1999: 27–8). Significant new information about the use and production of the photographs has been offered by Nhem En in interviews, but his claims to authorship of the photographs has not resulted in any public recognition appearing with the work. The other names not recorded on the walls of Gallery Three are those of prisoners identified by historians and the Photo Archive Group. Facsimile copies of five portraits included in the final exhibition were forwarded by the Photo Archive Group to MoMA with "the names we have" (Riley, 1997). To my knowledge, these names were not included in the exhibition.

The exhibition *Photographs from S-21* engaged New York audiences with images connected with a relatively less well known atrocity. But the museum also received criticism from visitors for presenting such artefacts as if it were simply necessary and desirable (in a moral or practical sense). It seems that visitors, not curators, struggled most with questions such as "whose memory is this?," "what form of memory?," and "how might these photographs be exhibited?" Suggestions that the S-21 photographs could have been recontextualized through the provision of maps, authority statements, or the involvement of diasporic Khmer communities are, however, equally problematic. The MoMA exhibition is not simply a case of images being removed from the geographical or institutional sites in which their testimony has meaning. The removal of the photographs from Cambodia was enabled by contemporary, internationalized discourses of humanitarian intervention and cultural memory, and an enthusiasm for specific cultural-geographical imaginaries. The S-21 photographs, their history already narrowed and overdetermined, arrived in a metropolitan art space which too readily gestured toward humanitarian sensibilities supposedly above political contestation.

NOTES

1   I wish to thank Susan Kismaric, Sarah Hermanson, and Rachel Crognale at the MoMA Department of Photography for their time, thoughts, and assistance during my visit to MoMA in January–February 2001.

2 The subject of this chapter is part of a larger research project based in Cambodia which examines memorials to the traumatic events and experiences of Democratic Kampuchea. In the course of this research I became interested in how and why the portrait photographs have become the undisciplined envoys of Cambodia's traumatic past, circulating on a global scale and through various media.

3 The United States and its allies had opposed Vietnam's 1979 "liberating" military incursion into Cambodia. For over a decade following 1979, Cambodia was denied significant Western food and medical aid. Vietnam's involvement in the reconstruction of Cambodia was perceived as a "Vietnamization" of the country in the West, and only the Soviet bloc gave aid to the People's Republic, despite mass media and scholarly exposure of the extreme privations effected by Cambodian genocide (see Klintworth, 1989; Evans & Rowley, 1990; Vickery, 1999).

4 In the early 1990s, Cornell University Library carried out a massive two-year project of microfiche copying at a number of archives in Phnom Penh.

5 Support was forthcoming from various sources in the United States, including funding from the Lucius and Eva Eastman Fund and private individuals, and photographic materials at discounted prices from various commercial photographic supplies groups.

6 David Chandler (1999: 170 n. 42) reports that an unknown number of portrait photographs disappeared during in the early years of the Museum.

7 The interest continued throughout the following year – the British Broadcasting Corporation shot a documentary about the work of the Photo Archive Group which aired on British television in 1996. The *Time* and *Photographers International* features were timed to commemorate the 20th anniversary of the Khmer Rouge's 1975 capture of Phnom Penh in April, 1995.

8 The film is also an important cultural representation for Cambodians, especially diasporic Khmer communities (see Smith, 1994: 153).

9 Two lounges and a low table at the center of Gallery Three provided those viewing *Photographs from S-21* with an opportunity to sit, write comments, and read from various books (including Niven and Riley's aforementioned book *The Killing Fields*).

10 The video showed the former leader being put on trial, denounced, and sentenced to life imprisonment by his own remnant Khmer Rouge forces. Two portrait photographs of Pol Pot, one taken in 1979 and the other a still from the video, appeared on the front page of *The New York Times* on July 29, 1997.

11 For example, the opening sentence of the wall text and press release accompanying the exhibition stated simply: "[I]n April 1975, Cambodia had just concluded five years of a disastrous civil war." No mention was made of the fact that this "civil war" was a conflict gravely exacerbated by the secret bombing campaigns visited on Cambodia by the United States during the later stages of its war in Vietnam, and by concurrent United States' support for the corrupt Lon Nol regime in Phnom Penh, against which the Khmer Rouge were able to rally a significant section of the country's population (see Kiernan, 1989, 1996; Chandler, 1991, 1996; and Vickery, 1999).

12 MoMA had previously exhibited works from other violent contexts: Gilles Peres's photographs of the 1994 violence in Rwanda; a show of overt political art entitled *The Path of Resistance*; and a show representing post-1960 works which critically explored ideas of counter-monuments and memory.

13 Some comments address co-visitors, others are directed towards the exhibition's curators, and some are explicitly self-addressing. A small number of comments suggest a deliberate visit to the *Photographs from S-21* exhibition, while other visitors report

coming upon the exhibition in the course of larger exploration of the photography galleries.

REFERENCES

Chandler, D. P. (1991). *The Tragedy of Cambodian History: War, Politics and Revolution since 1945*. New Haven: Yale University Press.

Chandler, D. P. (1996). *Facing the Cambodian Past: Selected Essays 1971–1994*. Sydney: Allen & Unwin.

Chandler, D. P. (1999). *Voices from S-21: Terror and History in Pol Pot's Secret Prison*. Chiang Mai: Silkworm Books.

Clifford, J. (1997). *Routes: Travel and Translation in the Late Twentieth Century*. Cambridge, MA and London: Harvard University Press.

Derrida, J. (1996). *Archive Fever: A Freudian Impression*. Trans. E. Prenowitz. Chicago: University of Chicago Press.

Dickerman, L. (2001). "Lenin in the Age of Mechanical Reproduction," in M. S. Roth and C. G. Salas, eds., *Disturbing Remains: Memory, History and Crisis in the Twentieth Century*. Los Angeles: Getty Research Institute.

Elsner, J. (1994). "A Collector's Model of Desire: The House and Museum of Sir John Soane," pp. 155–76 in J. Elsner and R. Cardinal, eds., *Cultures of Collecting*. London: Reaktion Books.

Evans, G. and Rowley, K. (1990). *Red Brotherhood at War: Vietnam, Laos and Cambodia since 1975*. London: Verso.

French, L. (2002). "Exhibiting Terror," in *Representation and Human Rights*. Rutgers University Press.

Griffin, T. (1997). "Photographs from S-21: 1975–1979," *Time Out New York*, Sept. 4–11, p. 50.

Hughes, R. (forthcoming). "Nationalism and Memory at the Tuol Sleng Museum of Genocide Crimes, Phnom Penh, Cambodia," in K. Hodgkin and S. Radstone, eds., *Contested Pasts*. London: Routledge.

Jackson, P. (1999). "Constructions of culture, representations of race: Edward Curtis' 'way of seeing'" in K. Anderson and F. Gale, eds., *Cultural Geographies*. Australia: Addison Wesley Longman.

Kiernan, B. (1989). "The American Bombardment of Kampuchea, 1969–1973," *Vietnam Generation* 1(1): 4–41.

Kiernan, B. (1996). *The Pol Pot Regime: Race Power and Genocide in Cambodia under the Khmer Rouge, 1975–79*. Chiang Mai: Silkworm Books.

*The Killing Fields* (1994). Warner Brothers (Enigma). Screenplay by B. Robinson; produced by D. Puttnam; directed by R. Joffé.

Kimmelman, M. (Aug. 27, 1997). "Hypnotized by Mug Shots That Stare Back: Are They Windows or Mirrors?," *The New York Times*, pp. C1 and C12.

Kirshenblatt-Gimblett, B. (1998). *Destination Culture: Tourism, Museums and Heritage*. Berkeley & Los Angeles: University of California Press.

Klein, K. L. (2000). "On the Emergence of *Memory* in Historical Discourse," *Representations* 69: 127–50.

Klintworth, G. (1989). *Vietnam's Intervention in Cambodia in International Law*. Canberra: Australian Government Publishing.

Ledgerwood, J. (1997). "The Tuol Sleng Museum of Genocidal Crimes: National Narrative," *Museum Anthropology* 21(1): 82–98.

Ly, D. and Muan, I. (2000*). The Legacy of Absence: A Cambodian Story*. Phnom Penh: Reyum Gallery.

McDowell, R. (Feb. 7, 1997). "Lens Captures Khmer Rouge Genocide," *The Bangkok Post.*

Museum of Modern Art (internal document, April, 1997). *Gallery Three*. Department of Photography MoMA files.

Museum of Modern Art (wall text and press release, May 1997). *Photographs from S-21: 1975–1979.* Department of Photography, MoMA files.

Nahas, D. (June 15, 1997). "Haunting Images of Impending Death," *The Critical State of Visual Art in New York Review,* pp.1–2.

Nancy, J.-L. (2000). *Being Singular Plural*. Stanford: Stanford University Press.

Niven, D. and Riley, C. (1996). *The Killing Fields..* Santa Fe: Twin Palms.

O'Sullivan, S. (June 28, 1997). "Critics' Choice: Photo," *Daily News.*

Photo Archive Group (unpublished, 1993). *Tuol Sleng Museum of Genocide Photo Archive Project Proposal,* CCC archive, Phnom Penh.

Photo Archive Group (unpublished, n.d.). *Tuol Sleng Museum of Genocide Project Summary,* Department of Photography, MoMA files.

Peters, G. (Oct. 12, 1994). "Restoration Project Immortalizes Haunting Images of S-21," *The Cambodia Daily,* p. 16.

Riley, C. (April 21, 1997). Facsimile communication to Adrienne Williams, MoMA Department of Photography files.

Smith, C. S. (Sept. 16, 1997). "Profiting From His Shots of Pol Pot's Terror," *The Wall Street Journal.*

Smith, F. (1994). "Cultural Consumption: Cambodian Peasant Refugees and Television in the 'First World,'" in M. Ebihara, C. Mortland, and J. Ledgerwood, eds., *Cambodian Culture Since 1975: Homeland and Exile.* Ithaca and London: Cornell University Press, pp. 141–59.

Soluri and Nolletti Productions (July 29, 1999). *Photographs from S-21*, facsimile of draft screenplay, Department of Photography, MoMA files.

Sontag, S. (1973). *On Photography.* New York: Farrar, Straus and Giroux.

Stewart, S. (1994). "Death and Life, in that Order, in the Works of Charles Willson Peale," in J. Elsner and R. Cardinal, eds., *Cultures of Collecting.* London: Reaktion Books, pp. 204–23.

Trebay, G. (June 3, 1997). "Killing Fields of Vision: Was Cambodia's Genocide Just a Moment of Photographic History?," *The Village Voice,* p. 34.

Vann Nath, (1998). *A Cambodian Prison Portrait: One Year in the Khmer Rouge's S-21.* Bangkok: White Lotus.

Vickery, M. (1999). *Cambodia 1975–1982.* Chiang Mai: Silkworm Books.

Williams, A. (July 7, 1997). Letter to William Dunlap and Linda Burgess, MoMA Department of Photography files.

Williams, A. (Aug. 31, 1998). Letter to Paul Ellis, MoMA Department of Photography files.

Zelizer, B. (1998). *Remembering to Forget: Holocaust Memory Through the Camera's Eye.* Chicago: University of Chicago Press.

# 34

## Sex Machine: Global Hypermasculinity and Images of the Asian Woman in Modernity

### L. H. M. Ling

Three visions of globalization currently dominate the popular imagination: "the West is best," "the West versus the rest," and "jihad versus McWorld."[1] All three treat globalization as a Westernizing assault with little input or agency from local, non-Western sources. This Western exceptionalism relies on two main assumptions: (1) global, Western forces subsume, if not destroy, local, non-Western ones, and (2) identity is singular and "hard." The logical conclusion is that much of the world faces a stark choice between globalization and localization.

This chapter proposes an alternative view: in order to succeed, globalization necessarily engenders a postcolonial mix of hybridity, simulacra, and other such global–local conversions. Together, these conversions provide a common, global context for diverse pursuits of markets, products, and profits in local contexts. This chapter further endorses the position that identity is multiple, layered, and malleable. One facet of identity that typifies this is a *global hypermasculinity* that is currently permeating the world political economy. In East Asia especially, this is dispersed through and disguised as modernization and internationalization.[2] Under the rubric of globalization, local and global media (backed by state and corporate capital, respectively) naturalize hypermasculinity as part and parcel of the economic development of manly states and manly firms.

Confirmed in this is a deepening of the globalist bias. In addition to a valorization of openness, globalization carries with it an association of capital-intensive, upwardly mobile hypermasculinity. This is opposed to an implicitly closed, localized, service-based, and socially regressive hyperfemininity. Hypermasculinity's promise and its appeal lie partly in its easy application to diverse contexts where it – and such notions as the manly state and the "bull market" – can be grounded in entrenched traditions of the patriarchal household. At the same time, hyper-masculinity cracks with internal contradictions as it pushes for greater and more intensive competition, often for the same (and thereby proportionately shrinking) objects of desire. Furthermore, by its very nature, global hypermasculinity contains "the Other" within. To demonstrate, I focus here on visual media (re)constructions of gender identity for women in East Asia.

## ■ Three Visions of Globalization ■

Francis Fukuyama claims that the "West is best" in terms of history and economy. He asserts that all countries will follow invariably a single path of development toward liberal capitalism, thereby instigating an "end to history." Although he laments a future when all passion, daring, idealism, and struggle "will be replaced by economic calculation, the endless solving of technical problems...and the satisfaction of sophisticated consumer demands," he concludes that world-order integration is an "inevitability."[3]

This line is reworked by Samuel P. Huntington into "the West versus the rest": the post-Cold War era, although no longer burdened with great economic or ideological struggles, presents a "clash" of civilizations, thereby counterposing "the rest" against "the West."[4] In particular, Huntington warns of threats from two civilizations with supposedly historic antipathies toward the West: the Confucian and the Islamic.

Finally, Benjamin J. Barber sees globalization as "jihad versus McWorld."[5] He bemoans the potential loss of democratic rights and freedom in two late modern juggernauts: "McWorld," a glitzy corporatization of global capitalism, which bull-dozes individual and communal rights in the name of profit, and "jihad," its fundamentalist counterpart, which does the same in the name of such primordial motivations as Allah and ethno-nationalism.

Despite their differences (including their suggested responses to these dangers), all three agree that globalization means one-sided Westernization. Fukuyama's West "wins," based on Hegel's notion of a world-encompassing superculture. Huntington, who already assumes the West's superculture status, offers a Machiavellian guide to maintaining this princely status by cementing relations with friendly nations while exploiting hostilities among the others. In Barber's variation, McWorld ultimately consumes jihad. He captures the either–or quality of all three of these arguments most succinctly: "[There is] no room in the mosque for Nintendo, no place on the Internet for Jesus.... Life cannot be both play and in earnest, cannot stand for the lesser gratification of a needy body and simultan-eously for the greater glory of a selfless soul. Either the Qu'ran speaks the Truth, or Truth is a television quiz show" (216).

Most provoking to this Western exceptionalism is East Asia. Fukuyama views the region as an exemplar of globalization where the local surrenders completely to the global. Japan and the region's newly industrializing countries (NICs), he writes, demonstrate "a truly universal consumer culture that has become both a symbol and an underpinning of the universal homogeneous state" (10). Even in Marxist-Leninist China, "the pull of the liberal idea continues to be very strong as economic power devolves and the economy becomes more open to the outside world" (11). Huntington, in contrast, sees Asia as culturally intransigent, weapons happy, and irremediably opposed to the West. The home of both Confucian and Islamic civilization has "power approach[ing] that of the West," even as it holds what he claims are fundamentally non-Western values (49).

Of these three, however, Barber finds Asia especially jarring. The region's McWorldian consumerist lifestyles clash noisily with jihadian cultural intolerance. China, for instance, is "huge, ancient, highly civilized, Communist, traditionally hostile to foreigners and their barbarian culture," yet it lurches almost giddily toward the hamburgers, discos, profits, and status of McWorld (190). The "Asian democracies" of Japan, India, and Korea face the opposite problem: they acknowledge the liberal politics of the West but fear its encroaching cultural imperialism. "An internal jihad," for example, brews within India among ethno-religious fundamentalists, and Japan's spiritual, cultural soul quakes before the next generation of hipsters, which identifies more closely with McWorld than with being "native Japanese."

Studies of women in Asia by Western feminists have sought to break out of related conventional analytical and cultural essentialisms; they instead speak from specific local, gendered perspectives on globalization. Nevertheless, many of these works still reify globalization as one-sided Westernization. Much of this literature, for example, highlights the structural oppression of Third World women, including those in East Asia, under global capitalism.[6]

The flattening of Third World women into oppressed victims or pawns of patriarchy effectively robs them of the very agency that Western feminists so cherish and advocate. It thus legitimates an implicit agenda of Western (white) feminists: "saving" their non-Western (nonwhite) sisters. This ethnocentrism caters to an ideological and sometimes economic defensiveness. A "new nationalism," Linda Y. C. Lim claims, allies Western feminists with local labor activists to boycott Asian economies that supposedly depress prices and eliminate jobs with their "cheap imports."[7] But this antidevelopmentalist sentiment among Western liberals risks playing into the hands of conservative local interests – Islamic, Confucian, or Catholic, for example – that seek to limit women's independence. Furthermore, the result may actually be worsened working conditions and wages for women in Asia – and the further legitimation of Western feminist imperialism.

"Systems of racial, class, and gender domination do not have *identical* effects on women in Third World contexts," Chandra Mohanty emphasizes.[8] Rather, we must attend to "the complex *relationality* that shapes our social and political lives" and which necessitates an emancipatory politics that cannot be reduced to "binary oppositions or oppressor/oppressed relations."

## ■ Global Hypermasculinity ■

I favor the dismantling of tiresome dualisms and commend calls for greater ethnological and ideological awareness from feminists and feminisms alike. This awareness can lead to a more comprehensive understanding of our contemporary world. But too often, the target of critique seems to be misplaced: though often guilty as charged, Western feminists are not the problem. The real enemy, I suggest, is a convergence of hypermasculine interests across cultural, spatial, and systemic divides.

The world seems remarkably uniform – and not fragmented into West–Rest or jihad–McWorld dichotomies – when women look up from their work in homes, fields, nurseries, factories, stores, schools, offices, hospitals, brothels, massage parlors, and myriad other locations. Globalization, by its very interaction with diverse local forces, necessarily requires identity – both global and local – to be open, organic, and unpredictable. Dynamic growth in East Asia brings new, especially entrepreneurial, opportunities for women in the region. But it also mires them in a local–global hegemony that I call "global hypermasculinity."

The term *hypermasculinity* was coined by Ashis Nandy.[9] The impact of British imperialism in India, Nandy says, was damaging to colonizer and colonized alike because both groups felt compelled to denigrate anything smacking of the "feminine" (including women, the poor, homosexuals, intellectual activity, and social welfare) in order to glorify the "masculine" (defined as aggression, achievement, control, competition, and power). What resulted was a reactionary, exaggerated form of masculinism, or hypermasculinity, which left in its wake a variety of psychosexual pathologies.

I extend this notion of hypermasculinity specifically to economic development and, more generally, to globalization. In East Asia's Confucian-based "miracle" economies, hypermasculinity adopts the traditional rhetoric of the state taking manly revenge against the West's (and later Japan's) emasculating imperialism in the past. Economic development, in particular, is the site of this enactment of hypermasculinity. By inflating the mantle of classical Confucian paternalism, the state locks society into a hyperfeminized position of classical Confucian womanhood, that is, into a role involving subordination, self-sacrifice, discipline, and deference. In this way, the state assumes that society *consents* to the imposition of the burdens and responsibilities of economic development – without its receiving commensurate concessions to political representation or even a political voice.

And as the exemplars of hyperfeminized society, women become the hypermasculine state's most obvious target. East Asia's economic growth was built on the backs of low-wage, unskilled, young female labor. Mass-manufacturing assembly plants targeted girls, usually from the countryside and aged 16 to 23, for their "nimble fingers" and "docile natures" – and paid these workers consistently less than their male counterparts. South Korea, until its recent financial crisis one of the world's fastest-growing economies, typifies the region: in 1971, female workers earned about 44 percent of men's wages; in 1985, this had improved to only 48 percent.[10] In 1990, Korean women's wages amounted to approximately 79 percent of men's wages in the service industries, 56 percent in clerical work, and 54 percent in manufacturing.[11]

Global hypermasculinity thus manufactures more efficiently and pervasively what Robert Young has characterized with regard to colonialism as a "machine of desire."[12] According to Young, colonialism sanctioned a "group fantasy" in which racist depictions of the Other simultaneously conveyed the colonizers' secret desire for the colonized even as it loudly proclaimed their revulsion. Likewise, hypermasculinity instills in local elites a group fantasy of righteous economic conquest and desire. But under the sway of the hypermasculine, desire engulfs as repulsion recedes. Indeed, global hypermasculinity builds on a colonial legacy of racialized, sexualized production and consumption, now billed as "modernity," "wealth," "mobility," "technological sophistication," and "internationalization." Moreover, today's capitalist globalization, as reified by Fukuyama and Barber (and to a lesser extent by Huntington), boldly pursues what colonialism dared not consider: transgressing national borders, integrating production, and unifying consumption. Toward these ends, the media play a critical, contributing role. This is evident in media (re)constructions of gender identity in East Asia, to which I now turn.

## ■ Gender, Media, and Globalization ■

The latest media market for hypermasculine developmentalism is China. Since 1978, China has shed the yoke of radical self-reliance and anticonsumerism. It fixates on state-run, capitalist economies such as Singapore as the preferred model of development. A recent survey of television commercials in Shanghai finds that local representations of gender identity increasingly conform to (Western) "international" ones. In particular, the Asian woman embodies "service" – for local and international media alike. But whereas international ads tend to sexualize this message (as in tourism ads that feature beautiful young Asian women in traditional dress enticing the male viewer/traveler to "visit"), local media frame it in traditional terms: married women are portrayed as "virtuous wives and good mothers" (*xianqi liangmu*) when they tend to their husbands and children at home, single women or young "misses" (*xiaojie*) reveal their "true selves" (*benlai mianmu*) as consumers in a market economy, and so on.

Accordingly, Shanghai television shows women in all those occupations deemed "feminine": doing the laundry, cooking or serving food, caring for children, applying makeup, washing hair, using household appliances. One commercial claims to document "all those important stages in a woman's life": graduating from school, landing a first job, getting married. When women are shown in offices or working outside the home, they bring the tea, carry the papers, do the typing, and attend to their male bosses' needs. Usually, these female characters dress in the latest international (that is, Western) fashion. Commercials that show women in traditional garb generally invoke historical figures – a well-known empress, concubine, or courtesan – or feature a beauty contestant such as "Miss China." But whether in Western or traditional garb, feminine deference typically marks these media images.

These images of Chinese women in the 1990s depart radically from the images of their precursors during the Cultural Revolution (1966–76). Then, women were depicted as authoritative cadres, devoted revolutionaries, unflinching guerrilla fighters, or "iron girls" (*tie guniang*). Today, Chinese media excoriate the "superwoman" (*nÿqiangren*) who may hold a doctorate, manage an enterprise, or run an office but who in her personal life aches for a husband and children. China's previous images also exploited women – for the party and state rather than the bottom line. But at least these images offered women the refreshing alternatives of becoming leaders and decision-makers, in charge of their own lives. Today, the Chinese media reiterate the same old bourgeois line heard around the world – that women matter only for their entertainment or (re)productive value.

Local constructions of Chinese masculinity are similarly "internationalizing." The "modern" Chinese man depicted in these commercials mirrors his Western counterpart. Instead of the ubiquitous blue Mao suit of yesteryear, he is now clad in snappy jacket and tie complemented by loafers and briefcase. When shown engaging in recreational or sporting activities, young men wear casually chic jeans with colorful T-shirts.

Indeed, Chinese commercials mirror those in the rest of East Asia. Media images of women in capitalist Taiwan also revolve around service, family, food, laundry, hair, and cosmetics. Masculinity, on the other hand, signifies progress, action, and achievement. Commercials focusing on single young women (e.g., for sanitary napkins) show them working in an office setting. The location of their desks, piled high with reams of paper, and their activities in the office (e.g., distributing mail) indicate that these women are clerical staff or other such underlings. They are clearly not in positions of authority. Commercials that feature young married women do not deviate from this norm. A car commercial begins with a handsome young couple, he in a tuxedo and she in a white wedding gown. In cinema-verité style, the couple is interviewed as they ride in the car. The viewer hears the following dialogue:

SALESMAN: Mr. Groom, please get in. You're about to be married in May. [This suggests that the couple is going through a trial run for the wedding ceremony as much as trying out the car. The salesman turns to the bride.]

SALESMAN: Sitting here now, do you think it's crowded in the back seat – especially when you're wearing such a big skirt?

BRIDE: No, not at all! In fact, it wouldn't matter if you added two or three children here. [She smiles knowingly.]

SALESMAN: Feel again our low steering frame and shock absorbers.

BRIDE [laughing]: You're too deep for me! We women don't understand such things.

The commercial ends with the happy couple holding a large banner of the car company's logo, smiling and waving goodbye.

Only mature women, it seems, receive any respect from Taiwan's media. But this respect derives from the stereotype of women existing to provide service, specifically in their primary function as mothers. A public-service announcement shows a woman in her late forties or early fifties busy with the demands of modern life – shopping for groceries, driving her car, drying dishes, spending time with her daughter. In a voice-over she reminds the audience that "watching one's daughter grow up is one of life's greatest joys." For this reason, she emphasizes (here, she turns directly to the viewer), regular checkups are a must: "I cannot afford to collapse."

Treating women as subordinate objects of desire is pervasive in news reports as well. In January 1997, one of Taiwan's morning news programs reported on a rash of assaults against women in southern small towns: men were randomly slashing the victims on their legs and necks with knives or razors, usually as the women were returning home from market, school, or work. The report ostensibly sought to show how women could defend themselves against such attacks. But the content and method of reporting reinforced the image of woman as helpless, hapless victim. The camera even took on a masculinized, voyeuristic gaze as it simulated these slashings. One actress wore a long, tight skirt with a high slit so that her shapely legs would receive ample exposure as she ran from her supposed attacker. Another actress's backside curiously commanded the camera's singular attention as she entered an elevator to find an old lech leering at her from within. Furthermore, these eroticized simulations suggested that only young and attractive women were victimized, when in actuality women of all ages and appearances were attacked.

The gender images apparent in the PRC and Taiwan reflect Japanese media stereotypes of women. With their high production values and well-established distribution networks, Japanese commercials dominate the region's broadcast and print media. Typically, the Japanese media market female consumers as cute schoolgirls (13 to 18 years old), hip cuties (18 to 22), single office workers (22 to 25), or sexy adults (25 to 35). An overlapping category of often older women is the "housewife." She falls into six types: the "broad-minded and almighty" woman, the "liberated and diplomatic" woman, the "woman of the house," the "harmonious wit and beauty," the "devoted and helpful" woman, and the "tranquil and prudent" woman.[13] Not surprisingly, these images of Japanese housewives often show them in traditional dress.

Occasionally, Japanese media images offer women a subtle source of resistance to patriarchal culture, but they invariably abide by the Japanese government's guideline for the normal course of a woman's life, which includes the edict: "a woman should also be ready to care for needy elderly in her family and for her husband when he retires."[14]

Significantly, these media images sell "internationalization," "class," or "sophistication" as combinations of Western and traditional ideals of beauty. For instance, Japanese advertisements often valorize the Western standard of longer legs, slimmer bodies, and fuller breasts in combination with indigenous claims of racial superiority in complexion and hair. An October 1992 cover of *An-An Magazine*, which is targeted toward women aged 20 to 35, exhibits "beautiful nudity" in the form of a young female gamboling naked on the beach. She appears trim and athletic with long, slim legs. Yet she is also relatively well endowed, despite her slenderness. Her short, wet hair bobs jauntily in the wind. Her face seems clear of makeup.

Compare this vision of feminine beauty with a description of the ideal woman during Japan's Heian period (794–1185):

> Gourd-shaped faces, high foreheads, plump and "shining" white faces (effected by an application of...chalky powder called *oshiroi*, along with a tint of rouge on the cheeks and eyelids), the removal of natural eyebrows and their replacement by daubs of black carbon high on the forehead, small noses, and circular red lips (only partially reddened with *beni* to give a flower-bud effect), which concealed black teeth that had been permanently dyed with *o-kane*, an iron acetate infusion. Their hair, however, was their most valued attribute. It was allowed to grow immensely long.[15]

Calendar posters from China from 1910 through the 1930s demonstrate this shift in gender aesthetics even more dramatically. Used to advertise products, these posters document the dominant ideals of beauty at the time. All the pictures portray well-dressed upper-class women. Indeed, their central appeal lies in vivid portrayals of dress, class, and environment. What these calendar images make clear is that as Chinese society internationalized, representations of the female body increasingly mixed Chinese and Western patriarchal standards of beauty.

For example, one of the earliest posters from this collection shows a woman in Manchurian dress with high collar, flat bodice, and full skirt. She sits formally, facing the viewer, with one arm crooked over the back of her chair. Her expression and demeanor convey a sense of calm and remote dignity. She seems to be a wife and mother somewhere in her thirties or forties. Only her face and hands are exposed to the viewer; her head is covered with an embroidered headdress. Two tiny slippers, suggestive of bound feet, peep from under her long skirt. Her relationship to the viewer is one of benign distance – the viewer's attention is flattering but incidental. This high-born lady would be her beautiful, contained self regardless of the viewer's existence.

By the 1930s, the ideal woman looks quite different. She wears a form-fitting, see-through dress with a long slit that exposes not only a glimpse of fetching leg but also lacy underwear. Inclined on a sofa with one leg crossed over the other, her head perched on one hand, she teases the viewer with a sidelong, dimpled glance. Her expression and attitude are playful, sexy, and inviting. In contrast to the depiction of her counterpart of the 1910s, this picture of the 1930s Chinese woman shows someone flaunting a curvaceous figure (with added shading to emphasize her voluptuousness). Her status is ambiguous: she could be a newlywed or a single woman-about-town. Definitely younger than her 1910s counterpart, this 1930s woman seems aged between 25 and 30. Interestingly, her relationship to the viewer has changed. Now, the woman wants and needs the attention of the viewer, who is, as can be inferred from her look and posture, male.

Upper-class Chinese women of this period saw modernization as their liberation. Removed from the more obvious strictures of traditional society, they were now free to show their bodies, be openly desirous and desired, and enjoy all the accoutrements of modernity: education, travel, physical exercise, romantic love. Leading intellectuals of the day, such as Ding Ling and Ba Jin, wrote searing critiques of the traditional Chinese family and its stultifying effects on society in general and women in particular. This was indeed a heady time for Chinese women, who, inspired by the trendy example set by Shanghai's Soong sisters, believed that their future lay in capitalist "internationalization." Little did they know that their new, liberated identity would be hyperfeminized into a sexualized and racialized stereotype that prevails to the present.

The West's powerful media machine now takes this hyperfeminized version to be the exclusive identity of Asian women. From high to popular culture, it perpetuates a colonial "group fantasy," in which the Asian woman embodies "service," especially for the white man. David Henry Hwang skewers this stereotype in his gender-bending play *M. Butterfly*, which is based on the true story of a French diplomat who somehow missed the fact that his Chinese mistress of 20 years was actually a man. For Hwang, this Frenchman personifies the Western ideological and emotional conviction that Asia must be a woman. At the end of the play (though not in real life), the diplomat commits suicide, unable to tolerate the possibility that his fantasy love mocked, not affirmed, his Western manhood.

The current mail-order-bride business feeds off of this image of the Asian woman. Men in richer economies not only exploit poor, desperate women who have little recourse to escape their circumstances except selling their conjugal "services,"[16] they also use this sexualized, racialized Asian woman to censure other, less subordinate women, regardless of race, as *feminists*. The largely visual techniques engaged to attract customers gloss over the underlying poverty, coercion, and violence that drive the Asian sex industry. Hypersexualized images conveniently overlook the physical and mental abuse suffered by prostitutes (many of whom are children), domestic workers, and mail-order brides at the hands of their clients, bosses, and husbands.

Several Filipina domestic workers have been killed or have committed suicide while working overseas. Others who have survived their indentured servitude have reported sexual abuse by employers who regarded them as private property. Mail-order brides do not even have the luxury of complaining. Some mail-order-bride services promise customers a 30-day "return policy" if not satisfied. And one source estimates that as many as 50,000 Filipinas living near US military bases in the Philippines have contracted the HIV virus.[17]

Critiques of media representations of women occur not only in the West. In March 1997, the All-China Women's Federation (Quanguo Funü Lianhehui, or Fulian) issued a protest against gender bias in PRC television ads. In a survey of 1,200 advertisements from major cities in China, the federation found that only 15 percent of the ads for science and technology products involved female images. A comparable percentage of advertisements featured scantily clad women. The overwhelming majority of the ads portrayed women as housewives, secretaries, and shoppers who also happened to be young and attractive; they appeared most often in advertisements for clothes and beauty products.

This protest, though important, missed the larger point: Hypermasculinity now sets the standard for successful globalization. As can be seen from the ads and television commercials that are displayed or broadcast in the region, both global and local media associate "modern," "international" men and women with stereotypically masculine traits: they are portrayed as upwardly mobile, well educated, well traveled, and well paid. Significantly, they are the managers, investors, bankers, and technocrats of the capitalist world economy. In stark contrast, the media assign stereotypically feminine traits to "traditional," "local" men and women, who are characterized as stagnant, ignorant, parochial, and scrounging for spare change. They are the subordinates, assistants, servers, guides, hawkers, and dependents of, or companions to, the world economy's masculinized subjects.

Within the saga of colonial relations, the image of the Asian female Other takes on a particularly interesting twist. To the white master, she is a potential ally as well as a handy maid. To the Asian male Other, she vacillates from sublime mother to the white master's profane whore. Yet, the Asian female also fulfills a common function for both. Her image embodies profits and fantasy, markets and sovereignty, globalism and colonialism, East and West. A 1996 ad for a posh new Hong Kong nightclub, Club Shanghai, exemplifies this attitude. Presumably backed by expat and local capital, the nightclub advertises itself in explicitly sexualized, racialized terms. With a whiff of colonial ennui enhancing its appeal, the slogan reads: "Shanghai in the '30s was an era of decadence and scandal. *The good old days are back*" (original emphasis). Underneath the caption is a large photograph showing two young Chinese women, hair slickly bobbed in the 1930s style, dressed in sexy cheongsams, dancing with each other. Each looks at the viewer with an inviting, seductive smile. Thus, we have come full circle from 1990s internationalization to 1930s bourgeois modernization.

## ■ Conclusion: Internal Contradictions ■

Despite its seeming opacity and omnipresence, global hypermasculinity may yet collapse under the weight of its own self-importance. As it structures globalization into competition for economic manhood, it provokes two concurrent counter-reactions: angry rebellion from prosperous heirs (e.g., the Japan/China/Korea that can say no) seeking recognition and authority for accomplishments made in the name of the capitalist white father; or open insurgency from wounded rebels (e.g., Iraq, Russia) coveting their fair share of hypermasculine globalism. For every instance of public deference (e.g., South Korea's Kim Dae Jung declaring in 1997 that his country would not deviate from the International Monetary Fund's demand for structural reforms "by one percent") there will be another of defiance (e.g., Malaysia's Mahathir Mohamad accusing Western financial institutions of a "new imperialism"). In either case, global hypermasculinity cannot maintain the status quo of its privilege without inviting open challenges to its own paternalistic authority.

In contrast to the three popular visions of globalization described at the beginning of this essay – visions reproduced, albeit more subtly, in much of the literature on East Asia – the present chapter reframes globalization as a postcolonial jumble. It assumes that (1) globalization needs to mix the global with the local to succeed, and (2) developmental frictions arise, but so do cultural borrowings, innovations, and (re)productions – precisely because identity, of all types, is open, multiple, layered, and organic. Such transformative possibilities excite, but they do not necessarily translate into changes for the better. Global hypermasculinity, for instance, fuses Western and Asian patriarchal traditions to rationalize "globalization." At the same time, global hypermasculinity suffers from debilitating internal contradictions, thereby generating opportunities for transformation.

While Fukuyama, Huntington, Barber, and other hypermasculine globalists depict the world as full of West/rest and jihad/McWorld binaries, the ultimate irony is, as global hypermasculinity demonstrates, such binaries no longer apply. Worse, they obscure the underlying convergences, compromises, negotiations, and alliances that protect both local and global patriarchal interests. These involve not just structural reorganizations (such as China's shift from a command to a market-driven economy) but a fundamental and constant reformulation of who we are, what we feel, how we live, and why we want the things we do.

Gender identity for women in Asia registers this ceaseless flow of identity manipulations. Feminists may be prompted to rephrase a Marxist manifesto: "Women of the world unite – you have nothing to lose but your chains!" The call to revolution, however, does not mean installing yet another set of alienating dichotomies that have been redrawn in gendered or racial terms. For just as the identities of nations, economies, and the world system are cross-linked, interconnected, and complicit, so are those of men and women. And women themselves cluster around different mobile configurations of race, class, level of development, and historical status. For example, while Japanese women suffer from stereotyping by the Japanese media, they also benefit from their economy's success at home and abroad. Similarly, women in Taiwan and Hong Kong enjoy a new ideological standing *vis-à-vis* China, given their media's feminization of the mainland as whore or spinster. But all these women are still subjugated by a common hypermasculine developmentalism.

What we need is a different starting point. Instead of positing the world in either/or terms – "West vs. rest," "jihad vs. McWorld," "us vs. them," "hypermasculinity vs. hyperfemininity" – let us trace the ambiguities, contradictions, and dilemmas that constitute our contemporary, late modern world. We may not resolve them. But in sorting through them, we may discover how deeply and irrevocably embedded we are in one another's lives, if not consciousness.

## NOTES

1 Here I focus on popular, rather than strictly academic, discussions of globalization, given the former's immediate impact on public opinion and policy-making. For a review of academic debates on globalization see L. H. M. Ling, "Globalisation and the Spectre of Fu Manchu: White Man's Burden as Dark Irony," in *Value Pluralism, Normative Theory, and International Relations*, eds. Stephan Fritz and Maria Lensu (London: Macmillan, 2003).

2 For antiglobalists in the West (e.g., militiamen), localization means opposing the so-called New World Order and international organizations such as the United Nations.

3 Francis Fukuyama, "The End of History?" *National Interest* 16 (summer 1989): 3–18.

4 Samuel P. Huntington, "The Clash of Civilizations?" *Foreign Affairs* 72(3) (summer 1993): 22–49; and Huntington, *The Clash of Civilizations and the Remaking of World Order* (New York: Simon and Schuster, 1996).

5 Benjamin J. Barber, *Jihad vs. McWorld: How Globalism and Tribalism Are Reshaping the World* (New York: Ballantine Books, 1996).

6 Three notable exceptions are edited volumes that include the perspectives of both Western and non-Western feminists. See Christina K. Gilmartin, Gail Hershatter, Lisa Rofel, and Tyrene White, eds., *Engendering China: Women, Culture, and the State* (Cambridge, MA: Harvard University Press, 1994); Tani Barlow, ed., *Gender Politics in Modern China: Writing and Feminism* (Durham, NC: Duke University Press, 1993); and Shirin Rai, Hilary Pilkington, and Annie Phizacklea, eds., *Women in the Face of Change: The Soviet Union, Eastern Europe, and China* (London: Routledge, 1992).

7 Linda Y. C. Lim, "Women's Work in Export Factories: The Politics of a Cause," in *Persistent Inequalities*, ed. Irene Tinker (New York: Oxford University Press, 1990), 117.

8 Chandra Talpade Mohanty, "Under Western Eyes: Feminist Scholarship and Colonial Discourses," in *Third World Women and the Politics of Feminism*, eds. Chandra T. Mohanty, Ann Russo, and Lourdes Torres (Bloomington: Indiana University Press, 1991), 13.

9 Ashis Nandy, *The Intimate Enemy: Loss and Recovery of Self under Colonialism* (Delhi: Oxford University Press, 1988).

10 Jeong-Lim Nam, "Women's Role in Export Dependence and State Control of Labor Unions in South Korea," *Women's Studies International Forum* 17(1) (Jan.–Feb. 1994): 57–67.

11 H. S. Paik, "Labor Market Segmentation and Male–Female Wage Differentials in Korea" (master's thesis, Sookmyung Women's University, 1993).

12 See Robert Young, *Colonial Desire: Hybridity in Theory, Culture, and Race* (London: Routledge, 1995).

13 Andrew A. Painter, "The Telepresentation of Gender in Japan," in *Re-Imaging Japanese Women*, ed. Ann E. Imamura (Berkeley and Los Angeles: University of California Press, 1996), 55–6.

14 N. R. Rosenberger, "Fragile Resistance, Signs of Status: Women between State and Media in Japan," in *Re-Imaging Japanese Women*, 14.

15 S. S. Deutsch, "An Abstract from 'Patchwork: A History of Women in Japan,'" in *The Feminine Image*, eds. S. S. Deutsch and H. A. Lind (Honolulu, Hawaii: Honolulu Academy of Arts, 1985), 10–25.

16 Today, mail-order brides are popular not only with men in North America, Western Europe, and Japan but also with men in the wealthier regional economies such as Taiwan and South Korea, where women from poorer economies such as China, Vietnam, Laos, and Kampuchea are much sought after.

17 "The Philippines' Shameful Export," *Nation*, April 17, 1995: 524.

# 35

# De-Eurocentricizing Cultural Studies: Some Proposals

## Robert Stam and Ella Shohat

Cultural studies undeniably constituted a progressive shift away from the high-art elitism of literature departments. Deploying a mode of scholarship which saw cultural products as embedded in a discursive and social continuum, Cultural Studies brought social theory into cultural analysis. Yet despite its radical credentials, Cultural Studies also risks becoming a Eurocentric form of Anglo-American navel gazing.[1] Although many Cultural Studies writers have disengaged the "complicitous critiques" to be found in the ever-evolving corpus of mass-cultural media productions, they have too often done so within the narrow frame of Anglo-American (and especially United Statesian) mass-culture. While stressing stratifications of power based on race, class, gender, and sexuality, Cultural Studies has not always sufficiently examined the *nationalist* premises undergirding some of its work. Too much Cultural Studies work remains insular and ethnocentric, showing little participatory (or even vicarious) knowledge of cultural production or intellectual critique generated from other sites. The privileging of the English language and Anglo-American popular culture robs work in Latin American, Asian, and African subjects of its theoretical aura; whatever does not belong to the Anglo-western world is peripheralized as "Area Studies." To merit institutional representation, it seems, Cultural Studies must trace its pedigree to London or Birmingham, New York or Urbana, Paris or Melbourne, but not to Sao Paulo, Mexico City, Lagos, Cairo, or New Delhi.

This unequal distribution of knowledge and prestige points to the necessity of de-Eurocentrizing and transnationalizing the field. In this chapter, we would like to argue for an analytical model that enacts relational connections across diverse cultural geographies. Our goal is to counterpoint usually ghettoized discourses within a transnational, multichronotopic form of analysis, using visual and media culture as cases in point. More specifically, our proposals bear on the following discussions (1) the basic terms of the debate; (2) the genealogies of the field; (3) the narrativization of modernism; (4) the examples of *modernismo* and tropicalia; and (5) the practice of *comparative* multiCultural Studies.

### ■ The Terms of Debate ■

By way of preamble, we should define what we mean by the two key terms "Eurocentrism" and "Multiculturalism." The former term points to the ideological substratum common to colonialist, imperialist, and racist discourse, one which still undergirds and permeates *contemporary* discourses even after the formal end of colonialism. The 500-year colonial domination of indigenous peoples, the capitalist appropriation of resources, the imperialist ordering of the world, all formed part of a massive globalizing movement that began with Columbus and reached its apogee at the turn of the twentieth century. While in the past "colonialist discourse" explicitly justified colonialist practices, Eurocentric discourse embeds, takes for granted, and "normalizes" the hierarchical power relations generated by colonialism. Eurocentrism's links to the colonizing process are obscured within a buried epistemology.

Within Eurocentrism, Europe – and here we mean Europe in the broadest sense to refer not to the continent but rather to Euro-hegemony around the world – is seen as the originary fountain from which all good things flow. From the time of Europe's "civilizing mission" and the "white man's burden" to the time of "globalization" and the "New World Order," Eurocentric discourse is diffusionist; it assumes that democracy, science, progress, and prosperity all emanate outward from a western source. Eurocentric discourse renders history as a North-by-Northwest sequence of empires: Pax Romana, Pax Hispanica, Pax Britannica, Pax Americana. One symptom of Eurocentrism is the tendency to trace the origins of all academic disciplines to ancient Greece (anachronistically constructed as "western"). Political Philosophy? Plato's *Republic*. Literary Criticism? Aristotle's *Poetics*. Science? Pythagoras. Yet a recent book – decidedly *not* by a multiculturalist – points out that the Babylonians developed the Pythogorean theorem 1,500 years before Pythagoras, that Indian mathematicians developed a proto-calculus a millennium before Europeans, that the Arab astronomer Ibn-al-Shatir explained planetary motion 150 years before Copernicus, that the Mayans created the number zero a few centuries after the death of Christ, and that third-century Chinese physicists summarized Newton's first law of motion.[2] In sum, Eurocentrism rigs the historical balance-sheet; it sanitizes western history while patronizing and even demonizing the nonwest; it thinks of itself in terms of its noblest achievements but of the nonwest in terms of its deficiencies, real or imagined. The double processes of self-idealization and other-demonization which places the US corporate/military elite as judge, jury, and policeman of global offenses merely updates and weaponizes the strategic operations of Eurocentric thinking.

The concept of "multiculturalism," meanwhile, has been a polysemic and conflicted term, subject to diverse political force-fields. In its more co-opted version, it evokes a state or corporate-managed pluralism whereby established power promotes ethnic "flavors of the month" for commercial or ideological purposes. Multiculturalism is above all protean, plural, conjunctural, existing in shifting relation to various institutions, discourses, disciplines, communities, and nation-states. As a "situated utterance," it can be top-down or bottom-up, hegemonic or resistant, or both at the same time. It all depends on who is multiculturalizing whom, from what social position, in response to what hegemonies, as part of what political project, by what means, for what ends, deploying what discourses, and so forth.

In the US the multiculturalist project unleashed virulent attacks from the right because it called for more egalitarian and democratic ways of writing history, teaching literature, hiring professors, curating art, programming films, organizing conferences, distributing monies and cultural resources, and, last but not least, doing Cultural Studies. Unfortunately, multiculturalism has not succeeded in defining itself. It has been defined by its enemies, whether by a Marxizing left which finds it too culturalist and ineffectual, or by a reactionary right which finds it too revolutionary. For the right, multiculturalism is 1960s radicalism in a new guise, while for a certain left it is a detour into a divisively narcissistic "identity politics" which distracts from "real" struggles over class and power. Many of the left critiques of multiculturalism, in our view, are premised on false dichotomies – political economy *or* culture, race *or* class, activism *or* scholarship. In a sense, "multiculturalism" has suffered the fate suffered earlier by "socialism," dismissed by the far left as too softly social-democratic and denounced by the right as merely communism in disguise. At the same time, the vagueness of the term facilitated recuperative deradicalization, which is why many of us have proposed qualifiers like "critical," "radical," "polycentric," and "antiracist" to distinguish our kind of multiculturalism from "corporate" and "co-optive" multiculturalism.[3]

What often gets lost in these debates is what might be called the "multicultural corpus," i.e. the actual scholarly work generated by the multiculturalist project. The term "multicultural corpus" refers to a loose affiliation of interdisciplinary research initiatives and political projects which "covers" a wide range of theories, discourses and areas of inquiry, practiced under diverse rubrics. The umbrella term "multicultural corpus" embraces such diverse formations (the groupings are admittedly arbitrary) as: revisionist history; Afro-diasporic cultural analysis; antiracist media critique; critical race theory; "whiteness" studies; subaltern studies; postcolonial discourse theory; transnational feminism; globalization critique; radical pedagogy; counter-Enlightenment philosophy; and "border" theory – as well as countless other forms of adversarial knowledge. Although some of this work might not be performed under the multiculturalist banner *per se*, and while there are tensions between and even within these diverse modes of critique, they all share a multidimensional and critical left engagement with the legacies of colonialism, slavery, imperialism, and racism. Unfortunately, there is no common rubric for such work. In France, work criticizing colonialism might go under the name simply of "history," as in the work of Louis Sala-Molins on slavery and the French Enlightenment, or of Benjamin Stora on the erasure of the Algerian War in French school books.[4]

Each of the possible terms to evoke such work is problematic. "Revisionist history" focuses too narrowly on a subfield of one discipline; "antiracist" studies is too locked into the same paradigm being combated; "postcolonial studies" is too academic and displays all the oft-noted problems about a "post" not yet really "post." "Whiteness studies," while usefully exnominating or "outing" whiteness, runs the risk of recentering it as well, and imposes Anglo-American categories of difference. "Identity politics" is the preferred term for the enemies of multiculturalism, whether from the right (e.g. conservatives) or from the putative left (deconstructionists, postmodernists), because it carries with it a whiff of an essentialist and narcissistic philosophy autocentered on "my" identity.

Despite its problems, the term "multiculturalism" served a number of strategic purposes; (1) its inclusiveness implies a broad progressive coalition, something lacking in terms like "black liberation" invoking only one band on the radical spectrum; (2) the term had embedded in it as historical memory the interwoven threads of two liberatory currents – anticolonial struggles in the third world and minority struggles in the first; (3) the term's very ambiguity made it useful for prodding institutions such as University administrations into making progressive gestures in the name of "diversity"; (4) both elements of the term were useful; the "multi" implied a constitutive heterogeneity based on multiple issues and axes of struggle and identification, while the word "culture" addressed a silent rebuke to the frequent Marxist blindness to culture and race as opposed to class. Putting "multi" and "culture" together enacted a coalitionary strategy that implicitly went beyond the binarism of "race relations" or "black studies" or "whiteness studies." The "ism" in multiculturalism, meanwhile, probably claimed too much by placing itself in the same paradigm as other "isms" referring to explanatory grids (Marxism), epochs (postmodernism), systems of production (capitalism) and ideologies (socialism). In any case, each term casts some light on a complex subject. The point is to deploy all the concepts in a differential, contingent, and relational manner, as part of a mobile set of grids, a more flexible set of disciplinary and cross-cultural lenses adequate to the complex politics of contemporary culture.[5]

## ■ Geneologies of Cultural Studies ■

The de-Eurocentrization of Cultural Studies might begin with the narrativization of the history of Cultural Studies itself. The conventional narrative tells us that "Cultural Studies" traces its roots to the 1960s work of such British leftists as Richard Hoggart (*The Uses of History*), Raymond Williams (*Culture and Society*), E. P. Thompson (*The Making of the English Working Class*), and later Stuart Hall, associated with the Centre for Contemporary Cultural Studies, founded in 1964 at the University of Birmingham. Conscious of the oppressive aspects of the British class system, the members of the Birmingham Center, many of whom were associated with adult education projects, deployed Gramscian categories to illuminate issues of class, looking both for aspects of ideological domination and for new agents of social change.

With all due respect for the extraordinary achievements of the Birmingham School, many (multi)cultural scholars came to the field through alternative itineraries not involving Birmingham. Although the catch-all term "Cultural Studies" must be credited to Birmingham, one can easily imagine a more diffuse and diasporized genealogy going back to such figures as Roland Barthes and Henri Lefebvre in France, Leslie Fiedler and James Baldwin in the United States, Aimé Césaire and Frantz Fanon in the Carribean and later France and North Africa, Ariel Dorfmann and Armand Mattelart in Chile, and C. L. R. James in his various peregrinations. Indeed, this body of work casts suspicion on the Anglo-diffusionist narrative that Cultural Studies "began" in England and then spread elsewhere. In our perspective, when James Baldwin spoke about gospel preaching and black reception of Hollywood films, when Roland Barthes spoke of the "mythologies" of empire, when Leslie Fiedler anatomized the myth of the "vanishing Indian" and found homoeroticism in *Huckleberry Finn,* when Henri Lefebvre analyzed the politics of everyday life, when Dorfmann/Mattelart discerned imperialism in Disney comics, and when C. L. R. James analyzed cricket and *Moby Dick,* they were all doing "Cultural Studies" *avant la lettre.*

Indeed, one could carry this archeological project even further, going back, in Europe itself, to the late 1920s and Bakhtin and Voloshinov in the Soviet Union and Benjamin and Kracauer (e.g. *The Mass Ornament*) in Germany. One could also call attention to some completely unsung "progenitors" of Cultural Studies from outside of Europe. One such neglected precursor is the brilliant Brazilian essayist, poet, novelist, anthropologist, and musicologist Mario de Andrade. A man of African, indigenous, and European ancestry, de Andrade both embodied and theorized "hybridity" long before the theme became fashionable. The subtitle of his 1928 novel *Macunaima* – "the hero without any character" – referred to the protagonist's racial, cultural, and ethical hybridity. A key participant in the Brazilian modernist movement in the 1920s, de Andrade mingled a wide spectrum of influences and sources – futurism, surrealism, Brazilian indianism, popular music, Afro-Brazilian candomble, indigenous legends – in a splendid *feijoada* of scholarship and creation. He took all of Brazilian cultural life, erudite and popular, as a legitimate object of study. Many practitioners of Cultural Studies in contemporary Brazil consciously build on the rich, anti-elitist inheritance left by Mario de Andrade.

Another "proto-cultural-studies" figure, writing a few decades later, was Frantz Fanon. A rereading of Fanon reveals him to be an important precursor for many currents within contemporary Cultural Studies. Although Fanon never spoke of "Orientalist discourse," for example, his critiques of colonialist imagery provide proleptic examples of anti-orientalist and postcolonial critique. Although often caricatured as a racial hardliner, Fanon anticipated the anti-essentialist critique of race. In Fanon's relational view in *Black Skin, White Masks,* the black man is obliged to be black "in relation to" the white man. The black man, as Fanon put it, "*is* comparison." Seeing race as languaged, situated, constructed, Fanon anticipated the "constructivist" current within Cultural Studies, yet his was a mobilizing sense of construction, one which embraced fluidity and ambivalence but without abandoning the struggle for such "constructs" as black solidarity, the Algerian nation, and Third World Unity.

Fanon was also one of the first thinkers to bring Lacanian psychoanalysis into film and cultural theory. Fanon saw racist films, for example, as a "release for collective aggressions." Fanon's work also fed into the theory and practice of "third cinema," in that many third-worldist films were influenced by or even quoted Fanon. The Argentinian film essay *The Hour of the Furnaces* (1968) not only quotes Fanon's adage that "Every Spectator is a Coward or a Traitor," but also orchestrates a constellation of Fanonian themes – the psychic stigmata of colonialism, the therapeutic value of anticolonial violence, and the urgent necessity of a decolonized culture. Many of the key third-Worldist cinema manifestos, most notably Solanas-Getino's "Towards a Third Cinema" and Glauber Rocha's "Aesthetic of Hunger" also resonate with Fanonian overtones. The whole question of Fanon and Cultural Studies comes full circle with the only film dedicated exclusively to Fanon – Isaac Julien's *Black Skin, White Mask* – where key figures in Cultural Studies such as Stuart Hall comment on Fanon's work. Although Fanon never used the talismanic phrase "Cultural Studies," in sum, he was its proleptic practitioner. Already in the 1950s he examined a wide variety of cultural forms – the veil, *transe*, language, radio, film – as sites of social and cultural contestation. Although never part of an explicit Cultural Studies project, he certainly practiced what now goes by that name.

Apart from Fanon, writers in Cultural Studies also tend to underestimate the impact of various anticolonial thinkers in the development of Cultural Studies itself. For example, the related movements of structuralism and poststructuralism clearly constituted key influences on Cultural Studies. But these movements did not spring forth unaided from the brain of Europe. Both had their long-term historical origins in a series of events that undermined the confidence of European modernity: the Holocaust (and in France the Vichy collaboration with the Nazis), and the postwar disintegration of the last European empires. Structuralist and poststructuralist thinking in some ways merely codified what anticolonial thinkers had been saying. The subversive work of "denaturalization" performed by the "left wing" of semiotics – for example Barthes' famous dissection of the colonialist implications of the *Paris Match* cover showing a black soldier saluting the French flag – had everything to do with the external critique of European master-narratives performed by Francophone decolonizers like Aimé Césaire and Fanon. Their decentering of Europe can now be seen as having both provoked and foreshadowed Derrida's claim (in "Structure, Sign and Play in the Discourse of the Human Sciences," 1966) that European culture has been "dislocated," forced to stop casting itself as "the culture of reference." There is "nothing fortuitous," Derrida wrote, "about the fact that the critique of [European] ethnocentrism . . . should be systematically and historically contemporaneous with the destruction of the history of metaphysics."[6] Many of the source thinkers of structuralism and poststructuralism, and thus of Cultural Studies, furthermore, as Robert Young points out, were biographically linked to what came to be called the Third World: Lévi-Strauss did anthropology in Brazil; Foucault taught in Tunisia; Althusser, Cixous, and Derrida were all born in Algeria, where Bourdieu also did his anthropological fieldwork.[7] Both the structuralist and the poststructuralist moments, in this sense, coincide with a veritable legitimation crisis, within Europe itself. Intellectual exchanges and circuitries, in sum, cannot be fully addressed within the straitjacket of nation-state or Euro-diffusionist thinking; the boundaries are much too porous, the influences too reciprocal.

## ■ The Narrativization of (Post)Modernism ■

Another area in which Cultural Studies could be internationalized is in terms of the narrativization of artistic modernism. Questions of modernism (and later post-modernism) are usually "centered" within the provincial frame of European-American art. Most writing on modernism restricts its attention to movements in European and North American capitals like Paris, London, New York, and Zurich while consigning to oblivion cognate movements in such places as Sao Paulo, Havana, Mexico City, and Buenos Aires (to speak only of Latin America). When acknowledged, these non-European modernisms are assumed to be pale copies of European originals, aesthetically inferior and chronologically posterior, mere latter-day echoes of pioneering European gestures. Yet from an aesthetic perspective, this temporality as belated repetition is quite problematic. Even the word "modernism" itself came to us via Latin America; it was coined by the Nicaraguan poet Ruben Dario in 1885. The word "postmodernism," similarly, first emerged not from Northern Europe but rather from the Hispanic world of the 1930s; Federico de Onis coined it a generation before its appearance in the Anglo-American world. The neologistic cultures of Latin America, as products of uneven development and of multifaceted transactions with other cultures, furthermore, can be seen as themselves the proleptic site of modernist and postmodernist practices. It was in this same spirit that Henry Louis Gates called blacks in the Americas the "first deconstructionists," or that Blackfoot-American philosopher Jamake Highwater explains that the multi-perspectivalism typical of indigenous cultures was introduced into European cultures under the name "postmodern."[8]

The dominant literature on modernism often regards Europe as simply absorbing "primitive art" as raw material to be refined and reshaped by European artists. This view prolongs the colonial trope which projected colonized people as body rather than mind, much as the colonized world was seen as a source of raw material rather than of mental activity or manufacture. Even such a generally acute theorist as Fredric Jameson, in his writings on Third World literature and film, tends to underestimate the radical revisioning of aesthetics performed by Third World and diasporic artists. Although he is (thankfully) inconsistent on this point, Jameson in his unguarded moments seems to conflate the terms of political economy (where he projects the Third World into a less developed, less modern frame) and those of aesthetic and cultural periodization (where he projects it into a "premodernist" or "pre-postmodernist" past). A residual economism or "stagism" here leads to the equation of late capitalist/postmodernist and precapitalist/pre-modernist, as when Jameson speaks of the "belated emergence of a kind of modernism in the modernizing Third World, at a moment when the so-called advanced countries are themselves sinking into full postmodernity."[9] Thus the Third World always seems to lag behind, not only economically but also culturally, condemned to a perpetual game of catch-up in which it can only repeat on another register the history of the "advanced" world. A more adequate formulation, in our view, would see all the "worlds" as coeval, interlinked, living the *same* historical moment (but under diverse modalities of subordination or domination). Temporality is scrambled and palimpsestic in all the worlds, with the premodern, the modern, the postmodern coexisting globally, although the "dominant" might vary from region to region. All societies and cultures are multiple, hybrid, heteroglossic, unevenly developed, characterized by multiple historical trajectories, rhythms, and temporalities.

The debt of European modernism and the avant-gardes to the arts of Africa, Asia, and indigenous America has been extensively documented. Leger, Cendrars, and Milhaud based their staging of "La Creation du Monde" on African cosmology. The British sculptor Henry Moore modeled his recumbent statues on the Chac Mool stone figures of ancient Mexico. Exposure to the artistic cultures of Africa and indigenous America helped liberate the European modernists from their own culture-bound aesthetic of realism. Thus while a Euro-diffisionist narrative makes Europe a perpetual fountain of artistic innovation, we would argue for a multidirectional flow of aesthetic ideas, with intersecting criss-crossing ripples and eddies. Just as the European avant-garde became "advanced" by drawing on the "archaic" and "primitive," so non-European artists have drawn on the most traditional elements of their cultures, elements less "pre-modern" (a term that embeds modernity as telos) than "para-modern." In the arts, the distinction archaic/modernist is often nonpertinent, in the sense that both share a refusal of the conventions of mimetic realism. It is thus less a question of juxtaposing the archaic and the modern than deploying the archaic in order, paradoxically, to modernize, in a dissonant temporality which combines a past imaginary communitas with an equally imaginary future utopia.

While much recent writing has been devoted to exposing the exclusions and blindnesses of Eurocentric representations and discourses, the actual cultural productions of non-Europeans have been ignored, a neglect which reinscribes the exclusion even while denouncing it. That is why we wish to call attention to alternative aesthetics which bypass the formal conventions of dramatic realism in favor of such modes and strategies as the anthropophagic, the magical realist, the archaic postmodernist.[10] These aesthetics are often rooted in nonrealist, often nonwestern or para-western cultural traditions featuring other historical rhythms, other narrative structures, other views of the body, sexuality, spirituality, and the collective life. Many incorporate nonmodern traditions into clearly modernizing or postmodernizing aesthetics, and thus problematize facile dichotomies such as traditional and modern, realist and modernist, modernist and postmodernist.[11]

These movements have also been fecund in neologistic aesthetics, literary, painterly, and cinematic: "*lo real maravilloso americano*" (Carpentier), "anthropophagy" (the Brazilian Modernists), the "aesthetics of hunger" (Glauber Rocha),

"Cine imperfecto" (Julio Garcia Espinosa), the "aesthetics of garbage" (Rogerio Sganzerla), "Tropicalia" (Gil and Caetano), "hoodoo aesthetics" (Ishmael Reed), the "signifying-monkey aesthetic" (Henry Louis Gates), "nomadic aesthetics" (Teshome Gabriel), and *santeria* aesthetics (Arturo Lindsay). Most of these alternative aesthetics revalorize by inversion what had formerly been seen as negative, especially within colonialist discourse. (Even "magic realism" inverts the colonial view of magic as irrational superstition.) At the same time, these aesthetics share the jiu-jitsu trait of turning strategic weakness into tactical strength. By appropriating an existing discourse for their own ends, they deploy the force of the dominant against domination.

## ■ Modernismo and Tropicalia ■

Although this is not the place to explore these movements in depth – we have done so elsewhere – here we would like to briefly sketch out the importance of just two (related) Brazilian movements: "Modernismo" in the 1920s, and Tropicalia (and its offshoot "the aesthetics of garbage") from the late 1960s to the present. As its name implies, the modernist movement in Brazil saw itself as allied to European modernist movements like Futurism, Dada, and Surrealism, but also in some ways went beyond those movements. The "Modern Art Week" held in Sao Paulo in February 1922 was an attempt by Brazilian poets, musicians, and visual artists to break with the Europhile academicism of the time. The currently fashionable talk of "hybridity" and "syncretism," usually associated with "postcolonial" theory, elides the fact that artists/intellectuals in Brazil were theorizing hybridity over six decades earlier. In two manifestos – "Manifesto of Brazilwood Poetry" (1924) and "Cannibalist Manifesto" (1928) – Oswald de Andrade pointed the way to an artistic practice at once nationalist and cosmopolitan, nativist and modern. Where colonialist discourse had posited the Carib as a ferocious cannibal, as diacritical token of Europe's moral superiority, Oswald called in the "Cannibalist Manifesto" for a revolution infinitely "greater than the French revolution," the "Carib revolution," without which "Europe wouldn't even have its meager declaration of the rights of man."[12] De Andrade saluted surrealism, in a self-mockingly patronizing and "stagist" manner, as one of the richest "pre-anthropophagic" movements.[13] The exoticizing metaphors of the European avant-garde had a strange way of "taking flesh" in the Latin American context, resulting in a kind of ironic echo effect between the European and Latin American modernisms. Thus Jarry's "neglected branch of anthropophagy" came to refer in Brazil to the putatively real cannibalism of the Tupinamba, and surrealist "transe writing" metamorphosed into the collective transe of Afro-Brazilian religions like *candomble*. Brazilian familiarity with the "madness" of carnival, with African-derived transe religions, thus made it easy for Brazilian artists to assimilate and transform artistic procedures that in Europe had represented a more dramatic rupture with ambient values and spiritual traditions.

Much later, the Modernist movement came to inflect Brazilian art through a recombinant cultural movement called "Tropicalia" or "Tropicalism," which emerged in Brazil in the late 1960s. In his autobiographical *Verdade Tropical* (Tropical Truth), writer, composer, singer, filmmaker, and pop star Caetano Veloso, a key founder of Tropicalia, repeatedly stressed the movement's links to Modernist Anthropophagy: "The idea of cultural cannibalism fit us tropicalists like a glove. We were 'devouring' the Beatles and Jimi Hendrix."[14] In the case of Tropicalia, it was a film – Rocha's *Terra em Transe* (Land in Anguish, 1967) – that catalyzed a new dynamism in Brazilian art. A stylized allegory about Brazilian politics in the wake of the 1964 right-wing coup d'état, *Land in Anguish* stages what Rocha himself called the "tragic carnival of Brazilian politics." In a layered discourse, the film counterpoints incommensurable cultural systems within a scrambled temporality which contemporizes Pedro Cabral (the Portuguese "discoverer" of Brazil in 1500) and Joao Goulart (the Brazilian president deposed by the right-wing coup d'état in 1964). Rocha's neo-baroque Afro-avant-gardist aesthetic is "trans/trance-Brechtian," i.e. it deploys the trance of west African possession religion to go beyond Brecht by tropicalizing, Africanizing, and carnivalizing his theories. In the film, the discontinuous, dissonant, fractured history of Brazil is figured through dissonant images and sounds and a feverish bricolage of styles, in violent, transgressive counterpoints where the tensions are highlighted rather than resolved or harmonized.

*Land in Anguish* had a catalytic effect on the arts in Brazil. As Caetano put it, "That whole Tropicalist thing became clear to me the day I saw *Terra em Transe*: My heart exploded during the opening sequence, when, to the sound of a candomble chant... an aerial shot of the sea brings us to the coast of Brazil."[15] Caetano hailed the film's invention of a different vision of life, of Brazil, and of the cinema.[16] Along with *Land in Anguish*, two other 1967 works inaugurated the Tropicalist movement – the play *Rei da Vela* (King of the Candle), and the installation "Tropicalia" by Helio Oiticica. The staging of *Rei da Vela*, a modernist, Ubuesque farce about the Brazilian elite based on an updated version of the 1930s Oswald de Andrade play, was deeply marked by Rocha's film, which provoked in theater director Ze Celso a sense that theater had been surpassed in aesthetic audacity by the cinema. The goal of the Oiticica installations, meanwhile, was to erase the frontiers between art and life by provoking an unpredictable, inter-active experience. He created *parangoles*, multicolored capes to be worn by specta-tors who thus *became* the artists. Carnival-like, the costumes invited the spectators to dance. The installation "Tropicalia," specifically, created a three-dimensional ambiance which mingled the feeling of Ipanema-style beaches with that of the favela. The work comprised two structures, on the one hand "penetrables" made of wood and brightly colored fabric, reminiscent of favela shacks, and on the other sand and pebble paths and tropical plants and parrots, culminating in a dark passage leading up to a television monitor.

The seminal "tropicalist" works share a number of common aesthetic features. First, all three anthropophagically devoured both national and international influ-ences. Rocha drew on the Brazilian popular culture of *cangaceiros* and *candomble* and samba but also on Shakespeare, Eisenstein, Brecht, and Godard. Caetano drew on the rural songs of the Northeast, but also on the hyper-sophisticated Brazilian "concrete poets," as well as on a wide international repertoire of popular and erudite music. Ze Celso formed part of the international "counterculture" of guerrilla theater and hallucinogenic experimentation. (His group collaborated with "The Living Theatre.") In the 1970s, Oiticica received a Guggenheim and moved to New York, where he was influenced by John Cage and Jack Smith. All three figures crossed over into other arts. Rocha drew sketches, and wrote poems and novels. Oiticica acted in Rocha's film *Cancer*, called his installations "*quasi-cinema*," and made a number of short films. Caetano began as a film critic and brought film criticism into his songs. The song "Cinema Novo" from *Tropicalia II* (written with Gil), for example, poetically encapsulates and critiques the entire history of the Brazilian film movement, and in the 1980s Caetano became a filmmaker with *Cinema Falado*.

The three seminal works of Tropicalia all shared what might be called an "aesthetic of mistakes," an aesthetic of transgression in which artistic language was liberated from the stifling norms of correctness. Such anticanonical work deconstructed not only the canon, but also the generating matrix that makes canons and grammaticality. Earlier, the Modernists had spoken of the "creative errors of the people," and in the 1960s, Bossa Nova proclaimed the right to be "desafinado," to sing "out of tune." Joao Gilberto's suavely shy guitar style was known as *gago* (stuttering), a stumbling, hesitant style which turned out to be even more beautiful than an academically correct style. Aesthetic "mistakes" thus keyed a transvaluation of the very idea of the beautiful. Cinema Novo directors, in the same vein, claimed the right to make ungrammatical films, "ugly, desperate films," in Rocha's words, film which broke formal as well as thematic taboos. The underground cinema of the late 1960s, working in the immediate aftermath of Tropicalia, spoke of an "aesthetics of garbage." In *Verdade Tropical*, Caetano evokes something like this aesthetic transvaluation of the negative when he speaks of a "transformation of the very criteria of taste."[17] Tropicalism, for Caetano, strives for an "equilibrio desequilibrado, feito samba," an awkward equilibrium comparable to the off-balance grace of samba or frevo. What impressed Caetano in Glauber's films was not "the attempt to do things correctly (or proving that one *could* do things correctly) but rather the making of mistakes and succeeding on a completely different level, from one's own point of view, according to a new set of criteria for judging what was correct and what was not."[18]

It took the "world music" phenomenon and postmodernism to finally call attention to Tropicalia as an artistic movement with contemporary relevance. Recently, Oiticica's installations have been exhibited in New York's New Museum and at the Guggenheim. And in 1989, David Byrne's Kuaka Bop label released *Beleza Tropical*, a successful compilation of Brazilian popular music that featured Tropicalist songs by Caetano and Gilberto Gil. In the mid-1990s tropicalist recordings from the late 1960s began to circulate among US musicians, winning praise from groups like Stereolab and singer-composers like Beck, who also wrote his own song, "Tropicalia." And in 2002, Caetano's memoir/analysis of Tropicalia, *Tropical Truth*, was published in English. Readers of the *New York Times* and *The Village Voice* were surprised to discover what Brazilians had long known, that the pop star

Caetano was an extremely sophisticated and international thinker/artist. Caetano could not only lead thousands of concert fans into collective jouissance, but also write like Proust and discourse knowingly about postmodernism, about the politics of popular culture, and about the comparabilities of race across the Americas.

Brazilian popular composers like Caetano, Gilberto Gil, and Chico Buarque de Holanda have managed to produce a utopian aesthetic synthesis at once Brazilian and international, popular and experimental, erudite and accessible, Africanized and cosmopolitan. Their lyrics offer poetry of the highest quality, while the music displays an anthropophagic capacity to absorb every kind of influence, while still being driven by an Africanized bass-note. "Popular" in both the box-office and the Bakhtinian carnivalesque sense, these artists constituted latter-day, singing and dancing versions of Gramsci's "organic intellectual." Caetano, for example, incarnates multicultural and polylingual cosmopolitanism. He sings "Cucurrucucu Paloma" in impeccable Spanish in Alamadovar's *Talk to Her*. He writes a song for Pasolini, in Italian. Musically, he slides easily between samba, bolero, rap, high life, and soul, even while his lyrics raise crucial cultural/political issues. The recent CD *Noites do Norte* constitutes an expanded musical/lyrical mediation on slavery and resistance, where the lyrics include long quotations from Brazilian abolitionists and where the drums provide what critic Jon Pareles calls "a life force, a conscience, and an ancestral memory" (see *New York Times* Nov. 27, 2002). The Caetano/Gil samba-reggae-rap "Haiti e aqui" constitutes a sophisticated statement about race and police brutality in the Americas. "Manyata" (a play on the Brazilian pronunciation of "Manhattan") poetically evokes New York as a multicultural metropolis with indigenous roots. In our view, musicians around the world could learn from the Brazilian pop artists, who demonstrate art's capacity to give pleasurable form to social desire, to open new grooves, to mobilize historical memory, to shake the booty-politic by appealing to deeply rooted but socially frustrated aspirations for new forms of festive community, crystallizing desire in a popular, mass-mediated form.

## ■ Toward Comparative (Multi)Cultural Studies ■

Another way of internationalizing Cultural Studies is to engage in "comparative (multi)Cultural Studies."[19] For example, multiculturalism clearly alters its valence in diverse national contexts. In countries like Canada and Australia the term designates official government programs designed to empower "minorities" through a modicum of representation. In Brazil, multiculturalism refers both to a taken-for-granted quality of Brazilian society and a name for what is seen as a United Statesian project. And in France, both right and left denounce multiculturalism, usually on the basis of no knowledge whatsoever, often in terms redolent of neoconservative discourse. For the center/right (Alain Finkelkraut, Pascal Bruckner) multiculturalism recycles 1960s third-worldist radicalism, while for the left (Bourdieu/Wacquant) it is a cunningly disguised form of American imperialism. This consensus denunciation sometimes leads to some very strange alignments, as when the "left" newspaper *Libération* turns, for an account of American multiculturalism, to none other than Dinesh d'Souza, the American neoconservative who argues in *The End of Racism* that slavery wasn't so bad, that segregation was well-intended, and that African Americans have reintroduced "barbarism into the midst of Western civilization." Thus the same intellectuals who denounce Bushism in political terms, endorse it in cultural terms.

Comparative (multi)Cultural Studies would engage such questions as the following: How does (multi)Cultural Studies "travel across diverse cultural geographies"? What happens in the back-and-forth movement from one cultural semantics into another, for example between Brazil and France and the US? How do these movements "translate"? What are the different vocabularies? Under what rubrics is (multi)cultural-style work performed? What happens when similar issues are seen through different national grids, or enter other "intellectual fields"? What can the various movements learn from one another? How are "out-of-place" ideas reinvoiced, indigenized, co-opted, contained, hybridized, cannibalized, recontextualized, resisted, transvocalized, misrecognized? What is elided, or added, or subtly changed, in the process of cross-cultural translation? In what ways do "debates about debates" in one nation-state allegorize debates about debates in another? What anxieties are projected onto "multiculturalism?" What are the mirrors and grids and prisms through which the debate is seen? What does the *refusal* of a discourse tell us about those who refuse it? What is the role of national exceptionalism and narcissism? What anxieties and utopias come into play when multiculturalism "travels"?[20]

Our current project, for example, has to do with a comparative study of how issues of race, identity, and multiculturalism are addressed in three sites: the United States, France, and Brazil. Despite the obvious differences, all three countries have a good deal in common. All three are Republics rooted both in the progressive side of the Enlightenment – democracy, the bill of rights, *les droits de l'homme* – and in the Enlightenment's seamy underside – colonialism, racism, and the slave trade. They are in this sense all "*Herrenvolk* democracies" – master-race democracies. In all three sites the "social contract" delineated by Enlightenment philosophy was doubled by an "antisocial contract" which served to dispossess the natives of the Americas and enslave Africans. All three countries wrestle, in different ways, with the sequels of slavery and colonialism in issues of discrimination, immigration, affirmative action. Each country has its narcissisms and exceptionalisms: "the city on a hill" in the US, *la République* in France, and "racial democracy" in Brazil. Yet both France and the US fall more onto the imperial, hegemonic side of the global divide, while Brazil falls on the subaltern, imperialized side. Yet Brazil too has its internal racial hegemonies embedded in the colonial past. First World/Third World and North/South binarisms, in this sense, hide commonalities, especially between Brazil and the US as New World settler states where European colonization led to the occupation of vast territories and the subjugation and dispossession of indigenous peoples, which practiced slavery, and which received parallel waves of immigrants from all over the world, ultimately forming complexly stratified multiracial societies.

In these cross-national debates, some thinkers crudely equate specific discourses with the nation-state from which they seem to emerge. For Pierre Bourdieu and Loïc Wacquant, multiculturalism is simply an "*American*" discourse, a symptom of imperialism alongside neoliberalism, globalization, and other forms of American hegemony. The syllogism seems to be: "America is imperialist. Multiculturalism is an American discourse. Multiculturalism is imperialist." While the right wing in the US demonizes multiculturalism as "anti-American," ironically, the two French sociologists demonize it as *only* American. Quite apart from the fact that Bourdieu and Wacquant seem *completely* unfamiliar with what we have called the " multicultural corpus," most of which is *anti*-imperialist, their equation is problematic on many levels. First, multiculturalism is not *a* discourse; it is a conflictual constellation of discourses. Like any other complex, heteroglossic intellectual movement, multiculturalism cannot be reduced simply to a national banner. Just as many ideas and thinkers traveled from the Third World to France to help shape "French" structuralism, many ideas and thinkers "traveled" to the US in order to mold multiculturalism. Not only is multiculturalism animated by scholars of the most diverse national origins, it also draws on a wide variety of intellectual sources, ranging from "dependency theory" (strongly associated with Latin America), "subaltern studies" (associated with India), poststructuralism (associated with France), hegemony theory (associated with Gramsci), along with all sorts of "Afro-diasporic" and "border" trends from around the Black Atlantic and the indigenous world. US academe, as George Yudice points out, has become a clearing house for varied intellectual tendencies, a magnet for "centripetal and centrifugal academic desires."[21] Postcolonial and multicultural theory are strong in US academe for precise historical reasons – for example, changes in immigration laws – but they were also well-received because other difference-affirming movements such as multiculturalism, black liberation, and native American liberation had created a hospitable space for them.

Unfortunately, various national narcissisms and exceptionalisms also operate within (multi)Cultural Studies, rendering international alliances more difficult. The most obvious form of national exceptionalism is that involved in work which is exclusively and complacently centered on Anglo-American mass culture. Although academics obviously have a right to teach their own national tradition, such work sometimes reinforces the monocultural assumptions of students who end up supporting the policies of the world's sole hyperpower. Those of us who teach in the US, for example, have a political and intellectual *obligation* to deprovincialize and internationalize those of our students who are monocultural. The problem is the asymmetrical, hierarchical, and unidirectional channeling of knowledge exchange. While intellectuals in Brazil or India are multilingual and generally aware of European and North American cultural currents, the reverse is not usually true.

Even in the more critical zones of US academe, the production of knowledge sometimes relays an implicit and even invisible US nationalism, giving us a rainbow chauvinism, a star-striped nationalism with a tan. Thus "diversity" committees speak of the "contribution of the world's cultures to *American* society," blithely unaware of the nationalist teleology undergirding their discourse. And while we have no quarrel with the idea of US uniqueness, we do quarrel with the idea that uniqueness is unique to the US. Every country has a palimpsestic uniqueness of its own, and along with that shared uniqueness, historical parallels and diasporic links between diverse national formations.

But national narcissisms and exceptionalisms are not a US monopoly. Narcissism also rears its head in some versions of Cultural Studies which reinscribe European elitist snobbery toward US culture, and which conveniently forget the past and present role of Europe in spreading racism and imperialism around the world. Some scholars resort to insults based on location. Terry Eagleton (admittedly not a friend of [multi]Cultural Studies) sprinkles his essays with sarcastic asides about those "sitting in Berkeley or Princeton," presumably impermeable to truths better grasped elsewhere. The self-flattering implication seems to be that "sitting in Oxford or Cambridge" does *not* entail any similar intellectual or political blind-spots. French scholar Serge Gruzinki, in *The Mestizo Mind*, similarly, also abuses American intellectuals on the basis of location: "everyone knows that many apologists of 'political correctness' and 'Cultural Studies,' from the shelter of the American empire's academic ivory towers, have developed the notion of a world rigidified into watertight, self-protecting communities."[22] Here Gruzinski mingles an anti-imperialist rhetorical gesture with a discourse that ironically buys into the right-wing imperialist caricature of multiculturalism as Balkanization. Like Eagleton's Oxford, Gruzinski's Ecole des Hautes Etudes is presumed to be untainted by any imperial stain. But French language and culture, too, still enjoy the fruits of a residual global prestige rooted in the longer colonial and imperial networks that guaranteed the dissemination of European ideas around the world.[23] Global structures of cultural power privilege both the Frenchman Pierre Bourdieu and the Americans Susan Sontag and Fredric Jameson (not to mention Harold Bloom and Denesh d'Souza) over the Brazilians Haroldo de Campos, Antonio Candido, and Marilena Chaui, brilliant intellectuals who have not even begun to get the international reputation they deserve.

In some Cultural Studies texts, a legitimate critique of US power and hegemony slides into an idealization of Europe and a blanket misrecognition of antihegemonic scholarship and movements in the US. A certain anti-Americanism sometimes becomes a form of scapegoating for Europeans, a way of saying that "we Europeans have nothing to do with all that racism and imperialism stuff – that's an American thing!" But such a view requires a very short memory. Although the US power-elite is clearly the current neo-imperial bully and the cutting-edge protagonist of the cruelest forms of globalization, the US did not invent colonialism, slavery, imperialism, or racism, or globalization; it merely fine-tuned what it inherited from Europe. The point is not to construct artificial hierarchies but to fight racism through an international alliance, to fight it both politically and through adversarial scholarship, whatever our location.[24]

Underlying all our proposals is the idea that Cultural Studies should be rethought as *multi*Cultural Studies, since all national cultures, especially in the age of the globalized mass-media, are inevitably touched and altered by the cultures of close or distant neighbors. Yet internationalizing is not simply a matter of "adding" new nations into the discussion, but rather of moving beyond monocultural and nation-state thinking generally. Rather than draw clear lines between nation-states as if they were impenetrable fortresses, our purpose here has been to suggest that any discussion of (multi)Cultural Studies must place often-ghettoized histories and discourses in productive relation. Rather than speak of cultural/racial/national groups in isolation, we have to speak of them "in relation." Within this multicultural critique, histories, geographies, and communities are mutually co-implicated, existing not as hermetically sealed entities but rather as part of a permeable interwoven relationality, particularly in a transnational age typified by the global "travel" of images, sounds, goods, and populations. On the one hand, it is important to speak about the power relations that underlie the circulation of ideas. On the other, it is imperative to interrogate the fixed lines drawn between "inside" and "outside," center and periphery, national and international. To draw such lines too rigidly is not only historically invalid, we have tried to suggest, but also theoretically, methodologically, and even politically calamitous.

## NOTES

1   This chapter combines revised versions of previously published materials – from our essay "Narrativizing Visual Culture: Towards a Polycentric Aesthetics," introductory essay to Nicholas Mirzoeff, ed., *The Visual Culture Reader* (London: Routledge, 1998), and "Travelling Multiculturalism: French Intellectuals and the US Culture Wars," in *Black Renaissance Noire* (Fall 2001) – along with new materials drawn from our current project, a study of (multi)Cultural Studies in three sites: Brazil, France, and the US.
2   See Dick Teresi, *Lost Discoveries: The Ancient Roots of Modern Science, From the Babylonians to the Maya* (New York: Simon and Schuster, 2002).
3   In a recent conversation, we were lamenting with Mary-Louise Pratt the left's tendency to flee from a word the minute it has been co-opted, rather than struggling to co-opt it back. Should the left abandon a slogan like "power to the people" because Richard Nixon tried to co-opt it?
4   To put it differently, there is no agreed-upon rubric to evoke the work of such diverse figures – here again the choices of names are somewhat arbitrary – as Enrique Dussel, Samir Amin, Yves Benot, Talal Asad, Peter Hulme, J. M. Blaut, Abdelwahab Meddeb, Benjamin Stora, Michel-Rolph Trouillot, Oren Lyons, Ward Churchill, Vine Deloria Jr, Ariel Dorfman, Mary-Louise Pratt, Patricia Williams, George Lipsitz, Robin Kelly, Abdias de Nascimento, Jean Franco, Edward Said, David Roediger, Ngugi wa Thiong'o, Manning Marable, George Yudice, Inderpal Grewal, Michael Hanchard, Arturo Escobar, Charles Mills, Chandra Mohanty, and Gloria Anzaldua.
5   For an extended discussion of these terms, see our *Unthinking Eurocentrism: Multiculturalism and the Media* (London: Routledge, 1994).
6   See Robert Young, *White Mythologies* (London: Routledge, 1990).
7   See James Tully, *Strange Multiplicity: Constitutionalism in an Age of Diversity* (Cambridge: Cambridge University Press, 1995), p. 25.

8   See e.g. Henry Louis Gates, Jr., *The Signifying Monkey* (New York: Oxford University Press, 1989); Jamake Highwater, *Dance: Rituals of Experience* (New York: Oxford University Press, 1996.

9   Fredric Jameson, *The Geopolitical Aesthetic: Cinema and Space in the World System* (Bloomington and London: Indiana University Press and BFI, 1992), p. 1.

10  We use the word "minoritarian" rather than "minority" because the latter term naturalizes what is historically produced and ideologically constructed through a project which constructs some groups as "major"and others as "minor." "Minoritarian" in our view, calls attention to the manufactured aspect of "minorities." Groups that are considered "minorities" were often "majorities" elsewhere or at another time, for example prior to conquest or colonization (e.g. the relation between Chicanos and Mexico).

11  For a comprehensive discussion of these alternative aesthetics, see our *Unthinking Eurocentrism*, esp. chs. 8 and 9.

12  For an English version of the "Cannibalist Manifesto," see Leslie Bary's excellent introduction to and translation of the poem in *Latin American Literary Review* 19(38) (July–Dec. 1991).

13  See Maria Eugenia Boaventura, *A Vanguarda Antropofagica* (Sao Paulo: Attica, 1985), p. 114.

14  Caetano Veloso, *Verdade Tropical* (Sao Paulo: Companhia das Letras, 1995), p. 247.

15  Ibid., p. 99.

16  Ibid., p. 105.

17  Ibid., p. 147.

18  Ibid., p. 101.

19  The book *Multicultural States: Rethinking Difference and Identity*, ed. David Bennett (London: Routledge, 1998), usefully maps out differences in a comparative way, largely within the English-speaking world.

20  The travel metaphor, as Caren Kaplan points out (e.g. in *Questions of Travel: Postmodern Discourses of Displacement* [Durham, NC: Duke University Press, 1996]), is not innocent. It conflates very different forms of travel: forced migration, modernist artistic exile, the imperial grand tour, and so forth. In complex criss-crossing movements, ideas constantly travel across borders; sometimes in the holds of ships, and sometimes in the first-class cabins, sometimes with their visas stamped and sometimes illegally.

21  See George Yudice, "A Globalizacao e a Difusao da Teoria Pos-Colonial," *Annals of Abalic* (1998).

22  Serge Gruzinksi, *The Mestizo Mind: The Intellectual Dynamics of Colonization and Globalization*, trans. Deke Dusinberre. (New York: Routledge, 2002), p. 3.

23  See Pascale Casanova, *La République mondiale des lettres* (Paris: Seuil, 1999).

24  Terms like "location" and "site" and "speaking position," while useful, encode a spatial metaphor that sometimes obscures issues of discourse and cultural politics. Thus some scholars essentialize intellectual trends as if they inhered in a national location or origin. In an otherwise stimulating recent essay Robert Young, in a symptomatic example, contrasts what he calls "the British model" of views on race with an American model presumed to be binaristic and essentialist.

> In the British model, identifiable with the positions of Stuart Hall...Paul Gilroy... Kobena Mercer...and Kwame Anthony Appiah...race is rejected as absolutist, biological, essentialist, or intrinsic.

This passage endorses anti-essentialism, but it does so, paradoxically, through an essentialist theory of national culture. A discourse of extremely diverse origins – anti-essentialism – is given a national name: "British." Thus British Cultural Studies, paradoxically, is seen as *essentially* anti-essentialist, while US Cultural Studies is seen as *essentially* essentialist. Yet three of the figures mentioned have often worked in the US, and the fourth is a frequently honored and influential visitor. And if the US is so essentially essentialist, why is the work of these figures so well-received in the US? And can one so neatly separate British and American Cultural Studies? Are they not mutually invaginated, mutually indebted? And where are the French anti-essentialists in all this? In any case, essentialist and anti-essentialist currents traverse every intellectual tradition. Therefore we should move beyond reductionist locationism when addressing issues of intellectual history and exchange, even while we together try to combat the imperialist policies of particular nation-states led by people like George Bush and (subordinately) Tony Blair.

# Part VIII

## Global Diasporas

# Introduction

## Ping-hui Liao

> Continent, city, country, society:
> the choice is never wide and never free.
> And here, or there ... No. Should we have stayed at home,
> Wherever that may be?"
>
> Elizabeth Bishop, "Questions of Travel"

In the summer of 2001, Phoebe Chang of the Harvard-Yenching Library took me to the home of Nelson Wu at Cambridge, Massachusetts. Professor Emeritus of Asian art history at the University of Washington-Missouri and a fiction writer whose work was ranked among the top 100 in contemporary Chinese literature, Wu is known in the Chinese-speaking world as Lu Qiao (Deer Bridge), a pen name he adopted at the age of 26 before going abroad in 1945 to study for an advanced degree at Yale University. Wu spent most of his life in the American mid-West, but nevertheless felt at home elsewhere. Readers from Taiwan still wrote to him and Chinese publishers kept urging him to sanction printing his novels in simplified characters on the ground that it was official policy that modern works should be made easily accessible to common folks. Few back in China knew of anything he did in America, where most of his friends and colleagues continued to address him as Nelson without realizing that Wu had assumed a diasporic identity. "To my neighbors, I am just a senile and useless Chinese immigrant ... However, my novels are re-issued and reach young people in many parts of the Chinese speaking world," Wu commented. Inhabiting more than one identity and not belonging to just one world, Wu exemplifies the stretched out geography of flows and connections that not only introduces split consciousnesses between "routes" and "roots," but produces disjunctive patterns of life through difficult fusions of different influences across different places – Beijing, Kunming, New Haven, San Francisco, Missouri, Cambridge, Taipei, and so on.

Elegant though frail, Wu and his wife were then in their early eighties. He died on March 19, 2002 – within a year of the interview – and did not live to see his novel *Wei-yang-ge* (Song of Youth) published in complex characters back in the homeland: China. Of course, pirated versions in simplified characters had long been available there, but Wu refused to authorize them. To him, Chinese traditional complex characters are more refined and nuanced in capturing what he wanted to express. He maintained over the years a critical distance from the country he was from; he was bitter about the outcome of the Cultural Revolution but was even more dismayed by the commercialization or "postmodern" turn in the PRC that tended to "sacrifice everything slow and thoughtful for speed and superficiality." That was partly why he and his wife did not want to go back to China or even to stay with their daughter (she and her family lived only a few blocks away). Wu's house was packed with boxes of books and painted scrolls; however, he had no problem finding an almanac he had brought with him when he left for the US some 60 years earlier. "In those days, everyone departing for strange shores would possess a copy like this and would hold on to it so long as the family name lived on. The almanac contained all the essential information one might need: a 10,000-year calendar, hexagrams, 100 most popular Chinese names, a copy of the Three Character Classic, a rhymed book of what to do and what not to do, of how to run a family according to Yuan Zhitui, etc. Most important was a lunar calendar marking the proper dates for ancestral worship, for marriages, family gatherings, funerals, and so forth." "As a departure talisman, this is a must even if one is illiterate or penniless," he went on to say.

Wu apparently consulted the almanac often and kept it as a family treasure – in spite of its tattered shape. I remember seeing similar almanacs at a Chinese restaurant in Milan, Italy; at an Asian American culture exhibit at the Smithsonian in Washington, DC, USA; and at a family shrine in Malaga, Malaysia. The almanac connects Chinese diasporas from street corners in Bamberg, Germany, to Chinatowns in San Francisco, Sydney, Leiden – all over the globe – charting the routes of travel and cultural translation that Aihwa Ong and Donald Nonini (1997) prematurely considered an "ungrounded" Chinese transnational empire on the basis of virtual capital and *guanxi*. In my view, the almanac functions not only as a symbolic link with one's imaginary homeland(s), but as a reminder that one has to develop a diasporic vision of the world from elsewhere. It marks, in the words of Salmam Rushdie (2002), "the very experience of uprooting, disjuncture and metamorphosis (slow or rapid, painful or pleasurable) that is the migrant condition, and from which, I believe, can be derived a metaphor for all humanity." As other exiled writers and postcolonial subjects – among them, for example, Derek Walcott or Eduard Glissant in discourses on the Caribbean – have also made clear, geographical and cultural displacements have increasingly informed our consciousness of local–global cultural dialectics, of the possibility of an alternative cartography of social space in response to traditional models of community that used to be isomorphic with nation and ethnicity. The diaspora metaphor is becoming a major theme in emergent world literature and international Cultural Studies, as there are reportedly more than 130 million migrants worldwide who find themselves struggling with problems of hospitality and hostility, of hybridization and ghettoization, of living in an interregnum caught between the old and the new, of reconciling the dweller (naturalized citizen) and the traveler (stranger).

## ■ The Uses and Abuses of Diaspora ■

An ancient and complex term, "diaspora" is derived etymologically from the Greek word *diasperin*, literally meaning scattering seeds across places (*dia*, "across"; *sperian*, "to sow seeds") and, by extension, dispersion of a population. It was notably used by the Greek historian Thucydides in *Peloponnesian War* (II: 27) to describe the displacement of the people of Aegina in the hands of Athenian cleruchs from 459 to 405 BCE. In *Deuteronomy* (28:25), the Hebrew *galut* was employed to refer to the forced exile of the Jews in Babylon (586 BCE). From 70 CE on, diaspora was predominantly associated with the dispersal of the Jews following the Roman conquest of Palestine and the destruction of Jerusalem, but the term has also had a much wider currency, being applied to other population dispersals, to the forced or unforced dislocation of the Armenians, Gypsies, Huguenots, Chinese, Indians, Irish, and the like (see Chaliand and Rageau, 1995). A recent trend has been to reinvent its critical genealogy and to confine its historical reference to the black African diaspora which resulted from the slave trade beginning in the sixteenth century and which took a worse colonial turn in the nineteenth (see Edwards, 2001; Gilroy, 1993).

While scholars have resorted to the diasporic framework in their discussion of the relatively unique histories of minority groups moving across national boundaries, they have tended to emphasize transnational connections and links to unsettle notions of modernity and identity. Though a condition of "terminal loss" (Said, 2001: 173), diaspora or exile is said to be able to make linkages that transect borderlands and open up new spaces or subject positions. This "partial linkage" discourse is often formed to the neglect of difficult transitions, especially for "children of immigration" (Suarez-Orozco and Suarez-Orozco, 2001), and of a tightening of patriarchal control over women in response to the social insecurities or moral ambivalences in the new "home" (Bhabha, 1996; Ifekuwingwe, 1999). Diaspora is thus celebrated in theories of culture traveling, of a displacement-dwelling dialectics (e.g. Clifford, 1997), or of realizing creative potentials and even triumphant achievements otherwise impossible (e.g. Said, 2001). It is understandable that critics from different camps have constantly cautioned against the uses and abuses of diaspora. However, the term is frequently evoked as a theoretical concept to frame questions of place, culture, memory, and identity in view of the unprecedented global flow of people, machinery, money, images, ideas, medical aids, entertainments and sports, and, not the least on the list, of travelers and indentured labor (see Appadurai, 1996; Behdad, 2000; Cohen, 1997).

W. E. B. Du Bois, Frantz Fanon, and many other thinkers of the Negritude movement helped promote the dissemination of a black diasporic consciousness, a theme reiterated in Paul Gilroy's (1993) seminal work *The Black Atlantic*. Within this transatlantic African diaspora framework, slavery and colonialism in many parts of North America, South America, the Caribbean, and elsewhere have been under scrutiny (see Okpewho et al., 1999). According to these thinkers, black African diaspora constituted a transnational network of countermodernity, for the slaves resuscitated their spiritual traditions in their new homes and thereby challenged the dominant trends of enchantment or enlightenment in the West. From the 1980s onwards, scholars have applied it to other religious or ethnic groups – Muslims or Sikhs (see Bates, 2001), for example – in their discussion of migration or deterritorization. The critical term has increasingly been associated with blacks across the Atlantic, with Asian immigrants, South American refugees, worldwide indentured labor, transnational mobility, postmodernism, globalization, minoritization, new ethnicity, cultural hybridity, nomadism, etc. The term no longer seems historically specific or even meaningful, as it is used indiscriminately with exile, migration, travel, and fluid identity formation. Cultural historians have understandably advised us to drop the term altogether. In China studies, for example, Wang Gungwu (2000) has cautioned about the politically centrifugal implications of the term in attenuating the sense of Chineseness, in undercutting the desire to return or to be reclaimed by China. "I have long resisted the use of *diaspora* to describe the Chinese overseas," he writes, "and am still concerned that it could acquire political overtones similar to those of *huaqiao*, which governments both inside and outside China have highlighted in the past" (Wang, 2000: 84 n. 4). Wang has argued against a "single Chinese diaspora" and suggests that we pay attention to the economic, political, and historical contextual specificities of variegated groups moving to different places across times. In opposition to Wang's stress on the ties to the motherland, several Asian American scholars have directed our attention to ways in which sinology has tended to freeze its object through the mechanism of writing the other (e.g. Chow, 1998), to racialized political economy of immigration acts and with them the tendency toward provincializing cultural internationalism (e.g. Lowe, 1996; Palumbo-Liu, 2002), or to ways in which Asian diasporas have developed and maintained crucial networks of material and symbolic exchange with their homelands as well as with various minority groups in receiving countries (e.g. Ong, 1999). They advocate a more worldly and contextual approach to the study of diaspora.

In many respects, Chinese diaspora study has benefited from the study of such particular cases as the black Atlantic (Gilroy); Aguilillans in Redwood City, California (Rouse, 1995); Koreans in Los Angeles (Abelmann and Lie, 1995); Caribbeans in New York (Scher, 2003), among others. Against these "Afrocentrist," cultural, or even "elitist" approaches, Ali Behdad (2000) has highlighted the layered, conflictive, and disjunctive nature of global movements by citing examples of southeast Asian guest workers in the Gulf states that join international circuits of migration to finance their home economies and to realize their hopes for better lives away from home, from famine, or from new terrorist regimes. Underneath this trajectory of empowerment, there is a peculiar form of what Benedict Anderson (1994) has called "long-distance nationalism," of upholding an alternative political culture back home. Filipino maids in Hong Kong certainly contribute to overseas national projects, to the political economy of diasporic aspirations (see San Juan, 1996). These case studies about diaspora attend to the particular configurations of power in sociocultural relations, and to the complexities of diasporic experiences triggered by the transnational flows of material and symbolic goods.

Of course, not all cultural critics agree that as a critical notion diaspora is politically useful. For instance, Bruce Robbins (1995) finds the term problematic as it highlights mobility to the neglect of intellectual and political engagement centering on questions of citizenship and racial inequality within the nation. To him, diaspora risks losing a historical specificity and critical edge. And if we review back issues of such journals as *Diaspora, New Formations, Positions, Public Culture,* and *Transitions,* the critical references to diaspora range from transnationality, the gay movement, ethnic communities abroad, consumerism, global contemporaneity, stateless and flexible citizenship, colonialisms, and alternative modernities, to return migration, foreignness, plurality, identity crisis, minority, exile, difference, exhibiting (Mexican) museum culture, etc. Apparently, diaspora has too many facets and does not adequately address concrete cultural issues. However, the term has been profitably expanded to cover the fractured trajectories not only of Africans and Jews exported or forced to move across the globe, but also of other ethnic groups in massive migration and their cultural representations from Algeria to Trinidad to New York and elsewhere (see Mirzoeff, 2000; Clifford, 1997). The general consensus finds the term useful as a concept so long as we take into consideration the complexities of diaspora experience and attend to the historical conditions that produce diasporic subjectivities. As Jana Braziel and Anita Mannur (2003) have pointed out in a recent anthology, diaspora does not "transcend differences of race, class, gender, and sexuality...nor can diaspora stand alone as an epistemological or historical category of analysis, separate and distinct from these interrelated categories" (5). Theorizing diaspora from the perspective of the discordant movements of modernity, they think of it as "a nomadic turn in which every parameter of specific historical moments are embodied...scattered and regrouped into new points of becoming" (3). To them, diaspora represents the lived experiences of peoples whose lives have unfolded in a myriad of diasporic communities across the globe, forcing us "to rethink the rubric of nation and nationalism, while refiguring the relations of citizens and nation-states" (7). It offers multiple dislocated sites of contestation to the hegemonic, homogenizing forces of globalization, challenging the rule relations of transnational empire, international economic exploitation and political disenfranchisement, and corporate capitalism or managerialism all over the world (10–11). While their critical enterprises very much echo what Michael Hardt and Antonio Negri (2000) have suggested in their conclusion to *Empire,* their discursive strategies of interethnic articulation and coordination are never clearly defined.

Historians and geographers have systematically used the term to mean dislocation or the existential predicaments resulting from such displacement. From the perspective of human geography and the migrant atlas, Gerard Chaliand and Jean-Pierre Rageau (1995) list the statistics of different ethnic groups scattered all over the world. Benedict Anderson (1997) opposes this sort of historical atlas; to him, real and imagined censuses fail to account for "phantom communities" which are created by imagination and no longer confined to the interiors of already-existing nation-states. "Is it necessary," he asks, "to underline that these countings were made by imperial state machineries for their own reasons and by their own peculiar logics, that it is quite uncertain how many of the 42,000 'Indians' in fact imagined themselves as such, and that there was every sort of ambiguity and arbitrariness involved in deciding who was a Jew in thirteenth-century Portugal?" (44–5). In other words, diaspora study has to consider qualitative transformations in relation to bound and unbound relationships with home. In an essay included in this section, James Clifford proposes that we view diaspora as a condition in which the displaced manage to form partial connection with homes – that is, with one far away and another in proximity. Diasporic consciousness operates in syncopated responses to differential communalities and temporalities, in modes of entanglement and cross-cutting time and space.

### ■ Signposts on the Diasporic Pathways ■

Diaspora has to do with dislocation, distanciation, difference, and disjunction. Diaspora involves forced exile and the inability to return except by the detour of symbolic acts, of tortured narratives to imaginary homelands. Anderson shows us how many people have been taken or traveled to foreign lands through indenture, kidnapping, migration, or even virtual tour. A recent account found there were nearly 30 million foreign-born people in the US. Forty-eight percent of all students in New York City schools come from immigrant-headed households that speak more than 100 different languages (Suarez-Orozco and Suarez-Orozco, 2001: 34–5). Asian immigrants alone reached up to 3 million around 1940 (Chan, 1991: 12). As for the Jews of the diaspora, from Italy to Iran, they "outnumbered those in the homeland" (Gruen, 2002: 233); this may also be true in the case of American Jews. As a result of such displacements, relationships between new home(s) and old homeland(s) have become entangled. In the selections below, Anderson raises issue of patriotism and long-distance nationalism; Clifford follows up Gilroy's account of black counter-modern projects to suggest comparative studies in diasporic communities and their partial connections with homelands; Naficy highlights the differential impacts homelands produce on exilic and diasporic filmmakers who situate their "identity performances" in relation to their desires to return or not to return; Eng considers the rise of queer discourses informed by a sense of castration, of being denied home and its symbolic order.

Distance from one's motherland generates a strong sense of loss, but it also introduces discrepant visions of the home and the new dwelling place, creating a split and trauma but also a poetics of re-vision, of looking backward and forward in differential temporalities. In the words of V. S. Naipaul, diaspora undermines a singular identity by cultivating a sense of "one out of many." It is disabling, in attenuating ties with one's home culture, language, and tradition. It unsettles systems of beliefs and a sense of security. However, it is in many ways enabling in a paradoxical structure of empowerment, offering new job or educational opportunities and even freedom from unjust persecution or discrimination at home. Though alienating and disturbing, distance provides comparative perspectives that see things anew, that engender borderland conditions in which one can transform relationships to lifeworlds and social habitus once taken for granted. Clifford and Naficy demonstrate the ways in which diaspora constituted new subjectivities and communities. Anderson directs our attention to the woman whose vision suddenly came into being when she was removed from home. Queer identity is posited by Eng as a discursive struggle to distanciate and to clear a space.

Diaspora is above all about difference, cultural, socio-economic, political, religious, sexual and gender. Works like *Wedding Banquet* (Ang Lee, 1993), *El Norte* (Gregory Nara, 1983), *Dictee* (Teresa Cha, 1995), or *The Journey* (Harish Saluja, 1997) show us the psychosocial experience of defeat and re-adjustment, of the arts of survival the characters deploy in the face of huge obstacles to success. This is a dominant theme in the age of multiculturalism and receives thorough discussion in the essays. In response to dislocation, distanciation, and difference, diasporas tend to form disjunctive subjectivities, often in the almost unrecognizable form of what Jacques Lacan terms "anamorphosis," of a contorted projection of hopes and fears into a distorted field of vision. Diasporas desire to belong while tortured by lack; their worldviews and discursive practices are informed by fetish desires to reproduce or to fill in the gap between the home and the new world.

While theoretically productive and politically useful, diaspora studies have yet to map new territories. The cases offered tend to focus on North America or the English-speaking Indian or Caribbean communities (cf. Bates, 2001; Verovec, 2000; Mishra, 1996). Comparative accounts have recently appeared (e.g. Cohen, 1997; Grewal, 1994; Hall, 1990; Israel, 2000; Sakai, 1997; among others), but they generally discuss global networks of capitalism initiated and controlled by the US. In the study of Chinese diasporas, for instance, a large proportion have been devoted to Asian Americans (Chan, 1991; Li, 1998; Lowe, 1996; Ma, 1998; Shih, 1997) or the notion of "Chineseness" (Cheah, 2001; Chow, 1993; Tu, 1994), with only a handful to the Chinese of Europe (Benton and Picke, 1998; Yue, 2000; Ma and Cartier, 2003), Australia (Ang, 2000), or southeast Asia (Wang and Wang, 1998). Drawing on diaspora and Cultural Studies, film critics continue to shed light on the formation of hybrid genres or accented cinema (Abbas, 1997; Hamamoto and Liu, 2000; Naficy, 2001). Gender studies have substantially contributed to our understanding of the difficult and confusing roles of women in diaspora, while queer studies have just begun to open up the field. An emergent area of research interest is the diasporic internet community and long-distance nationalism or network terrorism as manifested by such organizations as Izzawi's Cyber

Café, Falong Gong, or Al Qaeda (Nacify, 1999: 213–32; Anderson, 1997). However, a more nuanced critical genealogy of terms equivalent to diaspora in different cultures and communities is a path yet hardly taken, and should be a fruitful direction toward which our selections can serve as signposts.

## REFERENCES

Abbas, Ackbar. *Hong Kong: Culture and the Politics of Disappearance*. Minneapolis: University of Minnesota Press, 1997.

Abelmann, Nancy, and John Lie. *Blue Dreams: Korean Americans and the Los Angelos Riots*. Cambridge: Harvard University Press, 1995.

Anderson, Benedict. "Exodus." *Critical Inquiry* 20(2) (1994): 314–27.

Anderson, Benedict. *The Specters of Comparison*. New York: Verso, 1997.

Ang, Ien. "Identity Blues." In *Without Guarantees: In Honour of Stuart Hall*, eds. Paul Gilroy, Lawrence Grossberg, and Angela McRobbie. New York: Verso, 2000. 1–13.

Appardurai, Arjun. *Modernity at Large*. Minneapolis: University of Minnesota Press, 1996.

Bates, Crispin, ed. *Community, Empire and Migration: South Asians in Diaspora*. Basingstoke: Palgrave, 2001.

Behdad, Ali. "Global Disjunctures, Diasporic Differences, and The New World (Dis-)Order." In *A Companion to Postcolonial Studies*, eds. Henry Schwarz and Sangeeta Ray. Malden: Blackwell, 2000, 396–409.

Benton, Gregor, and Frank N. Picke, ed. *The Chinese in Europe*. Basingstoke: Palgrave, 1998.

Bhabha, Jacqueline. "Embodied Rights: Gender Persecution, State Sovereignty and Refugees." *Public Culture* 9(1) (1996): 3–32.

Braziel, Jana Evans and Anita Mannur, eds. *Theorizing Diaspora*. Malden: Blackwell, 2003.

Chaliand, Gerard, and Jean-Pierre Rageau. *The Penguin Atlas of Diasporas*. Trans. A. M. Berrett. New York: Penguin, 1995.

Chan, Sucheng. *Asian Americans: An Interpretive History*. New York: Twayne, 1991.

Cheah, Pheng. "Chinese Cosmopolitanism in Two Senses and Postcolonial National Memory." In *Cosmopolitan Geographies: New Locations in Literature and Culture*, ed. Vinay Dharwadker. New York: Routledge, 2001, 132–69.

Chow, Rey. *Writing Diaspora: Tactics of Intervention on Contemporary Cultural Studies*. Bloomington: Indiana University Press, 1993.

Clifford, James. "Diasporas." In *Routes: Travel and Translation in the Late Twentieth Century*. Cambridge, MA: Harvard University Press, 1997, 244–77.

Cohen, Robin. *GlobalDiasporas: An Introduction*. Seattle: University of Washington Press, 1997.

Eng, David L. *Racial Castration: Managing Masculinity in Asian America*. Durham, NC: Duke University Press, 2001.

Edwards, Brent Hayes. "The Uses of Diaspora." *Social Text* 66 (2001): 45–73.

Gilroy, Paul. *The Black Atlantic: Modernity and Double Consciousness*. Cambridge, MA: Harvard University Press, 1993.

Gilroy, Paul. "Diaspora." *Paragraph* 17(3) (1994): 207–12.

Grewal, Inderpal. "Autobiographic Subjects and Diasporic Locations: Meatless Days and Borderlands." In *Scattered Hegemonies: Postmodernity and Transnational Feminist Practices*, eds. Inderpal Grewal and Caren Kaplan. Minneapolis: University of Minnesota Press, 1994.

Gruen, Erich S. *Diaspora: Jews amidst Greeks and Romans.* Cambridge, MA: Harvard University Press, 2002.
Hall, Stuart. "Cultural Identity and Diaspora." In *Identity: Community, Culture, Difference,* ed. Jonathan Rutherford. London: Lawrence & Wishart, 1990, 222–37.
Hamamoto, Darrell Y. and Sandra Liu, eds. *Countervisions: Asian American Film Criticism.* Philadelphia: Temple University Press, 2000.
Hardt, Michael and Antonio Negri. *Empire.* Cambridge, MA: Harvard University Press, 2000.
Ifekuwingwe, Jayne O. *Scattered Belongings: Cultural Paradoxes of "Race," Nation and Gender.* New York: Routledge, 1999.
Israel, Nico. *Outlandish: Writing Between Exile and Diaspora.* Stanford: Stanford University Press, 2000.
Jaynes, Gerald D., ed. *Immigration and Race: New Challenges to American Democracy.* New Haven: Yale University Press, 2000.
Li, David Leiwei. *Imagining the Nation: Asian American Literature and Cultural Consent.* Stanford: Stanford University Press, 1998.
Lowe, Lisa. *The Immigrant Act.* Durham, NC: Duke University Press, 1996.
Ma, Laurence J. C. and Carolyn Cartier, eds. *The Chinese in Diaspora.* Oxford: Rowman and Littlefield, 2003.
Ma, Sheng-mei. *Immigrant Subjectivities in Asian American and Asian Diaspora Literatures.* Albany: State University of New York Press, 1998.
Mirzoeff, Nicholas, ed. *Diaspora and Visual Culture: Representing Africans and Jews.* New York: Routledge, 2000.
Mishra, Vijav. "The Diasporic Imaginary: Theorizing the Indian Diaspora." *Textual Practice* 10(3) (1996): 421–47.
Naficy, Hamid. *An Accented Cinema: Exilic and Diasporic Filmmaking.* Princeton: Princeton University Press, 2001.
Naficy, Hamid, ed. *Home, Exile, Homeland: Film, Media, and the Politics of Place.* New York: Routledge, 1999.
Naipaul, V. S. "One out of Many." In *Vintage Naipaul.* New York: Vintage, 2004.
Okpewho, Isidore, Carole Boyce Davies, and Ali A. Mazrui, eds. *African Diaspora: African Origins and New World Identities.* Bloomington: Indiana University Press, 1999.
Ong, Aihwa. *Flexible Citizenship: The Cultural Logics of Transnationality.* Durham, NC: Duke University Press, 1999.
Ong, Aihwa and Donald Nonini, eds. *Ungrounded Empires: The Cultural Politics of Modern Chinese Transnationalism.* New York: Routledge, 1997.
Palumbo-Liu, David. "Multiculturalism Now: Civilization, National Identity, and Difference before and after September 11th." *Boundary 2* 29(2) (2002): 108–27.
Robbins, Bruce. "Some Versions of U.S. Internationalism." *Social Text* 45 (1995): 97–123.
Rouse, Roger. "Thinking through Transnationalism: Notes on the Cultural Politics of Class Relations in the Contemporary United States." *Public Culture* 7(2) (1995): 353–402.
Rushdie, Salman. *Step Across This Line: Collected Nonfiction 1992–2002.* New York: Random House, 2002.
Said, Edward W. *Reflections on Exile.* Cambridge, MA: Harvard University Press, 2001.
Sakai, Naoki. *Translation and Subjectivity: On "Japan" and Cultural Nationalism.* Minneapolis: University of Minnesota Press, 1997.
San Juan, E., Jr. *From Exile to Diaspora: Versions of the Filipino Experience in the United States.* Boulder, CO: Westview, 1996.

Scher, Philip W. *Carnival and the Formation of a Caribbean Transnation.* Miami: University of Florida Press, 2003.

Shih, Shu-mei. "Nationalism and Korean American Writing: Theresa Hak-kyung Cha's *Dictee.*" In *Speaking the Other Self: American Women Writers,* ed. Jeanne Campbell Reesman. Athens: University of Georgia Press, 1997, 144–62.

Suarez-Orozco, Carola, and Marcelo M. Suarez-Orozco. *Children of Immigration.* Cambridge, MA: Harvard University Press, 2001.

Tololyan, Khachig. "Rethinking Diaspora(s): Stateless Power in the Transnational Moment." *Diaspora* 5(1) (1996): 3–36.

Tu, Wei-ming, ed. *The Living Tree: The Changing Meaning of Being Chinese Today.* Stanford: Stanford University Press, 1994.

Verovec, Steven. *The Hindu Diaspora: Comparative Patterns.* London: Routledge, 2000.

Wang, Gungwu. *The Chinese Overseas: From Earthbound China to the Quest for Autonomy.* Cambridge, MA: Harvard University Press, 2000.

Wang, Ling-chi and Wang Gungwu, eds. *The Chinese Diaspora: Selected Essays.* 2 vols. Singapore: Times Academic Press, 1998.

Yue, Ming-Bao. "On Not Looking German: Ethnicity, Diaspora and the Politics of Vision." *European Journal of Cultural Studies* 3(2) (2000): 173–94.

# 36

## Exodus

### Benedict Anderson

> I saw a place where English Cattle had been: that was a comfort to me, such as it was: quickly after that we came to an English Path, which so took with me, that I thought I could have freely lyen down and dyed. That day, a little after noon, we came to Squaukheag, where the Indians quickly spread themselves over the deserted English Fields.[1]

Thus, as remembered subsequently, was the experience of the 19-year-old, newly married Mary Rowlandson as her Narragansett abductors brought her with them through central Massachusetts – perhaps twenty miles north of today's turnpike – in mid-February 1675. One observes the strange, thoroughly creole crosscurrents in her words. On the one hand, she feels no need to explain to her readers where Squaukheag is located, let alone how to pronounce this strikingly un-European toponym. Her familiarity is not surprising; Squakheag is, so to speak, that place down the road, since she had been born and spent all her young life in the no less un-European Massachusetts. On the other hand, she sees before her "English Cattle," an "English Path," and "deserted English Fields," though she has never been within three thousand miles of England. These are not pluckings from the Cotswolds or the Downs – real places, as it were – but acts of imagination that would never have occurred to a young minister's wife in seventeenth-century Gloucestershire or Surrey. They are, in a way, getting ready to be "English" exactly because they are in Massachusetts, not in England, and are so because they bear for Mary the traces of her "English" people's agricultural labors. But we can also guess that up till the point of her abduction she had thought matter-of-factly about cattle as cattle and fields as fields. Her "nationalizing" moment comes when, in the power of the Narragansetts, she is torn out of the quotidian and – right in the very midst of her native Massachusetts – finds herself in fearful exile. She struggles along a path that becomes English at the exact juncture where she is sure she may not lie down and die upon it. When she is finally ransomed and returns to her community of origin, her "nationalist" frisson vanishes. For she has managed, more or less, to come home. But this home is Lancaster; it is not (yet) America.

The paradox here is that we today can without much trouble read Mary Rowlandson *as* American precisely because, in captivity, she saw English fields before her. Acton was on the mark when he wrote, two hundred years later, that "exile is the nursery of nationality."[2]

On the other side of the Atlantic, Mary Rowlandson's narrative was published within a year of the Massachusetts first edition and proved very popular, accumulating thirty editions over the eighteenth century.[3] A rapidly growing reading public in the recently united kingdom – Mary was captured two decades before Scotland – was becoming aware of anomalous English-writing women who had never been to England but who could be dragged through English fields by "savages." What were they? Were they really English? The photographic negative of "the colonial," the non-English Englishwoman, was coming into view.

Because the Spanish conquests in the Caribbean and southern Americas had begun a century before permanent English settlements in the North, non-Spanish Spaniards began to loom up very early. Already in 1612, the *madrileño* Dominican theologian Juan de la Puente was writing that "the heavens of America induce inconstancy, lasciviousness and lies: vices characteristic of the Indians and which the constellations make characteristic of the Spaniards who are born and bred there."[4] The creole was being invented figuratively, later to be realized culturally and politically. We can see here – especially if we recall the century-long rage at de la Puente made possible by the quiet two-way hiss of print across the Atlantic – the real historical origins of the "native," a persona that persists under sometimes other names well into our own times, in Europe as much as anywhere else.

For the native is, like colonial and creole, a white-on-black negative. The nativeness of natives is always unmoored, its real significance hybrid and oxymoronic. It appears when Moors, heathens, Mohammedans, savages, Hindoos, and so forth are becoming obsolete, that is, not only when, in the proximity of real print-encounters, substantial numbers of Vietnamese read, write, and perhaps speak French but also when Czechs do the same with German and Jews with Hungarian. Nationalism's purities (and thus also cleansings) are set to emerge from exactly this hybridity.

What set all these engines in motion? To put it a bit differently, what made Mary Rowlandson's – and in due course London's – unstable Englishness possible? The simple answer is capitalism, the institutions of which enabled the transportation, from the mid-sixteenth century on, of millions of free, indentured, and enslaved bodies across thousands of miles of water. But the materialities of this transportation – ships, fire-arms, and navigational equipment – were guided by the mathematically inspired Mercatorian map and the vast, accumulating knowledge stored and disseminated in print. It was also through print moving back and forth across the ocean that the unstable, imagined worlds of Englishnesses and Spanishnesses were created.

The essential nexus of long-distance transportation and print capitalist communications prepared the grounds on which, by the end of the eighteenth century, the first nationalist movements flowered. It is striking that this flowering took place first in North America and later in the Catholic, Iberian colonies to the south, the economies of all of which were *pre*-industrial. Nothing underlines this process better than the fact that in the second half of the eighteenth century there were more presses in colonial North America than in the metropole. So it was that by 1765, in the words of Michael Warner, "print had come to be seen as indispensable to political life, and could appear to such men as Adams to be the primary agent of world emancipation. What makes this transformation of the press particularly remarkable is that, unlike the press explosion of the nineteenth century, it involved virtually no technological improvements in the trade."[5]

These facts in themselves strongly suggest the untenability of Ernest Gellner's argument that *industrialism* was the historical source of nationalism's emergence.[6] (One might add that most of the zones in which early nineteenth-century European nationalisms became visible – say Ireland, Greece, Hungary, Poland, and Bohemia – were those most innocent of "industrial progress.") Nonetheless, industrialism did, at a later stage, become of signal importance for the spread and transformation of nationalism, first in Europe, afterwards in Asia and Africa. It did so by creating, directly and indirectly, new types of exile.

In his bizarre 1847 novel, *Tancred, or The New Crusade*, Benjamin Disraeli observed that "London is a modern Babylon."[7] In this oxymoron, the echoes of a captivity narrative are as loud as those of a proverbial trope for luxury and corruption. It sprang quite logically from the celebrated subtitle of *Sybil, or The Two Nations*, which Disraeli had published two years earlier. Deepening industrial capitalism had by then created within a single, very small territorial state – smaller, if we exclude Ireland, than Pennsylvania and New York combined – "two nations," however, that in no way corresponded to any putative ethnic or religious communities. When Friedrich Engels arrived in Manchester in 1842 and began his studies of the condition of the working class, George Stephenson had preceded him. The world's textile capital already had a railway station. The locomotive had begun its world-historical mission of transporting millions of rural villagers into urban slums, a mission scarcely less epochal than that which the transatlantic sailing ship had performed over the preceding three centuries.[8] Only a minority would return to end their days in those cemeteries where the rude forefathers of the hamlet slept. How the novel experience of industrial life radically transformed their lives and how this transformation made them, as it were, available for nationalism is splendidly described by Gellner, but his description should be read under the sign of exile. It was beginning to become possible to see "English fields" in England – from the window of a railway carriage.

Meanwhile, exile of another sort was emerging from the very wealth that industrial capitalism was producing for European states. For this wealth was making possible the spread of a centralized, standardized, steeply hierarchical system of public education. E. J. Hobsbawm reminds us that at the time of *Tancred*'s publication, on the eve of the upheavals of 1848, there were only 48,000 or so university students in all of Europe, a number substantially lower than the current enrollment at Ohio State University.[9] But in the second half of the century, ministries of education sprang up like mushrooms everywhere – Sweden in 1852, England in 1870, and France in 1882 – and children began to be compelled to migrate to schools.[10]

When the elderly Filipino Pedro Calosa was interviewed in the mid-1960s and asked to compare the conditions of that time with those of the uprising of 1931 that he had led against American colonialism, he observed with nostalgic satisfaction that "there were no teenagers" then.[11] For this new human type – nomad between childhood and working adulthood – was then only beginning to emerge from the imperialists' novel apparatus for mass education. More generally, however, the teenager was, from the second half of the nineteenth century, the site on which the state imposed its standardized vernacular. Whether this vernacular was a socially valorized dialect of a language widely understood among the state's subjects (say, the King's English), or a vernacular determined from among a multiplicity of vernaculars (say, German in Austria-Hungary), the effect was typically to restratify and rationalize the social and political hierarchy of vernaculars and dialects; all the more so in that the new education was increasingly linked to employment possibilities and opportunities for social mobility. Small wonder that people were becoming ever more self-conscious about their linguistic practices and the consequences of those practices. Quite often the effect was a kind of exile. The more a standardized vernacular ceased to be merely the internal language of officials and became the official language of a propagandizing state, the more likely became the emergence in Old Europe of something reminiscent of the creole or native: the not-really-German German, the not-quite-Italian Italian, the non-Spanish Spaniard. As in the Americas, a kind of unstable negativity appeared. Nothing, therefore, is less surprising than that the nationalist movements which transformed the map of Europe by 1919 were so often led by young bilinguals, a pattern to be followed after 1919 in Asia and Africa. How could a boy who learned Czech from his mother and German from his schooling unlearn a Czech that had left no contaminating traces on his German-speaking classmates? How could he not see his Czech as though in exile, through the inverted telescope of his German?

From the perspective sketched out so far, one might be inclined to view the rise of nationalist movements and their variable culminations in successful nation-states as a project for coming home from exile, for the resolution of hybridity, for a positive printed from a negative in the dark-room of political struggle. If one migrated from a village in the delta of the Ganges and went to schools in Calcutta, Delhi, and perhaps Cambridge; if one bore the indelible contaminations of English and Bengali; if one was destined to be cremated in Bombay, where was one intelligibly to be home, where could one unitarily be born, live, and die, except in "India"?

At the same time, for all the reasons just detailed, home as it emerged was less experienced than imagined, and imagined through a complex of mediations and representations. At the simplest level this imagining occurred through visual symbols such as flags, maps, statuary, microcosmic ceremonials; at a more profound level, through "self-" and "representative" government. The ingenuity of the mechanisms of popular suffrage seems to me to lie in the double duty they perform. Individually, legislators represent particular interests, localities, and prejudices; collectively and anonymously, as Parliament, Diet, or Congress, they represent a unitary nation or sovereignty.[12]

One can thus see why nation-statehood was so central to the nineteenth-century nationalist projects that destroyed the huge, polyglot, imperial-dynastic systems inherited from the age of absolutism. For it was felt both to represent, with its characteristically republican institutions, a newfound alignment of imagined home and imagined homeowners and to guarantee that stabilized alignment through the organized, systematic deployment of its powers and resources. Hence the plausibility of the Listian dream of the self-supplying national economy, guarded moat-like by the tariff. Hence too, one suspects, the Listian morphology of railway systems, mapped inward from state peripheries toward state capitals and often marked off, *zollverein* style, at borders by differential gauges.[13] If this surmise is right, one might view the locomotive along with the printed newspaper as the material points of juncture between the classical nation-state project and capitalism at the stage of primary industrialism.

The irony, however, is that, just as this classical nation-state project was coming fully into its own with the formation of the League of Nations in 1919, advancing capitalism was beginning to sap its foundations. As in an earlier age, the most visible transformations took place in the areas of transportation and communications. On land, motor vehicles increasingly displaced the locomotive, while the vast proliferation of macadamized road surfaces on which they sped were never gauge-calibrated to national frontiers. In the air, commercial aviation was, with the exception of a few very large and rich nations like the United States, primarily transnational from its earliest days. One flew to leave or to return to one's nation-state rather than to move about within it, and "national airspace" had only a short plausible life before the advent of the satellite made it obsolete. The pace and thrust of these changes is vividly demonstrated by the statistics on the admission of nonimmigrant aliens into historically immigrant America:

| | |
|---|---|
| 1931–40 | 1,574,071 |
| 1941–50 | 2,461,359 |
| 1951–60 | 7,113,023 |
| 1961–70 | 24,107,224 |
| 1971–79 | 61,640,389 |
| 1981–91 | 142,076,530[14] |

(The 1930s were the first decade in which nonimmigrants outnumbered immigrants, and they already did so by a ratio of three to one.)

Radio brought even illiterate populations within the purview of the mass media, and its reception was never effectively limited to nation-state audiences. No newspaper could ever hope to command the range of planetary acolytes that became available to the BBC or the Voice of America. Subsequently, the telephone and telex, film, television, cassettes, video recorders, and the personal computer accelerated and enormously magnified nearly everything that radio had initiated.

These developments have had and will continue to have vast consequences precisely because they are integral components of the transnationalization of advanced capitalism and of the steepening economic stratification of the global economy. As things now stand, less than 25 percent of the world's population appropriates 85 percent of world income, and the gap between rich and poor is steadily widening. Between 1965 and 1990 the difference between living standards in Europe and those in India and China increased from a ratio of forty to one up to seventy to one. In the 1980s, over 800 million people – more than the population of the United States, the European Community, and Japan combined – "became yet more grindingly poor, and one out of three children went hungry."[15] Yet, thanks to the airplane, the bus, the truck, and even the old locomotive, this inequality and misery is in all senses closer to privilege and wealth than ever before. Hence migration has moved not, as in earlier centuries, outwards to peripheries in the New World or the Antipodes but inwards toward the metropolitan cores.

Between 1840 and 1930, about 37,500,000 immigrants, overwhelmingly from Europe, came to the United States; approximately 416,000 per annum on average. In the 1970s, the annual figure was almost 500,000 and in the 1980s almost 740,000; 80 percent of the newcomers came from the "Third World."[16] Paul Kennedy notes that some demographers currently believe that as many as 15 million immigrants will enter America in each of the next three decades, that is, at an annual average rate of 1.5 million, double that of the 1980s.[17] Western Europe absorbed over 20 million immigrants in the three decades between the end of World War II and the oil crisis of the early 1970s. (The figure would have been much higher had it not been for the helpfulness of Stalin's iron curtain.) But in the latter part of the 1980s the numbers have swelled and will probably do so at least through the 1990s. Of Germany's 79 million inhabitants, 5.2 million (7 percent) are foreign immigrants; for France the figures are 3.6 (7 percent) out of 56 million; for the United Kingdom, 1.8 (2 percent) out of 57 million; for Switzerland, 1.1 (16.3 percent) out of 6.8 million.[18] (Even insular, restrictive Japan is said to have a million or so legal and illegal alien residents.) And the economic and political implosion of the Soviet Union is already moving people in a way that no *fin-de-siècle* continental system can stem.

At the same time, the communications revolution of our time has profoundly affected the subjective experience of migration. The Moroccan construction worker in Amsterdam can every night listen to Rabat's broadcasting services and has no difficulty in buying pirated cassettes of his country's favorite singers. The illegal alien, *Yakuza*-sponsored, Thai bartender in a Tokyo suburb shows his Thai comrades karaoke videotapes just made in Bangkok. The Filipina maid in Hong Kong phones her sister in Manila and sends money electronically to her mother in Cebu. The successful Indian student in Vancouver can keep in daily touch with her former Delhi classmates by electronic mail. To say nothing of an evergrowing blizzard of faxes. It is as if, were Mary Rowlandson alive today, she could see, in her small apartment bedroom, in perfect electronic safety on the screen beyond her toes, "truly" English fields and cattle.

But of course the meaning would have changed completely, not least because she can only see what the masters of the screen choose to let her see. Her eye can never gaze more widely than its frame. The "Englishness" of the fields comes not from within her but from a narrating voice outside her. More concretely, consider the well-known photograph of the lonely Peloponnesian *gastarbeiter* sitting in his dingy room in, say, Frankfurt. The solitary decoration on his wall is a resplendent Lufthansa travel poster of the Parthenon, which invites him, in German, to take a "sun-drenched holiday" in Greece. He may well never have seen the Parthenon, but framed by Lufthansa the poster confirms for him and for any visitor a Greek identity that perhaps only Frankfurt has encouraged him to assume. At the same time, it reminds him that he is only a couple of air hours from Greece, and that if he saves enough Lufthansa will be glad to assist him to have a fortnight's "sunny holiday" in his *heimat*. He knows too, most likely, that he will then return to exile in Frankfurt. Or is it that, in the longer run, he will find himself in brief annual exile in the Peloponnese? Or in both places? And what about his children?

Before turning to the political consequences of this broad sketch of post-1930s nomadism, two smaller but important related effects of post-industrial capitalism need briefly to be underscored. Consider the two most widely prevalent, quite modern official documents of personal identity: the birth certificate and the passport. Both were born in the nationalist nineteenth century and later became interlinked. It is true that in the Christianized regions of the world the registration of births long preceded the rise of capitalism. But these births were recorded locally and ecclesiastically in parish churches; their registration, foreshadowing imminent baptisms, signified the appearance of Christian souls in new corporeal forms. In the nineteenth century, however, registration was taken over by states that were increasingly assuming a national coloring. In industrially preeminent England, for example, the registrar general's office was created only in 1837. Compulsory registration of all births, whether to be followed by baptisms or not, did not come until 1876. Identifying each baby's father and place of birth, the state's certificates created the founding documents for the infant's inclusion in or exclusion from citizenship (through jus sanguinis or jus soli). (He or she was no longer born in the parish of Egham but in the United Kingdom.) The passport, product of the vectoral convergence of migration and nationalism in an industrial age, was ready to confirm the baby's political identity as it passed into adulthood.

The nexus of birth certificate and passport was institutionalized in an era in which women had no legal rights to political participation and the patriarchal family was the largely unquestioned norm. But in our time all this has radically changed. When the League of Nations was founded – and female suffrage was coming into its own – the ratio of divorces to marriages in the United States was about one to eight; today it is virtually one to two. The percentage of babies born to never-married mothers has increased spectacularly from 4.2 percent in 1960 to

30.6 percent in 1990.[19] The intranational as well as international nomadism of modern life has also contributed to making the nineteenth-century birth certificate a sort of counterfeit money. If, for example, we read that Mary Jones was born on 25 October 1970 in Duluth, to Robert Mason and Virginia Jones, or even Robert and Virginia Mason, we cannot nonchalantly infer that she was conceived in that same Duluth, was brought up there, or lives there now. We have no idea whether her grandparents are buried in Duluth, and, even if they were, we have few grounds for supposing that Mary will some day be buried alongside them. Is Virginia still a Mason? Or a Jones? Or something else again? What are the chances that Mary has much beyond periodic long-distance telephone contact with either Robert or Virginia? How far is she identifiable, also to herself, as a Duluthian, a Mason, or a Jones?

The counterfeit quality or, shall we say, the low market value of the birth certificate is perhaps confirmed by the relative rareness of its forgery. Conversely, the huge volume of passport forgeries and the high prices they command show that in our age, when everyone is supposed to belong to some one of the United Nations, these documents have high truth-claims. But they are also counterfeit in the sense that they are less and less attestations of citizenship, let alone of loyalty to a protective nation-state, than of claims to participation in labor markets. Portuguese and Bangladeshi passports, even when genuine, tell us little about loyalties or habitus, but they tell us a great deal about the relative likelihood of their holders being permitted to seek jobs in Milan or Copenhagen. The segregated queues that all of us experience at airport immigration barricades mark economic status far more than any political attachments. In effect, they figure differential tariffs on human labor.

Let me now turn finally to the political realm. The processes explicated above may be unraveling the classical nineteenth-century nationalist project – which aimed for the fullest alignment of habitus, culture, attachment, and exclusive political participation – on at least two distinct but related political sites.

The first site is more or less congruent with the postindustrial cores. During the nineteenth and early part of the twentieth centuries the so-called countries of immigration – the Americas, primarily, but also the antipodes – had a remarkable capacity to naturalize and nationalize their millions of immigrants. The names Galtieri, Eisenhauer, Fujimori, Van Buren, O'Higgins, and Trudeau tell the tale. But the birth certificate then had a primarily political significance, as we can see from the constitutional proviso that United States presidents be born inside that nation's borders. One was, thus, an American or one was not. Furthermore, military participation in the service of a state other than the United States was subject to the legal sanction of loss of citizenship, not that this was always rigidly enforced. When did this regime begin to weaken? Perhaps in our epochal 1930s, when Americans were permitted to join the International Brigade in the Spanish Civil War? Or in the later 1940s when Americans were tacitly permitted to participate in the defense of the infant state of Israel? But these breaks in the established rules were, I think, permissible precisely because of a confidence that these extralegal affairs were minor matters, concerning unimportant people with rather low visibility. Besides, the Americanness of the Americans involved was never seriously in question. These conditions began to change, however, after the middle of the 1960s. Andreas Papandreou started life as a Greek citizen, became an American citizen, and then, when opportunity beckoned, became again a Greek citizen and prime minister of Greece. A certain protocol is still evident in his progress. But what are we to make of the 1993 Cambodian presidential candidacy of self-made Long Beach millionaire Kim Kethavy? In the solemn words of the *New York Times*, he "carries an American passport.... The offices of his campaign headquarters bloom with American flags. (Under American immigration law, Mr. Kethavy would probably be forced to give up his United States citizenship in the unlikely event that he won.)"[20] Everything here is indicative: Mr. Kethavy's citizenship is in parentheses and the newspaper of record thinks that he will only "probably" be forced to give it up if he becomes Cambodia's president. Nothing suggests that the *Times* of the 1990s finds anything odd or discomforting in the behavior of Mr. Kethavy – or of the American government. After all, American citizens Milan Panic and Mohammed Sacirbey have recently served as premier of Serbia and Bosnian ambassador to the United Nations, while Rein Taagepera ran unsuccessfully for president of Estonia from a tenured professorship within the University of California at Irvine. Nor is this a uniquely American phenomenon; the Canadian citizen and computer systems capitalist Stanislaw Tyminski ran against Lech Walesa for the presidency of Poland.

The other side of this coin is the recent emergence in the United States and other older nation-states of an ethnicity that appears as a bastard Smerdyakov to classical nationalism's Dmitri Karamazov. One emblem of the American variant is perhaps the espionage trial of Jonathan Pollard a few years back. In the age of classical nationalism, the very idea that there could be something praiseworthy in an American citizen's spying on America for another country would have seemed grotesque. But to the substantial number of Jewish-Americans who felt sympathetic to Pollard, the resentful spy was understood as representing a transnational ethnicity. What else could so subversively blur American and Israeli citizenship? Another emblem is the colossal nonblack audience magnetized in 1977 by Alex Haley's TV miniseries *Roots*. (The final episode was watched by an astonishing 36,000,000 households.) The purpose of the program was to counter melting pot ideology by underlining the continuous "Africanness" that Haley's ancestors maintained as it were *despite* their Americanization. There can be little doubt that the popularity of *Roots* owed much to this transposable theme, given the rush, especially during the 1980s, of thoroughly American youngsters to lobby for various ethnic studies programs at universities and their eagerness to study languages that their immediate parents had so often been determined to abandon. Out of these and other impulses has emerged the ideological program of multiculturalism, which implies that a simple nineteenth-century version of Americanism is no longer adequate or acceptable.

The shift from, say, American through Armenian-*American* through *Armenian*-American is being accentuated both by the general revolution of transportation and communications discussed earlier, and by the recent disintegration of the

Soviet Union and Yugoslavia. Cleveland, for example, contains more people of Slovene descent than does Ljubljana, and now that Slovenia has become an independent state, being Slovene in Cleveland, and in the United States, assumes a heightened significance. Such ethnicities typically share a strongly fictive character with "Roots." We can easily be amused by the determinedly "Irish" Bostonian who knows no Irish literature, plays no Irish sports, pays no Irish taxes, serves in no Irish army, does not vote in Irish elections, and has only holiday conceptions of the Old Sow as she is today. It is less amusing, however, to reflect on the fact that the visible presence of gays and lesbians at St. Patrick's Day celebrations in Cork has done nothing to temper the passions surrounding sister celebrations in New York.

In Europe comparable tendencies are at work and may even be accentuated within the European Community by economic integration and the free movement of labor. The National Front, Le Pen's movement, and the rise of right-wing extremism in Germany are all signs of the "ethnicization" process.[21] For the thrust of their propaganda is essentially to draw a sharp line between the political nation and a putative original ethnos. Even if a black in the United Kingdom was born there, went to schools and university there, pays taxes there, votes there, and will be buried there, for the National Front he or she can never be genuinely English. Similarly in Le Pen's imagination, France is today teeming with aliens, not immigrants still carrying Algerian passports, but "non-French" citizens of political France. We could thus conceive of him looking out of the window of a railway carriage and seeing not fields, not even "French fields," but "dammit, French fields." In these movements racism is a very strong element, but I think the racism will prove in the longer run to be less important than ethnicization as Europeans circulate more massively around Europe.

The second type of political consequence of all the rapid changes I have been discussing concerns the migrants themselves. Not least as a result of the ethnicization of political life in the wealthy, postindustrial states, what one can call long-distance nationalism is visibly emerging. This type of politics, directed mainly toward the former Second and Third Worlds, pries open the classical nation-state project from a different direction. A striking illustration is the fateful recent destruction of the Babri mosque in Ayodhya, which has plunged India into her biggest crisis since Partition. The dismantling, which was carefully planned and involved extensive rehearsal and training by retired military and police personnel, was officially sponsored by the Vishwa Hindu Parishad (World Hindu Council), which "raised huge sums of money from its supporters in North America and Britain."[22] Needless to say, the vast majority of such supporters are Indians living overseas.[23] Many of the most uncompromising, fanatical adherents of an independent Khalistan do not live in the Punjab but have prosperous businesses in Melbourne and Chicago. The Tigers in Jaffna are stiffened in their violent struggles by Tamil communities in Toronto, London, and elsewhere all linked on the computer by Tamilnet. Consider the malign role of Croats not only in Germany but also in Australia and North America in financing and arming Franco Tudjman's breakaway state and pushing Germany and Austria into a fateful, premature recognition.

It would obviously be a mistake to assume that long-distance nationalism is necessarily extremist. There were substantial numbers of Filipinos outside the Philippines who contributed, not from *political* exile, to the struggle against Marcos; the Philippine economy today is heavily dependent on remittances sent in by such people from the Gulf, Italy, Saudi Arabia, England, California, Hong Kong, Japan, and Spain. Financial and other support for the democracy movement that culminated in the Tiananmen Square massacre also came from many Chinese not resident in China and often, indeed, citizens of other states.

Nonetheless, in general, today's long-distance nationalism strikes one as a probably menacing portent for the future. First of all, it is the product of capitalism's remorseless, accelerating transformation of all human societies. Second, it creates a serious politics that is at the same time radically unaccountable. The participant rarely pays taxes in the country in which he does his politics; he is not answerable to its judicial system; he probably does not cast even an absentee ballot in its elections because he is a citizen in a different place; he need not fear prison, torture, or death, nor need his immediate family. But, well and safely positioned in the First World, he can send money and guns, circulate propaganda, and build intercontinental computer information circuits, all of which can have incalculable consequences in the zones of their ultimate destinations. Third, his politics, unlike those of activists for global human rights or environmental causes, are neither intermittent nor serendipitous. They are deeply rooted in a consciousness that his exile is self-chosen and that the nationalism he claims on E-mail is also the ground on which an embattled ethnic identity is to be fashioned in the ethnicized nation-state that he remains determined to inhabit. That same metropole which marginalizes and stigmatizes him simultaneously enables him to play, in a flash, on the other side of the planet, national hero.

## NOTES

1 Mary Rowlandson, *A Narrative of the Captivity and Restauration of Mrs. Mary Rowlandson, 1682*, in *Narratives of the Indian Wars, 1675–99*, ed. Charles H. Lincoln (1913: New York, 1952), p. 132. Squaukheag is today Squakeag, near Bear's Plain. Northfield, Massachusetts.

2 John Dalberg-Acton, *Essays in the Liberal Interpretation of History*, ed. William H. McNeill (Chicago, 1967), p. 146.

3 See Nancy Armstrong and Leonard Tennenhouse, *The Imaginary Puritan: Literature, Intellectual Labor, and the Origins of Personal Life* (Berkeley, 1992), p. 204 and the references there cited.

4 Quoted in D. A. Brading, *The First America: The Spanish Monarchy, Creole Patriots, and the Liberal State, 1492–1867* (Cambridge, 1991), p. 200.

5 Michael Warner, *The Letters of the Republic: Publication and the Public Sphere in Eighteenth-Century America* (Cambridge, Mass., 1990), p. 32.

6 See Ernest Gellner, *Nations and Nationalism* (Ithaca, NY, 1983).

7 Benjamin Disraeli, *Tancred, or The New Crusade* (1847; London, 1894), p. 378; hereafter abbreviated as *T*. Regarding his England and his Europe as mortally threatened by

Enlightenment rationalism, bourgeois commercialism, and the heritage of the French Revolution, the young Lord Montacute sets off in his yacht for the Holy Land, seeking spiritual revival in "the only portion of the world which the Creator of that world has deigned to visit" (*T*, p. 421.) This quest leads him into proto-T. E. Lawrence political adventures in Palestine and Lebanon, in which he is guided by wise, courageous Hebrews and from which he has to be rescued by Mum and Dad, the Duchess and Duke of Bellamont. What is especially striking about the novel is the manner in which the Jewish Disraeli, Anglicized at his father's orders by baptism into the Church of England at the age of thirteen, discovers his "ethnicity" in Babylonian exile. Montacute, immensely rich, aristocratic, ur-English but, as it were, spiritually Jewish – Disraeli repeatedly insists that Christ and the Apostles were all Jews – is a hilariously snobbish self-projection of the future Conservative prime minister of the United Kingdom.

8   How quickly this profane mission was understood is entertainingly shown by the conversation in *Tancred* in which the hero suggests to Lady Bertie and Bellair that she and her husband join him on a pilgrimage to to Jerusalem:

> "That can never be," said Lady Bertie; "Augustus will never hear of it; he never could be absent more than six weeks from London, he misses his clubs so. If Jerusalem were only a place one could get at, something might be done; if there were a railroad to it for example."
> "A railroad!" exclaimed Tancred, with a look of horror. "A railroad to Jerusalem!"
>    "No, I suppose there can never be one," continued Lady Bertie in a musing tone. "There is no traffic." [*T*, p. 162]

9   See E. J. Hobsbawm, *The Age of Revolution, 1789–1848* (New York, 1962), pp. 166–7.

10  A characteristic industrial side to this process was the official invention of adult education in this era.

11  "An Interview with Pedro Calosa," in David Sturtevant, *Popular Uprisings in the Philippines, 1840–1940* (Ithaca, NY, 1976), p. 276.

12  Such is the general pattern, although there are significant exceptions, such as the House of Councillors in Japan and the Senate in the Philippines, where all members are elected from a single, nation-wide constituency.

13  To be sure, at least some railway systems, such as that of Germany, were substantially mapped for strategic military purposes. Differential gauges promised to bring one's own troops rapidly to one's threatened borders and at the same time block the enemy's railway penetration.

14  *Information Please Almanac, Atlas, and Yearbook, 1987* (Boston, 1987), p. 787, and *Information Please Almanac, Atlas, and Yearbook, 1993* (Boston, 1993), p. 830. These tables lack figures for 1980, which probably were somewhere between 8 and 9 million.

15  Perry Anderson, *A Zone of Engagement* (London, 1992), p. 353. See as well the sources there cited.

16  "Immigration," *The New Funk and Wagnalls Encyclopedia*, 25 vols. (New York, 1945–46), 19:6892; *The World Almanac and Book of Facts, 1992* (New York, 1992), p. 137.

17  See Paul Kennedy, "The American Prospect," *New York Review of Books*, 4 Mar. 1993, p. 50.

18  See "In Europe's Upheaval, Doors Close to Foreigners," *New York Times*, 10 Feb. 1993, pp. A1, A14. Note that these figures do not include an estimated 25 million political refugees around the world, mostly living in squalid, "temporary" dwellings outside their homelands.

19 Data drawn from Bureau of the Census figures cited in *The World Almanac and Book of Facts, 1992*, pp. 942, 944.

20 "For the Cambodian Vote, a Fourth of July Flavor," *New York Times*, 17 Feb. 1993, p. A4.

21 The Lega Lombarda of the late 1980s, now the Lega Nord, while not strictly analogous to these movements, nonetheless shows that something close to ethnicization can break down even a supposed core nation. For the Lega's attitudes to southern Italians are often rabidly contemptuous, as if the latter were of another, lesser breed.

22 Praful Bidwai, "Bringing Down the Temple: Democracy at Risk in India," *The Nation*, 25 Jan. 1993, p. 86.

23 The numbers of such people are very substantial. The total figure for South Asians outside South Asia is close to 8.7 million. The breakdown is as follows: Europe 1,482,034 (of which 1,260,000 are in the United Kingdom); Africa 1,389,722; Asia 1,862,654 (of which 1,170,000 are in Malaysia); Middle East 1,317,141, mostly in the Gulf states; Latin America and the Caribbean 957,330 (of which 730,350 are in Guyana and Trinidad); North America 728,500 (of which 500,000 are in the United States); and the Pacific 954,109 (of which 839,340 are in Fiji). Professor Myron Weiner kindly informs me that although this table counts South Asians, the major areas of emigration have long been inside the present borders of India. He also believes the figures to be too conservative: for example, the recent United States census shows the Indian population in America to be close to 900,000. Most likely, in his estimate, the true total for Indians living overseas is between 11 and 12 million. See Colin Clarke, Ceri Peach, and Steven Vertovec, "Introduction: Themes in the Study of the South Asian Diaspora," in *South Asians Overseas: Migration and Ethnicity*, ed. Clarke, Peach, and Vertovec (Cambridge, 1990), p. 2.

# 37

# Diasporas

## James Clifford

This essay asks what is at stake, politically and intellectually, in contemporary invocations of diaspora. It discusses problems of defining a traveling term, in changing global conditions. How do diaspora discourses represent experiences of displacement, of constructing homes away from home? What experiences do they reject, replace, or marginalize? How do these discourses attain comparative scope while remaining rooted/routed in specific, discrepant histories? The essay also explores the political ambivalence, the utopic/dystopic tension, of diaspora visions that are always entangled in powerful global histories. It argues that contemporary diasporic practices cannot be reduced to epiphenomena of the nation-state or of global capitalism. While defined and constrained by these structures, they also exceed and criticize them: old and new diasporas offer resources for emergent "postcolonialisms." The essay focuses on recent articulations of diasporism from contemporary black Britain and from anti-Zionist Judaism: quests for nonexclusive practices of community, politics, and cultural difference.

A few caveats are in order. This essay has the strengths and weaknesses of a survey: one sees the tips of many icebergs. Moreover, it attempts to map the terrain and define the stakes of diaspora studies in polemical and sometimes utopian ways. There is sometimes a slippage in the text between invocations of diaspora theories, diasporic discourses, and distinct historical experiences of diaspora. These are not, of course, equivalent. But in practice it has not always been possible to keep them clearly separate, especially when one is discussing (as I am here) a kind of "theorizing" that is always embedded in particular maps and histories. Although this essay strives for comparative scope, it retains a certain North American bias. For example, it sometimes assumes a pluralist state based on ideologies (and uneven accomplishments) of assimilation. While nation-states must always, to a degree, integrate diversity, they need not do so on these terms. Words such as "minority," "immigrant," and "ethnic" will thus have a distinctly local flavor for some readers. Local, but translatable. I have begun to account for gender bias and class diversity in my topic. More needs to be done here, as well as in other domains of diasporic complexity where currently I lack competence or sensitivity.

## ■ Tracking Diaspora ■

An unruly crowd of descriptive/interpretive terms now jostle and converse in an effort to characterize the contact zones of nations, cultures, and regions: terms such as "border," "travel," "creolization," "transculturation," "hybridity," and "diaspora" (as well as the looser "diasporic"). Important new journals, such as *Public Culture* and *Diaspora* (or the revived *Transition*), are devoted to the history and current production of transnational cultures. In his editorial preface to the first issue of *Diaspora*, Khachig Tölölian writes, "Diasporas are the exemplary communities of the transnational moment." But he adds that diaspora will not be privileged in the new journal devoted to "transnational studies" and that "the term that once described Jewish, Greek, and Armenian dispersion now shares meanings with a larger semantic domain that includes words like immigrant, expatriate, refugee, guest-worker, exile community, overseas community, ethnic community" (Tölölian 1991: 4–5). This is the domain of shared and discrepant meanings, adjacent maps and histories, that we need to sort out and specify as we work our way into a comparative practice of intercultural studies.

It is now widely understood that the old localizing strategies – by bounded *community*, by organic *culture*, by *region*, by *center and periphery* – may obscure as much as they reveal. Roger Rouse makes this point forcefully in his contribution to *Diaspora*'s inaugural issue. Drawing on research in the linked Mexican communities of Aguililla (Michoacán) and Redwood City (California), he argues as follows:

> It has become inadequate to see Aguilillan migration as a movement between distinct communities, understood as the loci of distinct sets of social relationships. Today, Aguilillans find that their most important kin and friends are as likely to be living hundreds or thousands of miles away as immediately around them. More significantly, they are often able to maintain these spatially extended relationships as actively and effectively as the ties that link them to their neighbors. In this regard, growing access to the telephone has been particularly significant, allowing people not just to keep in touch periodically but to contribute to decision-making and participate in familial events from a considerable distance. (Rouse, 1991: 13).

Separate places become effectively a single community "through the continuous circulation of people, money, goods, and information" (14). "Transnational migrant circuits," as Rouse calls them, exemplify the kinds of complex cultural formations that current anthropology and intercultural studies describe and theorize.[1]

Aguilillans moving between California and Michoacán are not in diaspora; there may be, however, diasporic dimensions to their practices and cultures of displacement, particularly for those who stay long periods, or permanently, in Redwood City. Overall, bilocale Aguilillans inhabit a *border*, a site of regulated and subversive crossing. Rouse appeals to this transnational paradigm throughout, giving it explicit allegorical force by featuring a photo of the famous wedding of Guillermo Gómez-Peña and Emily Hicks, staged by the Border Arts Workshop of San Diego–Tijuana at the point where the US–Mexico *frontera* crumbles into the Pacific. Border theorists have recently argued for the critical centrality of formerly marginal histories and cultures of crossing (Anzaldúa, 1987; Calderon and Saldívar, 1991; Flores and Yudice, 1990; Hicks, 1991; Rosaldo, 1989). These approaches share a good deal with diaspora paradigms. But borderlands are distinct in that they presuppose a territory defined by a geopolitical line: two sides arbitrarily separated and policed, but also joined by legal and illegal practices of crossing and communication. Diasporas usually presuppose longer distances and a separation more like exile: a constitutive taboo on return, or its postponement to a remote future. Diasporas also connect multiple communities of a dispersed population. Systematic border crossings may be part of this interconnection, but multilocale diaspora cultures are not necessarily defined by a specific geopolitical boundary: It is worth holding onto the historical and geographic specificity of the two paradigms, while recognizing that the concrete predicaments denoted by the terms "border" and "diaspora" bleed into each other. As we will see below, diasporic forms of longing, memory, and (dis)identification are shared by a broad spectrum of minority and migrant populations. And dispersed peoples, once separated from homelands by vast oceans and political barriers, increasingly find themselves in border relations with the old country thanks to a to-and-fro made possible by modern technologies of transport, communication, and labor migration. Airplanes, telephones, tape cassettes, camcorders, and mobile job markets reduce distances and facilitate two-way traffic, legal and illegal, between the world's places.

This overlap of border and diaspora experiences in late twentieth-century everyday life suggests the difficulty of maintaining exclusivist paradigms in our attempts to account for transnational identity formations. When I speak of the need to sort out paradigms and maintain historical specificity, I do not mean the imposition of strict meanings and authenticity tests. (The quintessential borderland is El Paso–Juárez. Or is it Tijuana–San Diego? Can *la ligna* be displaced to Redwood City, or to Mexican American neighborhoods of Chicago?) William Safran's essay in the first issue of *Diaspora*, "Diasporas in Modern Societies: Myths of Homeland and Return" (1991), seems, at times, to be engaged in such an operation. His undertaking and the problems he encounters may help us see what is involved in identifying the range of phenomena we are prepared to call "diasporic."

Safran discusses a variety of collective experiences in terms of their similarity to and difference from a defining model. He defines diasporas as follows: "expatriate minority communities" (1) that are dispersed from an original "center" to at least two "peripheral" places; (2) that maintain a "memory, vision, or myth about their original homeland"; (3) that "believe they are not – and perhaps cannot be – fully accepted by their host country"; (4) that see the ancestral home as a place of eventual return, when the time is right; (5) that are committed to the maintenance or restoration of this homeland; and (6) whose consciousness and solidarity as a group are "importantly defined" by this continuing relationship with the homeland (Safran 1991: 83–4). These, then, are the main features of diaspora: a history of dispersal, myths/memories of the homeland, alienation in the host (bad host?) country, desire for eventual return, ongoing support of the homeland, and a collective identity importantly defined by this relationship.

"In terms of that definition," Safran writes, "we may legitimately speak of the Armenian, Maghrebi, Turkish, Palestinian, Cuban, Greek, and perhaps Chinese diasporas at present and of the Polish diaspora of the past, although none of them fully conforms to the 'ideal type' of the Jewish diaspora" (84). Perhaps a hesitation is expressed by the quotes surrounding "ideal type," a sense of the danger in constructing, here at the outset of an important comparative project, a definition that identifies the diasporic phenomenon too closely with one group. Indeed, large segments of Jewish historical experience do not meet the test of Safran's last three criteria: a strong attachment to and desire for literal return to a well-preserved homeland. Safran himself later notes that the notion of "return" for Jews is often an eschatological or utopian projection in response to a present dystopia. And there is little room in his definition for the principled *ambivalence* about physical return and attachment to land which has characterized much Jewish diasporic consciousness, from biblical times on. Jewish anti-Zionist critiques of teleologies of return are also excluded. (These strong "diasporist" arguments will be discussed below.)

It is certainly debatable whether the cosmopolitan Jewish societies of the Mediterranean (and Indian Ocean) from the eleventh to the thirteenth centuries, the "geniza world" documented by the great historian of transnational cultures, S. D. Goitein, was oriented as a community, or collection of communities, primarily through attachments to a lost homeland (Goitein, 1967–93). This sprawling social world was linked through cultural forms, kinship relations, business circuits, and travel trajectories, as well as through loyalty to the religious centers of the diaspora (in Babylon, Palestine, and Egypt). The attachment to specific cities (sometimes superseding ties of religion and ethnicity) characteristic of Goitein's medieval world casts doubt on any definition that would "center" the Jewish diaspora in a single land. Among Sephardim after 1492, the longing for "home" could be focused on a city in Spain at the same time as on the Holy Land. Indeed, as Jonathan Boyarin has pointed out, Jewish experience often entails "multiple experiences of rediasporization, which do not necessarily *succeed* each other in historical memory but echo back and forth" (personal communication, October 3, 1993).

As a multiply centered diaspora network, the medieval Jewish Mediterranean may be juxtaposed with the modern "black Atlantic" described by Paul Gilroy, whose work will be discussed below. Although the economic and political bases of the two networks may differ – the former commercially self-sustaining, the latter caught up in colonial/neocolonial forces – the cultural forms sustaining and connecting the two scattered "peoples" are comparable within the range of diasporic phenomena. In Safran's prefiguration of a comparative field – especially in his "centered" diaspora model, oriented by continuous cultural connections to a source and by a teleology of "return" – African American/Caribbean/British cultures do not qualify. These histories of displacement fall into a category of quasi-diasporas, showing only some diasporic features or moments. Similarly, the South Asian diaspora – which, as Amitav Ghosh has argued (1989), is oriented not so much to roots in a specific place and a desire for return as around an ability to recreate a culture in diverse locations – falls outside the strict definition.

Safran is right to focus attention on defining "diaspora." What is the range of experiences covered by the term? Where does it begin to lose definition? His comparative approach is certainly the best way to specify a complex discursive and historical field. Moreover, his juxtapositions are often very enlightening, and he does not, in practice, strictly enforce his definitional checklist. But we should be wary of constructing our working definition of a term like "diaspora" by recourse to an "ideal type," with the consequence that groups become identified as more or less diasporic, having only two, or three, or four of the basic six features. Even the "pure" forms, as I've suggested, are ambivalent, even embattled, over basic features. Furthermore, at different times in their history, societies may wax and wane in diasporism, depending on changing possibilities – obstacles, openings, antagonisms, and connections – in their host countries and transnationally.

We should be able to recognize the strong entailment of Jewish history on the language of diaspora without making that history a definitive model. Jewish (and Greek and Armenian) diasporas can be taken as nonnormative starting points for a discourse that is traveling or hybridizing in new global conditions. For better or worse, diaspora discourse is being widely appropriated. It is loose in the world, for reasons having to do with decolonization, increased immigration, global communications, and transport – a whole range of phenomena that encourage multilocale attachments, dwelling, and traveling within and across nations. A more polythetic definition (Needham, 1975) than Safran's might retain his six features, along with others. I have already stressed, for example, that the transnational connections linking diasporas need not be articulated primarily through a real or symbolic homeland – at least not to the degree that Safran implies. Decentered, lateral connections may be as important as those formed around a teleology of origin/return. And a shared, ongoing history of displacement, suffering, adaptation, or resistance may be as important as the projection of a specific origin.

Whatever the working list of diasporic features, no society can be expected to qualify on all counts, throughout its history. And the discourse of diaspora will necessarily be modified as it is translated and adopted. For example, the Chinese diaspora is now being explicitly discussed.[2] How will this history, this articulation of travels, homes, memories, and transnational connections, appropriate and shift diaspora discourse? Different diasporic maps of displacement and connection can be compared on the basis of family resemblance, of shared elements, no subset of which is defined as essential to the discourse. A polythetic field would seem most conducive to tracking (rather than policing) the contemporary range of diasporic forms.

## ■ Diaspora's Borders ■

A different approach would be to specify the discursive field diacritically. Rather than locating essential features, we might focus on diaspora's borders, on what it defines itself against. And, we might ask, what articulations of identity are currently being replaced by diaspora claims? It is important to stress that the relational positioning at issue here is a process not of absolute othering but rather of entangled tension. Diasporas are caught up with and defined against (1) the norms of nation-states and (2) indigenous, and especially autochthonous, claims by "tribal" peoples.

The nation-state, as common territory and time, is traversed and, to varying degrees, subverted by diasporic attachments. Diasporic populations do not come from elsewhere in the same way that "immigrants" do. In assimilationist national ideologies such as those of the United States, immigrants may experience loss and nostalgia, but only en route to a whole new home in a new place. Such ideologies are designed to integrate immigrants, not people in diasporas. Whether the national narrative is one of common origins or of gathered populations, it cannot assimilate groups that maintain important allegiances and practical connections to a homeland or a dispersed community located elsewhere. Peoples whose sense of identity is centrally defined by collective histories of displacement and violent loss cannot be "cured" by merging into a new national community. This is especially true when they are the victims of ongoing, structural prejudice. Positive articulations of diaspora identity reach outside the normative territory and temporality (myth/history) of the nation-state.[3]

But are diaspora cultures consistently antinationalist? What about their own national aspirations? Resistance to assimilation can take the form of reclaiming another nation that has been lost, elsewhere in space and time, but that is powerful as a political formation here and now. There are, of course, antinationalist nationalisms, and I do not want to suggest that diasporic cultural politics are somehow innocent of nationalist aims or chauvinist agendas. Indeed, some of the most violent articulations of purity and racial exclusivism come from diaspora populations. But such discourses are usually weapons of the (relatively) weak. It is important to distinguish nationalist critical longing, and nostalgic or eschatological visions, from actual nation building – with the help of armies, schools, police, and mass media. "Nation" and "nation-state" are not identical.[4] A certain prescriptive antinationalism, now intensely focused by the Bosnian horror, need not blind us to differences between dominant and subaltern claims. Diasporas have rarely founded nation-states: Israel is the prime example. And such "homecomings" are, by definition, the negation of diaspora.

Whatever their ideologies of purity, diasporic cultural forms can never, in practice, be exclusively nationalist. They are deployed in transnational networks built from multiple attachments, and they encode practices of accommodation with, as well as resistance to, host countries and their norms. Diaspora is different from travel (though it works through travel practices) in that it is not temporary. It involves dwelling, maintaining communities, having collective homes away from home (and in this it is different from exile, with its frequently individualist focus). Diaspora discourse articulates, or bends together, both roots *and* routes to construct what Gilroy (1987) describes as alternate public spheres, forms of community consciousness and solidarity that maintain identifications outside the national time/space in order to live inside, with a difference. Diaspora cultures are not separatist, though they may have separatist or irredentist moments. The history of Jewish diaspora communities shows selective accommodation with the political, cultural, commercial, and everyday life forms of "host" societies. And the black diaspora culture currently being articulated in postcolonial Britain is concerned to struggle for different ways to be "British" – ways to stay and be different, to be British *and something else* complexly related to Africa and the Americas, to shared histories of enslavement, racist subordination, cultural survival, hybridization, resistance, and political rebellion. Thus, the term "diaspora" is a signifier not simply of transnationality and movement but of political struggles to define the local, as distinctive community, in historical contexts of displacement. The simultaneous strategies of community maintenance and interaction combine the discourses and skills of what Vijay Mishra has termed "diasporas of exclusivism" and "diasporas of the border" (1994).

The specific cosmopolitanisms articulated by diaspora discourses are in constitutive tension with nation-state / assimilationist ideologies. They are also in tension with indigenous, and especially autochthonous, claims. These challenge the hegemony of modern nation-states in a different way. Tribal or Fourth World assertions of sovereignty and "first-nationhood" do not feature histories of travel and settlement, though these may be part of the indigenous historical experience. They stress continuity of habitation, aboriginality, and often a "natural" connection to the land. Diaspora cultures, constituted by displacement, may resist such appeals on political principle – as in anti-Zionist Jewish writing, or in black injunctions to "stand" and "chant down Babylon." And they may be structured around a *tension* between return and deferral: "religion of the land"/"religion of the book" in Jewish tradition; or "roots"/"cut 'n' mix" aesthetics in black vernacular cultures.

Diaspora exists in practical, and at times principled, tension with nativist identity formations. The essay by Daniel and Jonathan Boyarin that I will discuss below makes a diasporist critique of autochthonous ("natural") but not indigenous ("historical") formulations. When claims to "natural" or "original" identity with the land are joined to an irredentist project and the coercive power of an exclusivist state, the results can be profoundly ambivalent and violent, as in the Jewish state of Israel. Indeed, claims of a primary link with the "homeland" usually must override conflicting rights and the history of others in the land. Even ancient homelands have seldom been pure or discrete. Moreover, what are the historical and/or indigenous rights of *relative* newcomers – fourth-generation Indians in Fiji, or even Mexicans in the southwestern United States since the sixteenth century? How long does it take to become "indigenous"? Lines too strictly drawn between "original" inhabitants (who often themselves replaced prior populations) and subsequent immigrants risk ahistoricism. With all these qualifications, however, it is clear that the claims to political legitimacy made by peoples who have inhabited a territory since before recorded history and those who arrived by steamboat or airplane will be founded on very different principles.

Diasporist and autochthonist histories, the aspirations of migrants and natives, do come into direct political antagonism; the clearest current example is Fiji. But when, as is often the case, both function as "minority" claims against a hegemonic/ assimilationist state, the antagonism may be muted. Indeed, there are significant areas of overlap. "Tribal" predicaments, in certain historical circumstances, are diasporic. For example, inasmuch as diasporas are dispersed networks of peoples who share common historical experiences of dispossession, displacement, adaptation, and so forth, the kinds of transnational alliances currently being forged by Fourth World peoples contain diasporic elements. United by similar claims to "firstness" on the land and by common histories of decimation and marginality, these alliances often deploy diasporist visions of return to an original place – a land commonly articulated in visions of nature, divinity, mother earth, and the ancestors.

Dispersed tribal peoples, those who have been dispossessed of their lands or who must leave reduced reserves to find work, may claim "diasporic" identities. Inasmuch as their distinctive sense of themselves is oriented toward a lost or alienated home defined as aboriginal (and thus "outside" the surrounding nation-state), we can speak of a diasporic dimension of contemporary tribal life. Indeed, recognition of this dimension has been important in disputes about tribal membership. The category "tribe," which was developed in US law to distinguish settled Indians from roving, dangerous "bands," places a premium on localism and rootedness. Tribes with too many members living away from the homeland may have difficulty asserting their political/cultural status. This was the case for the Mashpee, who in 1978 failed to establish continuous "tribal" identity in court (Clifford, 1988: 277–346).

Thus, when it becomes important to assert the existence of a dispersed people, the language of diaspora comes into play, as a moment or dimension of tribal life.[5] All communities, even the most locally rooted, maintain structured travel circuits, linking members "at home" and "away." Under changing conditions of mass communication, globalization, postcolonialism, and neocolonialism, these circuits are selectively restructured and rerouted according to *internal and eternal* dynamics. Within the diverse array of contemporary diasporic cultural forms, tribal displacements and networks are distinctive. For in claiming both autochthony and a specific, transregional worldliness, new tribal forms bypass an opposition between rootedness and displacement – an opposition underlying many visions of modernization seen as the inevitable destruction of autochthonous attachments by global forces. Tribal groups have, of course, never been simply "local": they have always been rooted and routed in particular landscapes, regional and interregional networks.[6] What may be distinctively *modern*, however, is the relentless assault on indigenous sovereignty by colonial powers, transnational capital, and emerging nation-states. If tribal groups survive, it is now frequently in artificially reduced and displaced conditions, with segments of their populations living in cities away from the land, temporarily or even permanently. In these conditions, the older forms of tribal cosmopolitanism (practices of travel, spiritual quest, trade, exploration, warfare, labor migrancy, visiting, and political alliance) are supplemented by more properly diasporic forms (practices of long-term dwelling away from home). The permanence of this dwelling, the frequency of returns or visits to homelands, and the degree of estrangement between urban and landed populations vary considerably. But the specificity of tribal diasporas, increasingly crucial *dimensions* of collective life, lies in the relative proximity and frequency of connection with land-based communities claiming autochthonous status.

I have been using the term "tribal" loosely to designate peoples who claim natural or "first-nation" sovereignty. They occupy the autochthonous end of a spectrum of indigenous attachments: peoples who deeply "belong" in a place by dint of continuous occupancy over an extended period. (Precisely how long it takes to *become* indigenous is always a political question.) Tribal cultures are not diasporas; their sense of rootedness in the land is precisely what diasporic peoples have lost. Yet, as we have seen, the tribal-diasporic opposition is not absolute. Like diaspora's other defining border with hegemonic nationalism, the opposition is a zone of relational contrast, including similarity and entangled difference. In the late twentieth century, all or most communities have diasporic dimensions (moments, tactics, practices, articulations). Some are more diasporic than others. I have suggested that it is not possible to define "diaspora" sharply, either by recourse to essential features or to privative oppositions. But it is possible to perceive a loosely coherent, adaptive constellation of responses to dwelling-in-displacement. The currency of these responses is inescapable.

## ■ The Currency of Diaspora Discourses ■

The language of diaspora is increasingly invoked by displaced peoples who feel (maintain, revive, invent) a connection with a prior home. This sense of connection must be strong enough to resist erasure through the normalizing processes of forgetting, assimilating, and distancing. Many minority groups that have not previously identified in this way are now reclaiming diasporic origins and affiliations. What is the currency, the value and the contemporaneity, of diaspora discourse?

Association with another nation, region, continent, or world-historical force (such as Islam) gives added weight to claims against an oppressive national hegemony. Like tribal assertions of sovereignty, diasporic identifications reach beyond mere ethnic status within the composite, liberal state. The phrase "diasporic community" conveys a stronger sense of difference than, for example, "ethnic neighborhood" used in the language of pluralist nationalism. This stronger difference, this sense of being a "people" with historical roots and destinies outside the time/space of the host nation, is not separatist. (Rather, separatist desires are just one of its moments.) Whatever their eschatological longings, diaspora communities are "not-here to stay." Diaspora cultures thus mediate, in a lived tension, the experiences of separation and entanglement, of living here and remembering/desiring another place. If we think of displaced populations in almost any large city, the transnational urban swirl recently analyzed by Ulf Hannerz (1992), the role for mediating cultures of this kind will be apparent.

Diasporic language appears to be replacing, or at least supplementing, minority discourse.[7] Transnational connections break the binary relation of "minority" communities with "majority" societies – a dependency that structures projects of both assimilation and resistance. And it gives a strengthened spatial/historical content to older mediating concepts such as W. E. B. Du Bois's notion of "double consciousness." Moreover, diasporas are not exactly immigrant communities. The latter could be seen as temporary, a site where the canonical three generations struggled through a hard transition to ethnic American status. But the "immigrant" process never worked very well for Africans, enslaved or free, in the New World. And the so-called new immigrations of non-European peoples of color similarly disrupt linear assimilation narratives (see especially Schiller et al., 1992).[8] Although there is a range of acceptance and alienation associated with ethnic and class variations, the masses of these new arrivals are kept in subordinate positions by established structures of racial exclusion. Moreover, their immigration often has a less all-or-nothing quality, given transport and communications technologies that facilitate multilocale communities. (On the role of television, see Naficy, 1991.) Large sections of New York City, it is sometimes said, are "parts of the Caribbean," and vice versa (Sutton and Chaney, 1987). Diasporist discourses reflect the sense of being part of an ongoing transnational network that includes the homeland not as something simply left behind but as a place of attachment in a contrapuntal modernity.[9]

Diaspora consciousness is thus constituted both negatively and positively. It is constituted negatively by experiences of discrimination and exclusion. The barriers facing racialized sojourners are often reinforced by socioeconomic constraints, particularly – in North America – the development of a post-Fordist, nonunion, low-wage sector offering very limited opportunities for advancement. This regime of "flexible accumulation" requires massive transnational flows of capital and labor – depending on, and producing, diasporic populations. Casualization of labor and the revival of outwork production have increased the proportion of women in the workforce, many of them recent immigrants to industrial centers (Cohen, 1987; Harvey, 1989; Mitter, 1986; Potts, 1990; Sassen-Koob, 1982). These developments have produced an increasingly familiar mobility "hourglass" – masses of exploited labor at the bottom and a very narrow passage to a large, relatively affluent middle and upper class (Rouse, 1991: 13). New immigrants confronting this situation, like the Aguilillans in Redwood City, may establish transregional identities, maintained through travel and telephone circuits, that do not stake everything on an increasingly risky future in a single nation. It is worth adding that a negative experience of racial and economic marginalization can also lead to new coalitions: one thinks of Maghrebi diasporic consciousness uniting Algerians, Moroccans, and Tunisians living in France, where a common history of colonial and neocolonial exploitation contributes to new solidarities. And the moment in 1970s Britain when the exclusionist term "black" was appropriated to form antiracial alliances between immigrant South Asians, Afro-Caribbeans, and Africans provides another example of a negative articulation of diaspora networks.

Diaspora consciousness is produced positively through identification with world-historical cultural/political forces, such as "Africa" or "China." The process may not be as much about being African or Chinese as about being American or British or wherever one has settled, differently. It is also about feeling global. Islam, like Judaism in a predominantly Christian culture, can offer a sense of attachment elsewhere, to a different temporality and vision, a discrepant modernity. I'll have more to say below about positive, indeed utopian, diasporism in the current transnational moment. Suffice it to say that diasporic consciousness "makes the best of a bad situation." Experiences of loss, marginality, and exile (differentially cushioned by class) are often reinforced by systematic exploitation and blocked advancement. This constitutive suffering coexists with the skills of survival: strength in adaptive distinction, discrepant cosmopolitanism, and stubborn visions of renewal. Diaspora consciousness lives loss and hope as a defining tension.

The currency of diaspora discourses extends to a wide range of populations and historical predicaments. People caught up in transnational movements of capital improvise what Aihwa Ong has termed "flexible citizenship," with striking differences of power and privilege. The range extends from binational citizens in Aguililla/Redwood City or Haiti/Brooklyn to the Chinese investor "based" in San Francisco who claims, "I can live anywhere in the world, but it must be near an airport" (Ong, 1993: 41). This pseudo-universal cosmopolitan bravado stretches the limit of the term "diaspora." But to the extent that the investor, in fact, identifies and is identified as "Chinese," maintaining significant connections elsewhere, the term is appropriate. Ong says of this category of Chinese immigrants: "Their subjectivity is at once deterritorialized in relation to a particular country, though highly localized in relation to family" (Ong, 1993: 771–2). Since family is rarely in one place, where exactly do they "live"?

What is the political significance of this particular crossing-up of national identities by a traveler in the circuits of Pacific Rim capitalism? In light of bloody nationalist struggles throughout the world, the investor's transnational diasporism may appear progressive. Seen in connection with exploitative, "flexible" labor regimes in the new Asian and Pacific economies, his mobility may evoke a less positive response. The political and critical valence of diasporic subversions is never guaranteed. Much more could be said about class differences among diasporic populations. In distinguishing, for example, affluent Asian business families living in North America from creative writers, academic theorists, and destitute "boat people" or Khmers fleeing genocide, one sees clearly that degrees of diasporic alienation, the mix of coercion and freedom in cultural (dis)identifications, and the pain of loss and displacement are highly relative.

Diaspora experiences and discourses are entangled, never clear of commodification. (Nor is commodification their only outcome.) Diasporism can be taken up by a range of multicultural pluralisms, some with quasi-official status. For example, the Los Angeles Festival of 1991, orchestrated on a grand scale by Peter Sellars, celebrated the lumpy US melting pot by giving the bewildering diversity of Los Angeles a global reach. The festival connected Thai neighborhoods with imported dancers from Thailand. The same was done for Pacific islanders and various Pacific Rim peoples.[10] Transnational ethnicities were collected and displayed in avant-garde juxtaposition, ostensibly to consecrate a non-Eurocentric art/culture environment. Los Angeles, successful host to the Olympics, could be a true "world city." The festival was well funded by Japanese and American corporate sponsors, and for the most part it delivered a nonthreatening, aestheticized transnationalism. The low-wage sweatshops where many members of the celebrated populations work were not featured as sites for either "art" or "culture" in this festival of diasporas.[11]

Reacting to trends in the US academy; bell hooks has pointed out that international or postcolonial issues are often more comfortably dealt with than antagonisms closer to home, differences structured by race and class (hooks, 1989, 1990; see also Spivak, 1989). Adapting her concern to the present context, we see that theories and discourses that diasporize or internationalize "minorities" can deflect attention from long-standing, structured inequalities of class and race. It is as if the problem were multinationalism – issues of translation, education, and tolerance – rather than of economic exploitation and racism. While clearly necessary, making *cultural* room for Salvadorans, Samoans, Sikhs, Haitians, or Khmers does not, of itself, produce a living wage, decent housing, or health care. Moreover, at the level of everyday social practice, cultural differences are persistently racialized, classed, and gendered. Diaspora theories need to account for these concrete, cross-cutting structures.

Diasporic experiences are always gendered. But there is a tendency for theoretical accounts of diasporas and diaspora cultures to hide this fact, to talk of travel and displacement in unmarked ways, thus normalizing male experiences. Janet Wolff's analysis of gender in theories of travel is relevant here (Wolff, 1993). When diasporic experience is viewed in terms of displacement rather than placement, traveling rather than dwelling, and disarticulation rather than rearticulation, then the experiences of men will tend to predominate. Specific diaspora histories, co-territories, community practices, dominations, and contact relations may then be generalized into gendered postmodern globalisms, abstract nomadologies.

Retaining focus on specific histories of displacement and dwelling keeps the ambivalent politics of diaspora in view. Women's experiences are particularly revealing. Do diaspora experiences reinforce or loosen gender subordination? On the one hand, maintaining connections with homelands, with kinship networks, and with religious and cultural traditions may renew patriarchal structures. On the other, new roles and demands, new political spaces, are opened by diaspora interactions. Increasingly, for example, women migrate north from Mexico and from parts of the Caribbean, independently or quasi-independently of men. While they often do so in desperation, under strong economic or social compulsion, they may find their new diaspora predicaments leading to renegotiated gender relations. With men cut off from traditional roles and supports, with women earning an independent, if often exploitative, income, new areas of relative independence and control can emerge. Life for women in diasporic situations can be doubly painful – struggling with the material and spiritual insecurities of exile, with the demands of family and work, and with the claims of old and new patriarchies. But despite these hardships, they may refuse the option of return when it presents itself, especially when the terms are dictated by men.

At the same time, women in diaspora remain attached to, and empowered by, a "home" culture and a tradition – selectively. Fundamental values of propriety and religion, speech and social patterns, and food, body, and dress protocols are preserved and adapted in a network of ongoing connections outside the host country. But like Maxine Hong Kingston (1976), who redeems the woman warrior myth from all the stories transmitted to her from China, women sustaining and reconnecting diaspora ties do so critically, as strategies for survival in a new context. And like the Barbadian women portrayed in Paule Marshall's *Brown Girl, Brownstones* (1981) – who work hard to make a home in New York while keeping a basic "aloofness" from "this man's country" – diaspora women are caught between patriarchies, ambiguous pasts, and futures. They connect and disconnect, forget and remember, in complex, strategic ways.[12] The lived experiences of diasporic women thus involve painful difficulty in mediating discrepant worlds. "Community" can be a site both of support and oppression. A couple of quotations from Rahila Gupta offer a glimpse of a South Asian ("black British") woman's predicament:

> Young women are … beginning to question aspects of Asian culture, but there is not a sufficiently developed network of Black women's support groups (although much valuable work has been done in this area) to enable them to operate without the support of community and family. This is a contradiction in which many women are caught: between the supportive and the oppressive aspects of the Asian community…
>
> Patriarchal oppression was a reality of our lives before we came to Britain, and the fact that the family and community acted as sites of resistance to racist oppression has delayed and distorted our coming together as women to fight this patriarchal oppression. (Gupta, 1988: 27, 29).

The book from which these quotations are taken, *Charting the Journey: Writings by Black and Third World Women* (Grewal, 1988), maps a complex overlapping field of articulations and disarticulations in contemporary Britain – what Avtar Brah has called a "diasporic space."[13] Grewal's anthology presents common experiences of postcolonial displacement, racialization, and political struggle, as well as sharp differences of generation, of region, of sexuality, of culture, and of religion. A possible coalition of diverse "black British" and "Third World" women requires constant negotiation and attention to discrepant histories.

Do diasporic affiliations inhibit or enhance coalitions? There is no clear answer. Many Caribbeans in New York, for example, have maintained a sense of connection with their home islands, a distinct sense of cultural, and sometimes class, identity that sets them apart from African Americans, people with whom they share material conditions of racial and class subordination. Scarce resources and the mechanisms of a hierarchical social system reinforce this response. It is not inevitable. On the one hand, feelings of diasporic identity can encourage antagonism, a sense of superiority to other minorities and migrant populations.[14] On the other, shared histories of colonization, displacement, and racialization can form the basis for coalitions, as in the anti-Thatcherite alliances of "black" Britain which mobilized Africans, Afro-Caribbeans, and South Asians in the 1970s. But such alliances fall apart and recombine when other diasporic allegiances come into focus – a loyalty to Islam in the Salman Rushdie dispute, for example. There is no guarantee of "postcolonial" solidarity. Interdiaspora politics proceeds by tactics of collective articulation *and* disarticulation. As Avtar Brah has written concerning the debates of the late 1980s surrounding terms for diasporic community in Britain. "The usage of 'black', 'Indian' or 'Asian' is determined not so much by the nature of its referent as by its semiotic function within different discourses. These various meanings signal differing political strategies and outcomes. They mobilize different sets of cultural and political identities, and set limits to where the boundaries of a 'community' are established" (Brah, 1992: 130–1).

## ■ The Black Atlantic ■

Diaspora communities, constituted by displacement, are sustained in hybrid historical conjunctures. With varying degrees of urgency, they negotiate and resist the social realities of poverty, violence, policing, racism, and political and economic inequality. They articulate alternate public spheres, interpretive communities where critical alternatives (both traditional and emergent) can be expressed. The work of Paul Gilroy sketches a complex map/history of one of the principal components of diasporic Britain: the Afro-Caribbean/British/American "Black Atlantic."

In *There Ain't No Black in the Union Jack* (1987), Gilroy shows how the diaspora culture of black settler communities in Britain articulates a specific set of local and global attachments. On one level, diaspora culture's expressive forms (particularly music) function in the defense of particular neighborhoods against policing and various forms of racist violence. On another level, they offer a wider "critique of capitalism" and a network of transnational connections. In Gilroy's account, the black diaspora is a cosmopolitan, Atlantic phenomenon, embroiled in and transcending national antagonisms such as Thatcherite England's "cultural politics of race and nation." It reinvents earlier strands of Pan-Africanism, but with a postcolonial twist and a 1990s British-European tilt. St. Clair Drake has distinguished "traditional" from "continental" Pan-Africanist movements (1982: 353–9). The former had its origins in the Americas, and it emerged strongly in the late nineteenth century through the work of black churches, colleges, and the political movements associated with Marcus Garvey and W. E. B. Du Bois. It was a transatlantic phenomenon. With the postwar emergence of African states. African nationalist leaders moved to the forefront, and Pan-Africanism's center of gravity moved to continental Africa. The allied political visions of Kwame Nkrumah and George Padmore would lead the way. Writing in the 1980s and 1990s in the wake of this vision's retreat, Gilroy returns the "black" cultural tradition to a historically decentered, or multiply centered, Atlantic space. In the process, he breaks the primary connection of black America with Africa, introducing a third paradigmatic experience: the migrations and resettlings of black British populations in the period of European colonial decline.

Gilroy's brilliantly argued and provocative new book, *The Black Atlantic: Modernity and Double Consciousness* (1993a), projects in historical depth a diverse black diaspora culture that cannot be reduced to any national or ethnically based tradition. This map/narrative foregrounds histories of crossing, migration, exploration, interconnection, and travel – forced and voluntary. A collection of linked essays on black intellectual history, *The Black Atlantic* rereads canonical figures in a transoceanic perspective, questioning their inscription in an ethnically or racially defined tradition: Du Bois in Germany; Frederick Douglass as ship caulker and participant in a maritime political culture; Richard Wright in Paris, connecting with the anticolonial Présence Africaine movement. Transnational culture-making by musicians is also given prominence, from the nineteenth-century Fisk University Jubilee Singers to contemporary reggae, hip-hop, and rap. Gilroy is preoccupied with ships, phonograph records, sound systems, and all technologies that cross, and bring across, cultural forms. The diaspora cultures he charts are thoroughly modern – with a difference.

Gilroy tracks moving vinyl, locally scratched and dubbed. But he roots – or routes – music in a wider transcultural and subaltern history of the Atlantic. Drawing on recent historical research by Peter Linebaugh and Marcus Rediker that uncovers a multiracial radical political culture spanning the eighteenth-century Atlantic (1990), Gilroy's account questions "national, nationalistic, and ethnically absolutist paradigms" (Gilroy, 1992a: 193), on both the Right and the Left. He counters reactionary discourses such as those of Enoch Powell (and a growing chorus) that invoke a "pure" national space recently invaded by threatening aliens, that assume the entanglement of Britain in black history to be a postwar, post-British Empire phenomenon (see also Shyllon, 1982). He also supplements E. P. Thompson's "making of the *English* working class" with the making of the *Atlantic* working class (a multiracial group), and challenges recent arguments from within the British labor movement for a popular "Left nationalism" to counter Thatcherism. Finally, Gilroy's black Atlantic decenters African *American* narratives, bringing the Caribbean, Britain, and Europe into the picture.

"The history of the black Atlantic," he writes, "... continually criss-crossed by the movement of black people – not only as commodities – but engaged in various struggles toward emancipation, autonomy, and citizenship, is a means to reexamine the problems of nationality, location, identity, and historical memory"

CLIFFORD: DIASPORAS

(Gilroy, 1992a: 193). Gilroy brings into view "countercultures of modernity," bringing "black" not only into the Union Jack but also into debates over the tradition of Enlightenment rationality. This "black" element is both negative (the long history of slavery, the legacy of scientific racism, the complicity of rationality and terror in distinctively modern forms of domination) and positive (a long struggle for political and social emancipation, critical visions of equality or difference that have been generated in the black diaspora).

If there is a utopian agenda in Gilroy's transnational counterhistory, it is counterbalanced by the antagonistic violence, displacement, and loss that are *constitutive* of the cultures he celebrates: the Middle Passage, plantation slavery, old and new racist systems of dominance, and economic constraints on travel and labor migration. In *There Ain't No Black in the Union Jack*, the long fifth chapter on music and expressive culture ("Diaspora, Utopia, and the Critique of Capitalism") follows and depends for its effect upon four chapters that establish the discursive, political power of racist structures in postwar Britain. Some version of this utopic/dystopic tension is present in all diaspora cultures.[15] They begin with uprooting and loss. They are familiar with exile, with the "outsiders" exposed terror – of police, lynch mob, and pogrom. At the same time, diaspora cultures work to maintain community, selectively preserving and recovering traditions, "customizing" and "versioning" them in novel, hybrid, and often antagonistic situations.

Experiences of unsettlement, loss, and recurring terror produce discrepant temporalities – broken histories that trouble the linear, progressivist narratives of nation-states and global modernization. Homi Bhabha has argued that the homogeneous time of the nation's imagined community can never efface discontinuities and equivocations springing from minority and diasporic temporalities (1990). He points to antiprogressive processes of repetition (memories of slavery, immigration, and colonization, renewed in current contexts of policing and normative education), of supplementarity (the experience of being "belated," extra, out of synch), and of ex-centricity (a leaking of the national time/space into constitutive outsides: "The trouble with the English," Rushdie writes in *The Satanic Verses*, "is that their history happened overseas, so they don't know what it means"). Diasporic "postcolonials," in Bhabha's vision, live and narrate these historical realities as discrepant, critical modernities. He invokes the "scattered" populations gathering in the global cities, the *diaspora* where new imaginings and politics of community emerge.[16]

Gilroy probes the specific "diaspora temporality and historicity, memory and narrativity that are the articulating principles of the black political countercultures that grew inside modernity in a distinctive relationship of antagonistic indebtedness" (1993a: 266). Arguing against both modernist linear progressivism and current projections of a continuous connection with Africanity, *The Black Atlantic* uncovers a "syncopated temporality – a different rhythm of living and being." Gilroy cites Ralph Ellison: "Invisibility, let me explain, gives one a slightly different sense of time, you're never quite on the beat. Sometimes you're ahead and sometimes behind. Instead of the swift and imperceptible flowing of time, you

■ 539 ■

are aware of its nodes, those points where time stands still or from which it leaps ahead. And you slip into the breaks and look around" (Gilroy, 1993a: 281). Ellison (via Gilroy) offers a black version of Walter Benjamin's practice of countermemory, a politics of interrupting historical continuities to grasp the "monads" (Ellison's "nodes"?) or "fissures" in which time stops and prophetically restarts (Benjamin, 1968). In syncopated time, effaced stories are recovered, different futures imagined.

In diaspora experience, the co-presence of "here" and "there" is articulated with an antiteleological (sometimes messianic) temporality. Linear history is broken, the present constantly shadowed by a past that is also a desired, but obstructed, future: a renewed, painful yearning. For black Atlantic diaspora consciousness, the recurring break where time stops and restarts is the Middle Passage. Enslavement and its aftermaths – displaced, repeated structures of racialization and exploitation – constitute a pattern of black experiences inextricably woven in the fabric of hegemonic modernity. These experiences form counterhistories, off-the-beat cultural critiques that Gilroy works to redeem. Afrocentric attempts to recover a direct connection with Africa, often bypassing this constitutive predicament, are both escapist and ahistorical. The "space of death" reopened by memories of slavery and in continuing experiences of racial terror casts a critical shadow on all modernist progressivisms. Gilroy supplements the analyses of Zygmunt Bauman (1989) and Michael Taussig (1986) on the complicity of rationality with racial terror. At crucial moments, the choice of death or the risk of death is the only possibility for people with no future in an oppressive system. Gilroy's reading of Frederick Douglass's struggle with the slave-breaker probes such a moment, paired with the story of Margaret Garner, whose killing of her children to spare them from slavery is retold in Toni Morrison's *Beloved*. The resulting sense of rupture, of living a radically different temporality, is expressed in an interview with Morrison quoted extensively in *The Black Atlantic*:

> Modern life begins with slavery...From a woman's point of view, in terms of confronting the problems of where the world is now, black women had to deal with post-modern problems in the nineteenth century and earlier. These things had to be addressed by black people a long time ago: certain kinds of dissolution, the loss of and need to reconstruct certain kinds of stability. Certain kinds of madness deliberately going mad in order, as one of the characters says in the book, "in order not to lose your mind." These strategies for survival made the truly modern person. (Gilroy, 1993a: 308)

Morrison's "modern person" is the result of struggle with a "pathology." "Slavery broke the world in half," she goes on to say. And not only for Africans: "It broke Europe." It made Europeans slave masters.

Diaspora cultures are, to varying degrees, produced by regimes of political domination and economic inequality. But these violent processes of displacement do not strip people of their ability to sustain distinctive political communities and cultures of resistance. Obviously the mix of destruction, adaptation, preservation, and creation varies with each historical case and moment. As counterdiscourses of modernity, diaspora cultures cannot claim an oppositional or primary purity. Fundamentally ambivalent, they grapple with the entanglement of subversion and the law, of invention and constraint – the complicity of dystopia and utopia. Kobena Mercer works with this constitutive entanglement in a penetrating essay, "Diaspora Culture and the Dialogic Imagination."

> There is no escape from the fact that as a diaspora people, blasted out of one history into another by the "commercial deportation" of slavery (George Lamming) and its enforced displacement, our blackness is thoroughly imbricated in Western modes and codes to which we arrived as the disseminated masses of migrant dispersal. What is in question [in recent black British film] is not the expression of some lost origin or some uncontaminated essence in black film-language, but the adoption of a critical "voice" that promotes consciousness of the collision of cultures and histories that constitute our very conditions of existence. (Mercer, 1988: 56)

There are important differences between Mercer's and Gilroy's conceptions of diaspora. Mercer's version is rigorously antiessentialist, a site of multiple displacements and rearticulations of identity, without privilege to race, cultural tradition, class, gender, or sexuality. Diaspora consciousness is entirely a product of cultures and histories in collision and dialogue. For Mercer, Gilroy's genealogy of British "blackness" continues to privilege an "African" origin and "vernacular" forms – despite his stress on historical rupture and hybridity and his assault on romantic Afrocentrisms (Mercer, 1990).[17] For Gilroy, Mercer represents a "premature pluralism," a post-modern evasion of the need to give historical specificity and complexity to the term "black," seen as linked racial formations, counterhistories, and cultures of resistance (Gilroy, 1993a: 32, 100).

I do not want to oversimplify either position in an important, evolving dialogue that is probably symptomatic of a moment in cultural politics and not finally resolvable. In this context it may be worth noting that, because the signifier "diasporic" denotes a predicament of multiple locations, it slips easily into theoretical discourses informed by poststructuralism and notions of the multiply positioned subject. Indeed, many of these discourses have been produced by theorists whose histories are, in varying degrees, diasporic. The approach I have been following (in tandem with Gilroy) insists on the routing of diaspora discourses in specific maps/histories. Diasporic subjects are distinct versions of modern, transnational, intercultural experience. Thus historicized, diaspora cannot become a master trope or "figure" for modern, complex, or positional identities, cross-cut and displaced by race, sex, gender, class, and culture.

Gilroy's specific map/history is certainly open to amendment and critique – for skewing "black Britain" in the direction of an Atlantic world with the Afro-Caribbean at its center, for focusing on practices of travel and cultural production that have, with important exceptions, not been open to women, for not giving sufficient attention to cross-cutting sexualities in constituting diasporic consciousness. Moreover, his diasporic intervention into black history reflects a specific predicament: what he has called "the peculiarities of the Black English"

(Gilroy, 1993b: 49–62). *The Black Atlantic* decenters, to a degree, a sometimes normative African *American* history. To a degree. The specific experiences of plantation slavery, emancipation, South–North mobility, urbanization, and race/ethnic relations have a regional, and indeed a "national." focus that cannot be subsumed by an Atlanticist map/history of crossings. Although the roots and routes of African *American* cultures clearly pass through the Caribbean, they have been historically shaped into distinct patterns of struggle and marks of authenticity. They are not transnational or diasporic in the same way or to the same degree. Important comparative questions emerge around different histories of traveling and dwelling – specified by region (for example, the "South" as a focus of diasporic longing), by (neo)colonial history, by national entanglement, by class, and by gender. It is important to specify, too, that black South America and the hybrid Hispanic/black cultures of the Caribbean and Latin America are not, for the moment, included in Gilroy's projection. He writes from a North Atlantic/European location.[18]

Gilroy is increasingly explicit about the limitations of his "strictly provisional" undertaking (1993a: xi), presenting it as a reading of "masculinist" diasporism and as a first step open to correction and elaboration. There is no reason his privileging of the black Atlantic, for the purposes of writing a counterhistory in some depth, should necessarily silence other diasporic perspectives. With respect to contemporary Britain, one can imagine intersecting histories based, for example, on the effects of the British Empire in South Asia, or on the contributions of Islamic cultures to the making and critique of modernity. Gilroy's work tactically defines a map/history in ways that may best be seen as "anti-antiessentialist," the double negative not reducible to a positive. If diaspora is to be something about which one could write a history – and this is Gilroy's politically pointed goal – it must be something more than the name for a site of multiple displacements and reconstitutions of identity. Like "black England," the black Atlantic is a historically produced social formation. It denotes a genealogy not based on any direct connection with Africa or foundational appeal to kinship or racial identity.

In the current theoretical climate of prescriptive antiessentialism, diaspora discourses such as Gilroy's refuse to let go of a "changing same," something endlessly hybridized and in process but persistently there – memories and practices of collective identity maintained over long stretches of time. Gilroy attempts to conceive the continuity of a "people" without recourse to land, race, or kinship as primary "grounds" of continuity.[19] What, then, is the persistent object of his history? How to circumscribe this "changing same"? The black Atlantic as a counterhistory of modernity is crucially defined by the still-open wound of slavery and racial subordination. It is also a "tradition" of cultural survival and invention out of which Gilroy writes. But before he can invoke the much-abused term "tradition" – site of a thousand essentialisms – he must redefine it, "wrench it open":

> [Tradition] can be seen to be a process rather than an end, and is used here neither to identify a lost past nor to name a culture of compensation that would restore access

to it. Here, too, it does not stand in opposition to modernity nor should it conjure up wholesome, pastoral images of Africa that can be contrasted with the corrosive, aphasic power of the post-slave history of the Americas and the extended Caribbean. Tradition can now become a way of conceptualizing the *fragile communicative relationships across time and space* that are the basis *not of diaspora identities but of diaspora identifications.* Reformulated thus, [tradition] points not to a common content for diaspora cultures but to evasive qualities that make inter-cultural, trans-national diaspora *conversations between them* possible. (Gilroy, 1993a: 276, emphasis added)

Identifications not identities, acts of relationship rather than pregiven forms: this *tradition* is a network of partially connected histories, a persistently displaced and reinvented time/space of crossings.[20]

## ▪ Jewish Connections ▪

Gilroy rejects "Africa" as privileged source (a kind of Holy Land) while retaining its changing contribution to a counterculture of modernity. His history of black Atlantic diversity and conversation echoes the language of contemporary Jewish diasporism, anti-Zionist visions drawn from both Ashkenazic and Sephardic historical experiences. As we shall see, their critique of teleologies of return to a literal Jewish nation in Palestine parallels Gilroy's rejection of Afro-centered diaspora projections. The ongoing entanglement of black and Jewish diaspora visions, often rooted in biblical imagery, is salient here, as are the shared roots of Pan-Africanism and Zionism in nineteenth-century European nationalist ideologies – the influence of Heinrich von Treitschke on Du Bois, or Edward Wilmot Blyden's interest in Herder, Mazzini, and Hertzl. Nor should we forget a common history of victimization by scientific and popular racisms / anti-Semitisms, a history that tends to be lost in current black–Jewish antagonisms. (For a corrective, see Philip, 1993; and West, 1993.) Gilroy confronts these connections in the last chapter of *The Black Atlantic*. Here I merely suggest a homology between defining aspects of the two diasporas. A full discussion of the differences, tensions, and attractions of the traditions is beyond my present compass.

When understood as a practice of dwelling (differently), as an ambivalent refusal or indefinite deferral of return, and as a positive transnationalism, diaspora finds validation in the historical experiences of both displaced Africans and Jews. In discussing Safran's constitution of a comparative field, I worried about the extent to which diaspora, defined as dispersal, presupposed a center. If this center becomes associated with an actual "national" territory – rather than with a reinvented "tradition," a "book," a portable eschatology – it may devalue what I called the lateral axes of diaspora. These decentered, partially overlapping networks of communication, travel, trade, and kinship connect the several communities of a transnational "people." The centering of diasporas around an axis of origin and return overrides the specific local interactions (identifications and ruptures, both constructive and defensive) necessary for the maintenance of diasporic social forms. The empowering paradox of diaspora is that dwelling *here* assumes a solidarity and connection *there*. But *there* is not necessarily a single place or an exclusivist nation.

How is the connection (elsewhere) that makes a difference (here) remembered and rearticulated? In a forcefully argued essay, "Diaspora: Generation and the Ground of Jewish Identity," Daniel and Jonathan Boyarin defend an interactive conception of genealogy – kinship not reducible to "race" in its modern definitions – as the matrix for dispersed Jewish populations (1993). They offer sustained polemics against two potent alternatives to diasporism: Pauline universalist humanism (we are all one in the spiritual body of Christ) and autochthonous nationalism (we are all one in the place that belongs, from the beginning, to us alone). The former attains a love for humanity at the price of imperialist inclusion/conversion. The latter gains a feeling of rootedness at the expense of excluding others with old and new claims in the land. Diaspora ideology, for the Boyarins, involves a principled renunciation of both universalism and sovereignty – an embrace of the arts of exile and coexistence, aptitudes for maintaining distinction as a people in relations of daily converse with others.

Permanent conditions of relative powerlessness and minority status justify and render relatively harmless ethnocentric survival tactics – for example, imposing marks of distinction on the body (special clothing, hairstyles, circumcision), or restricting charity and community self-help to "our people." In conditions of permanent historical exile – or what amounts to the same thing, in an exile that can end *only* with the Messiah – ethnocentrism is just one tactic, never an absolute end in itself. Rabbinical diasporist ideologies, developed over twenty centuries of dispersion and drawing on biblical traditions critical of Davidic monarchy and of all claims to authenticity in the "land," in effect continue the "nomadic" strand of early Judaism. For the Boyarins, this is the mainstream of Jewish historical experience. And they assert unequivocally that the Zionist solution to the "problem" of diaspora, seen only negatively as *galut* ("exile"), is "the subversion of Jewish culture and not its culmination... capturing Judaism in a state" (Boyarin and Boyarin, 1993: 722, 724). Drawing on the scholarship of W. D. Davies (1992) and others, they stress the ambivalence in Jewish tradition, from biblical times to the present, regarding claims for a territorial basis of identity. "Return," defined as exclusive possession of the "land," is not the authentic outcome of Jewish history. Against the national/ethnic absolutism of contemporary Zionism, Jonathan Boyarin writes, "we Jews should recognize the strength that comes from a diversity of communal arrangements and concentrations both among Jews and with our several others. We should recognize that the copresence of those others is not a threat, but rather the condition of our lives" (1992: 129).

The Boyarins' account of diaspora aspires to be both a model *of* (historical Jewish experience) and a model *for* (contemporary hybrid identities). This aim is apparent in the following passage:

Diasporic cultural identity teaches us that cultures are not preserved by being protected from "mixing" but probably can only continue to exist as a product of such mixing. Cultures, as well as identities, are constantly being remade. While this is true of all cultures, diasporic Jewish culture lays it bare because of the impossibility of a natural association between this people and a particular land – thus the impossibility of seeing Jewish culture as a self-enclosed, bounded phenomenon. The critical force of this dissociation among people, language, culture, and land has been an enormous threat to cultural nativisms and integrisms, a threat that is one of the sources of anti-Semitism and perhaps one of the reasons that Europe has been much more prey to this evil than the Middle East. In other words, diasporic identity is a disaggregated identity. Jewishness disrupts the very categories of identity because it is not national, not genealogical, not religious, but all of these in dialectical tension with one another. When liberal Arabs and some Jews claim that the Jews of the Middle East are Arab Jews, we concur and think that Zionist ideology occludes something very significant when it seeks to obscure this point. The production of an ideology of a pure Jewish cultural essence that has been debased by Diaspora seems neither historically nor ethically correct. "Diasporized," that is disaggregated, identity allows the early medieval scholar Rabbi Sa'adya to be an Egyptian Arab who happens to be Jewish and also a Jew who happens to be an Egyptian Arab. Both of these contradictory propositions must be held together. (Boyarin and Boyarin, 1993: 721)

The passage expresses a powerful and moving vision, especially for a world riven by absolute oppositions of Arab and Jew. It need not detract unduly from its force to ask whether Rabbi Sa'adya's disaggregated identity would have been restricted, or differently routed, if he had been a woman. How did women "mix" cultures? And how have they transmitted, "genealogically," the marks and messages of tradition? How have women embodied diasporic Judaism, and how has Judaism marked, empowered, or constrained their bodies?

The Boyarins, in this essay at least, are silent on such questions. They do briefly invoke feminist issues in the sentences that immediately follow the passage quoted above.

Similarly, we suggest that a diasporized gender identity is possible and positive. Being a woman is some kind of special being, and there are aspects of life and practice that insist on and celebrate that speciality. But this is not simply a fixing or a freezing of all practice and performance, of gender identity into one set of parameters. Human beings are divided into men and women for certain purposes, but that does not tell the whole story of their bodily identity. Rather than the dualism of gendered bodies and universal souls – the dualism that the Western tradition offers – we can substitute partially Jewish, partially Greek bodies, bodies that are sometimes gendered and sometimes not. It is this idea that we are calling diasporized identity. (Boyarin and Boyarin, 1993: 721)

Arguments from antiessentialist feminism are implicitly deployed here, and the figure of "woman" is joined to that of the Jew to evoke a model of identity as a performed cluster/tension of positionalities.[21] Would it make the same sense to say that a body was sometimes black, sometimes not, sometimes lesbian, sometimes not, sometimes poor, and so forth? Yes and no. For we approach a level of generality at which the specificities and tensions of diasporist, racialist, class, sex, and gender determinations are erased. Moreover, in this assertion of a common predicament we glimpse the hegemonizing possibilities of diasporist discourse. Skimmed over in the identification of "diasporized" gender identity are a series of historical specifications. "Human beings are divided into men and women for certain purposes." Whose purposes? What are the unequal dividing structures? How do these functional "purposes" appear from different sides of the gender divide? I have already argued that it is important to resist the tendency of diasporic identities to slide into equivalence with disaggregated, positional, performed identities in general. As they necessarily draw from antifoundationalist feminism, postcolonial critique, and various postmodernisms, contemporary diaspora discourses retain a connection with specific bodies, historical experiences of displacement that need to be held in comparative tension and partial translatability.

I have dwelt on one instance of too-quick diasporic equivalence in the Boyarins' essay to identify a persistent risk in "theoretical" comparisons, a risk that haunts my own project. Overall, the Boyarins maintain the specificity of their point of engagement, their "discrepant cosmopolitanism." As observing Ashkenazic Jews, they contest for a tradition, from within. But their theory and practice preclude this "inside" as an ultimate, or even principal, location. Perhaps, as they recognize, in allegorizing diasporism they run the risk of making Jewish experience again the normative model. But in the passage just cited, diaspora is portrayed in terms of an almost postcolonial vision of hybridity. Whose experience, exactly, is being theorized? In dialogue with whom? It is clear that the Boyarins have been reading and reacting to minority and Third World authors. And Paul Gilroy is a close student of Walter Benjamin. Moreover, Asian American diaspora theorists are reading black British Cultural Studies. Diasporas, and diaspora theorists, cross paths in a mobile space of translations, not equivalences.

The Boyarins do not, in fact, say very much about the specific mechanisms of "genealogy" (or "generation," as they also call it). Their chief effort is devoted to critical ground-clearing, making space for multifaceted, nonreductive transmissions of the marks and messages of peoplehood. Against Pauline spirituality, they insist on carnal, socially differentiated bodies. The bodies are gendered male, which is to say they are unmarked by gender – at least in this essay.[22] (Daniel Boyarin's *Carnal Israel* [1993b], as well as his work on Saint Paul [1993a], centrally engages feminist issues.) The Boyarins argue persuasively that the multiple social transmissions of genealogy need not be reduced to a "racial" matrix of identity. But in deploying the language of "generation" and "lineage," they risk naturalizing an androcentric kinship system. As in Gilroy's history, which leans toward the diasporic practices of men, there is considerable room for specification of gendered diaspora experiences.[23]

## ■ Diasporic Pasts and Futures ■

The Boyarins ground their defense of diaspora in two thousand years of rabbinical ideology, as well as in concrete historical experiences of dispersed community. They state: "We propose Diaspora as a theoretical and historical model to replace national self-determination. To be sure, this would be an idealized Diaspora generalized from those situations in Jewish history when the Jews were relatively free from persecution and yet constituted by strong identity – those situations, moreover, within which promethean Jewish creativity was not antithetical, indeed was synergistic with a general cultural activity" (Boyarin and Boyarin, 1993: 711). Jewish life in Muslim Spain before the expulsions – a rich, multireligious, multicultural florescence – is one of the historical moments redeemed by this vision. "The same figure, a Nagid, an Ibn Gabirol, or a Maimonides, can be simultaneously the vehicle for the preservation of traditions and of the mixing of cultures" (721). We enter, here, the whole "geniza world" of S. D. Goitein, the Mediterranean of the eleventh to the thirteenth centuries (and beyond) where Jews, Muslims, and Christians lived, traded, borrowed, and conversed in the process of maintaining distinct communities.[24]

There are no innocent periods of history, and the geniza world had its share of intolerance. Without reducing these centuries to a romanticized multiculturalism, one can recognize an extraordinary cosmopolitan network. As Goitein and his followers have shown, lines of identity were drawn differently, often less absolutely than in the modern era. For long periods and in many places, people of distinct religions, races, cultures, and languages coexisted. Difference was articulated through connection, not separation. In his book *After Jews and Arabs*, which draws generously on Goitein's research and vision, Ammiel Alcalay portrays a Levantine world characterized by cultural mixing, relative freedom of travel, an absence of ghettos, and multilingualism – the antithesis of current national, racial, and religious separations. A sweeping work of counterhistory and cultural critique, Alcalay's study begins to make room for women's histories, specified by class, in its world of intersecting cosmopolitan cultures. In this he builds on Goitein's awareness of "the chasm between the popular local subculture of women and the worldwide Hebrew book culture of the men" (quoted in Alcalay, 1993: 138). This "chasm" need not be taken to mean that men were cosmopolitan, and women not: affluent women, at least, traveled (sometimes alone), were involved in business, held property, crossed cultural borders – but in particular ways that Jewish diaspora studies have only begun to recognize and detail.

Alcalay's history gives "regional" concreteness to a diasporist Jewish history which, in the Boyarins' version, is not connected to a specific map/history. "Jewish history" is, of course, diverse and contested. In the present Israeli state, a division between Ashkenazic and Sephardic/Mizrahi populations reflects distinct diaspora experiences. As reclaimed in Alcalay's book, the Sephardic strand offers a specific counterhistory of Arab/Jewish coexistence and crossover. Sephardic/Mizrahi histories may also generate "diasporist" critiques by Arab-Jewish exiles within the Israeli "homeland" (Lavie, 1992; Shohat, 1988, 1989). Sephardic regional roots and emerging alliances with "Third World" or "Arab" movements can articulate networks that decenter both the diasporist figure of the "wandering Jew" and the overwhelming importance of the Holocaust as defining moment in modern "Jewish history." In Israel, a minority of European Jews have taken a leading role in defining an exclusivist Jewish state – predicated on religious, ethnic, linguistic, and racial subordinations. Sephardic/Mizrahi counterhistories question this state's hegemonic self-definition. Important as these struggles may be, however, one should not overgeneralize from current hierarchical oppositions in Israel. Both Sephardic and Ashkenazic traditions are complex, containing nationalist and antinationalist strands. There are strong resources for a *diasporist* anti-Zionism in pre-Holocaust Ashkenazi history. (Indeed, the recent signing of a fragile peace accord between Israel and the Palestine Liberation Organization makes this vision, these historical resources, seem less anachronistic. If a viable political arrangement for sharing the land of Palestine finally emerges, Jews and Arabs will need to recover diasporist skills for maintaining difference in contact and accommodation.)

Max Weinreich's historical research has shown that the maintenance of Ashkenazic Jewishness (*yidishkeyt*) was not primarily the result of forced, or voluntary, separation in distinct neighborhoods or ghettos. This relatively recent "ghetto myth" supports an ethnic absolutism (as Gilroy might put it) that denies the interactive and adaptive process of historical Jewish identity.

> Ashkenazic reality is to be sought between the two poles of absolute identity with and absolute remoteness from the coterritorial non-Jewish communities. To compress it into a formula, what the Jews aimed at was not isolation from Christians but insulation from Christianity. Although, throughout the ages, many Jews must be supposed to have left the fold, the community as a whole did succeed in surviving and developing. On the other hand, the close and continuous ties of the Jews with their neighbors, which used to be severed only for a while during actual outbreaks of persecutions, manifested themselves in customs and folk beliefs; in legends and songs; in literary production, etc. The culture patterns prevalent among Ashkenazic Jews must be classified as Jewish, but very many of them are specifically Ashkenazic. They are mid-course formations as those found wherever cultures meet along frontiers, in border zones or in territories with mixed populations. (Weinreich, 1967: 2204)

Weinreich's prime specimen of Ashkenazic border culture is Yiddish, the "fusion language" of which he is the preeminent historian. He also lays great stress on the open-ended process of Talmudic interpretation through which laws (*dinim*) and customs (*minhogim*) are continuously adapted and clarified anew in the light of the Torah (which, the Yiddish saying goes, "contains everything"). The defining loyalty here is to an open text, a set of interpretable norms, not to a "homeland" or even to an "ancient" tradition. I have been quoting from a summary essay of 1967 in which Weinreich characterizes Ashkenazic diasporic history without any mention of return, Holy Land, or Israel. The distinction of Jew and non-Jew is critical, but processual and nonessentialist: "It turns out that the very existence of a division is much more important than the actual location of the division line... More often than not, it appears, the distance between Jewish and non-Jewish patterns is created not by a difference in the ingredients proper but rather by the way they are interpreted as elements of the given system" (Weinreich, 1967: 2205). Difference, for Weinreich, is a process of continual renegotiation in new circumstances of dangerous and creative coexistence.[25]

What is at stake in reclaiming these different Ashkenazic and Sephardic diasporist visions, beyond their evident contribution to a critique of Zionism and other exclusivist nationalisms? An answer is suggested by my own belated route to the geniza world and the company of Goitein admirers: a remarkable hybrid work of ethnography/history/travel, *In an Antique Land,* by Amitav Ghosh (1992). An Indian novelist-cum-anthropologist, Ghosh writes of his fieldwork in the Nile Delta, and in the process uncovers a deep history of transnational connections between the Mediterranean, Middle East, and South Asia – a history onto which he grafts his own late-twentieth-century travel from one Third World place to another. In the dispersed Cairo geniza archive, he tracks the almost forgotten story of an Indian traveler to Aden, the slave and business agent of a Jewish merchant residing in Mangalore. (The history of this archive is itself an engrossing subplot.) Ghosh's search for his twelfth-century precursor opens a window on the medieval Indian Ocean, a world of extraordinary travel, trade, and coexistence among Arabs, Jews, and South Asians. Like Janet Abu-Lughod's important overview, *Before European Hegemony* (1989), and like the earlier world-historical visions of Marshall Hodgson (1993), Ghosh's account helps us remember/imagine "world systems," economic and cultural, that preceded the rise of an expansionist Europe. In the late twentieth century it is difficult to form concrete pictures of transregional networks not produced by and/or resisting the hegemony of Western techno-industrial society. These histories of alternate cosmopolitanisms and diasporic networks are redeemable (in a Benjaminian sense) as crucial political visions: worlds "after" Jews and Arabs, "after" the West and the "Rest," and "after" natives and immigrants.

Such visions and counterhistories can support strategies for nontotalizing "globalization from below." The phrase, paired with "globalization from above," is proposed by Brecher et al. (1993) to name transregional social movements that both resist and use hegemonizing technologies and communications. This constitutive entanglement is, I have argued, characteristic of modern diaspora networks. Entanglement is not necessarily cooptation. Recalling older histories of discrepant cosmopolitan contacts can empower new ways to be "traditional" on a more than local scale. Epeli Hau'ofa's recent recovery of a long history of Pacific travels in the projection of a new "Oceanian" regionalism ("our sea of islands") is a case in point (Hau'ofa et al., 1993).

The works I have been discussing maintain a clear, at times crushing, awareness of the obstacles to such futures, the constant pressure of transnational capital and national hegemonies. Yet they express, too, a stubborn hope. They do not merely lament a world that has been lost. Rather, as in diaspora discourses generally, both loss and survival are prefigurative. Of what? We lack a description and are reduced to the merely reactive, stopgap language of "posts." The term "postcolonial" (like Arjun Appadurai's "postnational") makes sense only in an emergent, or utopian, context.[26] There are no postcolonial cultures or places: only moments. tactics, discourses. "Post-" is always shadowed by "neo-." Yet "postcolonial" does describe real, if incomplete, ruptures with past structures of domination, sites of current struggle and imagined futures. Perhaps what is at stake in the historical projection of a geniza world or a black Atlantic is the "prehistory of postcolonialism." Viewed in this perspective, the diaspora discourse and history currently in the air would be about recovering non-Western, or not-only-Western, models for cosmopolitan life, nonaligned transnationalities struggling within and against nation-states, global technologies, and markets – resources for a fraught coexistence.

## NOTES

1   A comparable circuit, joining the Dominican Republic and New York, is treated in depth by Grasmuck and Pessar (1991). See also Brown (1991); Fischer and Abedi (1990); and Marcus and Fischer (1986; 94) for multi-locale ethnographic texts.
2   For example, see Pan (1990); also Chow (1992); Ong (1993); and Li (1993).
3   The distinction between immigrant and diasporic experiences, heightened for defin-itional clarity in this paragraph, should not be overdrawn. There are diasporic moments in classic assimilationist histories, early and late, as new arrivals maintain and later generations recover links to a homeland. Diasporic populations regularly "lose" members to the dominant culture.
4   On Jewish anti-Zionism, see, for example, the work of "diaspora nationalist" Simon Dubnow (1931, 1958), whose secular vision of "autonomism" projected a cultural/ historical/spiritual "national" identity beyond the territorial/political. In an (un)ortho-dox vein, Jonathan and Daniel Boyarin argue that a rigorous eschatology of "return" at the end of historical time can produce a radical critique of Zionist literalism (1993).
5   In *The Western Abenakis of Vermont, 1600–1800: War, Migration, and the Survival of an Indian People*, historian Colin Galloway (1990) argues that the survival of the Abenaki as a people was accomplished through "diaspora." The mobile family band, not the settled village, was the basic unit of group life. In response to conquest, many Abenaki bands moved to Canada and to sites all over the northeast United States, while some stuck it out in Vermont. When so many villages disappeared, it *seemed* to outsiders that the group had been fatally decimated. In Galloway's perspective, diasporic communities such as Mashpee – where displaced members of several Cape Cod communities came together – seem less aberrant.
6   Recent interest in the oxymoronic figure of the *traveling native* complicates and histor-icizes, though it does not eliminate, the tension between tribal and diasporic claims to legitimacy. I am drawing here on the insightful work of Teresia Teaiwa. She evokes a long history of Pacific Islander travels (linked to contemporary practices). This mobility can be traced along ancient routes of exchange, such as "the kula ring which linked the east

peninsula of mainland New Guinea with the Trobriand Islands and Louisiade Archipelago; the epic voyages between Hawai'i, Tahiti, and Actearca/New Zealand; the consistent migration and exchange within the Fiji–Tonga–Samoa triangle; and the exchange of navigational knowledge among Carolinian and Mariana Islanders. These, of course, are just a few of the circuits within which Pacific Islanders represented/performed their identities as both dynamic and specific – ways they thought about difference through connection" (Teaiwa, 1993; 12).

7 In the US academy, "minority" discourse has been theorized as a resistance practice (JanMohamed and Lloyd, 1990). It is often institutionalized in programs defined by ethnicity/race. Diasporic transnationalism complicates and sometimes threatens this structure, particularly when "minorities" have defined themselves in ethnically absolutist, or nationalist, ways. In Britain, the tension between minority and diaspora articulations of identity takes place in a different context: "minority discourse" has been largely an official discourse.

8 The distinction between old and new, European and non-European immigrants, while critical, should not be overdrawn. Immigrants from Ireland and from central, southern, and eastern Europe have been racialized. And anti-Semitism remains an often latent, sometimes explicit force. But generally speaking, European immigrants have, with time, come to participate as ethnic "whites" in multicultural America. The same cannot be said, overall, of populations of color – although region of origin, shade of skin, culture, and class may attenuate racist exclusion.

9 Edward Said has used the term "contrapuntal" to characterize one of the positive aspects of conditions of exile: "Seeing 'the entire world as a foreign land' makes possible originality of vision. Most people are principally aware of one culture, one setting, one home; exiles are aware of at least two, and this plurality of vision gives rise to an awareness of simultaneous dimensions, an awareness that – to borrow a phrase from music – is contrapuntal...For an exile, habits of life, expression or activity in the new environment inevitably occur against the memory of these things in another environment. Thus both the new and the old environments are vivid, actual, occurring together contrapuntally" (1984: 171–2; see also 1990: 48–50). These reflections on exile apply to experiences of diaspora, but with the difference that the more individualist, existential focus of the former is tempered by networks of community, collective practices of displaced dwelling, in the latter.

10 In a far-reaching historical critique of Pacific Rim discourse and liberal/neoliberal "free-trade" ideologies, Christopher Connery (1994) identifies a danger of imagining counterhegemonic sites of crossing/cosmopolitanism "within the dominant conceptual category of the Ocean, given that it is Capital's favorite myth-element." He calls for a careful historicizing of oceanic discourses, a concern that applies to Gilroy's projection of a black Atlantic, discussed below.

11 For diverse accounts and critiques of the Los Angeles Festival, see Getty Center (1991), particularly Lisa Lowe's comments on the depoliticizing effects of postmodern pluralism/multiculturalism.

12 Of course, men also select and strategize, within their own constraints and privileges. The difference between gendered diaspora predicaments is critical for an emerging comparative perspective. Ganguly's 1992 study of men's and women's memories in the South Asian US diaspora is exemplary; Bottomley (1992) provides an excellent treatment of gender and class articulation in a study of Greek migration as cultural process.

13 Brah (1993), Mohanty (1987), Hall (1988, 1990), Mercer (1988, 1990), and Radakrishnan (1991), among others, discuss this diasporic space of cross-cutting determinations.

14 On tensions between Caribbean and African American populations in New York, see Foner (1987). The analysis in Velez (1994) of a story by Puerto Rican writer Ana Lydia Vega, "Encancaranublado" (Vega, 1987), very acutely evokes the national/cultural/racial/linguistic differences separating Caribbean immigrants, as well as their common lumping together by the US racial order. Whether this latter repositioning will lead to new alliances or conflicts in the diasporic economy of struggle and scarcity is left open.

15 Here a parallel with border cultures could be developed, highlighting the constitutive, repeated violence of the arbitrary line, the policed border – and the desperate/utopic crossings that ensue. This ambivalence recalls Néstor García Canclini's conflicting, simultaneous images of transnational "border" cultures: the "airport" and the "garage sale," one institutional and disciplinary, the other popular and improvised (1992). The garage-sale image is derived from the portrayal of border cultures in Renato Rosaldo's *Culture and Truth* (1989: 44).

16 Bhabha tends to equate "diasporic" and "postcolonial" in his discussion. This raises an interesting question that I cannot develop fully here. To what extent are theorizations of postcoloniality projections of specific diasporas? Ella Shohat (1992) links articulations of hybridity in the name of a "postcolonial" condition to diasporic Third World intellectuals writing primarily in First World centers, and Arif Dirlik (1994) links them, in a functionalist account, with the needs of transnational capitalism. To be sure, South Asian theorists are strikingly prominent, notably in Britain and North America. Postcoloniality is not much heard from elsewhere – for example, in Latin America and Africa, where histories of de-, anti-, and neocolonialism are significantly different. If postcolonial theory is historicized in relation to South Asian diasporas, we might usefully distinguish, following Vijay Mishra (1983, 1994), two kinds: the first diaspora, in the late nineteenth century, involved the movement of indentured laborers to places such as Trinidad, Guyana, Surinam, Fiji, Mauritius, South Africa, and Malaysia; the second consisted of postwar "free" migrations to Britain, the United States, Australia, and Canada. The representative writer of the first would be V. S. Naipaul; that of the second, the moment of "postcolonial" visions, Salman Rushdie. Mishra's ongoing work will help flesh out this historicization in detail. Obviously, the substance of postcolonial theorizing is not entirely reducible to the histories of certain South Asian intellectuals. The key concept of hybridity, for example, rhymes with Latin American theorizations of *mestizaje*, or Caribbean *créolité*. These are not identical concepts, and they emerge from distinct historical situations; but they overlap and together denote a domain of complex cultural formations produced by, and partially subverting, colonial dichotomies and hierarchies.

17 *The Black Atlantic* guards, more explicitly, against the problems Mercer finds in Gilroy's concept of "populist modernism," with its implicit culture- and class-based authenticity test. The book's critical countertradition of modernity spans vernacular, "popular" forms and "high" cultural arguments (explicit and implicit) with Enlightenment philosophy.

18 *The Black Atlantic* is pointedly an intervention in the tradition of African *American* intellectual and cultural history. This tradition has canonically meant African *North*-American, including those areas of the Caribbean directly connected with the English-speaking United States. New Latino/Chicano readings of the Americas as

complex border zones question overly linear diaspora narratives. See, for example, José David Saldívar's reading of Ntozake Shange in terms of magical realism and *mestizaje* (1991: 87–104).

19 See Clifford (1988: 277–346, "Identity in Mashpee") for a similar attempt to portray an interactive culture/identity as something persistently, but not continuously, there. The differences concerning land, oral tradition, travel, racialization, and identity are of course salient. But the general approach to peoples who have managed to prevail through histories overdetermined by cultural, political, and economic power relations is comparable. See Gilroy (1991, 1992b) for the notion of a *changing same* (derived from Leroi Jones/Amiri Baraka). The phrase does not, I think, quite do justice to the tensions and violent discontinuities that are constitutive of the "tradition" he tracks. His most recent formulations struggle against the grain of various organicisms, while asserting a complexly hybrid *historical* continuity. Gilroy (1992b) is explicitly concerned not to privilege appeals to kinship or "family." Stefan Helmreich (1993) asserts the contrary but does not discuss *The Black Atlantic* or a wide range of Gilroy's recent work. Helmreich's suggestive etymological reading of the bias toward male genealogies built into the concept/metaphor of "diaspora" applies better to those strongly linear, genealogical visions of diaspora which Gilroy questions. Despite its general, but not exclusive, emphasis on men, Gilroy's work is not inherently closed to women's experiences or to complex intersections of gender, race, class, and sexuality. Etymology is not destiny. I fully agree with Helmreich's project of "set[ting] in motion to new meanings the term *diaspora*" (Helmreich, 1993: 248).

20 Gilroy's formulation of the interconnected diversity of historical "black" experiences is not reducible to the image of a tree – root, stem, and branches – proposed by St. Clair Drake (1982: 397). This difference distinguishes his diaspora from the "traditional" or "continental" forms evoked by Drake.

21 See Daniel Boyarin (1993a) for a historical account of the symmetrical discursive construction of "woman" and "Jew" in Pauline Christian universalism.

22 Their recent analysis of circumcision marks its subject matter and perspective explicitly as male (Boyarin and Boyarin, 1995).

23 Another area of specification I am not yet prepared to discuss: diasporic sexualities and/or sexualized diaspora discourses. In Brah's idea of "diasporic space," there is room for developing such analyses. And Mercer's work points the way, along with the productions of the Sankofa Film Collective. In commenting on a draft of this essay, Kathleen Biddick reminded me of Sankofa's *Passion of Remembrance* "and the strange place to which the film returns, with the voices and bodies of the man and woman fractured in interesting ways across it" (personal communication, 1993). Diasporic histories may not be necessary conditions for developing performative visions of gender, sexuality, race, and ethnicity, but their liminal spaces, displaced encounters, and tactical affiliations provide apt settings for such visions. In this vein, it would be interesting to historicize Audre Lorde's complex articulation of race, gender, and sexuality in *Zami: A New Spelling of My Name* (1982) with attention to New York City neighborhoods as diasporic spaces.

24 *Geniza*, in this context, refers to the "storeroom" of the synagogue at Fustat (Old Cairo), where a rich archive of records – business, personal, and religious in nature – survived from the tenth to the nineteenth century. These documents are the basis for Goitein's extraordinary vision of transregional, interactive Jewish life in the Middle Ages (see Goitein, 1967–93, vol. 1; also Ghosh, 1992; and Cohen, 1994).

25  In many places, Weinreich anticipates current contact perspectives on colonial and neocolonial border zones, processes of "transculturation" and interactive identity formation. Compare, particularly, Pratt's definition of "contact zone," also derived from ethnolinguistic "contact" or "fusion" languages (1992). See also Dubnow (1931) for a historically grounded Ashkenazi vision of interactive Jewishness that presupposes the permanence of diaspora.

26  In the past few years "postcolonial" and "postcoloniality" – terms that often confuse theoretical approaches and historical moments – have been subjected to searching, often skeptical, symptomatic critiques. See especially During (1987), Appiah (1991), Shohat (1992), Chow (1992), Frankenberg and Mani (1993), Miyoshi (1993), Dirlik (1994), and many of the papers in *Social Text*, 31–2 (1992). I cannot here engage the many unresolved issues raised by these arguments, except to say that I am persuaded by Frankenberg and Mani's insistence on a rigorously conjunctural understanding of different ways to be "postcolonial" (1993). Whatever the fate of this term, the sites of complex historical entanglement and agency it provisionally names should not be reduced to epiphenomena of postmodern fragmentation, neocolonial transnationality, or global capitalism. On the connection of postcoloniality with recent diaspora theories, see Frankenberg and Mani (1993: 302). Also for our current purposes, the three possible temporalities that Chow connects to the prefix *post*-are relevant, particularly the third: (1) "having gone through"; (2) "after"; (3) "a notion of time that is not linear but constant, marked by events that may be technically finished but that can only be fully understood with consideration of the devastation they left behind" (Chow, 1992: 152).

## REFERENCES

Abu-Lughod, Janet (1989). *Before European Hegemony: The World System A.D. 1250–1350.* Oxford: Oxford University Press.

Alcalay, Ammiel (1993). *After Jews and Arabs: Remaking Levantine Culture.* Minneapolis: University of Minnesota Press.

Anzaldúa, Gloria (1987). *Borderlands/La Frontera: The New Mestiza.* San Francisco: Spinsters/Aunt Lute.

Appiah, Kwame Anthony (1991). Is the Post in Postmodernism the Post in Postcolonial? *Critical Inquiry* 17(Winter): 336–57.

Bauman, Zygmunt (1989). *Modernity and the Holocaust.* Ithaca, NY: Cornell University Press.

Benjamin, Walter (1968). Theses on the Philosophy of History. In *Illuminations.* Hannah Arendt, ed. Harry Zorn, trans. Pp. 253–65. New York: Schocken Books.

Bhabha, Homi K. (1990). DissemiNation: Time, Narrative, and the Margins of the Modern Nation. In *Nation and Narration.* Homi K. Bhabha, ed. Pp. 291–322. London: Routledge.

Bottomley, Gillian (1992). *From Another Place: Migration and the Politics of Culture.* Cambridge: Cambridge University Press.

Boyarin, Daniel (1993a). Paul and the Genealogy of Gender. *Representations* 41 (Winter): 1–33.

——(1993b). *Carnal Israel: Reading Sex in Talmudic Culture.* Berkeley: University of California Press.

Boyarin, Daniel, and Jonathan Boyarin (1993). Diaspora: Generational Ground of Jewish Identity. *Critical Inquiry* 19(4): 693–725.

—— (1995). Self-Exposure as Theory: The Double Mark of the Male Jew. In *The Rhetorics of Self-Making*. Deborah Battaglia, ed. Berkeley: University of California Press.

Boyarin, Jonathan (1992). *Storm from Paradise: The Politics of Jewish Memory*. Minneapolis: University of Minnesota Press.

Brah, Avtar (1992). Difference, Diversity and Differentiation. In *'Race', Culture and Difference*. James Donald and Ali Rattansi, eds. Pp. 126–45. London: Sage.

—— (n.d.). *Diasporas and Borders*. University of California, Santa Cruz, unpublished manuscript.

Brecher, Jeremy, John Brown Childs, and Jill Cutler, eds. (1993). *Global Visions: Beyond the New World Order*. Boston: South End Press.

Brown, Karen McCarthy (1991). *Mama Lola: A Vodou Priestess in Brooklyn*. Berkeley: University of California Press.

Calderon, Hector, and José Saldívar, eds. (1991). *Criticism in the Borderlands: Studies in Chicano Literature, Culture, and Ideology*. Durham, NC: Duke University Press.

Canclini, Néstor García (1992). Museos, aeropuertos y ventes de garage. Paper presented at the Center for Cultural Studies, University of California, Santa Cruz, Borders/Diasporas Conference.

Chow, Rey (1992). Between Colonizers: Hong Kong's Postcolonial Self-Writing in the 1990s. *Diaspora* 2(2): 151–70.

Clifford, James (1988). *The Predicament of Culture*. Cambridge: Harvard University Press.

—— (1992). Traveling Cultures. In *Cultural Studies*. Lawrence Grossberg, Cary Nelson, and Paula Treichler, eds. Pp. 96–116. New York: Routledge.

Cohen, Robin (1987). *The New Helots: Migrants in the International Division of Labour*. Aldershot, England: Gower.

Connery, Christopher (1994). Pacific Rim Discourse: The Global Imaginary in the Late Cold War Years. *Boundary 2* 21(1).

Davies, W. D. (1992). *The Territorial Dimension of Judaism*. Minneapolis: University of Minnesota Press.

Dirlik, Arif (1994). The Postcolonial Aura: Third World Criticism in the Age of Global Capitalism. *Critical Inquiry* 20(2): 328–56.

Drake, St. Clair (1982). Diaspora Studies and Pan-Africanism. In *Global Dimensions of the African Diaspora*. Joseph E. Harris, ed. Pp. 341–404. Washington, DC: Howard University Press.

Dubnow, Simon (1931). Diaspora. In *Encyclopedia of the Social Sciences*. Pp. 126–30. New York: Macmillan.

—— (1958). *Nationalism and History: Essays in Old and New Judaism*. Philadelphia: Jewish Publication Society of America.

During, Simon (1987). Postmodernism or Post-Colonialism Today. *Textual Practice* 1(1): 32–47.

Fischer, Michael M.J., and Mehdi Abedi (1990). *Debating Muslims: Cultural Dialogues in Postmodernity and Tradition*. Madison: University of Wisconsin Press.

Flores, Juan, and George Yudice (1990). Living Borders/Buscando America. *Social Text* 24: 57–84.

Foner, Nancy (1987). West Indians in New York City and London: A Comparative Analysis. In *Caribbean Life in New York City: Sociocultural Dimensions*. Constance Sutton and Elsa Chaney, eds. Pp. 117–30. New York: Center for Migration Studies.

Frankenberg, Ruth, and Lata Mani (1993). Crosscurrents, Crosstalk: Race, "Postcoloniality," and the Politics of Location. *Cultural Studies* 7(2): 292–310.

Galloway, Colin (1990). *The Western Abenakis of Vermont, 1600–1800: War, Migration, and the Survival of an Indian People.* Norman: University of Oklahoma Press.

Ganguly, Keya (1992). Migrant Identities: Personal Memory and the Construction of Selfhood. *Cultural Studies* 6(1): 27–50.

Getty Center (1991). *New Geographies of Performance: Cultural Representation and Intercultural Exchange on the Edge of the 21st Century: Summary Report.* Los Angeles: Getty Center for the History of Art and the Humanities.

Ghosh, Amitav (1989). The Diaspora in Indian Culture. *Public Culture* 2(1): 73–8.

—— (1992). *In An Antique Land.* London: Granta Books.

Gilroy, Paul (1987). *There Ain't No Black in the Union Jack: The Cultural Politics of Race and Nation.* London: Hutchinson.

—— (1991). Sounds Authentic: Black, Music Ethnicity, and the Challenge of the *Changing Same. Black Music Research Journal* 11(2): 111–36.

—— (1992a). Cultural Studies and Ethnic Absolutism. In *Cultural Studies.* Lawrence Grossberg, Cary Nelson, and Paula Treichler, eds. Pp. 187–99. New York: Routledge.

—— (1992b). It's a Family Affair. *In Black Popular Culture: A Project by Michele Wallace.* Gina Dent, ed. Pp. 303–16. Seattle, WA: Bay Press.

—— (1993a). *The Black Atlantic: Double Consciousness and Modernity.* Cambridge: Harvard University Press.

—— (1993b). *Small Acts: Thoughts on the Politics of Black Cultures.* London: Serpent's Tail.

Goitein, Solomon Dob Fritz 1967–93 *A Mediterranean Society: The Jewish Communities of the Arab World as Portrayed in the Documents of the Cairo Geniza.* 6 vols. Berkeley: University of California Press.

Grasmuck, Sherri, and Patricia R. Pessar (1991). *Between Two Islands: Dominican International Migration.* Berkeley: University of California Press.

Grewal, Shabnam, ed. (1988). *Charting the Journey: Writings by Black and Third World Women.* London: Sheba Feminist.

Gupta, Rahila (1988). Women and Communalism, A Tentative Inquiry. In *Charting the Journey: Writings by Black and Third World Women.* Shabnam Grewal, ed. Pp. 23–9. London: Sheba Feminist.

Hall, Stuart (1988). New Ethnicities. *In Black Film, British Cinema.* Kobena Mercer, ed. pp. 27–30. London: Institute of Contemporary Arts.

—— (1990). Cultural Identity and Diaspora. *In Identity: Community, Culture, Difference.* Jonathan Rutherford, ed. Pp. 222–37. London: Lawrence and Wishart.

Hannerz, Ulf (1992). *Cultural Complexity: Studies in the Social Organization of Meaning.* New York: Columbia University Press.

Harvey, David (1989). *The Condition of Postmodernity: An Inquiry into the Origins of Cultural Change.* Oxford: Blackwell.

Hau'ofa, Epeli, Vijay Naidu, and Eric Waddell, eds. (1993). *A New Oceania: Rediscovering Our Sea of Islands.* Suva, Fiji: School of Social and Economic Development, The University of the South Pacific.

Helmreich, Stefan (1993). Kinship, Nation, and Paul Gilroy's Concept of Diaspora. *Diaspora* 2(2): 243–49.

Hicks, Emily (1991). *Border Writing: The Multidimensional Text.* Minneapolis: University of Minnesota Press.

Hodgson, Marshall (1993). *Rethinking World History.* Cambridge: Cambridge University Press.

hooks, bell (1989). Critical Interrogation: Talking Race, Resisting Racism. In *Traveling Theories, Traveling Theorists.* James Clifford and Vivek Dhareshwar, eds. Inscriptions 5: 159–64.

——(1990). *Yearning: Race, Gender, and Cultural Politics.* Boston: South End Press.

JanMohamed, Abdul, and David Lloyd, eds. (1990). *The Nature and Context of Minority Discourse.* New York: Oxford University Press.

Kingston, Maxine Hong (1976). *The Woman Warrior: Memoirs of a Girlhood among Ghosts.* New York: Knopf.

Lavie, Smadar (1992). Blow-Ups in the Borderlands: Third World Israeli Authors' Gropings for Home. *New Formations* 18: 84–106.

Linebaugh, Peter, and Marcus Rediker (1990). The Many Headed Hydra: Sailors, Slaves, and the Atlantic Working Class in the 18th Century. *Journal of Historical Sociology* 3(3): 225–352.

Lorde, Audre (1982). *Zami, A New Spelling of My Name.* Trumansburg, NY: Crossing Press.

Marcus, George, and Michael M. J. Fischer (1986). *Anthropology as Cultural Critique: An Experimental Moment in the Human Sciences.* Chicago: University of Chicago Press.

Marshall, Paule (1981). *Brown Girl, Brownstones.* New York: Feminist Press.

Mercer, Kobena (1988). Diaspora Culture and the Dialogic Imagination. *In Blackframes: Celebration of Black Cinema.* Mbye Cham and Claire Andrade-Watkins, eds. Pp. 50–61. Cambridge, MA: MIT Press.

——(1990). Black Art and the Burden of Representation. *Third Text* (Spring): 61–78.

Mishra, Vijay (1983). The Girmit Ideology Reconsidered. *In Language and Literature.* Satendra Nandan, ed. Pp. 240–53. Suva, Fiji: University of the South Pacific.

——(1994). "The Familiar Temporariness" (V.S. Naipaul): Theorizing the Literature of the Indian Diaspora. Paper presented at the Center for Cultural Studies, University of California, Santa Cruz, Feb. 2.

Mitter, Swasti (1986). *Common Fate, Common Bond: Women in the Global Economy.* London: Pluto Press.

Miyoshi, Masao (1993). A Borderless World? From Colonialism to Transnationalism and the Decline of the Nation-State. *Critical Inquiry* 19 (Summer): 726–51.

Mohanty, Chandra (1987). Feminist Encounters: Locating the Politics of Experience. *Copyright* 1 (Fall): 30–44.

Naficy, Hamid (1991). Exile Discourse and Televisual Fetishization. *Quarterly Review of Film and Video* 13(1–3): 85–116.

Needham, Rodney (1975). Polythetic Classification. *Man* 10: 349–69.

Ong, Aiwah (1993). On the Edge of Empires: Flexible Citizenship among Chinese in Diaspora. *Positions* 1(3): 745–78.

Pan, Lynn (1990). *Sons of the Yellow Emperor: A History of the Chinese Diaspora.* Boston: Little Brown.

Philip, Marlene Nourbese (1993). Black Jewish Relations. *Border/Lines* 29/30: 64–9.

Potts, Lydia (1990). *The World Labour Market: A History of Migration.* London: Zed Books.

Pratt, Mary Louise (1992). *Imperial Eyes: Travel Writing and Transculturation.* London: Routledge.

Radakrishnan, R. (1991). Ethnicity in an Age of Diaspora. *Transition* 54: 104–15.

Rosaldo, Renato (1989). *Culture and Truth: The Remaking of Social Analysis.* Boston: Beacon Press.

Rouse, Roger (1991). Mexican Migration and the Social Space of Postmodernism. *Diaspora* 1(1): 8–23.

Rushdie, Salman (1989). *The Satanic Verses.* New York: Viking.

Safran, William (1991). Diasporas in Modern Societies: Myths of Homeland and Return. *Diaspora* 1(1): 83–99.

Said, Edward (1984). Reflections of Exile. *Granta* 13: 159–72.

——— (1990). Third World Intellectuals and Metropolitan Culture. *Raritan* 9(3): 27–50.

Saldívar, José David (1991). *The Dialectics of Our America: Genealogy, Cultural Critique, and Literary History.* Durham, NC: Duke University Press.

Sassen-Koob, Saskia (1982). Recomposition and Peripherialization at the Core. *Contemporary Marxism* 5: 88–100.

Schiller, Nina Glick, Linda Basch, and Cristina Blanc-Szanton, eds. (1992). *Towards a Transnational Perspective on Migration: Race, Class, Ethnicity, and Nationalism Reconsidered.* New York Academy of Sciences, 645. New York: New York Academy of Sciences.

Shohat, Ella (1988). Sephardim in Israel: Zionism from the Standpoint of its Jewish Victims. *Social Text* 19/20: 3–45.

——— (1989). *Israeli Cinema: East/West and the Politics of Representation.* Austin: University of Texas Press.

——— (1992). Notes on the "Post-Colonial." *Social Text* 41/2: 99–113.

Shyllon, Folarin (1982). Blacks in Britain: A Historical and Analytical Overview. *In Global Dimensions of the African Diaspora.* Joseph E. Harris, ed. Pp. 170–94. Washington, DC: Howard University Press.

Spivak, Gayatri Chakravorty (1989). Who Claims Alterity? In *Remaking History.* Barbara Kruger and Phil Mariani, eds. Pp. 269–92. Seattle: Bay Press.

Sutton, Constance, and Elsa Chaney, eds. (1987). *Caribbean Life in New York City: Sociocultural Dimensions.* New York: Center for Migration Studies.

Taussig, Michael (1986). *Shamanism, Colonialism and the Wild Man: A Study in Terror and Healing.* Chicago: University of Chicago Press.

Teaiwa, Teresia (1993). Between Traveler and Native: The Traveling Native as Performative/Informative Figure. Paper presented at the University of California Humanities Research Institute, Minority Discourse II Conference, Santa Cruz, June.

Tölölian, Khachig (1991). The Nation State and its Others: In Lieu of a Preface. *Diaspora* 1(1): 3–7.

Vega, Ana Lydia (1987). Encancaranublado. In *Encancaranublado y otros cuentos de naufragio.* Pp. 73–9. Rio Piedras, PR: Editorial Antillana.

Velez, Diana L. (In press). Caribbean Counterpoint: The Stories of Ana Lydia Vega. Callaloo.

Weinreich, Max (1967). The Reality of Jewishness Versus the Ghetto Myth: The Sociolinguistic Roots of Yiddish. In *To Honor Roman Jakobson.* Pp. 2199–211. The Hague: Mouton.

West, Cornel (1993). *Race Matters.* Boston: Beacon Press.

Wolff, Janet (1993). On the Road Again: Metaphors of Travel in Cultural Criticism. *Cultural Studies* 7(2): 224–39.

Xiaoping Li (1993). New Chinese Art in Exile. *Border/Lines* 29/30: 40–4.

# 38

## Out Here and Over There: Queerness and Diaspora in Asian(-)American Studies

David L. Eng

To consider the hyphen in Asian American studies requires the investigation of diaspora as a function of queerness. This is queerness not only in the sense of sexual identity and sexual practices; it is also queerness in the sense of a critical methodology for evaluating Asian American racial formation across multiple axes of difference as well as in numerous local and global manifestations. How does queerness as a critical methodology provide a theoretical vantage point for thinking out past, present, and future Asian American political, economic, and cultural practices?

I want to approach these questions by juxtaposing two articles from recent issues of *Amerasia Journal.*[1] In the first volume, a special issue on lesbian, gay, and bisexual topics entitled "Dimensions of Desire: Other Asian and Pacific American Sexualities: Gay, Lesbian and Bisexual Identities and Orientation," Dana Y. Takagi notes in her lead article the potential of gay and lesbian sexual identities to dislodge the ossified masculinist notions of cultural nationalism. She eloquently argues for the need to recognize different sexual identities that also lay claim to the label *Asian American.* By doing so, Takagi insists, we can begin to rethink and reevaluate "notions of identity that have been used, for the most part, unproblematically and uncritically in Asian American studies" since its inception in the early 1970s around the tenets of cultural nationalism. She suggests that we ought to be talking seriously about the junctions of "gay and lesbian sexuality and Asian American Studies" because of the continued "theoretical trouble we encounter in our attempts to situate and think about sexual identity and racial identity" together.[2]

Takagi invokes gay and lesbian sexuality (she does not use the term *queer*) in the sense of sexual identity and practices that gain their meaning through the polarization of an oppositional heterosexuality and homosexuality.[3] To the extent that Asian American cultural nationalism was dependent on an unexamined notion of the "ideal" subject as male and heterosexual, the introduction of gay and lesbian sexuality into Asian American studies challenges this outdated conception of the "proper" Asian American subject by reconsidering racial formation through the lens of sexual multiplicity. However, in gesturing toward the possibility of a dynamic relationship between racial and sexual difference, Takagi's essay also points us in the useful direction of thinking about a potential (albeit unrealized) political project of queerness in Asian American studies neither restricted to nor exhausted by sexual identity and practices. How might we consider queerness as a critical methodology that intersects Asian American identity formation across multiple axes of difference and in highly dynamic ways?

Let me return for a moment to a passage from Lowe's *Immigrant Acts* discussed in the introduction to this volume. In this passage, Lowe notes the ways in which immigration exclusion laws and bars to citizenship not only racialized but also gendered the Asian American subject. "Racialization along the legal axis of definitions of citizenship," Lowe writes, "has also ascribed 'gender' to the Asian American subject. Up until 1870, American citizenship was granted exclusively to white male persons; in 1870, men of African descent could become naturalized, but the bar to citizenship remained for Asian men until the repeal acts of 1943–1952. Whereas the 'masculinity' of the citizen was first inseparable from his 'whiteness,' as the state extended citizenship to nonwhite male persons, it formally designated these subjects as 'male,' as well" (11). Lowe analyzes the ways in which social definitions of maleness are inextricably bound to hegemonic conceptions of whiteness. As such, she provides a provocative model for thinking about Asian American sexual and racial formation not as separate processes of identity formation. Sexuality and race cannot be restricted in singular isolation. To the contrary, they come into existence in and through a dialectical relationship with one another.

Lowe's model thus provides a theoretical grounding that can focus our attention on the dynamic relationship between sexuality and gender formation as they frame and are framed by Asian American racialization processes. The model provides a way for scholars in Asian American studies to consider queerness as a critical methodology based not only on content but on style and form. Thinking about queerness in this way highlights the need for those of us in Asian American studies to understand that legal and cultural discourses on "deviant" sexuality affect not merely those contemporary Asian American subjects who readily self-identify as gay or lesbian (a strict form of identity politics); rather, queerness comes to describe, affect, and encompass a much larger Asian American constituency – whatever their sexual identities or practices – whose historically disavowed status as US citizen-subject under punitive immigration and exclusion laws renders them "queer" as such.

I am sketching a conception of queerness in Asian American studies that exceeds the question of sexuality as a narrowly defined or singular category by considering the ways in which other critical and intersecting axes of difference give legibility to our social identities. From a slightly different angle, I am focusing on a politics of queerness that can function for Asian American studies as a wide method of racial critique, considering at once a network of social difference and political concerns as it dynamically underpins the formation of Asian American subjectivity. This focus on queerness, like our focus on the question of psychoanalysis, implicitly demands the investigation of Asian American racial formation through broad social categories and epistemologies, including (but not limited to) questions of sexuality and sexual identification.

Let me turn now to my second example from *Amerasia Journal* in order to consider how this expanded notion of queerness as a critical methodology for the examination of Asian American subject formation works in conjunction with diaspora in multiple global and local sites. In a special issue "Thinking Theory in Asian American Studies," published on the discipline's twenty-fifth anniversary in the academy, Takagi and Michael Omi (in their roles as guest coeditors) note in their introduction that the

> waning of radical political movements in the 1980s had attendant effects on theory and politics within Asian American Studies. We feel that the absence of a sustained and coherent radical theory of social transformation led to a retreat to more mainstream, discipline-based paradigmatic orientations. Contributing to this trend was the increasing "professionalization" of the field in academic settings, the demands of tenure and promotion for faculty members, and the entrance of newcomers to the field trained in specific disciplines who had not participated in the new social movements of the previous decades. The result of this has been the contraction of space for dialogue across the disciplines – one which could have critically interrogated disciplinary boundaries and fostered cross-disciplinary perspectives.[4]

How does this passage relate to Takagi's earlier claims for Asian American gays and lesbians as well as to my earlier remarks on queerness as a methodology not only attendant to content but to form and style? How might we evaluate Takagi and Omi's observations on the "waning of radical political movements" in Asian American studies in the 1980s against the emergence of queer activism and the AIDS movement during this same historical period?

That two Asian American critics as perceptive as Takagi and Omi fail to consider the historical contributions of Asian Americans to queer activism and the AIDS movement is indicative of the difficulties we still face in Asian American studies systematically to integrate not only issues of (homo)sexuality but issues of queerness into our critical vocabulary and theoretical discussions. This difficulty, I would also note, results from an intransigent failure on the part of mainstream gay and lesbian scholarship to consider queerness in the broader context I have sketched. In its consistent elision of race as a conceptual category for analysis, mainstream gay and lesbian scholarship fails to embrace queerness as a critical methodology for the understanding of sexual identity as it is dynamically formed in and through racial epistemologies. This integration is a crucial project given the alarming ways in which mainstream gay and lesbian political organizations have shaped, for example, current political claims and debates such as gay marriage as issues of civil and equal rights. This shaping, of course, is in opposition to the scaling back and massive attacks on affirmative action for people of color as special rights.)[5]

Takagi and Omi are certainly correct in their suggestion that the 1980s marked a demonstrable shift in Asian American political activism and the Asian American studies movement. Unquestionably, the apotheosis of global capital under the Reagan and Thatcher administrations, the collapse of communism in the Soviet Union and Eastern Europe, and the dismantling of prolabor movements and unions led to a concomitant shift in Asian American studies away from a traditional classbased critique of race.[6] Yet this shift, I would emphasize, might also be thought of as a displacement of progressive Asian American politics – and sustained class-based analyses of racial formation – into new realms of struggle rather than the disappearance or waning of radical political movements. This is not to say that issues of class should no longer be vigilantly pursued in their new global and local configurations but that our interrogation of Asian American racial formation must also be mediated by analyses of other forms of domination.

Globalization has shifted current frameworks of resistance. Therefore, we in Asian American studies cannot ignore the rise of queer activism (as well as critical debates on multiculturalism and Cultural Studies) in the 1980s as a visible and oppositional political movement.[7] If the global restructuring of capital in the 1980s dismantled a traditional class-based critique of race as the foundation for "radical political movements" in Asian American studies, we must consider how this attack on the field of progressive politics relates to the rise of queer activism and its critique of subject formation as a viable strategic alternative to a transformative Asian American political platform.[8] How does queer studies' critique of the subject come to function as a displaced marker for more traditional class-based analyses of race in Asian American studies?

To the extent that Takagi recognizes (in "Maiden Voyage") the dislodging of Asian American identity from its cultural nationalist moorings as a function of "gay and lesbian" sexualities, she offers a way for us to reconsider Asian American subjectivity in more capacious ways. Indeed, the now familiar critique of the subject of Asian American cultural nationalism as equating political efficacy not with particularity and difference but with similarity and unity as the basis for social action traces much of its theoretical roots to work done in queer (as well as feminist) activism and Cultural Studies during this time. Queerness, then, can help us to articulate how Asian American sexual, racial, and class formations come into existence in relation to one another. To the extent, however, that Takagi and Omi (in "Thinking Theory") overlook queer activism's ascendant role in oppositional politics in the 1980s, they miss the opportunity to understand queerness as it intersects with Asian American studies – queerness as a critical methodology that promises to open up a much broader set of Asian American identities as well as a more extensive set of Asian American concerns and locations.

How does Asian American queerness function not just in terms of identities but in terms of locations? If global restructuring of capital in the 1980s worked to clear the discursive field of oppositional class politics for a queer critique of the subject as one of progressive politics's new sites, then we must recognize and evaluate this displacement. This is a contemporary displacement, I reiterate, that emphasizes sexuality and globalization – queerness and diaspora – in Asian American studies. If earlier Asian American cultural nationalist projects were built on the political strategy of claiming home and nation-state through the domestic and the hetero-sexual, a new political project of thinking about this concept in Asian American studies today would seem to center around queerness and diaspora – its rethinking of home and nation-state across multiple identity formations and numerous locations "out here" and "over there." In the beginning of the new millennium, queerness and diaspora should be used not only to reevaluate the past but to orient the future development of Asian American political projects and strategies whose claims on a politics of social transformation can be acknowledged as such. This moment should be marked by a definitive shift away from a politics of cultural nationalism to a politics of transnational culturalism.

How might these various theoretical speculations on queerness and diaspora in Asian American studies appear in a material context? What might a queer Asian American in a globalized frame look like? I end this chapter with a brief analysis: Ang Lee's 1993 film, *The Wedding Banquet*.[9] Ang's transnational film provides us with one model for thinking about the possibilities – and ultimate limitations – of an emergent queer and diasporic Asian American male identity. [ ... ]

## ■ The Wedding Banquet ■

At first glance Gao Wai-Tung (played by Winston Chao) in Ang Lee's *The Wedding Banquet* provides what might be considered to be an unprecedented representation of Asian American male identity within the domestic sphere of the US nation-state. Considering the immigrant's queer and diasporic status with regard to his domes-tic situation in the urban metropole of New York City yields a rather startling picture that diverges from mainstream stereotypes of Asian American men as well as dominant portrayals of them in the popular gay press and media.[10]

Reviewing the film upon its release in 1993, I noted that *The Wedding Banquet* was the first wide-release motion picture in this country that significantly recon-figured the dominant Rice Queen dynamic so prevalent in the mainstream gay community. This stereotype, explored in chapter three's discussion of *M. Butterfly*, relies upon the racist coupling of passive gay Asian (American) men – the continu-ous recirculation of Puccini's *Madama Butterfly* fantasy – with objectionable Rice Queens – white men attracted to gay Asian (American) men through their orien-talized fantasies of submissive "bottoms."[11] That *The Wedding Banquet* signifi-cantly revises this Rice Queen dynamic, depicting a successful, savvy, and handsome Asian male who is not in a relationship of economic dependence with a homely white man twice his age, marks a laudable departure from the pervasive stereotype of the white daddy and the Asian houseboy endemic to mainstream gay culture. In my mind, Lee's innovative portrayal inaugurates a potential (though ultimately unfulfilled) shift of a stereotypical Asian American gay male image away from normative domestic representations toward a queer and diasporic formation. It is this detour through queerness, coupled with this turn toward the global, that takes us someplace new in terms of the dominant domestic image-repertoire. *The Wedding Banquet* challenges traditional stereotypes of Asian American men by instituting a new set of potentially enabling representations.

In light of our discussion about the vexed claims of both Asian Americans and queers on home and the nation-state, Wai-Tung's portrayal in *The Wedding Banquet* is notable for the fact that he is enfranchised as a US citizen. Given the long national history of Chinese exclusion and barriers to US citizenship, Lee's rendering of Wai-Tung as citizen verges on – indeed, becomes dependent upon – the queer. Through his ability to claim the domestic space of the US nation-state as a legitimate home – and through his ability to be legally recognized in his claims – queerness and diaspora emerge in Lee's film as a new and privileged form of Asian American male subjectivity. Earlier I asked what a diaspora organized in terms of sexuality, and not just racial or ethnic dispersion, might offer. This expansion of citizenship and legal claims through the combination of queerness and diaspora is one potential yield. Furthermore, it is important to note that not only is Wai-Tung enfranchised as a US citizen, it is through his diasporic queerness that Wei-Wei (played by May Chin) obtains her coveted green card and her own legal status – a reframing of Asian American identity outside of traditional heterosexual and white domestic familial configurations. This reconfiguration and reworking of kinship lines is another unexpected material consequence of queerness and diaspora's unpredictable combination. It is another way in which Lee's attention to a queer diaspora expands the conventional image-repertoire by reworking its representations through a challenge to its traditional exclusions.

Nevertheless, we must remember, it is also precisely because of the conflicted affiliations that constitute Wai-Tung's queer and diasporic positioning that he is impelled to accept a staged heterosexual marriage to Wei-Wei. Under the constant goading of his heir-demanding parents (played by Lung Sihung and Gua Ah-la), who still reside in Taiwan, Wai-Tung finally acquiesces to the fake marriage and tax break orchestrated by his white lover Simon (played by Mitchell Lichtenstein). Ultimately, the creation of a queer diaspora and a new multicultural queer family organized by and around this new type of Asian American male subjectivity are qualified by the demands of enduring heterosexual filiative imperatives. In this manner, *The Wedding Banquet* might better be thought of less as a film that inaugurates a successful queer and diasporic Asian American male subjectivity than as one that is set in motion by the very question of queerness and diaspora. Queerness and diaspora function as signs for the very confusion of Asian American identity that Lee's film strives to institute, investigate, and resolve.

Might we think of this rather unprecedented portrayal of Wai-Tung in the realm of the domestic space of the nation-state as one only purchased in the global arena of liberal capitalism through the rescripting of a quotidian patriarchal narrative? In a compelling reading of *The Wedding Banquet*, Mark Chiang considers the diasporic representations of the film in light of its domestic dimensions, noting that the film's resolution "depends most intently upon the disciplining of Wei-Wei as the figure of resistance, so that it is only Wai-Tung's impregnation of her, which turns out to be the mechanism of his control over her, that allows the ending to take place in a configuration that resolves the conflicts between the men. The consolidation of a transnational patriarchy of capital is fundamentally dependent upon the subordination of women and labor, and women and labor are conflated in the film, so that woman becomes the very sign of labor."[12] Wai-Tung's position as enfranchised citizen of the US nation-state (and a subject of capital) is made possible only through his subordination of the diasporic Third World woman (as an object of capital). Emancipation for Wei-Wei – her escape from the global underclass of undocumented workers and migrant laborers – comes up against emancipation for Wai-Tung, whose fulfillment of his Chinese father's paternal mandate demands her acquiescence to keep and not abort their (male) child.[13]

This purchase of queer Asian American citizenship is brokered on the level of the global, enabled only through Wai-Tung's complicit relationship with the transnational management of capital, resources, and labor.[14] This management of capital thus qualifies the potential of a progressive queer and diasporic political project for social transformation. After all, only by gaining control over Wei-Wei's material (Wai-Tung is her slumlord and thereby controls her claims on home) and reproductive labor is Wai-Tung able to secure his own claims within the borders of the US nation-state as a legitimate home. As such, queer and feminist discourses are also at odds when considered against the domestic and the diasporic dimensions of *The Wedding Banquet*. Wai-Tung's (potential) queerness comes to organize a host of conflicting differences – sexual, gender, race, class, and space – shutting down the position of the Third World woman through its expansion into both local and global capitalist arenas.

Like the earlier Asian American cultural nationalist project, Wai-Tung's access to the domestic space of a public US nation-state finally depends upon queer control over and possession of a devalued feminine realm – Wei-Wei's home, privacy, body, labor, and child. Hence, we might describe queer diaspora in *The Wedding Banquet* as a formation that rescripts a domestic patriarchal narrative of home and nation-state, of private and public, on a global scale. To think about the queer and diasporic formation of Asian American male subjectivity in *The Wedding Banquet* is to understand that the domestic tranquility that marks the end of the film has been purchased at a high price, one borne by the figure of the Third World woman. This is a model of queer and diasporic Asian American subjectivity that, as Sau-ling Cynthia Wong suggests, might be far more useful if critiqued as "*modes* rather than *phases*" of identity, a cleaving of queerness and diaspora that cannot be "lauded as a culmination" over the domestic or feminine, "a stage more advanced or more capacious."[15]

Ultimately, *The Wedding Banquet* provides a qualified model of a progressive queer and diasporic Asian American male subjectivity; queerness and diaspora in Lee's film do not constitute any inherent challenge to local and global status quos. *The Wedding Banquet* provides a new model for thinking about the numerous pitfalls of queerness and diaspora as an integral mode of Asian American domestic claims to home and nation-state at the turn of this past century. At the same time, this model requires vigilant critical scrutiny for the enabling positions as well as the disabling violences it effects. It is a tortured model that recontextualizes our very notions of Asian American citizenship in both the larger global arena and the domestic realm of a liberal, capitalist, US nation-state, which today is rapidly and urgently (re)consolidating itself as the preeminent and unforgiving bastion of economic freedom, straightness, and whiteness.

## NOTES

1   *Amerasia Journal* is one of the oldest serial publications in the field of Asian American studies. Founded at Yale University, it is now housed at UCLA's Center for Asian American Studies.

2   Dana Takagi, "Maiden Voyage: Excursions into Sexuality and Identity Politics in Asian America," *Amerasia Journal* 20.1 (1994): 2.

3   I use *gay* and *lesbian* to describe the largely identity-based political and academic movements that arose after Stonewall in response to the dominant, pathologizing medico-legal discourse of the "homosexual." In its publicness, as Rosalind Morris suggests, the notion of gay is often conflated with the issue of same-sex practices – practices that are often thought to be symptomatic of identity. I differentiate *gay* and *lesbian* from the term *queer*, which I believe eschews a political platform based exclusively on sexual identity and practices, and the polarization of homo- and heterosexuality. Use of the term *queer* is not just generational; as Michael Warner points out, " 'queer' gets a critical edge by defining itself against the normal rather than the heterosexual" (Introduction to *Fear of a Queer Planet: Queer Politics and Social Theory*, ed. Michael Warner [Minneapolis: University of Minnesota Press, 1993], xxvi). Initially a designation of terror and shame, *queer* in contemporary usage has been resignified in a rather open and capacious context – one that can be used simultaneously to discuss the politics of the personal, to question a spectrum of personal identities, to act against normalizing ideologies, and to resist the historical terror of social phobia and violence. We must remember that *gay*, *lesbian*, and *queer* are not mutually exclusive terms. Gayness might provide an ideal, though not exclusive, grounds for queer practices, and queers can often be "lesbians and gays in other contexts – as for example where leverage can be gained through bourgeois propriety, or through minority-rights discourse, or through more gender-marked language (it probably won't replace lesbian feminism)" (Warner, *Queer Planet*, xxviii). While *queer* has been used as a shorthand term to name a population of individuals with a stake in nonnormative, oppositional politics, the term also harbors homogenizing impulses that serve to erase some of the racial and gendered differences (lesbian feminism being one example) that I explore in this chapter.

4   Michael Omi and Dana Takagi, "Introduction: Thinking Theory in Asian American Studies," *Amerasia Journal*, 21(1) (1995): xiii.

5   Certainly not immune to similar accusations concerning the co-optation of special rights, members of mainstream gay and lesbian organizations must think through the particular political difficulties and contradictory agendas that national issues like gay marriage and affirmative action pose, both for individual queers of color who hold multiple affiliations with various political causes and for the politics of coalition building. The consideration of Asian American identity in a queer and diasporic

context is complicated by mainstream gay and lesbian activism's resistance to theorizing itself outside of US national borders. That the dominant focus of current gay and lesbian activism is on domestic issues and the claiming of equal rights obscures the international genealogy of queer activism and its reliance on the global. In claiming equal rights and access to the queer nation, queer activism reifies the US nation-state as the privileged site for oppositional politics in ways reminiscent of the Asian American cultural nationalist project, which calls for vigilant interrogation.

6 See Masao Miyoshi, "A Borderless World? From Colonialism to Transnationalism and the Decline of the Nation-State," *Critical Inquiry* 19 (1993): 726–51, for a concise summary of the economic and political shifts in the 1980s that allowed for the rampant spread of multinational capital and the global restructuring of these economic resources as transnational institutions.

7 However, given the current mainstreaming of the gay and lesbian movement and the waning public attention to the AIDS crisis, the future of queer activism looks rather bleak.

8 The gay and lesbian liberation movement that emerged following the Stonewall era was largely based on a politics restricted to sexual identity and practices. The new queer social movements are often based, instead, on the critique of identity politics and the discursive production of the subject. Queer activism's critique of the subject and its reorganization of coalitional interests along the lines of political goals needs to be considered in the context of racial differences.

9 *The Wedding Banquet*, dir. Ang Lee (Taipei: Central Motion Pictures Corporation, 1993).

10 See filmmaker Richard Fung's "Looking for My Penis: The Eroticized Asian in Gay Porn Video," in *How Do I Look?* ed. Bad Object Choices (Seattle: Bay Press, 1991), 145–60 (and chapter 18 in the present volume). Fung writes that in Western society "the Asian man is defined by a striking absence down there. And if Asian men have no sexuality, how can we have homosexuality?" (148). In the mainstream heterosexual community, Asian American men have had to contend with the pervasive stereotype of themselves as the "emasculated sissy" (Frank Chin's Charlie Chan and Fu Manchu syndrome). These mainstream portrayals of enervated Asian American members recirculate within gay communities, where queer Asian American men find themselves repositioned as passive and feminized "bottoms" – impotent Cio-Cio-Sans plucked from the orientalized stages of *Madama Butterfly*.

11 David L. Eng, "*The Wedding Banquet*: You're Not Invited and Some Other Ancillary Thoughts," *Artspiral* 7 (fall 1993): 8–10.

12 Mark Chiang, "Coming out into the Global System: Postmodern Patriarchies and Transnational Sexualities in *The Wedding Banquet*," in *Q & A: Queer in Asian America*, eds. David L. Eng and Alice Y. Hom (Philadelphia: Temple University Press, 1998), 383.

13 Chiang adds that the "multicultural, non-heterosexual family formed by Wai-Tung and Simon at the end of the film is in sharp contrast to the representation of women's liberation offered to Wei-Wei. Although it is unclear what kind of arrangement she and Wai Tung will eventually come to, the decision to keep the baby drastically reduces her options, foreclosing the possibility of withdrawal from the global system" (ibid., 384).

14 Leslie Sklair labels this class of global citizen the transnational capitalist class. See Leslie Sklair, *Sociology of the Global System*, 2d ed. (Baltimore: Johns Hopkins University Press, 1995).

15 Sau-ling C. Wong, "Denationalization Reconsidered: Asian American Cultural Criticism at a Theoretical Crossroads," *Amerasia Journal* 21(1) (1995): 17; Wong's emphasis.

# 39

# Situating Accented Cinema

## Hamid Naficy

## ▩ Accented Filmmakers ▩

The exilic and diasporic filmmakers discussed here are "situated but universal" figures who work in the interstices of social formations and cinematic practices. A majority are from Third World and postcolonial countries (or from the global South) who since the 1960s have relocated to northern cosmopolitan centers where they exist in a state of tension and dissension with both their original and their current homes. By and large, they operate independently, outside the studio system or the mainstream film industries, using interstitial and collective modes of production that critique those entities. As a result, they are presumed to be more prone to the tensions of marginality and difference. While they share these characteristics, the very existence of the tensions and differences helps prevent accented filmmakers from becoming a homogeneous group or a film movement. And while their films encode these tensions and differences, they are not neatly resolved by familiar narrative and generic schemas – hence, their grouping under accented style. The variations among the films are driven by many factors, while their similarities stem principally from what the filmmakers have in common: liminal subjectivity and interstitial location in society and the film industry. What constitutes the accented style is the combination and intersection of these variations and similarities.

Accented filmmakers came to live and make films in the West in two general groupings. The first group was displaced or lured to the West from the late 1950s to the mid-1970s by Third World decolonization, wars of national liberation, the Soviet Union's invasions of Poland and Czechoslovakia, Westernization, and a kind of "internal decolonization" in the West itself, involving various civil rights, counterculture, and antiwar movements. Indeed, as Fredric Jameson notes, the beginning of the period called "the sixties" must be located in the Third World decolonization that so profoundly influenced the First World sociopolitical movements (1984, 180). The second group emerged in the 1980s and 1990s as a result of the failure of nationalism, socialism, and communism; the ruptures caused by the emergence of postindustrial global economies, the rise of militant forms of Islam, the return of religious and ethnic wars, and the fragmentation of nation-states; the changes in the European, Australian, and American immigration policies encouraging non-Western immigration; and the unprecedented technological developments and consolidation in computers and media. Accented filmmakers are the products of this dual postcolonial displacement and postmodern or late modern scattering. Because of their displacement from the margins to the centers, they have become subjects in world history. They have earned the right to speak and have dared to capture the means of representation. However marginalized they are within the center, their ability to access the means of *reproduction* may prove to be as empowering to the marginalia of the postindustrial era as the capturing of the means of *production* would have been to the subalterns of the industrial era.

It is helpful, when mapping the accented cinema, to differentiate three types of film that constitute it: exilic, diasporic, and ethnic. These distinctions are not hard-and-fast. A few films fall naturally within one of these classifications, while the majority share the characteristics of all three in different measures. Within each type, too, there are subdivisions. In addition, in the course of their careers, many filmmakers move not only from country to country but also from making one type of film to making another type, in tandem with the trajectory of their own travels of identity and those of their primary community.

## Exilic filmmakers

Traditionally, exile is taken to mean banishment for a particular offense, with a prohibition of return. Exile can be internal or external, depending on the location to which one is banished. The tremendous toll that internal exile, restrictions, deprivations, and censorship in totalitarian countries have taken on filmmakers has been widely publicized. What has been analyzed less is the way such constraints, by challenging the filmmakers, force them to develop an authorial style. Many filmmakers who could escape internal exile refuse to do so in order to fight the good fight at home – a fight that often defines not only their film style but also their identity as oppositional figures of some stature. By working under an internal regime of exile, they choose their "site of struggle" and their potential social transformation (Harlow 1991, 150). When they speak from this site at home, they have an impact, even if, and often because, they are punished for it. In fact, interrogation, censorship, and jailing are all proof that they have been heard. But if they move out into external exile in the West, where they have the political freedom to speak, no one may hear them among the cacophony of voices competing for attention in the market. In that case, Gayatri Spivak's famous question "Can the subaltern speak?" will have to be reworded to ask, "Can the subaltern be heard?" Because of globalization, the internal and external exiles of one country are not sealed off from each other. In fact, there is much traffic and exchange between them.

In this study, the term "exile" refers principally to external exiles: individuals or groups who voluntarily or involuntarily have left their country of origin and who maintain an ambivalent relationship with their previous and current places and cultures. Although they do not return to their homelands, they maintain an intense desire to do so – a desire that is projected in potent return narratives in their films. In the meantime, they memorialize the homeland by fetishizing it in the form of cathected sounds, images, and chronotopes that are circulated intertextually in exilic popular culture, including in films and music videos. The exiles' primary relationship, in short, is with their countries and cultures of origin and with the sight, sound, taste, and feel of an originary experience, of an elsewhere at other times. Exiles, especially those filmmakers who have been forcibly driven away, tend to want to define, at least during the liminal period of displacement, all things in their lives not only in relationship to the homeland but also in strictly political terms. As a result, in their early films they tend to represent their homelands and people more than themselves.

The authority of the exiles as filmmaking authors is derived from their position as subjects inhabiting interstitial spaces and sites of struggle. Indeed, all great authorship is predicated on distance – banishment and exile of sorts – from the larger society. The resulting tensions and ambivalences produce the complexity and the intensity that are so characteristic of great works of art and literature. In the same way that sexual taboo permits procreation, exilic banishment encourages creativity.[1] Of course, not all exilic subjects produce great or lasting art, but many of the greatest and most enduring works of literature and cinema have been created by displaced writers and filmmakers. But exile can result in an agonistic form of liminality characterized by oscillation between the extremes. It is a slipzone of anxiety and imperfection, where life hovers between the heights of ecstasy and confidence and the depths of despondency and doubt.[2]

For external exiles the descent relations with the homeland and the consent relations with the host society are continually tested. Freed from old and new, they are "deterritorialized," yet they continue to be in the grip of both the old and the new, the before and the after. Located in such a slipzone, they can be suffused with hybrid excess, or they may feel deeply deprived and divided, even fragmented. Lithuanian filmmaker and poet Jonas Mekas, who spent some four years in European displaced persons camps before landing in the United States, explained his feelings of fragmentation in the following manner:

> Everything that I believed in shook to the foundations – all my idealism, and my faith in the goodness of man and progress of man – all was shattered. Somehow, I managed to keep myself together. But really, I wasn't one piece any longer; I was one thousand painful pieces. . . . And I wasn't surprised when, upon my arrival in New York, I found others who felt as I felt. There were poets, and film-makers, and painters – people who were also walking like one thousand painful pieces. (quoted in O'Grady 1973, 229)

Neither the hybrid fusion nor the fragmentation is total, permanent, or painless. On the one hand, like Derridian "undecidables," the new exiles can be "both and neither": the pharmacon, meaning both poison and remedy; the hymen, meaning both membrane and its violation; and the supplement, meaning both addition and replacement (quoted in Bauman 1991, 145–6). On the other hand, they could aptly be called, in Salman Rushdie's words, "at once plural and partial" (1991, 15). As partial, fragmented, and multiple subjects, these filmmakers are capable of producing ambiguity and doubt about the taken-for-granted values of their home and host societies. They can also transcend and transform themselves to produce hybridized, syncretic, performed, or virtual identities. None of these constructed and impure identities are risk-free, however, as the Ayatollah Khomeini's death threat against Salman Rushdie glaringly pointed out.[3]

Not all transnational exiles, of course, savor fundamental doubt, strive toward hybridized and performative self-fashioning, or reach for utopian or virtual imaginings. However, for those who remain in the enduring and endearing crises and tensions of exilic migrancy, liminality and interstitiality may become passionate sources of creativity and dynamism that produce in literature and cinema the likes of James Joyce and Marguerite Duras, Joseph Conrad and Fernando Solanas, Ezra Pound and Trinh T. Minh-ha, Samuel Beckett and Sohrab Shahid Saless, Salman Rushdie and Andrei Tarkovsky, Garcia Marquez and Atom Egoyan, Vladimir Nabokov and Raúl Ruiz, Gertrude Stein and Michel Khleifi, Assia Djebar and Jonas Mekas.

Many exilic filmmakers and groups of filmmakers are discussed in this book – Latin American, Lithuanian, Iranian, Turkish, Palestinian, and Russian. They are not all equally or similarly exiled, and there are vast differences even among filmmakers from a single originating country.

### Diasporic filmmakers

Originally, "diaspora" referred to the dispersion of the Greeks after the destruction of the city of Aegina, to the Jews after their Babylonian exile, and to the Armenians after Persian and Turkish invasions and expulsion in the mid-sixteenth century. The classic paradigm of diaspora has involved the Jews, but as Peters (1999), Cohen (1997), Tölölyan (1996), Clifford (1997, 244–77), Naficy (1993), and Safran (1991) have argued, the definition should no longer be limited to the dispersion of the Jews, for myriad peoples have historically undergone sustained dispersions – a process that continues on a massive scale today. The term has been taken up by other displaced peoples, among them African-Americans in the United States and Afro-Caribbeans in England, to describe their abduction from their African homes and their forced dispersion to the new world (Gilroy 1993, 1991, 1988; Mercer 1994a, 1994b, 1988; Hall 1988). In these and other recodings, the concept of diaspora has become much closer to exile. Consequently, as Khachig Tölölyan notes, "diaspora" has lost some of its former specificity and precision to become a "promiscuously capacious category that is taken to include all the adjacent phenomena to which it is linked but from which it actually differs in ways that are constitutive" (1996, 8).

Here I will briefly point out the similarities and differences between exile and diaspora that inform this work. Diaspora, like exile, often begins with trauma, rupture, and coercion, and it involves the scattering of populations to places outside their homeland. Sometimes, however, the scattering is caused by a desire for increased trade, for work, or for colonial and imperial pursuits. Consequently, diasporic movements can be classified according to their motivating factors. Robin Cohen (1997) suggested the following classifications and examples: victim/refugee diasporas (exemplified by the Jews, Africans, and Armenians); labor/service diasporas (Indians); trade/business diasporas (Chinese and Lebanese); imperial/colonial diasporas (British, Russian); and cultural/hybrid diasporas (Caribbeans). Like the exiles, people in diaspora have an identity in their homeland *before* their departure, and their diasporic identity is constructed in resonance with this prior identity. However, unlike exile, which may be individualistic or collective, diaspora is necessarily collective, in both its origination and its destination. As a result, the nurturing of a collective memory, often of an idealized homeland, is constitutive of the diasporic identity. This idealization may be state-based, involving love for an existing homeland, or it may be stateless, based on a desire for a homeland yet to come. The Armenian diaspora before and after the Soviet era has been state-based, whereas the Palestinian diaspora since the 1948 creation of Israel has been stateless, driven by the Palestinians' desire to create a sovereign state.

People in diaspora, moreover, maintain a long-term sense of ethnic consciousness and distinctiveness, which is consolidated by the periodic hostility of either the original home or the host societies toward them. However, unlike the exiles whose identity entails a vertical and primary relationship with their homeland, diasporic consciousness is horizontal and multisited, involving not only the homeland but also the compatriot communities elsewhere. As a result, plurality, multiplicity, and hybridity are structured in dominance among the diasporans, while among the political exiles, binarism and duality rule.

These differences tend to shape exilic and diasporic films differently. Diasporized filmmakers tend to be centered less than the exiled filmmakers on a cathected relationship with a single homeland and on a claim that they represent it and its people. As a result, their works are expressed less in the narratives of retrospection, loss, and absence or in strictly partisanal political terms. Their films are accented more fully than those of the exiles by the plurality and performativity of identity. In short, while binarism and subtraction in particular accent exilic films, diasporic films are accented more by multiplicity and addition. Many diasporic filmmakers are discussed here individually, among them Armenians. Black and Asian British filmmakers are discussed collectively.

## Postcolonial ethnic and identity filmmakers

Although exilic, diasporic, and ethnic communities all patrol their real and symbolic boundaries to maintain a measure of collective identity that distinguishes them from the ruling strata and ideologies, they differ from one another principally by the relative strength of their attachment to compatriot communities. The postcolonial ethnic and identity filmmakers are both ethnic and diasporic; but they differ from the poststudio American ethnics, such as Woody Allen, Francis Ford Coppola, and Martin Scorsese, in that many of them are either immigrants themselves or have been born in the West since the 1960s to nonwhite, non-Western, postcolonial émigrés. They also differ from the diasporic filmmakers in their emphasis on their ethnic and racial identity within the host country.

The different emphasis on the relationship to place creates differently accented films. Thus, exilic cinema is dominated by its focus on there and then in the homeland, diasporic cinema by its vertical relationship to the homeland and by its lateral relationship to the diaspora communities and experiences, and postcolonial ethnic and identity cinema by the exigencies of life here and now in the country in which the filmmakers reside. As a result of their focus on the here and now, ethnic identity films tend to deal with what Werner Sollors has characterized as "the central drama in American culture," which emerges from the conflict between descent relations, emphasizing bloodline and ethnicity, and consent relations, stressing self-made, contractual affiliations (1986, 6). In other words, while the former is concerned with being, the latter is concerned with becoming; while the former is conciliatory, the latter is contestatory. Although such a drama is also present to some extent in exilic and diasporic films, the hostland location of the drama makes the ethnic and identity films different from the other two categories, whose narratives are often centered elsewhere.

Some of the key problematics of the postcolonial ethnic and identity cinema are encoded in the "politics of the hyphen." Recognized as a crucial marker of ethnicity and authenticity in a multicultural America, group terms such as black, Chicano/a, Oriental, and people of color have gradually been replaced by hyphenated terms such as African-American, Latino-American, and Asian-American. Identity cinema's adoption of the hyphen is seen as a marker of resistance to the homogenizing and hegemonizing power of the American melting pot ideology. However, retaining the hyphen has a number of negative connotations, too. The hyphen may imply a lack, or the idea that hyphenated people are somehow subordinate to unhyphenated people, or that they are "equal but not quite," or that they will never be totally accepted or trusted as full citizens. In addition, it may suggest a divided allegiance, which is a painful reminder to certain groups of American citizens.[4] The hyphen may also suggest a divided mind, an irrevocably split identity, or a type of paralysis between two cultures or nations. Finally, the hyphen can feed into nativist discourses that assume authentic essences that lie outside ideology and predate, or stand apart from, the nation.

In its nativist adoption, the hyphen provides vertical links that emphasize descent relations, roots, depth, inheritance, continuity, homogeneity, and stability. These are allegorized in family sagas and mother-daughter and generational conflict narratives of Chinese-American films such as Wayne Wang's *Eat a Bowl of Tea* (1989) and *The Joy Luck Club* (1993). The filmmakers' task in this modality, in Stuart Hall's words, is "to discover, excavate, bring to light and express through cinematic representation" that inherited collective cultural identity, that "one true self" (1994, 393). In its contestatory adoption, the hyphen can operate horizontally, highlighting consent relations, disruption, heterogeneity, slippage, and mediation, as in Trinh T. Minh-ha's *Surname Viet Given Name Nam* (1985) and Srinivas Krishna's *Masala* (1990). In this modality, filmmakers do not recover an existing past or impose an imaginary and often fetishized coherence on their fragmented experiences and histories. Rather, by emphasizing discontinuity and specificity, they demonstrate that they are in the process of becoming, that they are "subject to the continuous 'play' of history, culture and power" (Hall 1994, 394). Christine Choy and Rene Tajima's award-winning film *Who Killed Vincent Chin?* (1988) is really a treatise on the problematic of the hyphen in the Asian-American context, as it centers on the murder of a Chinese-American by out-of-work white Detroit autoworkers who, resentful of Japanese car imports, mistook him for being Japanese.

Read as a sign of hybridized, multiple, or constructed identity, the hyphen can become liberating because it can be performed and signified upon. Each hyphen is in reality a nested hyphen, consisting of a number of other intersecting and overlapping hyphens that provide inter- and intraethnic and national links. This fragmentation and multiplication can work against essentialism, nationalism, and dyadism. Faced with too many options and meanings, however, some have suggested removing the hyphen, while others have proposed replacing it with a plus sign.[5] Martin Scorsese's *ITALIANAMERICAN* (1974) cleverly removes the hyphen and the space and instead joins the "Italian" with the "American" to suggest a fused third term. The film title by this most ethnic of New Hollywood cinema directors posits that there is no Italianness that precedes or stands apart from Americanness. In this book, I have retained the hyphen, since this is the most popular form of writing these compound ethnic designations.

The compound terms that bracket the hyphen also present problems, for at the same time that each term produces symbolic alliance among disparate members of a group, it tends to elide their diversity and specificity. "Asian-American," for example, encompasses people from such culturally and nationally diverse roots as the Philippines, Vietnam, Cambodia, Korea, Japan, Thailand, China, Laos, Taiwan, Indonesia, Malaysia, India, Bangladesh, and Pakistan. To calibrate the term, such unwieldy terms as "Southeast Asian diasporas" have also been created. Similar processes and politics of naming have been tried for the "black" British filmmakers.

Independent film distributors, such as Third World Newsreel, Icarus-First Run Films, and Women Make Movies, exploit the hyphen and the politics of the identity cinema by classifying these films thematically or by their hyphenated designation. Such classifications create targets of opportunity for those interested in such films, but they also narrow the marketing and critical discourses about these films by encouraging audiences to read them in terms of their ethnic content and identity politics more than their authorial vision and stylistic innovations. Several postcolonial ethnic and identity filmmakers are discussed individually and collectively.

Diaspora, exile, and ethnicity are not steady states; rather, they are fluid processes that under certain circumstances may transform into one another and beyond. There is also no direct and predetermined progression from exile to ethnicity, although dominant ideological and economic apparatuses tend to favor an assimilationist trajectory – from exile to diaspora to ethnic to citizen to consumer.

## ■ Mapping Accented Cinema's Corpus ■

It may be difficult to appreciate the geographic dispersion and the massive size of the accented cinema and the wide range of films that it has produced since the 1960s. To get a grip on this amorphous entity, I conducted a case study of Middle Eastern and North African accented filmmakers, a summary of which is presented in the following close-up section.

### Close-up: Middle Eastern and North African filmmakers

These filmmakers are a prime example of the new postcolonial, Third World, and non-Western populations in the West whose work forms the accented cinema. Although their emigration to Europe and the Americas is not new, there has been a massive surge in their transplantation since the 1960s. Accurate figures for their various population types (refugees, émigrés, exiles, etc.) are difficult to obtain and vary based on the definition of each type and the data sources that are consulted. In the United States, the 1990 Census Bureau data showed that the total number of those who trace their ancestry to the Middle East is nearly 2 million (exact figure: 1,731,000) out of a total US population of approximately 250 million. Among these, there are 921,000 Arabs, 308,000 Armenians, 260,000 Iranians, and 117,000 Israelis. The largest concentration of Middle Easterners in the United States, and in the Western world, some 300,000 people, is found in Los Angeles (Bozorgmehr, Der-Martirosian, and Sabagh 1996).

The Middle Eastern and North African filmmakers form a surprisingly large and diverse group, numbering 321 filmmakers from 16 sending countries who made at least 920 films in 27 receiving countries, mostly in Europe and North America.[6] In terms of output, Iranian filmmakers topped the list (with 307 films), followed by Armenians (235), Algerians (107), Lebanese (46), Palestinians (35), Turks (25), Moroccans (25), Tunisians (23), and Israeli/Jewish filmmakers (24). The majority of the filmmakers were men, reflecting the dominance of patriarchy within the sending nations and the general pattern of migrations worldwide, which have favored the emigration of men ahead of their families to establish a beachhead for chain migration. This gender imbalance also reflects the belief, common to many Middle Eastern and North African societies, that cinema is not a socially acceptable, religiously sanctioned, and economically feasible enterprise for women. The patriarchal ideologies of the receiving countries, too, contributed to women's underrepresentation.

The historical factors that caused the migration and the density, variety, and cultural and economic capital of the displaced populations in the receiving countries are factors that favored accented filmmaking. Algerian filmmakers made their films almost exclusively in France, the country that until 1961 colonized Algeria and to which Algerians emigrated in massive numbers after their independence. Likewise, the majority of Turkish filmmakers worked in Germany, where historical relationship favored Turkish guest workers. On the other hand, Armenians made films in a number of European and North American countries, commensurate with their worldwide diaspora. Likewise, a social revolution dispersed many affluent Iranians to North America, where they made most of their films. European countries with receptive immigration policies toward Iranians, such as France, Germany, Holland, and Sweden, also proved favorable to the filmmakers.

The accented filmmakers' films, too, form a highly diverse corpus, as many of them are transnationally funded and are multilingual and intercultural. They range widely in types, from amateur films to feature fiction films, and from animated films to documentaries to avant-garde video (television films and series were not considered).

The magnitude, diversity, and geographic reach of the Middle Eastern and North African immigration give us an idea of the larger scattering of the peoples across the globe and of the movement of cultural and intellectual capital from the Third World to the First World.[7] Clearly, we are facing a mammoth, emergent, transnational film movement and film style. However, unlike most film movements and styles of the past, the accented cinema is not monolithic, cohesive, centralized, or hierarchized. Rather, it is simultaneously global and local, and it exists in chaotic semiautonomous pockets in symbiosis with the dominant and other alternative cinemas.

## ■ The Stylistic Approach ■

How films are conceived and received has a lot to do with how they are framed discursively. Sometimes the films of great transplanted directors, such as Alfred Hitchcock, Luis Buñuel, and Jean-Luc Godard, are framed within the "international" cinema category.[8] Most often, they are classified within either the national cinemas of their host countries or the established film genres and styles. Thus, the films of F. W. Murnau, Douglas Sirk, George Cukor, Vincent Minnelli, and Fritz Lang are usually considered as exemplars of the American cinema, the classical Hollywood style, or the melodrama and noir genres. Of course, the works of these and other established directors are also discussed under the rubric of "auteurism." Alternatively, many independent exiled filmmakers who make films about exile and their homelands' cultures and politics (such as Abid Med Hondo, Michel Khleifi, Mira Nair, and Ghasem Ebrahimian) or those minority filmmakers who make films about their ethnic communities (Rea Tajiri, Charles Burnett, Christine Choy, Gregory Nava, Haile Gerima, and Julie Dash) are often marginalized as merely national, Third World, Third Cinema, identity cinema, or ethnic filmmakers, who are unable to fully speak to mainstream audiences. Through funding, festival programming, and marketing strategy, these filmmakers are often encouraged to engage in "salvage filmmaking," that is, making films that serve to preserve and recover cultural and ethnic heritage. Other exilic filmmakers, such as Jonas Mekas, Mona Hatoum, Chantal Akerman, Trinh T. Minh-ha, Isaac Julien, and Shirin Neshat, are placed within the avant-garde category, while some, such as Agnès Varda and Chris Marker, are considered unclassifiable.

Although these classificatory approaches are important for framing films to better understand them or better market them, they also serve to overdetermine and limit the films' potential meanings. Their undesirable consequences are particularly grave for the accented films because classification approaches are not neutral structures. They are "ideological constructs" masquerading as neutral categories (Altman 1989, 5). By forcing accented films into one of the established categories, the very cultural and political foundations that constitute them are bracketed, misread, or effaced altogether. Such traditional schemas also tend to lock the filmmakers into discursive ghettos that fail to reflect or account for their personal evolution and stylistic transformations over time. Once labeled "ethnic," "ethnographic," or "hyphenated," accented filmmakers remain discursively so even long after they have moved on. On the other hand, there are those, such as Gregory Nava, Spike Lee, Euzhan Palcy, and Mira Nair, who have made the move with varying degrees of success out of ethnic or Third World filmmaking and into mainstream cinema by telling their ethnic and national stories in more recognizable narrative forms.

One of the key purposes of this study is to identify and develop the most appropriate theory to account for the complexities, regularities, and inconsistencies of the films made in exile and diaspora, as well as for the impact that the liminal and interstitial location of the filmmakers has on their work. Occasionally, such a theory is explicitly embedded in the films themselves, such as in Jonas Mekas's *Lost, Lost, Lost* (1949–76), Fernando Solanas's *Tangos: Exile of Gardel* (1985), and Prajna Parasher's *Exile and Displacement* (1992). More often, however, the theory must be discovered and defined as the film moves toward reception, by marketers, reviewers, critics, and viewers. Such a deductive process presents a formidable challenge. It requires discovering common features among disparate products of differently situated displaced filmmakers from varied national origins who are living and making films in the interstices of divergent host societies, under unfamiliar, often hostile, political and cinematic systems. I have opted to work with a stylistic approach, designating it the "accented style."[9] Stylistic history is one of the "strongest justifications for film studies as a distinct academic discipline" (Bordwell 1997, 8). But stylistic study is not much in vogue today. Fear of formalism, lack of knowledge of the intricacies of film aesthetics and film production techniques, the importation of theories into film studies with little regard for the film's specific textual and spectatorial environments – all these can share the blame.

In the narrowest sense, style is the "patterned and significant use of technique" (Bordwell and Thompson 1993, 337). Depending on the site of the repetition, style may refer to a film's style (patterns of significant techniques in a single film), a filmmaker's style (patterns repeated in unique ways in a filmmaker's oeuvre), or a group style (consistent use of technique across the works of several directors). Although attention will be paid here to the authorial styles of individual filmmakers, the group style is the central concern of this book. In general, the choice of style is governed by social and artistic movements, regulations governing censorship, technological developments, the reigning mode of production (cinematic and otherwise), availability of financial resources, and the choices that individual filmmakers make as social and cinematic agents. Sometimes group style is formed by filmmakers who follow certain philosophical tendencies and aesthetic concerns, such as German expressionism and Soviet montage. The accented group style, however, has existed only in a limited, latent, and emergent form, awaiting recognition. Even those who deal with the accented films usually speak of exile and diaspora as themes inscribed in the films, not as components of style. In addition, the overwhelming majority of the many valuable studies of filmmaking in exile and diaspora have been narrowly focused on the works of either an individual filmmaker or a regional group of filmmakers. There are, for example, studies (both lengthy and brief) devoted to the filmmakers Raúl Ruiz, Fernando Solanas, Valeria Sarmiento, Amos Gitai, Michel Khleifi, Abid Med Hondo, Chantal Akerman, Jonas Mekas, Atom Egoyan, and Trinh T. Minh-ha, and there are studies centered on Chilean exile films, Arab exile cinema, *beur* cinema, Chicano/a cinema, Iranian exile cinema, and black African, British, and American diasporic cinemas. While these works shed light on the modus operandi, stylistic features, politics, and thematic concerns of specific filmmakers or of regional or collective diasporic films, none of them adequately addresses the theoretical problematic of an exilic and diasporic cinema as a category that cuts across and is shared by all or by many of them.[10] My task here is to theorize this cinema's existence as an accented style that encompasses characteristics common to the works of differently situated filmmakers involved in varied decentered social formations and cinematic practices across the globe – all of whom are presumed to share the fact of displacement and deterritorialization. Such a shared accent must be discovered (at least initially) at the films' reception and articulated more by the critics than by the filmmakers.

The components of the accented style include the film's visual style; narrative structure; character and character development; subject matter, theme, and plot; structures of feeling of exile; filmmaker's biographical and sociocultural location; and the film's mode of production, distribution, exhibition, and reception. I have devoted entire chapters to some of these components or their subsidiary elements, while I have dealt with others in special sections or throughout the book.

Earlier, I divided accented cinema into exilic, diasporic, and postcolonial ethnic films – a division based chiefly on the varied relationship of the films and their makers to existing or imagined homeplaces. Now I draw a further stylistic distinction, between feature and experimental films. The accented feature films are generally narrative, fictional, feature-length, polished, and designed for commercial distribution and theatrical exhibition. The accented experimental films, on the other hand, are usually shot on lower-gauge film stock (16mm and super-8) or on video, making a virtue of their low-tech, low-velocity, almost homemade quality. In addition, they are often nonfictional, vary in length from a few minutes to several hours, and are designed for nontheatrical distribution and exhibition. The feature films are generally more exilic than diasporic, and they are often made by older émigré filmmakers. On the other hand, the experimental films and videos are sometimes more diasporic than exilic, and are made by a younger generation of filmmakers who have been born or bred in diaspora. The experimental films also tend to inscribe autobiography or biography more, or more openly, than the feature films.[11] In them, the filmmakers' own voice-over narration mediates between film types (documentary, fictional) and various levels of identity (personal, ethnic, gender, racial, national). Although narrative hybridity is a characteristic of the accented cinema, the experimental films are more hybridized than the feature films in their intentional crossing and problematization of various borders, such as those between video and film, fiction and nonfiction, narrative and nonnarrative, social and psychic, autobiographical and national.[12]

## ■ Accented Style ■

If the classical cinema has generally required that components of style, such as mise-en-scène, filming, and editing, produce a realistic rendition of the world, the exilic accent must be sought in the manner in which realism is, if not subverted, at least inflected differently. Henry Louis Gates Jr. has characterized black texts as "mulatto" or "mulatta," containing a double voice and a two-toned heritage: "These texts speak in standard Romance and Germanic languages and literary structures, but almost always speak with a distinct and resonant accent, an accent that Signifies (upon) the various black vernacular literary traditions, which are still being written down" (1988, xxiii). Accented films are also mulatta texts. They are created with awareness of the vast histories of the prevailing cinematic modes. They are also created in a new mode that is constituted both by the structures of feeling of the filmmakers themselves as displaced subjects and by the traditions of exilic and diasporic cultural productions that preceded them. From the cinematic traditions they acquire one set of voices, and from the exilic and diasporic traditions they acquire a second. This double consciousness constitutes the accented style that not only signifies upon exile and other cinemas but also signifies the condition of exile itself. It signifies upon cinematic traditions by its artisanal and collective modes of production, which undermine the dominant production mode, and by narrative strategies, which subvert that mode's realistic treatment of time, space, and causality. It also signifies and signifies upon exile by expressing, allegorizing, commenting upon, and critiquing the conditions of its own production, and deterritorialization. Both of these acts of signifying and signification are constitutive of the accented style, whose key characteristics are elaborated upon in the following. What turns these into attributes of style is their repeated inscription in a single film, in the entire oeuvre of individual filmmakers, or in the works of various displaced filmmakers regardless of their place of origin or residence. Ultimately, the style demonstrates their dislocation at the same time that it serves to locate them as authors.

## Language, voice, address

In linguistics, accent refers only to pronunciation, while dialect refers to grammar and vocabulary as well. More specifically, accent has two chief definitions: "The cumulative auditory effect of those features of pronunciation which identify where a person is from, regionally and socially" and "The emphasis which makes a particular word or syllable stand out in a stream of speech" (Crystal 1991, 2). While accents may be standardized (for example, as British, Scottish, Indian, Canadian, Australian, or American accents of English), it is impossible to speak without an accent. There are various reasons for differences in accent. In English, the majority of accents are regional. Speakers of English as a second language, too, have accents that stem from their regional and first-language characteristics. Differences in accent often correlate with other factors as well: social and class origin, religious affiliation, educational level, and political grouping (Asher 1994, 9). Even though from a linguistic point of view all accents are equally important, all accents are not of equal value socially and politically. People make use of accents to judge not only the social standing of the speakers but also their personality. Depending on their accents, some speakers may be considered regional, local yokel, vulgar, ugly, or comic, whereas others may be thought of as educated, upper-class, sophisticated, beautiful, and proper. As a result, accent is one of the most intimate and powerful markers of group identity and solidarity, as well as of individual difference and personality. The flagship newscasts of mainstream national television and radio networks have traditionally been delivered in the preferred "official" accent, that is, the accent that is considered to be standard, neutral, and value-free.

Applied to cinema, the standard, neutral, value-free accent maps onto the dominant cinema produced by the society's reigning mode of production. This typifies the classical and the new Hollywood cinemas, whose films are realistic and intended for entertainment only, and thus free from overt ideology or accent. By that definition, all alternative cinemas are accented, but each is accented in certain specific ways that distinguish it. The cinema discussed here derives its accent from its artisanal and collective production modes and from the filmmakers' and audiences' deterritorialized locations. Consequently, not all accented films are exilic and diasporic, but all exilic and diasporic films are accented. If in linguistics accent pertains only to pronunciation, leaving grammar and vocabulary intact, exilic and diasporic accent permeates the film's deep structure: its narrative, visual style, characters, subject matter, theme, and plot. In that sense, the accented style in film functions as both accent and dialect in linguistics. Discussions of accents and dialects are usually confined to oral literature and to spoken presentations. Little has been written – besides typographical accentuation of words – about what Taghi Modarressi has called "writing with an accent":

The new language of any immigrant writer is obviously accented and, at least initially, inarticulate. I consider this "artifact" language expressive in its own right. Writing with an accented voice is organic to the mind of the immigrant writer. It is not something one can invent. It is frequently buried beneath personal inhibitions and doubts. The accented voice is loaded with hidden messages from our cultural heritage, messages that often reach beyond the capacity of the ordinary words of any language.... Perhaps it is their [immigrant and exile writers'] personal language that can build a bridge between what is familiar and what is strange. They may then find it possible to generate new and revealing paradoxes. Here we have our juxtapositions and our transformations – the graceful and the awkward, the beautiful and the ugly, sitting side by side in a perpetual metamorphosis of one into the other. It is like the Hunchback of Notre Dame trying to be Prince Charming for strangers. (1992, 9)

At its most rudimentary level, making films with an accent involves using on-camera and voice-over characters and actors who speak with a literal accent in their pronunciation. In the classical Hollywood cinema, the characters' accents were not a reliable indicator of the actors' ethnicity.[13] In accented cinema, however, the characters' accents are often ethnically coded, for in this cinema, more often than not, the actor's ethnicity, the character's ethnicity, and the ethnicity of the star's persona coincide. However, in some of these films the coincidence is problematized, as in the epistolary films of Chantal Akerman (*News from Home*, 1976) and Mona Hatoum (*Measures of Distance*, 1988). In each of these works, a filmmaking daughter reads in an accented English voice-over the letters she has received from her mother. The audience may assume that these are the voices of the mothers (complete coincidence among the three accents), but since neither of the films declares whose voice we are hearing, the coincidence is subverted and the spectators must speculate about the true relationship of the accent to the identity, ethnicity, and authenticity of the speaker or else rely on extratextual information.

One of the greatest deprivations of exile is the gradual deterioration in and potential loss of one's original language, for language serves to shape not only individual identity but also regional and national identities prior to displacement. Threatened by this catastrophic loss, many accented filmmakers doggedly insist on writing the dialogues in their original language – to the detriment of the films' wider distribution. However, most accented films are bilingual, even multilingual, multivocal, and multiaccented, like Egoyan's *Calendar* (1993), which contains a series of telephonic monologues in a dozen untranslated languages, or Raúl Ruiz's *On Top of the Whale* (1981), whose dialogue is spoken in more than a half dozen languages, one of them invented by Ruiz himself. If the dominant cinema is driven by the hegemony of synchronous sound and a strict alignment of speaker and voice, accented films are counterhegemonic insofar as many of them de-emphasize synchronous sound, insist on first-person and other voice-over narrations delivered in the accented pronunciation of the host country's language, create a slippage between voice and speaker, and inscribe everyday nondramatic pauses and long silences.

At the same time that accented films emphasize visual fetishes of homeland and the past (landscape, monuments, photographs, souvenirs, letters), as well as visual markers of difference and belonging (posture, look, style of dress and behavior), they equally stress the oral, the vocal, and the musical – that is, accents, intonations, voices, music, and songs, which also demarcate individual and collective identities. These voices may belong to real, empirical persons, like Mekas's voice narrating his diary films; or they may be fictitious voices, as in Marker's *Letter from Siberia* (1958) and *Sunless* (1982); or they may be accented voices whose identity is not firmly established, as in the aforementioned films by Akerman and Hatoum. Sergeï Paradjanov's four feature films are not only intensely visual in their tableau-like mise-en-scène and presentational filming but also deeply oral in the way they are structured like oral narratives that are told to the camera.

Stressing musical and oral accents redirects our attention from the hegemony of the visual and of modernity toward the acousticity of exile and the commingling of premodernity and postmodernity in the films. Polyphony and heteroglossia both localize and locate the films as texts of cultural and temporal difference.

Increasingly, accented films are using the film's frame as a writing tablet on which appear multiple texts in original languages and in translation in the form of titles, subtitles, intertitles, or blocks of text. The calligraphic display of these texts de-emphasizes visuality while highlighting the textuality and translational issues of intercultural art. Because they are multilingual, accented films require extensive titling just to translate the dialogues. Many of them go beyond that, however, by experimenting with on-screen typography as a supplementary mode of narration and expression. Mekas's *Lost, Lost, Lost,* Trinh's *Surname Viet Given Name Nam*, and Tajiri's *History and Memory* (1991) experiment with multiple typographical presentations of English texts on the screen linked in complicated ways to the dialogue and to the voice-overs, which are also accented in their pronunciation. In cases where the on-screen text is written in "foreign" languages, such as in Suleiman's *Homage by Assassination* (1991) and Hatoum's *Measures of Distance*, both of which display Arabic words, the vocal accent is complemented by a calligraphic accent. The inscription of these visual and vocal accents transforms the act of spectatorship, from just watching to watching *and* literally reading the screen.

By incorporating voice-over narration, direct address, multilinguality, and multivocality, accented films, particularly the epistolary variety, destabilize the omniscient narrator and narrative system of the mainstream cinema and journalism. Film letters often contain the characters' direct address (usually in first-person singular), the indirect discourse of the filmmaker (as the teller of the tale), and the free indirect discourse of the film in which the direct voice contaminates the indirect. Egoyan's *Calendar* combines all three of these discourses to create confusion as to what is happening, who is speaking, who is addressing whom, where the diegetic photographer and his on-screen wife (played by Egoyan and his real-life wife) leave off and where the historical persons Atom Egoyan and Arsinée Khanjian begin. The accented style is itself an example of free indirect discourse in the sense of forcing the dominant cinema to speak in a minoritarian dialect.

## Embedded criticism

As Dick Hebdige has noted, style – any style – is "a gesture of defiance or contempt, in a smile or a sneer. It signals a Refusal" (1979, 3). The accented film style is such a gesture, smile, or sneer of refusal and defiance. Although it does not conform to the classic Hollywood style, the national cinema style of any particular country, the style of any specific film movement or any film author, the accented style is influenced by them all, and it signifies upon them and criticizes them. By its artisanal and collective mode of production, its subversion of the conventions of storytelling and spectator positioning, its critical juxtaposition of different worlds, languages, and cultures, and its aesthetics of imperfection and smallness, it critiques the dominant cinema. It is also highly political because politics infuses it from inception to reception. For these reasons, accented cinema is not only a minority cinema but also a minor cinema, in the way that Deleuze and Guattari have defined the concept (1986).

However, this should not be construed to mean that the accented cinema is oppositional cinema, in the sense of defining itself primarily against an unaccented dominant cinema. Produced in a capitalist (if alternative) mode of production, the accented films are not necessarily radical, for they act as agents not only of expression and defiance but also of assimilation, even legitimization, of their makers and their audiences. As such, accented cinema is one of the dialects of our language of cinema.

## Accented structures of feeling

Since the accented style is not a programmatic, already formed style, one may speak of it as an emergent "structure of feeling," which, according to Raymond Williams, is not a fixed institution, formation, position, or even a formal concept such as worldview or ideology. Rather, it is a set of undeniable personal and social experiences – with internal relations and tensions – that is

> still in process, often indeed not yet recognized as social but taken to be private, idiosyncratic, and even isolating, but which in analysis (though rarely otherwise) has its emergent, connecting, and dominant characteristics, indeed its specific hierarchies. These are often more recognizable at a later stage, when they have been (as often happens) formalized, classified, and in many cases built into institutions and formations. (1977, 132)

The accented style is one such emergent category – not yet fully recognized or formalized. Its structure of feeling is rooted in the filmmakers' profound experiences of deterritorialization, which oscillate between dysphoria and euphoria, celibacy and celebration. These dislocatory feeling structures are powerfully expressed in the accented films' chronotopical configurations of the homeland as utopian and open and of exile as dystopian and claustrophobic.

In some measure, what is being described here is similar to the feeling structures of postmodernism. In speaking about the formation of a new mass audience for postmodernist art, Fred Pfeil notes that experiencing such art is characterized by "a very unstable play between a primal delight and primal fear, between two simultaneous versions of the primary aggressive impulse, that which seeks to incorporate the world into itself and that which struggles to prevent its own engulfment. This dialectic is the postmodern 'structure of feeling' (1988, 386). To the extent that the accented and postmodernist cinemas both immerse us in these dystopic and euphoric moments of unresolved polarity, they are similar. However, not all postmodernist films are diasporically or exilically accented, while all accented films are to some extent postmodernist. Accented films differ from other postmodernist films because they usually posit the homeland as a grand and deeply rooted referent, which stops the postmodernist play of signification. Since exile (more than diaspora) is driven by the modernist concerns and tropes of nationalism and state formation, which posit the existence and realness of the earth, mountains, monuments, and seas as well as of the peoples, histories, politics, and cultures of the homeland, many exilically accented films are intensely place-bound, and their narratives are driven by a desire either to recapture the homeland or to return to it. As a result, during the liminal period of displacement, the postmodernist playfulness, indeterminacy, and intertextuality have little place in exilic politics and cinema. The referent homeland is too powerfully real, even sacred, to be played with and signified upon. It is this powerful hold of the homeland that imbues the accented structures of feeling with such sadness and sense of terminal loss as described by Edward Said:

> Exile is strangely compelling to think about but terrible to experience. It is the unhealable rift forced between a human being and a native place, between the self and its true home: its essential sadness can never be surmounted. And while it is true that literature and history contain heroic, romantic, glorious, even triumphant episodes in an exile's life, these are no more than efforts meant to overcome the crippling sorrow of estrangement. The achievements of exile are permanently undermined by the loss of something left behind for ever. (1990, 357)

Sadness, loneliness, and alienation are frequent themes, and sad, lonely, and alienated people are favorite characters in the accented films.

Only when the grand return to the homeland is found to be impossible, illusory, or undesirable does the postmodernist semiosis set in. Then the nostalgia for the referent and the pain of separation from it may be transformed into a nostalgia for its synecdoches, fetishes, and signifieds – the frozen sounds and images of the homeland – which are then circulated in exilic media and pop culture (including wall calendars, as in Egoyan's *Calendar*).[14]

Multiple sites, cultures, and time zones inform the feeling structures of exile and diaspora, and they pose the representation of simultaneity and multisitedness as challenges for the accented films. Citing Sergei Eisenstein, George Marcus offered montage as a methodology that not only encodes multiple times and sites but also self-consciously problematizes the realist representation of the world. In the accented cinema, as in the multisited ethnography that Marcus describes, this is achieved by critical juxtapositions of multiple spaces, times, voices, narratives, and foci (1994).

## Tactile optics

The human body is experienced from both sides of the phenomenological divide: externally, by means of mirrors, photography, film, electronic sensors, and other peoples' reactions; and internally, by means of our own vision, organs of balance, and proprioception (Sobchack 1999). In traumatic forms of expulsion and exile, especially when they are coupled with racism and hostility in the new country, the certainty and wholeness of the body (and of the mind) are often put into doubt. The body's integrity, requiring a coincidence of inside and outside, is threatened, as a result of which it may be felt to be separated, collapsed, fractured, eviscerated, or pithed. The exilic dislocation can be experienced simultaneously both at quotidian and profound and at corporeal and spiritual levels. The impact of dislocation on language has already been discussed. The dominance of vision – an accepted fact of modernity (Jay 1993) – is attenuated for the exiles by the prominence of the other senses, which continually and poignantly remind them of their seemingly irrevocable difference, loss, or lack of fit. A particular fragrance on a hillside, a stolen glance in a restaurant, a body brush in a crowded street, a particular posture by a passenger in an elevator, a flash of memory during daily conversations, the sound of familiar words in one's native tongue heard from an adjoining car at a red traffic light – each of these sensory reports activates private memories and intensifies the feeling of *displacement,* a feeling that one may have suppressed in order to get on with life. However, just as frequently and powerfully, these very reports may serve the opposite function of restoration and *emplacement* – by reestablishing connections.

Since some of the most poignant reminders of exile are non-visual and deeply rooted in everyday experiences, they tend to emphasize tactile sensibilities. As formulated by Michael Taussig, the sense of everydayness includes "much that is not sense so much as sensuousness, an embodied and somewhat automatic 'knowledge' that functions like peripheral vision, not studied contemplation, a knowledge that is imageric and sensate rather than ideational" (1992, 8). This peripheral, distracted, tactile vision of the new location is replicated in the accented films' "tactile optics," that is, their nonlinear structure, which is driven by the juxtaposition of multiple spaces, times, voices, narratives, and foci – the montage effect. This effect, in turn, is propelled by the memory, nostalgic longing, and multiple losses and wishes that are experienced by the diegetic characters, exilic filmmakers, and their audiences. Significantly, such a distracted mode of being in the world is also characteristic of postmodern living. Given that distracted vision and glance are also characteristic of televisual viewing, as opposed to film spectatorship, which is largely gaze-driven, this may partially account for the affinity of the accented experimental filmmakers for televisuality.

In addition to the distracted aesthetics of montage, the tactile optics involves the style of filming. Some filmmakers force the audience to experience the diegesis by means of the texture of the film, video, and computer screens (as in Egoyan's *Next of Kin, Speaking Parts*, and *Calendar* and in Marker's *Sunless*). Some use long takes, which allow the spectators time to leisurely project themselves into the diegesis to the point of occupying it (as in Tarkovsky's *Nostalgia* and in Michael Snow's *Wavelength*, 1966–7). Single-frame filming and audio sampling capture fleeting moments of vision, memory, and voice, replicating distracted attention (as in Mekas's *Walden*, part of which is filmed in single frame, or in Trinh's *Reassemblage* (1982), in which unfinished words and sentences are repeated in different iterations). Texture is suggested by emphasizing aromatic and sensual experiences (as in Ang Lee's *Eat Drink Man Woman* [*Yinshi Nan Nu*] 1994); by showing nature's elemental forces (as in Artavazd Pelechian's *Seasons* [1982] and in Ivens and Loridan's *A Tale of the Wind* [1988]); or by inscribing extremely claustrophobic urban spaces (as in Yilmaz Güney's *The Wall* [1983], Tevfik Baser's *40 m² Germany* [1986], Sohrab Shahid Saless's *Utopia* [1982], Yuri Ilienko's *Swan Lake: The Zone* [1990], and Yilmaz Arslan's *Passages* [1982]). A thematic focus on journey, traveling, and nomadic wandering (as in Tarkovsky's *Stalker* [1979], Ulrike Ottinger's *Johanna d'Arc of Mongolia* [1989], and Rachid Bouchareb's *Cheb* [1990]) can also be a source of varying textures.[15]

Tactility is also promoted by the nonaudiovisual ways in which displaced people experience the audiovisual media. Located at the intersection of difference and alterity, they experience every film in the context of awareness of that difference. Certain images, sounds, characters, actors, accented speech, gestures, stories, locations, and quality of light within the film may remind exilic spectators of what Laura Marks calls their private "sense memories" (1994, 258), that is, each spectator's recollections of the images, sounds, smells, people, places, and times they have left behind.

The exilic structures of feeling and the tactile optics are reminiscent of Dudley Andrew's designation of "poetic realism" as an "optique" that characterizes the classic French films of the late 1930s. By his formulation, optique "suggests the ocular and ideological mechanisms of 'perspective,' both of which aptly play roles in the medium of film" (1995, 19). In its multiple contract with industry and audiences, optique is similar to genre, and in positing a spontaneous, idiosyncratic, and authentic relationship between films and their makers, it resembles style. The accented style is an exilic optique because it provides both an ocular and an ideological perspective on deterritorialization. The ocular is encoded in the tactile optics and the ideological in the structures of feeling and synaesthetic sensibilities of the style.

## Third cinema aesthetics

The genealogy of the accented style may be traced not only to the epochal shifts of postcolonialism and postmodernism but also to the transformation of cinematic structures, theories, and practices since the 1960s. Specifically, it begins with the emergence and theorization of a Latin-American cinema of liberation, dubbed "Third Cinema," and its later elaboration by Teshome H. Gabriel and others. Drawing upon the Cuban revolution of 1959, Italian neorealist film aesthetics, Griersonian social documentary style, and Marxist analysis, Brazilian filmmaker Glauber Rocha issued his passionate polemic, "The Aesthetics of Hunger," and Argentinean cinéastes Fernando Solanas and Spanish-born Octavio Getino, makers of the massive film *The Hour of the Furnaces* (*La Hora de los Hornos*, 1968), published their famous manifesto, "Towards a Third Cinema." These were followed by an avant-gardist manifesto, "For an Imperfect Cinema," written by the Cuban filmmaker Julio Garcia Espinosa.[16] Other "revolutionary" cinematic manifestos were issued in North Africa and the Middle East.[17] In France, the SLON (later ISKRA) and Dziga Vertov groups, among others, and in the United States, Newsreel and other groups picked up the clarion call of these manifestos and issued their own summons for new radical cinematic practices. The Latin-American polemics and manifestos in particular, including *The Hour of the Furnaces*, critiqued the mainstream, capitalist, "first cinema" and the petit bourgeois, authorial "second cinema"; in their place they proposed a new research category of "Third Cinema" – a cinema that is not perfect, polished, or professional.[18] Indeed, in its formal practices, *The Hour of the Furnaces* is a clear progenitor of the accented style.

The accented cinema is one of the offshoots of the Third Cinema, with which it shares certain attributes and from which it is differentiated by certain sensibilities. As Gabriel elaborated, although Third Cinema films are made chiefly in the Third World, they may be made anywhere, by anyone, about any subject, and in a variety of styles and forms, as long as they are oppositional and liberationist (1982, 2–3). As a cinema of displacement, however, the accented cinema is much more situated than the Third Cinema, for it is necessarily made by (and often for) specific displaced subjects and diasporized communities. Less polemical than the Third Cinema, it is nonetheless a political cinema that stands opposed to authoritarianism and oppression. If Third Cinema films generally advocated class struggle and armed struggle, accented films favor discursive and semiotic struggles. Although not necessarily Marxist or even socialist like the Third Cinema, the accented cinema is an engagé cinema. However, its engagement is less with "the people" and "the masses," as was the case with the Third Cinema, than with specific individuals, ethnicities, nationalities, and identities, and with the experience of deterritorialization itself. In accented cinema, therefore, every story is both a private story of an individual and a social and public story of exile and diaspora. These engagements with collectivities and with deterritorialization turn accented films into allegories of exile and diaspora – not the totalizing "national allegories" that Jameson once characterized Third World literature and cinema to be (1986).

Third Cinema and accented cinema are alike in their attempts to define and create a nostalgic, even fetishized, authentic prior culture – before contamination by the West in the case of the Third Cinema, and before displacement and emigration in the case of the accented cinema. Like *The Hour of the Furnaces*, accented films are hybridized in their use of forms that cut across the national, typological, generic, and stylistic boundaries. Similarly, many of them are driven by the aesthetics of provisionality, experimentation, and imperfection – even ama-teurness – and they are made in the artisanal, low-cost mode of "cinema of hunger." In sum, despite some marked differences, both accented films and Third Cinema films are historically conscious, politically engaged, critically aware, generically hybridized, and artisanally produced. The affinity of the two cinemas and the impact of the one on the other are paralleled in the lives of some of the filmmakers, such as Fernando Solanas from Argentina and Miguel Littín from Chile, who moved from the Third Cinema in the 1960s to the accented cinema of the 1980s and beyond.

## Border effects, border writing

Border consciousness emerges from being situated at the border, where multiple determinants of race, class, gender, and membership in divergent, even antagon-istic, historical and national identities intersect. As a result, border consciousness, like exilic liminality, is theoretically against binarism and duality and for a third optique, which is multiperspectival and tolerant of ambiguity, ambivalence, and chaos.

The globalization of capital, labor, culture, and media is threatening to make borders obsolete and national sovereignty irrelevant. However, physical borders are real and extremely dangerous, particularly for those who have to cross them. In recent years no region in the world has borne deadlier sustained clashes over physical (and discursive) borders than the Middle East and the former Yugoslavia. The collisions over physical and literal lands, even over individual houses and their symbolic meanings, are also waged in the accented films. Since their widely received formulation by Anzaldúa (1987), borderland consciousness and theory have been romanticized, universalized, and co-opted by ignoring the specific dislocatory and conflictual historical and territorial grounds that produce them. However, borders are open, and infected wounds and the subjectivity they engen-der cannot be postnational or post-al, but interstitial. Unequal power relations and incompatible identities prevent the wound from healing.

Since border subjectivity is cross-cultural and intercultural, border filmmaking tends to be accented by the "strategy of translation rather than representation" (Hicks 1991, xxiii). Such a strategy undermines the distinction between autoch-thonous and alien cultures in the interest of promoting their interaction and intertextuality. As a result, the best of the border films are hybridized and experi-mental – characterized by multifocality, multilinguality, asynchronicity, critical distance, fragmented or multiple subjectivity, and transborder amphibolic characters – characters who might best be called "shifters." Of these characteristics, the latter bears discussion at this point.

In linguistics, shifters are words, such as "I" and "you," whose reference can be understood only in the context of the utterance. More generally, a shifter is an "operator" in the sense of being dishonest, evasive, and expedient, or even being a "mimic," in the sense that Homi Bhabha formulated, as a producer of critical excess, irony, and sly civility (1994). In the context of border filmmaking, shifters are characters who exhibit some or all of these registers of understanding and performativity. As such, they occupy a powerful position in the political economy of both actual and diegetic border crossings. For example, in Nava's *El Norte*, a classic border film, the shifters consist of the following characters: the *pollo* (border-crossing brother and sister, Enrique and Rosa); the coyote (the Mexican middleman who for a fee brings the *pollo* across), the *migra* (the US immigration officers who chase and arrest Enrique); the *pocho* (Americans of Mexican descent who speak Mexican Spanish imperfectly, the man in the film who turns Enrique in to the immigration authorities); the *chola/cholo* and *pachuca/pachuco* (young inhabitants of the border underworld who have their own dialect called *caló*); and the US-based Mexican or Hispanic contractors who employ border crossers as day laborers (among them, Enrique).[19] The power of these border shifters comes from their situationist existence, their familiarity with the cultural and legal codes of interacting cultures, and the way in which they manipulate identity and the asymmetrical power situations in which they find themselves.

Accented films inscribe other amphibolic character types who are split, double, crossed, and hybridized and who perform their identities. As liminal subjects and interstitial artists, many accented filmmakers are themselves shifters, with multiple perspectives and conflicted or performed identities. They may own no passport or hold multiple passports, and they may be stranded between legality and illegality. Many are scarred by the harrowing experiences of their own border crossings. Some may be energized, while others may be paralyzed by their fear of partiality. Their films often draw upon these biographical crossing experiences.

*Themes*

Understandably, journeys, real or imaginary, form a major thematic thread in the accented films. Journeys have motivation, direction, and duration, each of which impacts the travel and the traveler. Three types of journeys are explored in this book: outward journeys of escape, home seeking, and home founding; journeys of quest, homelessness, and lostness; and inward, homecoming journeys. Depending on their directions, journeys are valued differently. In the accented cinema, westering journeys are particularly valued, partly because they reflect the filmmakers' own trajectory and the general flow of value worldwide. The westering journey is embedded, in its varied manifestations, in Xavier Koller's *Journey of Hope* (1990), Nizamettin Ariç's *A Cry for Beko* (1992), and Ghasem Ebrahimian's *The Suitors* (1989). In Nava's *El Norte*, a south-north journey lures the Mayan Indians from Guatemala to the United States.

There are many instances of empowering return journeys: to Morocco in Faridah Ben Lyazid's *Door to the Sky* (1989), to Africa in Raquel Gerber's *Ori* (1989), and to Ghana in Haile Gerima's *Sankofa* (1993). When neither escape nor return is possible, the desire for escape and the longing for return become highly cathected to certain icons of homeland's nature and to certain narratives. These narratives take the form of varied journeys: from the dystopic and irresolute journey of lostness in Tarkovsky's *Stalker* (1979) to the nostalgically celebratory homecoming journey in Mekas's *Reminiscences of a Journey to Lithuania* (1971–2) to the conflicting return journey to Japan and China in Ann Hui's *Song of the Exile* (1990).

Not all journeys involve physical travel. There also are metaphoric and philosophical journeys of identity and transformation that involve the films' characters and sometimes the filmmakers themselves, as in Mekas's films or in Ivens and Loridan's *A Tale of the Wind*.

## Authorship and autobiographical inscription

If prestructuralism considered authors to be outside and prior to the texts that uniquely express their personalities, and if cinestructuralism regarded authors as structures within their own texts, poststructuralism views authors as fictions within their texts who reveal themselves only in the act of spectating. Poststructuralist theory of authorship is thus embedded in theories of ideology and subject formation, and it privileges spectatorial reading over that of authoring. Roland Barthes went so far as to declare that "the birth of the reader must be at the cost of the death of the Author" (1977, 148). In this figuration, the author as a biographical person exercising parentage over the text disappears, leaving behind desiring spectators in search of an author. This author whom they construct is neither a projection nor a representation of a real author but a fictive figure within the text (Barthes 1975, 27). According to this formulation, the fictional structure or subject "Atom Egoyan" whom the spectators discover in the films of Atom Egoyan is not the same as, and does not necessarily map out onto, the empirical person named Atom Egoyan. Since texts create subject positions for both authors and spectators, poststructural theory must deal with the construction of both authors and spectators. Spectators, however, like authors, are not only subjects of texts but also – Barthes to the contrary – subjects in history, negotiating for positions within psychosocial formations, producing multiple readings and multiple author and spectator effects. The classical Hollywood cinema's invisible style creates filmic realism by promoting the impression of cohesiveness of time, space, and causality. As a result, diegetic reality appears to be authorless, natural, and mimetic, in an organic relationship to the profilmic world. As John Caughie notes, "The removal or suppression of the clear marks of 'authored discourse' transforms ideology from something produced out of a locatable, historical, determined position into something natural to the world" (1981, 202).

My project in this text is precisely to put the locatedness and the historicity of the authors back into authorship. To that extent, accented cinema theory is an extension of the authorship theory, and it runs counter to much of the postmodern theory that attempts to either deny authorship altogether or multiply the authoring parentage to the point of "de-originating the utterance."[20] However, film authors are not autonomous, transcendental beings who are graced by unique, primordial, and originary sparks of genius. Accented film authors are literally and figuratively everyday journeymen and journeywomen who are driven off or set free from their places of origin, by force or by choice, on agonizing quests that require displacements and emplacements so profound, personal, and transformative as to shape not only the authors themselves and their films but also the question of authorship. Any discussion of authorship in exile needs to take into consideration not only the individuality, originality, and personality of unique individuals as expressive film authors but also, and more important, their (dis)location as interstitial subjects within social formations and cinematic practices.

Accented films are personal and unique, like fingerprints, because they are both authorial and autobiographical. Exile discourse needs to counter the move by some postmodern critics to separate the author of the film from the enunciating subject in the film, for exile and authorship are fundamentally intertwined with historical movements of empirical subjects across boundaries of nations – not just texts.

To be sure, there are postmodern accented filmmakers, such as Egoyan and Caveh Zahedi, in whose films the relationship of the authoring filmmaker to both the text and the authoring structure within the text is one not of direct parentage but of convoluted performance. However, the questioning of the bond linking autobiography to authorship should not be used as a postmodernist sleight of hand to dismiss the specificity of exilic conditions or to defuse their subversive and empowering potentiality. Such a move comes at the very moment that, for the diasporized subalterns of the world, history, historical agency, and autobiographical consciousness have become significant and signifying components of identity, artistic production, and social agency. Accented authors are empirical subjects who exist outside and prior to their films.

In the accented cinema, the author is in the text in multiple ways, traversing the spectrum of authorship theories, from prestructuralism to poststructuralism. In a longitudinal and intertextual study of the films of individual filmmakers, we may discover certain consistencies from which we can construct an authorial presence within the films. It is thus that authors become discursive figures (Foucault 1977) who inhabit and are constructed not only by history but also by their own filmic texts. How they inhabit their films, or, in Bordwell's term (1989, 151–68), how they are "personified" varies: they may inhabit them as real empirical persons, enunciating subjects, structured absences, fictive structures, or a combination of these. In the accented films, determining the mode of habitation of the author within the text is a complex task, even in films in which the filmmakers appear as empirical persons and as themselves either audiovisually (Mekas's films, including *Lost, Lost, Lost*), or only visually (Suleiman's *Chronicle of Disappearance*), or only vocally and as the film's addressee (Akerman's *News from Home*), or as fictional characters (Egoyan's *Calendar*), or as author surrogates (Naderi's *Manhattan by Numbers* and Shahid Saless's *Roses for Africa*, 1991). In all these cases, filmmakers are engaged in the performance of the self. In short, because of their interstitiality, even in situations of self-inscription exilic authors tend to create ambiguity regarding their own real, fictive, or discursive identities, thus problematizing Phillipe Lejeune's "autobiographical pact," which requires that the author, the narrator, and the protagonist be identical (1989, 5).

Exilic authorship is also a function of the filmmakers' mode of production. In fact, in their multiple incarnations or personifications, the authors are produced by their production mode. If the cinema's dominant postindustrial production modes privilege certain kinds of authorship, then the artisanal accented production modes must favor certain other authorial signatures and accents. It is worth bearing in mind that such signatures or accents signify both the various incarnations of their authors and the conditions of exile and diaspora. The interpretation of these signatures and accents depends on the spectators, who are themselves often situated astride cultures and within collective formations. Hence, the figures they cut in their spectating of the accented filmmakers as authors are nuanced by their own extratextual tensions of difference and identity.

To further demonstrate the explanatory power of the accented style, a case study of Atom Egoyan's style is presented in the next close-up section, based on an examination of his feature films, a review of the literature by and about him, and my extensive discussions with him (Naficy 1997a). Although some of the components of Egoyan's accented style constitute his personal authorial signature, there are many components that he shares with other accented filmmakers.

## Close-up: Atom Egoyan's accented style

In the early 1990s, Atom Egoyan was considered to be the "most original" Canadian director next to David Cronenberg (Atamian 1991, 70; Ansen 1992). He was also called "the most accomplished Canadian director of his generation" (Johnson 1991, 68) and Canada's first multicultural feature filmmaker, "grant-magnet and prize pony" (Balley 1989, 46), a characterization he derided. His films occasionally received criticism on grounds of being "dishonest and posturing, more like intellectual masturbation" (Kempley 1990, D3), or for being "pretentious" and "elegantly empty" (Maslin 1989, C16). However, they were such a favorite of international film festivals and critics that he was regarded as "a child of the festival circuit" (Handling 1993, 8). It was at these festivals that his films received high praise and almost universal critical acclaim. Calling him one of the most talented directors at the 1987 Montreal Film Festival, Wim Wenders publicly turned over his $5,000 award for *Wings of Desire* (1988) to Egoyan for directing *Family Viewing* (1987). *The Adjuster* (1991) won the Special Jury Prize at the 1991 Moscow Film Festival, and the Cannes International Film Festival gave Egoyan the International Critics Prize for *Exotica* in 1993 and the Grand Prize for *The Sweet Hereafter* in 1997. With each film, both his cult following and his general popularity grew.

Egoyan was born in Egypt in 1960 to two artists, who were descendants of Armenian refugees. His parents ran a successful furniture store until the rising tide of Nasserist nationalism and the parochialism of the local Armenian community encouraged their emigration in 1962 to Victoria, British Columbia. Egoyan was three years old at the time. The only Armenian family in the area, they set up another furniture store called Ego Interiors (Atom Egoyan's film company is called Ego Film Arts). Although Egoyan spoke Armenian as a child, he gave it up when he entered kindergarten to forestall ethnic embarrassment and harassment. He also refused to speak Armenian at home, and whenever his parents spoke Armenian to him, he covered his ears. At eighteen, he moved to Toronto and became what he thought was a fully assimilated Canadian, graduating with honors in international relations from the University of Toronto. While there, he led a socially active life, writing plays, publishing film criticism in the school paper, and working on student films. Egoyan's first short film, *Howard in Particular* (1979), was made in Toronto and was followed by several more shorts. His contact at the university with nationalist Armenian students placed him on a trajectory of increased ethnic awareness.

Egoyan's output may be divided into three general categories: short films, television films and episodic series, and feature films. Despite the increasingly wide reception, even popularity, of some of his features and television films, so far Egoyan has remained an independent filmmaker, relying on a variety of funds from local and regional arts councils, private sources, his own earnings, and Canadian and European television networks. This independent and alternative mode of production is a characteristic of the accented film practice and is constitutive of its accented style. Another contributor to this style and to his authorship is Egoyan's multiple functions in his films: he has written and directed all of his features; edited several of them (*Next of Kin* [1984], *Family Viewing*, and *Calendar*); functioned as executive producer or producer in many of them (*Next of Kin, Family Viewing, Speaking Parts, Calendar, Exotica,* and *The Sweet Hereafter*); and acted in one feature (*Calendar*) and several shorts. He has also played the classical guitar sound track for two of his features (*Next of Kin* and *The Adjuster*). In addition, his wife, Arsinée Khanjian, has starred in all of his features and coproduced *Calendar* with him. Other on-camera talent and off-camera crew members have been regular participants in his films. As I discuss in the section on the mode of production, performing multiple functions and employing a repertory of talent and crew give accented filmmakers, such as Egoyan, fuller control over both the authorship and the cost of their projects. At the same time, however, this control deepens their interstitiality by limiting their options. As such, Egoyan's films tend to inscribe more fully his own biography, personal obsessions, and auteurist vision and style.

Issues of race, ethnicity, and submerged ethnicity are not limited to "ethnic" films. In fact, much of the mainstream Hollywood cinema is "saturated" with submerged ethnic and racial resonances (Shohat 1991, 219). On closer examination, it will be seen that Egoyan's films are also suffused with such submerged resonances and that his filmic career is one of increased ethnicization, which emerges fully in *Calendar*. His films embody many attributes of the accented style, including the inscription of closed and claustrophobic spaces both in the films' mise-en-scène and in the filming; ethnically coded mise-en-scène, characters, music, and iconography; multilinguality and accented speech by ethnic characters and actors; epistolarity by means of letters, video, and the telephone; tactile uses of video and technological mediation of all reality; slippery, guarded, and obsessive characters who camouflage or perform their identities and secret desires; ethnic characters who either are silent or are present but only on video; inscription of journeys of identity and of return journey to the homeland; the instability and persistence of memory that can be recorded, recorded over, remembered nostalgically, erased, and played back repeatedly; and fragmented structures of feeling and narratives.[21]

Certain Armenian sensibilities further accent Egoyan's films: looks, gestures, expressions, postures, and certain thematic concerns with family structures, Armenian history, religiosity, ethnicity, and diasporism. Added to these ethnocultural sensibilities are Egoyan's personal proclivities and his feeling structures as a subject inhabiting the liminal slipzones of identity, cultural difference, and film production practice. Another enabling component of his accented style is his expression of those sensibilities and feelings in certain juxtapositions, narratives, and themes that are at times so paradoxical as to require a knowing audience for their full appreciation. Like all accented speech, Egoyan's style has produced results that are fabulous and grotesque, charming and offensive.

These components of the accented style are present in the corpus of Egoyan's feature films, and to a large extent in each of his films. It is important to emphasize, however, that the identification of the accented style in his work in no way diminishes the heterogeneity of his films and the multiplicity of their meanings. My intention is not to reduce Egoyan to an essential exilic or ethnic subject. There is none! Rather, it is to analyze his accented style and the hitherto more or less latent currents, crosscurrents, and structures in his public image and films.[22] By neither conforming to nor exhausting the paradigm of the accented style, Egoyan's films confirm the importance of authorship as a marker of difference. His most glaring differences with the paradigm are his suppression of orality and his intense emphasis on the visual, vision, and voyeuristic structures of looking. In addition, although memory is significant in all his films, it does not particularly promote tactility or "tactile vision" (*Speaking Parts* excepted). There is almost no significant scene in any of Egoyan's films, except *Next of Kin*, in which the synaesthesia of meal preparation or of eating of food is figured. Likewise, open spaces, landscape, nature, and the human relation with them had no place in any of his feature films until *Calendar* – his most exilic work.

This examination of Egoyan's works also demonstrates the elasticity of the concept of style as a critical approach to exilic and diasporic cinema. Like many of the filmmakers discussed, both Egoyan and his cinema are nomadic and hybridized. The films combine aspects of exilic feature films and diasporic experimental films. His early features, especially the exilically pivotal *Calendar*, integrated the high-gloss, narrative-driven attributes of the former with the small-scale, experimental, home-video dimensions of the latter, while his later films – *The Adjuster*, *Exotica*, and *The Sweet Hereafter* – belong almost entirely to the feature film form. His wider critical and commercial success since *Exotica* is pushing him across another divide: away from the alternative and interstitial modes of production and toward the mainstream independent mode of production. By traveling across forms and modes, Egoyan himself is transformed. How he will respond to the undeniable allure of the big budgets, high gloss, and massive audience that the postindustrial cinema promises remains to be seen.

Like all approaches to cinema, the accented style attempts to reduce and to channel the free play of meanings. But this approach is driven by its sensitivity to the production and consumption of films and videos in conditions of exilic liminality and diasporic transnationality. The style designation also allows us to reclassify films or to classify certain hitherto unclassifiable films. Thus, Mekas's *Lost, Lost, Lost*, which has been variously regarded as documentary, avant-garde, or diary film, will yield new insights if reread as an accented film. If one thinks of Buñuel as an exilic filmmaker, as does Marsha Kinder (1993), further understanding about his films, hitherto unavailable, will be produced. Likewise, a rereading of Miguel Littín's docudrama *The Jackal of Nahueltoro* (*El Chacal de Nahueltoro*, 1969), turns it into a protoexilic film containing many components of the accented style in emergent form, even though at first blush the story does not warrant such an interpretation.

The accented style helps us to discover commonalities among exilic filmmakers that cut across gender, race, nationality, and ethnicity, as well as across boundaries of national cinemas, genres, and authorship. References to filmmakers in this text range far and wide, from Godard to Mekas, from Akerman to Med Hondo, and from Solanas to Trinh. Approached stylistically, films can be read, reread, and back-read not only as individual texts but also as sites of struggle over meanings and identities. By problematizing the traditional schemas and representational practices, this approach blurs the distinction, often artificially maintained, among various film types such as documentary, fictional, and avant-garde. All of these types are considered here.

The accented style is not a fully recognized and sanctioned film genre, and the exilic and diasporic filmmakers do not always make accented films. In fact, most of them would wish to be in Egoyan's place, to move out of marginal cinema niches into the world of art cinema or even popular cinema. Style permits the critics to track the evolution of the work of not only a single filmmaker but also a group of filmmakers. Asian Pacific American filmmaking has gradually evolved away from an ethnic focus toward diasporic and exilic concerns, while Iranian exilic film-makers have evolved toward a diasporic sensibility. These evolutions signal the transformation of both filmmakers and their audiences. They also signal the appropriation of the filmmakers, their audiences, and certain features of the accented style by the mainstream cinema and by its independent offspring. Because it goes beyond connoisseurship to situate the cinéastes within their changing social formations, cultural locations, and cinematic practices, the accented style is not hermetic, homogeneous, or autonomous. It meanders and evolves. It is an inalienable element of the social material process of exile and diaspora and of the exilic and diasporic mode of production.

## NOTES

1   I thank Bill Nichols for suggesting the parallel between exile and taboo. Also, see exile as "aesthetic gain" in Kaplan 1996, 33–41.

2   I have incorporated these and other attributes of exile and alterity to formulate a
    "paradigm of exile" (Naficy 1993).

3   If Rushdie is an example of exilic hybridity, F. M. Esfandiary is an example of exilic
    virtuality. In the 1960s, Esfandiary wrote novels from exile about the horror of life in
    his homeland Iran (*The Identity Card* [1966]), but in the late 1980s he changed his
    name to FM-2030 and developed the concept of transhumanism, which dismissed all
    usual markers of continuity and identity. To be a transhuman is to be a universal
    "evolutionary being" (FM-2030 1989, 205).

4   This is particularly true for the Japanese-Americans whose loyalty to the United States
    was questioned during World War II and to the Muslim Americans whose loyalty is
    often questioned in contemporary times.

5   Peter Feng suggests removing the hyphen from "Asian-American," while Gustavo
    P. Firmat recommends replacing it with a plus sign for "Cuban + American" (1994,
    16). Some insert a forward slash between the two terms. On the politics of the hyphen,
    especially for Asian-Americans, see Feng 1995, 1996; Lowe 1991.

6   These statistics should be understood in the following context. Many Middle Eastern
    filmmakers moved through several countries and across a number of identities. Some
    claimed multiple identities – both simultaneous and sequential – while others denied
    any form of particularistic identity. Some never returned, while others periodically
    visit their homelands, where they make films. Some moved among too many worlds,
    often leaving behind inadequately documented histories. A few deliberately obfuscated
    their history to conceal their tracks. Such fluidity and camouflaging, characteristic of
    exilic positionality, make it difficult to pin down some filmmakers' country of origin
    or residence, let alone their other markers of identity (such as their ethnic, religious,
    and political affiliations).

7   For sources on Middle Eastern and North African filmmakers in diaspora and exile, see
    the following: Arasoughly 1996; Armes 1996; Bodman and Bartholomew 1992; Bloom
    1995; Brossard n.d.; *CinémAction*, no. 7; *CinémAction*, no. 8; *CinémAction*, no. 24;
    *CinémAction*, no. 56; *Iransk Film i Exil* 1993; Kaufman et al. 1991; Omid 1367/1988;
    *Palestinian Film Week* 1992; Pflaum and Prinzler 1993; Radvanyi 1993; Salloum 1996;
    *The Second Festival for Iranian Films in Exile* 1995; Tavenas and Volard 1989; and
    Thomas 1990.

8   Although "international," even "transnational," these directors – whom Douglas
    Gomery (1991) labels "the individual as international film artist" – are not considered
    "exilic" or "diasporic" by the definition used here.

9   In an earlier publication, I explored the promise of theorizing these films as a
    transnational "genre" (Naficy 1996).

10  On regional exilic filmmaking, the following are notable studies: on Latin-American
    exile filmmakers, see Pick (1993, 157–85) and Burton (1986); on Chilean exile films,
    see King (1990); on Cuban exile films, see Lopez (1996); on cinemas of the black
    diaspora, see Martin (1995) and Ukadike (1994); on black British independent films,
    see Mercer (1994a), Diawara (1993b), and Fusco (1988); on black American diaspora
    films, see Diawara (1993a) and Reid (1991); on postcolonial and multicultural dia-
    sporic films, see Shohat and Stam (1994) and Sherzer (1996); on women and African
    and Asian diaspora films, see Foster (1997); on Caribbean exilic films, see Cham
    (1992); on Asian-American films, see Leong (1991); on Chicano/a cinemas, see
    Fregoso (1993) and Noriega (1992); on Middle Eastern exile films, see Friedlander
    (1995) and Naficy (1995); on Yiddish films, see Hoberman (1991); on Iranian exile

films, see Naficy (1993); on Turkish exile films, see Naficy (1996); on Soviet and Eastern European filmmakers in the West, see Petrie and Dwyer (1990); on exile and émigré cinema, particularly in France and Europe, including extensive filmographies, see the following special issues of *CinémAction* magazine: no. 7, "Cinéma contre racisme" (n.d.); no. 8, "Cinémas de l'émigration" (summer 1979); no. 24, "Cinémas de l'émigration" (n.d.); no. 56, "Cinémas métis: De Hollywood aux films beurs" (July 1990). On individual exilic filmmakers, consult the index or the close-up sections throughout the book.

11 On experimental diaspora cinema, see Marks 1994.

12 Even these two types of accented films are not fixed, for the works of some filmmakers may fall only partially into one or share attributes of both. This is another way in which these films are hybrid. For example, Solanas's *Tangos: Exile of Gardel* and Krishna's *Masala* may be categorized as hybrid films in their crossing of the boundaries and the mixing of elements of musical and melodrama, tragedy and comedy, narrative and nonnarrative, fictional and nonfictional, realism and surrealism, personal and national. However, both Solanas and Krishna make feature-length films, have high ambitions, and have large markets in mind. A key difference between them is that while *Masala* is a diaspora film, *Tangos* remains exilic, for it is focused solely on exile and on a binary relationship with the homeland. Likewise, Mekas's films share some of the characteristics of both feature films (their length) and experimental films (their aesthetics).

13 In the classical Hollywood cinema, the stars who retained their "foreign" accents fared differently. Some could not get parts because of their heavy accents. Scandinavian stars, particularly Greta Garbo, Sonja Henie, and Ingrid Bergman, were usually cast as European and Soviet foreign characters. Some British-born stars, such as Cary Grant, acquired a "transatlantic accent," so named perhaps because it was both readily comprehensible and hard to place (Jarvie 1991, 93).

14 For more on the phenomenon of exilic nostalgia and fetishization, see Naficy 1993, chap. 4.

15 A point should be made here about the "exilic" status of the filmmakers who worked in the former Soviet Union, such as Paradjanov, Tarkovsky, Ilienko, and Pelechian. Of these, only Tarkovsky lived in external exile, where he made his last two films. Paradjanov lived in internal exile, some of it spent in prison. Whatever their differences, these filmmakers made their films under the state-run mode of production, not a subversive interstitial mode. The presence of Armenian ethnicity and regional identity in the films of Paradjanov and Pelechian had a lot to do with Soviet cinematic politics of fostering the so-called friendship of the peoples. The filmmakers' choice of theme was often strategic. It might be more appropriate, therefore, to speak of filmmakers from the Soviet Union's "minority" republics as subaltern filmmakers instead of exilic filmmakers. I thank Susan Larsen for bringing these points to my attention.

16 These Latin-American and Third Cinema polemics and manifestos are collected in Martin 1997.

17 For some of these, see Willemen 1989, 5–6; for others, see Martin 1995.

18 There is disagreement over what constituted the first and second cinemas. Gabriel, for example, assigned First Cinema to the products of the mainstream film industry in capitalist market economies, while consigning Second Cinema to the products of the communist/socialist command economies (1982, chap. 1).

19  Other middlemen figures in the border drama include sanctuary movement advocates who assist potential refugees to gain asylum in the United States.

20  I have borrowed this phrase from Pfeil 1988, 387.

21  For "influences" on Egoyan, see Brady 1993.

22  For books on and by Egoyan, see Desbarats et al. 1993; Egoyan 1993, 1995. On recurrent themes in Egoyan's films, see Harcourt 1995; Porton 1997; and Naficy 1997.

## REFERENCES

Altman, Rick. 1989. *The American Film Musical.* Bloomington: Indiana University Press.

Andrew, Dudley. 1995. *Mists of Regret: Culture and Sensibility in Classic French Cinema.* Princeton, NJ: University of Princeton Press.

Ansen, David. 1992. "A Holiday from Hype." *Newsweek*, June 29, 64.

Anzaldúa, Gloria. 1987. *Borderlands/La Frontera: The New Mestiza.* San Francisco: Spinsters.

Arasoughly, Alia, ed. and trans. 1996. *Screens of Life: Critical Film Writing from the Arab World.* Vol. 1. Quebec: World Heritage Press.

Armes, Roy. 1996. *Dictionary of North African Film Makers.* Paris: Editions ATM.

Asher, R. E. ed. 1994. *The Encyclopedia of Language and Linguistics.* Vol. 1. New York: Pergamon Press.

Atamian, Christopher. 1991. "Emotion in Fast Forward: For Filmmaker Atom Egoyan, It's Veni, Video, Vici." *AIM*, August–September, 70.

Balley, Cameron. 1989. "Scanning Egoyan." *CineAction*, spring, 45–51.

Barthes, Roland. 1977. *Image, Music, Text.* Trans. Stephen Heath. New York: Hill and Wang.

——. 1975. *The Pleasure of the Text.* Trans. Richard Miller. New York: Hill and Wang.

Bauman, Zygmunt. 1991. "Modernity and Ambivalence." In *Global Culture: Nationalism, Globalization and Modernity*, edited by Mike Featherstone, 143–69. London: Sage.

Bhabha, Homi K. 1994. *The Location of Culture.* London: Routledge.

Bloom, Peter. 1995. "Locating Beur Cinema: Social Activism, Immigration Politics and the Naming of a Film Movement." Paper presented at the Tenth Triennial Symposium on African Art, New York University, New York, April.

Bodman, Ellen-Fairbanks, and Ronald L. Bartholomew. 1992. *Middle East and Islamic World Filmography.* Chapel Hill: University of North Carolina, Nonprint Materials Collection.

Bordwell, David. 1989. *Making Meaning: Inference and Rhetoric in the Interpretation of Cinema.* Cambridge, Mass.: Harvard University Press.

——. 1997. *On the History of Film Style.* Cambridge, Mass.: Harvard University Press.

Bordwell, David, and Kristin Thompson. 1993. *Film Art: An Introduction.* 4th ed. New York: McGraw-Hill.

Bozorgmehr, Mehdi, Claudia Der-Martirosian, and Georges Sabagh. 1996. "Middle Easterners: A New Kind of Immigrant." In *Ethnic Los Angeles*, edited by Roger Waldinger and Mehdi Bozorgmehr, 345–78. New York: Russel Sage Foundation.

Brady, Shirley. 1993. "Atom Egoyan Out of the Margins." *Shift* 1, no. 4: 10–13, 37.

Brossard, Jean-Pierre. N.d. "Dictionnaire des principaux cinéastes." In *L'Algérie vue par son cinéma*, 173–78. Locarno: Tisca Nova SA.

Burton, Julianne, ed. 1986. *Cinema and Social Change in Latin America: Conversations with Filmmakers.* Austin: University of Texas Press.

Caughie, John, ed. 1981. *Theories of Authorship: A Reader.* London: Routledge and Kegan Paul.

Cham, Mbye B. 1992. *Ex-Iles: Essays on Caribbean Cinema.* Trenton, NJ: Africa World Press.

Clifford, James. 1997. *Routes: Travel and Translation in the Late Twentieth Century.* Cambridge, Mass.: Harvard University Press.

Cohen, Robin. 1997. *Global Diasporas: An Introduction.* London: UCL Press.

Crystal, David. 1991. *A Dictionary of Linguistics and Phonetics.* 3d ed. New York: Blackwell.

Deleuze, Gilles, and Félix Guattari. 1986. *Kafka: Toward a Minor Literature.* Trans. Dana Polan. Minneapolis: University of Minnesota Press.

Desbarats, Carole, Daniele Riviere, Jacinto Lageria, and Paul Virilio, eds. 1993. *Atom Egoyan.* Paris and Toronto: Editions Dis Voir and Ontario Ministry of Culture, Tourism and Recreation.

Diawara, Manthia. 1993a. *Black American Cinema.* New York: Routledge.

——. 1993b. "Power and Territory: The Emergence of Black British Film Collectives." In *Fires Were Started: British Cinema and Thatcherism,* edited by Lester Friedman, 147–60. Minneapolis: University of Minnesota Press.

Egoyan, Atom, ed. 1995. *Exotica.* Toronto: Coach House Press.

——. 1993. *Speaking Parts.* Toronto: Coach House Press.

Feng, Peter. 1996. "Being Chinese American, Becoming Asian American: Chan Is Missing." *Cinema Journal* 35, no. 4: 88–118.

——. 1995. "In Search of Asian American Cinema." *Cinéaste* 21, nos. 1–2: 32–6.

Firmat, Gustavo Pérez. 1994. *Life on the Hyphen: The Cuban-American Way.* Austin: University of Texas Press.

Foster, Gwendolyn Audrey. 1997. *Women Filmmakers of the African and Asian Diaspora: Decolonizing the Gaze, Locating Subjectivity.* Carbondale: Southern Illinois University Press.

Foucault, Michel. 1977. *Language, Memory, Practice.* Ed. D. F. Bouchard. Oxford: Basil Blackwell.

Fregoso, Rosa Linda. 1993. *The Bronze Screen: Chicana and Chicano Film Culture.* Minneapolis: University of Minnesota Press.

Friedlander, Jonathan, ed. 1995. *The Cinema of Displacement: Middle Eastern Identities in Transition.* Los Angeles: UCLA Center for Near Eastern Studies.

Fusco, Coco. 1988. *Young British and Black: A Monograph on the Work of Sankofa Film/Video Collective and Black Audio Film Collective.* Buffalo, NY: Hallwalls.

Gabriel, Teshome, H. 1982. *Third Cinema in the Third World: The Aesthetics of Liberation.* Ann Arbor, Mich.: UMI Research Press.

Gates, Henry Louis, Jr. 1988. *The Signifying Monkey: A Theory of African-American Literary Criticism.* New York: Oxford University Press.

Gilroy, Paul. 1993. *The Black Atlantic: Modernity and Double Consciousness.* Cambridge, Mass.: Harvard University Press.

——. 1991. *"There Ain't No Black in the Union Jack": The Cultural Politics of Race and Nation.* Chicago: University of Chicago Press.

——. 1988. "Nothing But Sweat inside My Hand: Diaspora Aesthetics and Black Arts in Britain." *ICA Documents,* no. 7: 44–6. [Special issue on black film, British cinema.]

Gomery, Douglas. 1991. *Movie History: A Survey.* Belmont, Calif.; Wadsworth.

Hall, Stuart. 1994. "Cultural Identity and Diaspora." In *Colonial Discourse and Post-colonial Theory: A Reader,* edited by Patrick Williams and Laura Chrisman, 392–403. New York: Columbia University Press.

——. 1988. "New Ethnicities." *ICA Documents*, no. 7: 27–31. [Special issue on Black film, British cinema.]

Handling, Piers. 1993. "Allegories of Alienation: The Films of Atom Egoyan." *Cinematheque Ontario*, March 18–May 27, 8.

Harcourt, Peter. 1995. "Imaginary Images: An Examination of Atom Egoyan's Films." *Film Quarterly* 48, no. 3: 2–14.

Harlow, Barbara. 1991. "Sites of Struggle: Immigration, Deportation, Prison, and Exile." In *Criticism in the Borderlands*, edited by Héctor Caldrón and José David Saldívar, 149–63. Durham, NC: Duke University Press.

Hebdige, Dick. 1979. *Subculture: The Meaning of Style*. London: Methuen.

Hicks, D. Emily. 1991. *Border Writing: The Multidimensional Text*. Minneapolis: University of Minnesota Press.

Hoberman, J. 1991. *Bridge of Light: Yiddish Film between Two Worlds*. New York: Museum of Modern Art.

Jameson, Fredric. 1986. "Third-World Literature in the Era of Multinational Capitalism." *Social Text* 15 (fall): 65–88.

——. 1984. "Periodizing the 60s." In *The 60s without Apology*, edited by Sohnya Sayers et al., 178–209. Minneapolis: University of Minnesota Press.

Jarvie, Ian C. 1991. "Stars and Ethnicity: Hollywood and the United States, 1932–51." In *Unspeakable Images: Ethnicity and the American Cinema*, edited by Lester Friedman, 82–111. Urbana: University of Illinois Press.

Jay, Martin. 1993. *Downcast Eyes: The Denigration of Vision in Twentieth-Century French Thought*. Berkeley: University of California Press.

Johnson, Brian D. 1991. "Bleak Beauty." *Maclean's*, September 30, 68.

Kaplan, Caren. 1996. *Questions of Travel: Postmodern Discourses of Displacement*. Durham, NC: Duke University Press.

Kaufman, Deborah, Rena Orenstein, and Janis Plotkin, eds. 1991. *Independent Filmmakers: Looking at Ourselves. A Guide to Films Featured in the Jewish Film Festival*. Berkeley: Jewish Film Festival.

Kempley, Rita. 1990. "'Parts,' Video as Big Brother." *Washington Post*, February 3.

Kinder, Marsha. 1993. *Blood Cinema: The Reconstruction of National Identity in Spain*. Berkeley: University of California Press.

King, John. 1990. "Chilean Cinema in Revolution and Exile." In *Magic Reels: A History of Cinema in Latin America*, 169–87. New York: Verso.

Lejeune, Phillipe. 1989. *On Autobiography*. Ed. Paul Eakin. Minneapolis: University of Minnesota Press.

Leong, Russell, ed. 1991. *Moving the Image: Independent Asian Pacific American Media Arts*. Los Angeles: UCLA Asian American Studies Center.

Lopez, Ana M. 1996. "Greater Cuba." In *The Ethnic Eye: Latino Media Arts*, edited by Chon A. Noriega and Ana M. Lopez, 38–58. Minneapolis: University of Minnesota Press.

Lowe, Lisa. 1991. "Heterogeneity, Hybridity, Multiplicity: Making Asian American Difference." *Diaspora* 1, no. 1: 24–44.

Marcus, George E. 1994. "The Modernist Sensibility in Recent Ethnographic Writing and the Cinematic Metaphor of Montage." In *Visualizing Theory: Selected Essays from V.A.R., 1990–1994*, edited by Lucien Taylor, 37–53. New York: Routledge.

Marks, Laura, U. 1994. "A Deleuzian Politics of Hybrid Cinema." *Screen* 35, no. 3: 244–64.

Martin, Michael, ed. 1997. *New Latin American Cinema*. Vol. 1, *Theory, Practices and Transcontinental Articulations*. Detroit: Wayne State University Press.

——. 1995. *Cinemas of the Black Diaspora: Diversity, Dependence, and Oppositionality.* Detroit: Wayne State University Press.

Maslin, Janet. 1989. "On Forging Relationships by Electronic Intermediary." *New York Times*, September 29, C16.

Mercer, Kobena. 1994a. "Diaspora Culture and the Dialogic Imagination: The Aesthetics of Black Independent Film in Britain." In *Welcome to the Jungle: New Positions in Black Cultural Studies*, 53–68. London: Routledge.

——. 1994b. *Welcome to the Jungle: New Positions in Black Cultural Studies.* London: Routledge.

——. 1988. "Recoding Narratives of Race and Nation." *ICA Documents*, no. 7: 4–14. [Special issue on black film, British cinema.]

Modarressi, Taghi. 1992. "Writing with an Accent." *Chanteh* 1, no. 1: 7–9.

Naficy, Hamid. 1997. "The Accented Style of the Independent Transnational Cinema: A Conversation with Atom Egoyan." In *Cultural Producers in Perilous States: Editing Events, Documenting Change*, edited by George E. Marcus, 179–231. Chicago: University of Chicago Press.

——. 1996. "Phobic Spaces and Liminal Panics: Independent Transnational Film Genre." In *Global/Local: Cultural Productions and the Transnational Imaginary*, edited by Rob Wilson and Wimal Dissanayake, 119–44. Durham, NC: Duke University Press.

——. 1995 "Recurrent Themes in the Middle Eastern Cinema of Diaspora." In *The Cinema of Displacement: Middle Eastern Identities in Transition*, edited by Jonathan Friedlander, 3–63. Los Angeles: UCLA Center for Near Eastern Studies.

——. 1993. *The Making of Exile Cultures: Iranian Television in Los Angeles.* Minneapolis: University of Minnesota Press.

Noriega, Chon. 1992. *Chicanos and Film: Essays on Chicano Representation and Resistance.* New York: Garland.

O'Grady, Gerald. 1973. "Our Space in Our Time: The New American Cinema." In *The American Cinema*, edited by Donald E. Staples, 228–44. Washington, DC: US Information Agency.

Omid, Jamal. 1367/1988. *Farhang-e Sinema-ye Iran. Zendeginameh-ye Kargardanan, Tahiyehkonandegan, Filmnamehnevisan, Bazigaran, Filmbardaran, Tadvinkonandegan, Ahangsazan, Tarrahan-e Sahneh, va . . .* Tehran: Negah.

*Palestinian Film Week.* 1992. Jerusalem: Jerusalem Film Institute. [Film catalog.]

Peters, John. 1999. "Exile, Nomadism, and Diaspora: The Stakes of Mobility in the Western Canon." In *Home, Exile, Homeland: Film, Media, and the Politics of Place*, edited by Hamid Naficy, 17–41. New York: Routledge.

Petrie, Graham, and Ruth Dwyer, eds. 1990. *Before the Wall: Society and East European Filmmakers Working in the West.* Lanhan, MD: University Press of America.

Pfeil, Fred. 1988. "Postmodernism as a 'Structure of Feeling.'" In *Marxism and the Interpretation of Culture*, edited by Cary Nelson and Lawrence Grossberg, 381–403. Urbana: University of Illinois Press.

Pflaum, Hans Günther, and Hans Helmut Prinzler. 1993. *Cinema in the Federal Republic of Germany.* Bonn: Inter Nationes.

Pick, Zuzana M. 1993. "Exile and Displacement." In *The New Latin American Cinema: A Continental Project*, 157–85. Austin: University of Texas Press.

Porton, Richard. 1997. "Family Romances: An Interview with Atom Egoyan." *Cinéaste* 23, no. 2: 8–15.

Radvanyi, Jean, ed. 1993. *Le Cinéma Arménien.* Paris: éditions du Centre Pompidou.

Reid, Mark A. 1991. "African and Black Diaspora Film/Video." *Jump Cut*, no. 36: 43–6.

Rushdie, Salman. 1991. *Imaginary Homelands: Essays and Criticism, 1981–1991*. London: Granta.

Safran, William. 1991. "Diasporas in Modern Societies: Myths of Homeland and Return." *Diaspora* 1 no. 1: 83–99.

Said, Edward W. 1990. "Reflections on Exile." In *Out There: Marginalization and Contemporary Cultures*, edited by Russell Ferguson, Martha Gever, Trinh T. Minh-ha, and Cornel West, 357–66. Cambridge, Mass.: MIT Press.

Salloum, Jayce, ed. 1996. *East of Here: (Re)Imagining the "Orient."* Catalogue of an exhibition held at YYZ Artists' Outlet, Toronto, November 20–December 14.

*The Second Festival for Iranian Films in Exile, 6–13 October.* 1995. Göteborg: Sweden: Exile-Film Festival.

Sherzer, Dina, ed. 1996. *Cinema, Colonialism, Postcolonialism: Perspectives from the French and Francophone World*. Austin: University of Texas Press.

Shohat, Ella. 1991. "Ethnicities-in-Relation: Toward a Multicultural Reading of American Cinema." In *Unspeakable Images: Ethnicity and the American Cinema*, edited by Lester D. Friedman, 215–250. Urbana: University of Illinois Press.

Shohat, Ella, and Robert Stam. 1994. *Unthinking Eurocentrism: Multiculturalism and the Media*. London: Routledge.

Sobchack, Vivian. 1999. "'Is Any Body Home?': Embodied Imagination and Visible Evictions." In *Home, Exile, Homeland: Film, Media and the Politics of Place*, edited by Hamid Naficy, 45–61. New York: Routledge.

Sollors, Werner. 1986. *Beyond Ethnicity: Consent and Descent in American Culture*. New York: Oxford University Press.

Spivak, Gayatri Chakravotry. 1988. "Can the Subaltern Speak?" In *Marxism and the Interpretation of Culture*, edited by Cary Nelson and Lawrence Grossberg, 271–313. Urbana: University of Illinois Press.

Taussig, Michael. 1992. "Tactility and Distraction." In *Reading Cultural Anthropology*, edited by George E. Marcus, 8–14. Durham, NC: Duke University Press.

Tavenas, Stéphane, and François Volard. 1989. *Guide of European Cinema*. Trans. David Clougher. Paris: éditions Ramsey/Eurocinéma.

Thomas, Nicholas, ed. 1990. *International Dictionary of Films and Filmmakers*. 2d ed. Chicago: St. James Press.

Tölölyan, Khachig. 1996. "Rethinking Diaspora(s): Stateless Power in the Transnational Moment." *Diaspora* 5, no. 1: 3–36.

Ukadike, Nwachukwu Frank. 1994. *Black African Cinema*. Berkeley: University of California Press.

Willemen, Paul. 1989. "The Third Cinema Question: Notes and Reflections." In *Questions of Third Cinema*, edited by Jim Pines and Paul Willemen, 1–29. London: British Film Institute.

Williams, Raymond. 1977. "Structure of Feeling." In *Marxism and Literature*, 128–35. London: Oxford University Press.

# Part IX

## Cities and the Urban Imaginary

# Introduction

## Ackbar Abbas

What can urban theory tell us about the "Asian City" today? It is with this question in mind that the texts in this section have been chosen. It is not a matter of asking what is specifically "Asian" about Asian cities, or of giving these cities a greater prominence than they deserve, or of concentrating exclusively on writings about Asia. It is rather a matter of testing the assumption that the urban concepts useful for thinking the Asian city are likely to be the concepts crucial for an understanding of urbanism today.

The focus on the Asian city seems justifiable for at least two reasons. In the first place, while there is a large body of work on the social and economic aspects of the Asian city, there is as yet not enough work that relates these aspects in an interdisciplinary way to cultural issues; especially if we agree that in performing such a task, recourse to an ahistorical and reified notion of "Asian Values" is hardly adequate. On the other hand, works that do make interesting links between cities and culture, like Peter Hall's in many ways magisterial volume *Cities in Civilization*,[1] do not feel the need to discuss the contribution of Asian cities to urban culture. With the exception of Tokyo, Asian cities do not figure at all in his book.

However, besides trying to redress an imbalance, there is a second and more important reason for focusing on the Asian city: because it seems likely that that is where some of the more radical urban and cultural experiments of the twenty-first century will be taking place. Asian cities are the most challenging urban sites today because they are the most problematic. Transformed at unprecedented speed by new forms of capital, politics, media, and technology, the Asian city today threatens to outpace our understanding of it. More so perhaps than cities elsewhere, the Asian city reminds us that the city exists not just as a physical, political, and economic entity that can be accurately documented, but also as a cluster of images, a series of discourses, an experience of space and place, and a set of practices that do not necessarily add up.

This unevenness constitutes a novel form of "uneven development" that is taking place not just between different cities, but also within each city itself. Different parts of the city undergo change at different speeds, resulting in a kind of spatial anamorphosis that Anthony Vidler calls a "warped space."[2] Such a space challenges traditional recognitions, even when, *especially* when, it looks "traditional." Beijing, Shanghai, Guangzhou, Shenzhen, Hong Kong, Taipei, Kuala Lumpur, Mumbai – each of these cities is like a kind of jigsaw puzzle of the mind, made up of cognitive/experiential fragments, of historical residues and aspirations. When some of the bits and pieces click into place in relation to one another, as they sometimes do, a kind of *urban epiphany* takes place, and we believe for a fugitive moment that we see the city whole; but more often than not, these bits and pieces stubbornly refuse meaning and defy comprehension. Hence these cities are never simply "interesting" or "boring"; rather, our experience of them is split right down the middle: moments of heightened intensity and breathless expectation alternate with periods of boredom, apathy, and hopeless repetition.

It is often said that Asian cities present "a mixture of the old and the new," of the old and familiar co-existing picturesquely with the new and unfamiliar. However, this cliché does not begin to describe their historical complexity. For example, new architecture in Beijing and Shanghai may disorient our perceptions of these cities; but just as disorienting is the trend towards "preserving" old buildings to stimulate tourism. One effect of preservation is to make us experience the "old" as itself unfamiliar. While the physical building may remain recognizable, the grids and coordinates by which we make sense of it are more elusive. Hence the need not only to provide new terms to describe Asian cities and cities elsewhere, but also to rethink old terms. And this brings us now to the texts in this section.

In her essay "Cultural Intersections: Re-visioning Architecture and the City in the Twentieth Century," Zeynep Çelik rightly sees colonialism as central to urban history, but colonialism is also one of those terms that need to be rethought. In an opening passage, she argues that "it is essential to understand modernism as a universal phenomenon in the twentieth century and not as something that belongs solely to the 'West.' To expand on these concepts, a closer look at colonialism is indispensable." Furthermore, as an architectural historian, she is concerned with the way colonialism embodies itself in built forms: "Among cultural formations, architecture occupies a prominent position because it bears the potential to express social relation and power structures at certain critical moments in crystallized forms." The "colonial city" redirects attention to cities in Asia, Africa, and South America and reserves a place for them in urban history. Çelik begins by quoting Frantz Fanon's famous depiction of the colonial city as essentially a dual structure, designed to separate as starkly as possible the space of the colonizer from the space of the colonized. She goes on to show how this stress on segregation is achieved through colonial town planning; for example, the creation of parks and green areas as so many *cordons sanitaires*, the emphasis on edges and contours, the introduction of zoning laws, and so on. However, "colonialism" also has the ability to transform itself and adapt to changing economic, cultural, and political situations. It is one thing in the era of imperialism, and something else (perhaps unrecognizable) in the era of globalism. At the same time, urban forms are transmuted. The later part of the chapter therefore focuses not on examples of spatial segregation but on the building of skyscrapers in postcolonial Asian cities like Kuala Lumpur and Shanghai, largely by American architectural firms who are thereby invested with "a great deal of authority and power to give architectural and aesthetic expression to cultural and national identities elsewhere... Colonial structures thus survive (albeit in renewed forms), and the superordinates and the subordinates remain unchanged even if building activity has shifted to the East." But something has changed, and it is an open question, as Çelik realizes, whether it is possible today to speak of "colonialism" without very careful qualifications. As cities take on new spatial forms, so domination and control follow a different spatial logic.

This brings us to the important writings of Manuel Castells. In a body of work that powerfully combines theory and empirical evidence, he shows us that while cities today are of very different kinds, they all share a spatial logic specific to the Information Age: the logic of the space of flows. One direct result of this logic is the creation of megacities. Megacities are not just big or dispersed; what is distinctive about them is the new way in which they are organized: they are "globally connected and locally disconnected." What is distinctive about the space of flows, whose unit is the network, is that it allows *simultaneously* for centralization and decentralization; locational concentration can go together with territorial sprawl. Thus the network permits command and control units to be centralized in head offices located in New York or London, while back offices or production units can be decentralized to the suburbs or to other cities. The space of flows therefore makes possible "the simultaneity of social practices without territorial contiguity"; i.e., it makes possible action (in time) at a distance, which is a new form of spatial control. The megacity too is a kind of expansion and control of space, and Castells' prediction is that this type of city "is likely to become the most representative urban face of the twenty-first century."

Nevertheless, Castells goes on to argue that the space of flows is not the whole story; there is also the space of places. People, he argues, still tend to construct their lives around places even when places no longer imply a sense of community. So while dominant activities are organized around the space of flows, most of experience and social interaction are organized around the space of places. In other words, the network society is not a closed system, characterized by "domination" alone; it can be penetrated by "grassroots" groups capable of constructing alternative meanings within the system. And here we come to the crux of the argument: the possibility of agency, or of resistance to the dominant. "Where there is domination," Castells writes, "there is resistance," and he points out that the "grassroots of societies do not cease to exist in the Information Age." Castells goes on to outline a number of ways for "grassrooting the space of flows," to make it a plural and contested space. Above all, what grassrooting has to contest is exactly the separation of flows and places, because it is by working on their *interface* that agency returns.

Rem Koolhaas's writings on the city are very different from Castells', in that they offer us a playful but nonetheless serious take on contemporary urban mutations. His essay "The Generic City" consists of 17 numbered sections of witty aphorisms and observations, not detailed arguments or empirical evidence.[3] In one respect, though, his work impinges on Castells', and that is when he describes the "generic city" as "what is left after large sections of urban life crossed over into cyberspace"; however, the implications he draws from this fact cannot be more different. Instead of asking how agency and identity can be retained, Koolhaas takes the opposite tack and asks what the *disadvantages* of identity are and what the advantages of blankness. His thesis is that the Generic City – many examples of which can be located in Asia (Singapore, the cities of the Pearl River Delta) – has overcome any fixation on identity; and furthermore, that this shedding of identity is seen not as loss but as liberation: "What if the seemingly accidental – and usually regretted – homogenization were an intentional process, a conscious movement away from difference toward similarity? What if we are witnessing a global movement: 'down with character!'" The great "originality" of the generic, he goes on to say, is "simply to abandon what doesn't work"; in other words, it travels light, pragmatically unburdened by any "history" that might constrict identity. Hence, the Generic City is "the city without history," in that what it represents is a major urban mutation: "The generic city is all that remains of what used to be the city. The Generic City is the post-city being prepared on the site of the ex-city."

Like Koolhaas, Mario Gandelsonas also directs our attention to urban mutation. What he calls X-Urbanism is the latest stage in the history of the American city. However, in a short, tantalizing footnote, he suggests that X-Urbanism, first developed in America, can now be exemplified in many cities in Asia, like Shanghai and Shenzhen. In his book, Gandelsonas gives us, through drawings and text, a history of urban mutations in America in 7 scenes, each scene more traumatic than the one before.

It is the final scene, what Gandelsonas calls Scene X, that concerns us most, the mutation of the suburban city into the X-Urban City. The suburbs' development into the suburban city is made possible by, among other things, the motorcar and TV: one extends the suburban house to the city, the other brings the city to the house. The urban scene is now doubled, consisting of the pairing of the urban and the suburban. By contrast, the X-Urban city came into being when global finance institutions and the service industries began to relocate their offices to the suburbs. However, unlike the suburban city, X-Urbia does not develop in opposition to the center, but in contiguity and in tandem to it. We find then an urbanism that does not oppose fringe to center, home to workplace, but rather an urbanism that is multicentered, decentered, or fractal. X-Urbia does not so much supplement as supplant the suburbs, changing them from the inside out.

It is perhaps through TV and films that the difference between suburbia and X-Urbia can best be grasped. For example, in 1950's sitcoms like the classic *I Love Lucy*, the suburbs are experienced as the site of normalcy and quiet green spaces, however wacky Lucille Ball may be. By contrast, in the X-Urban, this same scene of white picket fences and manicured lawns is, in David Lynch's *Blue Velvet*, the scene of perversion and paranoia, where X marks the scene of a crime. Gandelsonas's two most striking images of the X-Urban are, first, the new gated communities where X-Urbanities hide paranoically behind their electronic surveillance and alarm systems; and secondly, the TV docudrama *Cops*, where the automobile is morphed from a privileged means of transport into the police car on the prowl for crime that lurks everywhere. As prefix, "X" suggests not just the unknown; it also suggests the figure of chiasmus, a critical point of cross over, where old boundaries are blurred, and everything needs to be reformulated, including ideas about the authentic and the fake.

Perhaps it could be argued that one symptom of the X-Urban is precisely the fake goods that are so readily available in Asian cities. If the X-Urban is the metropolitan face of a new global economy, then the fake is the local face of the global commodity. The trade in fakes contributes quite significantly to the creation of a "shadow economy" in the places where they are sold, though there are understandably no exact figures. The shadow economy has no CEOs, no management boards, no archive, no statistics, no accountants. Nevertheless, one of the conditions for the production of fakes is the electronic media that make the dissemination of information fast and economical. In other words, the fake too belongs to the history of information, and to the moment when information itself is the most important commodity. We can think of the fake then – quite aside from its all too obvious factitiousness – as a response at a local and apparently trivial level to the process of globalization.

One of the most striking chapters in Ziauddin Sardar's *The Consumption of Kuala Lumpur* is the chapter about the night market on Petaling Street. This is one of the many night markets of the developing world where millennial dreams jostle with economic reality and where: fakes are sold. Sardar's argument is that the fake is a form of resistance, even a form of "gentle subversion," against exclusion from the global world order. When "slight Malay bodies" dress themselves in fake goods, Sardar writes, "they are *in*-cluded, fashion and fancy, and not *ex*-cluded, marginalized onlookers. In the international politics of self and style they are fully empowered." Sardar is pointing to a kind of value in fake goods; but to make the point, it is perhaps enough to see the fake as symptom rather than as subversion. Its value as symptom is that it gives in shabby, damaged form, the negative imprint of a global world. Through a kind of maniacal imitation, the fake sometimes catches the global system off-guard, and provides a kind of crazing of the smooth mirror of global production. That is the *countervalue* of the counterfeit.

NOTES

1   Sir Peter Hall, *Cities in Civilization: Culture, Innovation, and Urban Order* (London: Weidenfeld and Nicolson, 1998).

2   Anthony Vidler, *Warped Space: Art, Architecture and Anxiety in Modern Culture* (Cambridge, MA: MIT Press, 2000).

3   Similarly, Koolhaas's other text on cities in the Pearl River Delta (the site of one of Castells' megacities) takes us on a guided tour of the urban condition he calls the generic city. Hence it is not too surprising that in that text (part of the ongoing collaborative "Harvard Project on the City"), when Koolhaas describes the Chinese cities of the Delta – specifically Shenzhen, the Gordon Wu highway, Dongguan, and Zhuhai – he sounds a little like Alice describing the Looking-Glass world. And like Alice talking to Humpty-Dumpty, he is conscious of "a need to overhaul the vocabulary at our disposal. The contemporary language for talking about the city is lacking when it comes to naming and interpreting its mutations." Hence Koolhaas says, perhaps tongue-in-cheek: "We have introduced seventy-five new terms to account for the specific characteristics encountered here; these will be published in copyrighted form to make their ownership clear." See Rem Koolhaas, "PRD Pearl River Delta," in *Mutations: Rem Koolhaas, Harvard Project on the City* (Barcelona: ACTAR, 2000), 309–35.

# 40

# Cultural Intersections: Re-visioning Architecture and the City in the Twentieth Century

## Zeynep Çelik

■ Homogeneity and Cultural Difference ■

Architecture and urbanism at the end of the century reveal a hitherto unwitnessed globalization. Cultural boundaries can no longer be neatly drawn and notions such as "purity" and "authenticity" have become obsolete. Echoing Paul Ricoeur's observation that "everywhere throughout the world, one finds the same bad movie, the same slot machines, the same plastic or aluminum atrocities, the same twisting of language by propaganda,"[1] urban forms and architecture have increasingly become universalized. At the end of the century, the suburbs of Boston, Houston, and Paris, the heights of Algiers, the hills of the Bosphorus in Istanbul, and the center of Taipei share the slick, uniform, and interiorized environments of shopping malls, where similar or even identical products are enthusiastically consumed. Steel and glass skyscrapers transform urban landscapes everywhere; they overshadow previous layers of history with their sheer size and signify new directions in the economic structure. This architecture belongs to the era of transnational corporations that "represent neither their home countries nor their host nations but simply their own corporate selves" which began to dominate the world economy from the 1970s on, creating a specific culture and a privileged, transnational class of professionals who live a global lifestyle.[2] Furthermore, boundaries and borders are increasingly being replaced by interface as access to the contemporary city through electronic systems, global information, and capital networks begin to devalue the physical idea of space.[3]

If the new transnational class represents one end of the spectrum in homogenizing cities throughout the world, poverty is the equalizer at the other end. Social segregation according to class and ethnicity divides cities into fragments, with the formal characteristic of the residential quarters of low-income groups, for example, displaying striking similarities despite geographic distances. Not only do the squatter settlements around Bombay, Rabat, Brasilia, Caracas, Algiers, and Paris (the last prominent in the 1960s, now cleared) display similar configurations and architectural and constructional features, but the housing "solutions" aimed to prevent such developments follow the same formulas, creating strikingly similar environments in disparate parts of the globe. The edges of many cities during the last decades of the century consist of sprawls of housing blocks, unanimously inadequate measures against the towering shortage of decent housing, united in their visual anonymity and the sad barrenness of the spaces separating them.

The anonymity that marks the end-of-the-century city is accompanied by an immense pressure for an expression of identity. In the 1990s – torn with ethnic and neonationalist struggles and deep conflicts over cultural, ethnic, and racial differences – this urge may hark back to the artistic and literary productions of the "third world" in the aftermath of the Second World War, when nationalism became a trope for "belonging," "bordering," and "commitment."[4] Nevertheless, the expression of cultural identity now takes on new meanings and is absorbed into the logic of today's global markets. As observed by one cultural critic in specific reference to Benetton advertisements, the global markets now not only acknowledge but also depoliticize cultural differences by presenting them in "categorical rather than relational terms."[5] Although reaching a peak at the end of the century, the two interlocked and seemingly contradictory paradigms of homogeneity and expression of cultural difference in architecture and urbanism run throughout it, shifting in form and meaning within a complex web of social, cultural, political, and economic entanglements. Modernism – understood according to Marshall Berman's definition as "a struggle to make ourselves at home in a constantly changing world" that "implies an open and expansive way of understanding culture" – constitutes the broad framework for the entire century.[6]

Even at moments when expression of identity emerges as the leading drive, notions such as "purity" and "authenticity" remain obsolete due to the complexities of cultural interchange.[7] Nonetheless, the discourse on architecture and urbanism still pursues the nineteenth-century compulsion to classify, categorize, and frame: empire-building techniques linger, pigeonholing societies and cultures according to familiar hierarchies. It often glosses over the porous nature of present-day borders or capitalizes upon them to emphasize a one-way traffic that ends up reiterating the supremacy of certain cultures over others. The systematic repetition of tired formulas continues to coalesce into a seemingly coherent and authoritative "truth." The division of the world into "first" and "third" (with the clouded "second" disappearing ever faster), "developed" and "underdeveloped," "central" and "peripheral," "Western" and "non-Western," culminates in the contrived debate between (Western) modernism and the traditions of others and is reduced to a paradigm, memorably summarized by Rasheed Araeen as "our Bauhaus, others' mudhouse." Araeen suggests that, as important as it is to understand the construction of the other by the dominant culture, a more interesting question is how this other subverts the assumptions on which it is based.[8] Regardless of where and how it originated, it is essential to understand modernism as a universal phenomenon in the twentieth century and not as something that belongs solely to the "West." To expand on these concepts, a closer look at colonialism is indispensable.

With its powerful nineteenth-century legacies, colonialism has continued to play a crucial role in defining relationships between societies and cultures during our century as well. Cultural production was fundamental in establishing the colonial condition, because, as Edward Said argued, culture enabled the formation of the idea of imperiality, which depended on "the enterprise of empire."[9] Yet cultural formations responded during the arduous process of decolonization, resisting notions of imperiality and subverting the order of the world (if not changing it). Among cultural formations, architecture occupies a prominent position because it bears the potential to express social relations and power structures at certain critical moments in crystallized forms: as physical frame to all human activity and because of its experiential qualities that engage everybody, architecture constitutes an essential part of the human experience. It expresses cultural values and is firmly grounded in material and daily life. Its connection to the everyday world is so substantial that if it can never be divorced from worldly associations; neither can it transcend them.

## ■ Colonialism and Cities ■

The sheer scope of building activity, as well as the innovative, varied, and experimental nature of architectural and urban projects undertaken in the colonies in the twentieth – as well as the nineteenth – century call for a more extensive analysis than the discipline of architectural history has dedicated to the topic so far. The history of modernism cannot be abstracted from the architectural and urban practices in the colonies scattered to all corners of the world, and the study of colonialism cannot be treated separately from that of the *métropole* or treated as a subtext to it. The interlocked nature of the *métropole* and the colony was well understood at the height of the colonial age and underlined by two prominent French figures. Louis Hubert Gonzalve Lyautey, the resident general of the French protectorate in Morocco, in a widely-quoted statement called the colonies "the laboratories for modernism," and Albert Sarraut (former governor of Indochina and minister of colonies) explained the phenomenon with a modernist architectural metaphor: "Henceforth, the European edifice rests on colonial *pilotis*."[10]

Regardless of the shifts in colonial policies adopted by different powers and at different times, the architecture of European quarters in colonized territories relied upon the newly developing concepts of modernism, as well as on nineteenth-century traditions (themselves forming the basis for modernist notions). To refer to a few memorable case studies, in Rabat – called by Lyautey the "Washington, DC of Morocco" – Henri Prost created a road network in the 1910s that combined radial and orthogonal avenues; these spatial avenues highlighted the public and monumental structures by framing them with vistas, and the whole system was "aired" by parks and gardens. A decade later in French Indochina, Ernest Hébrard's addition to Hanoi, a monumental administrative center, emulated the diagonal and grid street network and incorporated into it spacious green areas. In 1913 Sir Edwin Lutyens designed the showcase of British colonialism, New Delhi, according to another complex plan of diagonals and grids, and very deliberately utilized grand vistas to highlight the buildings that symbolized the British Empire. In colonial Manila (1906–14), Daniel Burnham was able to realize his City Beautiful *par excellence*, surpassing in scale and coherence of design any of his projects in the United States. In the Belgian Congo, the city of Goma, built in the 1920s and 1930s, displayed another ambitious design with converging avenues.

If the colonial city planners' designs shared similarities, the architecture built in each city was different. In the French colonies the nineteenth-century practice of equating the "conqueror's style" with public buildings as a blatant political statement gave way in the early years of this century to a more flexible attitude reflecting "tolerance" toward local cultures in accordance with new experiments in colonial policies: the move from "assimilation" to "association."[11] This trend resulted in many notable buildings that combined Beaux-Arts principles with decorative programs derived from local architecture and endowed each colonial city with its own image. Landmarks in two French colonial cities – the Hôtel de Ville in Sfax, Tunisia, by Raphaël Guy, clad in neo-Islamic elements, and the Musée d'histoire Louis Finon in Hanoi by Ernest Hébrard, with Indochinese details, both designed in the 1920s – exhibit this attitude, which can be interpreted as the absorption of the colonies into the cultural repertoire of the empire, albeit in a controlled and tamed manner. The architectural references in Lutyens's New Delhi operate in a similar frame.

Colonial cities came in different shapes and scales but shared one prominent characteristic: a dual structure that clearly delineated the separation of the colonizer from the colonized. During the most intense phase of decolonization struggles, Frantz Fanon described the generic "colonial city" as being composed of two irreconcilable parts:

> The zone where the natives live is not complementary to the zone inhabited by the settlers. The two zones are opposed, but not in the service of a higher unity. Obedient to the rules of pure Aristotelian logic, they both follow the principle of reciprocal exclusivity. No conciliation is possible, for of the two terms, one is superfluous. The settler's town is a strongly built town, all made of stone and steel. It is a brightly lit town; the streets are covered with asphalt, and the garbage cans swallow all the leavings, unseen, unknown and hardly thought about.... The settler's town is a well-fed town, an easygoing town; its belly is always full of good things....
>
> The town belonging to the colonized people, or at least the native town, the Negro village, the medina, the reservation, is... a world without any spaciousness; men live there on top of each other, and their huts are built one on top of the other. The native

town is a hungry town, starved of bread, of meat, of shoes, of light. The native town is a crouching village, a town on its knees, a town wallowing in the mire.[12]

The dichotomy was not an accident, but a deliberate creation. Following nineteenth-century practices, "European" cities were built adjacent to "native" towns in all corners of the world, with long-term consequences that have contributed to the endurance of bipolar cultural and societal formulas even now, at the end of the twentieth century. Guillaume de Tarde, a former secretary general of the Protectorate of Morocco, expressed the need for a revised understanding of the dual-city pattern in his report to the International Congress of Urbanism in the Colonies, held in conjunction with the 1931 Colonial Exposition in Paris:

> Separation should exist, but this should not be a radical separation. The issue is not to establish distance with an attitude of contempt toward the indigenous town ... but to the contrary, to maintain a discreet separation of two towns otherwise closely united. ... In summary, the European town should be sufficiently far from the indigenous town in order not to absorb it, but close enough to it so that it can live off it to some measure.[13]

In Morocco during the 1910s and the 1920s, under the leadership of Marshal Lyautey and his chief architect, Henri Prost, this duality was explained within a philosophy of tolerance as a protective measure to save the architectural and urbanistic heritage of the medinas. Moroccan cities, varying from major settlements such as Rabat, Fez, and Marrakesh, to smaller centers like Tétouan and Meknèz, thus remained untouched by colonial interventions but were subjected to another kind of pressure from the planned new developments outside their boundaries.[14] In Tunisia, the municipality of Tunis commissioned architect Victor Valensi in 1920 to devise a *projet d'aménagement, d'embellissement, et d'extension* with a specification to "conserve carefully the medina and especially the zone of the souks" and extend the European city according to modern concepts.[15]

The recommendation that a green zone – a *cordon sanitaire* – be placed whenever possible between the two parts of the city revealed concerns other than "tolerance" behind the physical separation. As an urban design feature, this item became transcribed into the "wish list" of participants in the 1931 congress on colonial urbanism in order to ensure the maintenance of ethnic segregation.[16] Le Corbusier's unrealized Obus projects for Algiers (1931–42) re-interpreted the same notion and took it to an extreme by making the new European city bridge over the intact Casbah, transforming the greenbelt into an air band and reversing the horizontality of the former into a vertical element. The implications of these designs extended the colonial premise farther: Le Corbusier's plans established constant visual supervision over the local population and clearly marked the hierarchical social order onto the urban image, with the dominating located above and the dominated below.[17]

The meticulous order and imperial facade of Lutyens's New Delhi contrasted with the dense and "chaotic" fabric of historic Delhi nearby. The Italian planners working under Mussolini also followed the familiar formula. In Tripoli, Libya, for example, a monumental piazza separated the Muslim town from the new Italian quarters while bringing a touch of Venice: two pillars on the waterfront act as the "gate" to the city.[18] In the "functional" plan developed for Addis Ababa, Ethiopia, the officially stated principle was segregation. According to a 1937 report, the first problem to be resolved (rather, "disciplined") in a colonial city was "coexistence of metropolitans and natives...so profoundly different in terms of race, religion, and (above all) civilization." Therefore, indigenous markets and living quarters were relegated to the edges of the city (which also contained the industries); the administrative center and European residential and commercial areas were in the center.[19]

The separation of Europeans from the colonized population was camouflaged with a more "scientific" and "technical" tone following the new methodologies developed in urban planning; "zoning" emerged as the key term. In the plans for the extension of Hanoi, for example, the dual structure was presented in terms of residential and commercial "zones" for Europeans and the "indigenous," in addition to industrial, administrative, military, and recreational zones. In French Equatorial Africa, defined as a "new country" whose urbanistic, hygienic, and residential development had to happen "at once" (*d'un seul coup*), Brazzaville had become "unrecognizable" within the short period of three years. Brazzaville was "separated from [the indigenous settlements to the southwest and northeast] in order to radically isolate illness in case of an epidemic." With its "beautiful arteries...that connected the important points, the train stations, and the harbors," the city was divided into clear zones: civic center, military and colonial establishments, commercial activities, harbor and warehouses, and residential neighborhoods of the *nouvelle ville*.[20] In this order, the "indigenous villages" were presented as an additional zone. Another striking example of this trend is a generic "Belgian colonial town," designed in 1949 in an ideal and linear configuration along a rail line. The five alternative schemes are divided into European, indigenous, commercial, and industrial zones, with the European and the indigenous quarters divided either by a commercial or an industrial buffer. Two of the schemes are further complicated by the presence of a third group, the *évolués*, who were zoned away from the *non-évolués* by commerce and placed next to the Europeans, though separated from them by the railroad.[21] These are only a few among the myriad examples that illustrate the marriage between the hierarchical order of colonial thinking and the principles of modern planning. [...]

## ■ Modernism and the New Capitals ■

While one group of modernist architects was finding inspiration in "non-Western" vernacular forms, modern architecture in its purest "Western" manifestation was being adopted by many "developing" countries because of its symbolic significance: its association with technological advancement and contemporary civilization. This is perhaps most clearly expressed in the creation of new capital cities.

The earliest modernist example of a brand-new showcase is Ankara, made the capital of the Republic of Turkey in 1923. The Turkish Republic, declaring a radical departure from the Ottoman Empire upon whose ashes it was built, undertook a series of reforms aimed to bring the country to the level of technological and cultural development achieved in the Western world. These reforms, qualified by one historian as "Westernizing despite the West," extended to urbanism and architecture.[22] With a goal defined as the creation of a "civilized and healthy" city in the "Western style," Ankara's design was entrusted to German planners early in the process, and the master plan drawn in 1927 by Herman Jansen of Berlin was put into effect despite pressing economic problems faced by the new state.[23] The image sought for Ankara, with its location in the center of the country carrying symbolic and practical significance, was deliberately very different from that of Istanbul, the capital of the Ottoman Empire for almost five centuries. Istanbul's impressive monumental complexes, strategically situated on the hills of the city and complementing them with their domes and minarets, expressed the image of a once-powerful empire still imbued with religious values in the early twentieth century. In contrast, Ankara's monumentality would be defined by government, administrative, and educational buildings designed in a rational formalism, representing the essence and dynamism of the young and secular republic and its desperate longing to belong to the modern world.

Similar disassociations from the past surfaced frequently in the design of other capital cities, though much later than in Ankara. Brasilia, designed by Lucia Costa and Oscar Niemeyer in the late 1950s and early 1960s, was situated in the heart of Brazil in response to a desire to integrate the country geopolitically,[24] the city plan also corresponded to the modernization reforms undertaken during the same period under the democratic government of Juscelino Kubitschek. The plan was a grand gesture very much inspired by Le Corbusier's theoretical schemes and the practical dictums of numerous CIAM charters. What mattered was the construction of an image of modernity with large blocks and vast open spaces, with each zone clearly delineated according to function – at the expense of public space.[25] Costa and Niemeyer thus turned away from the historic precedents of Latin urbanism, which organized the life of a city around a central plaza and provided for the needs of the individual as well as social interaction within the urban public spaces. Yet, despite all its shortcomings, the city embodied the hopes of many Brazilians and "in particular, their desire for modernity."[26]

This longing for modernity accounts largely for the forms and images of numerous new capitals built for nations that have gained their independence since the 1960s. Islamabad, the capital of Pakistan designed by Doxiadis Associates in the early 1960s, embodied, according to its military ruler General Ayub Khan, "the sum total of the aspirations, the life and the ambitions of the people of the whole of Pakistan."[27] Intended by Doxiadis as a "dynapolis" – a dynamic city with its own impetus of growth provided by a master plan – Islamabad was organized in a rectilinear pattern along a central axis, a ceremonial avenue that culminated at the government complex; the buildings that filled the grid further enhanced the image of modernity. Another example is Abuja, planned in 1975 as Nigeria's new capital. Its geographical location in the center of the country was in accord with another official attempt to unite heretofore disconnected regions physically (by means of an extensive transportation network) and symbolically (by implying peace and harmony among the numerous tribes). Abuja's master plan, prepared by Kenzo Tange, also has a predominant axis with an impressively scaled "mall" that centers on the parliament. The plan may be reminiscent of the City Beautiful plans of the turn of the century, but the imagery is that of the space age defined by impressive frame structures filled in with modular components. Despite the designers' insistence on the "indigenous" roots of their inspiration (based on their study of many Nigerian cities), the scheme projects the aesthetics of a late twentieth-century modernity. Perhaps it was the future-oriented (yet ambivalent) quality of this image that made the project symbolically appropriate to surpass the many schisms in the country.

In these master plans the governmental buildings are situated at the vistas of the principal axes; they dominate the city as visual reflections of the all-mighty state and its control mechanisms. They hence follow in the footsteps of colonial urban designs that also mapped a hierarchical order. However, such schematic metaphors evince conflicts regarding the essence of modernism. In modern regimes, power is not centralized; disciplinary practices are broken into small mechanisms that are disseminated in a different pattern than that of a centralized, singular political authority with its institutions radiating power.[28] Therefore, the contemporary and modern façades of the new capitals are about appearance and aspirations; consideration of their urban design principles exposes other realities.

Even more complex is the choice of Ralph Lerner's project for the Indira Gandhi National Center for Arts in New Delhi. The 1987 competition for the center outlined a complicated and extensive program for a compound to be built on the Central Vista green in the administrative core of New Delhi. The framework was Lutyens's imperial design; the project was to complete it, but the nature of the completion was not obvious. How would a building complex intended to promote all aspects of Indian culture fit into an urban design scheme that represented the colonial past of India? The controversy was voiced by certain critics who challenged the appropriateness of an international competition for a center devoted to Indian art and who argued that it should be open only to Indian architects. However, Prime Minister Rajiv Gandhi insisted and, referring to Mahatma Gandhi's statement about artistic boundaries not being restricted by national boundaries, he accused the critics of myopia.[29]

Lerner, an American architect and an outsider to Indian culture, followed a formalistic approach and almost innocently overlooked India's recent history and the memory of the colonial period. While he explained his project as inspired by Hindu, Moghul, and classical architecture and as a synthesis of the two traditions of planning in New Delhi – the monumental and axial planing of Lutyens and the treatment of the city as an extensive garden[30] – the project largely reflects Lutyens's design and adheres to it both on urban-design principles and architectural style. The references to the local heritage are very much in accord with Lutyens's own incorporation of the "Indian" styles into his classical architecture, thereby making

Lerner's addition a continuation of the imperial style – with perhaps a touch of the "western fashions and stylistic preoccupation" of the 1980s.[31] In this case, then, unlike those of the other capitals discussed above, it is not the apparent modernity of the proposal that appealed to the jury, but rather its straightforward continuity with colonial monumentality.

In contrast to Lerner's scheme, the second-prize winner, Indian architect Gautam Bhatia, opted for an oppositional design that answered back to Lutyens's open and ceremonial vistas, to his architectural rendering of power relationships and hierarchies. Bhatia proposed an asymmetrical *parti* for the organization of the site, a metaphor that saw "Rajpath [the main avenue that the site faces] as a river, with the city taking the form of a journey along the river." He pursued the symbolism by developing the project as a "ghat" (a bathing place by a river, an important component of Indian life and religion) that faced onto the "Rajpath River."[32] Anchoring himself in the historic heritage of India and following the standards set by the sophisticated and by now truly mature experiments of Indian architects, he proposed an architecture that turned inward, that compartmentalized the program into smaller units, and that privileged modesty over monumentality.[33] At the same time, with this intervention he disrupted the order imposed on the city by Lutyens.

The unanimous choice of Lerner's scheme over Bhatia's opens up a web of questions related to end-of-the-century issues of cultural identity as represented through architecture.[51] Is the colonial past so overwhelming that it imposes a continuity on its cultural and artistic products? Do the forms of this past overshadow those of modernism, with its potential for neutrality and its future-oriented symbolism? Or can it be argued that four decades after independence, cultural products of colonialism can be forcefully appropriated into the rich and multilayered history of contemporary India and that they can be reshaped to reflect its new image? Is there a charged reciprocity between Lutyens's appropriation of Indian motifs and the preference for a scheme that reappropriated Lutyens's forms? Is this another way of talking back and metaphorically claiming the power that previously belonged to the colonizer?

## ■ Uniformity or Hypercomplexity? ■

The universalization that dominates urban centers in the twentieth century marks the end of an era: local and "pure" cultural identities as the evocation of difference by the juxtaposition of cultures now gives way to a dispersed heterogeneity. Borders, fragments, cultures, and hybrids interpenetrate and redefine the urban space everywhere. However, as Henri Lefebvre points out in his analysis of "social space," this is not a simple juxtaposition that leads to the disappearance of the "local" space: "the worldwide does not abolish the local." The combinations, superpositions, and even collisions in question do not lead to the absorption of the local, but to the creation of "innumerable places" within the urban space, resulting in a hypercomplexity that is crisscrossed by a myriad of currents. The analysis of urban space thus becomes further complicated as a result of such interpenetrations and superpositions that subject each fragment to a host of social relationships.[34]

A much-publicized building complex is already acknowledged as a signifier of end-of-the-century architecture. The Petronas Twin Towers in Kuala Lumpur, Malaysia (1997), present a curious and extreme case study and help to reveal the multiplicity of forces that lead to a hypercomplexity, with the local and the universal interpenetrating in a most visible (if reductive) formula. Designed by Cesar Pelli and Associates for the headquarters of the Petroliam Nasional Berhad (Petronas), the 88-story towers have been hailed as the world's tallest skyscrapers. They were commissioned with a clear agenda to make a worldwide statement about Malaysia's goal to become a fully industrialized nation by the year 2020 according to Prime Minister Mahathir Mohamad's economic program, "Vision 2020."

The towers utilize a complicated technology: the vertical loads are supported by a central concrete core and concrete columns on the periphery; the semicircular and triangular floor extensions that cantilever beyond the perimeter columns are carried by prefabricated steel trusses; and a two-story steel skybridge joins the two towers. The technological sophistication is reflected on the exterior: the towers are completely clad with horizontal rows of glass and stainless steel.[35] Yet a techno-logical statement was not sufficient for the image sought for twenty-first-century Malaysia. As emphasized by the administrative cadres of Petronas, the architecture had to be "Malaysian." In the words of Cesar Pelli, "The new towers should not look as if they could have been built in America or Europe, but as somehow belonging to Malaysia. The most important objective, therefore, was to design towers with their own character, belonging to the place."[36]

Two "Malaysian" sources — one Buddhist, the other Islamic – inspired the design. The tapered and faceted outline of the towers was derived from Kek Lok Si, the country's (and Southeast Asia's) largest Buddhist temple, hence a most obvious local monument. Pelli also equated "Malaysian" with what he called "Islamic geometric traditions," thus lumping the entire world of Islam and its long history into the prosaic formula that geometric patterns are much more important in "Islamic countries" than in the West and that "they are perceived and appreciated by everyone in their society." Arguing that he and his team worked hard not to create a "cultural pastiche," Pelli maintained the resulting design responded to "the sense of form and patterning that I could perceive in traditional Malaysian buildings and objects." Utilizing what the architects identified as the most important geometric forms underlying "Islamic designs," the architectural *parti* became two interlocking squares that were rotated in horizontal levels and filled in with small circular elements. The "Islamic" nature of the building was underlined further by characteristic "colors, patterns, traditions, and crafts"; the geometric patterns of the lobby floors, the wooden screens on the lobby windows accentuated, according to one report, "the complex's imaginatively Malaysian character."[37] Furthermore, a flavor of Chinese culture was interjected by a steel skybridge inspired by Chinese philosopher Lao Tse, who, Pelli claims, "taught us that the reality of a hollow object is in the void and not in the walls that define it." The rationale for the placement of a conference room, executive dining room, and mosque in this "portal to the sky" remains obscure.[38]

The corporate image presented by the Petronas Twin Towers is in accord with the customary representation of a transnational business and thus reflects its prominent position in the world market. At the same time, the emphasis put on technology expresses the construction of a national image and makes a statement about the level of development and modernity aimed at by the government; it recalls the modernist imagery sought after in the building of new capitals. Nevertheless, a sense of locality (which is another level of belonging) is also required by the clients. In today's configuration of power and culture this does not conflict with the mentality of transnational corporations that function in a "color-blind" manner, seamlessly reducing notions of difference to a simple kit of selected symbols – in the case of the Petronas towers, a tapered silhouette and geometric patterns.

The choice of the architect for the towers indicates the continuing authority of the technically advanced Western world. As a senior architect at Cesar Pelli and Associates puts it with self-confidence, tall buildings are considered the specialty of large American firms that have developed a reputation to "design them efficiently and with an artistic intention." Another American architect who works in China adds that "in China, it is assumed that if you're an American firm, you're qualified to do all kinds of work."[39]

This reputation provides American architects with opportunities not available in the United States during the last decade of the twentieth century and invests them with a great deal of authority and power to give architectural and aesthetic expression to cultural and national identities elsewhere – a pattern reminiscent of the colonial era. Like colonial architects, but often with less patience to study the culture and architecture of the place they are designing for ("time is money"), they rely on stereotypical and quick formulas about cultures and architectural forms unfamiliar to them and use them to adorn corporate high-technology structures.

Colonial structures thus survive (albeit in renewed forms), and the superordinates and the subordinates remain unchanged even if building activity has shifted to the East. The global organization of the profession reflects this condition. Recent computer technologies have totally transformed the professional scene, giving much greater fluidity to architectural ideas and their efficient dissemination – and contributing further to the inequity between the "developed" and the "developing" worlds. Consider the recent scheme by a major American firm, Hellmuth, Obata & Kassabaum (HOK), to establish a centralized production office in India for all their East Asian operations, with the ability to keep the workshops open for twenty-four hours (in shifts) to handle the office's European work as well. At a forum organized by *Progressive Architecture*, a spokesman for HOK presented the plan diplomatically, emphasizing the office's high regard for the training of architects in India, while leaving out another primary factor in the decision: salary levels.[40]

In summary, the end of the century is marked by a break with the past. Highly affected by new developments in media and the recent patterns of displacement, the notions of national space and identity are ruptured and modernity is re-written by a globalization that is vernacular. Nevertheless, the divide with the past is not absolute and globalization is not equal to homogenization.[41] The continuity manifests itself in several realms. The former power relationships still survive, although their centralized mechanisms are now dispersed and sometimes even intangible. Large American architectural firms thus dominate the international construction market and furthermore, empowered with new technologies, can employ "third world" architects on low salaries. The search for cultural identity continues as well. In some instances, it is absorbed by the globalized market structure – as in the case of the Petronas Towers; in others, it redefines space and urban image by appropriation and hybridity – as in the transformation of Paris by its new immigrant populations.

The Institut du Monde Arabe (1987), one of the most celebrated buildings of the late twentieth century, stands in its prominent location in Paris as the embodiment of the leading themes in cultural intersections today, as well as their links to the past. Rightly considered one of the highlights of the recent Parisian *grands projects*, Jean Nouvel's design has been hailed by critics as a particularly sensitive response to the site, context, materials, and modernism at large. The Insitut du Monde Arabe is also an intriguing visual symbol of Islam in the heart of Europe. The building's main concept is duality: its modern facade overlooking the Seine is juxtaposed with its back that represents Arab culture by means of stylized *mushrabiyyas*. The front and the back are separated from each other by a narrow, dead-end "street" that ends up in a courtyard – in obvious reference to two spatial "signs" that defined Islam to the West for a long time. Nevertheless, all visual references to Arab culture are appropriated by a powerfully expressed high technology which corrects and incorporates them into the architectural repertory of the late twentieth century, while underlining their otherness.

The Institut du Monde Arabe's global and corporate imagery absorbs and tames cultural difference, but maintains much of the past associations, thereby calling for further reflection on Miyoshi's argument that this is "an age of... intensified colonialism, even though it is under an unfamiliar guise."[42]

## NOTES

1   Paul Ricoeur, "Universal Civilization and National Cultures," in *History and Truth*, trans. C. A. Kelbley (Evanston, Il.: Northwestern University Press, 1965), 276–7.

2   Masao Miyoshi, "A Borderless World? From Colonialism to Transnationalism and the Decline of the Nation-State," *Critical Inquiry* 19 (Summer 1993): 739–42.

3   Ackbar Abbas, "Building on Disappearance: Hong Kong Architecture and the City," *Public Culture* 6 (1994): 443.

4   Timothy Brennan, "The National Longing for Form," in *Narration and Nation*, ed. Homi Bhabha (London and New York: Routledge, 1990), 47.

5   Henry A. Giroux, "Consuming Social Change: The 'United Colors' of Benetton," *Cultural Critique* (Winter 1993–4): 15.

6 Marshall Berman, *All That Is Solid Melts into Air: The Experience of Modernity* (New York: Viking Penguin, 1988), 5–6.

7 This notion was articulated as early as 1950 by Aimé Césaire: "Ce n'est pas une société morte que nous voulons faire revivre. Nous laissons cela aux amateurs de l'exotisme." See Aimé Césaire, *Discours sur le colonialisme* (Paris and Dakar: Présence africaine, 1989), 29.

8 Rasheed Araeen, "Our Bauhaus, Others' Mudhouse," *Third Text* 6 (Spring 1989): 3–14.

9 Edward Said, *Culture and Imperialism* (New York: Alfred Knopf, 1993), 11–12.

10 Albert Sarraut, *Grandeur et servitude coloniales* (Paris: Editions du Sagittaire, 1931), 220–1.

11 See François Béguin, *Arabisances: décor architectural et tracé urbain en Afrique du Nord, 1830–1850* (Paris: Dunod, 1983).

12 Frantz Fanon, *The Wretched of the Earth*, trans. Constance Farrington (New York: Grove Press, 1963), 38–9.

13 Guillaume de Tarde, "L'Urbanisme en Afrique du Nord," in Jean Royer, ed., *L'Urbanisme aux Colonies et dans les pays tropicaux* (Delayance: La Charité-sur-Loire, 1932), v. 1, 29–30.

14 A considerable literature has developed on French colonial planning in Morocco within the last fifteen years or so. I consider Janet L. Abu-Lughod's *Rabat: Urban Apartheid in Morocco* (Princeton, NJ: Princeton University Press, 1980), by far the best study on the topic.

15 "L'Urbanisme à Tunis" in Royer, *L'Urbanisme aux colonies*, v. 1, 54.

16 Henri Prost, "Rapport Général," ibid., 22. See also Abu-Lughod, *Rabat*, 145.

17 For an analysis of Le Corbusier's Algiers projects within the framework of colonial policies, see Zeynep Çelik, "Le Corbusier, Orientalism, Colonialism," *Assemblage* 17 (April 1992): 58–77.

18 For Tripoli under Mussolini, see Krystyna von Henneberg, "Piazza Castello and the Making of a Fascist Colonial Capital," in *Streets: Critical Perspectives on Public Space*, eds. Zeynep Çelik, Diane Favro, and Richard Ingersoll (Berkeley and Los Angeles: University of California Press, 1994), 135–50.

19 Mia Fuller, "Wherever You Go, There You Are: Fascist Plans for the Colonial City of Addis Ababa and the Colonizing Suburb of EUR '42," *Journal of Contemporary History* 31 (1996): 403–6. Fuller argues that even the terminology revealed the segregation: "natives" lived in "quarters," whereas Italians lived in the "city" or the "center."

20 Ernest Spanner, "L'Urbanisme en Afrique Equatoriale Française," in Royer, *L'Urbanisme aux colonies*, 160.

21 Bruno DeMeulder, *Reformisme, thuis en oversee: Geschiedenis van de Belgische planning in een kolonie* (Ph.D. diss., Katholieke Universiteir te Leuven, 1990), vol. 2.2, fig. 13.5.

22 Tarik Zafer Tunaya, "Devrim Hareketi İçinde Atatürk ve Atatürkçülük," *Siyaset Ilmi Serisi* (Istanbul) 14 (1964): 122, quoted in Inci Aslanoğlu, *Erken Cumhuriyet Dönemi Mimarlıği* (Ankara: ODTÜ Mimarlik Fakültesi, 1980), 8–9. Tunaya used this phrase to underline the dilemmas of the reformers who passionately believed in the model set by Western powers, despite the fact that the declaration of the new Turkish state was met with hostility by European powers who wanted to establish exclusive control over the Ottoman Empire defeated in World War I.

23 Aslanoğlu, *Erken Cumhuriyet Dönemi Mimarlıği*, 12.

24 Ankara was also chosen to be the capital due to its location in the geographical center of Anatolia.

25  For critical evaluations of Brasilia, see: David G. Epstein, *Brasilia, Plan and Reality: A Study of Planned and Spontaneous Urban Development* (Berkeley and Los Angeles: University of California Press, 1973); Norma Evenson, "Brasilia: 'Yesterday's City of Tomorrow,'" in *World Capitals: Toward Guided Urbanization*, ed. H. Wenthworth Eldredge (Garden City, NY: Anchor Press, 1975); and James Holston, *The Modernist City: An Anthropological Critique of Brasilia* (Chicago: University of Chicago Press, 1989).

26  Berman, *All that Is Solid Melts into Air*, 7.

27  Ayub Khan, quoted in Glenn Stephenson, "Two Newly-Created Capitals: Islamabad and Brasilia," *Town Planning Review* 41 (October 1970): 323. For new capitals, also see Lawrence J. Vale, *Architecture, Power, and National Identity* (New Haven, Conn., and London: Yale University Press, 1992), 128–62.

28  Partha Chatterjee, "The Disciplines in Colonial Bengal" in *Texts of Power: Emerging Disciplines in Colonial Bengal*, ed. Partha Chatterjee (Minneapolis and London: University of Minnesota Press, 1995), 23.

29  *Architectural Record* 175, no. 3 (March 1987): 62.

30  For Lerner's explanation of the project, see J. P. Partenaires, "Concours international pour le Centre National d'Arts Indira Gandhi," *L'Architecture d'aujourd'hui*, no. 249 (February 1987): vi.

31  Ibid. iv.

32  Ibid., vi.

33  The list of Indian architects who synthesized local and historic forms with modern principles in most impressive experiments is long. Among the best known are Balkrishna Doshi, Charles Correa, and Raj Rewal.

34  Henri Lefebvre, *The Production of Space*, trans. Donald Nicholson-Smith [Oxford, UK, and Cambridge, Mass.: Blackwell, 1991 (French ed. 1974)], 86–8.

35  The structure is designed by the Thornton-Tomasetti Engineers of New York City, in collaboration with the Malaysian engineering firm of Ranhill Bersekutu. For a technical exposé, see *Architecture* 85, no. 9 (September 1996): 160–1.

36  Quoted in "A Monumental Achievement for Malaysia: Petronas Towers, 'The Tallest of 'em all'," *Islamic Horizons* (July–August 1996): 22.

37  Philip Langdon, "Asia Bound," *Progressive Architecture* 76, no. 3 (March 1995): 47.

38  "A Monumental Achievement for Malaysia: Petronas Towers," 22.

39  Langdon, "Asia Bound," 45.

40  Larry Self, chief operating officer and executive director of European and Middle Eastern operations, HOK, St. Louis, Missouri, "The Impact of the Mega Firm," presented at the *Progressive Architecture* forum "New Directions in Architectural Practice," Washington, DC, 23 September 1995.

41  Arjun Appadurai, *Modernity at Large*, (Minneapolis and London: University of Minnesota Press, 1996) (especially the chapter titled "Here and Now," 1–23).

42  Miyoshi, "From Colonialism to Transnationalism," 720.

# 41

## Grassrooting the Space of Flows

### Manuel Castells

■ Introduction ■

Our historic time is defined fundamentally by the transformation of our geo-graphic space. This is a key dimension of the multilayered social and technological transformation that ushers in the so-called Information Age. To understand such a spatial transformation, I proposed ten years ago the concept of space of flows. The aim at that point was to acknowledge the reality and the significance of the transformation without yielding to the simplistic notions of futurologists announcing the death of distance and the end of cities.

Empirical evidence showed – and shows – that new information and communi-cation technologies fit into the pattern of flexible production and network organization, permitting the simultaneous centralization and decentralization of activities and population settlements, because different locations can be reunited in their functioning and in their interaction by the new technological system made out of telecommunications, computers, and fast reliable transportation systems, as well as dispatching centers, nodes, and hubs. So new communication technologies allow for the centralization of corporate activities in a given space precisely because they can reach the whole world from the City of London and from Manhattan without losing the dense network of localized, ancillary firms as well as the opportunities of face-to-face interaction created by territorial agglomeration.

At the same time, back offices can decentralize into the suburbs, newly developed metropolitan areas, or in some other country and be part of the same system. New business centers can be created around the country and around the world, always following the logic of clustering and decentralizing at the same time, of concentrating and networking, so creating a selective worldwide web of business services. As well, the new industrial space is characterized by its similar pattern of the spatial dispersion of activities and concentration of innovation and strategic decision-making – around what Peter Hall and I propose to label as "milieux of innovation," following the evidence gathered by a series of studies undertaken in the 1980s at Berkeley by the Institute of Urban and Regional Development. The new media have also become built around the double process of globalization of capital and customization/networking of information and images that respond to the localization of markets and segmentation of audiences. In territorial terms, in fact, the age of information is not just the age of spatial dispersal, it is the age of generalized urbanization. In the next decade it is likely that most people of the world will be, for the first time, living in the cities. Yet cities are, and will be, of very different kinds, depending on cultures, institutions, histories, and economies, but they share, and they will share in the foreseeable future, a spatial logic that is specific to the Information Age. This logic is characterized by the combination of territorial sprawl and locational concentration. Thus intrametropolitan, interregional, and international networks connect with global networks in a structure of variable geometry that is enacted and modified by flows of information and electronic circuits and fast, information-based, transportation systems. In the last decade, studies by Peter Hall, Peter Daniels, AnnaLee Saxenian, Michael Batty, Jim Wheeler, Barry Wellman, Jeff Henderson, Roberto Camagni, Stephen Graham, Simon Marvin, Amy Glasmeier, and so many other scholars have substantiated, empirically, the emergence of a new spatial structure. This structure is defined by articulated territorial concentration and decentralization in which the unit is the network. This particular model of spatial organization, which seems to be characteristic of the Information Age, is the model that I tried to conceptualize, ten years ago, as the space of flows.

## ■ The Space of Flows ■

By space of flows, I understood, and I understand, the material arrangements that allow for simultaneity of social practices without territorial contiguity. It is not a purely electronic space. It is not what Batty has called a cyberspace, although cyberspace is a component of the space of flows. It is made up first of all of a technological infrastructure of information systems, telecommunications, and transportation lines. The capacity and characteristics of this infrastructure and the location of its elements determine the functions of the space of flows and its relationship to other spatial forms and processes.

The space of flows is also made of networks of interaction, and the goals and task of each network configurate a different space of flows. Thus financial markets, high-technology manufacturing, business services, entertainment, media news, drug traffic, science and technology, fashion design, art, sports, or religion constitute a specific network with a specific technological system and various territorial profiles. So they all operate on the logic of the space of flows but they specify this logic.

Second, the space of flows is made up of nodes and hubs. These nodes and hubs structure the connections and the key activities in a given locale or locales. For instance, Wall Street or Ginza are such nodes, as well as Cali and Tijuana in their specific trade, or Berkeley, Stanford, and MIT in computer sciences. Hubs are communication sites, airports, harbors, train, or bus stations that organize exchanges of all kinds, as they are increasingly interconnected and spatially related. However, what characterizes the new role of these hubs and nodes is that they are dependent on the network, that their logic depends on their place in the network, and that they are sites to process signals that do not originate from any specific place but from endless recurrent interactions in the network.

Third, the space of flows is also made of habitats for the social actors who operate the networks, be it residential spaces adjacent to the nodes, spaces of consumption, protected and secluded, or global corridors of social segregation separating these corridors from the surrounding places around the globe (VIP lounges, the virtual office, computing on the run, standardized international hotels).

Fourth, the space of flows comprises electronic spaces such as Web sites, spaces of interaction, as well as spaces of one-directional communication, be it interactive or not, such as information systems. A growing proportion of activity is from the Web, and the visual design of Web sites, as well as the structure of an operation of their content, is becoming a fundamental frame for decision-making, information making, and communication.

## ■ Space of Places ■

I have sketched out the new spatial structure of the Information Age, the space of flows. But we really need to know that not all space is organized around the space of flows. As has been the case throughout the whole history of humankind, most people live, work, and construct their meaning around places. I defined, and I define, a place, as the locale whose form, function, and meaning are self-contained within the boundaries of territorial contiguity. People tend to construct their life in reference to places, be they their homes, their neighborhoods, their cities, their regions, their countries. Now this is not to say that the local community is thriving. In fact, research shows that all over the world, there has been a process of individualization and atomization of place-based relationships. The loss of community is, in fact, the founding theme of urban sociology, since the Chicago School. Yet you may have no community and still refer to your place as your main source of experience. Social organization and political representation are also predominately place-based. And cultural identity is often built on the basis of sharing historical experience in a given territory.

So, when analyzing spatial transformation in the Information Age and showing the emergence of a new spatial form, the space of flows, I also emphasized the persistence of the space of places as the most usual form of spatial existence for humankind. And I observed that while most dominant activities were constructed around the space of flows, most experience and social interaction was and still is organized around places. For dominant activities, I refer to financial flows and to the management of major corporations in services and manufacturing, as well as to their ancillary networks of firms, to media, entertainment, professional sports, science and technology, institutionalized religion, military power, the global criminal economy. Thus I added that, in fact, the constitution of the space of flows was in itself a form of domination, since the space of flows, even in its diversity, is interrelated and can escape the control of any locale, while the space of places is fragmented, localized, and thus increasingly powerless vis-à-vis the versatility of the space of flows, with the only chance of resistance for localities being to refuse landing rights for overwhelming flows – only to see that they land in the locale nearby, inducing therefore the bypassing and marginalization of rebellious communities.

This was my analysis some time ago, presented in various publications during the last decade. I still sustain most of this analysis, and I think it can be backed up empirically. However, what was an analysis of transformation of the space in a given historical moment – that is, the moment of the dawn of the Information Age – should not be cast in stone as an iron rule of spatial development. Yes, there are two different forms of space: flows and places. Yes, the space of flows is historically new in its overwhelming prevalence because it can deploy its logic through a new technological medium. Yes, dominant activities in our society are organized around the logic of the space of flows, while most forms of autonomous construction of meaning and social and political resistance to the powers that be are being constructed, for the time being, around places. But two major qualifications may be introduced:

First, the space of flows includes some places. Indeed, the space of flows is not simply an electronic space. Electronic spaces – such as the Internet or global communication media – are but one dimension, however important, of the space of flows.

Second, both electronic spaces and the space of flows at large are not exclusively organized around and by social/economic/cultural domination. Societies are not closed systems, they are always open processes, characterized by conflict. History, in fact, is a very tiresome experience. It never ends, against the claims of the neoliberal illusion. Wherever there is domination, there is resistance to domination. Wherever there is imposition of meaning, there are projects of construction of alternative meaning. And the realms of this resistance and this autonomous meaning are ubiquitous – which means, concretely, that while the space of flows has been produced by and around dominant activities and social groups, it can be penetrated by resistance and can be diversified in its meaning. The grass roots of societies do not cease to exist in the Information Age. And after an initial moment of exclusion and confusion, people and values of all kinds are now penetrating and using the space of flows, Internet and beyond, in the same way as the Parisian Champs-Élysées dreamed by Hausman to escape the populace of the *rive gauche*, have become, in the 1990s, the hangout place for the festive and multiethnic young people of the Paris *banlieues* (suburbs). While the space of flows remains the space in which dominant activities are spatially operated, it is experiencing at the same time the growing influence and pressure of the grass roots and the insertion of personal meaning by social actors, in a process that may alter the cultural and political dynamics of our societies and ultimately may alter the space of flows itself. So let me review the main dimensions of this grassrooting of the space of flows.

## ■ The Space of Flows and the Grass Roots ■

First, I will refer to a series of dimensions of autonomous expression of social meaning in the space of flows, with emphasis on electronic spaces but in inter-action with the space of places. First is personal interaction – people using the Net for themselves and electronic mail as recuperating letter writing as a form of communication. And people are finding ways to be together with much more diversity and importance than has been the experience before in history: chat groups, multidimensional communication, cultural expressions of all kinds, people building their Web sites. People build their fantasies, but they also experience their needs and exchange their information. They are inhabiting the space of flows and thus transforming it. Am I talking maybe about a small global elite? Well not so small, and not so elite.

A second dimension for autonomous expression is represented by purpo-sive, horizontal communication, not just personal feelings of casual communi-cation. Horizontal communication occurs among people and across countries, and establishes information systems that are alternative to the media. And they are in fact doubling the media. There is, indeed, much gossip and irresponsible infor-mation. As you know, the news that triggered one of the latest scandals relating to President Clinton was first sent from the Internet through a news bulletin that is a one-man operation out of his home office in Los Angeles, while *Newsweek* was considering publication of the story. There are people and institutions very con-cerned about the lack of control of information on the Net. Many governments are terrified of losing control of information, a fundamental source of power through-out history. They usually argue in terms of controlling child pornography. I think child pornography is terrible. But what happens in countries like France or Spain, for instance, is that it is perfectly legal to sell child pornography – it is not legal to produce the images, and it is not legal to hire or kidnap the children to do it, but selling it is not a problem. But you cannot do it on the Internet. Why? Because the Internet is a mass medium, or so the statist argument goes. The fact is that horizontal communication on the Internet, by bypassing both media and govern-ment controls, is becoming a most fundamental political issue which, ultimately, reflects who we are collectively, as a society. And if some of us are enjoying child pornography, if we are this kind of monster, this appears reflected on the Internet. The Internet brings us face to face with the mirror of who we actually are. So I would rather work on ourselves than close down the Net. The fight is against the self, not against the Net.

Third, there is a fast growth of networks of solidarity and cooperation on the Internet, with people bringing together their resources to live and to survive. To give an example, Senior Net in the United States not only brings information (for instance, to counter the monopoly of medical information by doctors) and resources together: it also develops solidarity ties between senior people, thus reinforcing the group to which all of us belong – or will belong if we are lucky. Thus, at the time the welfare state, at least as constructed in the last half-century, is being challenged economically and politically, people are reconstructing networks of solidarity and reflecting and debating about them at the same time.

The fourth dimension is social movements. The Net is increasingly used by social movements of all kinds as their organizing ground and as their privileged means to break their isolation. The greatest example here, and one that has become a classic, is the Zapatistas in Chiapas, Mexico. Without fully presenting the case, on which I have written in my latest book, let me remind you of some interesting facts about this social movement. The Zapatistas organized solidarity groups around the world on the Internet. And they used the Internet very effectively to diffuse their information and to obtain interactive communication between their different solidarity groups. They have also used the Internet as a protective way to fight repression when, in February 1995, there was a major military offensive that forced them to escape to the forest. They sent a message over the Internet asking everybody to flood the White House with messages, because at that point the White House had put money into the Mexican bailout. A major crisis in Mexico would jeopardize the entire stability of the region, ultimately wasting US taxpayers' money. So in one day more than 30,000 messages came to the White House. That does not mean that street demonstrations in front of the White House are not important; they continue to be important, but you cannot organize them in twenty-four hours, and in this particular case it was a matter of life and death in these twenty-four hours. This ability of the Zapatistas to work on the Net does not come from Sub-commandante Marcos, as people say, whether he was a communications professor or from the Indian communities. It came from women's groups in Mexico. In 1993, women's groups organized an Internet network in Mexico to support women's solidarity funded by the Catholic Church and organized instrumentally by the Institute of Global Communication in San Francisco, a group of progressive, computer people in Silicon Valley. The institute and the women's groups sent several people to Chiapas, and they organized an extension of the women's network that was called La Neta. La Neta is an interesting expression because on the one hand it is the Spanish feminine term for the Net, but in Mexican slang it also means the truth. So this La Neta network organized by women's groups branched out and trained a number of people in Chiapas who, through human rights groups, were the ones who were able to link up with the Zapatistas and provide both the technological and the knowledge support for their Internet operations.

However, not only progressive movements are on the Internet. Everybody is on the Internet, and our societies are on the Internet. The Internet has played a major role in the development of American militia groups. The Internet is as real as life itself. Increasingly, global movements of solidarity, environmentalists, and human rights and women's groups are organized on the Internet, again on the basis of local/global connection. One of the greatest and latest examples in the United States was the fall 1997 One Million Women March organized by two black women in Philadelphia. There was practically no organization, no sponsorship, and yet a small group of women in Philadelphia went on the Net and called a demonstration, obtaining an extraordinary level of support and mobilization. But going to a place, I think is the most interesting thing. The space of flows is not just being on the Net, it is organizing on the Net to be in Philadelphia on a given day; that is, using the Net to control space.

Fifth, linkages are a development to which we have to pay close attention, increasing linkages between people and institutions in an interactive process. The creation of what some people call virtual cities is renewing local governments and citizen democracy. May I say that we have some relatively old experiments, such as in 1986, when Santa Monica's PEN program allowed public debate between citizens, including debates on major issues such as homelessness in Santa Monica, with the homeless themselves being able to get into the debate. European cities are organizing participation in information systems. Graham and Aurigi have studied these experiments and they say that they are usually one-directional information systems. So it is still not a full-fledged participatory democracy; it is more information than participation and democracy, but still evolving and changing.

And there is a potential for much more. I am personally struck by the experience of Amsterdam's Digital City, an autonomous group originally supported by the municipality of Amsterdam. It is a private foundation that has organized a system of citizen participation and citizen interaction. You have to register to take part – anyone can visit the site, but to really participate to go to the homes, you have to be registered. By 1998, they had 80,000 fully registered participating "residents." They have activities organized around different squares: bigger squares and then micro squares. Each square relates to different activities, cultural politics, sports, business, then homes. People have built their homes, they also sometimes have marriages between the families that live in these homes; they do recall elections, they certainly do debates, and from time to time they link this to real life in a very close interaction. So the Digital City experience has shown the possibility of mobilizing the population at dramatically different levels, from the most political activist level to chat groups. What strikes me too is how much the group is connected to the local, political, and spatial experience in Amsterdam. On the one hand, this is a movement that grew out of the squatters movement in Amsterdam. Caroline Nevejan and Marlene Strikker, the two women who lead the movement and who lead this program, were members of this squatters movement and, in their own view, they have not changed their values much. They have continued their ability to mobilize people and change society through the new medium without abandoning the idea of the city as a place. Even symbolically, the city has ceded to them as their headquarters one of the most historic buildings in Amsterdam, the Waag, the building that in the sixteenth century used to close the canals for trade when the ships were coming to Amsterdam. This building also housed the School of

Medicine where autopsies were performed that were illegal because of the church's repression. In that building, there is a room where Rembrandt painted his famous "Anatomy Lesson." In this very room is located the Digital City server. I think this kind of historical continuity, this linkage between history and information flows, place and electronic networks, is representative of something new happening in the space of flows.

Another example of this linkage between institutions, civil society, and grass roots groups, something that is less known because it is only in the project stage, is the Barcelona Internet Citizen Project. This project is being sponsored by the city of Barcelona and is linked to a megaproject they called Forum 2004. It is in fact a good example of connecting the global to the local, Internet to grass roots. Remember that the 1992 Olympic games created a great transformation in Barcelona. Among other things, Barcelona opened up to the sea by building a whole new neighborhood connecting to the harbor, seaside promenade, and beaches. Now a group of local leaders, with the support of the municipality, have conceived a new project, an Olympics of sort: the Forum 2004, with the sponsorship of UNESCO and the Pope. Over the course of the next six months, the project will make plans to bring in half a million young people from all over the world into Barcelona in 2004 to discuss what to do with the world in the twenty-first century. And of course they need to build a city to organize this project – therefore another 20 kilometers of seaside development.

Furthermore, the project includes the idea of linking up the world to these thousands of youth and sharing the debate on the Net. To ensure Barcelona citizens are up to the task, there is a project to set up an Internet citizen center to train and diffuse the uses of the Internet to people at large. Most people in Barcelona are unaware of the potential uses of the Internet, so a literacy campaign directly linked to an event and with the purpose of participating in a global debate could be key in bringing Barcelona as a whole into the Information Age.

As you can see, there is a gradual opening up of the Information of Age to different avenues. So through a blossoming of initiatives, people are taking on the Net without uprooting themselves from their places. And through this practice they transform both forms of the space. However, are we talking about only a small elite? Are people not in fact being massively excluded from the Net? Well, first of all, the recent data show there is a large elite – about 128 million users in 1998. Yes, data are shaky, but the same shaky data were indicating about 30 million users in 1995/6. What seems to be a little bit more solid is the rate of diffusion among users, which seems to be nearly doubling every year. By the end of 2000, we should be approaching 500 million Internet users. Serious experts in the communication business predict about 1 billion users by the middle of the first decade of the twenty-first century, considering a slowdown in the rate of diffusion when less-advanced countries and less-educated and less-affluent groups become the new frontier of expansion. Computer capacity and telecommunications capacity are already there; the issue is how to bring people onto the Net. And for what?

Yet there is certainly a social bias in terms of who uses the Internet. There is a gender bias, with the proportion of men to women being 3 to 1. There is also an ethnic bias, with ethnic minorities having much lower rates of Internet use, although in the case of Hispanics in the United States, the rates of incorporation are extremely high. There is a country bias too. In fact, Scandinavia is advancing over everybody else. Finland has decided to become the first information society in the world. In 1998 there was one Web site for every ten people in Finland, and projections are that by 2000 there will be more Web sites in Finland than Finnish people. Still, in absolute terms, there is a dominance of the Internet by American users.

However, more importantly, the bias is not only in terms of use, but use for what purpose, that is the level of education required to look for and retrieve information. I have proposed a notion that we are living in a world that is made up of the interactive and the interacted. We interact, but many people are just interacted. For many people the Net may become an extension of a multimedia-based, one-directional system, so that they may receive some basic information to which they just have to react, as in some marketing device. However, if we look historically into the diffusion of information, and the diffusion of technology, and the ability to upgrade the level of consciousness and the level of information, there has always been a connection between open-minded, educated social groups and the uneducated masses who, through this connection, become educated. In the historic example of the development of the labor movement, printing workers were critical in that they knew how to read, whereas most workers did not know how to read nor want to read. Printing workers were the ones who, in many countries, created the basis for self-training, self-development, and self organization of these uneducated masses. And this is happening now in many countries. Low income communities are being brought onto the Internet in different ways by local community groups.

I also personally know of some important experiences that are highly developed, such as in the working class periphery of Barcelona, an area called the Lower Llobregat, in which the unions and the municipalities decided that they have to move into the Information Age and develop social struggles and social consciousness. They have created a cultural organization and a network of Internet-based, publicized activities around a journal titled *La Factoria* that you can access on the Net. Thus they have started a process of mass education and social debate, mixing print, the Net, the city, and the factory, and ultimately grass-rooting the Net.

Finally, even if there is still a minority of users (but a minority that is going to be numbered in the hundreds of millions), their eruption on the Net, with the creative cacophony of their social diversity and the plurality of their values and interests expressed on the Net, and the linkage between places and information flows transform the logic of the space of flows and make it a contested space – a plural and diversified space.

## ■ Conclusion ■

Whither the theory of the space of flows? Not necessarily. This is because it was always based on the linkage between electronic space and places through networks of flows – and this is becoming increasingly the space in which most important activities operate in our societies. There is interaction; there is connection. Moreover, it remains true, I think, and can be empirically sustained that strategically dominant activities are operated essentially through the space of flows, and that global elites ensure their domination in this process, bypassing segmented, isolated localities. And trenches of resistance to the domination of flows of capital and information are being built primarily around places.

However, a new dynamics is operating, a dynamics of interpenetration of uniformity and autonomy, of domination and resistance, of instrumentality and experience, within the space of flows. So, historically produced forms of space, even as complex and new as the space of flows, by their very existence are transformed through the process of their enactment. They become contested spaces as well, freedom is carved in their hallways, and cultural identity is built and affirmed on the Net. So the geography of the new history will not be made, after all, of the separation between places and flows, but out of the interface between places and flows and between cultures and social interests, both in the space of flows and in the space of places. The attempt by capital, media, and power to escape into the abstraction of the space of flows, bypassing democracy and experience by confining them in the space of places, is being challenged from many sources by the grass-rooting of the space of flows.

# 42

# The Generic City

## Rem Koolhaas

**1. Introduction 1.1** Is the contemporary city like the contemporary airport – "all the same"? Is it possible to theorize this convergence? And if so, to what ultimate configuration is it aspiring? Convergence is possible only at the price of shedding identity. That is usually seen as a loss. But at the scale at which it occurs, it *must* mean something. What are the disadvantages of identity, and conversely, what are the advantages of blankness? What if this seemingly accidental – and usually regretted – homogenization were an intentional process, a conscious movement away from difference toward similarity? What if we are witnessing a global liberation movement: "down with character!" What is left after identity is stripped? The Generic? **1.2** To the extent that identity is derived from physical substance, from the historical, from context, from the real, we somehow cannot imagine that anything contemporary – made by us – contributes to it. But the fact that human growth is exponential implies that the past will at some point become too "small" to be inhabited and shared by those alive. We ourselves exhaust it. To the extent that history finds its deposit in architecture, present human quantities will inevitably burst and deplete previous substance. Identity conceived as this form of sharing the past is a losing proposition: not only is there – in a stable model of continuous population expansion – proportionally less and less to share, but history also has an invidious half-life – as it is more abused, it becomes less significant – to the point where its diminishing handouts become insulting. This thinning is exacerbated by the constantly increasing mass of tourists, an avalanche that, in a perpetual quest for "character," grinds successful identities down to meaningless dust. **1.3** Identity is like a mousetrap in which more and more mice have to share the original bait, and which, on closer inspection, may have been empty for centuries. The stronger the identity, the more it imprisons, the more it resists expansion, interpretation, renewal, contradiction. Identity becomes like a lighthouse – fixed, overdetermined: it can change its position or the pattern it emits only at the cost of destabilizing navigation. (Paris can only become more Parisian – it is already on its way to becoming hyper-Paris, a polished caricature. There are exceptions: London – its only identity a lack of clear identity – is perpetually becoming even less London, more open, less static.) **1.4** Identity centralizes; it insists on an essence, a point. Its tragedy is given in simple geometric terms. As the sphere of influence expands, the area characterized by the center becomes larger and larger, hopelessly diluting both the strength and the authority of the core; inevitably the distance between center and circumference increases to the breaking point. In this perspective, the recent, belated discovery of the periphery as a zone of potential value – a kind of pre-historical condition that might finally be worthy of architectural attention – is only a disguised insistence on the priority of and dependency on the center: without center, no periphery; the interest of the first presumably compensates for the emptiness of the latter. Conceptually orphaned, the condition of the periphery is made worse by the fact that its mother is still alive, stealing the show, emphasizing its offspring's inadequacies. The last vibes emanating from the exhausted center preclude the reading of the periphery as a critical mass. Not only is the center by definition too small to perform its assigned obligations, it is also no longer the real center but an overblown mirage on its way to implosion; yet its illusory presence denies the rest of the city its legitimacy. (Manhattan denigrates as "bridge-and-tunnel people" those who need infrastructural support to enter the city, and makes them pay for it.) The persistence of the present concentric obsession makes us *all* bridge-and-tunnel people, second-class citizens in our own civilization, disenfranchised by the dumb coincidence of our collective exile from the center. **1.5** In our concentric programming (author spent part of his youth in Amsterdam, city of ultimate centrality) the insistence on the center as the core of value and meaning, font of all significance, is doubly destructive – not only is the ever-increasing volume of dependencies an ultimately intolerable strain, it also means that the center has to be constantly *maintained*, i.e., modernized. As "the most important place," it paradoxically has to be, at the same time, the most old and the most new, the most fixed and the most dynamic; it undergoes the most intense and constant adaptation, which is then compromised and complicated by the fact that it has to be an unacknowledged transformation, invisible to the naked eye. (The city of Zurich has found the most radical, expensive solution in reverting to a kind of reverse archaeology: layer after layer of new modernities – shopping centers, parking, banks, vaults, laboratories – are constructed underneath the center. The center no longer expands outward or skyward, but inward toward the center of the earth itself.) From the grafting of more or less discreet traffic arteries, bypasses, underground tunnels, the construction of ever more *tangentiales*, to the routine transformation of housing into offices, warehouses into lofts, abandoned churches into nightclubs, from the serial bankruptcies and subsequent reopenings of specific units in more and more expensive shopping precincts to the relentless conversion of utilitarian space into "public" space, pedestrianization, the creation of new parks, planting, bridging, exposing, the systematic restoring of historic mediocrity, all authenticity is relentlessly evacuated. **1.6** The Generic City is the city liberated from the captivity of center, from the straitjacket of identity. The Generic City breaks with this destructive cycle of dependency: it is nothing but a reflection of present need and present ability. It is the city without history. It is big enough for everybody. It is easy. It does not need maintenance. If it gets too small it just expands. If it gets old it just self-destructs and renews. It is equally exciting – or unexciting – everywhere. It is "superficial" – like a Hollywood studio lot, it can produce a new identity every Monday morning. **2. Statistics 2.1** The Generic City has grown dramatically over the past few decades. Not only has its size increased, its numbers have too. In the early seventies it was inhabited by an average of 2.5 million official (and $\pm$ 500,000 unofficial) residents; now it hovers around the 15 million mark. **2.2** Did the Generic City start in America? Is it so profoundly unoriginal that it can only be imported? In any case, the Generic City now also exists in Asia, Europe, Australia, Africa. The definitive move away from the countryside, from agriculture, to the city is not a move to the city as we knew it: it is a move to the Generic City, the city so pervasive that it has come to the country. **2.3** Some continents, like Asia, aspire to the Generic City; others are ashamed by it. Because it tends toward the tropical – converging around the equator – a large proportion of Generic Cities is Asian – seemingly a contradiction in terms: the over-familiar inhabited by the inscrutable. One day it will be absolutely exotic again, this discarded product of Western civilization, through the resemanticization that its very dissemination brings in its wake...**2.4** Sometimes an old, singular city, like Barcelona, by oversimplifying its identity, turns Generic. It becomes transparent, like a logo. The reverse never happens...at least not yet. **3. General 3.1** The Generic City is what is left after large sections of urban life crossed over to cyberspace. It is a place of weak and distended sensations, few and far between emotions, discreet and mysterious like a large space lit by a bed lamp. Compared to the classical city, the Generic City is *sedated*, usually perceived from a sedentary position. Instead of concentration – simultaneous presence – in the Generic City individual "moments" are spaced far apart to create a trance of almost unnoticeable aesthetic experiences: the color variations in the fluorescent lighting of an office building just before sunset, the subtleties of the slightly different whites of an illuminated sign at night. Like Japanese food, the sensations can be reconstituted and intensi-fied in the mind, or not – they may simply be ignored. (There's a choice.) This pervasive lack of urgency and insistence acts like a potent drug; it induces a *hallucination of the normal*. **3.2** In a drastic reversal of what is supposedly the major characteristic of the city – "business" – the dominant sensation of the Generic City is an eerie calm: the calmer it is, the more it approximates the pure state. The Generic City addresses the "evils" that were ascribed to the traditional city before our love for it became unconditional. The serenity of the Generic City is achieved by the *evacuation* of the public realm, as in an emergency fire drill. The urban plane now only accommodates necessary movement, fundamentally the car; highways are a superior version of boulevards and plazas, taking more and more space; their design, seemingly aiming for automotive efficiency, is in fact surpris-ingly sensual, a utilitarian pretense entering the domain of *smooth* space. What is new about this locomotive public realm is that it cannot be measured in dimensions. The same (let's say ten-mile) stretch yields a vast number of utterly different experiences: it can last five minutes or forty; it can be shared with almost nobody, or with the entire population; it can yield the absolute pleasure of pure, unadulterated speed – at which point the sensation of the Generic City may even become intense or at least acquire density – or utterly claustrophobic moments of stoppage – at which point the thinness of the Generic City is at its most noticeable. **3.3** The Generic City is fractal, an endless repetition of the same simple structural module; it is possible to reconstruct it from its smallest entity, a desktop computer, maybe even a diskette. **3.4** Golf courses are all that is left of otherness. **3.5** The Generic City has easy phone numbers, not the resistant ten-figure frontal-lobe crunchers of the traditional city but smoother versions, their middle numbers identical, for instance. **3.6** Its main attraction is its anomie. **4. Airport 4.1** Once manifestations of ultimate neutrality, airports now are among the most singular, characteristic elements of the Generic City, its strongest vehicle of differentiation. They have to be, being all the average person tends to experience of a particular city. Like a drastic perfume demonstration, photomurals, vegetation, local costumes give a first concentrated blast of the local identity (sometimes it is also the last). Far away, comfortable, exotic, polar, regional, Eastern, rustic, new, even "undiscovered": those are the emotional registers invoked. Thus conceptually charged, airports become emblematic signs imprinted on the global collective unconscious in savage manipulations of their non-aviatic attractors – tax-free shopping, spectacular spatial qualities, the frequency and reliability of their connections to other airports. In terms of its iconography/performance, the airport is a concentrate of both the hyper-local and hyper-global – hyper-global in the sense you can get goods there that are not available even in the city, hyper-local in the sense you can get things there that you get nowhere else. **4.2** The tendency in airport gestalt is toward ever-greater autonomy: sometimes they're even practically unrelated to a specific Generic City. Becoming bigger and bigger, equipped with more and more facilities unconnected to travel, they are on the way to replacing the city. The in-transit condition is becoming universal. Together, airports contain populations of millions – plus the largest daily workforce. In the completeness of their facilities, they are like quarters of the Generic City, sometimes even its reason for being (its center?), with the added attraction of being hermetic systems from which there is no escape – except to another airport. **4.3** The date/age of the Generic City can be reconstructed from a close reading of its airport's geometry. Hexagonal plan (in unique cases penta-or heptagonal): sixties. Orthogonal plan and section: seventies. Collage City: eighties. A single curved section, endlessly extruded in a linear plan: probably nineties. (Its structure branching out like an oak tree: Germany.) **4.4** Airports come in two sizes: too big and too small. Yet their size has no influence on their performance. This suggests that the most intriguing aspect of all infrastructures is their essential elasticity. Calculated by the exact for the numbered – passengers per year – they are invaded by the countless and survive, stretched toward ultimate indeterminacy. **5. Population 5.1** The Generic City is seriously multiracial, on average 8% black, 12% white, 27% Hispanic, 37% Chinese/Asian, 6% indeterminate, 10% other. Not only multiracial, also multicultural. That's why it comes as no surprise to see temples between the slabs, dragons on the main boulevards, Buddhas in the CBD (central business district). **5.2** The Generic City is always founded by people on the move, poised to move on. This explains the insubstantiality of their foundations. Like the flakes that are suddenly formed in a clear liquid by joining two chemical substances, eventually to accumulate in an uncertain heap on the bottom, the collision or confluence of two migrations – Cuban emigrés going north and Jewish retirees going south, for instance, both ultimately on their way someplace else – establishes, out of the blue, a settlement. A Generic City is born. **6. Urbanism 6.1** The great originality of the Generic City is simply to abandon what doesn't work – what has outlived its use – to break up the blacktop of idealism with the jackhammers of realism and to accept whatever grows in its place. In that sense, the Generic City accommodates both the primordial and the futuristic – in fact, *only* these two. The Generic City is all that remains of what used to be the city. The Generic City is the post-city being prepared on the site of the ex-city. **6.2** The Generic City is held together, not by an over-demanding public realm – progressively debased in a surprisingly long sequence in which the Roman Forum is to the Greek agora what the shopping mall is to the high street – but by the *residual.* In the original model of the moderns, the residual was merely green, its controlled neatness a moralistic assertion of good intentions, discouraging association, use. In the Generic City, because the crust of its civilization is so thin, and through its immanent tropicality, the vegetal is transformed into *Edenic* Residue, the main carrier of its identity: a hybrid of politics and landscape. At the same time refuge of the illegal, the uncontrollable, and subject of endless manipulation, it represents a simultaneous triumph of the manicured and the primeval. Its immoral lushness compensates for the Generic City's other poverties. Supremely inorganic, the organic is the Generic City's strongest myth. **6.3** The street is dead. That discovery has coincided with frantic attempts at its resuscitation. Public art is everywhere – as if two deaths make a life. Pedestrianization – intended to preserve – merely channels the flow of those doomed to destroy the object of their intended reverence with their feet. **6.4** The Generic City is on its way from horizontality to verticality. The skyscraper looks as if it will be the final, definitive typology. It has swallowed everything else. It can exist anywhere: in a rice field, or downtown – it makes no difference anymore. The towers no longer stand together; they are spaced so that they don't interact. Density in isolation is the ideal. **6.5** Housing is not a problem. It has either been completely solved or totally left to chance; in the first case it is legal, in the second "illegal"; in the first case, towers or, usually, slabs (at the most, 15 meters deep), in the second (in perfect complementarity) a crust of improvised hovels. One solution consumes the sky, the other the ground. It is strange that those with the least money inhabit the most expensive commodity – earth; those who pay, what is free – air. In either case, housing proves to be surprisingly accommodating – not only does the population double every so many years, but also, with the loosening grip of the various religions, the average number of occupants per unit halves – through divorce and other family-dividing phenomena – with the same frequency that the city's population doubles; as its numbers swell, the Generic City's density is perpetually on the decrease. **6.6** All Generic Cities issue from the tabula rasa; if there was nothing, now they are there; if there was something, they have replaced it. They must, otherwise they would be historic. **6.7** The Generic Cityscape is usually an amalgam of overly ordered sections – dating from near the beginning of its development, when "the power" was still undiluted – and increasingly free arrangements everywhere else. **6.8** The Generic City is the apotheosis of the multiple-choice concept: all boxes crossed, an anthology of *all* the options. Usually the Generic City has been "planned," not in the usual sense of some bureaucratic organization controlling its development, but as if various echoes, spores, tropes, seeds fell on the ground randomly as in nature, took hold – exploiting the natural fertility of the terrain – and now form an ensemble: an arbitrary gene pool that sometimes produces amazing results. **6.9** The writing of the city may be indecipherable, flawed, but that does not mean that there *is* no writing; it may simply be that *we* developed a new illiteracy, a new blindness. Patient detection reveals the themes, particles, strands that can be isolated from the seeming murkiness of this Wagnerian *ur*-soup: notes left on a blackboard by a visiting genius 50 years ago, stenciled UN reports disintegrating in their Manhattan glass silo, discoveries by former colonial thinkers with a keen eye for the climate, unpredictable ricochets of design education gathering strength as a global laundering process. **6.10** The best definition of the aesthetic of the Generic City is "free style." How to describe it? Imagine an open space, a clearing in the forest, a leveled city. There are three elements: roads, buildings, and nature; they coexist in flexible relationships, seemingly without reason, in spectacular organizational diversity. Any one of the three may dominate: sometimes the "road" is lost – to be found meandering on an incomprehensible detour; sometimes *you see no building*, only nature; then, equally unpredictably, you are surrounded only by building. In certain frightening spots, all three are simultaneously absent. On these "sites" (actually, what is the opposite of a site? They are like holes bored through the concept of city) public art emerges like the Loch Ness Monster, equal parts figurative and abstract, usually self-cleaning. **6.11** Specific cities still seriously debate the mistakes of architects – for instance, their proposals to create raised pedestrian networks with tentacles leading from one block to the next as a solution to congestion – but the Generic City simply enjoys the benefits of their inventions: *decks, bridges, tunnels, motorways* – a huge proliferation of the paraphernalia of connection – frequently draped with ferns and flowers as if to ward off original sin, creating a vegetal congestion more severe than a fifties science-fiction movie. **6.12** The roads are only for cars. People (pedestrians) are led on rides (as in an amusement park), on "promenades" that lift them off the ground, then subject them to a catalog of exaggerated conditions – wind, heat, steepness, cold, interior, exterior, smells, fumes – in a sequence that is a grotesque caricature of life in the historic city. **6.13** There *is* horizontality in the Generic City, but it is on the way out. It consists either of history that is not yet erased or of Tudor-like enclaves that multiply around the center as newly minted emblems of preservation. **6.14** Ironically, though itself new, the Generic City is encircled by a constellation of New Towns: New Towns are like year-rings. Somehow, New Towns age very quickly, the way a five-year-old child develops wrinkles and arthritis through the disease called progeria. **6.15** The Generic City presents the final death of planning. Why? Not because it is not planned – in fact, huge complementary universes of bureaucrats and developers funnel unimaginable flows of energy and money into its completion; for the same money, its plains can be fertilized by diamonds, its mud fields paved in gold bricks... But its most dangerous *and* most exhilarating discovery is that planning makes no difference whatsoever. Buildings may be placed well (a tower near a metro station) or badly (whole centers miles away from any road). They flourish/perish unpredictably. Networks become over-stretched, age, rot, become obsolescent; populations double, triple, quadruple, suddenly disappear. The surface of the city explodes, the economy accelerates, slows down, bursts, collapses. Like ancient mothers that still nourish titanic embryos, whole cities are built on colonial infrastructures of which the oppressors took the blueprints back home. Nobody knows where, how, since when the sewers run, the exact location of the telephone lines, what the reason was for the position of the center, where monumental axes end. All it proves is that there are infinite hidden margins, colossal reservoirs of slack, a perpetual, organic process of adjustment, standards, behavior; expectations change with the biological intelligence of the most alert animal. In this apotheosis of multiple choice it will never be possible again to reconstruct cause and effect. They work – that is all. **6.16** The Generic City's aspiration toward tropicality automatically implies the rejection of any lingering reference to the city as fortress, as citadel; it is open and accommodating like a mangrove forest. **7. Politics 7.1** The Generic City has a (sometimes distant) relationship with a more or less authoritarian regime – local or national. Usually the cronies of the "leader" – whoever that was – decided to develop a piece of "downtown" or the periphery, or even to start a new city in the middle of nowhere, and so triggered the boom that put the city on the map. **7.2** Very often, the regime has evolved to a surprising degree of invisibility, as if, through its very permissiveness, the Generic City resists the dictatorial. **8. Sociology 8.1** It is very surprising that the triumph of the Generic City has not coincided with the triumph of sociology – a discipline whose "field" has been extended by the Generic City beyond its wildest imagination. The Generic City *is* sociology, happening. Each Generic City is a petri dish – or an infinitely patient black-board on which almost any hypothesis can be "proven" and then erased, never again to reverberate in the minds of its authors or its audience. **8.2** Clearly, there is a proliferation of communities – a sociological zapping – that resists a single overriding interpretation. The Generic City is loosening every structure that made anything coalesce in the past. **8.3** While infinitely patient, the Generic City is also persistently resistant to speculation: it proves that sociology may be the worst system to capture sociology in the making. It outwits each established critique. It contributes huge amounts of evidence for and – in even more impressive quantities – against each hypothesis. In *A* tower blocks lead to suicide, in *B* to happiness ever after. In *C* they are seen as a first stepping stone toward emancipation (presumably under some kind of invisible "duress," however), in *D* simply as passé. Constructed in unimaginable numbers in *K*, they are being exploded in *L*. Creativity is inexplicably high in *E,* nonexistent in *F. G* is a seamless ethnic mosaic, *H* perpetually at the mercy of separatism, if not on the verge of civil war. Model *Y* will never last because of its tampering with family structure, but *Z* flourishes – a word no academic would ever apply to any activity in the Generic City – because of it. Religion is eroded in *V,* surviving in *W,* transmuted in *X.* **8.4** Strangely, nobody has thought that cumulatively the endless contradictions of these interpretations prove the richness of the Generic City; that is the one hypothesis that has been eliminated in advance. **9. Quarters 9.1** There is always a quarter called Lipservice, where a minimum of the past is preserved: usually it has an old train/tramway or double-decker bus driving through it, ringing ominous bells – domesticated versions of the Flying Dutchman's phantom vessel. Its phone booths are either red and trans-planted from London, or equipped with small Chinese roofs. Lipservice – also called Afterthought, Waterfront, Too Late, 42nd Street, simply the Village, or even Underground – is an elaborate mythic operation: it celebrates the past as only the recently conceived can. It is a machine. **9.2** The Generic City had a past, once. In its drive for prominence, large sections of it somehow disappeared, first unlamented – the past apparently was surprisingly unsanitary, even dangerous – then, without warning, relief turned into regret. Certain prophets – long white hair, gray socks, sandals – had always been warning that the past was necessary – a resource. Slowly, the destruction machine grinds to a halt; some random hovels on the laundered Euclidean plane are saved, restored to a splendor they never had... **9.3** In spite of its absence, history is the major preoccupation, even industry, of the Generic City. On the liberated grounds, around the restored hovels, still more hotels are con-structed to receive additional tourists in direct proportion to the erasure of the past. Its disappearance has no influence on their numbers, or maybe it is just a last-minute rush. Tourism is now independent of destination... **9.4** Instead of specific memories, the associations the Generic City mobilizes are general memories, memories of memories: if not all memories at the same time, then at least an abstract, token memory, a déjà vu that never ends, generic memory. **9.5** In spite of its modest physical presence (Lipservice is never more than three stories high: homage to/revenge of Jane Jacobs?) it condenses the entire past in a single complex. History returns not as farce here, but as *service*: costumed merchants (funny hats, bare midriffs, veils) voluntarily enact the conditions (slavery, tyranny, disease, poverty, colony) – that their nation once went to war to abolish. Like a replicating virus, worldwide, the colonial seems the only inexhaustible source of the authentic. **9.6** 42nd Street: ostensibly the places where the past is preserved, they are actually the places where the past has changed the most, is the most distant – as if seen through the wrong end of a telescope – or even completely eliminated. **9.7** Only the memory of former excess is strong enough to charge the bland. As if they try to warm themselves at the heat of an extinguished volcano, the most popular sites (with tourists, and in the Generic City that includes everyone) are the ones once most intensely associated with sex and misconduct. Innocents invade the former haunts of pimps, prostitutes, hustlers, transvestites, and to a lesser degree, artists. Paradoxically, at the same moment that the information highway is about to deliver pornography by the truckload to their living rooms, it is as if the experience of walking on these warmed-over embers of transgression and sin makes them feel special, alive. In an age that does not generate new aura, the value of established aura skyrockets. Is walking on these ashes the nearest they will get to guilt? Existentialism diluted to the intensity of a Perrier? **9.8** Each Generic City has a waterfront, not necessarily with water – it can also be with desert, for instance – but at least an edge where it meets another condition, as if a position of near escape is the best guarantee for its enjoyment. Here tourists congregate in droves around a cluster of stalls. Hordes of "hawkers" try to sell them the "unique" aspects of the city. The unique parts of all Generic Cities together have created a universal souvenir, scientific cross between Eiffel Tower, Sacre Coeur, and Statue of Liberty: a tall building (usually between 200 and 300 meters) drowned in a small ball of water with snow or, if close to the equator, gold flakes; diaries with pockmarked leather covers; hippie sandals – even if real hippies are quickly repatriated. Tourists fondle these – nobody has ever witnessed a sale – and then sit down in exotic eateries that line the waterfront: they run the full gamut of food today: *spicy*: first and ultimately maybe most reliable indication of being elsewhere; *patty*: beef or synthetic; *raw*: atavistic practice that will be very popular in the third millennium. **9.9** Shrimp is the ultimate appetizer. Through the simplification of the food chain – and the vicissitudes of preparation – they taste like english muffins, i.e., noth-ingness. **10. Program 10.1** Offices are still there, in ever greater numbers, in fact. People say they are no longer necessary. In five to ten years we will all work at home. But then we will need bigger homes, big enough to use for meetings. Offices will have to be converted to homes. **10.2** The only activity is shopping. But why not consider shopping as temporary, provisional? It awaits better times. It is our own fault – we didn't think of anything better to do. The same spaces inundated with other programs – libraries, baths, universities – would be terrific; we would be awed by their grandeur. **10.3** Hotels are becoming the generic accommodation of the Generic City, its most common building block. That used to be the office – which at least implied a coming and a going, assumed the presence of other important accommodations *elsewhere*. Hotels are now containers that, in the expansion and completeness of their facilities, make almost all other buildings redundant. Even doubling as shopping malls, they are the closest we have to urban *existence*, 21st-century style. **10.4** The hotel now implies imprisonment, voluntary house arrest; there is no competing place left to go; you come and stay. Cumula-tively, it describes a city of ten million all locked in their rooms, a kind of reverse animation – density imploded. **11. Architecture 11.1** Close your eyes and imagine an explosion of beige. At its epicenter splashes the color of vaginal folds (unar-oused), metallic-matte aubergine, khaki-tobacco, dusty pumpkin; all cars on their way to bridal whiteness... **11.2** There are interesting and boring buildings in the Generic City, as in all cities. Both trace their ancestry back to Mies van der Rohe: the first category to his irregular Friedrichstadt tower (1921), the second to the boxes he conceived not long afterward. This sequence is important: obviously, after initial experimentation, Mies made up his mind once and for all against interest, for boredom. At best, his later buildings capture the spirit of the earlier work – sublimated, repressed? – as a more or less noticeable absence, but he never proposed "interesting" projects as possible buildings again. The Generic City proves him wrong: its more daring architects have taken up the challenge Mies abandoned, to the point where it is now hard to find a box. Ironically, this exuberant homage to the interesting Mies shows that "the" Mies was wrong. **11.3** The architecture of the Generic City is by definition beautiful. Built at incredible speed, and conceived at even more incredible pace, there is an average of 27 aborted versions for every realized – but that is not quite the term – structure. They are prepared in the 10,000 architectural offices nobody has ever heard of, each vibrant with fresh inspiration. Presumably more modest than their well-known colleagues, these offices are bonded by a collective awareness that something is wrong with architecture that can only be rectified through *their* efforts. The power of numbers gives them a splendid, shining arrogance. They are the ones who design without any hesitation. They assemble, from 1,001 sources, with savage precision, more riches than any genius ever could. On average, their education has cost 30,000 dollars, excluding travel and housing. 23% have been laundered at American Ivy League universities, where they have been exposed – admittedly for very short periods – to the well-paid elite of the other, "official" profession. It follows that a combined total investment of 300 billion dollars ($300,000,000,000) worth of architectural education ($30,000 [average cost] × 100 [average number of workers per office] × 100,000 [number of worldwide offices]) is working in and producing Generic Cities at any moment. **11.4** Buildings that are complex in form depend on the curtain-wall industry, on ever more effective adhesives and sealants that turn each building into a mixture of straitjacket and oxygen tent. The use of silicone – "we are stretching the facade as far as it will go" – has flattened all facades, glued glass to stone to steel to concrete in a space-age impurity. These connections give the appearance of intellectual rigor through the liberal application of a transparent spermy compound that keeps everything together by intention rather than design – a triumph of glue over the integrity of materials. Like everything else in the Generic City, its architecture is the resistant made malleable, an epidemic of yielding no longer through the application of principle but through the *systematic* application of the unprincipled. **11.5** Because the Generic City is largely Asian, its architecture is generally air-conditioned; this is where the paradox of the recent paradigm shift – the city no longer represents maximum development but borderline underdevelopment – becomes acute: the brutal means by which universal conditioning is achieved mimic inside the building the climatic conditions that once "happened" outside – sudden storms, mini-tornadoes, freezing spells in the cafeteria, heat waves, even mist; a provincialism of the mechanical, deserted by gray matter in pursuit of the electronic. Incompetence or imagination? **11.6** The irony is that in this way the Generic City is at its most subversive, its most ideological; it elevates mediocrity to a higher level; it is like Kurt Schwitter's *Merzbau* at the scale of the city: the Generic City is a *Merzcity*. **11.7** The angle of the facades is the only reliable index of architectural genius: 3 points for sloping backward, 12 points for sloping forward, 2-point penalty for setbacks (too nostalgic). **11.8** The apparently solid substance of the Generic City is misleading. 51% of its volume consists of atrium. The atrium is a diabolical device in its ability to substantiate the insubstantial. Its Roman name is an eternal guarantor of architectural class – its historic origins make the theme inexhaustible. It accommodates the cave-dweller in its relentless provision of metropolitan comfort. **11.9** The atrium is void space: voids are the essential building block of the Generic City. Paradoxically, its hollowness insures its very physicality, the pumping up of the volume the only pretext for its physical manifestation. The more complete and repetitive its interiors, the less their essential repetition is noticed. **11.10** The style of choice is postmodern, *and will always remain so.* Postmodernism is the only movement that has succeeded in connecting the practice of architecture with the practice of panic. Postmodernism is not a doctrine based on a highly civilized reading of architectural history but a method, a mutation in professional architecture that produces results fast enough to keep pace with the Generic City's development. Instead of consciousness, as its original inventors may have hoped, it creates a new unconscious. It is modernization's little helper. Anyone can do it – a skyscraper based on the Chinese pagoda *and/or* a Tuscan hill town. **11.11** All resistance to postmodernism is anti-democratic. It creates a "stealth" wrapping around architecture that makes it irresistible, like a Christmas present from a charity. **11.12** Is there a connection between the predominance of mirror in the Generic City – is it to celebrate nothingness through its multiplication or a desperate effort to capture essences on their way to evaporation? – and the "gifts" that, for centuries, were supposed to be the most popular, efficient present for savages? **11.13** Maxim Gorky speaks in relation to Coney Island of "varied boredom." He clearly intends the term as an oxymoron. Variety cannot be boring. Boredom cannot be varied. But the infinite variety of the Generic City comes close, at least, to making variety normal: banalized, in a reversal of expectation, it is repetition that has become unusual, therefore, potentially, daring, exhilarating. But that is for the 21st century. **12. Geography 12.1** The Generic City is in a warmer than usual climate; it is on its way to the south – toward the equator – away from the mess that the north made of the second millennium. It is a concept in a state of migration. Its ultimate destiny is to be tropical – better climate, more beautiful people. It is inhabited by those who do not like it elsewhere. **12.2** In the Generic City, people are not only more beautiful than their peers, they are also reputed to be more even-tempered, less anxious about work, less hostile, more pleasant – proof, in other words, that there *is* a connection between architecture and behavior, that the city can make better people through as yet unidentified methods. **12.3** One of the most potent characteristics of the Generic City is the stability of its weather – no seasons, outlook sunny – yet all forecasts are presented in terms of imminent change and future deterioration: clouds in Karachi. From the ethical and the religious, the issue of doom has shifted to the inescapable domain of the meteorological. Bad weather is about the only anxiety that hovers over the Generic City. **13. Identity 13.1** There is a calculated (?) redundancy in the iconography that the Generic City adopts. If it is water-facing, then water-based symbols are distributed over its entire territory. If it is a port, then ships and cranes will appear far inland. (However, showing the containers themselves would make no sense: you can't particularize the generic through the Generic.) If it is Asian, then "delicate" (sensual, inscrutable) women appear in elastic poses, suggesting (religious, sexual) submission everywhere. If it has a mountain, each brochure, menu, ticket, billboard will insist on the hill, as if nothing less than a seamless tautology will convince. Its identity is like a mantra. **14. History 14.1** Regret about history's absence is a tiresome reflex. It exposes an unspoken consensus that history's presence is desirable. But who says that is the case? A city is a plane inhabited in the most efficient way by people and processes, and in most cases, the presence of history only drags down its performance... **14.2** History present obstructs the pure exploitation of its theoretical value as absence. **14.3** Throughout the history of humankind – to start a paragraph the American way – cities have grown through a process of consolidation. Changes are made on the spot. Things are improved. Cultures flourish, decay, revive, disappear, are sacked, invaded, humiliated, raped, triumph, are reborn, have golden ages, fall suddenly silent – all on the same site. That is why archaeology is a profession of *digging*: it exposes layer after layer of civilization (i.e., city). The Generic City, like a sketch which is never elaborated, is not improved but abandoned. The idea of layering, intensification, completion are alien to it: it *has* no layers. Its next layer takes place somewhere else, either next door – that can be the size of a country – or even elsewhere altogether. The archaeologue (= archaeology with more interpretation) of the 20th century needs unlimited plane tickets, not a shovel. **14.4** In exporting/ejecting its improvements, the Generic City perpetuates its own amnesia (its only link with eternity?). Its archaeology will therefore be the evidence of its progressive forgetting, the documentation of its evaporation. Its genius will be empty-handed – not an emperor without clothes but an archaeologist without finds, or a site even. **15. Infrastructure 15.1** Infrastructures, which were mutually reinforcing and totalizing, are becoming more and more competitive and local; they no longer pretend to create functioning wholes but now spin off functional entities. Instead of network and organism, the new infrastructure creates enclave and impasse: no longer the *grand récit* but the parasitic swerve. (The city of Bangkok has approved plans for three competing airborne metro systems to get from A to B – may the strongest one win.) **15.2** Infrastructure is no longer a more or less delayed response to a more or less urgent need but a strategic weapon, a prediction: Harbor $X$ is not enlarged to serve a hinterland of frantic consumers but to kill/reduce the chances that harbor $Y$ will survive the 21st century. On a single island, southern metropolis $Z$, still in its infancy, is "given" a new subway system to make established metropolis $W$ in the north look clumsy, congested, and ancient. Life in $V$ is smoothed to make life in $U$ eventually unbearable. **16. Culture 16.1** Only the redundant counts. **16.2** In each time zone, there are at least three performances of *Cats*. The world is surrounded by a Saturn's ring of meowing. **16.3** The city used to be the great sexual hunting ground. The Generic City is like a dating agency: it efficiently matches supply and demand. Orgasm instead of agony: there *is* progress. The most obscene possibilities are announced in the cleanest typography; Helvetica has become pornographic. **17. End 17.1** Imagine a Hollywood movie about the Bible. A city somewhere in the Holy Land. Market scene: from left and right extras cloaked in colorful rags, furs, silken robes walk into the frame yelling, gesticulating, rolling their eyes, starting fights, laughing, scratching their beards, hairpieces dripping with glue, thronging toward the center of the image waving sticks, fists, overturning stalls, trampling animals... People shout. Selling wares? Proclaiming futures? Invoking Gods? Purses are snatched, criminals pursued (or is it helped?) by the crowds. Priests pray for calm. Children run amok in an undergrowth of legs and robes. Animals bark. Statues topple. Women shriek – threatened? Ecstatic? The churning mass becomes oceanic. Waves break. Now switch off the sound – silence, a welcome relief – and reverse the film. The now mute but still visibly agitated men and women stumble backward; the viewer no longer registers only humans but begins to note spaces between them. The center empties; the last shadows evacuate the rectangle of the picture frame, probably complaining, but fortunately we don't hear them. Silence is now reinforced by emptiness: the image shows empty stalls, some debris that was trampled underfoot. Relief... it's over. That is the story of the city. The city is no longer. We can leave the theater now...                                   **1994**

# 43

# Scene X: The Development of the X-Urban City

## Mario Gandelsonas

A new urban restructuring took place in the 1970s and acquired full speed in the 1980s, as expressions of the growth and the dominance of the service industry in general, and the globalization of the finance industry in particular. One of the symptoms of this process was the development of exurban "office campuses," which blurred the opposition of suburbs versus central city that had symbolically structured the suburban city. As part of the restructuring of the workplace, the white-collar workforce, which now included a high percentage of women, was moved to secondary offices in less expensive locations. The post-World War II suburbs that had been exclusively residential now became part of clusters including offices, shopping malls, and entertainment centers, where the new exurbanites could work, shop, and play. This change defines a new multiuse urbanity, with a very low density and a total dependence on the automobile. X-Urbia (*Ex*: out of; *exurbia*: out of the city) has transformed America into a colossal urbanized territory.[1] Where are these new developments located? Besides the office campuses, most of the new housing is being developed in the outer edges of the suburban city, in the one-mile grid or in the intersections of the freeway system.

The semiautonomy of these urban clusters provides them with a certain independence from the core city, which becomes one more semiautonomous urban "village" in the metropolitan constellation of X-Urban centers. However, this process of "sprawl" accounts for only one side of the X-Urban city. In the downtowns of the old cities, the exclusive light industrial districts also experience a transformation through processes of gentrification and preservation. While the processes of "voiding" the residential buildings from the center city continued, buildings in light industrial districts were gentrified; that is, transformed into residential buildings and with that came new shopping and entertainment repeating the X-Urban processes in the edges of the metropolitan area. In other words, the gentrification of decayed neighborhoods and light industrial districts, and the X-Urbanization of residential suburban areas into a car-dependent, low-density urbanity, are two sides of the same coin. In both cases, the major apparent changes occur at the level of programming while there seems to be very little visible change at the physical and formal level.

However, a major change takes place in downtowns throughout America at a morphological level: fields of parking, with object-buildings and/or fragments of urban fabric sitting on them become the dominant landscape. The freeway also enters and disrupts the downtowns, producing urban fields of parking and isolated object-buildings and/or islands of fabric. The city of Des Moines, Iowa, is one of hundreds of cities where the downtown has become an office park where commuters that live in exurbia work. A very dense and compact downtown business district where clusters of office buildings and parking structures are linked in this particular case with a hermetic skywalk system, is surrounded by over one hundred acres of parking on ground. The persistence of these dense downtowns have falsified the predictions of the 1960s planners about the disappearance of the city: the downtowns grow more during the 1980s than in any period since the end of World War II.[2] The economic restructuring of the 1980s requires both the dense downtown business districts and the sparse X-Urban office campuses.

The changes brought by the X-Urban city define a new urbanity not organized anymore in oppositional terms such as center versus periphery but as a multicenter city, not as a dominant totality versus subordinated parts but as a nonhierarchical fragmented urbanized territory. While all the other mutations entertain an oppositional relationship with the previous cities, the current mutation is developing by contiguity to the urban/suburban city. As such, the X-Urban city supplements the suburban city programmatically but also supplants the previous city. This new city is something added to make up for a deficiency; for instance, major European cities lack massive, structured, touristic consumption, a shortcoming that is remedied by their conversion to theme parks such as the Parisian Louvre. However this addition ends up taking the place of the previous city, which in turn is integrated as part of the theme parks or as neutral, picturesque or invisible background. For example, in Battery Park City in Manhattan, Wall Street becomes a background for a space that collapses and brings together gentrified and X-Urban space. The changes affect not just the city but also the buildings nor just the exterior but also their interiors, redefine and multiply the public and the private spheres and displace the public space into the house and the private space into the streets.[3]

The X-Urbia of the 1990s is produced by the *condensation* of the programs left behind by the suburban city (the workplace and entertainment), located in "points," in the proximity of existing or new residential X-Urban neighborhoods. Office campuses and multiplex cinemas come to the suburbs, transforming them into disjointed or scattered cities with the car as the predominant mode of transportation. The suburbs of the 1950s, the scattered neighborhoods of the suburban city, have not changed; they become older and start to decay. They become one of the elements of the new X-Urban scattered city.

The old city center, the urban city, and exurbia are depicted in terms of two opposing *fantasies: the urban fantasy and the X-Urban fantasy*. In the latter "edge city," one of the names given to X-Urbia, is seen as a necessary stage in the process of urban growth, an economic inevitability. While the center city is seen as an impossible condition, the very picture of present disaster, edge city is described as a green Edenic space. Urbanism, associated with tall buildings and "too much asphalt," is worse than parking lots.[4] While edge city is structured around the individual freedom, the go-anywhere provided by the car, the center city depends on the less desirable centralized mode of transportation of mass transit.[5] What this view suppresses is the question of government support that sustains the X-Urban development.[6] In the former fantasy, the center, seen as the repository of history, identity, diversity, and the realm of culture, stands in opposition to X-Urbia, which is determined solely by economics. The condition of the center is attributed to its relationship (or lack thereof) with suburbia. The sprawl, where X-Urbia flourishes, is where the blame is placed. The metaphor of the wall depicts both conditions, "cramming the poor into the constricted center cities, while the suburbs maintain its wall of segregation," or "boundaries that cordon off the core city from the suburban territory."[7] While edge city is presented in a negative way, leading towards some future environmental and social catastrophe, the center city is seen as a "possible future" in the development of the megalopolis. This prediction of a "possible future" is supported by the fact that opening those walls to produce the interdependence of city-suburbs exurbs produces positive results: the better center-city incomes compare to the suburbs the better the economic regional perform-ance.[8] And the way to make this happen is by systematically annexing new growth areas and creating cities without suburbs.

Both fantasies deny the contingent, the violent emergence of something that defies the limits of the established field, the limits of what one holds for "possible," where possible is, so to speak, a pacified contingency. An example of this contin-gency is the entrance of women into the labor market and its effects, which marks the end of the suburban fantasy and the beginning of the X-Urban fantasy. This fact, the new role played by women, shattered the stability of the suburban order, exposing the repressed antagonism in the fixed gender roles structured by the suburban fantasy, and produced the conditions for the emergence of the X-Urban city. This fact never figured into the planning "theories" and predictions of the 1960s. We are now facing an unexpected massive entrance into the virtual city and the possibilities of active participation (in commercial rather than political activ-ities) given by the World Wide Web. With these possibilities come the opening of new opportunities, the emergence of new desires, of new unreachable objects that will affect urbanity in unexpected ways.

Kenneth Jackson establishes a continuity between suburbia and exurbia, exurbia as an intensification of suburbia in a view that looks at the urban/suburban dichotomy as a stable relationship where the two terms complement each other, where the positive and negative signs alternate; for instance, when the contemporary situation is seen as a reversal of the flight to the suburbs, a "back-to-downtown," which is his desire. However, neither the 1980s downtown nor the suburbs are the same as the original terms of the suburban city. One could actually reverse Jackson's theory and propose the suburban city as a transitory stage of the X-Urban city in the process that starts with the gridding of America.[9]

"Scene X" or "X-Urbia," which is being constructed and multiplied while I write, is a scene where two similar objects, the television set and the computer monitor, which belong to two different systems, analogic versus digital, define two different cities, the suburban and the exurban. Television became the window[10] that allowed the view of the urban city and brought it to the suburban city and is now being challenged and perhaps superseded by the computer monitor's opening of X-Urbia to the global city, erasing national boundaries and consolidating the X-Urban fantasy. However, while national boundaries are being blurred, local boundaries are being built. The process of destabilization of the suburban city and the emergence of the X-Urban city was overdetermined by the development of a black middle class that started to move into the suburbs, blurring the oppositions city versus suburbs correlated to the opposition black versus white. A new fantasy fuels the centrifugal impulse exploited by the developers of the newest X-Urban gated communities: *the suburbs are now the stage where crime takes place.*

Gated communities are the new X-Urban armored residential developments being built at the outer edges of the megacities throughout America insulated from the outside with implied or sometimes literal walls. These paranoid exurban walls are opposed to the ecological walls or boundaries that the urbanites want to impose in the constantly expanding process of *sprawl*.[11]

These changes are taking place not only at the level of the urban object but also (and perhaps primarily) at the level of the urban subject, a subject defined by the X-Urban city. It is through an example born of the transformation of the suburban residential areas from imaginary suburban landscapes into a territory of imaginary violence that we can begin the construction of this subject. This example is not about the way in which these spaces are configured, but rather about the way in which these spaces are perceived though the media, specifically as seen through the television program *Cops*.[12]

*Cops* is a television show that airs daily and presents itself as a documentary. Each episode is structured around three events located in different cities. During each event the camera follows a team of police officers from the point when they are about to apprehend a criminal. Although the action is not staged, the program is rigorously edited and constructed. For instance, the action always takes place in the suburbs, of which an aerial view is shown in the presentation. First, the camera inside the car alternates between the profile of the cop driving his car while explaining the "case," and the view from behind the windshield where the viewer is placed in the position of the cop. The scene where the criminal is subject to police intervention usually takes place in X-Urban terrain (trailer parks and other deteriorated suburban environments), or inside a suburban house or apartment building. The suburbs are now the stage where crime takes place. The criminals are mostly white, lower-middle-class suburbanites involved in drugs and violence; most often the programs are about domestic disputes, which stand in sharp contrast to the 1950s depiction of family life.

What is interesting about *Cops* is that we find in the 1990s the same elements that define the suburbia of the 1950s: the suburban *house*, the *car*, the *television*. However these elements are articulated in two very different series of equivalencies. In the first situation, the 1950s suburb, the car and the TV represent the drastic restructuring of relations between private/public and interior/exterior that differentiates suburbia from the classical city: the emphasis on privatization and interiorization. While the car becomes the extension of the house and the windshield becomes a new type of (private) window that frames the exterior (public) space, the television screen acts as the gate for the public to invade the interior domestic space.

While in the 1950s suburban city, the car and the television are different means to *see*, for *viewing*, in the 1990s the exurban observer is *being seen*. In *Cops*, the car represents the eye of the law, and the television frames the house. While the suburban observer is defined as a driver, through the windshield viewing at a certain speed, in contrast to the slow pace of pedestrian urban observer of the classical city, the X-Urban observer, a *subject* who can travel through electronic space at any time, who zaps through hundreds of television channels and surfs the World Wide Web, is defined at the same time as the *object* of constant surveillance.

The technological-political changes of the 1990s transform private space, which is now increasingly constituted by a mechanism (telephone-fax-email-Internet) that augments and extends the fluid circulation of private information. However, there is a painful paradox in the coextensivity of the democratization of information and of the field of the police and the state: the extension of the power of the police parallels the democratic permeability and transparency of personal communication. The same technology that constitutes and circumscribes a new privately controlled space is the same that opens it up to intrusion.[13]

The practice of surveillance affects the boundaries between public and private: they become transparent. Furthermore, this practice does not just affect the existing fixed spatial boundaries. The permanent flow of the police car produces a mobile temporal boundary, an implied wall pierced by the horizontal windows produced by the movement of the car. This implied wall that the police surveillance produces in the suburbs is correlated to the literal wall of the new X-Urban armored communities that are being built at the outer edges of megacities throughout America.

Why this pathological return of the wall? At the imaginary level, the wall is a defensive gesture, a reaction to X-Urban violence. Since the private is violated or fantasized as such, the privatizing reaction that follows (familial, nationalizing, ethnocentric) is expected.[14] However, while these walls are useless, or always subject to actual or visual piercing in reality, they fulfill a role at a fantasy level and at the same time they indicate a new articulation of the symbolic field in X-Urbia. While the symbolic world of the suburban city is structured in terms of the separation and reconnection of city and suburb, of the urban and suburban cities, the X-Urban city problematizes the (ever-extending) object's edge, the subject's gaze. While the connecting suburban mechanisms (the car, the TV) transform the private/public/–/interior/exterior relationships, the marking of boundaries in the X-Urban city transforms the private/public/–/actual/virtual relationships.

From an architectural point of view, the symbolic role of these walls might be the marking and the materialization on the vertical plane of what is lacking on the horizontal plane. The continuing expansion of the megacity brings up the question of the edge, the lack of an edge, and, at the symbolic level, the return of the frontier as a major signifier that replaces the garden, the major signifier in the suburban city. Since sprawl blurs the edge of the megacity, the marking of edges becomes an obsession: gated communities, urban frontiers,[15] bounded natural preserves. While the suburban relation is internal to the city (urban–suburban) the frontier that separates civilization from savagery (that is, unruly uncooperative nature[16]), is present in different ways in the urban, the suburban, and the X-Urban. The frontier in the city is established between the "inner city population" as a "natural element" and the gentrifying forces of "urban pioneers" that advance on the basis of internal differentiation of an existing fabric. In the suburbs the frontier is established by circulating police cars that construct the imaginary safety wall in the television docudrama *Cops*. And, in X-Urbia, the frontier is materialized with the wall (literal or imaginary) of the new communities that separate them from the external world and that are populated with wild animals instead of urban or suburban pets: crocodiles in Florida, deer and foxes in New York and New Jersey, and dangerous insects such as deer ticks (that attack the body) instead of suburban termites (that attack the house).

The walls are perhaps the result of a symbolic identification with downtown, the place without literal walls (or material walls, as with the Internet). They are the return on the vertical plane of what is lacking in the horizontal plane; they are the return in the material world of what is lacking in the virtual world. The wall of surveillance, as we know can both protect but also invade our privacy. In the X-Urban city, the two possibilities given by centralized surveillance or generalized access to surveillance define two very different models: the scary one where police control surveillance, or the other, proposed by *Cops*, as a fantasy where the police themselves are always potentially subject to surveillance, where the police are being watched.

## ■ Architecture Inhabits the City ■

While the 1970s were most notably dedicated to theoretical production, the 1980s were about building with many urban-scale projects being initiated, particularly in Europe (Paris, Barcelona, Berlin), but also in Asia. However, these interventions are still designed in the spirit of early modernism or a post-modernism that ignores the X-Urban city. In fact, most architecture ignores the X-Urban city.

## ■ The City Inhabits Architecture ■

The fact that the "architecturally resistant" X-Urban city is spreading – not only across the American territory, but across the world – opens up a problematic concerning both the city and architecture that has not yet been theorized: the question of the identity of the American city, the role that architecture plays in its construction and the related questions concerning architecture's insistence in this role or, in other terms, the city's persistent role as the object of architecture.

While the suburban city proposed a spatial opposition between two types of cities – one, European and classical, the other, American and modern – the X-Urban city proposes a relationship to the previous American urban mutations that takes place both in the temporal as well as in the spatial dimension. While expanding the definition of the city, the X-Urban city appears as the latest stage in a process of construction of urban identity that involves the three previous American cities: the gridded city, the city of skyscrapers, and the suburban city.

Since the X-Urban city rejects architecture the way we know it and, since architecture nevertheless insists on the possibility of an articulation with "the city" (a signifier for a different urban entity that has been radically restructured multiple times), the possible strategies for the articulation of architecture and the X-Urban city need to include a previous historization and theorization of their relationship that goes back to the constitutive moments of architecture itself.

NOTES

1  Mario Gandelsonas, "Conditions for a Colossal Architecture," in *Cesar Pelli: Buildings and Projects 1965–1990* (New York: Rizzoli, 1990).
2  See Sassen, *The Global City* (Princeton: Princeton University Press, 1991).
3  The changes also affect the field of vision: different computer techniques such as computer-aided design and animation, virtual-imaging helmets, and magnetic reson-ance imaging destabilize the notion of representation and relocate vision by separating it from the human observer. Today vision is situated in an electromagnetic terrain of bits as opposed to both classical perception and the twentieth-century analog media such as photography, film, and television.
4  Joel Garreau, *Edge City: Life on the New Frontier* (New York: Doubleday, 1991), 45.
5  However the question is not just about private versus public transportation but about the eruption of desire in relation to movement and transportation, which was essentially functional since the days when walking and horseback riding were the primary modes of transportation.
6  National laws for taxation, highways, and environmental protection favor the suburbs.
7  Neal R. Peirce, *Citistates: How Urban America Can Prosper in a Competitive World* (Santa Ana, Calif.: Seven Locks Press, 1993), 119.
8  Ibid., 19.
9  Kenneth T. Jackson, *Crabgrass Frontier: The Suburbanization of the United States* (New York: Oxford University Press, 1985).

10   Thomas Keenan, "Windows of Vulnerability," in Bruce Robbins, ed., The Phantom Public Space (Minneapolis: University of Minnesota Press, 1993), 121–41.

11   The exurban city is the physical manifestation of a process that produces constantly expanding boundaries.

12   This television show was the research topic chosen by Joseph Cho, a graduate student in my urbanism seminar at the Princeton University School of Architecture in Princeton, New Jersey.

13   Jacques Derrida, "Questions d'Etranger," in Anne Dufourmantelle Invite Jacques Derrida à Répondre, de l'Hospitalité (Paris: Calman-Levy, 1997), 57.

14   Ibid., 51. See also M. Christine Boyer, Cybercities: Visual Perception in the Age of Electronic Communication (New York: Princeton Architectural Press, 1996).

15   Urban frontiers protect the gentrified areas from the neighboring slums. See Neil Smith, The New Urban Frontier: Gentrification and the Revanchist City (New York and London: Routledge, 1996).

16   Smith, The New Urban Frontier.

# 44

# On the Political Economy of the Fake

## Ziauddin Sardar

I go to the Mall to buy a specific product. On the first floor, buried inside a record store, is the shop of my friend Jimmy. It is very easy to miss him: the loud audio and visual output of the record shop does not allow anyone to focus on anything, pick out the detail and perceive that there is a shop within a shop. Behind the façade of the real economy, there is another economy. One manifestation of postmodernism in Kuala Lumpur is the strong political economy of the fake. If there is no difference between the real and the imaginary, the object and its image, as postmodernism maintains, than the real is as good as the fake. And the fakes that one finds in KL, and the region in general, are not just any fakes – they are genuine fakes. It is not marketing hype. Digital music sounds exactly the same whether it is on a real CD – that is, the one sold by its manufacturer – or on a fake CD, the copied version sold everywhere by street vendors and hawkers. This underground economy has played an important, although unrecognized, part in the development of Kuala Lumpur. Jimmy sells fake films.

Even though his shop cannot be seen easily, Jimmy can spot his potential customers the instant they appear on his floor. He will cleverly manoeuvre you into his secret enclave – all the time dropping the names of the latest Hollywood blockbusters. Jimmy sells three distinct varieties of fakes and an experienced customer will insist on knowing the pedigree of the imitation. The commonest type is the film that has actually been refilmed. This involves smuggling a Super-8 video camera inside a cinema and recording the proceedings. Invariably, the sound quality of the copies tends to be bad. Often you get only part of the film. It is not that the entire performance has not been recorded, just that the secret recorder got a seat too near and a bit off-centre of the big screen, so physics being physics, not all the action fits into the lens of his Super-8. But this is compensated by an added value: the postmodern experience of observing the observers, witnessing audience reactions and enjoyment – or not – of the film. One can hear the audience laughing, booing, hissing and gasping with fear or excitement as well as witness their excursions to buy popcorn or visits to the toilet. The added value is invaluable material for the truly critical viewer.

The next sort is the film that is not quite yet a film. This is what one would imagine to be the final, pre-release director's cut and it comes complete with time codes at the bottom of the screen. The visual and sound quality of these copies is rather good but that is not their main strength. They have an extra postmodern dimension that the real video does not contain. The ending in these 'fake films' can sometimes be different from the commercially released version, or contain scenes that do not make it to the cinema. There is a logical explanation to this mystery. Initial audience previews, before a film is released, sometimes cause the director or the studio to change the ending or trim the running time. This, of course, is not only an invaluable asset for students of film but also an economic boon for Jimmy. Sometimes, he sells his pre-release fake with one ending and cheap at the price together with the released version at inflated market prices. The world of fakes is a win–win world.

The last type of fake film in Jimmy's lair is the film that is more than a film. This variety is copied on video from a laser disc, so here we have digitized picture and sound. The video comes in two parts, divided by several minutes of blank screen – this is where the laser discs are being changed. This is not the only change involved. In pirate videos the sound is always recorded in reverse – the main channel carries the music and sound effects and the dialogue is demoted to the secondary channel. This is not surprising really, since the Southeast Asian audiences are, on the whole, more interested in bang, bang, wham than banter, banter, silence. So the film jumps out of the screen every time a gun is fired, a car crashes or a punch is thrown – and then fades back into background noise that can just about be distinguished as dialogue. There are added dimensions to the picture as well. It could slow down, freeze up, speed up or burst into billions of pixels and then morph into its original digital form. All this means the laser disc copies invariably tend to be longer than the original films. So you get, as Jimmy says, more for your less money.

Now Jimmy is not just any merchant: he is a philosopher-merchant, a Chinese businessmen who is also intensely Malaysian. Buying from Jimmy is not a transaction; it is a social relationship. A real film buff, Jimmy is much more than a *Halliwell's* on two feet. The famed Bible of the film world only covers the films of Hollywood. Jimmy can talk with equal facility about American, Hong Kong, Taiwanese, Indian, Indonesian and Malaysian cinema. He introduced me to the films of the Hong Kong director John Wu, and action actor, Chow Yun-Fat, long before they became cult figures in the West. Both, Jimmy predicted, would migrate to Hollywood and lose their poetic edge. He has proved right on both accounts. Jimmy's philosophy is rather simple: he is a die-hard believer in free speech and free trade. And you get plenty of both at his shop. His regular customers are showered with a generous dose of abuse directed at the ignorantly applied prurience of the local censors, drowned in reportage of the local political scene and how it is destroying the indigenous film and media industry, and drenched with liberal references to Malay proverbs. There is one that Jimmy cites more than frequently: 'one should never interfere with another man's rice bowl'. When he has repeated this proverb more than once in less than ten minutes, you know the counterfeit police have been around. But Jimmy takes these raids in his stride. He is constantly under threat of being closed down, run out of business or having his contraband confiscated. But the threat is as fake, or indeed real, as the films he sells. Jimmy is scrupulously honest and more than generous to his regular customers. If he thinks it is a bad film and if he knows the copy to be poor, he will sell you a film only reluctantly and then only if you insist. So buying a film from Jimmy is not a simple affair – the ritual involves three distinct steps. First, you ask if he has the film that will be released in New York in a couple of weeks. 'Got, got,' he will reply enthusiastically and then launch into a colourful critique quoting advance reviews and gossip he has acquired over the Internet, before giving his own verdict: 'story no good, *lah*'. Jimmy likes films with strong narratives, meandering, cyclic plots that, in the final analysis, like *Sejarah Malayu*, have something to say. It is not surprising, then, that he dislikes most of the films he actually sells. So we move to the second part of the process. Does he actually have a decent copy of this film with a rotten story? 'Copy no good, *lah*! Two weeks, two weeks. Good copy in two weeks.' If you insist he will actually slip the film in the video set up at the corner of his shop and let you decide for yourself. We thus move to the final phase. Can I have a lousy copy of this lousy film, please? It is at this point that Jimmy disappears. He grabs a carrier bag and runs out of the shop at great speed. Ten, fifteen, twenty minutes later he reappears triumphantly holding a reasonably watchable copy – invariably with added value. 'Bring it back if you don't like it!', he says, as he slips the naked video into a flashy, shrink-wrapped cover. He means it. When I don't like a film, when the yarn is not to my taste, I take it back and Jimmy exchanges it for a film that I think I would like.

Like Jimmy's added-value films, there is more to this business than meets the eye. The world of fake goods is not limited to music and films. All manner of designer products – from watches, sunglasses to clothes and shoes, as well as computer software, spare parts for cars and machinery – are available as real fakes. The Mall, where Jimmy carries on his enterprise, looks and feels like a place of genuine imitation. But genuine imitation is actually the guarantee loudly proclaimed by the stall-holders of Petaling Street, in the heart of KL's Chinatown, a place that positively reeks of history, thanks mostly to the oldest drains in the city. 'Come, look, genuine imitation, real fakes!', the smiling young purveyors of fake watches cry as they lure tourists to their stalls. Petaling Street is a traditional thoroughfare lined with Chinese shop-houses, selling all variety of merchandise, the covered pavements and mouths of alleyways host hawker food stalls, around which cluster tables and chairs for the diners. Negotiating your way along Petaling Street would be a sufficient obstacle course without the addition of what brings everyone here, the real front of the fake economy. For the street is double-parked with market stalls. To visit the stalls you must walk in the roadway as traffic snakes and snarls and jostles among the shoppers. Around 6 p.m. everyday the cars are banished and Petaling Street becomes the most famous and populous night market in KL. Two more lines of edge-to-edge stalls are set up in the middle of the road and crowds of shoppers negotiate their way from stall to stall in an enclosed, heaving and sweaty mass. As well as the real imitations, there are stalls selling fruit, stalls selling sweets – at least that is how they appear to the casual observer; on examination they turn out to be things such as sour plums that are both salty and sour with a background of sweetness. There are stalls selling refreshing drinks: sea coconut and cat's eye juice (it's a fruit) at one end of the street and at the other a real sugar cane juice outfit. This delectable juice requires peeled trimmed lengths of raw sugar cane. The sticks are fed through a contraption that looks and operates exactly like an old-fashioned mangle, the kind people used to use to wring out their washing. From one part of the device comes the pulp of the mangled sticks and from another the green and delicious juice, the best thirst-quencher known to man. Petaling Street looks, feels, tastes and smells like another world. It is old Asia, populous and alive, a part of the old Indian Ocean world, one with the spirit of that world that kept on trying to subvert and reorganize around the fringes of the colonial order and the growth of industrial modernity, from which it was excluded. Petaling Street continues the resistance.

Southeast and East Asia are where cheap electronics and the high-tech ingredients of all information technology as well as much else are manufactured in bulk. It is also counterfeit country. There is no contradiction here. Those who labour in the factories to produce all the consumer desirables often earn too little to buy the genuine branded end products, which, despite local component production, end up as costly imports from other countries. In KL low-income groups need never suffer from the true definition of poverty, which is not absolute absence of disposable income, but the socially more cutting and cruel fate of not being able to participate in the consumerist illusions of the postmodern era. The fake economy, the inability to tell the real from the imitation, enables those with little money to keep themselves in the game of social presentation and fashion permutations. Slight Malay bodies clad in fake designer jeans, fake T-shirts, wrists adorned with fake designer watches, clutching fake designer bags and cloned mobile phones look as if they have wandered straight out of Beverly Hills for the pittance the get-up cost them. They are *in*-cluded, fashion and fancy, and not *ex*-cluded, marginalized onlookers. In the international politics of self and style they are fully empowered. And the transformation can be accomplished within the ambience and precincts of living history.

Kuala Lumpur is not unlike Jimmy's different categories of videos, underpinned by the spirit of Petaling Street. Development, after all, is fundamentally, philosophically, entirely about imitation. Kuala Lumpur strategizes genuine imitation for itself and the whole nation. It looks to the glamour and glitter not merely of Hollywood but also of Japan, Korea, Taiwan and Singapore. Development, as many have learned, can be a real fake. So genuine imitation requires that the provenance of the process be scrutinized with a practised eye. The economy of genuine imitation requires skills, artifice and considerable acumen both ancient indigenous and modern imported. Old skills and facilities are essential to making the process possible and what is possible is to appear and in many senses to be part of a new order, a postmodern reordering of global realities. KL has a foothold in all the stages, expressions and appearances of each and every stage from the old Indian Ocean dynamic to the forefront of the future of globalized cyberspace. In many instances its stories have or seek different endings from the branded product, and one can prefer an alternative scenario. Genuine imitation is also subtle subversion allowing authentic local ideas and imperatives to be included and empowered in ways not designed for, intended for or even to the taste of audiences elsewhere. Kuala Lumpur is involved in many ways, on many levels in the international politics of style and self. It achieves its sense of place through enterprise and artifice that retains, employs and works through institutions, organizations and ideas that are distinctively its own and not beholden to anyone else's patternbook. And sometimes its labours are just a fraud.

# Index